# THE ITALIANS OF DALMATIA:
# FROM ITALIAN UNIFICATION TO WORLD WAR I

Located on the eastern coast of the Adriatic Sea, the area known as Dalmatia, part of modern-day Croatia and Montenegro, was part of the Austrian Empire during the nineteenth and twentieth centuries. Dalmatia was a multicultural region that traditionally had been politically and economically dominated by its Italian minority. In *The Italians of Dalmatia*, Luciano Monzali argues that the vast majority of local Italians were loyal to and supportive of Habsburg rule, desiring only a larger degree of local autonomy. An Italian national consciousness developed only in response to pressure from Slavic national movements and was facilitated by the emergence of a large, unified, and independent Italian state.

Using little-known Italian, Austrian, and Dalmatian sources, Monzali explores the political history of Dalmatia between 1848 and 1915, with a focus on the Italian minority, on Austrian-Italian relations, and on the foreign policy of the Italian state towards the region and its peoples.

(Toronto Italian Studies)

LUCIANO MONZALI is an associate professor in the Faculty of Political Science at the University of Bari.

# The Italians of Dalmatia
## From Italian Unification to World War I

LUCIANO MONZALI

Translated by Shanti Evans

UNIVERSITY OF TORONTO PRESS
Toronto Buffalo London

© University of Toronto Press Incorporated 2009
Toronto Buffalo London
www.utpublishing.com
Printed in Canada

ISBN 978-0-8020-9931-0 (cloth)
ISBN 978-0-8020-9621-0 (paper)

Printed on acid-free paper

Toronto Italian Studies

---

**Library and Archives Canada Cataloguing in Publication**

Monzali, Luciano
The Italians of Dalmatia : from Italian unification to World
War I / Luciano Monzali ; translated by Shanti Evans.

(Toronto Italian studies)
Translation of: Italiani di Dalmazia : dal Risorgimento alla Grande Guerra.
Includes bibliographical references and index.
ISBN 978-0-8020-9931-0 (bound).   ISBN 978-0-8020-9621-0 (pbk.)

1. Italians – Croatia – Dalmatia – History – 19th century.   2. Italians –
Croatia – Dalmatia – History – 20th century.   3. Dalmatia (Croatia) –
History – 19th century.   4. Dalmatia (Croatia) – History – 20th century.
I. Evans, Shanti   II. Title.   III. Series: Toronto Italian studies

DR1625.5.I8M6613 2009      949.7'202      C2009-902317-2

---

This book has been published with the help of a grant from the Società
Dalmata di Storia Patria-Venezia.

University of Toronto Press acknowledges the financial assistance to its
publishing program of the Canada Council for the Arts and the Ontario
Arts Council.

University of Toronto Press acknowledges the financial support for its
publishing activities of the Government of Canada through the Book
Publishing Industry Development Program (BPIDP).

# Contents

# Foreword

Viola. What country, friends, is this?
Captain. This is Illyria, lady.
Viola. And what should I do in Illyria?

(Shakespeare, *Twelfth Night*, I, ii)

What should she do, indeed? To Shakespeare's contemporaries in Renaissance England, Illyria was not only a quasi-mythical land of bright sunshine, excellent food, fine wine, and good government but also a place where wayfarers might be shipwrecked by sudden storms, siblings separated, genders switched, identities confused, and strangers mistaken for pirates. In Shakespeare's *Twelfth Night* it all eventually ended happily with several marriages and good socio-economic arrangements for all the main characters, except for Malvolio, whose obsessive interest in himself alone led to his ridicule and demise.

Illyria is the ancient name for Dalmatia, the land along the eastern coastline of the Adriatic Sea that separates the Italian peninsula from what we now call the former Yugoslavia. For modern travellers it is, as it was for Shakespeare, an idyllic place. It is, however, also a place of deep-rooted conflicts and tensions. Today, the pirates that so troubled merchant ships in the Middle Ages and in the Renaissance have given way to nationalist extremists who, over the past century and a half, have turned modern-day Dalmatia into a hub of ethnic violence and historical revisionism. In a way, these extremists are the modern Malvolios, but unfortunately their selfish interests have had tragic consequences for their idyllic land and the people who inhabit it.

Why is there such ethnic tension in Dalmatia and how did it all start? As far back as the seventh century CE, when the first Slavic tribes crossed the Dinaric Alps and began to settle among the Latin and Il-lyrian populations that inhabited these coastal regions, Dalmatia has been home to a multicultural and multilingual population that lived in relative peace and mutual tolerance. Then something went wrong, and by the mid-twentieth century its various ethnic groups were murdering and expelling each other, so much so that by the end of the century the world community was obliged to intervene. This was not a millenarian hatred that suddenly exploded into genocidal rage but a fairly recent development that was the fruit of political and ideological movements that started in the nineteenth century. In fact, the tensions that charac-terize modern-day Dalmatia and, with it, the entire region of the former Yugoslavia can be laid firmly at the feet of two recent phenomena: nine-teenth-century Italian and Slavic nationalisms and their counterpart, Habsburg imperial politics. Were it not for these antithetical, but in this case complementary, forces – one a nascent ideology determined to give birth to a new world system, and the other a moribund political system determined to retain power at whatever cost – modern-day Dalmatia might well have been spared the civil wars, genocides, and population displacements it so violently suffered in the twentieth century.

By focusing on the history of Dalmatia in the seventy years that pre-ceded the outbreak of World War I, Luciano Monzali is able to chart the collapse of its ethnic peace and the rise of the various nationalisms that, on at least three occasions during the twentieth century, tore the region apart. He is also able to document the central role played in the late nineteenth century by the Austrian governing class in fomenting the ethnic divisions that persist to this day in the former Yugoslavia, which was once part of the Austro-Hungarian Empire. Gone is the image of a benevolent Emperor Francis Joseph and a fair and balanced Austrian government – the idea that 'Austria was an orderly country,' still so much alive today in certain parts of Italy, Istria, and Dalmatia and so charmingly depicted in Lino Carpinteri and Mariano Faraguna's popu-lar series Le Maldrobìe that featured volumes such as *L'Austria era un paese ordinato* (Austria Was an Orderly Country; 1996), *Noi delle vecchie provincie* (We from the Old Provinces; 1997), *Viva l'A.* (Long Live A.; 1998), *Povero nostro Franz* (Our Poor Franz; 2002). In its place we dis-cover, instead, a paternalistic emperor and an entrenched conservative governing class who, in order to keep a newly unified Italian state at bay and out of their shop, were prepared to put their thumb on the scales of Dalmatian life and tilt them in favour of what they assumed would be their own political advantage – a move that eventually had disastrous consequences for the region, the empire, and the Habsburg family itself.

These political manoeuvres on the part of the Austrian ruling class were not at all surprising. Austria's short war with the Kingdom of Piedmont in 1859 had disastrous consequences for the Habsburgs, who lost much of the northern Italian territories they controlled – Lombardy, the duchies of Parma and Modena, and the grand-duchy of Tuscany – all of which were annexed (by force or by plebiscite) into the Kingdom of Piedmont, together with the papal legations of Ferrara, Bologna, and the Romagna. Austria then sat powerless as the audacious general Giuseppe Garibaldi conquered the Kingdom of the Two Sicilies and gave it gratis to King Victor Emmanuel II of Piedmont (1860). The following year, the Piedmontese parliament proclaimed Victor Emmanuel king of a unified Italian state that stretched along the length of the peninsula. Italy had been born, and this in spite of Piedmont's lack-lustre military exploits. In fact, the 1859 gains in northern Italy had been made on the strength of direct French military assistance; the 1860 conquest of southern Italy had been facilitated by the earlier withdrawal of Swiss mercenaries from Naples and by an armistice in Sicily brokered by English diplomacy. Meanwhile the 1866 acquisition of Venice and the Veneto was owed entirely to German victories on Austria's northern front and not to Italian military gains on the southern front. In short, Austria soon found itself with a rapidly expanding neighbour at its borders, a neighbour who, though normally not victorious in war, was nonetheless constantly victorious in the aftermath of war.

From the perspective of the Hofburg Palace in Vienna, the newly formed Kingdom of Italy was a clear threat to the long-standing Habsburg Empire. Those parts of the diminishing empire that contained significant Italian-speaking populations – the Trentino, the Alto Adige, Venezia Giulia, Istria, and Dalmatia – were now viewed as territories that needed to be protected from the growing menace of Italian expansionism. Vienna's tactic was thus to undermine Italian nationalist sentiments in these territories and, in the case of the last three regions, to foster instead their Slavic elements (Slovenian, Croatian, Serbian). This, Vienna hoped, would sap the strength from Italian culture in the region and weaken any irredentist movement that might be developing there. The tactic seemed perfect at the time, but history has exposed its serious flaws. By playing the nationalist game the Hofburg helped to set the stage for the break-up of its own empire and for the ethnic conflicts that, over the past century, have led to so much bloodshed in these regions.

Austria was, however, neither the only player nor the only culprit. The new Kingdom of Italy, which had started off in Count Camillo di Cavour's mind as a union of northern Italy states, had unexpectedly ended up as a union of the entire peninsula. As a result, Italy's geopolitical concerns had been drastically altered. Its eastern border now ran the entire length of the Adriatic Sea and was difficult to defend from attack by the powerful Austrian navy. If Italy could annex the territories on the northeastern shores of the Adriatic on the grounds that they were *Italia irredenta* and thus part of a single Italian nation, then Austria would lose its sea accesses at Trieste, Pola, and Fiume, and this would turn the Adriatic once again into a *mare nostrum* (our sea), as it had been at the time of the Venetian republic. By closing off the Adriatic to Austria, Italy could better protect its eastern seaboard. For reasons of national security, and not really for reasons of cultural integrity, Italy began to pay closer attention to the Italian-speaking populations in Istria and Dalmatia and to help them maintain their language and culture in the face of growing Slavic influence in the region.

The seemingly unstoppable rise of various Slavic nationalisms also contributed to this warming cauldron. Slavic nationalists played themselves off against the Italian element in Istria and Dalmatia in order to gain further concessions and preferment from Vienna, and they did this very successfully – so much so, in fact, that Emperor Francis Joseph II and the entire Austrian ruling class were soon favouring their Slavic subjects over their Italian ones. The growing disenchantment of the Italian-speaking populations in the region with the cultural politics emanating from Vienna soon began to turn the previously loyal subjects of the Habsburg emperors into aspiring subjects of the House of Savoy. Finding themselves passed over and often undermined by Vienna, the Italian population of Istria and Dalmatia turned to Rome for support. Italian irredentism was thus born.

The growth of a pan-Slavic movement and of an Italian irredentist movement soon spelled the demise of Dalmatian culture as it had existed for centuries, if not for thousands of years. Dalmatian culture had developed since ancient times as a blend of various ethnicities and languages and remained strong well into the nineteenth and twentieth centuries. Until at least the middle of the twentieth century, Dalmatians considered themselves to be culturally distinct both from their Italian neighbours across the sea and from their Slavic neighbours across the

Dinaric Alps. Drawing from both neighbouring cultures and from their own deep ancestral roots in the region, Dalmatians proudly claimed their own unique identity. Most, if not all, could switch easily from the local Italian dialect to its Croatian or Serbian counterpart, and some even spoke the local indigenous idiom, Dalmatian, a Romance language that had three distinct dialectical subgroups: Istrioto (in Istria), Veglioto (in northern Dalmatia), and Ragusan (in the south). While Istrioto is still spoken today by a small native population in places such as Rovigno (Rovinj) and Dignano (Vodnijan), Veglioto became extinct at the end of the nineteenth century when its last native speaker, Antonio Udina (called 'Burbur'), died from a land mine explosion in 1898; Ragusan had disappeared long before, having been replaced in the sixteenth century by the Venetian dialect.

In the late nineteenth century the strength of this Dalmatian cultural identity animated a number of Dalmatian leaders who adamantly argued against an incorporation of Dalmatia into Croatia, a move fondly wished by Croatian nationalists intent on defining their future nation, and warmly welcomed by the Austrian ruling class intent on defending itself against Italian irredentism. The argument for a distinct Dalmatia within the various national units that comprised the Habsburg Empire was eventually lost, and the region was folded into greater Croatia, where it remains to this day, a victim of nineteenth-century nationalisms.

Monzali's detailed analysis of political developments in Dalmatia from the revolutions of 1848 to the outbreak of World War I in 1914 carefully charts the vertiginous rise of ethnic nationalisms in the region and the consequent downward spiral of peace. It sets the stage for the tragedies that would unfold during and immediately after World War II and then again in the 1990s, when unspeakable atrocities were perpetrated against neighbours and fellow citizens for the sake of an untenable goal of ethnic homogeneity. To narrate this story with a carefully balanced view of all sides in the conflict, the author has examined government documentation from Italy, Austria, Croatia, and Serbia, as well as from other European countries such as England, France, Germany, Switzerland, and Belgium. His thesis that Croatian national consciousness and its territorial ambitions in Dalmatia were fostered by external forces, such as Austrian imperial politics in response to Italian unification or rising Serbian nationalism in anticipation of a collapse of the Ottoman Empire, may well prove controversial, especially with readers more accustomed to hearing about the supposed 'resentment' of the

Slavic populations at the centuries-long 'oppression' they had suffered at the hands of their Venetian and Italian 'overlords.' Monzali discounts this interpretation and proposes, instead, a more recent and pragmatic set of factors that are much more in line with the *Realpolitik* of late-nineteenth-century imperialists than with the historical revisionism of twentieth-century nationalists.

His conclusions will certainly be viewed by many as considerably more favourable to an Italian-Dalmatian perspective than one is currently accustomed to read, but this should not come as a surprise, nor should it be unwelcome. A corrective to the current philo-Slavic interpretation of this history is very much in order. Since the end of World War II, the entire question of an Italian presence on the eastern shores of the Adriatic has been highly politicized, and discussion of it has been fraught with peril. First in the old republic of Yugoslavia and now in the new republic of Croatia, the official position speaks of an overwhelming Slavic majority oppressed for centuries by a minuscule Italian minority that was augmented, but never to the point of becoming a majority, by proactive immigration from the Italian peninsula during the Fascist regime of the 1920s to the 1930s. It speaks of just cause, national identity, and the quest for freedom. In post-war Italy, the entire question has been either silenced completely or discussed in muted tones that echo the Yugoslav/Croatian party line to the point of servility. Until the late 1990s, the Italian government, its educational system, the press, and even the general population avoided thinking, let alone talking, about what had happened in five of its provinces from the 1920s to the 1950s and carefully ignored the wholesale executions of Italians carried out by the partisan soldiers and kangaroo courts of the Yugoslav dictator Marshal Josip Broz ('Tito') or the massive exile and complete dispersal of the indigenous Italian population of Istria and Dalmatia.

The silence has finally been broken. Since the late 1990s there has been an awakening, in Italy at least, to the tragic history that engulfed the Italian population of Istria and Dalmatia in the twentieth century and led to its dispersion, an event of biblical proportions that will shortly lead to the extinction of this population and its culture. While there is now a growing body of works in Italian on this history, there still is very little available in English.[1] A recent contribution has been

---

1 See, for example, Giuseppe Praga, *History of Dalmatia*, ed. Franco Luxardo, trans. Edward Steinberg (Pisa: Giardini, 1993), which begins with the Greeks and goes up to the Italian wars of independence in the nineteenth century.

the publication, by the University of Toronto Press, of Arrigo Petacco's *A Tragedy Revealed: The Story of the Italian Population of Istria, Dalmatia, and Venezia Giulia, 1943–1956* (2005), a work of investigative journalism by one of Italy's most eminent and respected senior journalists. Luciano Monzali's careful analysis of the background to this tragedy is another corrective. Firmly anchored in archival and government documents, it sets the stage for scholarly discussion and opens the way for further research on this troubled question.

Coming, as it did, from a multicultural and multilingual area, the exiled Italian population of Istria and Dalmatia has adapted to its new circumstances on the Italian peninsula, in other European countries, in North and South America, in South Africa, and in Australia, as have adapted those few Italians who remained on their ancestral soil. Perhaps there is no point in discussing their story further or in recalling a painful past. However, when we look around and see that atrocities are still being committed in the name of ethnic and nationalist agendas, then it becomes obvious that we still need to look deeply into our history and identify the steps that lead a people to the brink of such an abyss. Monzali's volume charts these steps in the case of Dalmatia. It points to the growing rumble of nationalist sentiments, to the weakening strength of central governments, and to the ineffective solutions of victimized populations, and it teaches a lesson that has still not been appreciated in our post-modern world.

Konrad Eisenbichler
Victoria College
University of Toronto

# Preface

Since its foundation in 1926, the Società Dalmata di Storia Patria has been committed to keeping alive the identity of the Adriatic regions whose cultures were deeply influenced for centuries by the presence of autochthonous Latin, Venetian, and, later, Italian populations and their institutions, art, and literature. This aim has been and is being pursued through academic seminars, scholarships, publications, and a specialized library of over 12,000 titles pertaining to Dalmatia.

With the advance of European integration our objectives have broadened, and we have begun to support works aimed at an international readership, either in English, such as *History of Dalmatia* by G. Praga and *The Fruitful Impact: The Venetian Heritage in the Art of Dalmatia* by G. M. Pilo, or in Croatian, such as *Zadar: Od bombardiranja do izgnanstva 1943–1947* by G. E. Lovrovich, or in both languages, such as *They Came From the Sky ...* by O. Talpo and S. Brcic. It was therefore natural to support the translation and the publication of this academic work, the first of a series of three by Professor Luciano Monzali on the Italian inhabitants of Dalmatia. His documentary approach based on Italian, Austrian, and Croatian archives has marked an awakening of Italian historiography on the theme and sheds a new, stimulating light on the personalities and events experienced by our ancestors, distant and recent.

The attentive reader will also discover that Professor Monzali has written not just a regional history, but in many pages he also analyses the foreign policies in the Balkans and in Eastern Europe of the great players of the '800 (Austria-Hungary, Italy, Turkey, Germany, Russia, France). Thus it becomes easier to understand why the political decisions taken over 100 years ago still have an impact on today's situation in cases such as Bosnia and Kosovo.

The forced departures after World War I and the 'ethnic cleansing' after World War II have left only a few hundred Italians scattered among a half million Croats and Serbs. Their legacy, however, remains in each sculpted stone on the coast and in books like this.

There used to be an old saying: the sea does not separate but it unites. I trust that this contribution does the same and helps new generations, in Europe and overseas, to become better acquainted with their roots in order to avoid the errors of the past and to build a shared future.

Franco Luxardo, President
Società Dalmata di Storia Patria
Venice

# Introduction

The aim of *The Italians of Dalmatia: From Italian Unification to World War I* is to reconstruct the fundamental phases in the history of the Italians of Dalmatia during the last decades of Habsburg rule and to analyse the progressive emergence of a political relationship between liberal Italy and the Italian minority in Dalmatia in the years preceding the outbreak of World War I.

Italian linguistic and cultural groups had settled in the main urban centres of the Dalmatian coast since the Early Middle Ages and had lived for centuries in harmony with the other nationalities of Dalmatia (Croats, Serbs and Albanians). The spread of nationalist (pan-Croatian, pan-Serbian, and Yugoslavian) ideologies within Dalmatian society over the course of the nineteenth century triggered political struggles that were increasingly dominated by nationalistic values: a conflict arose between Slavophile nationalists, who wanted a union of Dalmatia with Croatia and Slavonia within the Habsburg Empire and a drastic reduction in the role of the Italian language and culture, and Italophile liberal autonomists, who defended the political and cultural autonomy of Dalmatia, seen as an Italo-Slav land.

Since on the political plane the majority of Italian Dalmatians identified with the autonomist liberal movement, writing the history of the Italian minority in the last decades of Habsburg Dalmatia signifies studying the fortunes of this party, which was set up in 1860 to combat any plan for Dalmatian-Croatian union, in the name of the regionalist ideal of a Dalmatian nation, and then was transformed into a movement in defence of not just the multi-ethnic identity of Dalmatia but also the Dalmatian Italians persecuted by pan-Croatian nationalism.

For several years the Autonomous Liberal Party was the dominant political force in Dalmatia, thanks to the support it received in the urban centres of the coast. However, this dominance proved to be fragile. Even though the vast majority of the Italian Dalmatians were loyal to and supportive of Habsburg rule and hostile to any form of political irredentism, the emergence of a large, independent, and unified Italian state gradually turned the Italian and Italian-speaking populations of the Eastern Adriatic into potential threats to the security of the empire in the eyes of a substantial part of the Austrian ruling class. From the 1870s onward, the Autonomous Liberal Party and the Italian minority in Dalmatia saw a severe retrenchment of their role and influence as a result of the strengthening of pan-Croatian nationalism with the backing of the authorities of the Habsburg state. The Italian Dalmatians started to fall victim to a policy of assimilation and 'Croatization' on the part of the Croatian nationalists who held sway in the province. This favoured the emergence of a new Italian liberal national ideology in the Autonomous Party and among the Italian Dalmatians, which in turn led them to identify increasingly with the Italian national state – at one and the same time a model of liberal society and a possible political protector.

Liberal Italy had shown little interest in Dalmatia in the first few years after unification. However, the naval defeat at Lissa (Vis), the evolution of relations with the Habsburg Empire, and the Austro-Hungarian conquest of Bosnia-Herzegovina made the Italian ruling class aware of the strategic importance of the political set-up in the Eastern Adriatic. Dalmatia was now seen as the territory whose control permitted the assertion of Austro-Hungarian naval supremacy in the Adriatic Sea, a situation regarded as incompatible with the security of the Italian state. The flare-up of nationalistic conflicts in Dalmatia and the deterioration in the living conditions of Italians in Austria prompted a growing interest in the fate of the Italian minority in Dalmatia on the part of public opinion in the kingdom. The government in Rome started to intervene directly in Dalmatian politics through the Dante Alighieri Association, supporting the Italian Autonomous Liberal Party financially; thus, toward the end of the nineteenth century political ties were established between the Italians of Dalmatia and the government. The Italian minority used these ties not to cultivate secessionist designs but to keep their own educational and cultural institutions alive and to strengthen their hand in a very difficult and hostile political situation.

The outbreak of World War I marked a turning point for the Italian minority in Dalmatia and the foreign policy of liberal Italy. The government in Rome saw the conflict as a great opportunity to establish political borders capable of ensuring the strategic security of the national state; the control of part of Dalmatia was considered an indispensable element in Italian plans of expansion. This had a decisive influence on the fortunes of the Italian peoples in the Eastern Adriatic. The stepping up of persecution by the Croatian and Serbian nationalist parties and the inclusion of part of Dalmatia in Italy's plan of territorial conquest persuaded the leaders of the Italian Autonomous Party to abandon the legalist policy of mere national defence and throw themselves instead into the struggle for the break-up of the Habsburg Empire. Finally, with the exile to Italy of Roberto Ghiglianovich, one of the leaders of the Italians in Zara (now Zadar), the Italian Autonomous Party was transformed into a movement whose central plank was the struggle for the union of Dalmatia with Italy.

In order to promote a complete understanding of the history of the Italian minority in Dalmatia we have reconstructed the main developments in Dalmatian politics between the middle of the nineteenth century and the outbreak of World War I, using as principal sources the Dalmatian press of the period, the minutes of the sessions of the Dalmatian provincial diet, and published and unpublished Italian and Habsburg diplomatic records. As Dalmatia was a component of the Austrian part of the Habsburg Empire, it has also been necessary to carry out a wide-ranging analysis of the politics of Cisleithania, which always had a decisive influence on the evolution of the political situation in Dalmatia.

One of the fundamental propositions of this study has been the idea that the fate of the Italian minority in Dalmatia was heavily conditioned by the state of the relations between Italy and the Habsburg Empire and by shifts in the balance of power in central and eastern Europe. There arises the need to reconstruct, on the basis of a careful study of Italian, Austrian, and European diplomatic sources, the policies of the great European powers in the Balkans, the mutable nature of the diplomatic relations between Italy and the Habsburg Empire, and the change in the attitude of the ruling class of liberal Italy toward the Dalmatian question from the time of the Risorgimento to World War I.

Studying the history of Dalmatia in the late Habsburg period means carrying out historical research that is truly European in its scope, in so far as it requires analysis of the fortunes of various European nationalities (Austrians, Italians, Croats, and Serbs). Writing this book has required long periods of study in many Italian, Austrian, and Croatian libraries and archives, in particular the Archivio Storico of the Italian Ministry of Foreign Affairs, the Archivio Centrale dello Stato, the Archivio Storico of the Società 'Dante Alighieri,' the Biblioteca Nazionale and the Fondo Mario Toscano in the Department of Political Sciences of La Sapienza University in Rome; the Biblioteca Marciana and the Biblioteca della Scuola Dalmata dei Santi Giorgio e Trifone in Venice; the Biblioteca Statale Isontina in Gorizia; the Haus-, Hof- und Staatsarchiv and Österreichische Nationalbibliothek in Vienna; and the Sveučilišna Knjižnica in Split. A fundamental contribution to the realization of this work came from the two grants that I received from the Austrian and Italian governments in 1999 and 2000, which allowed me to go twice to Vienna for periods of study.

I would like to thank a number of people who have helped me to carry out this work. I am very grateful to Professor Italo Garzia, who holds the History of International Relations chair at the University of Bari, for his continual support of my inquiries and the great deal of useful advice that he has given me. My gratitude also goes to Professor Alessandro Duce for the encouragement and advice I received during the years of my collaboration with him at the University of Parma. My thanks go as well to Professor Pietro Pastorelli, who passed on to me the teachings of his great master, Mario Toscano, during the time I was working on my research doctorate; to professors Gianluca Andrè and Anton Giulio de' Robertis for the kindness they showed me; to Professor Carlo Ghisalberti for his interest in my writings; and to Professor Lothar Höbelt of the University of Vienna for the suggestions and advice that facilitated my research into Austrian politics. In addition I am grateful to Professor Antonio Donno, Professor Francesco Perfetti, and Franco Luxardo for the interest they have shown in this work of mine.

My friends Massimo Bucarelli, Francesco Caccamo, Luca Micheletta, and Luca Riccardi have read various parts of the text, offering me useful advice and criticism, for which I am deeply grateful.

I would also like to thank my parents, Mirella Valli and Giustino Monzali, who have supported me through these years of hard and demanding study, and Jadranka Miočić for her assistance in my bibliographic research at Split. The volume is dedicated to my wife, Estera, who has helped me with so much love to understand better the history and culture of her homeland, Dalmatia.

# Abbreviations

| | |
|---|---|
| ACS | Archivio Centrale dello Stato, Rome. |
| ADP-BI | *Atti della Dieta Provinciale Dalmata/Brzopisna Izvješća Zasjedanja Pokrajinskoga Sabora Dalmatinskoga.* Zara, 1861–. |
| AP | *Atti parlamentari. Camera dei deputati.* Rome, 1861–. |
| APP | *Die auswärtige Politik Preußens, 1858–1871.* Berlin: Stalling-Oldenbourg, 1933–9. |
| ARC POL | Archivio Politico (1861–87). |
| ARG | Archivio Riservato di Gabinetto (1906–11). |
| ASF | Archivio di Stato di Forlì. |
| ASMAE | Archivio storico del Ministero degli Esteri Italiano, Rome. |
| BD | *British Documents on the Origins of the War, 1898–1914.* London: HMSO, 1927–. |
| BL | Biblioteca Comunale di Lucera, Foggia. |
| BS | Biblioteca del Senato, Rome. |
| Carte Depretis | Agostino Depretis Papers, Archivio Centrale dello Stato, Rome. |
| Carte Ghiglianovich | Roberto Ghiglianovich Papers, Biblioteca del Senato, Rome. |
| Carte Giolitti | Giovanni Giolitti Papers, Archivio Centrale dello Stato, Rome. |
| Carte Luzzatti | Luigi Luzzatti Papers, Istituto Veneto di Scienze, Lettere e Arti, Venice. |
| Carte Salandra | Antonio Salandra Papers, Biblioteca Comunale di Lucera. |

| | |
|---|---|
| Carte Tornielli | Giuseppe Tornielli Papers, Archivio di Stato di Forli. |
| *Commissiones:* | *Monumenta spectantia historiam slavorum meridionalium. Commissiones et Relationes Venetae,* Academy of Sciences and Arts, Zagreb 1876-. |
| CP | *British Documents on Foreign Affairs: Reports and Papers from the Foreign Office, Confidential Print.* Washington: University Publications of America, 1983–. |
| DA | Archivio Storico della Società Dante Alighieri, Rome. |
| DB | *Die Belgischen Dokumente zur Vorgeschichte des Weltkrieges, 1885–1914.* Berlin: Deutsche Verlagsgesellschaft für Politik, 1925. |
| DD | *Die Deutschen Dokumente zum Kriegsausbruch 1914.* Berlin: Deutsche Verlagsgesellschaft für Politik, 1921. First published 1919. |
| DDF | *Documents diplomatiques français, 1871–1914.* Paris: Imprimèrie Nationale, 1929–. |
| DDI | *Documenti diplomatici italiani.* Rome: Libreria dello Stato-Istituto Poligrafico dello Stato, 1952–. |
| DDS | *Documents diplomatiques suisses / Documenti diplomatici svizzeri / Diplomatische Dokumente der Schweiz 1848–1945.* Bern: Benteli Verlag, 1979–. |
| EMB VIENNA | Italian Embassy in Vienna. |
| GP | *Die Grosse Politik der Europäischen Kabinette, 1871–1914.* Berlin: Deutsche Verlagsgesellschaft für Politik und Geschichte, 1922–7. |
| HHSTA | Haus-, Hof- und Staatsarchiv, Vienna. |
| IB | *Die Internationalen Beziehungen im Zeitalter des Imperialismus.* Berlin, 1934–42. |
| IVSLA | Istituto Veneto di Scienze, Lettere e Arti, Venice. |
| KA | Kriegsarchiv, Vienna. |
| MR | *Die Protokolle des Österreichischen Ministerrates, 1848–1867. V Abteilung: Die Ministerien Rainer und Mensdorff; VI Abteilung: Das Ministerium Belcredi.* Vienna: Österreichischer Bundesverlag für Unterricht, Wissenschaft und Kunst, 1971–. |

| | |
|---|---|
| *Nachlass* Macchio | Karl Macchio Papers, Vienna. |
| *Nachlass* Rodich | Gabriel Rodich Papers, Vienna. |
| OEU | *Österreich-Ungarns Aussenpolitik von der Bosnischen Krise 1908 bis zum Kriegsausbruch 1914.* Vienna: Österreichischer Bundesverlag, 1930–. |
| OUS | *Österreich-Ungarn und Serbien 1903–1918: Dokumente aus Wiener Archiven.* Belgrade: Historisches Institut, 1973–89. |
| PA | *Politisches Archiv.* |
| RB | *Diplomatic Documents relating to the Outbreak of the European War.* New York: Oxford University Press, 1916, pp. 127–346. |
| SP | Serie Politica. |
| TEL GAB | Archivio Telegrammi di Gabinetto. |

THE ITALIANS OF DALMATIA:
FROM ITALIAN UNIFICATION TO WORLD WAR I

# 1  A Slav-Italian Nation: The Italian Dalmatians and the Birth of Autonomist Liberalism

## 1.1. Dalmatia and Its Peoples

Dalmatia emerged as a historical and political concept in the Roman era. Augustus created a Roman province named after the Dalmati, Delmata or Delmatae, an Illyrian tribe that lived on the eastern coasts of the Adriatic. This province incorporated the central and western Balkans – not just the east coast of the Adriatic from eastern Istria to the Drina River but also a vast hinterland that was bounded to the north by the southern part of the territory traversed by the Sava River and that comprised the modern regions of Bosnia, Herzegovina, and Montenegro, and much of Albania and Serbia. The province was inhabited by Illyrian tribes, of Indo-European stock, who left a deep ethnic mark on the peoples of the Balkans.[1] In the period prior to the Roman conquest, small Hellenic urban centres had formed on the Dalmatian coast, and these were to be some of the keystones in the process of the Romanization of Dalmatia, along with the numerous military colonies that the empire established for political and strategic reasons in various parts of its territory.

Dalmatia underwent a marked Romanization on the ethnic and linguistic plane, especially in the urban centres and on the coast,[2] but the

---

1 Wilkes, *The Illyrians.*
2 On the Roman rule of Dalmatia see Wilkes, *Dalmatia*; Praga, *Storia di Dalmazia*, translated as *History of Dalmatia*; Novak, *Povijest Splita*, vol. 1; *Prošlost Dalmacije*, vol. 1, pp. 38 et seq; Mustilli, *La conquista romana*; Rinaldi Tufi, 'La Dalmazia,' pp. 471–6; Tamaro, *La Vénétie Julienne et la Dalmatie*, vol. 2, *Histoire de la Nation italienne sur ses frontières orientales*, pp. 73–104; Alföldy, 'La Dalmazia nella storia dell'impero romano,' pp. 113–31; Santini, *Dall'Illirico romano alla Jugoslavia moderna.*

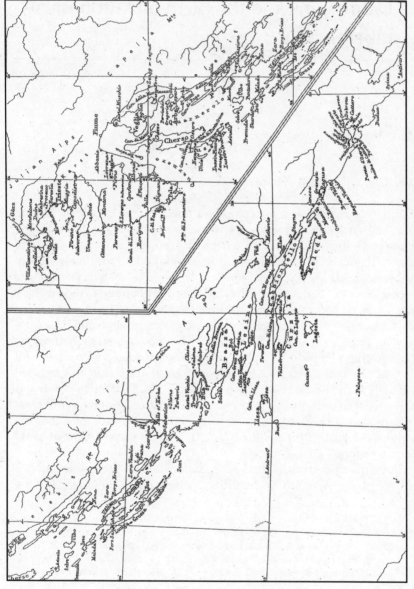

*The Shores of the Adriatic, the Austrian Side* by Frederick Hamilton Jackson (New York, 1908)

Illyrian element undoubtedly remained present, especially in the poor and inaccessible zones of the Dinaric Alps. So, ever since the Roman era, Dalmatia has experienced an ethnic and linguistic split, stemming from the existence of various peoples in the same territory.

With the definitive separation of the Roman Empire into an eastern and a western part on the death of Theodosius I in 395, the Balkans were divided into two zones. Macedonia and much of the Illyrian region were assigned to the Eastern Roman Empire, ruled by Theodosius's son Arcadius, while the eastern Adriatic coast remained under the control of the Western Empire, ruled by Honorius. The Balkan region was separated by a line that ran from the Danube along the Drina River, across what is now Montenegro, and to the Adriatic. As Georg Ostrogorsky has pointed out, 'a borderline was traced between East and West that over time would come to mark ever more clearly the boundary between the Western cultural world, of Rome, and the Eastern and Byzantine one.'[3]

Dalmatia was linked politically to the Italian peninsula for many decades, even if it was under the de facto influence of the Eastern Roman Empire. Odoacer annexed Dalmatia to the barbarian kingdom of Italy, and Dalmatia stayed united with Italy throughout the Ostrogoth period and the time of the Byzantine reconquest. The Longobard invasion of the Italian peninsula led to a first political separation between the Dalmatian coast, which remained a Byzantine dominion, and the greater part of central and northern Italy, which was subjugated by the Longobards. The political set-up of Byzantine Dalmatia was disrupted by the invasions of the Avars and the Slavs. Between the second half of the sixth century and the beginning of the seventh many Slav tribes settled in Pannonia, Moesia and Dalmatia.[4] Numerous Roman towns

---

3 Ostrogorsky, *History of the Byzantine State*, trans. from the German by Joan Hussey (New Brunswick, NJ: Rutgers University Press,1969). The passage has been translated from the Italian edition, *Storia dell'impero bizantino* (Turin: Einaudi,1993), p. 47. On Dalmatia in the late Roman era see Ferluga, *L'amministrazione bizantina in Dalmazia*, p. 35 et seq.
4 On the arrival of the Slavs in Dalmatia see Obolensky, *The Byzantine Commonwealth*; Ferluga, *L'amministrazione bizantina*, p. 86 et seq.; Jirecek, 'L'eredità di Roma nelle città della Dalmazia durante il Medioevo,' p. 37 et seq.; Novak, *Prošlost Dalmacije*, vol. 1, p. 93 et seq.; Lucio, *Storia del regno di Dalmazia e di Croazia* (Trieste: Lint, 1983), p. 93 et seq. (this is a reprint, under the auspices of the Società Dalmata di Storia Patria in Venice, of the first, 1896, Italian edition of the work published in Latin by the historian from Traù in the seventeenth century); Šišić, *Pregled povijest hrvatskoga naroda*, p. 67 et seq.; Ostrogorsky, *History of the Byzantine State*, p. 85 et seq.

and cities were wiped out. Solin (Salona), the main centre of Roman Dalmatia, was totally destroyed; the surviving Latin inhabitants fled to the islands and then migrated to Diocletian's former fortified villa at Asphalatos (Spalato [Split]), between 638 and 641.[5] In fact, the Latin populations in general took refuge in fortified cities or on the islands of Dalmatia; Ragusa (Dubrovnik) and Traù (Trogir) were originally small islands just off the coast, while Zara (Zadar) was an easily defended peninsula.

The arrival of the Slavs led to a retrenchment of the Byzantine presence in the western Balkans. The Byzantines maintained direct rule over the islands of the eastern Adriatic and parts of the coast, but the interior of Roman Dalmatia, in what are now Croatia, Bosnia-Herzegovina, Serbia, and Montenegro, was settled by Slav tribes who organized themselves autonomously on the political plane, while formally recognizing the sovereignty of the Eastern Roman Empire.[6] This marked the beginning of a process of political and cultural diversification between the eastern coast of the Adriatic and the inland regions that was to last, with few interruptions, for many centuries. With the passing of time the name *Dalmatia* came to be used not for the vast territories of Roman Dalmatia but for the stretch of the eastern Adriatic coast clearly delimited geographically by the mountain ranges of Velebit and the Dinaric Alps.

The urban communities on the coast, remaining under the feeble protection of the Byzantine empire (which structured its Dalmatian possessions into first an archonship[7] and then a theme[8]), reorganized themselves on the model of the old Roman municipium but adapted it to meet the new political and economic conditions.

In those years the town of Jadera (Zara or Zadar), an old Roman settlement that had withstood the impact of the Slav invasions better than others had, assumed particular significance. Jadera was chosen by the Byzantines as the political and military capital of their Dalmatian

---

5 Praga, review of Ferdo Šišić, *Povijest Hrvata u vrijeme narodnih vladara*, in *Atti e Memorie della Società dalmata di storia patria*, vol. 2, pp. 213 et seq.; Thomae, 'Historia salonitarorum pontificum atque spalatensium a s. Domnio usque ad Rogerium († 1266),' p. 40.
6 On the relations between the Byzantine empire and the Slav peoples see Ostrogorsky, *History of the Byzantine Stat.*; Obolensky, *The Byzantine Commonwealth*.
7 Ferluga, *L'amministrazione bizantina in Dalmazia*, pp. 134–5.
8 Ibid., pp. 165 et seq.

province since it was 'strategically better situated and closer to the outposts of the empire in Istria and at Venice.'[9] With the weakening of the Byzantine grip on Dalmatia over the course of the tenth and eleventh centuries, small city-republics were established at Zara (Zadar), Arbe (Rab), Spalato (Split), Traù (Trogir) and Dubrovnik (Ragusa) that were de facto independent, even though from time to time subjected to rule by the Byzantines, the Venetians, or the Croatian and Serbian principalities of the interior. These communes were essentially oligarchic republics dominated by a few aristocratic families. The communes were led by a prior (later called *rector* and *count*), a number of judges, and a council of patricians.

On the level of the social structure, the development of maritime and commercial activities produced a slow internal diversification. While the hegemony of the *maiores*, the old aristocracy of Roman origin, was uncontested until the tenth century, from the year 1000 onward the economic and political clout of a new mercantile class, distinguishing itself from the working and lower classes, began to grow. This new class, made up of merchants, navigators, sailors, and craftsmen, played a leading role in the trade in which Dalmatia was becoming increasingly involved, within the economic area that developed in the Early Middle Ages between central and western Europe, Italy, the Balkans and the Near East.[10]

The Dalmatians who lived on the islands and in cities like Spalato, Zara, Traù and Ragusa were descendents of the Latin settlers and the autochthonous Illyrian tribes that had been progressively Romanized. The Dalmatians of Roman origin spoke a local Romance language, Dalmatian, which bore some resemblance to Friulian and survived on the island of Veglia (Krk) until the end of the nineteenth century.[11] Surrounded by a hinterland inhabited by Slav peoples who needed to establish trading links with the Italian peninsula, the Romance-speaking natives of Dalmatia were naturally obliged to permit a slow penetration of Slavs and Italians into their towns and cities. The need to develop

---

9   Praga, *Storia di Dalmazia*, p. 53; Ferluga, *L'amministrazione bizantina in Dalmazia*, pp. 100–1, 159. On the history of Zara in the Early Middle Ages see Brunelli, *Storia della città di Zara*.

10  Praga, *Storia di Dalmazia*, cit., pp. 68 et seq.

11  On the Dalmatian language see Bartoli, *Il Dalmatico*; 'Due parole sul neolatino indigeno di Dalmazia,' pp. 201 et seq.; Maver, 'Discorso sul dalmatico,' pp. 102 et seq.; Zamboni, 'Note linguistiche dalmatiche,' pp. 9 et seq.

political and economic relations with the country around the urban settlements in order to obtain agricultural produce, create commercial ties, and allow the political survival of the communes favoured the intensification of contacts between Dalmatians of Roman origin, Slavs, and Albanians, and the emigration of Slavs to the urban centres. Villages inhabited by Slav farmers and shepherds began to spring up near the Latin cities and would later become their suburbs. The practice of mixed marriages spread, not only amongst the poorer segments of the population but also in the ruling class; from the tenth century onward, Slav personal names appear among the noble urban families in the documents conserved in the historical archives of the oldest Dalmatian communes.[12] Croatian and Serbian aristocrats took up residence at Ragusa, Zara, and Spalato, in part because these cities had a clear interest in forming and improving ties with the Slav rulers of the interior.[13]

For the Dalmatian free cities, as Bruno Dudan shrewdly pointed out, the basic criterion for the acceptance of new inhabitants was their utility and loyalty to communal interests, and certainly not their nationality or language, elements that were of no political significance in the pre-modern era: 'The idea of the city, if not that of the family, decidedly outweighed any concept that had emerged of a greater national community. Control over ethnic elements in terms of nationality was secondary, since any threat they represented was secondary. More important was the man and his loyalty, to his family and his origin, to his city and its interests.'[14]

Between 1100 and the middle of the fifteenth century there was a degree of economic prosperity in the Dalmatian cities, inserted into the major Mediterranean and European commercial networks that were dominated by the Venetians and the Italian republics. The majestic churches and cathedrals, and the handsome palaces of Zara, Traù, Spalato, Sebenico (Šibenik), and Cattaro (Kotor), indicate the existence of significant levels of wealth in those cities. Economic growth created a need for labour and therefore immigration. The most skilled work-

---

12 Jirecek, 'L'eredità di Roma,' pp. 141–51.
13 On the multi-ethnic character of the Dalmatian urban classes in the medieval period see Krekić, *Dubrovnik, Italy and the Balkans in the Late Middle Ages*; Budak, 'Elites cittadine in Dalmazia nel Tre-Quattrocento,' pp. 163–80.
14 Bruno Dudan, 'Continuità nazionale negli ordinamenti municipali della Dalmazia,' in Bruno Dudan and Antonio Teja, *L'italianità della Dalmazia negli ordinamenti e statuti cittadini*, p. 47.

ers came from Italy, as certain professions (physicians, pharmacists, notaries, registrars, teachers) were often reserved for Italians from the peninsula.[15] Many Dalmatians also emigrated to Italy in the hope of improving their fortunes or for the purpose of commerce and study. Affinities of culture, language, and geographical proximity encouraged these flows of people.[16]

The inhabitants of the Dalmatian free cities realized that their own economic development was dependent on a constant strengthening of commercial relations with the Italian states, the point of contact with western Europe; these trade links led the cities of Dalmatia to acquire the natural products of the Balkan hinterland in order to sell them in the West and Italy, and to obtain in exchange manufactured goods for resale to the Slav populations of the interior.[17] All this favoured the spread of the Italian language throughout the Dalmatian coast, even in the period prior to the definitive establishment of Venetian rule over much of Dalmatia in the fifteenth century. The intensity of the trade links between the Italian peninsula and Dalmatia, the similarity of culture and lifestyle between the populations of the two territories, and the emigration of many Italians to the Dalmatian cities were the reasons for this diffusion. Italian was also the lingua franca of Mediterranean commerce, which obviously promoted its use all over the Mediterranean basin and its role in the Dalmatian society, economically dependent on Venice from the eleventh century onward.[18] Progressively, Italian, and the Venetian dialect in particular, and the Slav dialects became the languages spoken in the cities and on the islands of Dalmatia, while Dalmatian, from the thirteenth century on, gradually lost its importance and began to disappear.[19] In short the Dalmatian communes turned into Italo-Slav cities, characterized by a multilingualism

---

15 Krekić, 'Venezia e l'Adriatico,' pp. 51–85.
16 Spremić, 'La migrazione degli Slavi nell'Italia meridionale e in Sicilia alla fine del Medioevo,' pp. 3 et seq.
17 In this connection see the considerations of Brunelli, *Storia della città di Zara*, p. 553.
18 On the economic and commercial relations between Venice and the Dalmatian cities see Hocquet, *Il sale e la fortuna di Venezia*, pp. 49 et seq., 174 et seq. On the spread of the Italian language in the Mediterranean over the course of the Middle Ages see Silva, *Il Mediterraneo dall'Unità di Roma all'impero italiano*, pp. 96 et seq.; Volpe, *Il Medioevo*; 'Italiani fuori d'Italia fra XI e XVI secolo.'
19 On the spread of Venetian and Serbian and Croatian dialects in coastal and insular Dalmatia see Praga, 'Elementi neolatini nella parlata slava dell'insulario dalmato,' pp. 129–58.

that led the Dalmatians of the sea-coast to speak in Venetian and in Serbian and Croatian dialects and to write in Latin and Italian. In the central and northern parts of the Dalmatian coast a specific Croatian language developed, *čakavo* or Chakavian, which was characterized by the assimilation of a large number of Dalmatian and Italian words and came into widespread use.[20] At Ragusa and Cattaro, the proximity of the Serbs and Montenegrins favoured the spread of a *štokavo* or Shtokavian dialect, while Antivari (Bar) and Dulcigno (Ulcinj), other old Romance-speaking communes, saw the penetration of Albanian. It can be presumed that there was a phase in which Dalmatian and Italian vernacular coexisted, giving rise to a linguistic hybrid that mixed up Venetian idioms, words from old Dalmatian, and Slavic expressions[21] and was used in the private contracts of medieval Dalmatia; however, this hybrid was subsequently displaced by Venetian.

Between the tenth and eleventh century new figures emerged in the politics of Dalmatia. Weakened by internal strife, the young kingdom of Croatia, which had been established just inland of the Dalmatian coast, subjugating much of it, was absorbed by the powerful kingdom of Hungary between 1091 and 1097. Coloman (Koloman), king of Hungary, seized Zara, Traù, Spalato, Arbe, and Veglia between 1105 and 1108, and although the cities preserved their domestic autonomy and freedom to trade, they had to recognize Magyar sovereignty.[22] This marked the beginning of the Hungarian presence in Dalmatia, which was to last, with phases of greater and lesser fortune, until the fifteenth century.

Venice was the great adversary of Hungarian rule over Dalmatia for several centuries. The city of St. Mark had begun to play a leading role in the political and military affairs of the Adriatic in the eighth century when its fleet, as part of the Byzantine naval forces, had been a protagonist in Constantinople's wars against the Longobards and the Franks. Between the eighth and the tenth century the Byzantine grip on Venice started to slacken and eventually lost hold altogether, though there con-

---

20  Cronia, *Storia della letteratura serbo-croata*.
21  Brunelli, *Storia della città*, p. 577.
22  On the Hungarian presence in Dalmatia see Tombor, 'L'alleanza della Repubblica di Genova,' pp. 221–45; 'La formazione e lo sviluppo dell'autonomia comunale,' pp. 241–74; Praga, *Storia di Dalmazia*, p. 89 et seq.; Teke, 'L'Ungheria e l'Adriatico all'epoca del re Sigismondo,' pp. 141–9.

tinued to be strong commercial and cultural ties between the lagoon city and Constantinople. The growing lack of Byzantine interest in events in the Adriatic facilitated the assertion of Venice's political and military power in Dalmatia,[23] with the Venetians presenting themselves as the heirs and successors of the Byzantine empire, ready to take over its ancient role of protector of the Latin cities of the Adriatic. Anxious to gain control of various bases on the eastern coast of the Adriatic, along which passed the traditional route of ships headed for Constantinople and in search of raw materials, the Venetians had an autonomous presence in Dalmatia from the end of the tenth century. In this connection the naval expedition led by Doge Pietro II Orseolo, which resulted in the creation of strong political links between Venice and several Dalmatian cities, has taken on mythical proportions.[24] Faced with the growing problem of Croatian piracy, which was damaging the commercial interests of Venice and the Dalmatian cities, Doge Pietro Orseolo organized a naval expedition to Istria and Dalmatia in 1000, destroyed various Neretvan and Croatian bases, and established close relations of a political and military character between the Latin-Dalmatian communes and Venice. It was the beginning of a Venetian political presence in the eastern Adriatic that was to last for many centuries.

Thus the history of Dalmatia in the period from 1000 to the end of the fifteenth century was characterized by the struggle between Venice, Hungary, and the various Croatian and Serbian principalities of the hinterland (which were often walking a tightrope between subjection to Hungary and a substantial independence) for political hegemony in the region. The Dalmatian seafaring republics sought to maintain their independence and autonomy by turning the rivalry between these

---

23 For an analysis of the Dalmatian question in Venetian policy the reader is referred to Romanin, *Storia documentata di Venezia*; Cessi, *La Repubblica di Venezia e il problema adriatico*; *Storia della Repubblica di Venezia*; Praga, *Dalmazia*; Pederin, *Mletačka uprava, privreda i politika u Dalmaciji (1409–1797)*; Novak, *Povijest Splita*, 1 and 2; Bogović, *Katolička Crkva i pravoslavlije u Dalmaciji za mletačke vladavine*. Interesting material on Venetian rule in Dalmatia is to be found in the collections of Venetian documents published by the Academy of Sciences and Arts in Zagreb: *Monumenta spectantia historiam slavorum meridionalium*, vol. 6, *Commissiones et relationes venetae* (henceforth *Commissiones*), parts 1, 2 and 3 edited by Simeon Ljubić, parts 4, 5, 6, 7 and 8 edited by Grga Novak (Zagreb: Akademija Znanosti i Umjetnosti, 1876–).

24 On the Venetian expedition to Dalmatia in the year 1000 see Romanin, *Storia documentata di Venezia*, pp. 193 et seq.; Praga, *Dalmazia*, pp. 71 et seq.; Cessi, *La Repubblica di Venezia*, pp. 29 et seq.; Manfroni, *Storia della Marina italiana*, vol. 1, pp. 76 et seq.

powers to their own advantage. The Venetian political domination of coastal Dalmatia, often successfully opposed by the Hungarians and the Croatian and Serbian principalities, was fairly intermittent up until the early years of the fifteenth century, but the economic and commercial superiority of Venice in the region remained strong; the might of the Venetian navy and Venice's ability to strangle any excessively hostile city economically limited the freedom of action of the Dalmatian republics and Magyar policy. On top of this the Dalmatian communes were weakened by their fierce rivalry, which rendered any lasting policy of co-operation impossible, and by the small size of the territories controlled by these city-states, which often consisted of no more than an urban centre and a tiny area of surrounding countryside.

A determined opponent of Venetian hegemonic designs over Dalmatia throughout the medieval period was the city of Zara, which succumbed to Venetian rule several times between the twelfth and the fourteenth century and frequently rebelled against it. Zara had an important role as a mainland port of call on the Venetian sea lanes; whence the repeated Venetian efforts to establish a permanent dominance of the city, which frequently clashed with the highly independent spirit of its inhabitants, who were anxious to preserve their political and economic autonomy.

Driven out of Dalmatia following the defeat inflicted by Louis I the Great in the 1350s, and having survived the fierce struggle with Genoa, Venice succeeded in reconquering its positions in the eastern Adriatic and annexing the whole of the Dalmatian coastline, with the exception of Ragusa and its territory. Taking advantage of dynastic struggles in the kingdom of Hungary, Venice conquered Zara (1409) and Spalato (1420) and further strengthened its own bases in Dalmatia, subsequently annexing the mouth of the Narenta (Neretva) as well as Macarsca (Makarska), Budua (Budva), and Veglia (Krk). For Zara, Spalato, and the other cities of central and northern Dalmatia the definitive assertion of Venetian sovereignty in 1420 marked the beginning of a very long period of political subjection to the republic of St. Mark that was to last until the suppression of the independent Venetian state by Napoleon Bonaparte in 1797.

Although the Venetians maintained a constant presence for almost four centuries in Spalato, Sebenico, Zara, and Cattaro, the domination of Venice over much of Dalmatia was much more discontinuous and fragile, especially in the regions of the Dinaric hinterland and the Neretva shoreline; in fact, the appearance of the Ottoman state in the

The Balkans at the end of 1400

Balkans created difficulties for Venice in the Aegean Sea and Dalmatia.
The expansion of the Ottoman Turks became irresistible over the course
of the fifteenth century, and Serbia, Albania, Bosnia, and Herzegovina
were incorporated into the Turkish empire. It was only in Dalmatia that
the Ottoman advance began to falter, although it was not to be halted,
thanks to the dogged resistance of Venice.[25] Over the course of a long
series of wars spanning the fifteenth and sixteenth centuries, Venice
suffered heavy losses of territory in Greece, Albania, and Dalmatia itself but was able to use the strength of its navy, which was capable of
closing the Adriatic to Turkish ships and guaranteeing the continuity of

25  On the Ottoman invasion of Dalmatia in the fifteenth century and the Venetian reac-
    tion see De' Benvenuti, *Storia di Zara dal 1409 al 1797*, pp. 52 et seq.; Novak, *Prošlost
    Dalmacije*, I, pp. 187 et seq.

supplies to its dominions, to preserve an important part of its colonial empire in the Adriatic.[26]

The arrival of the Turks disrupted the social, economic, and ethnic structure of Dalmatia. From the second half of the fifteenth century until the beginning of the eighteenth century the Dalmatian territories became a borderland between the Christian west and the Islamic east, a field of battle and war, alternating with periods of unstable and uneasy peace. The Ottoman armies conquered much of inland Dalmatia between 1525 and 1540, wresting from Venice almost all of the hinterland of Zara and Spalato and taking the cities of Tenin (Knin), Obrovazzo (Obrovac) and Clissa (Klis). Spalato and Zara became small Venetian enclaves between Turkish dominions, with the border just a few kilometres from the urban centres and the coast.

The Turkish conquest impoverished the Dalmatian cities, depriving them of their surrounding rural areas and creating a situation of political instability that brought about a deep crisis in the Dalmatian economic system. The flight of the inhabitants from the territories conquered by the Turks resulted in the depopulation of the countryside and a slump in local agriculture. Economic activities like weaving, fishing, the production of salt, and the sea trade, which had flourished for centuries in Dalmatia, went into rapid decline. This was exacerbated by the Venetian policy of monopoly, which blocked an intensification of trade between the Dalmatian cities and the rest of Italy. It was the beginning of a period of economic stagnation in Dalmatia that was to last for hundreds of years.

The appearance of the Turkish threat altered the nature of the relations between the cities of Dalmatia and Venice. While over the course of the Middle Ages the republic of St. Mark had been a little-loved master, from the fifteenth century onward Turkish expansionism transformed Venice into a protective force, the only power capable of ensuring the freedom and survival of the Dalmatian peoples. The Venetians were no longer regarded as harsh oppressors of communal liberties but

---

26 A substantial proportion of the Venetian diplomatic records of the political relations between Venice and the Ottoman Empire in the sixteenth century has been published: Alberi, *Relazioni,* series 3, vols. 1, 2, and 3; for example, *Relazione dell'Impero Ottomano del clarissimo Giacomo Soranzo, ritornato ambasciatore da sultano Amurat li 8 novembre 1576,* in Alberi, *Relazioni,* vol. 2, pp. 193 et seq. On Turkey as a political and cultural problem for the Venetian ruling class see Preto, *Venezia e i Turchi.*

as benevolent defenders of the Dalmatian identity. As a consequence, Venetian rule in Dalmatia received greater local support.

Spalato and Zara, like the rest of Dalmatia, were badly shaken by the changes that the Turkish invasion brought to the Adriatic and Balkan regions.[27] The military security of Spalato, which had always been guaranteed by control of the encircling mountains, was profoundly undermined by the Turkish conquest in 1537 of Clissa (Klis), the gateway to the small area of flat country that surrounded the Dalmatian city[28]; for over a century the Turks maintained a military presence just two miles from Spalato.[29] The erosion of the countryside rendered Spalato's economic situation precarious for many decades, causing it great difficulties in the supply of food and making it highly dependent on Venice.

Zara, capital of the Venetian dominion in Dalmatia and seat of the high political and military command in the region, found itself in a similar condition. Zara was subjected to siege by the Turks several times, with a hinterland that remained a no man's land for centuries, a battlefield between Venetian and Ottoman soldiers and subjects.

The published Venetian documents allow us to make an accurate assessment of the living conditions and social structure of the cities of Dalmatia over the course of the sixteenth century. The overall picture is that of profound desolation and grave economic and social crisis. The sole exception was Ragusa (Dubrovnik), independent of Venice and paying tribute to Ottoman Turkey; its ability to act as a commercial intermediary between the Turks and Christian Europe brought it great prosperity in that period.[30] In comparison with wealthy Ragusa,

---

27  On the history of Spalato see Kečkemet, *Prošlost Splita*; Madirazza, *Storia e costituzione dei comuni dalmati*, pp. 163 et seq.; Novak, *Povijest Splita*, vols. 1 and 2; Devich, 'Documenti per la storia di Spalato'; Marcocchia, 'Lineamenti della storia di Spalato,' pp. 3–17; Selem, 'Tommaso Arcidiacono e la storia medievale di Spalato'; Cvitanic, *Pravno uredjenje splitske komune po statutu iz 1312 godine*, pp. 11–28; Paci, *La 'Scala' di Spalato*.

28  Alacevich, 'Il forte di Clissa ed il conte Nicolò Cindro,' pp. 1–5.

29  *Relatione fatta alla Serenissima Signoria della città di Spalato per il nob. Homo Alvise Loredan, Commissiones*, part 4, p. 227 et seq.; Paci, *La 'Scala' di Spalato*, pp. 31 et seq. A good history of the Jews of Spalato can be found in Kečkemet, *Židovi u povijesti Splita*. See too Kečkemet, 'Židovi u Splitu,' pp. 316–31.

30  On Ragusa see Tenenti, *Il prezzo del rischio*; Mitic, *Dubrovačka država u medjunarodnoj zajednici*; Krekić, *Dubrovnik, Italy and the Balkans*; Di Vittorio et al., *Ragusa (Dubrovnik) una Repubblica adriatica*.

which was the largest city in Dalmatia in the sixteenth and seventeenth centuries with 30 000 inhabitants, Venetian Dalmatia was depopulated and depressed. The Venetian documents of the mid-sixteenth century declare that Zara had 8100 inhabitants, Sebenico 6350, and Spalato just 2100.[31] The population of Dalmatia was in constant decline and growing poorer. At Zara and Spalato the nobles were very poor, having lost their estates in the hinterland following the Turkish conquests. The internal divisions in the various cities remained strong, marked by strife between the nobility and the common people, with the latter more favourable to Venetian rule.

Various nationalities coexisted in these centres, and there was a substantial bilingualism of Italian and Slav. In the eyes of the Venetian administrators Zara and Veglia stood out as places in which the Italian cultural and linguistic influence was stronger, inasmuch as the inhabitants – noted a Venetian official – 'are closer than the others to us, the nearer they come to the customs of Italy.'[32] At Spalato and in central Dalmatia, on the other hand, the Slav presence was more substantial; according to Giovanni Battista Giustiniano, 'the customs of Spalato are all in the Slav tradition ... It is true that the citizens all speak lingua franca [Italian], and some dress in the Italian manner; but the women do not speak anything but their mother tongue.'[33]

Zara had a more markedly Italian character, partly because as capital of the province it attracted many Italians from the Veneto and Venetian Lombardy.[34] However, there was also a strong influx of Slav peoples into the city from the inland regions, who were fleeing the Turks and came to constitute part of the less affluent classes. Quite a few of these fugitives were 'schismatics,' that is, Serbs and Vlachs of the Orthodox faith, to whom the Venetian government conceded certain rights in the religious field.[35] It was at this time that Serbian peoples began to make their way into northern Dalmatia.

On the political plane the long wars between Venice, Turkey, and

---

31  *Relatione de noi Michiel Bon e Gasparo Erizzo già sindici in Dalmazia* (MDLIX), *Commissiones*, III, pp. 112–36.

32  *Itinerario di Giovanni Battista Giustiniano maggio 1553*, *Commissiones*, II, p. 262.

33  Ibid., p. 215.

34  On the history of Zara in the Venetian period see De Benvenuti, *Storia di Zara*; Raukar et al., *Zadar pod Mletačkom upravom 1409–1797*.

35  De Benvenuti, *Storia di Zara*, pp. 59, 107, 216. On the religious problem in Dalmatia in the seventeenth and eighteenth centuries see Bogović, *Katolička Crkva*.

Austria during the course of the seventeenth century and the early eighteenth century (the Venetian-Turkish war over Candia (Crete) from 1645 to 1669; the Venetian participation in the hostilities between Austria, Poland, and Turkey that led to the Treaty of Carlowitz in 1699; and the 1714–18 war),[36] caused by the struggle between the Habsburgs and the Ottomans for hegemony in the Danubian region and the Turkish attempts to drive the Venetians out of the Aegean Sea, marked the beginning of the decline of the Ottoman Porte and of the Venetian republic itself. On the other hand, these wars saw the rise of a new great power in the Balkans and the Adriatic, the Habsburg state, which conquered Hungary, Danubian Croatia, and Transylvania and began to consolidate its possessions in the Adriatic, giving a new value to the ports of Trieste and Fiume on the commercial and maritime plane.

The positive consequence for Dalmatia was the Venetian conquest of large areas of the hinterland. The long war over Crete, which had begun brilliantly for the Venetians on the Dalmatian front, had left the borders of Venetian Dalmatia almost unchanged with respect to those drawn after Lepanto, apart from the annexation of Clissa. The border treaty of 1671 followed the confines of the so-called Acquisto Vecchio (Old Acquisition), that is, the territories that had been under Venetian control for centuries, with minor adjustments: it comprised all the Dalmatian islands to the north of Curzola (Korčula), and the cities of Zara, Sebenico, Traù, Spalato, Almissa (Omiš), Cattaro, and Perasto (Perast), all with an extremely limited hinterland; inland Dalmatia and the long stretch of coast around Makarska remained in Turkish hands, separating the Venetian dominions from the northern boundary of the republic of Ragusa for several tens of kilometres. It was only with the Venetian involvement in the Austro-Turkish wars fought between the end of the seventeenth century and the beginning of the eighteenth century that the territorial set-up of Dalmatia changed radically. While the treaties of Carlowitz (Sremski Karlovci) (1699) and Passarowitz (Požarevac) (1718) marked the definitive decline of the Venetian presence in the eastern Mediterranean, they also tripled the size of the Venetian territory in Dalmatia; the whole of inland Dalmatia as far as the geographic

---

36 On the Venetian-Turkish wars in Dalmatia in the seventeenth and eighteenth century see Jacov, 'Le guerre veneto-turco del XVII secolo in Dalmazia'; Praga, *Dalmazia*, pp. 196 et seq.; Romanin, *Storia documentata di Venezia*, vol. 7, pp. 243 et seq., vol. 8, pp. 28 et seq.

frontiers of the Dinaric Alps, with the centres of Benkovac, Knin, Dernis (Drniš), Signi (Sinj), and Imoschi (Imotski), came under Venetian control, as did the coastline to the south of Omiš.

With the peace treaty of Passarowitz a new Dalmatia took on shape and substance, very different on the ethnic, cultural, and social plane from the country that had been tied politically and/or economically to Venice for centuries. The borders that the Venetian negotiators and soldiers had sought to establish were the result of the quest for military and strategic security. There were no concerns about the national identity of the subjects acquired because, as was the Venetian tradition, the only thing that mattered was the utility of the new territories and their inhabitants. It was no accident that since the sixteenth century the Venetian government had tried to settle the depopulated regions of Istria and Dalmatia with Serbs, Croatians and Vlachs fleeing Ottoman rule.[37]

These Venetian policies contributed to the creation of a new ethnonational and socio-economic balance in Dalmatia. Finally two profoundly different historical and cultural realities came into contact and began to mingle with a previously unknown intensity: the realities of the coastal cities, inhabited by mixed Italian and Slav populations with a tradition of municipal and urban civilization quite distinct from those of other Danubian and Balkan peoples; and the realities of the barren lands of the interior, ruled by the Turks for almost two centuries and inhabited by shepherds and farmers who were either Slavs or Slavicized Vlachs (the so-called Morlachs), remote from and alien to the maritime culture of the coast. There was a definitive shift in the demographic balance from the eighteenth century onward. While the population of Venetian Dalmatia was 50 000 in 1650, it had risen to 108 090 by 1718 and reached the level of 288 320 by the end of the eighteenth century. It was the rural Slavic-speaking population that grew out of all proportion. Certainly, we can go along with Giuseppe Praga to some extent when he claims: 'The addition of the newly acquired populations and the transplant of the Morlachs resulted in an ever increasing imbalance in favor of the Slav majority, but it was still the Italian cities, reinvigorated by a notable influx of industrialists, professionals, and craftsmen, especially from Bergamo, Romagna, and the Marche, that de facto

---

37  Nicolich, 'Colonie di slavi di Dalmazia nell'Istria,' pp. 126–36.

and de jure represented, controlled, and managed the whole life of the province.'[38]

Nevertheless it is a fact that the new Dalmatia molded by Venice as a result of the wars against the Turks was a profoundly different social and national reality from the Dalmatia of the previous centuries. It now had a marked Slav character. Simply placing the ancient Italo-Slav cities of the coast and the inland territories under a single government considerably facilitated the progressive Slavicization of the urban societies of the coast, which was completed over the following decades under the impetus of flows of immigrants and through intensification of relations with the peoples of the hinterland.

After 1718 the Venetian government found itself ruling a territory that for centuries had been chiefly a battlefield for armies and bands. It tried to lay the foundations for gradual economic development of the province by building some roads and organizing its new dominions on the juridical and administrative level. Notwithstanding these efforts, however, the overall picture in Dalmatia remained that of a poor and backward territory where the rapid demographic growth posed serious problems for the sustenance of the population. Yet it should be noted that in the eighteenth century Venetian Dalmatia was the most developed and advanced region of the Balkans on the cultural and political plane. Even in the darkest periods of the wars and outbreaks of plague, an indigenous cultural activity had continued to exist in the urban centres, and it took on new vigour in the eighteenth century. Thanks to Venetian and Italian culture the Dalmatians were in touch with the intellectual currents that were emerging in Europe. Several bilingual or Italian-speaking Dalmatian intellectuals operated at Spalato and Zara – Rados Antonio Michieli Vitturi, Leonardo Grussevich, and Girolamo Bajamonti – who demonstrated the cultural vitality of Dalmatian society, however poverty stricken it was. They initiated the renewal of traditional Dalmatian municipal culture by bringing it into contact with the new ideas of the Enlightenment and studying the social problems of Dalmatia; for instance, the improvement of agriculture or ways of fostering economic growth in the region.[39] The cultural and national

---

38  Praga, *Dalmazia*, p. 213. On eighteenth-century Dalmatia see too Wolff, *Venice and the Slavs*; Paladini, *Un caos'che spaventa*.

39  On the Enlightenment in Dalmatia see Novak, *Povijest Splita*, II, pp. 320–5; Znanstveni Skup, *Splitski Polihister. Julije Bajamonti* (Split: Književni Krug, 1996);

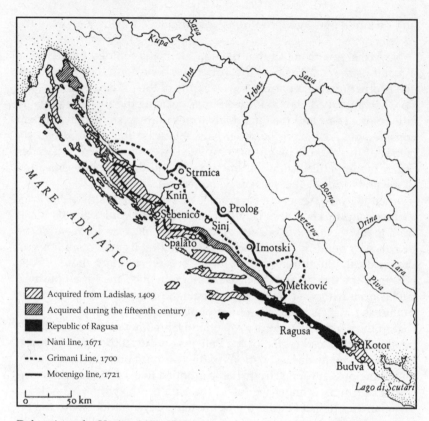

Dalmatia under Venice, 1409–1797

identity of these writers was founded on the concept of a 'Dalmatian nation,' distinct from the Italian world as well as from the Slav, Croatian or Serbian worlds. The idea of a Dalmatian nationality effortlessly integrated and reconciled Adriatic Slavism and Italian spirit, making it possible to explain and justify on the intellectual and political plane the multi-ethnic and multilingual nature of Dalmatian urban society,

Tamborra, 'Problema sociale e rapporto città-campagna in Dalmazia alla fine del sec. XVIII,' pp. 3–13; Venturi, *Settecento riformatore*, vol. 5, part 2, pp. 347 et seq.; Duplancić, 'Dopune zivotopisu i bibliografiji Julija Bajamontija,' pp. 157 et seq.; Cella, 'Studi, pregiudizi e polemiche della fine del '700,' pp. 73–85; Foretić, 'L'uomo dell'illuminismo in Dalmazia con particolare riferimento a Dubrovnik,' pp. 61 et seq.; Pantić, 'Illuminismo a Ragusa nel Settecento,' pp. 41–51.

the product of civic communities that had existed for over a thousand years.[40]

It was from this markedly Dalmatian cultural tradition, which was bilingual, municipalist, and particularist, and yet capable of absorbing influences coming from Italy, the west, and the Germanic and Slav worlds, that the Dalmatian autonomist liberalism of Antonio Bajamonti and Luigi Lapenna developed in the political sphere over the course of the nineteenth century.

## 1.2.  The Habsburgs in Dalmatia

At the end of the fifteenth century, owing to the rise of Habsburg expansionist aims toward Italy and the Adriatic, a political and economic rivalry had emerged between the republic of Venice and the Austrian state, triggering numerous border wars. The Venetian state had proved incapable of establishing secure political boundaries from a strategic viewpoint; its attempts to win control of the Isonzo, the Julian Alps, and part of the Italian Tyrol in the second half of the fifteenth century and at the beginning of the sixteenth century had come to naught and had left the republic of Venice in a position of great military weakness with respect to the Habsburg states of Spain and Austria. Throughout the sixteenth and seventeenth centuries Venice's great naval power and economic prosperity, which permitted the recruitment of large armies, allowed it to maintain hegemony in the Adriatic and guarantee its security. However, Venice's economic and political enfeeblement following the numerous wars with the Turks facilitated the increase in Habsburg influence in the Adriatic. The conquest of Hungary, Croatia, and Transylvania under the leadership of Eugene of Savoy[41] at the end of the seventeenth century transformed the Austrian state into the dominant power of Danubian Europe and reawakened interest in the problems of the Adriatic. After all, Hungary had ruled Dalmatia and Bosnia for centuries, and the Habsburgs presented themselves as heirs to that

---

40  With regard to the existence of the idea of Dalmatian nationality in Dalmatian writers: Vrandečić, *Dalmatinski autonomistički pokret u XIX stoljeću*, pp. 25 et seq.; 'What Did the Merchant's Son Francis of Assisi Say to Thomas?'; Zorić, 'Marco Casotti e il romanticismo in Dalmazia,' pp. 201–3; 'Romantički pisci u Dalmaciji na talijanskom jeziku,' pp. 339 et seq.

41  On the figure of Eugene of Savoy see Srbik, *Aus Österreichs Vergangenheit von Prinz Eugen zu Franz Joseph,* pp. 7 et seq.

political and state tradition. Precise signals of the Austrian determination to tolerate Venetian political and commercial hegemony in the Adriatic no longer were the unilateral Habsburg proclamation that navigation in the Adriatic Sea was 'safe and free,' with the consequent violation of the Venetian ban on free shipping trade (1717), and the creation of free ports at Trieste and Fiume (1719).[42]

The eighteenth century saw the progressive decline of the Venetian state, unable to reshape itself internally and find new economic vitality. The French invasion of Italy in 1796 laid bare Venice's weakness. Venetian neutrality was a poor fig leaf for its military impotence and was very soon made to look ridiculous by the arrogant and aggressive policy of republican France. The French government – anxious to put an end to a war with Austria that had gone on for too long and to gain control of important Habsburg territories like Lombardy and Austrian Flanders – decided to offer to the Habsburgs the Venetian Istria, Dalmatia, and much of the Venetian mainland between the Oglio River, the Po River, and the Austrian borders as recompense; this was the substance of the Austro-French preliminaries to peace signed at Leoben on 18 April 1797. The territorial exchanges were later confirmed by the peace treaty signed at Campo Formio on 25 October 1797, which also ceded the city of Venice to Austria.[43]

Despite the efforts of the Venetian administration to improve the conditions of life in the province, eighteenth-century Dalmatia was a poor and under-developed region on the economic level. This made it easier for the Habsburgs to consolidate their rule in Dalmatia, which met with no resistance from the local population.[44] Habsburg sway was interrupted by a brief period of French control, only to be re-established after the fall of Napoleon I. The republic of Ragusa also lost its independence in the Napoleonic period and, after a short period of French rule, was annexed by the Austrians.[45]

---

42 Tamaro, *Storia di Trieste*, vol. 2; Cova, *Commercio e navigazione a Trieste*, pp. 27–150.
43 On the subject of the end of Venetian rule in Dalmatia and the treaties of Leoben and Campo Formio: Romanin, *Storia documentata di Venezia*, X, pp. 51 et seq.; Cessi, *Campoformido*; Ghisalberti, *Da Campoformido a Osimo*, pp. 15–28.
44 On the advent of Austrian rule in Dalmatia and the attitude of the local populations: Erber, 'Storia della Dalmazia dal 1797 al 1814'; Bauer, *Drei Leopardenköpfe in Gold*, pp. 134 et seq.; Novak, *Prošlost Dalmacije*, II, pp. 265 et seq.
45 On French rule in Dalmatia at the beginning of the nineteenth century: Erber, 'Storia della Dalmazia'; Novak, *Prošlost Dalmacije*, II.

The annexation by Austria seemed to open up new prospects for Dalmatia, uniting the province to a great and vast empire and thus linking it no longer to just the Italian peninsula, but also to Danubian and Germanic Europe. A region lacking capital and with a surplus of population, Dalmatia ought to have benefited greatly from inclusion in the Habsburg realm, which provided a possible outlet for emigration and a motor for revival of the economy. In reality, for many decades the Austrian government seemed to show no particular interest in far-off Dalmatia.[46] The Dalmatian region was certainly important to the Habsburg ruling class in strategic terms, as was demonstrated by the fact that for many years the governors of this province were military men. With its control Austria became the dominant maritime power in the Adriatic and came into possession of a base for a possible expansion into the Turkish territories (Bosnia-Herzegovina, Serbia and Montenegro, and Albania) bordering on Dalmatia. However, for the whole of the first half of the nineteenth century Vienna appeared to have no aims of expansion into the Balkans. Clemens Metternich and the Habsburg rulers were interested chiefly in the maintenance of Austrian hegemony in Italy and Germany and considered the annexation of poor and backward territories in the Balkans of little value. It is no accident that the central plank of Metternich's Balkans policy was the preservation of the political and territorial status quo and the development of peaceful and friendly relations with the Turkish empire, now a power in decline and therefore no longer a dangerous and threatening neighbour.[47]

This lack of political interest in the Balkans led to a static and conservative approach to government in Dalmatia, careful not to upset the traditional social and economic order. For several decades there were no incisive initiatives of administration and investment that would have helped to bring about strong economic growth in Dalmatia. The

---

46 On the Austrian administration in Dalmatia in the first half of the nineteenth century: Bauer, *Drei Leopardenköpfe*, pp. 134 et seq.; Novak, *Prošlost Dalmacije*, II, pp. 265 et seq.; Kratzik, *Die nationalen Auseinandersetzungen in Dalmatien*, pp. 7 et seq.

47 On Austrian Balkan policy in the first half of the nineteenth century and the lines of Metternich's foreign policy: Beer, *Die orientalische Politik Oesterreichs seit 1774*; Bridge, 'Österreich(-Ungarn) unter den Grossmächten,' pp. 196 et seq.; Vocelka, 'Das osmaniche Reich und die Habsburgermonarchie 1848–1918,' pp. 247–55; Srbik, *Metternich; Deutsche Einheit*: pp. 217 et seq.; Schroeder, 'Metternich Studies since 1925,' pp. 237 et seq.; *Metternich's Diplomacy at Its Zenith 1820–1823*.

only significant improvement was a certain resurgence of shipping activity, stimulated by the initiatives that the entrepreneurs of Trieste undertook to turn the city into a major commercial port and the Austrian merchant navy into a leading player in Mediterranean trade.[48] Under the impetus of the strengthening of Trieste's economic role in the Adriatic, not just the commercial relations but also the cultural and social relations between the city and Dalmatia intensified, while Venice moved progressively toward a lasting decline. Trieste, economic and cultural capital of the eastern Adriatic, and Vienna, centre of the Habsburg empire, attracted many Dalmatians and became indispensable points of reference for the political and cultural life of Dalmatia over the course of the nineteenth century.

Spalato experienced constant, even if fairly slow, demographic growth;[49] the city began to draw people over the course of the eighteenth century, attaining a population of around 12 000 in the second half of the nineteenth century. It remained a place inhabited by populations of different languages and religions: Italians, Croatians, and Serbs; Catholics, Jews, and Orthodox. The long rule of Venice had left a deep mark on the city's life, making the Veneto dialect the most widely spoken tongue among its citizens. On the urbanistic plane the city was divided into two precise and distinct parts: the old city, which was ringed by Venetian walls, built on the remains of Diocletian's palace, and inhabited by aristocrats, the middle class, artisans, and traders, and in which the element of Italian origin or Italian speakers was predominant (although not exclusive as many bilingual Slavs were also present); and the villages (Luciaz, Manuš, Pozzobon, and Borgo Grande) that had grown up outside the walls, which were inhabited by Slavs.[50]

Zara too, confirmed in its role of capital of the province by the Austrian rulers, developed into a multi-ethnic city.[51] Here, however, the Italian and Italian-speaking element was stronger than in Spalato, making

---

48  In connection with Trieste and its economic development in the eighteenth and nineteenth centuries: Tamaro, *Storia di Trieste*, II, pp. 133 et seq.; Cusin, *Appunti alla storia di Trieste*, pp. 177 et seq.; Apih, Sapelli, and Guagnini, *Trieste*; Cervani, *La borghesia triestina nell'età del Risorgimento; Momenti di storia e problemi di storiografia giuliana*; Coons, *Steamships, Statesmen and Bureaucrats*.

49  Paci, *La 'Scala' di Spalato*, pp. 145–6.

50  Ganza-Aras, 'Prilog upoznavanju društva splitskog kraja u doba pohrvacenja splitske opcine,' p. 180. On nineteenth-century Spalato: Monzali, 'Dalmati o Italiani?' pp. 419 et seq.

51  On Zara in the nineteenth century: De' Benvenuti, *Storia di Zara dal 1797 al 1918*; Monzali, 'Oscar Randi scrittore di storia dalmata,' pp. 648–50.

up the greater part of the population until World War II, with a percentage ranging from 60 to 90 percent. This Italian majority coexisted with various national groups, in particular Croatians and Serbs, whose numbers were continually fed by a solidly Slav hinterland. A significant role in the life of the city was also played by the Albanian population of Borgo Erizzo (Arbanasi),[52] which had emigrated to Zara at the beginning of the eighteenth century.

The Italian population in Dalmatia had variegated and diverse ethnic origins and was dominated by a markedly particularistic and provincial spirit that led it to show little interest in political developments on the Italian peninsula until the end of the nineteenth century. A minority element in a region like Austrian Dalmatia, which was inhabited chiefly by Slav peoples, the Italian population was concentrated in the cities on the coast and the islands, where it constituted an important part of the urban scene. Fishermen, craftsmen, merchants, public officials, lawyers, sailors, and landowners were the principal components of the Dalmatian Italian minority. They were joined by a constant influx of Italians from the peninsula that remained strong throughout the nineteenth century. All of this and the influence of Italian culture on the Slav peoples of the coastal region explained the persistence of the Italo-Slav character of the Dalmatian cities even after the end of Venetian rule.

An important contribution to this was made by the bilingual Slav Dalmatians, a social and national group with confused and contradictory characteristics. Italian and Croat or Serb languages and cultures coexisted among these people, usually resident in the urban centres, without great tensions for the whole of the nineteenth century. Faithful to their own local identity, they remained for a long time untouched by the various national ideologies that emerged in the Balkan and Adriatic world over the course of that century. Rather than Croatian, Serbian or Italian, they felt themselves to be Dalmatian, proud of being Adriatic Slavs but also determined defenders of the maintenance of an important role for the Italian language in Dalmatian society, for they considered it part of their own tradition, as well as a useful economic tool. The Italian element and the bilingual Slav element were the social and ethnic base from which sprang Dalmatian autonomist liberalism, the main political movement of the Italian Dalmatians between the second half of the nineteenth century and World War I.

---

52 On the Albanians of Borgo Erizzo: Erber, 'La colonia albanese di Borgo Erizzo presso Zara'; Maserati, 'Attività nazionali della comunità di Borgo Erizzo,' pp. 117–38.

## 1.3. The Attitude of Italian Dalmatians to the Political Upheavals of 1848–49

A first and partial foreshadowing of the political alignments that were to characterize Dalmatia in the second half of the nineteenth century emerged over the course of the crisis of 1848–9. The revolutions that took place in the Habsburg empire during 1848 and 1849[53] permitted the first open manifestation of the cultural tendencies that existed in Dalmatia. Owing to its brevity, this did not allow the rise of true political parties, but it did herald the positions that would be the source of conflict within Dalmatian society between 1859 and 1914.

Events that had an echo in Dalmatia included the end of the absolute state in March 1848; the rebirth of the independent republic of Venice through the efforts of the liberals led by Daniele Manin; the creation of an autonomous Hungarian government and an Austrian parliament which included Dalmatian residents; the Austro-Piedmontese war; and the outbreak of struggles between Hungarian National liberals and German, Croatian, and Serbian conservative loyalists, led by Alfred Windischgraetz and Josip Jelačić (Jellachich), with the final defeat of the Hungarians by czarist troops.[54] The internal disorder of those years per-

---

53 On the political events in the Habsburg Empire and the Sardinian-Austrian wars in 1848–9: Kiszling, *Die Revolution im Kaisertum Österreich 1848–49*, with essays by J. Diakow, M. Ehnl, G. Hubka, and E. Steinitz, 2 vols.; Macartney, *The Habsburg Empire*; Dudan, *La monarchia degli Asburgo*, vol. 1, pp. 236 et seq.; Kann, *History of the Habsburg Empire: 1526–1918*; Srbik, *Deutsche Einheit*, II, p. 7 et seq.; Hantsch, *Die Geschichte Österreichs*, vol. 2, pp. 337 et seq.; Schiffrer, *Le origini dell'irredentismo triestino*, pp. 74 et seq.; Lutz, *Zwischen Habsburg und Preussen*; Sked, *The Decline and Fall of the Habsburg Empire*; Lippert, *Felix Fürst zu Schwarzenberg*; Bianchi, *Storia documentata della diplomazia europea in Italia*, vols. 5 and 6; Spellanzon and Di Nolfo, *Storia del Risorgimento*, vols. 3, 4, 5, 6.

54 Regarding Dalmatian politics in 1848–9: Novak, *Prošlost Dalmacije*, II, pp. 334 et seq.; *Povijest Splita*, pp. 107 et seq.; Praga, *Dalmazia*, p. 239 et seq.; Clewing, *Staatlichkeit und nationale Identitätsbildung*; Vrandečić, *Dalmatinski autonomistički pokret u XIX stoljeću*, pp. 85 et seq.; Camizzi, 'La Dalmazia e il Risorgimento italiano (1815–1866),' pp. 193 et seq.; Praga and Zink, 'Documenti del 1848–49 a Zara e in Dalmazia'; Petrović, 'Il problema dell'Unione della Dalmazia con la Croazia nel 1848,' pp. 137 et seq. Of great interest is the collection of documents published by Obad, *Dalmacija revolucionarne 1848/49 Godine*. On the absence of irredentist tendencies in the Italians of Dalmatia in those years: Salvemini and Maranelli, 'La questione dell'Adriatico,' in Salvemini, *Dalla guerra mondiale alla dittatura (1916–1925)*, pp. 285 et seq., especially pp. 353–4.

mitted the brief emergence of a political life in coastal Dalmatia, which found partial expression in a number of local newspapers.[55] Among the middle class and aristocrats of the coastal cities there were many who rejoiced at the liberal shift of the Habsburg empire, seeing the establishment of a constitutional and parliamentary political system as a positive development. However, a deep split emerged within nascent Dalmatian liberalism due to the emergence of the national question. After decades of cultural and linguistic revival stimulated by the movement of Illyrism, in 1848 and 1849 pan-Croatian nationalism[56] began to take on a complete form in Zagreb and northern Croatia, finding its standard bearer in the ban, Josip Jelačić.[57] In addition to the struggle against Magyar hegemony, one of the most important of the Croatian demands, which was put forward by the National Assembly at Zagreb in a public manifesto on 25 March 1848, was the union of Dalmatia with the rest of the Croatian lands, within an administrative entity belonging to the Habsburg empire that would have linked Croatia, Slavonia, Dalmatia, Fiume, and the Military Frontier.

These Croatian demands prompted contrasting reactions in Dalmatia: they were supported by some Dalmatians who believed that the region's future lay in an ever closer union with the other Slav lands of the Habsburg south; they were opposed by many others who were hostile to such an aim and eager to maintain the separation of Dalmatia and Croatia.

A group of Dalmatian students living in Vienna – headed by Augusto Antonio Grubissich from Spalato, who was director of the Italian Church in Vienna, and some of the future leaders of Dalmatian autonomism like Luigi Lapenna, Giacomo Ghiglianovich, and Girolamo Alesani – protested against the requests for the unification of Dalmatia

---

55 Kasandric, *Il giornalismo dalmato dal 1848 al 1860*.
56 On the origins of the Croatian national movement and its various political ideologies in the middle of the nineteenth century: Tamborra, *L'Europa centro-orientale nei secoli XIX e XX (1800–1920)*, part 2, pp. 472 et seq.; Gross, *Die Anfänge des modernes Kroatien*; Jelavich, 'The Croatian Problem in the Habsburg Empire in the Nineteenth Century,' pp. 83–115; Krizman, 'The Croatians in the Habsburg Monarchy in the Nineteenth Century,' vol. 3, pp. 116–158; Rothenberg, 'Jelačić, the Croatian Military Border, and the Intervention against Hungary in 1848,' vol. 1, pp. 45 et seq.; Stančić, 'Das Jahr 1848 in Kroatien,' pp. 103–28; Sked, 'Jelačić in the Summer of 1848,' pp. 129–64; Suppan, 'Die Kroaten,' vol. 3, part 1, in particular pp. 714 et seq.; Salvi, *Il movimento nazionale*.
57 Görlitz, *Jelačić Symbol für Kroatien*.

with Croatia and Slavonia that had been advanced by a Croatian deputation to the Austrian government, and they presented a declaration to
the emperor in which they contested the right of Croatian politicians
to speak in the name of Dalmatia.[58] This sparked a debate in the Dalmatian newspapers that was to last until the following year, when the
reassertion of absolutism in Austria essentially put an end to any freedom of the press and to any openly pluralistic political action.

The municipality of Spalato, headed in those years by the mayor
Leonardo Dudan, played a leading role among those who were opposed to any plan for union between Dalmatia and Croatia. When Josip
Jelačić, ban of Croatia, was appointed governor of Dalmatia in December 1848, the municipal assembly of Spalato protested publicly against
this act, which seemed to presage Dalmatia's unification with Croatia.
In a public petition of 28 December, the municipality of Spalato, after
pointing out that Dalmatia, unlike Croatia, was a mixed nation, 'a Slav-
Italian nation,' asked that no decision be taken on union without consulting the Dalmatian municipal assemblies and that the rights of the
Dalmatians be protected.[59]

Any plans for Croatian-Dalmatian unification soon foundered, notwithstanding the appointment of Jelačić. On December 11, the Dalmatian representatives in the Austrian parliament (the so-called Diet
of Kremsier) had protested against Jelačić's appointment as governor
and declared their opposition to any possible union with Croatia.[60] The
constitution granted by the new Habsburg emperor Francis Joseph in
March 1849 decided nothing in this regard, limiting itself to providing in Article 73 for the possibility of future negotiations between the
Croatian diet and the Dalmatian parliamentary representatives over
union between Croatia-Slavonia and Dalmatia, but reserving the final
decision on the matter for the Austrian government. The suspension
of the constitution and the reintroduction of absolute rule blocked any
possible application of this article, maintaining the separation between
Dalmatia, part of Austria, and Croatia, included in the kingdom of
Hungary.[61]

The political and military developments in Italy during 1848 and

---

58   Kasandric, *Il giornalismo dalmato.*
59   Novak, *Povijest Splita*, vol. 3, p. 142.
60   Bauer, *Drei Leopardenköpfe in Gold*, p. 163; Praga, *Dalmazia*, cit., p. 245.
61   Bauer, *Drei Leopardenköpfe in Gold*, pp. 160–4.

1849, and in particular the brief resurrection of the Venetian Republic, had few direct political consequences on Dalmatia.[62]

It has to be stressed that in the years 1848 and 1849, which were the first moments of strong political expression of the Italian national liberal movement involving a large part of the peninsula, there was no thorough debate over the territorial limits that the Italian national revolution should have to the north and the east. It was only men from the Adriatic regions (Veneto, Friuli, and the Marche) who attempted to raise the question, although the answers they came up with were highly discordant.

The liberal uprising of 1848 in Venice had a strongly municipalist character. Many Venetians were more interested in getting rid of the Austrians in order to restore the republic of Venice than in founding a unified Italian state in the future – a republic of Venice that would perhaps have been able to get back some of its former provinces, such as Venetian Istria and Dalmatia. In March, appeals were published in Venice calling for the reconstitution of the republic of St. Mark and inviting the Venetians' Istrian and Dalmatian brothers to take part in the rebirth of the 'Queen of the Adriatic Sea.'[63] It is no coincidence that in the spring of 1848 there were attempts by the Venetian government to stir up insurrections in Istria and Dalmatia, with the aim of weakening and dividing the military forces of the Habsburgs.[64] However, these efforts were in vain. No revolt against the Austrians broke out in Dalmatia: as Vincenzo Marchesi has pointed out: 'If there were feelings of sympathy for the Italian cause in Dalmatia, ... the majority of the Slav population was devoted to the emperor.'[65] Many Dalmatians (it suffices

---

62 On the republic of Venice in 1848–9: Marchesi, *Storia documentata della Rivoluzione*; Spellanzon and Di Nolfo, *Storia del Risorgimento*, vols. 3, 4, 5, 6; Tommaseo, *Venezia negli anni 1848 e 1849*; Pierazzi (Pirjevec), 'Studi sui rapporti italo-jugoslavi (1848–49),' pp. 181–249; Pirjevec, *Niccolò Tommaseo tra Italia e Slavia*, pp. 114 et seq.; Ciampini, *Vita di Niccolò Tommaseo*; Sanzin, *Federico Seismit Doda nel Risorgimento*); Silva, *Il 1848*; Ginsborg, *Daniele Manin and the Venetian Revolution of 1848–49*.

63 'Invito all'Istria e alla Dalmazia ad unirsi a Venezia,' 29 March 1848, in Diritto d'Italia, doc. 163. See too the appeal by Cristoforo Negri to the Istrians and Dalmatians to send representatives to the legislative councils of the republic of Venice, dated 2 April 1848, reproduced in Diritto d'Italia, doc. 169.

64 Marchesi, *Storia documentata della Rivoluzione*, pp. 160–1. Tommaseo was also convinced that it would be easy to organize pro-Venetian revolts in the eastern Adriatic: Tommaseo, *Venezia*, pp. 105–7.

65 Marchesi, *Storia documentata della Rivoluzione*, p. 209.

to mention Tommaseo and Federico Seismit Doda) participated in the Venetian revolution of 1848–9; but often those who had moved permanently to Italy and the Veneto fought for the freedom of Venice and Italy, not for the union of Dalmatia with a future Italian nation state.

Among the Italian liberals who took an interest in the Adriatic question in 1848, it is worth mentioning Pacifico Valussi and Terenzio Mamiani in particular. The writer Pacifico Valussi was a Friulian who had lived for a long time in Trieste, contributing to the local newspaper *La Favilla*, which was the principal mouthpiece of pre-1848 Italian liberalism in Trieste, and he therefore had a clear understanding of the ethnic make-up and the economic and political problems of the regions of Venezia Giulia and Dalmatia. In 1848 and 1849 he set out the idea that, since Italy was not strong enough to take over the Italian cities of the eastern Adriatic, it would be opportune to create a neutral Italo-Slav state, which would comprise Trieste, Istria, and Dalmatia and constitute, like Switzerland and Belgium, a political buffer between great nation states.[66]

Terenzio Mamiani was an intellectual from Pesaro who was at first close to Giuseppe Mazzini and then adopted a moderate liberal stand;[67] he served for several months as papal prime minister. Mamiani also paid some attention to the problem of the new Italy's future eastern border. From 1848 onward he put forward arguments grounded in a realistic analysis of the political and military needs of a future Italian state that, in the 1860s, would come to be shared and supported by much of the liberal political world. In several open letters sent to the newspapers *Lega Italiana* and *Epoca* in March and April 1848, at the moment when the war between the Sardinian-Piedmontese army and the Austrians was at its height, Mamiani pointed out that the Julian Alps had marked the borders of Italy ever since the time of Augustus, and he invited Charles Albert of Savoy to occupy Trieste and Istria and make the Julian Alps into 'the inexpugnable wall of Italy.'[68] In

---

66  On Valussi's thinking about the Adriatic in 1848–49: Schiffrer, *Le origini dell'irredentismo triestino*, pp. 58–63; Tamborra, *Cavour e i Balcani*, pp. 53–4.

67  On the figure of Terenzio Mamiani, one of the most important political thinkers of the national liberalism of the Risorgimento, there is a fine study by Pincherle, *Moderatismo politico e riforma religiosa in Terenzio Mamiani*.

68  'Terenzio Mamiani al direttore della "Lega Italiana,"' 28 March 1848, in Diritto d'Italia, doc. 161. See too 'Mamiani ai signori direttori dell''Epoca," 11 April 1848, in Mamiani, *Scritti politici*, pp. 263–5.

Mamiani's view, therefore, Italy should aim to expand to its Alpine geographical confines, occupying Istria, which was considered indispensable to the defence of the peninsula from foreigners. On the other hand, it was necessary to renounce territorial designs on Dalmatia, an Italo-Slav land whose control was not vital to Italian independence. Here is what the politician from Pesaro had to say on this question:

> With regard, then, to Illyria and Dalmatia, it suffices for now to note that those provinces are inhabited by a people in whose discretion lies the decision whether to declare themselves for the Italian cause or for that of the Slav peoples; although by descent they are born Slav, by custom, letters, and government they feel Italian. All that matters to us is this, that they are not and do not wish to be Austrian, and Austria cannot go on causing us continual affronts and inconveniences in the ports of Dalmatia.[69]

In Mamiani's opinion, Italy had to carry out a policy of economic and cultural penetration of Dalmatia, as well as Hungary, Croatia, and the Balkans, aiming to set up a customs and commercial union that would permit the revival of trade between the Italian peninsula and the Danubian and Mediterranean east. On the political and territorial plane Italy should 'desire and expect solely what nature has given her, i.e., her natural frontiers from the Varo to the Quarnero; of the rest, not ask anything but good neighborliness and friendship.'[70]

Thus the positions that Italian liberalism took toward the Adriatic question in 1848–9 were extremely diverse and contrasting, a consequence of the heterogeneous character of the Risorgimento movement in those years, which was still a confused coalition of supporters of a unified republic, federalists, and municipalists, along with Savoy monarchists and liberals loyal to the old Italian states. It was not until the second half of the 1850s, with the rise to power of Camillo Cavour in the Savoy state, that the Italian national liberal program began to assume a coherence and homogeneity, a realism and pragmatism on the political plane that, as we shall see, would also be applied to the Adriatic question.[71]

---

69  Mamiani, *Scritti politici*, p. 265.
70  'Mamiani a Carlo Zucchi,' 20 April 1848, in Mamiani, *Scritti politici*, pp. 269–72. On the subject: Tamborra, *Cavour*, p. 73.
71  Here we echo the views of Tamborra, *Cavour*, and Cervani, 'Cavour e gli slavi' in

## 1.4. The War of 1859, Constitutional Reforms in Austria, and the Birth of Dalmatian Autonomist Liberalism

The military defeat suffered by Austria in Italy in 1859 at the hands of the Franco-Piedmontese alliance forced Emperor Francis Joseph to abandon the system of absolutist rule. Although the absolutist regime and police repression, while incapable of solving the grave political and national problems that had evidently emerged in 1848 and 1849, had been able to cow the populations ruled by the Habsburgs during the 1850s, the defeat in Italy rekindled dissent within the empire, stirring up again the many national conflicts that troubled it. The events in Italy (the military debacle, the loss of Lombardy, and the annexation of the Habsburg states of Modena and Tuscany to the kingdom of Savoy in the name of the principle of national self-determination) appeared to undermine the very legitimacy of the Habsburg monarchy, triggering nationalistic uprisings that were stoked by the empire's enemies. In 1858, Cavour, head of the government in Turin, began to forge links with members of the intransigent and radical wing of the Hungarian national liberal movement (Lajos Kossuth and György Klapka, who were in exile in France) and the Serbian and Romanian governments, seeking to organize insurrections in the Danubian plain.[72] With the foundering of any possibility of a restoration of Habsburg rule in Modena and Tuscany, envisaged by the preliminary peace of Villafranca and the treaties of Zurich,[73] and with the establishment of the new kingdom of Northern Italy in the spring of 1860, Cavour continued, up until his death in 1861, to nurse the hope of fomenting national strife within the Habsburg empire and provoking revolts in Hungary,

---

un articolo poco noto di Francesco Ruffini,' in *Momenti di storia*, pp. 167 et seq. On Cavour's foreign policy the following are still fundamental: Romeo, *Cavour e il suo tempo*; Valsecchi, *L'Europa e il Risorgimento*; Di Nolfo, *Europa e Italia nel 1855–1856*; Bianchi, *Storia documentata della diplomazia europea*, vols. 7 and 8.

72  Tamborra, *Cavour e i Balcani*; Romeo, *Cavour e il suo tempo*, vol. 3, pp. 554–7, 773 et seq.; Cavour to Nigra, 17 December 1858, in *Il Carteggio Cavour-Nigra*, vol. 1, doc. 172.

73  Ample documentation of the genesis of the Zurich treaty in *La conferenza e la pace di Zurigo nei documenti diplomatici francesi; Il problema veneto*, vol. *Austria*, docs. 10 et seq. On the Italian question in European politics during 1859 and 1860: Deutsch, *Habsburgs Rückzug aus Italie.*; Valsecchi, *L'Italia del Risorgimento e l'Europa delle nazionalità*; Srbik, *Deutsche Einheit*, vol. 2, pp. 333 et seq., vol. 3; Romeo, *Cavour e il suo tempo*, vol. 3; Malinverni, *La Germania e il problema italiano*; Berti, *Russia e stati italiani*.

with a view to weakening the Austrian state in preparation for a war aimed at the conquest of Venice and its territories.[74]

Awareness in the ruling circles of Vienna of the existence of these Italian plans and the grave threat that all this implied drove the Habsburgs to concede internal reforms. As early as 15 July 1859, in a proclamation made after the defeat at Solferino, Francis Joseph promised the Habsburg subjects reforms and changes in legislation and administration.[75] Over the following months, under contrasting pressures from the reformist minister Karl Ludwig Bruck[76] and the leaders of the new government (which was headed by the Polish aristocrat Agenor Goluchowski, with Johann Bernhard Rechberg as foreign minister), the process of liberalization slowly got underway. A patent issued on 5 March 1860 set up the Council of the Empire, which was composed largely of councillors appointed by the emperor (some of them representing the various provinces), who were assigned general advisory powers, the right to block the introduction of new taxes, and the task of preparing the draft of a new constitution.

Convened at the end of May 1860, the Council of the Empire remained active until September 28 of the same year. The council was dominated by the so-called federalists, who 'desired a decentralization of state power and respect for the "historico-political individualities of the countries of the monarchy."'[77] The representatives of Bohemia, the Tyrol, and Croatia and the conservative Hungarian and Polish legitimists took a federalist stand.

In the course of the discussions that took place in the council, the question of the union of Dalmatia (a province of Austria) with Croatia (part of the kingdom of Hungary) was openly raised by the Croatian councillors. The representative of Dalmatia, Francesco Borelli, opposed

---

74  Cavour to d'Azeglio, 16 March 1860, in *Cavour e l'Inghilterra*, vol. 2, part 2, doc. 1313.
75  On the constitutional reforms in Austria in 1860–61: Alessandro Dudan, *La monarchia degli Asburgo*, vol. 2, pp. 32 et seq.; Kolmer, *Parlament und Verfassung*, pp. 39 et seq.; Macartney, *The Habsburg Empire*; Sestan, 'Le riforme costituzionali austriache del 1860–61,' in *La crisi dell'impero austriaco*, pp. 63–91; Lutz, *Zwischen Habsburg*; Rogge, *Oesterreich von Vilagos bis zur Gegenwart*, vol. 2; Brauneder, 'Die Entstehung des Parlamentarismus 1861/1867,' in *Österreichs Parlamentarismus*, pp. 83 et seq.; 'Die Verfassungsentwicklung in Österreich 1848 bis 1918,' in *Die Habsburgermonarchie*, vol. 7, part 1, pp. 145 et seq.
76  On Bruck: Agnelli, *La genesi dell'idea*, pp. 87 et seq.; Goodman, 'The Nachlass of Karl Ludwig Freiherr von Bruck,' in *Austrian History Yearbook*, vol. 25, pp. 185–93.
77  Dudan, *La monarchia degli Asburgo*, vol. 2, p. 46.

any idea of a Dalmatian-Croatian union, asserting that Croatia had no historical right in this respect since Dalmatia had submitted spontaneously to Habsburg sovereignty at the time of the disappearance of the republic of Venice in 1797. Borelli asked for the future Austrian constitution to provide for the autonomy of the kingdom of Dalmatia within the Habsburg empire; he admitted that the majority of Dalmatians were 'Slav in language, spirit, and heart,' but this did not mean that the Dalmatians wanted to lose their own identity in a union with Croatia and Slavonia.[78]

Josip Strossmayer, the bishop of Đakovo and a member of the council, disputed Borelli's arguments, asking for the unification of Dalmatia with the kingdom of Croatia and Slavonia. After the separation of Dalmatia from the rest of the Croatian lands, according to Strossmayer, foreign non-Slav elements had established themselves in that region, incapable of speaking the language of the majority of Dalmatians but dominating local politics and culture. Since a provincial Dalmatian diet would have been controlled by this foreign and non-Slav element, unable to represent the interests of the Dalmatian Slavs, there was no point in setting up the diet.[79]

The imperial diploma of 20 October 1860 was the first attempt to give a new constitutional order to the empire in line with the views of the council's federalist majority, but it did not resolve the question of Dalmatia, avoiding it on the legislative plane. The diploma sought to create a constitutional system in which the importance of the emperor's authority was reasserted, but many legislative and judicial powers were devolved to the provincial diets, to be reconstituted on the basis of the old regional and provincial constitutions, or to be created *ex novo*.

Despite various concessions by the emperor in administrative mat-

78 Speech by Francesco Borelli, Vienna 1872, in *Verhandlungen des österreichischen verstärkten Reichsrates*, pp. 231–6.
79 Speech by Josip Juraj Strossmayer, in *Verhandlungen des österreichischen verstärkten Reichsrates*, pp. 236–40. On the debate over the union between Dalmatia and Croatia in the Council of the Empire: Novak, *Prošlost Dalmacije*, vol. 2, pp. 358–9; Kratzik, *Die nationalen Auseinandersetzungen*, pp. 54 et seq. On the figure of Strossmayer, the driving spirit behind the Yugoslav brand of Croat nationalism: Šišić, ed., *Korespondencija Rački-Strossmayer*, vols. 1 and 2; Vitezić, 'Die roemisch-katholische Kirche,' in *Die Habsburgermonarchie*, vol. 4, pp. 350 et seq.; Rohrbacher, 'Bishop J. J. Strossmayer's Yugoslavism,' pp. 343 et seq.; Šidak, 'Josip Juraj Strossmayer,' pp. 195–7; Tamborra, *Imbro I. Tkalac e l'Italia*, pp. 127 et seq.

ters, which were guaranteed by the imperial autographs of 20 October, there was great dissatisfaction among Hungarian liberals, who were demanding the restoration of the constitution of 1848. In Croatia, however, the imperial law, accompanied by the convocation of the Croatian diet, was favourably received. In the diet of Croatia and Slavonia, the Croatian representatives again called for union with Dalmatia, emphasizing the ties of language and blood between Croatians and Dalmatians. In those same weeks, a delegation from Zagreb went to Vienna to plead for Croatian-Dalmatian union.[80]

In response to Croatian pressure, an imperial autograph of 5 December 1860 created a ministry for Croatia-Slavonia at the court in Vienna, reintroduced the Croat language in the administration of those territories, and declared that the requests for reconstitution of the Croatian-Slavonian-Dalmatian 'triple kingdom' were being taken into account, while deferring a final decision until Dalmatia, which still lacked a provincial diet, would be able to express its own political will.[81] Nevertheless, it was decided that a Dalmatian delegation would be sent to Zagreb to discuss the problem of Croatian-Dalmatian union at a conference chaired by the ban of Croatia, the highest political authority of the Croatian-Slavonian territory.[82]

The imperial autograph, Vienna's first partial acceptance of Croatian requests for the annexation of Dalmatia, prompted remonstrations and protests in many Dalmatian cities. The municipal assembly of Spalato, headed by Antonio Bajamonti, complained the loudest about any plan for immediate union. Antonio Bajamonti[83] was a wealthy landowner whose family had emigrated to Dalmatia from Italy in the seventeenth century. After studying medicine in Padua, he had returned to Spalato,

---

80  Novak, *Prošlost Dalmacije*, vol. 2, pp. 360 et seq.; Gross, *Die Anfänge des modernes Kroatien*, pp. 75 et seq.
81  Dudan, *La monarchia degli Asburgo*, vol. 2, pp. 58–9.
82  Pirjevec, *Niccolò Tommaseo*, p. 185.
83  On the figure of Antonio Bajamonti: *Onoranze funebri ad Antonio Bajamonti*; Randi, *Antonio Bajamont,*; Monzali, 'Dalmati o Italiani?' pp. 419 et seq.; Russo, *Antonio Bajamonti; L'epopea dalmatica e il suo Eroe*; Solitro, *Antonio Bajamonti il podestà mirabile di Spalato*; Smerchinich, *Antonio Bajamonti*; Tamaro, *La Vénétie Julienne*, vol. 3; Soppelsa, 'Antonio Bajamonti,' p. 409 et seq.; Camizzi, 'Figure dell'irredentismo dalmata.' Among the contributions by Croatian historians: Novak, *Povijest Splita*, vol. 3, pp. 186 et seq.; Vrandečić, *Dalmatinski autonomistički pokret u XIX stoljeću*, pp. 90 et seq.; Kečkemet, "Associazione dalmatica' i pad Ante Bajamontija,' pp. 75–116; *Bajamonti I Split*.

already drawing attention to himself in the years 1848 and 1849 as a liberal sympathizer[84] and supporter of civil and political reform in Austria. Over the course of the 1850s he had emerged as the leader of a group of young aristocrats and bourgeois in Spalato who supported a liberal program in the economic and political field. The program was characterized by a strong municipalism and the aim of fostering a process of capitalistic modernization in Dalmatia that would make Spalato one of the main ports of the Balkans. Appointed mayor of Spalato by the Austrian government at the beginning of 1860, Bajamonti assembled his councillors on 7 December of the same year and published a public declaration that was sent to the other Dalmatian municipalities and the governor of Dalmatia. With this declaration the mayor called on the city council to organize a special delegation and send it to the emperor with the aim of persuading him to 'suspend any decision on the aggregation of Dalmatia to Croatia until the Dalmatian Diet had met, in conformity with the Diploma of 20 October 1860, and the thoughts and wishes of the Dalmatian people been expressed through it.'[85] The resolution was to be communicated to the other Dalmatian municipalities, and the governor of Dalmatia, Lazarus von Mamula, would be asked to head the provincial delegation to Vienna.[86]

In the face of the governor's opposition to this initiative, around the middle of December Bajamonti and his councillors Vincenzo Degli Alberti, Pietro Illich, and Giorgio Giovannizio decided to send an appeal to Francis Joseph. They asked for the creation of a Dalmatian provincial diet before any decisions were to be taken over the position of Dalmatia within the empire, as any such step had to be an 'expression of the votes of the Dalmatian People, and the result of mature and conscientious consideration of our true interests.'[87] In the eyes of Bajamonti

---

84  Preserved in the archives of the information service of the Austrian Foreign Ministry are notes from the years between 1853 and 1856 that describe Bajamonti as a liberal sympathizer hostile to the absolutist government: HHSTA, *Kartei des Informationsbüros*, 1853, 1855, 1856, file 'Bajamonti Anton.' Further Austrian documentation on Bajamonti has been published by Bruno Franchi, who regards, in our view erroneously, the politician from Spalato as an Italian irredentist: Franchi, 'Per la storia della Dalmazia nel Risorgimento,' *La Rivista dalmatica*, 1938, no. 4, p. 15, 1939, no. 1, pp. 13–17.
85  *Relazione della Congregazione*, annex A, pp. 18–19.
86  Ibid.
87  'Allegato C,' in *Relazione della Congregazione*, pp. 21–6.

and his followers, Croatia had no historical and legal claim over the Dalmatians, a *popolo deditizio* who had submitted of their own accord to Habsburg sovereignty in 1797. 'The land of Dalmatia,' proclaimed Bajamonti and the councillors of Spalato, 'may have been Slav, but the people knew of other life, and if the Nation had been asked to vote at the time, it would perhaps have responded that even if the Dalmatian were Slav, he would never be Croatian by choice!'[88]

Bajamonti reasserted his opposition to any idea of forced annexation of Dalmatia to Croatia at the meeting of the Spalato city council on 23 December. After recalling the struggle that the Dalmatians had carried out in 1848–9 against plans for annexation, he confirmed his rejection of any unilateral Croatian imposition; while in the future Dalmatia might find that its prospects lay in 'throwing itself into the arms of the Croatians and Slavonians,' carrying out the union in the way planned by the Croatians would lead to their dominance over the Dalmatians.[89]

The initiatives undertaken by Bajamonti and the liberals of Spalato against annexation caused a great stir throughout Dalmatia, receiving the support of many Dalmatian municipalities. The mayor of Spalato published his anti-annexationist speeches and petitions in a pamphlet,[90] which helped the spread of his ideas and arguments and made him one of the leaders of emerging Dalmatian autonomism. However, the principal ideologue of the Dalmatian autonomists was Niccolò Tommaseo. Although absent for many years from the place of his birth, the writer from Sebenico had maintained close ties with his homeland. Considered the greatest Dalmatian intellectual of the day, he was invited to intervene publicly in the struggle against Croatian annexationism and, from January 1861 onward, wrote repeatedly in support of the autonomist struggle. According to Tommaseo, the Dalmatians were a people with an identity of their own, different from the Croatians of the north; too rapid and premature a union of Dalmatia and Croatia would distort the identity of Dalmatian culture, which had been founded on the meeting of Slavs and neo-Latins. For the moment it would be better for Dalmatia to remain autonomous within the Habsburg empire and, thanks to its

---

88 Ibid.
89 *Relazione della Congregazione*, pp. 15–16.
90 *Relazione della Congregazione*. On Bajamonti's political ideas see too Bajamonti, *Nello inaugurare la pubblicità; Dell'amministrazione del Comune*.

capacity for intermediation between Italy and the Slav world, to aim to play a civilizing role among the Balkan nations.[91]

Following Bajamonti's example, most of the Dalmatian city councils refused to send representatives to Zagreb to discuss the plan for a union of Croatia and Dalmatia, deciding instead, in February 1861, to dispatch a delegation of Dalmatian autonomists to Vienna, led by the mayor of Spalato and the magistrate Luigi Lapenna, to plead against annexation.[92]

The evolution of domestic politics in the Habsburg Empire proved of considerable help to the Dalmatian autonomists. The October diploma, which envisaged a decentralized structure of the state, was never put into effect, owing to the fierce opposition of the Hungarian and Austro-German liberals.[93] The Hungarian liberals, led by Ferencz Deak and Gyula Andrássy, demanded the reinstatement of the constitution of 1848, while the Germans were afraid that the October diploma would lead to a weakening of their dominance and the break-up of the empire.

Members of court circles close to Francis Joseph shared the fear that assigning too broad powers to the provincial diets would unleash centrifugal nationalist forces and undermine the authority of the emperor and the central bureaucracy. Anton von Schmerling, the former president of the supreme court who was appointed minister of the interior in December 1860, became the standard bearer of the demands of Austro-German liberalism and centralism.[94] The federalist stance within the government increasingly lost ground. On 4 February 1861, Archduke Rainier of Habsburg, a supporter of liberal centralism, was appointed prime minister, and the position of Schmerling, who was determined to reconcile the liberal demands of the German middle classes with Francis Joseph's absolutism, was strengthened.

Over the course of February 1861 numerous meetings of the Austrian

---

91  On Tommaseo's thinking with regard to the Dalmatian question: Tommaseo, *Ai Dalmati*; *La questione dalmatica*; *Via Facti*; Ciampini, *Vita di Niccolò Tommaseo*, pp. 653 et seq.; Pirjevec, *Niccolò Tommaseo tra Italia e Slavia*, pp. 182 et seq.; Camizzi, 'Il dibattito sull'annessione,' pp. 225 et seq.

92  On the emergence of the autonomist movement: De' Benvenuti, 'I riflessi della crisi dell'impero in Dalmazia,' pp. 305–13; Vrandečić, *Dalmatinski autonomistički pokret u XIX stoljeću*, p. 103 et seq.

93  Dudan, *La monarchia degli Asburgo*, vol. 2, pp. 62 et seq.

94  On the figure of Schmerling: Höbelt, ed., *Österreichs Weg zur Konstitutionellen Monarchie*; Somogyi, *Vom Zentralismus zum Dualismus*, pp. 5 et seq.

cabinet were held at which the problem of Dalmatia and its possible union with Croatia were discussed at length. Ivan Mažuranić, president of the *kroatisch-slawonischen Hofdikasterium*, did everything he could to persuade the cabinet and the emperor to go ahead with the unification of Croatia and Dalmatia and to not allow the creation of a Dalmatian provincial diet. It is interesting to note how the events of 1859 in Italy influenced the attitude of many Habsburg politicians and led them to see Dalmatia as a political problem linked to Italian unification. Mažuranić and Count Johann Bernhard von Rechberg, the Austrian minister of foreign affairs and a strenuous defender of the Croatian arguments, regarded the union of Dalmatia and Croatia as indispensable not just as a counterweight to Hungarian demands but also to avert the presumed threat of the 'Italianisierung Dalmatiens.' It was necessary, explained Rechberg, to strengthen politically the Slav element in Dalmatia, loyal to Austria, against the possible secessionist designs of an extremely active Italian minority.[95] Moreover, reinforcement of the Slav element in Dalmatia might prove useful to Austria's policy in the Balkans, constituting a magnet for the Slav Christians under Turkish rule.[96]

In fact, from the summer of 1859 onward, Habsburg policy on the Italian question[97] was shaped by Rechberg's fear that the claims of the Savoy monarchy to Veneto and Venezia might be a prelude to or a fig leaf for the intention of conquering the former Venetian domains in Istria and Dalmatia as well. In August, Rechberg made it clear to the Habsburg plenipotentiary Franz von Colloredo Wallsee, who was entrusted with the task of negotiating a definitive peace treaty with the French after the war in Italy, that Austria could accept the idea of an Italian confederation only with the participation of the still Austrian part of the Lombardo-Venetian kingdom; it was necessary, on the other hand, to insist on the exclusion of South Tyrol, Istria, and Dalmatia from the Lombardo-Venetian kingdom in order to ensure the Habsburg empire's retention in the future of 'both the Italian part of the

---

95 Meeting of 14 February 1861, in MR, section V, 1, pp. 26–9; meeting of 20 February 1861, p. 91.
96 Meeting of 12 February 1861, in MR, section V, 1, p. 20; meeting of 14 February 1861, pp. 26–9.
97 *Il problema veneto*, Austria, docs. 10, 94, 99, 101, 153, 169; *Quellen*, vol. 1, docs. 320, 374, vol. 2, doc. 979. On Rechberg's foreign policy: Deutsch, *Habsburgs Rückzug aus Italie*; Clark, *Franz Joseph and Bismarck*; Blaas, 'L'Austria di fronte al problema veneto,' pp. 49–77; Engel-Janosi, *Graf Rechberg*.

Tyrol and the former Venetian provinces on the east coast of the Adriatic.'[98] Over the course of 1860 Rechberg sought to win British support by using the presumed Italian threat to Istria and Dalmatia to justify rejection of the peaceful surrender of the Veneto. Renunciation of the Veneto by the Habsburgs would have given further encouragement to the expansionistic designs of the Savoy state, which was eager to obtain control of other lands inhabited by Italians or previously ruled by the Venetians. In the view of the Austrian minister, the government in Turin had plans of conquest that were aimed at the creation of a large Italian empire comprising the whole of the Adriatic coast as far as Cattaro, and the Alpine territories as far as the Brenner Pass, which would have undermined the status quo in the Balkans and the Mediterranean, strengthened France, and caused grave damage to British interests.[99]

The fact that Rechberg's arguments were specious is demonstrated by an analysis of Cavour's attitude to the question of Dalmatia. Throughout the political process that had led to the creation of the unified Italian state, Dalmatia had remained absent from the territorial goals of first the kingdom of Sardinia, and then the kingdom of Italy. Cavour, outlining the program of the constitution of a kingdom of Northern Italy and then a unitary Italian state, wanted to avoid the direct involvement of Prussia and Great Britain in defence of the Habsburg positions on the peninsula. Consequently, he had limited immediate Sardinian territorial ambitions in the northeast to the conquest of the Lombardo-Venetian kingdom (which was not part of the German confederation), reserving the creation of secure borders through annexation of the Italian Tyrol, Trieste, and Istria for a more distant future. Very well aware of the dangers that the proliferation of maximalist territorial claims might pose to the Italian cause, and conscious both of the hostility of many German states, especially Bavaria and Prussia,[100] toward any idea of Savoy annexation of Trent and Trieste, and of Russian and British suspicion of

---

98  Rechberg to Colloredo, 19 August 1859, *Il problema veneto*, Austria, doc. 10.

99  Rechberg to Apponyi, 29 June 1860, *Il problema veneto*, Austria, doc. 99; see too docs. 94, 101, 153, 169.

100 On the attitude of the German states toward Savoy expansionism in 1860 and the birth of the kingdom of Italy: APP, II, 1, docs. 17, 54, 116, 119, 183, 273; APP, II, 2, docs. 320, 350, 397, 412, 424; *Quellen*,1, docs. 279, 282, 286, 374, 392, 548; *Quellen*, 3, doc. 1122; Blaas, 'L'Austria e la proclamazione del regno d'Italia,' pp. 331–61; Benedikt, 'Le relazioni italo-austriache dal 1861 al 1870,' pp. 219–23; Malinverni, 'L'Unificazione,' pp. 444–61.

any Italian plan of reconquest of the former Venetian possessions in the Adriatic and the Mediterranean, the Piedmontese prime minister imposed a renunciatory and prudent character on Savoy policy in the Adriatic. While sympathizing with the irredentist activity of the exiles from Trentino and Venezia Giulia, Cavour was always careful not to increase the fears of the great powers. The Savoy prime minister reacted to Prussian protests over a decree that seemed to claim Trieste belonged to Italy, by writing in December 1860 to the commissioner for the Marche, Lorenzo Valerio, to tell him to avoid any declaration that might give the impression that the new Italian state aspired to conquer 'not just the Veneto but also Trieste with Istria and Dalmatia.' Cavour went on to say:

> I am not unaware that in the cities on the coast there are centres of Italian population by race and aspirations. But in the countryside the inhabitants are of the Slav race, and any sign of wishing to remove all outlet to the Mediterranean from such a vast part of Central Europe would seriously alienate the Croats, the Serbs, the Magyars, and all the Germanic populations. Any rash statement of this kind is a terrible weapon in the hands of our enemies, who would use it to try to turn against us Great Britain herself, which would also look unfavourably on the possibility that the Adriatic should once again become, as it was in the times of the Venetian Republic, an Italian lake.[101]

The Italian governments that followed the one headed by Cavour (who died in June 1861) were led by Bettino Ricasoli, Urbano Rattazzi, Marco Minghetti, and Alfonso La Marmora and to a great extent continued to pursue the guidelines of international policy shaped by the founder of the unified Italian state. They sought to weaken the Habsburg empire by improving relations with Prussia and Russia; by supporting Hungarian, Serbian, and Romanian secessionist tendencies within Austria; and by strengthening political ties with the small Balkan states (Greece, Serbia, Montenegro, and the Danubian principalities). No claims were

---

101  Cavour to Valerio, 28 December 1860, in Chiala, *Camillo Cavour,* IV, doc. 1089, and in *Cavour, la liberazione del Mezzogiorno,* IV, doc. 2839. On the protests of the German states against Valerio's decree: APP, II, 2, docs. 299, 301, 303, 304; *Quellen,* 1, doc. 301, 320. On Cavour's attitude toward the Adriatic question: Stefani, *Cavour e la Venezia Giulia;* Cervani, 'Cavour e gli slavi,' pp. 167–95.

made to Dalmatia; it was regarded exclusively as a territory from which to launch, on the initiative of Italy, a future insurrection against Austria that would have its heart in Hungary and the Danubian lands inhabited by Serbs and Croats. This view of Dalmatia as Austria's Achilles' heel stemmed from the awareness that the Ottoman presence in Bosnia and Herzegovina rendered the Austrian positions in the Adriatic insecure.[102]

In any case, Dalmatia's political and strategic importance for Austria increased from 1859 onward, and Rechberg's words to the cabinet reflected the Austrian determination to foment national strife in order to strengthen imperial power, even though there was no Italian irredentism on Dalmatian soil at the time. As early as 1861, therefore, Austrian policy toward the Italian-speaking population of Dalmatia was influenced by motivations of international politics, and a link, which was desired neither by the Italian government nor by the Italian Dalmatians but was a consequence of changes in the European balance of power, was created between the existence of a unified Italian national state and the fate of the Italian and Italian-speaking Dalmatian populations.

The positions of the Dalmatian autonomist liberals were defended strenuously by German liberal politicians in the cabinet, especially Schmerling, finance minister Ignaz von Plener, and minister without portfolio Joseph Lasser. In Plener's view, the union of Dalmatia with Croatia was not in the empire's interest, and so it was better to proceed with caution before making any decision on it.[103] Schmerling and the liberal ministers succeeded in persuading a dubious Francis Joseph to put off any decision about the constitutional status of Dalmatia and to convene the Dalmatian provincial diet with the mandate of starting

---

102 Fundamental with regard to Italian foreign policy in the early 1860s are volumes 1–6 of the first series of the DDI; amongst the historical literature we recommend: Mori, *La questione romana 1861–1865*; Cialdea, *L'Italia nel concerto europeo (1861–1867*; Anchieri, 'Il riconoscimento del regno d'Italia,' in *Il sistema diplomatico europeo: 1814–1939*; Di Nolfo, 'Il problema di Roma nella politica dell'Italia'; Silva, 'La convenzione di settembre secondo i documenti ufficiali francesi,' in *Figure e Momenti di storia italiana*, pp. 305–35; Vigezzi, 'L'Italia dopo l'Unità: liberalismo e politica estera,' in *L'Italia*, pp. 1–54; Case, *Franco-Italian Relations 1860–1865*; Tamborra, *Cavour e i Balcani*; 'Russia, Prussia, la questione polacca,' pp. 147 et seq.; Decleva, 'Il compimento dell'Unità e la politica estera,' pp. 113 et seq.; Mugnaini, *Italia e Spagna nell'età contemporanea*, pp. 211 et seq.
103 Meeting of 14 February 1861, in MR, section V, 1, p. 29.

negotiations with Croatian representatives on the possibility of unification.[104]

On the advice of Schmerling and the German liberals, the emperor issued a patent on 26 February 1861 that modified some of the provisions of the October diploma.[105] An imperial parliament (made up of a senate and a house of representatives) with broad legislative powers was created, while the law-making areas reserved for the provincial diets were drastically reduced. The February patent approved fifteen statutes of the reconstituted provincial diets, with their associated regulations, providing for an electoral system that gave the right to vote to only those who possessed a certain amount of property, albeit minimal. The electoral system was based on four curias, representing different social groups; in Dalmatia they were called the constituency of the highly assessed (owners of a large amount of property), the constituencies of the cities, those of the chambers of commerce, and those of the rural communes. The electoral system was designed to favour the middle class and the aristocracy, as well as the urban populations over those populations living in the countryside, since it gave greater parliamentary representation to property owners and the inhabitants of towns and cities. In much of the empire this strengthened the political clout of the German group, which was more advanced socially and economically and often concentrated in the cities. In the regions of the Adriatic the system favoured the populations of Italian language and culture, which were strong in the cities of the coast of Istria, the Quarnero (Kvarner), and Dalmatia.[106]

The patent of February 1861 met the demands of the Dalmatian autonomist liberals, blocking for the moment any plans for Dalmatian-Croatian union and permitting the creation of a Dalmatian provincial diet, for which elections were held between 24 and 30 March 1861.[107] The result was a dramatic victory for the autonomist liberal movement, which won the majority of seats in the diet.

---

104 Meeting of 20 February 1861, ibidem, pp. 29–30.
105 On the genesis of the February patent: Kann, *History of the Habsburg Empire*; Macartney, *The Habsburg Empire*. A precise analysis of the contents of the February patent in Dudan, *La monarchia degli Asburgo*, II, pp. 66–90.
106 On the Austrian electoral system and its effects on political life: Höbelt, 'Die Vertretung der Nationalitäten im Reichsrat,' in *Österreichs Parlamentarismus*, pp. 185 et seq.
107 On this: Maschek, *Manuale del regno di Dalmazia*, p. 11.

However, the Rainier-Schmerling government had said nothing final about Dalmatia's constitutional status in the empire, limiting itself to leaving the problem of the Dalmatian province undecided and declaring the kingdom of Dalmatia provisionally part of Austria, and not Hungary as the Croatians had requested. Over the following months fierce debate on the problem of the union of Dalmatia with Croatia continued in the cabinet, with various attempts by Mažuranić, Rechberg, and Strossmayer to persuade the government to impose union on the Dalmatians, attempts that were blocked by the action of the German liberal ministers, who were favourable to the arguments of the Dalmatian autonomists.[108]

The ability to express the feelings and positions of the populations of the Dalmatian cities, who were attached to their municipal identity and hostile to pan-Croatian and pan-Serbian nationalism, was one of the reasons for the success of the autonomist movement in the elections for the provincial diet in March 1861. Another crucial element was the electoral system created by the Austrian government. As has already been pointed out, the right to vote was based on property, favouring the aristocracy, bourgeois, and merchant classes. Out of forty-three members of the provincial diet, ten were elected by the wealthiest property owners, eight by the cities, three by the chambers of commerce, and twenty by the rural districts; an automatic right to a seat in the diet was given to the metropolitan of the Greek rite of Zara and to the Catholic archbishop of Dalmatia.[109]

It was the geographical distribution of the seats, however, more than the restrictions on the right to vote, that favoured the liberal autonomists. The Slavophile Dalmatian nationalists complained for years that, on the basis of the Austrian electoral system, the 400 000 inhabitants of the countryside and villages, the vast majority of whom were Serbs and Croatians, could elect only twenty representatives, while the 40 000 inhabitants of the Italo-Slav cities had twenty-one.[110] It was easy for the autonomists, deeply rooted and numerous in the urban centres of the coast and the islands, to win a majority in the diet (twenty-seven rep-

---

108  See, for example: meeting of 16 March 1861, in MR, section V, 1, pp. 168–73; meeting of 1 May 1861, in MR, section V, 2, pp. 3–7; meeting of 6 May 1861, in MR, section V, 2, pp. 28–33.

109  On the electoral system in force in Dalmatia: Dudan, *La monarchia degli Asburgo*, II, pp. 73 et seq.

110  *Il Nazionale*, 16 February 1867; Pirjevec, *Niccolò Tommaseo*, p. 198.

resentatives out of forty-one) and keep it in the subsequent provincial elections of 1864 and 1867.[111]

As in much of the Habsburg Empire, the authorities exercised a decisive influence on the outcome of the elections in Dalmatia. The vote was not secret,[112] and this, in a restricted electorate, permitted a great deal of pressure and interference. In a poor and underdeveloped province like Dalmatia the weight and influence of the state administration on the whole of society was immense, and it was hard for officials of the state and the local governments to go against the wishes of their leaders. Over the course of the 1860s this government influence on the elections favoured the Dalmatian autonomists, who were loyal to Austria and closely linked to the Austro-German liberals in power in Vienna. However, in the years following the war of 1866 the reinforcement of a Slavophile tendency in court circles and in the Habsburg armed forces led to interference in Dalmatian politics on behalf of the nationalists.

The victory in the elections of March 1861 showed that the strongholds of Dalmatian liberal autonomism were the main cities of former Venetian Dalmatia: Zara, Spalato, and Sebenico. The winners in Zara were the autonomists Spiridione Petrovich (Petrović) (a Serb lawyer who was president of the diet for several years),[113] Natale Filippi (a lawyer), Giacomo Ghiglianovich (the father of Roberto Ghiglianovich, future leader of Italian irredentism), Francesco Borelli, (a descendant of a Bolognese family that had emigrated to Dalmatia), and Cosimo de Begna Possedaria (the mayor of the city). At Spalato and Traù, Bajamonti was elected, along with his friends Giorgio Giovannizio (a lawyer), Leonardo Dudan, Vincenzo Degli Alberti, Antonio Radman, and Count Antonio Fanfogna. Other important autonomists who won seats were Luigi Lapenna, Antonio Galvani (a Sebenico notary), Giovanni Marassovich (the mayor of Scardona/Skradin), and Giovanni Smerkinic (the mayor of Curzola and the founder of a political dynasty, the Smerkinics (Smerchinichs), who were the leaders of autonomism on Curzola for many years).

---

111  On the electoral results in Dalmatia in the 1860s: Ivo Perić, *Dalmatinski Sabor 1861– 1912 (1918) God.* (Zadar: Centar Jugoslavenske Akademije Znanosti i Umjetnosti, 1978), pp. 17 et seq.; Novak, *Prošlost Dalmacije*, II, pp. 384 et seq.; Buczynski, 'Der Dalmatinische Landtag,' in *Die Habsburgermonarchie*, vol. 6, part 1, pp. 1951 et seq.
112  Dudan, *La monarchia degli Asburgo*, II, pp. 84–5.
113  On Petrovich: Bellumore, *I nostri onorevoli.* pp. 46 et seq.

The Croatian-Serbian nationalists managed to get good results in the rural constituencies. The notary Stefan Ljubiša and Juraj Pulić and Michele (Mihovil) Klaić, teachers at the high school in Zara, became representatives for the regions of Cattaro and Ragusa, while the priest Pavlinović was elected in the district of Metković and Makarska. It was in southern Dalmatia, from Makarska to Cattaro, a more backward area in socio-economic terms and one where the Italian element was less strong, that the Croatian-Serbian nationalists received the greatest support.[114]

The Dalmatian autonomist liberals openly expressed their fervent loyalty to Austria from 1861 onward. The setting up of the provincial diets in that year raised the problem of electing representatives of the individual diets to the imperial parliament and sending them to the newly created Abgeordnetenhaus in Vienna. The constitutional laws of 1861 envisaged a Reichsrat with two functions: that of an enlarged Reichsrat representing all the peoples of the empire (including the Hungarians) with the sole exception of the inhabitants of Veneto; and that of a reduced Reichsrat or parliamentary body for those parts of the Habsburg state not included in the kingdom of Hungary. In reality, the boycott by the Hungarian, Croatian, and Transylvanian parties[115] prevented the Reichsrat from carrying out any activity as a broad parliamentary institution, limiting its function to that of a restricted body representing the non-Hungarian Habsburg domains.

In order to assert their links with the Italian world and their own demands for autonomy, the Italian liberal parties of Istria and the Trentino attempted to boycott the reduced Reichsrat, refusing to send parliamentary representatives to Vienna. The Istrian provincial diet, dominated by liberals who already espoused an Italian national ideology and were eager to demonstrate Istria's own desire to be incorporated into the Austrian part of the Lombardo-Venetian kingdom, refused to elect representatives for Vienna, writing 'No One' on the ballot papers. As a result of this act of insubordination toward Austrian central authority,

---

114  Information on those elected to the Dalmatian provincial diet in March 1861 in *Atti della Dieta Provinciale Dalmata* (henceforth ADP-BI), year 1861 (Zadar, 1861), personal status, p. 20; Vrandečić, *Dalmatinski autonomistički pokret u XIX stoljeću*, pp. 167 et seq.

115  Berchtold, 'Die politischen Parteien,' p. 139; Höbelt, 'Die Vertretung der Nationalitäten im Reichsrat,' pp. 185–222, in particular p. 187; Corsini, 'Deputati delle terre italiane ai Parlamenti viennesi,' p. 65.

the Istrian diet was dissolved and new elections were held. Influenced by the government, these elections produced a pro-government majority in the diet.[116]

The Italian liberals of Trentino also decided not to take part in the meetings of the Abgeordnetenhaus for several years as a protest against Tyrolean centralism, which was opposed to the provincial autonomy of Trentino, and against the political order created after 1859, which placed Trentino or the Italian Tyrol under the institutional dominance of the German Tyrol and separated its people from the other Italian provinces of the empire.[117]

By contrast, once the Dalmatian provincial diet had met between 8 April and 24 April 1861, the Dalmatian autonomists, who were enthusiastic supporters of Austrian political liberalization, loyal Habsburg subjects and in possession of a majority in the assembly, immediately elected the five members of the parliament in Vienna: four members represented the constitutional-autonomist majority, that is, Lapenna, Vincenzo Degli Alberti (from Spalato), Giovanni Machiedo from Lesina (Hvar), and Simone Bujas of Sebenico; one member, the Serb Ljubiša, represented the Dalmatian Serbian-Croatian National Party.[118]

Another important resolution that was passed by the Dalmatian provincial diet on 18 April 1861 was the refusal to send a delegation to Zagreb to discuss the possibility of a union of Croatia and Dalmatia. The autonomists Antonio Galvani and Antonio Bajamonti, while not excluding the hypothesis of a Dalmatian-Croatian union in the distant future, argued forcefully against any plan for immediate and hasty unification. Galvani pointed to the many things that separated Dalmatians and Croatians: they had different cultural identities that were the product of distinct histories; the great barriers of the mountain ranges had constituted a major obstacle to Croatian-Dalmatian relations for

---

116  On Italian liberalism and the national question in Istria in the second half of the nineteenth century: Quarantotto, *Figure del Risorgimento in Istria; Uomini e fatti del patriottismo istriano*; Sestan, *Venezia Giulia*; Stefani, *Cavour e la Venezia Giulia*, pp. 336 et seq.; Riccardi, *Francesco Salata tra storia*, pp. 22 et seq.

117  Benvenuti, *L'autonomia trentina al Landtag*, pp. 27 et seq.; Corsini, 'Correnti liberali trentine tra Italia, Austria e Germania,' in Lill and Matteucci (eds.), *Il liberalismo in Italia e in Germania*, pp. 507 et seq.

118  Information on the Dalmatian members of the Austrian Reichsrat between 1861 and 1918: Knauer, *Das oesterreichische Parlament von 1848–1966*.

centuries; the Dalmatian Slav language was more like the one spoken in Serbia and Bosnia than that in Croatia, and in any case the Croatians spoke a different language from the Dalmatians. He did not rule out the possibility of a future union of Dalmatia and Croatia, after the Croatian nation had undergone a complete cultural and political regeneration that would allow it to find the right relationship with Hungary, but to discuss the annexation of Dalmatia to Croatia at that moment was premature and dangerous as there was no guarantee that the rights of the Dalmatians to liberty, autonomy, and their own customs and 'idioms' would be preserved. In addition, an immediate union would have given the Croatians undisputed superiority over the Dalmatians.[119] Bajamonti, on the other hand, disputed Croatia's presumed historical rights over Dalmatia. The cities of the Dalmatian coast, in his view, had never belonged to the Croatians. The Dalmatians would have gained no advantage from union with Croatia. A confederation would have entailed the risk of dominance by the larger and more populous province (Croatia) over the smaller one (Dalmatia); in the event of annexation and incorporation, which would have meant annexation to a Croatia that was still an integral part of Hungary, the Dalmatians would have run the risk of losing the rights to the individual and collective freedom guaranteed by the Austrian constitution. According to the mayor of Spalato, Dalmatian-Croatian union could not be invoked in the name of the principle of nationality. While Dalmatia was largely Slav, this did not mean that it was Croat; whence the rejection of the annexation to Croatia.[120]

The diet approved by a clear majority the motion presented by Galvani, which reaffirmed its opposition to the annexation of Dalmatia to Croatia and its refusal to send representatives to Zagreb to discuss the possibility of a union.[121] On 24 April, the diet passed a declaration that was hostile to the union with Croatia, to be sent to Emperor Francis Joseph, and in the following days both the representatives of the annexationist National Party and those of the autonomist movement went to Vienna to argue their cases.

---

119  Speech by Galvani, meeting of 18 April 1861, in ADP-BI, p. 11.
120  Speech by Bajamonti, meeting of 18 April 1861, in ADP-BI, p. 12. On Bajamonti's position with regard to the national question in Dalmatia: Monzali, 'Dalmati o Italiani?' pp. 443 et seq.
121  Meeting of 18 April 1861, in ADP-BI.

The imperial cabinet resumed discussion of the question of a Dalmatian-Croatian union between 1 May and 6 May 1861. The Croatian political position in Vienna was weakened over the course of the spring. The refusal of the diet in Zagreb to send its own representatives to the imperial Reichsrat had annoyed both Schmerling and the emperor. Still favourable to the idea of a Dalmatian-Croatian union at the end of 1860, the emperor had begun to grow irritated with the repeated Croatian requests to incorporate or participate in the administration of the Militärgrenze (Military Frontier), disrupting the system of government of that Danubian region, which was the main source of recruits for the armed forces. On 1 May, Schmerling presented to cabinet the case of the Dalmatian autonomists, that is, their refusal to send a delegation to Zagreb to discuss the hypothesis of a union between Dalmatia and Croatia, and asked that the question of the position of the kingdom of Croatia and Slavonia with respect to Hungary be settled first.[122]

Emperor Francis Joseph attended the next cabinet meeting on 6 May, and Josip Strossmayer, the true leader of the Croatian National Party, was invited to take part. Strossmayer defended the Croatian requests for the incorporation of Dalmatia and for representation of the Militärgrenze at the diet in Zagreb, but he now found himself facing a hostile attitude from the emperor. Francis Joseph, with the support of the minister of war, restated his determination to keep the Militärgrenze separate from Croatia and declared that he found Dalmatian fears with regard to possible annexation to Hungary legitimate and reasonable; therefore, he invited the Croatian diet to send a deputation to the Reichsrat in Vienna that would be able to negotiate on the various questions.[123]

Schmerling proposed that the representatives of the Dalmatian and Croatian diets meet in Vienna and discuss the question of union under the emperor's protection. Francis Joseph accepted Schmerling's idea and, to facilitate the negotiations, received delegations from both the Dalmatian and the Croatian diets in the Austrian capital on 8 May.[124] The Croatian delegation was headed by Strossmayer, and the Dalmatian delegation was made up of Stefan Knezevich, who was the Serbian Orthodox bishop of Zara and a supporter of autonomy, and Petrovich,

---

122  Meeting of 1 May 1861, in MR, section V, vol. 2, p. 6.
123  Meeting of 6 May 1861, in MR, section V, vol. 2, pp. 31–2.
124  Ibid.

Bajamonti, Lapenna, Bujas, Degli Alberti, and Ljubiša. However, the encounter between the two delegations, which took place on 12 May, came to nothing, the sides being unable to reach an agreement.[125]

Faced with the inability of the two diets to find a solution to the problem of union by mutual consent, the Austrian cabinet realized that it was impossible to take a decision that would satisfy both sides, and it chose to preserve the status quo, that is, to leave Dalmatia as an integral part of Austria and constitutionally separate from Croatia and the kingdom of Hungary. On 8 June, following the failure of the negotiations, the emperor, while declaring that he did not wish to jeopardize the possibility of Croatian-Dalmatian unification in any way, gave the go-ahead for the activation of the Landesausschusses (provincial council) in Dalmatia, thereby setting the administrative and legislative machinery of the province in motion for autonomy without yielding powers to Zagreb.[126]

The struggle against the annexation of Dalmatia to Croatia proved a temporary success for the Dalmatian autonomists, who had been able to head off Strossmayer's attempts to persuade the imperial government to accept the requests for union. Decisive to this success had been the alliance with the German liberals, who exercised great political influence in Vienna in those years. Unlike the Czechs, Hungarians, and Croatians, who abstained from parliamentary sittings for the first half of the 1860s, the Dalmatian autonomists were always present at the parliament in Vienna between 1861 and 1867,[127] supporting the political and legislative action of Schmerling and Beust and then voting in favour of the laws on the Ausgleich (the Austro-Hungarian compromise of 1867).[128]

Luigi Lapenna was the undisputed leader of the Dalmatian autonomist representatives in Vienna and a leading player in Austrian politics,

---

125  Novak, *Prošlost Dalmacije*, II, pp. 376–7.
126  Meeting of 8 June 1861, in MR, section V, vol. 2, , pp. 111–12.
127  On the representatives of the Dalmatian autonomists at the Austrian Reichsrat: *Namen-Verzeichniss der p.t. Herren Mitglieder des Abgeordnetenhauses*, p. 58; *Reichs-raths-Almanach für die Session 1867*, p. 20. The most active liberal autonomist in the Austrian parliament was Lapenna, a skilled orator in German and an able jurist; for example: *Stenographische Protokolle*, 4 June 1867, pp. 106–7; 5 June 1867, pp. 171–2. See too Kratzik, *Die nationalen Auseinandersetzungen*, pp. 90–5.
128  Speech by Luigi Lapenna, *Stenographische Protokolle*, 13 November 1867, pp. 1372–4; Kolmer, *Parlament und Verfassung*, I, pp. 355–7.

without doubt the most powerful Italian in the empire in those years.[129] He was descended from a family that had emigrated from Puglia to Dalmatia in the eighteenth century; born at Signi (Sinj) in 1825, he attended high school in Zara and then university in Vienna, where he graduated in law in 1849. Lapenna married a Viennese woman and embarked on a brilliant career as a magistrate that took him from Vienna to Spalato to Ragusa to Zara. In Habsburg Austria, many functionaries of the state typically played an active part in political life. A skilled orator with a gift for languages (in addition to Italian, he spoke fluent German, Serbo-Croatian, and French), Lapenna was not just one of the founders of Dalmatian autonomism but also the player of an important political role in Vienna. He had established close ties with the leaders of Austrian liberalism – Karl Giskra, Ignaz von Plener, Eduard Herbst, and Anton von Schmerling – and earned the esteem of the emperor. Over the course of the 1860s he succeeded in becoming vice-president of the parliamentary club of the Left (a grouping of all the German, Italian, and Ruthenian liberals) and vice-president of the Austrian elective assembly.[130] A member of the Reichsrat and of the Dalmatian provincial diet, the president of the provincial court in Zara, and then a judge of the supreme court in Vienna, Lapenna was a very powerful politician in Dalmatia and Austria throughout the liberal period.

## 1.5. The Dalmatian Autonomist Liberal Movement: Ideology and Organization

The struggle against the initiatives of the provincial diet in Zagreb and the Dalmatian pan-Croatian annexationist movement was the event that provoked, as we have seen, the rise of an organized political group that was hostile to any plan of unification, the Dalmatian autonomist liberal movement, which was to dominate the political and cultural life of Dalmatia for about two decades.

In reality, during the 1860s and 1870s, the Dalmatian autonomist lib-

---

129  There is no satisfactory study of Luigi Lapenna's life. For some perfunctory data: *Il Dalmata*, 8 and 11 April 1891; *Reichsraths-Almanach für die Session 1867*, p. 120; Randi, 'Luigi Lapenna e l'autonomia dalmata'; Soppelsa, 'Luigi Lapenna,' pp. 428–9; Bellumore, *I nostri onorevoli*, pp. 67–70; Vrandečić, *Dalmatinski autonomistički pokret u XIX stoljeću*, pp. 116–18.

130  On Lapenna's high standing in Austrian governing circles during the 1860s: Meeting of 6 June 1863, MR, section V, vol. 6, pp. 78–9.

erals usually referred to themselves as the autonomous and constitutional party: *autonomous* because the party fought for the maintenance
of Dalmatia's autonomy, separate from Croatia and Slavonia, within
Austria; and *constitutional* because, following the example of the Austro-German liberals, the autonomists believed that the conquest and
defence of a constitutional and pluralistic political system founded on
the individual and collective civil, political, and religious liberties that
had been granted and guaranteed by the 1861 patent and subsequent
Austrian legislation of liberal inspiration was an indispensable element
of their own program.

The autonomist liberals, reflecting the ethnic, religious, and cultural
complexity of the Dalmatian cities, were always a fairly heterogeneous
political group: in ethnic and national terms because, rejecting any idea
of Italian or Croatian nationalism and grounded in local municipalist
values, they included Italian Dalmatians, Croatians, and Serbs; and in
political terms because they were split between the conservative liberals (for example, Nicolò Trigari from Zara) who were linked to the
Catholic tradition and were willing to accept the persistence of strong
absolutistic tendencies in Austrian politics, and the progressive liberals
(like Antonio Bajamonti) who were anticlerical and inclined to a gradual shift in the political system toward democracy.

The character and ideology of Dalmatian autonomous liberalism has
frequently been misunderstood by Croatian and Serbian historians,
their vision distorted by anti-Italian stereotypes that have too often led
them to make moral and ideological condemnations of Italian political
and cultural activity in Dalmatia.[131] The majority of Italian historians
have displayed grave limitations as well, being almost always ready
to accept a certain posthumous irredentist political mythology and to
interpret in terms of Italian nationalism figures and circles that are not

---

131 Even the best of the Dalmatian Croatian historians, Grga Novak, author of works
fundamental to the understanding of the history of Dalmatia (for example, *Povijest
Splita*), while aware that autonomist liberalism had a Slav side as well, was often
motivated by a passionate Croatian nationalism, leading to an ideological rejection
of the idea of Dalmatia as a multi-ethnic and multinational land; thus his writing
is almost always centred on a nationalistic identification of the Dalmatian and
Croatian character. On the other hand, in his recent book on Dalmatian autonomism Josip Vrandečić deserves praise for an effort to go beyond the traditional
nationalistic categories of Croatian historiography: Vrandečić, *Dalmatinski autonomistički pokret u XIX stoljeću*.

susceptible to simplistic explanations based on national and ethnic uniformity.[132]

In the first place, Dalmatian autonomism can be defined as a regionalist political movement, infused with a visceral municipalist particularism. The Dalmatian autonomists were strongly opposed to the annexation of their land to Croatia because they felt themselves to be Dalmatian, not Croatian. According to the autonomist representative of Sebenico, Antonio Galvani, who did not reject the possibility of a future fusion of Croatians and Dalmatians, the inhabitants of Dalmatia had their own customs, history, and idioms; the Croatians spoke a language that was 'bastardized by foreign voices with the result that a Dalmatian finds it hard to understand.'[133]

The autonomists believed in the existence of a specific Dalmatian identity, shaped by particular historical, cultural, and geographical factors and characterized to a great extent by the encounter and fusion of neo-Latin and Slav peoples. Antonio Bajamonti compared the Dalmatians to the Swiss, a mix of three different peoples speaking three different languages who had been driven to live together as brothers by various historical events, by geographic conditions, and by a common interest, eventually becoming a nation. The Dalmatian case was similar: the Dalmatians, whether 'Italian or Slav, have been bound together for centuries not just by ties of love, but by the more lasting ones of interest. Living in the same land, rather than reuniting with their mother countries, they believed it more opportune for them to live in the same family, which the centuries and misfortunes ... gave the right to consider itself a nation.'[134]

This regionalistic sentiment, which led many autonomists to speak of the existence of a Dalmatian nation founded on a shared civilization that united different races and ethnic groups, helps to explain the multi-ethnic character that Dalmatian autonomism had for much of its

---

132 Despite the many years that have passed and the extremely dated and politicized character of his works, the Dalmatian writings of Attilio Tamaro remain a point of reference in the Italian historical literature devoted to Dalmatian autonomism; on the strengths and limitations of Tamaro's historiography: Cervani, 'La "Storia di Trieste" di Attilio Tamaro,' in *Momenti di storia*, pp. 107–44; Monzali, 'Tra irredentismo e fascismo,' pp. 267 et seq.

133 Speech by Galvani, meeting of 18 April 1861, ADP-BI.

134 Speech by Bajamonti, meeting of 18 April 1861, ADP-BI. See too Monzali, 'Dalmati o Italiani?' pp. 443 et seq.

history. Lapenna rightly recalled that the autonomist members of the first Dalmatian provincial diet in 1861 included both Slavs and Italians and that a Dalmatian Serb, Petrovich, was elected by his political allies as speaker of the assembly for many years.[135] Among the most important exponents of autonomous liberalism were (in addition to the Italian-speaking Dalmatians Bajamonti, Lapenna, Galvani, Trigari, Borelli, and Begna Possedaria) several bilingual Slav Dalmatians: Spiridione Petrovich (Petrović); Marassovich, the mayor of Scardona; and Smerkinic (Smerchinich), a landowner from Curzola. In addition, Stefan Knezevich, the Serbian Orthodox bishop of Zara, openly sympathized with the autonomists and agreed to be their representative at the Reichsrat in Vienna in 1867.[136]

So it is a mistake to define the Dalmatian Autonomist Liberal Party as an exclusively Italian movement, just as it is wrong to interpret the political and cultural situation in Dalmatia in the second half of the nineteenth century on the basis of rigid and homogeneous opposing national alignments. As Tommaseo has acutely pointed out, for many centuries the Dalmatians had been a separate people, the product of the meeting and fusion of Italian and Slav races and cultures: 'Not only have the stocks been mixed, and the glories and the sorrows, the benefits and the hopes intertwined; but the very names have been exchanged. Italian families that have died out, live on in Slav ones, and leave to the Slavs the heritage of their memories and their fortunes; Slav families assumed Italian names; so that those who hate the name of Italy can be said to doubly hate their country, disowning themselves.'[137]

Tommaseo, Bajamonti, Lapenna, Galvani, and the Dalmatian autonomists believed that there was a Dalmatian nation, founded on values that were not so much ethnic as historical and cultural, and produced by the mingling of Slavs and Italians and by the historical separation of Dalmatia and Croatia. The specificity of the lifestyle, mentality, culture, and languages of the Dalmatians legitimized their struggle for the defence of a political and administrative autonomy of Dalmatia within the Habsburg Empire.

---

135  L. [Luigi Lapenna], 'La situazione,' in *Il Dalmata*, 7 February 1885.
136  For a profile of the bishop: *Reichsraths-Almanach für die Session 1867*, p. 116.
137  Niccolò Tommaseo, *La questione dalmatica nei suoi nuovi aspetti: Osservazioni*, quoted in Camizzi, 'Il dibattito sull'annessione della Dalmazia,' p. 240.

For many years the position taken by Vincenzo Duplancich, a journalist from Zara who later emigrated to Italy and who tended (unlike Tommaseo, Galvani, and Lapenna) to identify Dalmatian culture with the Italian culture and to separate and distinguish Slavism from the Italian spirit, was shared only by a small minority of Italian Dalmatians and supporters of the liberal autonomist movement.[138]

An important element of Dalmatian autonomist regionalism and a source of its nourishment was, as we have pointed out, the municipalism that was widespread among the urban populations of Dalmatia. In fact, one of the reasons for the great success of autonomism at the polls had been its ability to express the municipalist and regionalist sentiments of the urban classes of Dalmatia. Throughout the nineteenth century the inhabitants of Zara, Spalato, and Sebenico identified themselves chiefly with the traditional culture of their cities rather than with vague and abstract feelings of nationalism; they felt themselves to be citizens of Zara, Spalato, or Sebenico rather than Croatians or Italians. This municipalist particularism was a central part of the autonomist ideology; Bajamonti, for example, compared the struggles against Croatian annexationism with those of the Dalmatian city-states in defence of their independence in the Middle Ages, and he saw the ancient municipal traditions of the cities of Dalmatia as the origin of autonomist liberalism.

However, municipalism, the product of centuries of Dalmatian urban civilization, which was lacking among the other Balkan peoples, was also the source of innumerable disagreements within the autonomist movement and undermined its organizational cohesion. During the second half of the nineteenth century Dalmatian autonomism was not so much a true party along the lines of modern political parties with mass appeal, as it was a confederation of fairly independent groups headed by local notabilities. The autonomous movement lacked an undisputed central political leadership in Dalmatia as a whole; rather, in every Dalmatian town and city there was an autonomist group led by one or more prominent local figures (usually landowners, doctors, notaries, state officials, teachers, and above all, lawyers) who mobilized their own followers and clients for political events and elections.

---

138 Novak, *Povijest Splita*, III, pp. 248–250; Paoli Palcich, 'Vincenzo Duplancich', pp. 169 et seq.

Reading circles, cafés, sports, and music societies were the hubs around which the activity of the Dalmatian autonomists was organized.[139]

Thus family dynasties were formed within Dalmatian autonomist liberalism and remained at the head of the autonomist groups of the various cities until the outbreak of World War I: the Ghiglianovichs in Zara, the Galvanis and the Fenzis at Sebenico, the Marassovichs at Scardona, the Fanfognas at Traù, the Smerchinich family at Curzola, the Serraglis in Ragusa, and the Botteris at Cittavecchia (Stari Grad) on Lesina.[140]

This political and organizational fragmentation facilitated the pro-liferation of personal and municipal rivalries within the autonomist movement. The party never had a single political leader but was al-ways guided by groups of often quarrelsome individuals. For several years the leadership of Luigi Lapenna, undoubtedly the most brilliant and gifted personality in the movement and a representative of its Zara wing, seemed to predominate, but Bajamonti, head of the autonomists in Spalato, never accepted his primacy and tried repeatedly to establish himself as the undisputed leader.

These personal clashes were often fuelled by municipal rivalries, and the political and economic competition between Zara and Spalato, for example, was one of the causes of the weakening of the autonomist movement over the course of the 1870s.

An important part of the difference between the Dalmatians and the Croatians was their use of the Italian language. Although for many years the vast majority of the Dalmatian autonomists did not define themselves as Italians on the political and national plane, but simply as Dalmatians, they always vigorously defended the use and spread of the Italian language and culture in Dalmatia. At the root of this position, in our view, there was a precise awareness of the needs of Dalmatian soci-ety, located between Italy and the Balkans. As Tommaseo observed, the Italian language and culture had an extremely important role to play on the Dalmatian coast since they could foster the cultural and economic progress of the population and the connection of the Dalmatians with

---

139 On autonomist associations in Spalato between the middle of the nineteenth century and World War I: Skunca, *Glazbeni život Splita od 1860–1918*. On autonomist associations in Zara: De' Benvenuti, *Storia di Zara dal 1797 al 1918*, pp. 380 et seq.; Maserati, 'Simboli e riti nell'irredentismo dalmata,' pp. 63–78.
140 For a list of the principal autonomist families in Dalmatia at the beginning of the 1890s: *Onoranze funebri ad Antonio Bajamonti*, pp. 37 et seq.

Europe and the rest of the world. The same concept was often stressed by Bajamonti: the Italian language was 'the means best suited to expressing our feelings, as a way of keeping ourselves in the sphere of those positive interests that can best make up for the deficiency of our economic factors, as the best vehicle to carry us in the direction of civil progress.'[141]

Defence of the use of Italian did not signify for the autonomists a denial of the predominantly Slav character of Dalmatian society as a whole. Contrary to the negative anti-autonomist stereotypes spread by nationalist Croatian and Yugoslav journalism and historiography, the autonomists were not opposed to encouraging the use of the Slav language. The linguistic policy of the Italian liberals in Trieste and Istria must not be confused with that of the Dalmatian Italo-Slav liberals. The Dalmatian autonomists were determined supporters of bilingualism. At the first session of the Dalmatian provincial diet the autonomist majority proclaimed the freedom of use of Italian and Serbo-Croatian in the assembly, in so far as both languages were spoken in Dalmatia. The autonomist municipal administrations sought to promote education of the people through the creation of schools with two media of instruction, Italian and Serbo-Croatian. This policy was contested by the Croatian and Serbian nationalists who, after declaring their acceptance of bilingualism for several years, began to see Italian as a harmful legacy of Venetian colonialism. For the editors of *Il Nazionale* (later *Narodni List*), the main Dalmatian nationalist newspaper, there was no Italian nationality in Dalmatia, and the use of the Italian language was 'the symbol of foreign rule, symbol of the privileged races of the past and ... symbol of privilege in the present day.'[142] Once they had achieved political dominance in Dalmatia, the Serbo-Croatian nationalists had Italian eliminated as a language of instruction in the schools, and it was taught merely as a foreign language, on a par with French and English.

In favour of bilingualism, the autonomists were opposed to an immediate and radical introduction of the use of Croatian in all sectors of public life, preferring a gradual approach in order to avoid upheavals in Dalmatian society.[143] The temporary predominance of Ital-

---

141 Bajamonti, *La società politica dalmata*, p. 11.
142 *Il Nazionale*, 18 December 1867.
143 There is a great deal of material on the linguistic question in the proceedings of the Dalmatian provincial diet; for example: speeches by members Kapović (Capovic)

ian was recognized, but hopes were expressed for a more complete bilingualism in the future. Antonio Bajamonti, who as mayor of Spalato favoured the setting up of popular Slav schools in the city, pointed out that Italian and Croatian were not incompatible: 'Let us live, let us develop the elements in which our homeland is not so lacking, and we, on our own initiative, will push ahead the language of our people, which is the Tuscan of Slavia, and we, on our own initiative, will add our stone to the rebirth of the Slav peoples by using and not wasting one of the best factors, Italian civilization, which must in fact contribute to that glorious work.'[144]

Thus bilingualism was a resource for Dalmatian society, and its defence for the autonomists did not mean denying the predominantly Slav character of the Dalmatians. The autonomists did not repudiate the Slav component of their culture but, on the contrary, declared themselves its supporters and defenders. Tommaseo's concept of the Dalmatians as the guiding nation of the Slav peoples was very widely aired in autonomist political journalism. Moreover, the Croatian language, in its Chakavian or Shtokavian dialects, was used in the autonomist press (which was mostly in Italian), and articles and letters in Slav were carried by the main autonomist liberal newspapers, *Il Dalmata* of Zara and *L'Avvenire* and *La Difesa* of Spalato. Attempts were made to defend bilingualism in education: the autonomist mayor of Scardona, Giovanni Marassovich, pointed out in 1867 that pupils at the girls school in his town were taught in the Italian and Slav languages, 'this in homage to Scardona's Italian culture and its Slav nationality.'[145]

Another fundamental element of autonomist political ideology was liberalism. The Dalmatian autonomists enthusiastically backed the policy of granting individual civil, religious, political, and cultural freedoms and of partially limiting the absolute power of the sovereign and the state, which was introduced by Austro-German liberalism over the course of the 1860s; they were also resolute supporters of the February patent and the constitutional laws of 1867. This identification with

---

and Messa, meeting of 14 December 1885, ADP-BI, pp. 228–32; speeches by the Nationalist representatives Klaić and Zore and by the autonomist Bajamonti, meeting of 17 December 1886, pp. 325–46,

144  Speech by Bajamonti, meeting of 18 April 1861, ADP-BI; Monzali, 'Dalmati o Italiani?' pp. 444–5.

145  *Il Nazionale*, 19 January 1867. On the figure of Marassovich: Vrandečić, *Dalmatinski autonomistički pokret u XIX stoljeću*, pp. 174 et seq.

Austro-German liberalism stemmed in part from the liberal convictions of the Dalmatian autonomists and in part from the awareness that the laws of 1861 and 1867 sanctioned the separation of Dalmatia from Croatia.

Political and economic liberalism was the ideology of the mercantile and administrative classes (who comprised the majority of the autonomist electorate), an important part of the autonomist ruling class (which was made up of liberal members of the bourgeoisie and the aristocracy). These social groups welcomed the liberalization of the Austrian political and economic system, deriving prosperity and advantages as well as growing political influence in a society dominated by imperial absolutism and the traditionalist aristocracy.

Dalmatian liberalism, like equivalent movements in much of Europe during that period, was founded on an elitist and oligarchic vision of society in which participation in political power was based on wealth, property, and the ability to pay taxes. In Dalmatia this oligarchic perspective was combined with a belief that the culture of the urban populations was superior to that of the country people. The gravity of the rural question in Dalmatia (a region characterized by a poor and backward agricultural economy and dominated by large landed estates that were often owned by people of Italian language and culture who lived in the city, but were cultivated by poverty-stricken Slav, Serbian or Croatian peasants) and the inability of the autonomist liberal movement to deal with the rural world of the hinterland and set down political roots in it were elements that seriously weakened Dalmatian autonomism in the long term. Autonomist liberalism remained a movement rooted in the cities, able to muster support even from parts of the urban working class (sailors, artisans, farmers from the immediate surroundings and the suburbs, and labourers) on the basis of patronage and a common project of economic progress that was centred on municipalism. It was not capable of giving convincing answers to a restless and impoverished peasant class, and in the countryside the nationalist and populist values upheld by the National Party, whose most fervent support came from many Catholics and Orthodox priests, proved more attractive. Attempts to alter farming contracts and leases to the advantage of peasants were denounced by the autonomist press as efforts by 'ultra-Slav demagogues' to subvert social order.[146] Even Antonio Bajamonti, expo-

---

146  'Il Comunismo in Dalmazia,' in *L'Avvenire*, 26 July 1875.

nent of the most progressive wing of the liberal autonomist movement and founder of the first workers' benefit society in Spalato,[147] and who had always tried to bring various elements of the city's working classes into his movement, never saw the question of relations with the rural world as a serious political problem; he dismissed the successes of Croatian nationalism in inland Dalmatia as the result of the work of 'a few fanatical priests' and the acts of violence of a rabble that forced 'the constitutionalists to back off during elections in order not to see their homes burned, their vineyards destroyed.'[148]

For the autonomists, in short, the peasants of Dalmatia were a passive element in Dalmatian society that ought to remain outside politics. The attitude of the autonomists toward the rural world is summed up well by an anonymous columnist of Il Dalmata who, criticizing the election of many farm workers to the city council of Sebenico in 1903, wrote ironically: 'Poor and deluded countryman! Your place is not on councils, in civic bodies; the wretched politics that are practised today are harmful to your naturally honest character, accustomed to the harmony of the fields, to salubrious labour on the fragrant and fertile land! In the fields, that is your place, there you are king.'[149]

The regionalistic identity and the alliance with Austrian liberal constitutionalism had significant repercussions on the political choices made by the Dalmatian Autonomist Liberal Party. For several decades the Dalmatian liberals rejected and fought any suggestions of detachment of Dalmatia from the Habsburg Empire and of union with Italy, and were faithful subjects of Austria. The autonomist press of the 1860s and 1870s was filled with glorifications of the Austrian military victories in 1866.[150] In 1876, Antonio Bajamonti was able to claim with every right the loyalty of the Dalmatian Autonomous Liberal Party to the Habsburgs, recalling the support that the population and the municipal administration of Spalato had given to the Habsburg navy during

---

147   Il Nazionale, 7 August 1867. On the progressive tendencies of autonomist liberalism in Spalato: Vrandečić, Dalmatinski autonomistički pokret u XIX stoljeću, pp. 176 et seq.
148   Bajamonti, Discorso pronunziato alla Camera, p. 12.
149   'I podestà di Sebenico,' in Il Dalmata, 25 February 1903 (the anonymous author of the article was probably Emanuele Fenzi, leader of the Autonomist Party in Sebenico).
150   Bajamonti, his right-hand man Giovannizio, and the autonomist city council of Spalato sent congratulations to the emperor of Austria for the victory at Lissa: Il Nazionale, 23 January 1867.

the war against Italy ten years earlier.[151] In the 1890s the autonomists were still singing the praises of the Austrian and Dalmatian heroes of the battle of Lissa (Vis).[152]

An opposite attitude was taken by the Italian liberals of the Trentino and Venezia Giulia, who had displayed an explicit political and cultural identification with the nascent Italian national state ever since the conflict of 1859, an identification that had been long absent from Dalmatian autonomism.[153] In June 1866 the Italian consul in Sarajevo, Cesare Durando, observed the total identification between the Autonomist Party and Habsburg institutions and the distrust that had arisen between the Dalmatian nationalists and autonomists over the rumours of possible Italian designs on the annexation of Dalmatia.[154] The Italian consul in Trieste, Giovanni Domenico Bruno, shrewdly noted the profound political difference between the liberals of Venezia Giulia and the Dalmatian autonomists, declaring in a report of 1869:

> The Autonomist Party of Dalmatia should not be confused with the so-called Italian Party of Trieste and Istria. Aspiring to union with Italy, the latter has hope in the future and is trying to prepare for it. The Autonomist Party of Dalmatia, on the contrary, is far from any thought of union with Italy ... and has no aspiration at all to separate Dalmatia from the Austro-Hungarian Empire, but only to prevent its union with Croatia and Hungary. It rejects unification with Croatia because, having a Latin culture and

---

151  Bajamonti, *Discorso pronunziato alla Camera*, pp. 19–20.
152  Speech by Antonio Smirich, meeting of 16 February 1894, ADP-BI.
153  Our interpretation draws on the arguments, taking them further and providing them with a documentary base, for the non-existence of Italian irredentism in Dalmatia in 1866 that Gaetano Salvemini and Carlo Maranelli had put forward in the political pamphlet *La questione dell'Adriatico*, now reproduced in Salvemini, *Dalla guerra mondiale alla dittatura (1916–1925)*, pp. 285 et seq. Italian irredentist political journalism and the historiography inspired by it have sought instead to demonstrate the existence of Dalmatian aspirations to unification with Italy since the middle of the nineteenth century: Tamaro, *Italiani e Slavi nell'Adriatico*; Praga, *Dalmazia*; Randi, *Bajamonti*. On the loyalty to Austria of the Dalmatian autonomists in 1866: Vrandečić, *Dalmatinski autonomistički pokret u XIX stoljeću*, pp. 133 et seq.
154  Durando to the foreign minister, 18 June 1866, ASMAE, ARC POL, 1861–1887, Divisione Legazioni, portfolio 906. A selection of reports by Durando from Bosnia, but lacking the most interesting documents written by the Italian diplomat on the Yugoslav question, had been published in *Izvještaji italijanskog konzulata u Sarajevu (1863–1870)*.

civilization, it does not want to merge with a province that has only just emerged from barbarism.[155]

One should not be surprised at this loyalty to the Habsburgs on the part of the Italophile Dalmatian autonomist liberals. Liberal autonomism was an expression of the urban middle classes of former Venetian coastal Dalmatia, who looked with favour on Dalmatia's belonging to the Habsburg Empire. In the wake of Habsburg economic growth after 1849 and Austria's expansion into the Balkans, these Dalmatian Italo-Slavs hoped to make Dalmatia the great trading centre of the region and regarded pro-Habsburg constitutional liberalism as fully in keeping with their own values. The Dalmatian autonomists were strong supporters of Habsburg expansionism in the Balkans, in which they saw a possible source of commercial and financial advantage. Even in the 1860s Antonio Bajamonti argued for the necessity of the Habsburg conquest of Bosnia and Herzegovina, territories that in his view should be united with Dalmatia.[156] The autonomist press vigorously defended the actions of the Habsburg government during the Balkan crisis of 1875–8 and applauded the occupation of the Bosnian provinces.[157]

## 1.6.  Autonomist Liberalism and the Serbo-Croatian National Party in Austrian and Dalmatian Politics During the First Half of the 1860s

The year 1861 had sanctioned the triumph of the autonomist movement in Dalmatia. The provincial elections had demonstrated the consensus that the autonomists enjoyed in the main Dalmatian cities. Even the evolution of Austrian politics seemed to favour the autonomists. The victory of Schmerling and the Centralist liberals was welcomed by the Dalmatian autonomists. Lapenna's strategy – consolidation of the alliance between Dalmatian autonomism and Austro-German liberalism, with a view to checking the rise of Slav nationalism and ensuring the support of the state authorities for his movement – had proved to be a success.

---

155  Bruno to Menabrea, 23 August 1869, DDI, I, 11, doc. 525.
156  See Bajamonti's platform at the provincial elections of 1867, reproduced in *Il Nazionale*, 23 March 1867.
157  On this: 'L'Austria e l'Oriente' in *Il Dalmata*, 24 July 1878; *Il Costituzionale*, 13 May 1877.

However, the Autonomist Party turned out to be a not very harmonious and united group, with a strong propensity for internal conflict. Political rivalries between its leaders were constant throughout its existence. The personal disagreements often had their origin in municipalism. Since 1861, disputes had emerged between the autonomists of Zara, led by Possedaria and Lapenna, and those of Spalato over the question of the railroad. Bajamonti's plan to build a railroad that would connect Spalato with Belgrade through Bosnia prompted protests from the inhabitants of Zara, who feared economic damage to their city and asked for links between Zara, Fiume, and Zagreb.[158] Then there were differences between Bajamonti and the autonomists of Zara over the presumed attempts by the politician from Spalato to obtain the status of free port for his city and make it the administrative capital of Dalmatia.[159]

Over the course of 1863 the conflicts between the autonomists of Spalato and Zara worsened. On the occasion of a by-election for the provincial diet that was held at Signi in January 1863, Lapenna and the Zara autonomists supported the candidature of Girolamo Alesani, a government official in Spalato and a friend of Lapenna, thereby clashing with the followers of Bajamonti who were in favour of Giuseppe Piperata, also from Spalato. Alesani won, but his election was annulled by the diet in March 1863 for breaches of the rules. The rivalry between Alesani, who was the highest authority of the state in Spalato, and Bajamonti became more and more intense, reaching its peak in 1864 when Alesani accused the mayor of excessive expenditure and budget irregularities and had the Spalato city council dissolved and Bajamonti dismissed.[160]

---

158  On Bajamonti's railroad schemes: Bajamonti, *Nello inaugurare la pubblicità delle sessioni municipali in Spalato*, pp. 12–13; *Dell'amministrazione del comune di Spalato*, pp. 55–7. On the disagreements between Zara and Spalato over the routes of the future Dalmatian railroads: *Il Nazionale*, 26 November 1862, 11 February 1863, 1 July 1863; on the disputes inside the Autonomist Party: Vrandečić, *Dalmatinski autonomistički pokret u XIX stoljeću*, pp. 116 et seq.

159  *La Voce Dalmatica*, 15 October 1862 and 10 January 1863; Palcich, *Vincenzo Duplancich.* p. 208.

160  *Il Nazionale*, 28 and 31 January 1863, 12 and 19 March 1864, 25 June 1864; Degli Alberti, *Memoria intorno lo scioglimento del municipio di Spalato*; Bajamonti, *Dell'amministrazione del comune di Spalato*, pp. 107 et seq.; Lanza, *Sopra le relazioni dell'amministrazione del comune di Spalato*; Novak, *Povijest Splita*, III, pp. 317 et seq.; Vuličević, *Partiti e lotte in Dalmazia*, pp. 67 et seq.

The growing disputes with the Zara autonomists and the dissolution
of the municipal administration of Spalato convinced Bajamonti and
his followers of the need to approach the Serbo-Croatian nationalists
and form a political alliance with them.

After several years of political and organizational weakness, the example and the political and financial assistance of the Croatian nationalist movement led by Bishop Strossmayer, which called for unification
within the Habsburg Empire of all the lands inhabited by Croatian and
Serbian populations (Croatia, Slavonia, the Military Frontier, Istria,
Fiume, and Dalmatia), had stimulated the birth of a Slav unionist nationalist party of the south in Dalmatia, the so-called National Party.[161]

The Dalmatian nationalists, desiring the annexation of Dalmatia to
Croatia and the promotion of the use of the Croatian and Serbian languages, were at the outset a composite and heterogeneous political formation comprising Croats, Serbs, and Italians; atheists, Catholics, and
Orthodox; liberals, and clericalists. What kept such a diverse range of
groups together for many years was a Slavophile national and populist
ideology that claimed the existence of a single nationality in Dalmatia,
which was generically declared Slav and proclaimed identical to that
of the peoples who lived in the southern territories of the Habsburg
Empire (Croatia, Bosnia, Herzegovina, Serbia, and Montenegro). The
editors of *Il Nazionale*, official organ of the Narodnjaci (the followers of
the National Party) over the course of the 1860s and 1870s, argued in
1863 that 'morally Dalmatians, Serbs, and Croatians form a single nation, and ... their language is one, as their origin is one, their appearance
in Europe contemporary, and their history not very different.'[162]

Regarding the linguistic differences between the populations of the
coast and those of the hinterland and the use of the Italian language
as negative and pernicious, the National Party advocated the spread
of the so-called Slav language and the dominance of the Croatian-Serbian nationality throughout Dalmatia. According to Costantino (Kosta)

161  On the Slav national movement in Dalmatia in the second half of the nineteenth
    century: Novak, *Prošlost Dalmacije*, II, pp. 334 et seq.; Petrović, *Nacionalno pitanje
    u Dalmaciji u XIX stoljeću*; Perić, *Dalmatinski Sabor*; Foretić, ed., *Dalmacija 1870*;
    Ivanišević, *Narodni Preporod u Dalmaciji*; Schödl, *Kroatische Nationalpolitk und 'Jugo-
    slavenstvo'*. On the contacts between Strossmayer and the Dalmatian nationalists:
    Šišić, ed., *Korespondencija Rački-Strossmayer*, vol. 1, docs. 31, 37, 216, 304, 305, 322.
162  *Il Nazionale*, 14 January 1863.

Vojnović, one of the principal Dalmatian Slavophile intellectuals, Dalmatia was part of the 'Slav-Hellenic' peninsula and was populated exclusively by the 'Slav race'; there were no Italians in Dalmatia, and so it was necessary to 'nationalize' the schools, the administration, and the courts in order to erase the traces left by Venetian rule and the damage it had caused. The Italian culture could survive only within the limits of the Slav national character of the country and, in any case, without any recognition as an autochthonous element of Dalmatian society.[163]

This Dalmatian Slav nationalist ideology presented several problematic aspects. It was based on certain concepts founded on clear dichotomies (Slav/Italian, patriot / foreigner or traitor) that did not match the actual reality of Dalmatian urban society, in which an ethnic mixture prevailed and a rigid separation into national groups was not possible. However, this abstractness was also a point of strength since, thanks to a generic Slav populism, it avoided tackling the question of the relationship between the Croatian and Serbian nationalities and was able to attract and unite not just Croats and Serbs but also Dalmatians of ethnic Italian origin who were inspired by a Slavophile and populist political consciousness.

Among the leaders and founders of the Croatian-Serbian national movement in Dalmatia were several intellectuals, including the high-school teachers Michele (Miho) Klaić,[164] Natko Nodilo, Đuro (Juraj) Pulić, Don Ivan Danilo, and Don Michele (Miho) Pavlinović, and the lawyers Stefan Ljubiša and Kosta Vojnović. A few Dalmatians of Italian language, culture, and origin also played an important role in the emergence of Yugoslav nationalism in Dalmatia. Particularly interesting is the figure of one of the most brilliant Dalmatian nationalist intellectuals, Lorenzo (Lovre) Monti, who was a lawyer from Knin and the author of various writings in support of annexation; he later became a member of the provincial diet and the Reichsrat.[165] Despite his Italian origins, he held that 'a people cannot belong to two nations but

163 Costantino (Kosta) Voinović, 'La sola conciliazione possibile,' in *Il Nazionale*, 19 March 1862; 'Della missione della civiltà italiana in Dalmazia,' ibidem, 2 and 5 April 1862.
164 On Miho Klaić: *Enciklopedija Jugoslavije*, vol. 5, p. 252.
165 For information on Lorenzo Monti: Novak, *Povijest Splita*, III, pp. 229–31; see too the work with which Monti announced his retirement from politics on the grounds of his disagreement with the purely Croatian direction taken by the National Party at the end of the 1870s: Monti, *Zašto sam istupio iz Sabora i iz Carevinskoga Vijeća*.

must, on pain of its fortune and its honour, stick closely to what it can rightly call its own.' According to Monti, two nationalities cannot live in a single country, 'one inside and the other outside the walls of a few cities, clearly distinct from one another'; as the predominant nationality in Dalmatia was 'Illyro-Serb,' Dalmatians of Italian ancestry had to sacrifice their language and their origin to their native land and become Slavic.[166] For Italian Dalmatians like Monti the assertion of Slav national ideals was the only way to bring together and merge the rural and urban populations and thereby further the cultural and political development of Dalmatia.

There were numerous Italian Dalmatians in the National Party in Spalato, including its founders Edoardo Tacconi and Vito (Vid) Morpurgo. Until the rise of the political star of Gajo Filomeno Bulat, Tacconi, son of a Lombard who had emigrated to Dalmatia in the first half of the nineteenth century, was one of the undisputed leaders of the opposition to Bajamonti.[167] Morpurgo, a bookseller, publisher, and businessman from a Jewish family of Italian language and culture in Spalato, was an indefatigable promoter of the nationalist movement in that city.[168]

Despite electoral defeat at the first provincial elections of 1861, the National Party had shown itself to be the predominant political force in southern Dalmatia and the countryside, but it was weak in the central and northern cities (Zara, Sebenico, Spalato) and the islands. Over the following years it strengthened its presence in the main urban centres. A fundamental boost to the reinforcement of the party's organizational structure came from the opening of national reading societies (*Narodne Čitaonice*), which made it possible to carry out cultural and political activities in the Slav language in cities still dominated by the Italian language and culture; in 1863 Slav reading societies were set up in Zara, Ragusa, and Spalato, and in the following years in Jelsa, Cittavecchia, Traù, Sebenico, Curzola, Knin, Obrovac, and Pučišća.[169]

---

166  Monti, *Considerazioni sull'annessione del regno di Dalmazia a quelli di Croazia e Slavonia*.
167  On the Tacconi family: Tacconi, ed., *Antonio e Ildebrando Tacconi*. On Edoardo Tacconi and his many decades of militancy in the National Party, which came to an end in 1885 as a result of personal disagreements with Bulat: *Narod*, 22 July and 3 October 1885.
168  Kečkemet, *Vid Morpurgo i Narodni Preporod u Splitu*.
169  On the national *čitaonice*: Petrović, *Nacionalno pitanje u Dalmaciji u XIX stoljeću*, pp. 213 et seq.; Ivanišević, *Narodni Preporod u Dalmaciji*, pp. 52–4.

The crucial element in the development and success of the National Party in Dalmatia, however, was its capacity to attract and mobilize numerous members of the Catholic and Serbian-Orthodox clergy.[170] For centuries in Dalmatia, especially after the collapse of the economy that was triggered by the Turkish invasion and the decline of the coastal cities, the clergy constituted a fundamental part of the intelligentsia and the ruling class. Its importance was increased by the fact that it offered, along with trade, one of the few possibilities of upward mobility in Dalmatia's static and rigid society; as a result, a considerable number of men of rural and peasant origin entered the Dalmatian clergy. They were often alien to the bilingual and Italophile culture of the coastal cities, where the wide range of possible economic activities made a career in the church less attractive. Particularly significant was the role and influence of the clergy in the Dalmatian countryside, where the local priest was frequently the only educated person in an extremely poor and illiterate population. The emergence of pluralist politics, founded on elections for representative institutions, gave the parish priests great political influence, which they wielded on behalf of the National Party, becoming its leaders and organizers in many places. With regard to the clout of the clergy in Dalmatian political life the autonomist leader Lapenna declared: 'The population of the countryside is not yet fully mature enough to grasp its own interests and to appreciate the influence that the constitutional system and the parliamentary mechanism exercise on it, and meekly follows the path indicated to it by its Parish Priest, and with all the more trust since the majority of Priests in Dalmatia are recruited from the rural population.'[171] Moreover, numerous Narodnjaci leaders were priests: Pavlinović, Juraj Biankini, Ivo Prodan, Frane Bulić, and Pulić.

Aware of the growing strength of the National Party, Bajamonti, in contrast to the autonomists of Zara and Lapenna, started to make political overtures to the nationalists, which lead to the creation of the so-called Liberal Union, an alliance between autonomist liberals and Slav national liberals.[172] The alliance arose for reasons of political con-

170 In this connection see the considerations of Novak, *Prošlost Dalmacije*, II, pp. 372–3; see too Vitezić, 'Die roemisch-katholische Kirche bei den Kroaten.'
171 L. [Luigi Lapenna], 'La situazione,' in *Il Dalmata*, 21 February 1885.
172 The most important source on the Liberal Union is the nationalist newspaper *Il Nazionale*, which between 1863 and 1864 took a very favourable attitude toward

venience: on the one hand, Bajamonti needed to regain control of the municipality of Spalato, whose council and mayor had become elective offices following the reforms implemented by the government in Vienna in 1864; and on the other hand, the Narodnjaci desired to increase their own influence in the main city of central Dalmatia. Bajamonti, however, justified his new political strategy from the perspective of both program and ideology. Starting out with the idea of an Italo-Slav, multi-ethnic, and bilingual Dalmatian nation, he announced that if the nationalists were to renounce any plan of union with Croatia and declare themselves ready to respect the Italian language and culture, the conditions would exist for a collaboration between national liberals and autonomist liberals.[173] He repeated this in a speech to the Dalmatian diet on 5 April 1864; stating that the autonomists were hostile not to the Slav language and nationality of Dalmatia but only to its annexation to Croatia, Bajamonti launched what was to become his famous slogan, 'Slavs tomorrow even, Croatians never!' For Bajamonti it was necessary to overcome the difference of nationality, seeking to find harmony and goodwill and abandoning the idea of annexation to Croatia. With this program it was possible to merge the liberal members of the nationalist and autonomist movements to give rise to a single liberal party, which would bring together all Dalmatians above and beyond national divisions.[174]

Bajamonti and many of the autonomists believed that the Dalmatians had a civilizing role to play in the Balkan world, based on the idea that the Latin-Slav symbiosis at the root of the society of coastal Dalmatia gave it a cultural superiority that justified a future Dalmatian supremacy over other Slav and Balkan peoples. This entailed an acceptance of the possibility of a progressive Slavicization of Dalmatian society, but the process should involve the preservation of the Italian cultural tradi-

Bajamonti, becoming in practice his mouthpiece; see too the minutes of the Dalmatian provincial diet for the years 1863 and 1864. The writings of Grga Novak are useful: Novak, *Povijest Splita*, III; *Prošlost Dalmacije*, II, pp. 388–93; 'Političke prilike u Dalmaciji 1862–1865,' pp. 5–34; Monzali, 'Dalmati o Italiani?' pp. 446 et seq.; Vrandečić, *Dalmatinski autonomistički pokret u XIX stoljeću*, pp. 116 et seq.

173 Letter from Antonio Bajamonti to the editorial staff of *Il Nazionale*, in *Il Nazionale*, 7 March 1863.

174 Speech by Antonio Bajamonti to the Dalmatian provincial diet on 5 April 1864, statement published in *Il Nazionale*, 9 April 1864. On this speech see too: Novak, *Povijest Splita*, III, p. 280; Peric, *Dalmatinski Sabor*, pp. 77–8.

tion, which was considered a fundamental element of the region's identity, and guarantee the institutional autonomy and political hegemony of the Italo-Slav Dalmatians. In the view of Bajamonti and his followers, the political and national compromise with the Slav nationalists and the Liberal Union were elements in the scheme to make Dalmatia the vital centre of the Balkan world in the future, a bridge between the Slavic east and the Latin-Germanic west.

With these programs (abandonment of the demand for the union of Dalmatia with Croatia, increased use of the Slav language in schools and institutions, full achievement of constitutional liberty, and struggle against 'the many exorbitances of the governing party'[175]), Bajamonti and some nationalist representatives, Klaić and Ljubiša, set up the Liberal Union in the spring of 1864. Thus Bajamonti's need to find allies in Spalato to regain control of the municipal council led to a split in the autonomist movement. At the elections for the diet in July, Bajamonti's liberals presented themselves in alliance with the nationalists, clashing with the independent autonomists led by Lapenna, but without much success: the Liberal Union won only thirteen seats (nine for nationalists and four for followers of Bajamonti), while Lapenna's autonomists, backed by Vienna, gained a majority in the diet with twenty-four seats.[176]

The Liberal Union fared better at the municipal elections in Spalato, where Bajamonti, who could rely on widespread support, was able to win back the office of mayor in August 1865.

Analysis of these events reveals the powerful influence of personal clashes and municipal rivalries on the political actions of the Dalmatian autonomists. In those early years the question of nationality was not considered a crucial element of political division and conflict; nationality was seen as something dynamic and mutable, a cultural choice or a political ideology that could be assumed and then abandoned without traumatic effects, especially in a situation like that of Dalmatia, which was characterized by bilingualism and a medley of ethnic groups.

Redefinition of the Dalmatian political panorama on the base of the confrontation between the Liberal Union and the independent autono-

---

175  On these: Degli Alberti, *Memoria intorno lo scioglimento del municipio di Spalato*, p. 21.
176  Novak, *Povijest Splita*, III, p. 283.

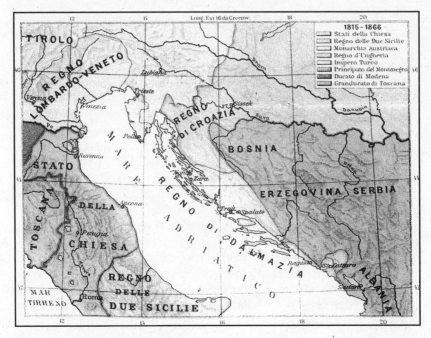

The Adriatic regions, 1815–66. The Kingdoms of Lombardo-Veneto, Croatia, and Dalmatia were part of the Austrian Empire. The regions indicated as Bosnia, Erzegovina, Serbia, and Albania were part of the Ottoman Empire.

mists was short lived. In 1866 fierce disagreements arose between the nationalists and Bajamonti in Spalato when they lost patience with the mayor's excessive power.[177] The final blow to the Liberal Union, however, was dealt by developments in international and Austrian politics during the years 1866 and 1867.

---

177  *Il Nazionale*, 12 and 16 May 1866, 23 January 1867.

# 2 The War of 1866 and the Emergence of the Italian National Question in Dalmatia

## 2.1. The War of 1866, the Austro-Hungarian Compromise, and the Shift in the Political Balance of Power in Dalmatia

The growing rivalry between Prussia and Austria within the German Confederation was the political development that allowed the kingdom of Italy to challenge the Habsburg Empire on the battlefield in 1866.[1]

---

1 Many diplomatic documents on the origin and course of the Austro-Prussian War have been published. In addition to the collection of Italian diplomatic papers (DDI, I, vols. 5, 6 and 7), the correspondence of Victor Emmanuel II (*Le lettere di Vittorio Emanuele II*, edited by Francesco Cognasso, 2 vols., in particular vol. 2, pp. 869 et seq.) and the Austrian, French, and British documentation published in *Il problema veneto*, we should mention the collection of papers edited by Hermann Oncken (*Rheinpolitik*, vols. 1 and 2), comprising Austrian, Prussian, and southern German documents; *Les origines diplomatiques*, vols. 6, 7, 8, 9, 10, 11, and 12 (collection of French diplomatic papers); APP (this collection, which includes not just Prussian diplomatic papers but also Sardinian/Italian, Austrian, Russian, British, and French papers, ceased publication with vol. 6, devoted to the period from April 1865 to March 1866); the publication edited by Heinrich von Srbik, *Quellen*, vols. 4 and 5, which contains Habsburg diplomatic papers. Amongst the literature devoted to the political and military events of the war of 1866: Chiala, *Ancora un po' più di luce sugli eventi politici e militari dell'anno 1866* (reproduces documents from the La Marmora and Govone papers); Srbik, *Deutsche Einheit*, in particular vol. 4; Beiche, *Bismarck und Italien*; Blaas, 'Vom Friauler Putsch in Herbst 1864 bis zur Abtretung Venetiens 1866,' pp. 264–338; *Die italienische Frage und das österreichische Parlament*, vol. 22, pp. 151–245; 'L'Austria di fronte al problema veneto,' pp. 49–77 (essays that help to explain Austrian policy toward Italy); Wandruszka, *Schicksaljahr 1866*; Riccardi, *Francesco Salata*, pp. 32 et seq.; Silva, *Il Sessantasei*; 'La politica italiana di Napoleone III,' *Nuova Rivista Storica*, 1927, no. 1/2I, pp. 1–51; 1927, no. 3/4, pp. 242–85, in particular pp. 260 et seq.; Lefebvre d'Ovidio, 'Napoleone III, l'Austria e la questione del Veneto,' pp. 85–124; De' Robertis, *La*

Between 1863 and 1865, with the backing of Great Britain, which saw the problem of the Veneto as a source of instability in European politics,[2] Italian diplomacy had tried to find a peaceful solution to the Venetian question but without concrete results. In the face of deteriorating Franco-Russian relations, provoked by the violent suppression of the uprising in Poland, Marco Minghetti's government had sent Count Giuseppe Pasolini on a secret mission to London and Paris in the summer of 1863 to propose a grand alliance between France, Great Britain, Italy, Sweden, and the Habsburg Empire. The objective was to prepare for a war against Russia in order to re-establish an independent Polish state. In exchange for its participation Italy would be given the Veneto, while Austria would receive the Danubian principalities. The Italian plan, which intended to reform the coalition that had defeated Russia in the 1850s, came to nothing, meeting with a firm rejection from Habsburg diplomacy.[3]

The Italian government also tried to persuade Vienna to sell the Veneto for a very large sum of money. With this objective Count Alessandro Malaguzzi Valeri travelled to the Austrian capital in the fall of 1865; a native of Reggio Emilia, he had spent many years in Vienna as court chamberlain and had extensive contacts in the Habsburg aristocracy. There Malaguzzi proposed to the government a reconciliation between Italy and Austria that would be sanctioned by the peaceful transfer of the Veneto and by a marriage between an Austrian archduchess and the crown prince of Italy, but the Italian offers were turned down by Emperor Francis Joseph.[4]

diplomazia italiana e la frontiera settentrionale nell'anno 1866; Gall, Bismarck, the White Revolutionary; Lill, 'L'alleanza italo-prussiana,' pp. 79–98; Dethan, 'La France et la question de Venise en 1966,' pp. 109–19; Di Nola, 'La Venezia nella politica europea,' in Nuova Rivista Storica,' 1961, no. 1, pp. 109–39; 1961, no. 2, pp. 230–279; Wawro, The Austro-Prussian War.

2 Il problema veneto, Inghilterra, docs. 575, 690, 761, 778, 907.

3 On this: DDI, I, 3, docs. 556, 567, 606; DDI, I, 4, docs. 52, 61, 64, 71, 80, 81, 97, 98, 99, 105, 126, 128, 146, 150, 159, 174, 214, 215, 220, 225; Palmerston to Hudson, 13 August 1863, Il problema veneto, Inghilterra, doc. 592; Funaro, L'Italia e l'insurrezione polacca; Mori, La questione romana 1861–1865, pp. 178–81; Cialdea, L'Italia nel concerto europeo (1861–1867), pp. 301 et seq.

4 On the Malaguzzi mission: La Marmora to Malaguzzi, 9 October 1865, DDI, I, 6, doc. 159; Luzio, 'La missione Malaguzzi a Vienna nel 1865–66 per la cessione del Veneto,' in Il Risorgimento Italiano, 1922, nos. 1–2, pp. 125–200; 1922, nos. 3–4, pp. 414–48; 1923, nos. 1–2, pp. 213–60.

Faced with the impossibility of a diplomatic solution to the Venetian question, the government in Florence decided, with the backing of the French emperor, Napoleon III, to respond favourably to the overtures of Prussian Chancellor Otto von Bismarck, which were aimed at the conclusion of an Italo-Prussian alliance against Austria. The Italo-Prussian negotiations were held in the early months of 1866 in a difficult and ambiguous political atmosphere. As Pietro Silva has pointed out,[5] the mutual suspicion between Italians and Prussians heavily influenced the outcome of the negotiations and the relations between the two powers. Italy was afraid that Bismarck would use the talks as a means of exerting pressure on Austria and that he intended to abandon the government in Florence at the first opportunity; the Prussian diplomats suspected that the Italian government was just a tool of French foreign policy, eager to provoke an Austro-Prussian war in order to make territorial gains.

Thus the secret treaty signed on 8 April 1866 was the product of tough negotiations that saw Italian diplomacy cave in to Bismarck's conditions. In the case of victory in a war against Austria, Prussia would guarantee Italy acquisition of the Austrian part of the Lombardo-Venetian kingdom, that is, the Veneto and Friuli, but any hypothesis of surrender of the Trentino and the Italian Tyrol, which belonged to the German Confederation, was rejected.

The war between Austria, Prussia, and Italy broke out in the summer of 1866 and led to an unsatisfactory outcome for the Italian army. In contrast to Prussia's victories in Bohemia, Italy met with repeated defeats, first at Custoza and then at Lissa. Thanks to the overwhelming superiority of his army Bismarck was able to force the Habsburg Empire on 26 July to sign preliminaries to a peace treaty that gave Italy possession of the Venetian part of the Lombardo-Venetian kingdom but excluded any support for its claims on the Tyrol, Trieste, and Istria. In the absence of backing from the Prussians and the French and with the threat of a resumption of hostilities on the part of Austria, the government in Florence withdrew from the occupied territories in Trentino and on the Isonzo (Soča) and signed an armistice with Austria at Cormons on 12 August, accepting what had already been agreed between France, Prussia, and Austria, that is, the return of the Veneto and Friuli to Italy as a gift from France. The Italo-Austrian peace treaty was signed in Vienna on 3 October 1866.

---

5  Silva, *Il Sessantasei*, pp. 26 et seq.

Dalmatia remained absent from Italian territorial designs in those years. In 1866, the Italian government saw the Dalmatian coast not as a future conquest but as a possible battlefield on which to launch a diversionary attack, with a Garibaldian-type expedition  or a maritime offensive by the Italian navy. There was nothing new about this, in that King Victor Emmanuel II of Savoy had been cherishing plans since 1861–2 of staging landings in Dalmatia to provoke a revolution against the Habsburgs in Hungary.[6]

From 1861 onward, however, aspirations to the annexation of the Italian Tyrol and the Trieste coast had grown stronger in Italy, largely because of the incessant activities of the community of émigrés from the Veneto, Venezia Giulia, and Trentino. With regard to the Adriatic area alone, writers like Pacifico Valussi, Carlo Combi, and Tomaso Luciani had devoted their efforts to demonstrating the Italian character of the Istrian cities and Trieste and pointing out the strategic importance of the establishment of an eastern border on the Julian Alps and Monte Maggiore (Mount Učka).[7]

Nothing of this kind was put forward in favour of the annexation of Dalmatia between 1861 and 1866. Study of the Italian diplomatic papers shows that any idea of such annexation was excluded from the territorial plans that were drawn up by the government in Florence for the Austro-Italo-Prussian war. Alfonso La Marmora's government, which handled the diplomatic preparations for the war of 1866, conceived plans of conquest that envisaged the annexation of the Venetian part of the former Lombardo-Venetian kingdom (rounded off in the east, for strategic reasons, at the Isonzo River) and the conquest of the so-called Italian Tyrol as far as the watershed of the Alps.[8] They were extremely moderate aims, which left out any possible claims not just to Dalmatia but also to Trieste and Istria, and therefore differed from the views of a

---

6  On this subject: Mori, *La questione romana*, pp. 72–3. On the plans for an invasion of Dalmatia with the aim of triggering a revolt in Hungary: Komaromy and Csaky to Minghetti, 27 August 1864, DDI, I, 5, doc. 167.

7  In this connection it is very useful to read the correspondence of Alberto Cavalletto, political leader of the irredentist Venetian émigrés in the kingdom of Italy: *Carteggio Cavalletto-Luciani 1861–1866*; *Carteggio Volpe-Cavalletto 1860–1866*; *Carteggio Cavalletto-Meneghini 1865–1866*. On the plans for the borders of Italy cherished by the émigrés from Venezia Giulia: Tamborra, *Cavour*; Riccardi, *Salata*; Quarantotto, *Figure del Risorgimento*.

8  DDI, I, 6, docs. 159, 427, 450, 669. On the question of the Italian territorial claims in 1866 see the fine work of De' Robertis, *La diplomazia italiana*.

large section of Italian public opinion that wanted to see the conquest of Trieste and Istria and the establishment of an eastern border on the Julian Alps.[9]

It is no coincidence that the subsequent Bettino Ricasoli government, with Emilio Visconti Venosta in the post of foreign minister, expanded the Italian territorial claims in the belief that it was vital to conquer Trieste and Istria on the battlefield if they were going to be assigned to Italy in the future peace treaty.[10]

During the 1866 war there were several Dalmatians living in Italy, such as Vincenzo Solitro from Spalato, who urged the government to conquer Dalmatia. Solitro wrote to Ricasoli on 9 July 1866 to remind him of the importance of the annexation of Dalmatia, an 'Italian province in custom, language and heart,'[11] but there was no response on the part of the Italian ruling class.

In any case, despite the lack of Italian expansionistic designs on the Dalmatian coast, the war of 1866 had profound repercussions not only on the territorial set-up of Europe and on Austrian domestic policy, leading to the reorganization of the Habsburg Empire with the Austro-Hungarian institutional compromise, but also on politics in Dalmatia.

Italy's attack on Austria and the attempted invasion of Dalmatian territory by the Italian fleet, culminating in the defeat at Lissa, strengthened xenophobic and anti-Italian sentiments among the Slav nationalists in Dalmatia. The Serbian and Croatian nationalist groups began, unwarrantedly but skilfully, to persuade people increasingly to identify the Autonomist Party with Italy, and tried to undermine the political role of the autonomists by attributing to them presumed irredentist sympathies with secular and anti-Catholic Italy. On 4 August 1866, after the battle of Lissa, *Il Nazionale* published an article entitled 'The Consequences of the Battle of Lissa.' The nationalist newspaper exalted the Austrian victory off the island of Lissa, presenting it as a great triumph for the Slavs as well, and invited the imperial government to draw a lesson from the events of the war. To permanently avert the

---

9  This was also the hope of Costantino Nigra, influential Italian representative in Paris. In June 1866, Nigra responded to Napoleon III's advice that Italy, once it had obtained the Veneto, should renounce future claims on the Tyrol and Trieste, by saying that 'if the war goes well for Italy, she will reclaim and hold the whole Italian side of the Alps' (Nigra to La Marmora, 12 June 1866, DDI, I, 6, doc. 740).

10  DDI, I, 7, docs. 75, 115, 244.

11  *Carteggi di Bettino Ricasoli*, vol. 22, doc. 296.

danger of Italian expansionism in the Adriatic, it was necessary to raise 'an insurmountable national frontier between Dalmatia and Italy,' the political role of the Italian element in Dalmatia had to be cut back, and Italian cultural and linguistic influence in the region had to be reduced. The Slav national element had to be helped to develop fully and 'obtain the respect and the position to which it [was] entitled.'[12]

This article marked the beginning of an anti-Italian campaign waged in the press for several decades by *Il Nazionale* and by many nationalist politicians, such as Pavlinović and Klaić, who accused the autonomists ever more openly of wanting to Italianize Dalmatia and who urged the Austrian government to combat autonomist and Italophile influence in the region. For Pavlinović (an advocate of the need for strong solidarity among the Slav peoples, the true defenders of Christianity), hostility to a liberal Italy, which was considered an enemy of the papacy and its temporal power, easily blended with resentment against the Dalmatian autonomists, whom he considered renegade Slavs and supporters of a civic and oligarchic liberalism antithetical to the values of the Slav people of Dalmatia.[13]

In short, the Serbo-Croatian nationalists in Dalmatia sought to exploit the war of 1866 in order to compel the Austrian government to implement a policy favourable to Croatian nationalism. It was a further step in the radicalization of the political struggle in Dalmatia and in its slow but steady shift in a nationalist direction.

The specious and groundless nature of this attack on the Italian element should be emphasized. Over the course of 1866 the Dalmatian autonomists, whether members of Lapenna's faction or Bajamonti's, had displayed unswerving loyalty to Austria, unlike some of the liberals of Trentino and Istria, and had rejected any irredentist plans.[14] Later a number of Italian writers claimed that there had been contacts between Bajamonti, his followers, and the government in Rome with a

---

12 'Le conseguenze della battaglia di Lissa,' in *Il Nazionale*, 4 August 1866. In this connection see too Novak, 'Političke Prilike u Dalmaciji G. 1866–76,' pp. 35–65, in particular pp. 37–8.

13 On Pavlinović's anti-Italian political ideology: speech by Pavlinović to the Slav reading society in Zara, in *Il Nazionale*, 2 and 5 January 1867; speech by Pavlinović to the Dalmatian provincial diet, in *Il Nazionale*, 16 January 1867; speech by Pavlinović at Imotski, in *Il Nazionale*, 26 March, 2, 16, and 23 April 1870; Pavlinović, *Misao Hrvatska i Misao Srbska u Dalmaciji*.

14 Vrandečić, *Dalmatinski autonomistički pokret u XIX stoljeću*, pp. 133 et seq.

view to organizing the Italian occupation of Spalato.[15] In reality there is no evidence to support the existence of these irredentist schemes. On the basis of the information contained in the press of the time we know, in fact, that the outbreak of the war caught Antonio Bajamonti in Vienna, and he did not return to Spalato until after the end of the war and the drawing up of the Italo-Austrian peace treaty, preferring to spend the tempestuous months of the conflict in the Habsburg capital[16] and steering clear of anti-Austrian initiatives. His right-hand man, Giorgio Giovannizio, was the administrator of the municipality of Spalato during the months of war, and Bajamonti's followers collaborated closely on the defence of Dalmatia that was organized by the Austrian state. As soon as the war between Italy and Austria broke out, the municipality of Spalato made a public declaration of allegiance to Austria,[17] and over the following months Giovannizio demonstrated his absolute loyalty to the Habsburgs. After the war and Bajamonti's return from Vienna, the Spalato city council met, praised Giovannizio's efforts, and sent a message of congratulations to Emperor Francis Joseph for the Austrian victory at Lissa, which had been achieved by a fleet manned to a great extent by Dalmatians.[18]

So the Dalmatian autonomists displayed a fervent loyalty to the Habsburgs during the Italo-Austrian war. Yet the events of 1866 reinforced the old suspicions about the untrustworthiness of the Italian and Italophile element and the danger it posed to the empire in many Austrian political circles (among military commanders, in the conservative aristocracy, and in the imperial family). It was a suspicion that had been shared by several Austrian politicians (Johann Bernhard Rechberg, for example) since the war of 1859, and that the new conflict seemed to confirm. After 1866 the distrust by the conservative sections of the Habsburg ruling class of Austria's Italian population began to turn into open hostility.

The minutes of the Habsburg cabinet at the end of 1866 show the intensity of the emperor's hostility toward the Italians and the nature of his political directives in this connection. Francis Joseph was fully converted to the idea of the general disloyalty of the Italian and Italian-speaking element to the Habsburg dynasty. At the meeting of the

---

15  For example Russo, *L'epopea dalmatica e il suo Eroe*, p. 65.
16  On Bajamonti's presence in Vienna: *Il Nazionale*, 27 June 1866 and 23 January 1867.
17  *Il Nazionale*, 27 June 1866.
18  *Il Nazionale*, 23 January 1867.

Council of Ministers on 12 November 1866, he gave the express order to 'decisively oppose the influence of the Italian element still present in some *Kronländer*, and to aim unsparingly and without the slightest compunction at the Germanization or Slavicization – depending on the circumstances – of the areas in question, through a suitable entrustment of posts to political magistrates and teachers, as well as through the influence of the press in South Tyrol, Dalmatia, and the Adriatic Coast.' All the central authorities were instructed to proceed systematically in this direction.[19]

These anti-Italian sentiments expressed by the emperor, which were to have heavy political consequences in Dalmatia in the following years, were particularly strong in the army, which had fought many wars in Italy and was eager for revenge. Considering the preponderant role of the military in the government of Dalmatia, this was extremely dangerous for the Dalmatian autonomists.

The new course of foreign policy adopted by the Habsburg Empire at the end of the 1860s also served to strengthen Italophobic tendencies. On the international plane, Count Friedrich Ferdinand von Beust, the new foreign minister, who was conscious of the stability of the kingdom of Italy and the strength of Prussia in Germany, outlined a new strategy aimed at the conquest of political and economic spaces in the Balkans.[20] Driven out of the German and Italian plains, Austria was forced to dust off its old mission of civilization of the Balkan east. It was a policy that, through a painstaking effort of economic penetration of the Ottoman Empire, would pave the way in the long term for dominance in the Balkans. The consequence of this strategy was the emergence of the idea, very popular among the military, that it was necessary to carry out a

---

19 Meeting of 12 November 1866, MR, section VI, vol. 2, p. 297. This passage has also been quoted by: Novak, 'Prilike 1866–76,' pp. 40–1; *La campagna del 1866 nei documenti militari austriaci*, pp. 396 et seq.; Corsini, 'Gli italiani nella monarchia asburgica dal 1848 al 1948,' in *Problemi di un territorio di confine*, p. 27. The passage here is based on Corsini's translation.

20 On the significance of Balkan questions in Beust's foreign policy, centred on the one hand on the attempt to counter the assertion of Prussian hegemony in southern Germany, and on the other hand on a pragmatic quest for new political alternatives: Diószegi, *Österreich-Ungarn und der französisch-preussische Krieg 1870–1871*; Lutz, *Österreich-Ungarn und die Gründung des Deutschen Reiches*; der Bagdasarian, *The Austro-German Rapprochement, 1870–1879*; Bridge, *From Sadowa to Sarajevo*; Beust, *Trois quarts du siècle*, in particular vol. 2. Interesting documents on the Balkan policy pursued by Beust in *Les origines diplomatiques*, vol. 14, docs. 4075, 4160, 4211, 4283.

Slavophile policy in Dalmatia in order to win the sympathies of the Serb and Croat populations of Bosnia and Herzegovina for Austria.[21]

In the ambit of this Austrian international strategy, Dalmatia took on growing importance as a springboard for Habsburg penetration of the Balkans. Naturally this favoured the Dalmatian nationals, who were ardently loyal to the Habsburgs and ready to play the new role that the shift in Austrian policy seemed to be offering them. From 1866 onward Croatian nationalists began to receive more and more support from the conservative Austrian establishment, which considered them more faithful to imperial authority than the Italians.

The weakening of imperial autocracy resulting from the military defeat of 1866, and the consequent resumption of the process of internal reforms, slowed to some extent the application of the anti-Italian policy desired by Francis Joseph and the Austrian military.

The rise to power of Beust produced the political reorganization of the Habsburg Empire. With the backing of Austro-German liberalism,[22] Beust was able to reach a general agreement with the Hungarian liberals, in the so-called Ausgleich,[23] modifying the constitution of the empire. The Ausgleich redefined the functions and structure of the Habsburg state, which was split into two parts – the empire of Austria (Cisleithania) and the kingdom of Hungary (Transleithania) – that were held together and united by a single ruler and several common ministries (foreign affairs, armed forces, finance). The Austro-Hungarian compromise was also a major success for the Dalmatian autonomist liberals: Dalmatia's inclusion in the Austrian part of the empire was confirmed, making impossible the union with Croatia, which was incorporated into the kingdom of Hungary. So it was no surprise that the Dalmatian liberals strongly backed the Austro-Hungarian compromise and, thanks to an agreement reached with Beust,[24] voted in fa-

21 On the Slavophile policy pursued by the Austrian representatives in Bosnia-Herzegovina in the 1860s, see the interesting considerations of the Italian consul in Sarajevo, Durando: Durando to the foreign minister, 27 June 1865, ASMAE, ARC POL, 1861–1887, legations division, portfolio 906.

22 On the positions of the German Liberals with regard to Beust in the 1860s: Somogyi, *Vom Zentralismus zum Dualismus*, pp. 78 et seq.

23 On the Austro-Hungarian Ausgleich: Berger, *Der österreichisch-ungarische Ausgleich von 1867*; Holodik, *Der österreichisch-ungarische Ausgleich 1867*; May, *The Hapsburg Monarchy 1867–1914*; Kolmer, *Parlament und Verfassung in Österreich*, pp. 202 et seq.

24 Kolmer, *Parlament und Verfassung in Österreich*, I, pp. 355–7.

vour of the laws that applied it. Speaking in the Abgeordnetenhaus, Lapenna declared with force that it was the wish of the Dalmatians to remain part of Austria and that Croatia and Hungary had no historical and legal claim to Dalmatian territory. Consequently the autonomists supported the new constitutional laws that named Dalmatia as one of the territories that would have its own representatives in the Austrian Reichsrat.[25]

Thus the Austro-Hungarian compromise and the new constitutional laws of 1867 ratified an autonomous political and administrative set-up for Dalmatia, separate from Croatia and Slavonia, that would last until 1918 and the break-up of the Habsburg Empire.

On the plane of internal equilibrium the Austro-Hungarian compromise guaranteed, with the transitory consent of the emperor, the dominance of German liberalism in Cisleithania and of the Hungarian nation in Transleithania. On the political level this was a defeat for the clerical conservative parties, who were in favour of strong decentralization, and for the Slav nationalists. In particular the Croatian nationalists, still allied with the Austrian Serbs in the National Party, were penalized: not only had they failed to obtain the unification of Croatia, Slavonia, the Military Frontier, and Dalmatia, but their interests were damaged by the new constitutional laws that assigned Dalmatia to Austria and the rest of Croatia to Hungary. Not surprisingly the National Party led by Strossmayer opposed the Ausgleich, and the Dalmatian national representative in Vienna, Ljubiša, voted against the new constitutional laws. However, the Ausgleich strengthened the power of the Dalmatian autonomist liberals, in so far as it placed the Austrian government in the hands of their allies, the German liberals.

Dalmatian politics after 1866 were shaped by the split in the Liberal Union and the return to the old conflict between nationalists and autonomists. Bajamonti became reconciled with Lapenna, and their renewed co-operation gave the autonomists an easy victory in the 1867 elections to the diet: the liberal autonomists won twenty-six seats, the nationalists only fifteen.[26] The diet then appointed five new deputies to the Austrian chamber – four representing the Autonomist Party (Bajamonti, Lapenna, the Orthodox bishop Stefan Knezevich, and Simeone

---

25  *Stenographische Protokolle*, 13 November 1867, pp. 1372–4.
26  On the 1867 elections: *Il Nazionale*, 2, 6, and 9 February 1867; Novak, 'Prilike 1866–76,' pp. 41–2.

de Michieli-Vitturi), and one the nationalists (Ljubiša).[27] In Vienna the autonomist deputies joined the parliamentary group of the empire's southern territories, to which the representatives of all the Habsburg Italian provinces also belonged, much to the irritation of the nationalists, who accused Bajamonti, Lapenna, and Knezevich of Italian sympathies and being false Dalmatians.[28]

In 1869 a revolt broke out in southern Dalmatia that disrupted the political panorama of the Adriatic region. The introduction of a compulsory draft throughout the empire had caused great resentment among the Serbian and Montenegrin mountain people of the Bocche di Cattaro (Gulf of Cattaro), who had been exempt from military service for centuries. In October 1869 an insurrection broke out in the Krivošije region, spreading throughout the territory around Cattaro in the following weeks. The Habsburg troops suffered a series of defeats, which scandalized the Austro-Hungarian public who were surprised by the difficulties encountered in putting down such uprisings.[29]

Criticized for his inability to solve the crisis in southern Dalmatia, the province's governor, General Johann Wagner, was dismissed, and in February 1870 the functionary Joseph Fluck de Leidenkron, with conservative leanings, was placed in charge temporarily. Fluck ran the province until the office was assumed by the new governor, General Gabriel (Gavrilo) von Rodich (Rodić), who suppressed the revolt in the Bocche di Cattaro.[30]

The revolt triggered widespread debate in Vienna over the policy to be pursued in the Balkans, and focused attention on Dalmatia. Criticism of the attitude taken toward the Slavs by the liberal government grew in conservative circles. The autonomist position was further weakened in 1870 with the fall of the liberal government in Vienna and the ascent to power of the Polish conservative Alfred Potocki. Potocki's objective, shared by the emperor, who had appointed the extremely loyal Eduard Taaffe as minister of the interior, was to reach a political accord with the Czech and Slav national parties of the south who had remained

27 *Reichsraths-Almanach für die Session 1867*, p. 20.
28 'I quattro a Vienna,' in *Il Nazionale*, 21 December 1867.
29 On the revolt in southern Dalmatia in 1869: Sosnosky, *Die Balkanpolitik Österreich-Ungarns seit 1866*, pp. 71 et seq.
30 'La Dalmazia e il luogotenente provvisorio,' in *Il Nazionale*, 2 February 1870; 18 May 1870; Novak, 'Prilike 1866–76,' p. 53.

opposed to the Ausgleich, in order to consolidate the internal stability of the state.[31]

The Potocki government believed that the political set-up in Dalmatia had to be changed as it was too favourable to the autonomists and disadvantageous to the Croatian and Serbian nationalists. Klaić, Danilo, and Ljubiša were ready to respond to the new signals coming from Vienna and the lieutenancy of Zara; they began to moderate the intransigence of their opposition to the constitutional laws of 1867. They went on fanning the flames of Italophobia, denouncing the presumed threat of Dalmatian autonomism to the territorial integrity of the empire.

To bring about a readjustment of the political situation in Dalmatia in favour of the nationalists, the Potocki government dissolved the Dalmatian diet ahead of time. Fluck, faithful executor of the emperor's new pro-Slav directives, intervened actively in the electoral campaign for the new provincial diet. For the first time many nationalist candidates were backed by the government authorities.

The elections of July 1870 brought a reversal in the balance of power in Dalmatia as the National Party was able to gain a majority in the provincial diet, winning twenty-four seats (with Klaić elected in two constituencies), as opposed to sixteen for the autonomists. The nationalists prevailed in the vast majority of the rural districts (seventeen out of twenty) and, while remaining a minority in the coastal cities, managed to win enough of them (eight out of twenty-one) to ensure a majority in the diet.[32]

The nationalist victory in 1870 was without doubt a significant event in Dalmatian political history, but not yet a decisive turning point. The nationalists would not become the dominant political force in Dalmatia until the years from 1879 to 1885, with the defeat of the autonomists in the elections for the Reichsrat in 1879 and 1885 and the municipal elections in Spalato in 1882. In any case, the autonomist liberals lost their undisputed political sway in Dalmatia and found themselves facing a new and much more difficult and confused situation, where their tradi-

---

31  On the Potocki government: Engel-Janosi, 'Österreich-Ungarn im Sommer 1870,' pp. 207 et seq.; Kolmer, *Parlament und Verfassung in Österreich*, vol. 2, pp. 60 et seq.

32  On the elections for the Dalmatian provincial diet in 1870: *Il Nazionale*, 11, 15, 18, and 29 June, 6 and 13 July 1870; Novak, 'Prilike 1866–76,' pp. 53–5; Foretić, 'Izbori za Sabor Dalmacije 1870,' in *Dalmacija 1870*, pp. 125–46; Vrandečić, *Dalmatinski autonomistički pokret u XIX stoljeću*, pp. 148 et seq.

tional nationalist adversaries were beginning to gain the support of an important part of the Habsburg establishment.

With the winning of a majority in the provincial diet the xenophobic and anti-pluralistic tendency of Croatian and Serbian nationalism in Dalmatia quickly came to the surface. Since their majority in the diet was small and fragile, with more of the elected members (for example, Giuseppe Antonietti) owing their allegiance to the government than to the National Party, the nationalists decided not to confirm the election of many autonomist representatives, which led to bitter clashes in the diet and the abstention of the autonomists from the work of the assembly for several years.[33] Then the Narodnjaci, anxious to undermine the political influence of autonomism at the state level, chose to break with the tradition of including a member of the opposition among the representatives to the parliament in Vienna. In 1870 five nationalist members (Giuseppe Antonietti, Ivan Danilo, Giorgio Vojnović, Pietro Budmani, and Stefan Ljubiša) were elected to the Reichsrat, thereby eliminating any autonomist representation in Vienna.[34]

Over the following years the policy of Croatization of schools got underway. Taking advantage of the control exercised by the provincial diet over such matters, the nationalists abandoned their merely theoretical acceptance of bilingualism in the past and began, despite the protests of the autonomists, to change the medium of instruction in various schools and to discriminate against the Italian language; Italian was no longer recognized as a native language and was dropped as a medium of instruction in the schools. The Italian gymnasia of Sebenico and Curzola were abolished, and in most Dalmatian schools Croatian became the sole medium of instruction, with Italian studied only as a foreign language.[35]

As we have already pointed out, this anti-Italian educational policy stemmed from the nationalist conviction that the use of Italian in Dal-

---

33 'Un pretesto mal scelto,' in *Il Nazionale*, 7 September 1870. See too the minutes of the Dalmatian provincial diet: ADP-BI, 1870, sessions of 31 August, 1 September and 2 September 1870.

34 *Il Nazionale*, 3 September 1870.

35 On the policy of wholesale Slavicization of the cultural institutions implemented by the National Party in Dalmatia: 'Dietro alle quinte,' in *Il Dalmata*, 21 January 1874; 'Il ginnasio reale di Curzola soppresso,' in *Il Dalmata*, 13 September 1876. See too Marcocchia, 'Sessant'anni di storia della scuola in Dalmazia,' pp. 60 et seq.

matia was solely a colonial legacy, the result of centuries of foreign rule. For the nationalists there was only one national language in that region, Serbo-Croatian, spoken by the vast majority of the population; there was no indigenous Italian element in Dalmatia, only Italianized Slavs who had to be reconverted to their presumed original identity, whether they liked it or not, in the name of the development of the Serbo-Croat nationality; this nationality, given its weakness and fragility, did not brook the existence of rivals or alternative cultures.[36]

This view of the national question in Dalmatia was superficial and distorted by the political requirements of the moment, more the product of ideology than of careful reflection on the history and needs of Dalmatian society. The Dalmatian nationalists, whose political ideology was the fruit of the encounter between the political and cultural model of the liberal nationalism of Risorgimento Italy and a Slavism steeped in religious mysticism, attempted to create a homogeneous and uniform national culture; they forgot that Dalmatian society was completely different from Italian society as the Dalmatians were diverse on the ethnic, linguistic, religious, and cultural planes. The desire to impose on Dalmatia a model of society founded on an ethnically pure and uniform nationalism meant doing violence to that culture, fuelling conflicts that were to characterize the history of the eastern Adriatic until the end of the twentieth century. Moreover, it was a nationalism with grave cultural limitations; for example, interpreting the presence of the Italian culture and language as simply the result of Venetian colonialism was to fail to understand that Italo-Slav bilingualism answered to deep needs in Dalmatian society, a society whose prosperity had always been dependent on its capacity to play a role of cultural and commercial mediation between the Balkans, the East, and Italy. The cultural and political weaknesses of the Yugoslav national myth, that is, the idea that Serbs and Croats formed a single nationality, a contention that dominated Dalmatian nationalism in the 1860s and 1870s, would be demonstrated a few years later with the split in the National Party and the formation of a political movement by the Serbs of Dalmatia.

The Slav nationalist policy in Dalmatia, notwithstanding the support of many people in the army and at court, as well as the National Party of Croatia, encountered stubborn resistance from the autonomists. The

---

36  A clear exposition of the Slav nationalist point of view on the question of the language in Dalmatia is in *Stenographische Protokolle*, 13 March 1874, parliamentary question raised by Monti, pp. 1078–80.

latter took advantage of their alliance with the Austro-German liberals, who were still strong in the parliament in Vienna and who, on the fall of the conservative Hohenwart government in 1871,[37] regained executive power for several years with the Adolf von Auersperg ministry.

Exploiting the uncertainty of the political situation in Vienna, where a hard battle between liberals and conservatives was being waged, Lapenna launched a campaign in the Viennese newspapers in defence of the Dalmatian autonomists and against the actions of Fluck.[38] Over the course of the summer of 1870 there were lengthy negotiations in Vienna between the Austrian government, Lapenna, several nationalist leaders, and General Rodich (the new governor of Dalmatia) aimed at finding a way of pacifying the province, which was being shaken by fierce struggles between the Dalmatian parties. The Dalmatian autonomists asked the new nationalist majority to take a moderate stance on the linguistic question and to refrain from pursuing policies in favour of annexation to Croatia; they also wanted room to be made in the provincial administration and the executive board of the diet for men to the liking of the Autonomist Party.[39] These negotiations, which are amply recorded in Rodich's diaries,[40] went nowhere. The nationalists did not want to make concessions to the autonomist minority, who were excluded from any participation in the administration of the province and were denied any representation in the Reichsrat. The new governor preferred to follow his own line, relying on the full confidence of Francis Joseph, Archduke Albert von Habsburg, and the commanders of the imperial army.

Gavrilo Rodich, governor of Dalmatia from 1870 to 1881, was the master of Dalmatian politics in those years. Born in 1812 in the territories of the Military Frontier (at Vrginmost in what is now Croatia),[41]

---

37  On the Hohenwart government: Fischer, 'New Light on German-Czech Relations in 1871,' pp. 177 et seq.; Lutz, *Österreich-Ungarn*, pp. 416 et seq.; Somogyi, *Der gemeinsame Ministerrat der österreichisch-ungarischen Monarchie 1867–1906*, pp. 217 et seq.

38  On this: *Il Nazionale*, 19 and 29 October 1870.

39  On the negotiations between the autonomists, Rodich, Potocki, Taaffe, and the nationalists, there is much information in a letter from Lapenna, 15 October 1870, *Neues Fremden-Blatt*.

40  KA, *Nachlass Rodich*, portfolio 14, months of August and September 1870.

41  An insight into Rodich's personality and life can be found in the general's unpublished autobiographical writings conserved among his personal papers: KA, *Nachlass Rodich*, portfolio 38; Gabriel Rodich, *Sechzehn Jahre in Dalmatien*, ibidem, portfolio 36; *Feldzeügmeister Gabriel Freiherr von Rodich*. The best biographical profile of Rodich is the one by Kiszling, 'Gabriel Freiherr von Rodich,' pp. 127–36. See too: Kiszling, *Die Revolution*, vol. 2, p. 162; Wandruszka, *Schicksaljahr*, pp. 251–84.

from whence came the best units of the Austrian army, Rodich was a southern Slav of Orthodox faith[42] who, like many high-ranking Habsburg officers of Serb and Croatian birth in the Military Frontier, had become progressively Germanized, absorbing the German language and culture but not forgetting his origins. A loyal and able soldier, he had fought alongside Jelačić in 1848–9 to defend the integrity of the state against Hungarian separatists, and then he went on to spend several years in Italy, taking part in the war of 1866. He was considered to be one of the best Austrian commanders and to have an excellent understanding of Balkan affairs; he was not a Croat, Serb, or Yugoslav nationalist but an Austrian Slav, convinced that the interests of the empire and of the southern Slavs coincided. For Rodich the future of the Habsburg state lay in expansion into the Balkans and the absorption of the Slav peoples; therefore, it was necessary to have a pro-Slav policy in Dalmatia, with a view to attracting the Slavs of Bosnia, Herzegovina, and Montenegro. It is no accident that Rodich was one of the planners of the Austrian conquest of Bosnia-Herzegovina.[43]

In Rodich's eyes, the Dalmatian autonomists were an untrustworthy political force in that they were liberal in outlook and no friend of the armed forces. He was worried by the pro-Italian leanings of the autonomists, a possible indication of future secessionist temptations. Thus Rodich's constant objectives were destruction of the autonomist political hegemony, strengthening of Slavophile forces, and increasing the influence and role of the Serbian and Croatian languages in Dalmatia. However, it would be a mistake to interpret the policy of the Habsburg general in terms of simple Yugoslav nationalism; in reality he pursued an Austrian policy, which utilized nationalisms to the advantage of imperial authority. Rodich did not want the total destruction of the Italian and Italophile element but wanted the end of its political and cultural dominance in Dalmatia, considered a potential threat to the empire after 1866.

The autonomists, under Lapenna's leadership, tried to counter the

---

42  In the Dalmatian press Rodich was described as Slav or Croatian, but Kiszling says that he belonged to the Orthodox faith: Kiszling, 'Gabriel Freiherr von Rodich,' pp. 130, 133.

43  On the expansionist ideas of Rodich and his role in the Habsburg conquest of Bosnia and Herzegovina: Rupp, *A Wavering Friendship*, pp. 30, 78; Diószegi, *Die Aussenpolitik der Oesterreichisch-Ungarischen Monarchie 1871–1877*; Kos, *Die Politik Oesterreich-Ungarns während der Orientkrise 1874/75–1879*.

influence of the nationalists and Rodich in Vienna by making the most of their links with the Auersperg government. Dominated by Austro-German liberals, the government was opposed to the strengthening of Slavophile tendencies in Austria. The Autonomist Party also exploited the growing divisions within the Narodnjaci. Rodich's desire to turn the nationalists into a party of government, totally subjugated to the interests of the empire, temporarily threw the nationalist movement into crisis. When the five nationalist members of the Reichsrat voted in favour of the law reforming the imperial electoral system in 1873, at Rodich's instigation and against the instructions of their leaders in the province, who were opposed to any legal and political recognition of the separation of Dalmatia from Croatia, the result was a split in the Nationalist Party.[44] Ljubiša, who was a loyal Habsburg Serb and a friend of Rodich, set up a new nationalist party (which took its name from *Zemljak*, the newspaper that represented the new movement); a more moderate group, it accepted the constitutional laws of 1867.[45]

With the introduction of direct election of representatives to the Vienna parliament and the raising of the number of Dalmatian members to nine, new elections for the imperial parliament were called in 1873. The autonomists achieved great success, winning five seats, as opposed to the nationalists winning three and Zemljak one. Lapenna and Bajamonti went back to Vienna to represent the autonomist liberals, along with the newly elected Odoardo Keller, Marino Bonda, and Cosimo Begna-Possedaria; the nationalists managed to elect Klaić, Monti, and Pavlinović; and Zemljak elected only Ljubiša.[46]

The Dalmatian autonomist representatives, who had always sided with the Austro-German liberal parties (*Verfassungsparteien*), joined the parliamentary grouping of the German Liberal Left (the so-called Club der Linken), to which important liberals like Karl Giskra and Eduard Herbst also belonged. Lapenna was appointed its vice-president. At the same time, together with various representatives of Istria, Trieste, Gorizia, and the Italian Tyrol, they set up a 'Free Conference of the Members for the Southern Provinces' that was intended to provide a basis

---

44  *Il Dalmata*, 26 and 29 March 1873; Perić, *Dalmatinski Sabor*, p. 102.
45  *Il Dalmata*, 19 April 1873; Perić, *Dalmatinski Sabor*.
46  On the elections to the Reichsrat in 1873: *Il Dalmata*, 8, 15, and 22 October 1873; 'Abbiamo vinto!' ibidem, 29 October 1873; Vrandečić, *Dalmatinski autonomistički pokret u XIX stoljeću*, pp. 184 et seq. On the Dalmatian members of the Reichsrat after the 1873 elections: *Reichsraths-Almanach für die Session 1873–1874*.

for encouraging co-operation, however limited, among the southern Italian-speaking regions. As testimony to his prestige in Vienna, Lapenna was elected chairman of this committee of southern members of parliament.[47]

So the autonomist liberals strove to consolidate their alliance with German liberalism. The strength of this alliance was confirmed at the time of the vote on the new Austrian confessional laws in 1874, which curbed the privileges and powers of the Catholic Church in Austria. The autonomists and Ljubiša voted in favour of the laws of liberal inspiration, while the intransigent Croatian and Serbian nationalists opposed them.[48]

The great success of the autonomists in the elections of 1873 seemed to open up new political prospects in Dalmatia. The division among Serbo-Croatian nationalists increased the political weight of the autonomists, who made overtures to the moderates of Zemljijak. Lapenna and Bajamonti also tried to persuade the government in Vienna to dissolve the Dalmatian provincial diet and call new elections in the province, but their efforts were in vain.[49]

Just as the political situation in Dalmatia seemed to be improving for the autonomists, the movement was faced with a grave crisis of leadership. In 1875, Lapenna, who had been appointed Austrian representative to the Commission of the Egyptian Public Debt in Alexandria by the government in Vienna, withdrew from political activity and resigned his parliamentary seat, moving to Egypt for several years. This was a serious loss for the autonomists, who found themselves without their most able and respected leader, a man of unquestioned loyalty to Austria who had been capable of reconciling the different wings of the party and had the ear of liberals as well as conservatives in Viennese political circles. In the same year, Keller gave up his seat in the Vienna parliament too, which meant the holding of two by-elections.[50]

The autonomist liberal movement split over the choice of candidates to succeed Lapenna and Keller; the old disagreements between Zara

---

47 'Cronaca parlamentare,' in *Il Dalmata*, 22 November 1873.
48 'Le leggi confessionali,' in *Il Dalmata*, 18 March 1874. On the Austrian confessional laws of 1874, the denunciation of the concordat, and the political confrontation that arose between the Holy See and Austria-Hungary: Engel-Janosi, *Österreich und der Vatikan 1846–1918*, vo. 1, pp. 188 et seq.; *Die politiche Korrespondenz der Päpste mit den oesterreichischen Kaisern 1804–1918*, pp. 280 et seq.
49 *Il Dalmata*, 10 December 1873.
50 *Il Dalmata*, 26 September and 6 October 1875.

and Spalato resurfaced, and a fierce rivalry emerged between Antonio Bajamonti, who wanted to become the undisputed head of the movement for the whole of Dalmatia, and Nicolò Trigari, the new mayor of Zara.[51] The autonomists of Zara refused to support the candidates with ties to the mayor of Spalato and formed an alliance with Zemlijak under the auspices of Governor Rodich to elect the state official Antonietti, who was close to the moderate nationalists although he was Italian in language and culture. The two by-elections were won by the Serbo-Croatian nationalists and Zemlijak, who returned Antonietti and Fluck, the provisional governor of Dalmatia in 1870 who had turned to politics.[52] Dalmatian autonomism split into two factions, one led by Trigari that was strong in Zara and maintained good relations with the governor and the Catholic Church, and one headed by Bajamonti that held a majority in central and southern Dalmatia and included the more progressive and anticlerical autonomist liberal currents.[53]

Rent by personal and municipal rivalries, the autonomists presented two separate lists at the elections to the Dalmatian provincial diet in 1876[54] and were heavily defeated, winning only eleven seats: three for Bajamonti's group (Bajamonti, Antonio Radman, and Gian Antonio Botteri, the mayor of Cittavecchia) and eight for the candidates loyal to Trigari (Trigari, Giuseppe Messa, Pietro Abelich, Cosimo Begna, Cesare Pellegrini-Danieli, Gustavo Ivanics, Giovanni Smerchinich, and Luigi Frari). The Serbo-Croatian National Party gained a clear majority, demolishing the moderates of Zemlijak.

While Trigari, who had good relations with Governor Rodich, embarked on a policy of dialogue with the nationalist majority, which agreed to make him deputy speaker of the diet, Bajamonti radicalized his political stand from 1875 onward. The politician from Spalato tried to weaken Trigari's position by setting up a newspaper (*Il Costituzionale*) and his own group of supporters in Zara, but he failed to make a

---

51  On Trigari: Vanni Tacconi, 'Nicolò Trigari,' in Semi and Tacconi, *Istria e Dalmazia*, vol. 2, pp. 429 et seq.

52  *Il Dalmata*, 23 and 30 October, 3 November 1875, and 1 January 1876; 'L'intrigo elettorale del 20 ottobre,' in *L'Avvenire*, 25 October 1875; 15 November 1875; Novak, 'Političke Prilike,' pp. 59–60; Perić, *Dalmatinski Sabor*, p. 105.

53  On the disputes within the Autonomous Liberal Party: Bajamonti, 'Lettera al redattore,' in *L'Avvenire*, 20 December 1875; *Il Costituzionale*, 5 and 11 March 1877; 'I nostri onorevoli,' ibidem, 18 and 25 March, and 1 April 1877.

54  On the 1876 elections for the provincial diet: *Il Dalmata*, 25 October, 15, 18 and 22 November 1876; Perić, *Dalmatinski Sabor*, pp. 219–20.

dent in Trigari's grip on the Dalmatian capital.[55] Bajamonti then began
to attack Rodich publicly, accusing him of rigging the elections against
the autonomists and liberals and pursuing an anti-Italian policy,[56] and
in general assumed a more aggressive attitude toward the Nationalist
Party.

The climax of Bajamonti's offensive against Rodich and his pro-Slav
policy came with an uncompromising speech he gave in the Austrian
parliament in December 1876.[57] The autonomist representative accused
Rodich of having turned Dalmatia into a land without law and order
where the constitution and the principles of freedom were not respected
and the administration was in thrall to the ideas of groups hostile to liberal values: 'We have no governor, since General Rodich is not a worthy
representative of His Majesty but a party leader who sometimes sows
the seeds of hatred and partiality, ostracism and favouritism, to the
point of offending the most instinctive of human virtues – decency.'[58]

In Bajamonti's view, Rodich had created 'a pashadom in a constitutional state.' The governor's objective was to 'pervert the nature of Dalmatia – which naturally derives a mixed character from the two races
that inhabit it – and give it a purely Slav character' in order to facilitate the Habsburg conquest of Bosnia and Herzegovina; therefore, his
action was aimed at weakening the constitutional Autonomist Party,
'composed of Italians and many Slavs who either speak Italian or share
the political convictions of the former.'[59]

The public attacks on Rodich and the increasing radicalization of
the struggle of Bajamonti's group against the nationalists resulted in

---

55  *Il Costituzionale*, edited by Antonio Boniciolli, was published from March 1877 to
    February 1878; the leader of the autonomist liberal faction in Zara close to Bajamonti
    was the magistrate Giuseppe Piperata, originally from Spalato but resident in Zara.
    On the innumerable disputes between the followers of Bajamonti and Trigari: 'Il
    deputato d.r. Ivanich nazionale-autonomo-costituzionale,' in *Il Costituzionale*, 11
    March 1877; Ildebrando Tacconi , 'Biografia di Vitaliano Brunelli,' pp. 9 et seq.
56  Statements by Bajamonti, session of 22 January 1877, ADP-BI, pp. 5–17; session of
    25 January 1877, pp. 19–26; *L'Avvenire*, 8 July 1875; 'Dopo cinque anni,' ibidem, 12
    August 1875.
57  Bajamonti, *Discorso pronunziato alla Camera dei deputati dall'on*. The speech was made
    in Italian and, since the stenographers did not know the language, was not tran-
    scribed in the proceedings of the Abgeordnetenhaus: *Stenographische Protokolle*, 9
    December 1876, p. 7329. On this speech by Bajamonti: Monzali, 'Dalmati o Italiani?'
    p. 449.
58  Bajamonti, *Discorso pronunziato alla Camera dei deputati dall'on*, p. 6.
59  Ibid., p. 9.

a worsening of political tension in the province, with the occurrence of incidents and brawls between followers of the autonomists and nationalist militants in Zara, Sebenico, and Spalato.[60] Bajamonti's strategy, aimed at forcing the liberal government in Vienna to intervene on behalf of its autonomist allies, proved counterproductive. Rodich represented imperial authority, and the policy he had implemented was intended to serve precise objectives of Austrian foreign policy (the occupation of Ottoman territories inhabited by Christian Slavs) and enjoyed Francis Joseph's total support. Attacking Rodich in such an ostentatious manner signified, therefore, contesting government policy and the emperor himself. Even in Spalato the strength of the autonomists began to dwindle, with the nationalists managing to put down roots in the city under a new and able leader, the lawyer Gajo Filomeno Bulat. Bulat[61] was a paradoxical and complex figure that was hard to interpret. A typical member of the nineteenth-century urban bourgeoisie in Dalmatia, Italian by language and culture, he was for decades the leader of Croatian nationalism in Spalato, even though he was incapable of speaking correctly and writing in Croatian. Bulat succeeded in encroaching on the privileged relationship that Bajamonti had with the middle and business class in Spalato, criticized the extremism of the autonomist liberal

---

60 The minutes of the Dalmatian provincial diet, characterized by harsh verbal clashes between members and between them and part of the public, well reflect the climate of political tension that held sway in Dalmatia in those years: ADP-BI, sessions of 22 and 29 January 1877.

61 On Bulat: Bulat, *Izabrani spisi*; Perić, 'Mesto i Uloga Gaje Bulata u politici dalmatinske narodne stranke,' in *Politički portreti iz prošlosti Dalmacije*, p. 157; Monzali, 'Dalmati o Italiani?' pp. 450 et seq. An analysis of the minutes of the provincial diet and the Dalmatian press allows us to present a more complicated image of Bulat than the picture of the Croatian national hero typically painted by Croatian historians. Elected a nationalist member of the diet for many years, he continued to speak exclusively in Italian; obliged for reasons of expediency to make speeches in Croatian, he had them written by a journalist and then he read them in public. His poor pronunciation in reading and frequent grammatical blunders when forced to extemporize in Croatian were the object of mockery among his Serbian and autonomist adversaries, who accused him of being a traitorous Italian who had joined the Croatian nationalists to further his career and to marry Klaić's sister. It should be pointed out that Bulat, Slav by ideology, always claimed to believe in the existence of a single Serbo-Croatian Dalmatian nationality despite siding with the Croatian majority after the breakaway of the Serb element from the Dalmatian National Party in 1879–80.

mayor and his incompetence in administrative matters, and accused him of placing his own interests before those of the city.[62]

In general, over the course of the 1870s the National Party, ably led by Klaić, overcame the crisis of the breakaway of Zemlijak and acquired increasing political credibility among Austrian conservative and Catholic circles in Vienna and Dalmatia, presenting itself as a movement respectful of traditional values and the established order, loyal to the Habsburgs, and ready to contribute to the further expansion of Austria-Hungary in the Balkans.

## 2.2. The Habsburg Conquest of Bosnia-Herzegovina, the Taaffe Era, and the Decline of Dalmatian Autonomist Liberalism

As has been pointed out, the second half of the 1870s was characterized by the emergence of a serious crisis in Dalmatian autonomism. Despite retaining majority support in many Dalmatian cities, the movement proved incapable of regaining control of the provincial diet and countering the initiatives of the nationalists in Dalmatia and Vienna. However, the most decisive factor in the downfall of Dalmatian autonomism was the evolution in the international and domestic policy of the Habsburg Empire.

In the aftermath of the war of 1866, the government in Vienna had begun to pay new attention to the problems of the Balkans. The political and territorial arrangements established by the peace treaties of Prague and Vienna had sanctioned Prussian hegemony in the Germanic world and the consolidation of the Italian state. The geopolitical areas in which the Habsburgs had held sway between the sixteenth and nineteenth centuries (Italy and Germany) were now dominated by other states. The military and political defeats of 1866 obliged the Habsburg Empire to turn eastward again and to resume the policy of expansion that had been masterminded by Eugene of Savoy but had ceased to be a priority of Austrian foreign policy following the disastrous outcome of the war with Turkey in 1733–8.[63]

---

62 On Bulat's harsh attack on the Bajamonti administration and the response to it from the autonomist politician: Novak, *Povijest Splita*, vol. 3, pp. 336 et seq.; Randi, *Bajamonti*; Kečkemet, 'Associazione dalmatica i pad Ante Bajamontja,' pp. 75 et seq.; 'Il d.r. Bajamonti e i suoi detrattori,' in *L'Avvenire*, 1 July 1875.
63 Hantsch, *Die Geschichte Österreichs*, vol. 2; Kann, *History of the Habsburg Empire*; Beer, *Die orientalische Politik Oesterreichs seit 1774*.

For several years Beust tried to prepare the ground for a possible Habsburg resurgence in Germany, constructing an alliance with Napoleonic France and nurturing the particularism of the southern German states to counter the consolidation of Prussian power. However, the Habsburg minister was also very careful to outline a new strategy of political and economic penetration in the Balkans. In his view, the Austrian government, while formally respecting the integrity and independence of the Turkish empire, should pursue a more active and dynamic policy in the region, becoming the protector of the interests of the Christian populations of the Balkans and a force for economic modernization in those territories. Through the construction of railroad lines linking Austria with the Ottoman lands and fostering the creation of strong economic ties between the Habsburg Empire and the Balkan peoples, the foundations would be laid for Habsburg hegemony in the region and for a prospective conquest.[64] This new importance of the Balkans in Habsburg policy was underlined by a long journey that Francis Joseph made to Constantinople and Egypt, passing through the Balkan region, in 1869.[65]

The Habsburg strategy of penetration of the Ottoman Empire and in particular the hinterland of Dalmatia, that is, Bosnia, Herzegovina, and Albania, was stepped up over the course of the 1870s. The outcome of the Franco-Prussian war put an end to any dream of revenge against the Hohenzollerns. The policy of expansion in the Balkans was strongly supported by the so-called *Hofpartei* (the conservative and traditionalistic groups with influence at the Habsburg court), military circles, Archduke Albert, and Rodich himself. For many in the army the honour of the monarchy had been dented by the defeats of 1859 and 1866; a new territorial conquest and a victorious war were needed to restore the prestige of the armed forces, lynchpin of the empire, and return Aus-

---

64  On Habsburg foreign policy between the end of the 1860s and the beginning of the 1870s: Beust, *Trois quarts de siècle*, vol. 2; Lutz, *Österreich-Ungarn*; Bagdasarian, *The austro-german rapprochement*; Diószegi, *Österreich-Ungarn und der französich-preussische Krieg*; Engel-Janosi, 'Die römische Frage in den diplomatischen Verhandlungen 1869–1870,' in *Geschichte*, pp. 143 et seq.; Bridge, *From Sadowa*; Mori, *Il tramonto del potere temporale 1866–70*, pp. 354 et seq.; Di Nolfo, 'Austria e Roma nel 1870,' pp. 409–36; Di Nolfo, 'Monarchia e governo durante la crisi diplomatica dell'estate 1870,' pp. 107–42; Halperin, *Diplomat under Stress*.

65  Beust, *Trois quarts de siècle*, vol. 2, pp. 261 et seq.

tria to the rank of a great European power.[66] Bosnia and Herzegovina were a natural objective of expansion; inhabited largely by Christian Croat and Serb populations that chafed under the Ottoman yoke and by Bosnian Muslims, they were regions rich in mineral and agricultural resources, control of which would consolidate the territorial holdings of the empire, eliminating an awkward and dangerous wedge inserted between Croatia, Hungary, and Dalmatia. In June 1866 the Italian consul in Sarajevo, Cesare Durando, had discerned the emergence of serious political interest on the part of the Habsburg Empire in the Bosnian provinces, where Vienna could count on the sympathies of the Catholic element. In the Italian diplomat's opinion, Austria would gain great advantages from the conquest of Bosnia and Herzegovina, strengthening its naval position and revitalizing Dalmatia, 'a long strip of land, or rather of rocks, backed by a rich and extensive countryside but shut in by state borders.'[67]

In January 1875, well before the insurrection in Herzegovina, the highest authorities of the Habsburg state declared themselves in agreement over the necessity of expansion in the Balkans. At the imperial conference of 29 January the foreign minister, the Hungarian Gyula Andrássy[68] who had succeeded Beust in 1871, proclaimed himself convinced of the importance of a Habsburg conquest of Bosnia-Herzegovina in order to avoid the formation of dangerous and threatening national states on the southern borders of the empire. Francis Joseph showed that he shared these concerns and designs and declared the urgent need to take control of an adequate hinterland for Austrian Dalmatia by occupying the whole of Bosnia and Herzegovina.[69]

Some members of the Habsburg armed forces (for instance, General

---

66  On the political ideas of the *Hofpartei* and Austrian military circles: Stickler, *Erzherzog Albrecht von Österreich*; Holzer, *Erzherzog Albrecht 1867–1895*; Schober, 'L'arciduca Alberto alla corte d'Asburgo,' pp. 301 et seq.; Ledel, 'Konservativismus und das Haus Habsburg,' pp. 183 et seq.; Broucek, 'Konservativismus in den Armeen des Hauses Österreich und der Republik Österreich,' pp. 163 et seq.

67  Durando to the foreign minister, 12 June 1866, ASMAE, ARC POL, 1861–1887, Divisione Legazioni, portfolio 906.

68  On the figure and life of Gyula (Julius) Andrássy: Schmidt, *Graf Julius Andrássy*; Wertheimer, *Graf Julius Andrássy*; Diószegi, *Die Aussenpolitik*; *Bismarck und Andrássy*.

69  *Protokoll über die am 29 Jänner 1875 unter dem Allerhoechsten Vorsitze Seiner Majestät des Kaisers abgehaltene Konferenz*, reproduced in Diószegi, *Die Aussenpolitik*, pp. 321–32. In this connection see too: Haselsteiner, 'Zur Haltung der Donaumonarchie in der orientalischen Frage,' pp. 227–43.

Friedrich Beck, head of the imperial military chancellery) regarded the conquest of the Bosnian provinces as the first step in a progressive expansion that would lead to Austrian control of Old Serbia, part of Albania, and Macedonia and to the extension of the empire's boundaries as far as the Aegean Sea.[70] The governor of Dalmatia, Rodich, played a prominent role in the preparations for the Austrian conquest; in fact, he persuaded Francis Joseph to pay a long visit to Dalmatia in 1875 with the aim of demonstrating Austrian concern over the fate of the Dalmatian and Bosnian Slav populations. Over the course of his visit the emperor received numerous delegations of Croats and Serbs from Bosnia and Herzegovina and presented himself as protector of the Christian Slavs.[71] The political significance of the journey was clear from the outset. In May 1875 the Italian consul in Trieste, Giovanni Domenico Bruno, noted that it now appeared evident that the Vienna government was thinking about expansion in the Balkans, and the emperor's visit to Dalmatia was 'the first step toward carrying out this design.'[72]

Partly as a result of instigation from the government in Vienna, a revolt against Turkish role broke out in Herzegovina in the summer of 1875, gradually spreading to other regions. It was the beginning of an international crisis that led to the Serbian and Montenegrin war against Turkey, the Russian-Turkish war, and the subsequent Habsburg occupation of Bosnia-Herzegovina and the sanjak of Novi Pazar.

In the light of the most recent historiography on Habsburg foreign policy it appears that the outbreak of the Herzegovinian insurrection triggered a debate in the imperial government not over the expediency of a policy of expansion into the Ottoman provinces (a strategy on which all, Andrássy included, agreed) but over the tactics to be followed in the conquest of Bosnia and Herzegovina. On the one hand, there were the ambitions of the court and military circles, who were eager to bolster the uprising so that it could be turned to the advantage

---

70  Diószegi, *Die Aussenpolitik*, pp. 139–40. On the Habsburg plans for expansion in the Balkans: Rupp, *A Wavering Friendship*; Kos, *Die Politik Oesterreich-Ungarns*; Medlicott, *Bismarck, Gladstone and the Concert of Europe*, pp. 47–8; Langer, *European Alliances and Alignments, 1871–1890*.

71  On Rodich's role in Austrian Balkan policy and the imperial visit to Dalmatia: Rupp, *A Wavering Friendship*; Sumner, *Russia and the Balkans 1870–1880*, pp. 138 et seq.; Diószegi, *Die Aussenpolitik*; DDI, II, 6, docs. 184, 202; Kos, *Die Politik Oesterreich-Ungarns*, pp. 49–50.

72  Bruno to Visconti Venosta, 16 May 1875, DDI, II, 6, doc. 202.

of the Habsburg state with a rapid military conquest; on the other hand, various members of the two Austrian and Hungarian executives and the foreign minister, Andrássy, were aware of the international repercussions that an isolated Austrian action might bring and wanted to obtain the approval of the great powers for a Habsburg initiative. It was Andrássy's line that prevailed and that attained British and German assent to the occupation of the Bosnian provinces, with the attempt to find a difficult agreement with Russia, sanctioned on the international plane with the Austro-Russian accords of Reichstadt and Budapest.[73]

Over the course of the 1870s, therefore, Dalmatia's importance in Austrian foreign and domestic policy increased. It was the base for the campaign of Austrian expansion in Bosnia and the Balkans and, at the same time, a proving ground for schemes designed to alter the internal political structure of Austria. As has been pointed out, the plan of the conservative Austrian ruling class to embark on a policy of concessions to the Slav nationalities, who were considered more loyal to the empire and willing to accept the authority of the emperor and the Habsburg aristocracy, found its first field of application in Dalmatia.

The Balkan crisis seemed to confirm the realism of this political design, in which the various Slav nationalisms were tools of Austrian expansion, and the policy toward the empire's nationalities became an element of its international strategy. This connection was clearly grasped by the consul Bruno, who had the following to say about Austrian policy in Dalmatia as early as 1875:

The appointment of the Croatian general Rodich as Governor in Dalmatia, his policy aimed at constantly favouring the Slav element of that province, the great efforts that the official Austro-Hungarian press has been making for some time to draw Europeans' attention to the sad treatment of the populations of Herzegovina and Bosnia by the Ottoman Authorities and the protection and assistance that exiles from those provinces find on Austro-Hungarian soil are, in my view, so many elements which demonstrate that the Austro-Hungarian Government, while not yet resolutely determined to take advantage of the first favourable circumstance to liber-

---

73 On the Balkan accords between Austria-Hungary and Russia reached in 1876 and 1877: Langer, *European Alliances*, vol. 1, pp. 148 et seq.; Sumner, *Russia and the Balkans*, pp. 155 et seq.; Mackenzie, *The Serbs and Russian Panslavism 1875–1878*, pp. 106 et seq.; Stojanović, *The Great Powers and the Balkans 1875–1878*, pp. 74 et seq.; Kos, *Die Politik Oesterreich-Ungarns*, pp. 134 et seq.

ate those provinces and annex them to the Empire, has adopted a policy that is directed toward this end.[74]

Within Austria the various Polish, Czech, Slovene, and Croat parties extolled and supported the conquest of the Ottoman territories inhabited by Christian Slavs. The Dalmatian nationalists, in particular, exploited the Bosnian crisis to win ever greater sympathy in Vienna, presenting themselves as ardent defenders of Austrian expansion in the Balkans, which would be a work of civilization and liberation of the Christian Slav peoples and, above all, an undertaking that would unify all Croatians within the Habsburg Empire.[75] Klaić and the leaders of the Dalmatian National Party, backed by Strossmayer in Zagreb, set up committees in support of the Herzegovinian and Bosnian rebels.[76] The representative Lorenzo (Lovre) Monti called for the Austrian conquest of Bosnia and Herzegovina and expressed his hope for a Austro-Russian collaboration that would drive the Turks out of Europe and permit the emergence of Slav states in the Balkans; on the domestic plane the government should eliminate the oppressive system of dualism and foster the free development of the Slav nationality, perfectly compatible with the greatness of the Habsburg Empire.[77]

In these years the idea of trialism began to take hold in Croatian political circles, that is, the scheme of annexing Bosnia and Herzegovina to Croatia and Dalmatia and creating a unitary Croatian political entity that would form a third state and territorial component within the Habsburg Empire.[78] To facilitate the realization of this plan the Dalmatian nationalists did not hesitate to resort to the highly effective bugbear of Italian irredentism in Dalmatia. In a speech to the parliamentary delegations in December 1878, Klaić made a virulent attack on the policy pursued by the Vienna government in Dalmatia in the past, which

---

74 Bruno to Visconti Venosta, 16 May 1875.
75 On the pressure exerted by the Slav parties in favour of an Austrian conquest of Bosnia: DDF, I, 2, docs. 2, 5, 7. On Strossmayer's attitude toward the Bosnian question: Rohrbacher, 'Bishop J. J. Strossmayer's Yugoslavism,' pp. 343 et seq.
76 On the attitude of the Dalmatian National Party toward the revolt in Bosnia and Herzegovina: Grabovac, *Dalmacjia u oslobodilačkom pokretu hercegovačko-bosanske raje 1875–1878.*
77 Speech by Lorenzo Monti to parliament in Vienna, 21 January 1879, reproduced in *Il Dalmata*, 5 February 1879.
78 See the observations of the French ambassador in Vienna, de Vogüé, on the matter: DDF, I, 2, docs. 163, 356.

he considered too pro-Italian, and asserted that the best defence against the possibility of Italian irredentism was the national reawakening of the Slav peoples.[79]

The Balkan crisis put the Dalmatian autonomists in an awkward situation. They had always been in favour of Austrian expansion in the Balkans, inasmuch as they thought it would help the economic growth of Dalmatia. Even in the years 1875–8 they supported imperial policy and praised the occupation of Bosnia.[80] However, some of them, including Bajamonti, followed the example of the Austro-German and Hungarian liberals and began to fear the consequences that the conquest of these territories would have on Austrian domestic policy, given the strengthening of conservative groups and the Slav nationalists. In a speech made in December 1876 Bajamonti noted that the prospective annexation of Bosnia and Herzegovina to Dalmatia could only be welcomed by all Dalmatians, but it was necessary to avoid any disruptions of the internal set-up of Austria, such as a Croatian-Dalmatian union.[81]

The emperor's decision to conquer Bosnia-Herzegovina had devastating effects on the balance of power in Austria. The opposition of many Austrian and German liberals to the policy of expansion in Bosnia, and their desire for parliament to have a say in foreign policy, which was considered the exclusive and unchallenged domain of the emperor, led to a head-on clash with Francis Joseph. In March 1878 many liberals voted against supplementary funding of future military operations, much to the emperor's irritation. The funding was approved, but the rift between the imperial court and the Liberal Party was now irremediable.[82]

79 'Il discorso dell'onorevole Klaich,' in *Il Dalmata*, 18 December 1878.
80 On the support of the Dalmatian autonomous liberal press for the Habsburg policy of expansion in the Balkans: 'La guerra d'Oriente e la pace,' in *Il Dalmata*, 6 February 1878; 'Si vis pacem para bellum,' in *Il Dalmata*, 12 June 1878; 'L'Austria e l'Oriente,' in *Il Dalmata*, 24 July 1878. In August 1879 the autonomist administration of Zara, headed by Mayor Trigari and the councilor Luxardo, organized a collection among the citizens on behalf of the Austrians wounded and killed during the war of occupation of Bosnia and Herzegovina: *Il Dalmata*, 21 August 1878.
81 Bajamonti, *Discorso pronunziato alla Camera dei deputati*, pp. 25–6; see too 'L'insurrezione dell'Erzegovina,' in *L'Avvenire*, 26 August 1875. There are some references to the position of the Dalmatian autonomist liberals in Grabovac, *Dalmacjia u oslobodilačkom pokretu hercegovačko-bosanske raje*, pp. 76 et seq.
82 On the Austrian political crisis of 1878–9 the reader is referred to: Bled, *François Joseph*, pp. 415 et seq.; Jenks, *Austria under the Iron Ring*, pp. 28 et seq.; Höbelt, 'Parteien und

The Balkans after the Berlin Congress, 1878

The breakdown in relations between the liberals and the emperor, and the divisions within Austrian liberalism itself, prompted the Auersperg government to resign in the fall of 1878. It was succeeded in the following spring by the Karl Stremayr government, a coalition of liberals and conservatives formed to satisfy the emperor, in which the key role was played by Eduard Taaffe, who took over the Ministry of the Interior. An aristocrat with conservative leanings and a personal friend of Francis Joseph, who had already served as minister of the in-

Fraktionen im Cisleithanischen Reichsrat,' in *Die Habsburgermonarchie*, vol. 7, tome 1, pp. 924 et seq.; DDI, II, 9, docs. 549, 567, 623; II, 11, docs. 225, 329, 539; II, 12, docs. 151, 240; DDF, I, 2, doc. 351.

terior and as governor of the Tyrol from 1871 to 1879,[83] Taaffe became the vehicle for the emperor's new domestic policy. As minister of the interior he had a powerful influence on the parliamentary elections that were held in July 1879. At the same time he opened negotiations with the 'feudal' Bohemian Right and the moderate Nationalist Party of the 'Old Czechs,' which had refused to participate in the work of the chamber for several years; his aim was to persuade them to come back to the Reichsrat and co-operate in the formation of a future 'right-wing' government, opposed to the liberals and well disposed toward the Catholic world and the Slav parties. Taaffe reached an accord with the Czech Bohemians, who agreed to return to the Reichsrat after the new elections in exchange for future concessions on their national rights.

Piloted by Taaffe, who favoured the Croatian nationalists in Dalmatia, the elections of 1879 left the German liberal groups in a minority and saw the emergence of a new majority in the parliament, centred on the German clerical conservatives and the Czech, Croat, Slovene, and Polish nationalists. Together with liberal groups loyal to the emperor, they supported the Taaffe ministry, which would dominate Austrian politics until the 1890s.

In Dalmatia the autonomist liberals entered the 1879 elections under difficult conditions. The fall of the liberal government in Vienna deprived them of the ally that had allowed them to counter Rodich's Slavophile policy, which had been inspired by the *Hofpartei*. The policy of rapprochement with the Slav parties that was implemented by Taaffe in Dalmatia increased the indulgence of the state administration toward the National Party. The other two political forces in Dalmatia found themselves in profound difficulties: Zemljiak collapsed on the death of Ljubiša at the end of 1878, and the autonomists were split between the factions headed by Trigari and Bajamonti.

Trigari, at odds with the mayor of Spalato's opposition to Rodich and with the anticlericalism of the liberals led by him, stood for election with a very moderate and pragmatic platform, founded on loyalty to the emperor and the importance of the Catholic religion. In his view it was necessary to focus on improvement of the economic conditions in Dalmatia and foster harmony among the Dalmatian people, 'as they are all sons of the same soil and brothers.'[84]

---

83 Still of value on the figure of Taaffe, Jenks, *Austria under the Iron Ring*, pp. 29 et seq.
84 *Il Dalmata*, 28 June 1879. On the 1879 elections in Dalmatia: Perić, *Dalmatinski Sabor*,
   p. 106.

Not only did Bajamonti's and Trigari's autonomists run for election without any electoral accord, but they did so in suicidal competition. In the constituency of the cities of Zara, Sebenico, Lesina, Cittavecchia, and Curzola, in which Trigari stood as candidate, Bajamonti put up Gian Antonio Botteri, the leader of the autonomists in Cittavecchia, despite knowing that he had no possibility of winning.[85] Very curious was the case of the constituency of the highly assessed, where Trigari's autonomist liberals put forward Francesco Borelli, one of the founders of the autonomist movement. In 1879 Borelli again made clear to the voters his opposition to the annexation to Croatia, as this would have reduced Dalmatia to a state of servitude; what he wanted to see, instead, was Dalmatia at the centre of the southern Slav world, annexing Bosnia, Herzegovina, and even Croatia.[86] There was no hint of Italian nationalism in Borelli, for he remained faithful to Tommaseo's idea of Dalmatia's role as an intermediary between the Western world and the Slavs of the south. The Croatian nationalists decided to put forward Francesco's son Count Manfredo Borelli as their candidate in the same constituency; also Italian by language and culture, he was a supporter of the nationalists and ready to accept the program of Croatization of the schools called for by the Narodnjaci.[87]

The elections for the Reichsrat saw the triumph of the National Party, which won eight seats out of nine. The nationalists sent Manfredo Borelli, Lorenzo Monti, Bulat, Raffaele Pozza from Ragusa, Giorgio Vojnović, Pavlinović (who later resigned in favor of Klaić), Doimo Rendić Miočević, and Antun Šupuk (the mayor of Sebenico) to Vienna.[88] The autonomists were only able to elect one representative, Gustavo Ivanics, a relative of Trigari, in the rural constituency of Zara.[89] Split between Bajamonti's faction based in Spalato and Trigari's group in Zara, and stripped of government support, the autonomists were soundly beaten.

The 1879 elections marked the end of Dalmatian autonomism as the majority party in Dalmatia, and in particular they also sanctioned the division of the National Party into two separate groups, Serbian and Croatian.

---

85 *Il Dalmata*, 12 July 1879.
86 Letter from Francesco Borelli, *Il Dalmata*, 23 July 1879. On the Borelli family, originally from Bologna: Peričić, 'Vranski feud i obitelj Borelli,' pp. 389–412.
87 'Il programma del 'Narodni List," in *Il Dalmata*, 28 June 1879.
88 *Namen-Verzeichniss der Mitglieder des Abgeordnetenhauses*, p. 109.
89 On the electoral results of 1879 in Dalmatia: *Il Dalmata*, 9 and 23 July 1879.

Over the course of the 1870s the ideological influence of the Catholic clerical element inside the National Party had grown. The clergy had played a fundamental role in giving an organizational structure to the nationalists. In many inland parts of Dalmatia the nationalist associations were headed by priests, who exercised an important function at elections, mobilizing the electorate and drumming up support and votes. The main national newspapers in Dalmatia were edited by priests: *Il Nazionale (Narodni List)* by Don Juraj Biankini and the *Dalmazia Cattolica (Katolička Dalmacija)* by Don Ivo Prodan. The nationalist Catholic priests Pavlinović, Biankini, and Prodan launched a new political message centred on an identification of religious faith and national consciousness, leading to the progressive abandonment of Yugoslav ideology by the Dalmatian nationalists and the assertion of a purely Croatian nationalist ideal. Men like Pavlinović accepted the idea of an ethnic and cultural commonality between Croatians and Serbs but felt that the Catholic faith was the mark of the Croatians' superiority to the Orthodox and Serb population, which had to be redeemed on the religious and national plane through a process of conversion and assimilation that would make them Catholic and therefore Croatian. Pavlinović argued forcefully that only Slavs lived in Dalmatia and that these Slavs were all Croatians. He denied not just the existence of an element of Italian language and culture in Dalmatia but also the legitimacy of the Serb presence. Italians and Serbs had only one alternative: to become Croatian or to leave.[90] The Balkan crisis of the 1870s and the question of the fate of Bosnia-Herzegovina intensified this progressive ideological divergence and aggravated the conflicts among the Dalmatian nation-

---

90  Pavlinović's political thinking has naturally been interpreted in contrasting ways
in Croatian, Serb, and Yugoslav historiography. In general the anti-Italian attitude
of the Croatian politician has always been praised and defended, while his anti-
Serbian ideas have produced more varied assessments: Petrović, for example, drew
attention to their xenophobic character (Petrović, *Nacionalno pitanje u Dalmaciji u XIX
stoljeću*, pp. 343 et seq.), while others, like Stančić, have explained them as a reaction
to the arguments in favour of a Greater Serbia that were being put forward in some
Serbian political circles (Nikša Stančić, 'Misaoni razvoj Mihovila Pavlinovića u
šezdesetim godinama XIX st.,' in Foretić, *Dalmacija 1870*, pp. 243 et seq.). In general,
with the break-up of Yugoslavia and the birth of an independent Croatia, figures like
Pavlinović and Prodan, supporters of an anti-Serbian and anti-Italian pan-Croatian
nationalism, have undergone a positive historical and political reappraisal: Diklić,
'Mihovil Pavlinović i pojava pravaštva u Dalmaciji,' pp. 15 et seq.; Nikša Stančić,
"Hrvat i Katolik'. politička misao Mihovila Pavlinovića,' in Pavlinović, *Izabrani
politički spisi*, pp. 9–70.

alists. Between 1875 and 1878 the leader of the National Party, Klaić, and many Dalmatian Croats worked to have Bosnia and Herzegovina conquered by Austria, while many Dalmatian Serbs hoped that the Serbian and Montenegrin states would also make substantial territorial gains in Bosnia.[91]

It was on the occasion of the elections for the Vienna parliament in 1879 that the breach between Croatians and Serbians within the Dalmatian National Party widened. Klaić decided to stand in the rural constituency of Zara, which comprised many towns and villages with a majority of Serb inhabitants. The Serbian leaders of northern Dalmatia tried to impose the candidature of Vladimiro Simić (Simich), mayor of Obrovac, on the National Party, and when this was rejected by the Croatians, they struck a deal with the autonomists of Zara to block Klaić's election, giving the seat to the autonomist Gustavo Ivanics.[92] Klaić's defeat was the straw that broke the camel's back. The National Party split, and the following years saw the foundation of a Serbian Party of Dalmatia, taking a national-liberal position; its strongholds would be the centres of Knin and Benkovac and the Bocche di Cattaro. At the beginning of 1880, the National Party assumed the name of Hrvatska Narodna Stranka (Croatian National Party), abandoning any Yugoslav ideology and espousing a purely Croatian nationalism.

The results of the 1879 elections marked an important shift in the political balance in the whole of Cisleithania. The Austro-German liberals won forty-nine less seats than they had held in the previous legislature, and with the simultaneous reduction in the numbers of their Dalmatian autonomist and Ruthenian or Ukrainian allies, this meant the loss of their majority in the parliament. The clericalist and conservative Right, comprising the clericalists of the Austrian Alps and the Slovenian, Croatian, and Romanian nationalists, won fifty-seven seats. The Czech and Polish parties also achieved a good result, with fifty-four and fifty-seven seats respectively.[93]

---

91  On the disagreement between the Croats and Serbs of Dalmatia over the future of Bosnia: Petrović, *Nacionalno pitanje u Dalmaciji u XIX stoljeću*, pp. 343 et seq.
92  On these events: *Il Dalmata*, 9 July 1879; 'Il dr. Gustavo Ivanics e il "Narodni List,"' *Il Dalmata*, 26 July 1879; 'La "Politik" e la caduta del dr. Klaich,' *Il Dalmata*, 2 August 1879. See too Perić, *Dalmatinski sabor*, p. 106.
93  On the 1879 elections in Austria: Jenks, *Austria under the Iron Ring*, pp. 35–6; Bled, *François Joseph*, pp. 419 et seq.; Macartney, *The Habsburg Empire*; Höbelt, 'Parteien und Fraktionen,' pp. 928 et seq.

Thus the German liberals and their Dalmatian, Italian, and Ruthenian allies lost their majority in the elected chamber. Tired of having to
deal with unreliable politicians who wanted to limit the prerogatives of
imperial power, Francis Joseph now had a lot of room to manoeuvre.
He gave the post of prime minister to Taaffe, who formed a distinctly
conservative government linked to the feudal, Catholic, and federalist
aristocracy. Taaffe worked to put together a majority in parliament in
support of the new executive, a true 'government of the emperor.'

In the face of Francis Joseph's initiatives the German liberal movement split definitively and found itself in crisis. Taaffe succeeded in
creating a new parliamentary coalition, made up of Czechs, Slovenes,
Croatian Dalmatians, Poles, clericalist Germans, and a few groups of
liberals who were particularly loyal to the emperor, and he took the
government in a decidedly conservative direction. This shift took on a
definitive form in 1881 with a complete rupture between the German
liberals and the parliamentary majority; it consisted of the 'Iron Ring,'
an alliance between Austro-German conservatism, with its strongholds
in Tyrol and Styria, and the Slav nationalist parties (Czech, Polish, Slovene, and Croat).[94]

The political consequences of the swing to the right in the Austrian
part of the Habsburg Empire from 1878 onward were particularly heavy
for the Italian inhabitants of the eastern Adriatic Coast. The Taaffe government made political and cultural concessions to the various Slav
parties in order to win their support. In Bohemia and Moravia it tried
to meet the demands of the Czech nationalists by, for instance, split-
ting the University of Prague into two separate institutions, German
and Czech, in 1881.[95] On the coast of Venezia Giulia and in Dalmatia it
pursued a policy more favourable to the Slovene and Croat parties, at
the expense of the Italian and Italophile liberals, who were considered
untrustworthy and a potentially treacherous element.

The growing anti-Italian bias shown by the Habsburg government
on the Adriatic coast after 1878 was motivated not just by domestic
considerations but also by foreign policy: a pro-Slav domestic policy
served the interests of Habsburg expansionism in the Balkan territories

---

94 On the formation of the Taaffe government and its domestic policy: Jenks, *Austria
under the Iron Ring*, pp. 37 et seq.
95 Ibid., pp. 71 et seq.

inhabited by Slav peoples.[96] At the same time, anything that helped to weaken the Italian and Italophile groups in Trieste, Gorizia, Istria, and Dalmatia represented a further obstacle to any designs of conquest on the part of the kingdom of Italy.[97]

The link between domestic and foreign policy in the Habsburg action in Dalmatia was clearly grasped by an anonymous journalist in *Il Dalmata*. Writing in December 1879, he attributed the shift in the strategy of the Austrian government to the empire's new objectives of foreign policy in the Balkans: 'The reawakening of Slav national feeling, so keenly fostered by government, is happening not so much out of a respect for national freedom, as with the aim of forming a powerful centre within the boundaries of the empire, capable of attracting the bordering Slav populations, who loathe the Turkish yoke.'[98]

In short, according to the view of the autonomous liberal newspaper, national struggles were being exploited by Austrian leaders; in Dalmatia the cultural and national rights of the Croats were favoured in order to detach the region definitively from Venetian and Italian lands, even though there was no trace of any territorial claim on Dalmatia in Italian public opinion. The journalist of *Il Dalmata* pointed out that, as a result of this political calculation, the Italian-speaking populations of Dalmatia, notwithstanding their loyalty to Austria, had been left by the government in Vienna at the mercy of the anti-Italian policy of Croatian nationalism; they who had demonstrated their devotion to the Habsburg dynasty so many times were being 'basely mistreated for reasons of foreign policy.'[99]

The irredentist agitations that took place in Italy between 1878 and 1880 in the name of the exaltation of the Trentino and Giulia regions' Italian character, and the Italian diplomatic activity aimed at contain-

---

96 On Austria-Hungary's Balkan policy in the 1880s: Langer, *European Alliances*; Palotás, *Machtpolitik und Wirtschaftsinteressen*; Bridge, *From Sadowa to Sarajevo*; Albertini, *The Origins of the War of 1914*; *Die Habsburgermonarchie 1848–1918*, vol. 6, part 2, in particular the essays by Branislav Vranešević, Virginia Paskaleva, Milčo Lalkov, and Marija Wakounig.

97 On the difficult Italo-Austrian relations between 1875 and 1880: Petrignani, *Neutralità e alleanza*, pp. 66 et seq.; Sandonà, *L'irredentismo nelle lotte politiche e nelle contese diplomatiche italo-austriache*, vol. 1; Salvatorelli, *La Triplice Alleanza*, pp. 29 et seq.

98 'Nazionalità,' in *Il Dalmata*, 17 December 1879 (the author is anonymous but may have been the newspaper's editor, Vincenzo de Benvenuti).

99 Ibid.

ing Austrian influence in Serbia, Albania, Montenegro, and Romania,[100] were often used to justify a series of political and administrative initiatives by the Stremayr and Taaffe governments. Such initiatives in favour of the Slovene and Croat elements included dissolution of city councils in the hands of Italophile parties (for example, those of Trieste in November 1878[101] and Spalato in 1880), Slavicization of schools, and promotion of the linguistic rights of the Slav-speaking populations. Their aim was to weaken the political, economic, and cultural ties between the eastern Adriatic coast and Italy. The Italian ambassador to Vienna, Carlo Felice Nicolis di Robilant, declared in 1879, in connection with the anti-Italian policy pursued by the Austrian authorities in Trieste: 'The agitation on behalf of "unredeemed Italy" that has occurred in Italy has united Government and subjects in Austria-Hungary in a single thought, that of retaining at any cost to the Empire that gem of the Monarchy which is its splendour and indeed its life. To attain that end the aim of *de-Italianizing* Trieste is shared by all.'[102]

As has already been pointed out, the shift to the right in the domestic policy of Cisleithania and the formation of the Iron Ring weakened the Dalmatian autonomists, who lost their last ally, the Austro-German liberals, in the struggle against the nationalists. For their part, the nationalists, abandoning any Yugoslav ideal and espousing a determined Croat nationalism, became a party of government. The Croatian representatives of Dalmatia joined the parliamentary group that supported Taaffe and was led by Karl Sigmund von Hohenwart, who was federalist and clerical in orientation.[103] The Austrian premier rewarded the Croatian nationalists for their parliamentary support by helping them in their struggle to establish their dominance in Dalmatia once and for all.

Crucial in this respect was the winning of control of Spalato and the cities of central Dalmatia. The autonomist liberals, despite having lost

---

100  On the irredentist agitations in Italy at the end of the 1870s: Chiala, *Pagine di storia contemporanea dal 1858 al 1892*, pp. 1–72. See too: Petrignani, *Neutralità e alleanza*, pp. 185 et seq.

101  On this: Veronese, *Vicende e figure dell'irredentismo giuliano*, pp. 51–3; *Ricordi d'irredentismo*, pp. 67–70; Tamaro, *Storia di Trieste*, vol. 2, p. 414.

102  Robilant to Cairoli, 12 August 1879, DDI, II, 12, doc. 100,. On the anti-Italian policy of the Stremayr and Taaffe governments see: DDI, II, 11, docs. 26, 42, 102; DDI, II, 12, doc. 116. In this connection see too Sandonà, *L'irredentismo*, vol. 1, pp. 252 et seq.

103  On the political collaboration between the Dalmatian nationalists, Hohenwart, and Taaffe: Morović, 'Pisme Miha Klaića uredniku "Narodnog Lista" Jurju Biankiniju,' pp. 273–306, in particular docs. 20, 22, 26, and 27.

their majority in the provincial diet and having only one member in the imperial parliament, still held the majority of the governments of the coastal and island cities of central and northern Dalmatia.

The hub of the Dalmatian political struggle in those years was Spalato, the biggest city in central Dalmatia, where Antonio Bajamonti had been in power since 1860. On the base of a political platform that blended liberalism and municipalism, he had been able to gather support from all of the city's social and national components. The Taaffe government made some concessions to the nationalists in order to strengthen their position in Spalato: at the beginning of 1880, at the request of the nationalists, the government decided to make Croatian the medium of instruction in the high schools of Spalato,[104] relegating Italian to the status of a second, and therefore foreign, language. Nothing came of the protest by the autonomist municipal government, which wanted to keep Italian as the medium of instruction in the schools and sent a deputation to Vienna made up of several Dalmatian university professors and scholars (Adolfo Mussafia, Antonio Lubin, and Luigi Cesare Pavissich) to plead the cause of the Italian language. Put under pressure by Vienna and attacked by the Croatian nationalists, who accused him of serious irregularities in the administration of the city's finances,[105] Bajamonti made the mistake of accepting the radicalization of the political confrontation and fell victim to a series of provocations.

The events of the summer of 1880 were decisive. During August and September, street clashes took place in Spalato between autonomist sympathizers and Croatian soldiers of the imperial army, culminating in the knifing of Arturo Colautti, the editor-in-chief of the local autonomist newspaper, by Croatian soldiers and officers. Bajamonti and his supporters criticized the armed forces, accusing them of political bias, but in doing so they brought the linch-pin of the Habsburg Empire into question and made things easier for the Croat nationalists, who were quick to denounce the presumed subversive aims and Italophile tendencies of the Dalmatian autonomists.[106] With the assent of the em-

---

104 'Il conte Taaffe e la sua politica,' in *Il Dalmata*, 31 March 1880; 'Le scuole medie di Spalato I, II,' *Il Dalmata*, 3 and 7 April 1880; 'La deputazione di Spalato,' in *L'Avvenire*, 17 May 1880; *L'Avvenire*, 24 May 1880.
105 On this: Monzali, 'Dalmati o Italiani?' p. 453.
106 'I disordini di Spalato,' in *Il Dalmata*, 25 August 1880; 'In Austria?' *Il Dalmata*, 29 September 1880; 'Nuove mistificazioni,' *Il Dalmata*, 2 October 1880; Novak, 'Kako je došlo do pobjede Hrvata u Splitu god. 1882,' pp. 7–54, in particular pp. 36 et seq.

peror and the government in Vienna, Bajamonti's old enemy Governor
Rodich dissolved the city council of Spalato in November 1880, thereby
satisfying the demands of the Croat nationalists.[107]

Two years went by before new municipal elections were held, time
that helped to strengthen support for the Nationalist Party, which now
enjoyed strong backing from all government authorities. The Dalmatian autonomist liberals proved incapable of rising to the political chal-
lenges that threatened their existence. Lacking a strong and unified
organization and sapped by internal rivalries, they were unable to defend their positions in Spalato. At the beginning of 1880, the Dalmatian
autonomist liberals were essentially isolated at the state level; the only
people they could call on for help were the German liberals,[108] with
whom, however, relations had cooled to some extent as a consequence
of the German nationalistic attitude assumed by many Austrian liberals.[109] It is no coincidence that in those years the only Dalmatian autonomist member of the Reichsrat, Ivanics, left the parliamentary groups
of the German Left and joined the Liberal-Conservative Centre headed
by Francesco Coronini, an aristocrat from Gorizia and a personal friend
of Francis Joseph. Apart from the publication of various articles in the
*Neue Freie Presse* in defence of their old allies, the German liberals closest to the Dalmatian autonomists (Herbst, Ignaz von Plener, and Johann
von Chlumecky) could or would do nothing.[110]

The autonomists, in short, victims of the shift in Habsburg domestic
and foreign policy, were incapable of reacting to a new situation that
was distinctly hostile to them. Opposing them was the Croatian Nationalist Party, united under the leadership of Klaić and Bulat, which
was ruthless, strong, and fully able to grasp and exploit the changes
and evolution in Austrian policy. With the contemporaneous support of
the Czech and German clericalist press, which were opposed to the Ital-

107 'Lo scioglimento del Comune di Spalato,' in *Il Dalmata*, 6 November 1880; 'Un po'
di luce,' *Il Dalmata*, 13 November 1880.
108 Appeals for solidarity between German and Dalmatian liberals were made in 'Il
Parteitag tedesco-austriaco,' in *Il Dalmata*, 24 November 1880; 'Siamo Uniti!' in *Il
Dalmata*, 27 November 1880.
109 On the ideological shift toward German nationalism among Austrian liberals:
Höbelt, *Kornblume und Kaiseradler*; 'Die Deutschliberalen Altösterreichs als Verfassungsbewegung 1848–1918.'
110 On the sympathy of the Austrian liberal press, whose principal organ was the *Neue
Freie Presse*, for the Dalmatian autonomists see, for example, *L'Avvenire*, 21 May and
23 September 1881.

ian parties, Klaić, while fully aware that there was no Italian irredentism in Dalmatia, launched a violent campaign in the Croatian press on the presumed links between Dalmatian autonomists and the circles of 'irredentist Italy' and on the danger to Austria of a strong autonomist presence in Dalmatia.[111]

Held in a heated political atmosphere, the elections of July 1882 saw the nationalists win a majority on the city council of Spalato, putting an end to twenty years of unchallenged dominance by Bajamonti[112] and dealing a heavy blow to the political fortunes of Dalmatian autonomist liberalism.

The defeat in Spalato was a significant moment in the history of Dalmatian autonomism as it marked the beginning of the movement's political decline. Within the space of a few years, the autonomists lost control of the principal municipalities of central Dalmatia. Cittavecchia on the island of Lesina, an autonomist stronghold, met the same fate as Spalato, when its council was dissolved by government decree in 1885,[113] and the nationalists won a majority in the subsequent elections. The other important autonomist liberal municipality in central Dalmatia, Traù, was taken over by the Croatian nationalists in 1887.[114]

The elections to the Dalmatian provincial diet also saw a series of defeats for the autonomists. In the elections of 1883 only eight of their candidates won seats (Messa, Michele Capovic, Trigari, Smerchinich, Enrico Pezzi, Radman, Ivanics, and Luigi Serragli), and these seats were reduced to six in the elections of 1889. Now in control solely of Zara, the party was only able to win in the constituencies of the highly assessed, the city, and the chamber of commerce that were reserved for the capital of the province. From the second half of the 1880s until the outbreak of World War I, the Autonomist Party was able to hold on to no more than the six provincial seats assigned to Zara.[115]

---

111 On these polemics: 'Liquidazione,' in *Il Dalmata*, 24 March 1880; 'All'erta dalmati!' *Il Dalmata*, 22 January 1881; 'I delatori,' *Il Dalmata*, 29 January 1881; 'Irredentismo?' *Il Dalmata*, 19 April 1882.

112 *Il Dalmata*, 26 July and 9 August 1882. In Croatian historiography the best analysis of the victory of the Narodnjaci in Spalato is the one by Grga Novak: Novak, *Povijest Splita*, vol. 3, pp. 341 et seq.; 'Kako je došlo do pobjede Hrvata u Splitu god. 1882,' pp. 7–54; see too Monzali, 'Dalmati o Italiani?' pp. 453–5; Randi, *Antonio Bajamonti*.

113 'Il comune di Cittavecchia,' *Il Dalmata*, 21 July 1885.

114 'A Traù,' *La Difesa*, 27 January 1887.

115 Perić, *Dalmatinski sabor*, pp. 220–5; Vrandečić, *Dalmatinski autonomistički pokret u XIX stoljeću*, pp. 223 et seq.

The autonomists were weakened not only by the hostility of the Austrian government and the organizational and political superiority of the Croatian National Party but also by the electoral reform of 1882, which favoured the Croatian nationalists by broadening the suffrage; with the help of the rural clergy, the nationalists were able to mobilize many voters who had no ties with the Italo-Slav culture of the coastal cities.

In an effort to revive their dying movement, the autonomist leaders Trigari and Bajamonti, now forced into reconciliation by the general collapse of Dalmatian autonomism, persuaded its former head, Luigi Lapenna, to return to politics.

As has already been said, Lapenna had retired from active politics in 1875 when he was appointed the Austrian member of the international Commission of the Egyptian Public Debt in Alexandria. Returning to Austria in 1880, he was rewarded for his work with the post of president of the supreme court and the title of baron; in 1881 he was asked to draw up a plan for the organization of the judiciary in Bosnia-Herzegovina.[116] In short, despite the general decline of liberalism, the former autonomist leader had remained a man of the imperial establishment, a Habsburg loyalist who had links to its highest echelons. His return to the political scene was an attempt by the autonomist ruling class to curry favour in Vienna.

Unquestionably the most brilliant and significant political figure in Dalmatian autonomist liberalism, Lapenna threw himself energetically into the electoral campaign. In the face of the political and ideological crisis that had overtaken the autonomist movement, he decided to publish a series of articles reflecting on the past and speculating about the future of Dalmatian autonomist liberalism, in *Il Dalmata* in February 1885.[117] Lapenna praised what, in his view, were the underlying values of autonomist liberalism in Dalmatia. He forcefully denied that there was an Italian party in Dalmatia. The Autonomist Party had always been multi-ethnic, made up of both Italian-speaking and Slav-speaking

---

116  *Il Dalmata*, 29 January and 1 October 1881.
117  'La situazione,' in *Il Dalmata*, 7, 10, 14, 17, 21, and 24 February 1885. These articles were published anonymously under the initial *L* but were immediately attributed by the Dalmatian press to Lapenna, who provided implicit confirmation that he was their author by publishing comments on the controversy generated by his writings in *Il Dalmata*: cf. *Il Dalmata*, 4 April 1885; 'Gli articoli del dr. Lapenna,' *Narod*, 7 March 1885.

Il Dalmata (1866–1916)            Pravi Dalmatinac (1897–1907)
L'Avvenire (1875–82)              Il Risorgimento (1908–1914)
La Difesa (1884–87)

Newspapers of the Autonomist Party in Dalmatia

Dalmatians: 'So *Italian or Slav* nationality is not the distinctive character of the parties in Dalmatia, but the question of the *annexation* to Croatia or the *autonomy* of the kingdom. It is true that the Autonomist Party which combats Croatian aspirations also defends the Italian element and culture; but it is not the *exclusivity* of this element that lies at the top and bottom of its program, but provincial autonomy and respect for both the languages, Italian and Slav, and the development of the culture of *both*.'[118]

The Autonomist Party, in Lapenna's opinion, rejected nationalistic ideas and believed in the unifying power of people seeing themselves as Dalmatian, in 1861 as in 1885: 'It did not know then, as it does not know today, any distinction of race, religion or social status; it proclaimed then, as it proclaims today, that all Dalmatians are children of the same motherland, given that their ancestors in the many changes of rule and the even greater numbers of movements of peoples came from over the mountains or over the seas a more or less long time ago to make it their home and to devote to it their affections, their intelligence, their labor, their interests, their fortune.'

Another fundamental element of Dalmatian autonomist ideology was, according to the magistrate, belief in the liberal values of the Austrian constitution: 'When the Autonomist representatives found themselves in a majority in the Reichsrat, they sat on the left. Nor could they have done otherwise. The left represented the principle of the unity of the empire, held the Austrian flag high, defended the constitution, fought federalism and made itself the champion of Liberal ideas and of reform of the laws in order to bring about progress and modern civilization.'

After stressing the relevance and validity of the basic principles of autonomist liberalism, Lapenna attempted to outline a new political strategy. On the one hand, he strove to reaffirm the moderate character of his movement and its loyalty to the main political and religious institutions, that is, the Austrian government and the Catholic Church. Criticizing the nationalist drift of German liberalism, which had abandoned 'the principle of equality of all the state's languages and nationalities, and [had replaced] the flag of the unity of the empire with the German national flag,' Lapenna defended the new centrist position of autonomism; he was ready to hold a pragmatic dialogue with the Taaffe

---

118 'La situazione,' *Il Dalmata*.

government since the autonomists shunned both 'the approach of opposition at any cost, and on the other hand what is summed up in the dilemma *your purse or your life.'* As for the Catholic Church, while deploring the fact that there were priests who preached 'intolerance and racial antagonism' and that there had been a lack of respect for the ecclesiastic world on the part of the autonomists, the Dalmatian politician denied that they were hostile to the Church and underlined its importance for the well-being and development of Dalmatian society, especially in the poorer and more backward areas. On the other hand, Lapenna argued for the necessity of a close and staunch alliance between autonomists and Serbian Dalmatians. Confronted by the increasingly aggressive and intolerant character of Croatian nationalism, which tended to stifle the linguistic and cultural rights of Dalmatians of Italian and Serbian language and culture, these Dalmatians needed to unite in a grand alliance on the basis of a program founded on rejection of the annexation to Croatia, on true liberalism 'which wants respect for the rights of all, the individual as well as the nationality,' on equal recognition of the various languages spoken in Dalmatia, and on a political action that would give absolute priority to the material progress of the province.

In essence Lapenna reasserted the traditional themes of liberal autonomist thinking (Dalmatian patriotism, liberalism, and loyalty to Austria), while trying to adapt to the new political context in Austria at the end of the century. It is interesting, however, to note that the long struggle of the Croatian nationalists against the Italian element in Dalmatia (for more than a decade) obliged even him, so remote from any Italian national or nationalistic political ideology, to assign growing importance to defending the rights of the Italian culture in Dalmatia. Lapenna condemned in the harshest tones the Croatian nationalist persecution of the Italian language, which by making Dalmatia exclusively Croatian, was aimed at facilitating its annexation to Croatia. In his view, the presence of the Italian language, an irreplaceable part of the Dalmatian identity, had not just a spiritual function but also an economic one, which could not be renounced. Without the Italian language and culture ('this bond that still unites us morally with the civilized world'), the commercial and economic activities of Dalmatia would be very seriously damaged. As Lapenna observed, even if 'we were to forget that knowledge of the Italian language opens up vast possibilities for work, honour and profit in foreign countries for our diligent youth, solely its material advantages for our merchant navy and our trade, which also favours agricultural production, would and should have held today's

Croatian dictators back from the vandalism that they are carrying out. The Italian language is an inestimable treasure for Dalmatia, ... it is a treasure that we possess and it would be a crime against the love of our country if it were to disappear from the heritage of our native land.'[119]

Despite the return of Lapenna and the alliance with the Dalmatian Serb party, the autonomists did not succeed in electing a single candidate in the elections for the Reichsrat of 1885. Lapenna, who stood in the constituency of the cities of Zara and Sebenico, was defeated (836 votes against 1130) by the nationalist mayor of Sebenico, Šupuk, while the Ragusan Marino Bonda was beaten in the constituency of the cities of Spalato, Ragusa, and Cattaro by the Croatian Lovro Borčić (525 votes against 791). The leader of the Serb party, Savo Bjelanović, supported by the autonomists in the rural constituency of Zara, Benkovac, Arbe, and Pago, was defeated by Klaić (99 votes against 167). The Croatian National Party won all nine seats for the parliament in Vienna.[120]

Yet the strategy of the Serb-Autonomist alliance, the union of two weaklings against the excessive power of the Croatian National Party,[121] did serve to preserve autonomous liberalism as a political force with a certain weight in some Dalmatian cities. In those years the Serb-Autonomist coalition won control of the city councils of Ragusa and Cattaro, retaining it up until the second half of the 1890s.[122] It was also thanks to this alliance that in the 1888 by-election for a seat in the Reichsrat in the constituency of the wealthiest property owners, the autonomists and the Dalmatian Serb party were able to elect Luigi Lapenna. But Lapenna, falling gravely ill a year later, retired from active politics; he died in 1891,[123] the same year as the other founder of Dalmatian autonomist liberalism, Antonio Bajamonti, passed away.[124]

---

119  Ibid.
120  On the 1885 electoral campaign and its results: *Narod*, 23, 27, and 30 May 1885, 10 June 1885; *Il Dalmata*, 19 May, 9 and 23 June 1885.
121  On the collaboration between Serbs and autonomists in Dalmatia: Rajčić, 'Odnos "Srpskog Lista (Glasa)" prema autonomašima u Dalmaciji 80-ih godina XIX stoljeća,' pp. 375–87; Vrandečić, *Dalmatinski autonomistički pokret u XIX stoljeću*, pp. 238 et seq.
122  On the Serb autonomist administration headed by Francesco Gondola in Ragusa: Vrandečić, *Dalmatinski autonomistički pokret u XIX stoljeću*, pp. 242 et seq.
123  *Il Dalmata*, 8 and 11 April 1891.
124  On the subject of Bajamonti's death and the significance of his role in the political life of Spalato: 'Chi succede?' in *Narod*, 27 January 1891; *Onoranze funebri ad Antonio Bajamonti*.

In the subsequent elections for the Reichsrat in 1891, the Serb-Autonomist alliance was again able to win the constituency of the highly assessed. The vote reserved for the wealthiest people in the province gave more strength to the Autonomous Liberal Party, which reflected the views of much of the aristocracy and middle class of the cities on the Dalmatian coast. The Ragusan Marino Bonda was elected,[125] even receiving support from certain ministerial circles owing to the weakening of the Iron Ring coalition and the return of various German liberals to the Austrian government.[126] The nobleman from Ragusa, who joined Coronini's Liberal-Conservative Club in the Abgeordnetenhaus,[127] just as Lapenna had done in 1888, was the last representative of the Dalmatian autonomists elected to the Austrian parliament. From the end of the 1890s the Serbs were eager for a rapprochement with those Croatian parties that seemed to be muting their anti-Serbian views and rediscovering the idea of a Croatian-Serbian solidarity in order to challenge Hungarian and German hegemony within the empire. With the weakening of the alliance with the Serbs, Bonda failed to win a seat at the elections of 1897. His defeat marked the final eclipse of the Dalmatian Liberal Autonomist Party, which ceased to play a significant role in Austrian politics and became just a small regional party.

## 2.3.  Italy and Austria in the Adriatic After 1866

While the outcome of the Italo-Austrian war of 1866 guaranteed the kingdom of Italy the conquest of the Veneto and much of Friuli, it did not fully satisfy the expectations of the Italian ruling class. The objective of the conflict had been not just the national liberation of the Veneto but also the establishment of secure borders from a strategic viewpoint, ensuring that Italy would be able to defend itself easily against any military attack from the north or east. The failure of the war on the military plane (with the defeats at Custoza and Lissa) and the scanty Prussian support for Italian territorial claims forced the government in

---

125  On the 1891 elections: *Il Dalmata*, 18 and 21 March 1891.
126  On this: Höbelt, 'Die Linken und die Wahlen von 1891,' pp. 270–301. See too: Bonda to Chlumecky, 14 March 1891, *Chlumecky Nachlass*, Brno, portfolio 15 (I am grateful to Professor Höbelt for supplying me with a copy of this letter).
127  On Bonda's parliamentary activity in Vienna: *Stenographische Protokolle*, vol. 11 (1894), p. 13 264; vol. 18 (1896), pp. 22 907, 23 022; Vrandečić, *Dalmatinski autonomistički pokret u XIX stoljeću*, p. 242.

Florence to sign an armistice on 11 August 1866 that respected the terms of the Italo-Prussian treaty of April 1866 and left Austria in control of the whole of the Italian Tyrol, the region of Gorizia, Trieste, and Istria.[128]

Italian diplomacy strove untiringly over the course of the negotiations for the conclusion of the Italo-Austrian peace treaty, conducted by Luigi Federico Menabrea in Vienna, to persuade the Habsburg government to concede further significant territorial adjustments in Tyrol and eastern Friuli, promising in exchange large indemnities, financial compensation, and the beginning of a new era in the relations between Italy and the Habsburg Empire.[129] In the face of the Habsburg refusal, Menabrea asked for control of the whole region of Lake Garda and the line of the Isonzo, but once again met with opposition from Vienna.[130] The Habsburg government saw control of the Tyrol and eastern Friuli as a central plank of its own security, as well as a means of keeping the Italian state in a position of strategic weakness, which it believed would greatly limit the country's independence and political power.

Faced with the alternative of concluding a treaty that did not meet expectations but guaranteed control of the Veneto, or resuming military hostilities in a situation of international isolation, since neither France nor Prussia backed the Italian demands, Italy chose to sign the peace treaty in Vienna on 3 October 1866.[131]

In Italian political circles the political and territorial set-up created by the treaty of Vienna was considered unsatisfactory from both the strategic and military viewpoint (as it did not give Italy secure borders) and the national viewpoint (as it left substantial groups of Italian and Italian-speaking people outside the territory of the kingdom). Giuseppe Mazzini, spiritual father of the National Liberal Left, in strong language denounced the territorial situation produced by the war of 1866: 'And

---

128 On this: Visconti Venosta to Nigra, 29 July 1866, DDI, I, 7, doc. 244; docs. 245, 254, 276, 286, 302, 343; *Carteggi di Bettino Ricasoli*, vol. 22, docs. 92, 243, 269, 352, 358; *Le lettere di Vittorio Emanuele II*, vol. 2, pp. 895 et seq.; De' Robertis, *La diplomazia italiana*; Silva, *Il Sessantasei*; Lefebvre d'Ovidio, 'Napoleone III'; Dassovich, *I molti problemi dell'Italia al confine orientale*, pp. 9–13.

129 Foreign Minister Visconti Venosta's instructions to the plenipotentiary for peace with Austria Menabrea, 10 August 1866, DDI, I, 7, doc. 337; Visconti Venosta to Menabrea, 26 August 1866, doc. 431; Menabrea to Visconti Venosta, 2 September 1866, doc. 455.

130 Visconti Venosta to Menabrea, 6 September 1866, DDI, I, 7, doc. 466; Visconti Venosta to Nigra, 6 September 1866, doc. 467.

131 DDI, I, 7, docs. 596 and 603; *Les origines diplomatiques*, 12, docs. 3637, 3646, 3687.

the peace – but this does not matter as much as the dishonour – is ruinous for the country. Dug in on this side of the Alps, master of Istria, key to our eastern frontier, master of poor betrayed Trentino, key to Lombard-Veneto, master of the passes that always lead it into our midst, the enemy can watch out for and seize the propitious moment, the moment that the difficult conditions of Italy must inevitably bring about, to swoop down on us. The peace as it is condemns us to the necessity of another war.'[132]

For Carlo Felice Nicolis di Robilant, a soldier and diplomat close to Cavour's Piedmontese Right, as well as a conservative and a fervent supporter of entente between the Habsburg Empire and the Savoy kingdom, the border produced by the war of 1866 was totally unsatisfactory. He wrote to the president of the council and foreign minister Menabrea in December 1867: 'The present frontier between the Veneto and Austria does not meet any of the conditions that one normally looks for in borderlines: it does not satisfy the ethnographic conditions of the two countries, nor their geographic conditions, nor the requirements of military defence, nor even, for much of its length, does it meet the most obvious and common needs of the economic life of the state.'[133]

On this judgment there was unanimity within Italian national liberalism. However, views varied on the possible strategies and forecasts of the time that would be needed for a revision of the borders between Italy and Austria. On the Cavourian Right, the dominant force until 1876, it was believed that the political priority for Italy was internal consolidation. This was an argument that Emilio Visconti Venosta, foreign minister several times between 1867 and 1876 and a man with close ties to Minghetti, often put forward in his dispatches. In his opinion, Italy was a country that had to reform and reorganize its administration, finances, and armaments; peace was a necessity, inasmuch as the nation required it, 'after its long period of unrest, in order to constitute its political, social, and economic forces';[134] and it was the Italian ruling class's duty 'not to jeopardize the immense results achieved by tackling extremely grave crises before our political edifice is completely

---

132  Mazzini, 'Alleanza repubblicana,' in *Scritti politici*, vol. 3, pp. 545 et seq., citation
    p. 550. On Mazzini's assessment of the outcome of the war of 1866: Sarti, *Mazzini*.
133  Robilant to Menabrea, 24 December 1867, DDI, I, 10, doc. 1. On the figure of Robilant, plenipotentiary minister and then ambassador to Vienna in the 1870s and
    1880s: Chabod, *Italian Foreign Policy*.
134  Visconti Venosta to Launay, 7 March 1871, DDI, II, 2, doc. 230.

consolidated.'[135] Revision of the borders with Austria was an objective
to be pursued in the long term; it was necessary to try to establish close
political co-operation with Vienna, going along with possible Habsburg
plans of expansion in Germany or the Balkans; and it could be hoped
that in exchange for Italian support the government in Vienna might be
persuaded to peacefully cede several Austrian territories desired by the
Savoy kingdom.[136] All this went hand in hand, for representatives of
the Liberal Right like Minghetti, Robilant, and Costantino Nigra, with a
vision of the positive role Austria could play in European politics as an
element of stability, an obstacle to Russian and Prussian expansionistic
designs in central and southern Europe, and a font of civilization for
the peoples of the Balkans.[137] Even the swing toward liberalism in the
Habsburg state and its internal reorganization, with the reaching of the
Austro-Hungarian Compromise and the consequent end of Hungarian
secessionism, seemed to facilitate Italian political designs. The attenu-
ation of the ideological differences between the two states and the co-
opting of many Magyar liberals (some of whom had shown sympathy
for Italian national liberalism in the past) into the Habsburg ruling class
could provide the basis for the emergence of a close collaboration between Italy and the Habsburg Empire.[138]

Amongst the liberal Left in opposition, on the other hand, bellicose echoes of the Mazzinian tradition prevailed for many years. The
Habsburg Empire was seen as the sworn enemy of the Italian national
movement, an adversary that had to be fought openly and destroyed,
with a view to establishing Alpine borders and helping the national
emancipation of the Slav peoples, whom Mazzini considered to be op-

---

135  Instructions of the foreign minister, Visconti Venosta, to the minister in London,
     Cadorna, for the London conference, 28 December 1870, DDI, II, 1, doc. 765.
136  On foreign policy ideas on the Italian Liberal Right: Vigezzi, 'L'Italia dopo l'Unità,'
     pp. 1–54; Chabod, *Italian Foreign Policy*; Berselli, *Il governo della Destra*, in particular
     pp. 359 et seq.; Petrignani, *Neutralità e alleanza.*; Decleva, *L'Italia e la politica internazi-
     onale dal 1870 al 1914*; Halperin, *Italy and the Vatican at War*
137  On this: Chabod, *Italian Foreign Policy*, pp. 537–8; Minghetti, *Discorsi parlamentari*,
     vol. 5, session of 24 April 1872, p. 259; vol. 7, session of 17 March 1880, pp. 483 et
     seq.
138  On the influence of liberalism on Italo-Austrian relations in the Beust period:
     Vigezzi, 'L'Italia dopo l'Unità,' pp. 246–7. On the friendly nature of the political re-
     lations between Italy and Austria-Hungary in the years after 1866: DDI, I, 11, docs.
     233, 237, 583; DDI, I, 12, docs. 186, 200; *Die Rheinpolitik*, 3, docs. 644, 648; *Les origines
     diplomatiques*, 20, doc. 7388; DDF, I, 1, doc. 192.

pressed by Habsburg rule.[139] It was this view that underpinned the fervent support of the liberal, monarchist, and republican Left for political irredentism among the Italians of Austria and the hope that Prussian expansionism would bring about a disintegration of the Habsburg state, of which Italy too would be able to take advantage.[140]

The Italian diplomatic corps and the political leaders of the liberal Right, Minghetti, Menabrea, Visconti Venosta, and Gioacchino Napoleone Pepoli, sought in every way to improve relations with the Habsburg Empire after 1866, with the aim of establishing forms of political co-operation that would strengthen Italy's international position.[141] The evolution of European politics appeared to favour Italian designs. The eruption of rivalry between France and Prussia over hegemony in Europe, and French attempts to block the process of German unification by supporting the particularism of the southern German states and forging close political links with Vienna, seemed to offer the Habsburg Empire (Austria-Hungary from 1867) a great opportunity to redress the balance with Prussia. From 1867 onward France and Austria-Hungary began to co-operate on the political level in a clear attempt to counter Prussia's expansionism.[142] This international context rendered Italy's position significant; its adherence to the emerging Franco-Austrian alliance would have strengthened the Habsburg Empire by freeing it from the potential threat of a repetition of the events of 1866, in other words a joint attack from Italy and Prussia.

Between 1868 and 1869 negotiations were held over the conclusion of an alliance between France, Austria-Hungary, and Italy.[143] It is not our

---

139 On Mazzini's vision of the Habsburg Empire and the Slav peoples refer to: Mazzini, 'La guerra. Al direttore del "Dovere,"' in *Scritti politici*, vol. 3, pp. 538–44; 'Alleanza repubblicana'; 'La guerra franco-germanica,' in *Scritti di politica e di economia*, vol. 2, pp. 290–9; 'Politica internazionale,' in *Scritti di politica e di economia*, vol. 2, pp. 300–12; Levi, *Mazzini*, pp. 223–7; Giusti, *Mazzini e gli Slavi*; Agnelli, 'Mazzini e le giovani nazioni nel centenario della morte di Giuseppe Mazzini,' pp. 9–34.

140 Decleva, *L'Italia e la politica internazionale*.

141 Minghetti's statements on the subject to parliament in April 1872: Session of 24 April 1872, in Minghetti, *Discorsi parlamentari*, vol. 5, pp. 259–61.

142 A large number of documents on Franco-Austrian relations between 1867 and 1870 have been published: for instance, *Les origines diplomatiques*, vols. 14–29; *Die Rheinpolitik*, 2, docs. 327, 328, 506, 537; *Die Rheinpolitik*, 3, docs. 611, 656, 669, 671.

143 A great deal of documentation on these negotiations has been reproduced in: DDI, series I, vols. 10, 11, and 12; *Les origines diplomatiques*, vols. 20, 21, 22, 23, 24, 25, and 26; *Die Rheinpolitik*, vols. 2 and 3; *Le lettere di Vittorio Emanuele II*, vol. 2.

intention to reconstruct in detail the Franco-Austro-Italian talks, which have already been studied in depth by Renato Mori[144] and Friedrich Engel-Janosi.[145] Yet it is interesting to analyze the political objectives that lay at the root of Florence's willingness to join the alliance with Paris and Vienna. In exchange for its support for Habsburg and French expansionistic designs in the Germanic world, Italy aimed to obtain approval for the annexation of what was left of the Papal States and hoped to modify the Italo-Habsburg border that had been ratified by the Treaty of Vienna in October 1866. Not coincidentally, in exchange for participation in a war against Prussia, the government in Florence asked for the Italian Tyrol, a small territory in the eastern Adriatic, and the border on the Isonzo.[146] All this indicated a strong desire on the part of Italy to adjust its borders with Austria in its favour.

As is well known, the tripartite alliance did not get beyond an exchange of non-committal letters between the three rulers, never assuming a concrete political efficacy. When the Franco-Prussian war broke out, Italy and Austria-Hungary remained neutral despite the entreaties of the French, developing a mutual diplomatic collaboration aimed at co-ordinating their respective positions.[147]

The emergence of political co-operation between Italy and Austria-Hungary, which was of considerable help to the Italian conquest of the Papal State, proved incapable of turning into a stable and close alliance over the course of the 1870s, notwithstanding the sincere efforts of the government, now in Rome, to embark on a new phase in its relations with Vienna.

A serious and formidable obstacle to the creation of an alliance was the refusal of the Habsburg ruling class to accept the Italian political

---

144 Mori, *Il tramonto del potere temporal*.
145 Engel-Janosi, 'Die römische Frage in den diplomatischen Verhandlungen 1869–1870.' See too: Lutz, *Österreich-Ungarn und die Gründung des Deutschen Reiches*; Halperin, *Diplomat under Stress*.
146 DDI, I, 11, docs. 59 and 121. The Italian demands for compensation with Austrian territories were looked on with favour by the French government but met with great resistance in Vienna: *Die Rheinpolitik*, III, docs. 648 and 669.
147 On Italian policy during the Franco-Prussian war of 1870: Di Nolfo, 'Monarchia e governo durante la crisi diplomatica dell'estate del 1870,' pp. 107–42; 'Austria e Roma nel 1870,' pp. 409–36. See too Halperin, *Diplomat under Stress*. For an in-depth reconstruction of Beust's policy in those months: Dioszegi, *Österreich-Ungarn und der französich-preussische Krieg*; Lutz, *Österreich-Ungarn und die Gründung des Deutschen Reiches*.

design that was founded on the link between Austrian expansion in the Balkans and the ceding of territory to Italy. A very clear enunciation of the Habsburg point of view came in May 1874 with the presentation of a note, signed by the foreign minister Andrássy, to the government in Rome and to Robilant, the Italian minister plenipotentiary in Vienna.[148] The Andrássy note (also called the Wimpffen note after the Habsburg minister plenipotentiary in Rome, Felix Wimpffen, who delivered the document to Visconti Venosta) was the product of the decision by Austro-Hungarian diplomacy to clarify Italo-Habsburg relations at a moment highly favourable to Vienna. Austria's rapprochement with Germany and Russia, reflected in the meetings between their rulers in the spring and summer of 1873 and the conclusion of the Alliance of the Three Emperors,[149] had enormously strengthened the international position of Austria-Hungary with regard to an isolated Italy; the latter was viewed with distrust by Bismarckian Germany and considered an ungrateful and hostile power by France owing to the policy of neutrality adopted during the war of 1870. Faced with an increasingly uncertain scenario in the Balkans[150] as a consequence of a weakening of the Ottoman grip, the government in Vienna, which for years had been preparing to expand in the Balkans at the expense of the Ottoman Empire, decided, on the pretext of some irredentist agitations that had taken place in the peninsula, to communicate to Italy a peremptory refusal to consider any possible compensation for the Savoy state in the case of a shift in the *status quo* in the Turkish territories to the advantage of the Habsburg Empire. In the note Andrássy observed there were groups in Italy that hoped to obtain 'a territorial readjustment' to the detriment of Austria-Hungary. These people, according to the Hungarian minister, did not realize that the Habsburg Empire was no longer a weak and isolated entity as it had been at the time of Napoleon III; Austria's domestic and international position had strengthened enormously. The Habsburg Empire had given up any claim on its former Italian posses-

---

148  On the events connected with the presentation of the Andrássy note: Sandonà, *L'irredentismo*, vol. 1, pp. 104 et seq.; Petrignani, *Neutralità e alleanza*, pp. 66 et seq.; Berselli, *Il governo della Destra*, pp. 379 et seq. The text of the Andrássy note is reproduced in DDI, II, 5, note 1 to doc. 413, pp. 432–4, and in Sandonà, *L'irredentismo*, vol. 1, pp. 106–11.

149  On this: Langer, *European Alliances*; Diószegi, *Die Aussenpolitik*; Der Bagdasarian, *The Austro-German Rapprochement*, pp. 114 et seq.

150  DDI, II, 5, docs. 331, 611, 625 and 639.

sions and held that a respect for the existing frontiers should be the unalterable basis for the maintenance of good relations between Italy and Austria-Hungary; even modification of the borders through 'a friendly arrangement' was out of the question. To justify this position Andrássy presented the convenient argument that any territorial change made on the basis of ethnic principles would have provoked centrifugal tendencies in many of the empire's nationalities and created tension and unrest throughout Europe: 'The day we accept such a readjustment on the basis of an ethnographic delimitation, similar claims might be made by others and it would be almost impossible to reject them. In fact we would not be able to cede to Italy populations that are linked to her by language without provoking in the nationalities located on the frontiers of the empire a centrifugal movement toward their sister nationalities bordering in our States. This movement would face us with the alternative of resigning ourselves to the loss of these provinces or, still following the system of nationalities, incorporating neighbouring lands into the Monarchy.'[151]

In reality, behind the Habsburg refusal to accept the hypothesis of territorial rewards for Italy there were also other motivations than those of the defence of the empire's integrity and the maintenance of peace in Europe. The aim of the Italian territorial claims was not just to unite Italian-speaking populations with the Savoy state but also, and above all, to attain secure borders. Increasing the security of the Italian state was, however, something unacceptable to Austria-Hungary, which was not disposed to lose the great military advantages that the border of 1866 had given it and to deal with Italy on completely equal terms. The Austrian disdain for and sense of superiority over the *Welschen* were combined with fear of the new Italian kingdom, which was regarded as a constant military threat to the empire and a state whose vitality and prospects of economic and political development were apparent to the more far-sighted Habsburg leaders. Surrender of the Trentino region would have strengthened Italy by weakening the strategic position of the Habsburg state on its southern flank and rendering it even more exposed to political pressure from the Italians in the south and the Russians in the northeast. Thus making territorial concessions to Italy signified drastically reducing the international influence and role of

---

151  Sandonà, *L'irredentismo*, I, pp. 108–9.

Austria-Hungary, transforming it into a secondary power with respect to Germany, Russia, and Italy.[152]

The reaction of Italian diplomacy to the Andrássy note was fairly superficial and non-committal. On receiving the note from Wimpffen, Foreign Minister Visconti Venosta only stressed the intention to maintain good relations with Vienna and pointed out that the government was not responsible for articles of an irredentist character in the press.[153] Robilant, minister plenipotentiary in Vienna since 1871, commented on Andrássy's move by explaining it as a signal of Habsburg determination to prepare for a division of the Ottoman Empire: 'It is probably a matter of forearming themselves against us so that, should that day come, it will already be clear that Austria does not intend to reward Italy with the Trentino, and still less with Trieste. I agree that in practical terms this will not prevent Italy, on the day that the aforesaid takes place, from demanding what will be reasonable, and essentially what we will find ourselves in a position to demand. Nonetheless, I would not be at all surprised if this consideration has not weighed in the balance.'[154]

Robilant's comment is significant because it illustrates the Italian attitude to the question of the borders between Italy and Austria-Hungary. Despite the clear Austrian warnings that the opposite was true, the government in Rome and a substantial part of the country's ruling class were convinced (in 1874 and over the following decades) that the strategy of support for Habsburg eastward expansion in exchange for territorial rewards could be a successful one. It was a misjudgment that stemmed from a superficial assessment of the values and attitudes of the dominant classes in Austria-Hungary, but one that would nonetheless condition Italian foreign policy for decades, since, as Rinaldo Petrignani has rightly pointed out, 'the majority of Italians continued to delude themselves that an adjustment of borders would be offered by Austria should certain conditions be met. This perpetuated a misunderstanding detrimental to Italo-Austrian relations.'[155]

The other problem that made Italo-Austrian relations increasingly

152  On this: Stickler, *Erzherzog Albrecht*, in particular pp. 422 et seq.; Holzer, *Erzherzog Albrecht*, pp. 57 et seq.
153  Visconti Venosta to Robilant, 18 June 1874, DDI, II, 5, doc. 413; Sandonà, *L'irredentismo*, vol. 1, pp. 112–13.
154  Robilant to Visconti Venosta, 28 June 1874, DDI, II, 5, doc. 421.
155  Petrignani, *Neutralità e alleanza*, p. 84.

difficult was the antagonism between Rome and Vienna in the Balkan peninsula, much of it still ruled by the Ottoman Empire.

The Italian diplomatic corps and ruling class had paid a great deal of attention to the Balkan world throughout the period of the Risorgimento, seeking constantly to bring about, for reasons of ideology or political expediency, a link between Italian emancipation and national struggles in the territories belonging to the Habsburg and Ottoman empires.[156] However, the uncertainty that characterized the relations between the Habsburg Empire and Italian liberalism, see-sawing between total hostility and hopes of political co-operation, had a decisive influence on the Balkan policy of unified Italy, giving it an ambivalence and an inconsistency of aims. Following the tradition of Cavour, Italian diplomacy after 1861 pursued an ambiguous Balkan policy: on the one hand, it supported ideologically and politically, whenever useful and expedient, moves toward independence on the part of the nationalities under Habsburg and Ottoman rule; on the other hand, the Italian government showed itself to be not only amenable to an alliance with Vienna and a diplomatic solution to the dispute between Italy and Austria, but also not opposed to maintenance of the *status quo* in the Balkans. The Italian culture of the time did not have a Manichaean and superficial vision of the Ottoman world, in part because for centuries (it suffices to think of the tradition of the Venetian Republic) the relations between them had been not exclusively of conflict but often entailed political and commercial co-operation. In the 1860s and 1870s the survival of the Ottoman Empire was regarded as extremely useful by Italian diplomacy, in that Turkish rule of the Balkans, Egypt, and North Africa was considered less dangerous than potential and uncontrollable expansion by the Russians, Habsburgs, British, or French.[157] In addition, the *status*

---

156  There is an extensive literature on the relationship between the Italian Risorgimento and the Balkan and Danubian world; some classic texts that have looked at the Balkan problem and the more general question of the East in the attitude of Italian national liberalism toward international policy are Tamborra, *Cavour e i Balcani*; Spellanzon and Di Nolfo, *Storia del Risorgimento*, vols. 4, 5, 6, 7; Di Nolfo, *Europa e Italia nel 1855–1856*; Valsecchi, *L'Europa e il Risorgimento*; Romeo, *Cavour e il suo tempo*, vol. 3; Giusti, *Mazzini e gli slavi* ; Pirjevec, *Tommaseo*. On Italy's Balkan policy in the early years after Unification: Cialdea, *L'Italia nel concerto europeo*; Giannini, 'I rapporti italo-ellenici (1860–1955),' pp. 389 et seq.

157  See for example: Menabrea to Maffei, 29 January 1869, DDI, I, 11, doc. 57; Menabrea to Pepoli, 29 January 1869, doc. 58; Menabrea to Maffei, 26 April 1869, doc. 278.

*quo* would allow Italy to develop its own commercial and cultural influence in those regions.[158]

Italy's Balkan policy in the 1860s and 1870s was very timid and cautious  because the kingdom, while obliged to deal with the political and cultural reawakening of many nationalities 'without a history' and with the eruption of rivalry between the great powers, was focused on the problem of the liberation of the national territory from Habsburg rule, on the question of Rome, and on the problems of internal consolidation. In this ambit no political concern over Dalmatia and its national problems had emerged, partly because of the absence of irredentist tendencies among the Italian Dalmatians, a large number of whom were followers of the Autonomist Party, which was an ardent supporter of the Habsburg Empire. The war against Austria in 1866 could have provided the opportunity for the enunciation of a plan of expansion into Dalmatia but, as has been seen, the highest territorial objective of the Italian ruling class of the time was to take the geographical borders of the country as far as the Brenner Pass and the Julian Alps, including the Italian Tyrol and Istria but excluding Fiume and Dalmatia. Even Mazzini, who represented the most radical position in Italian national liberalism, held that Italy's goal had to be the establishment of geographical borders in the Alps, and therefore control of the Italian Tyrol and Istria, while the eastern Adriatic coast beyond Monte Maggiore ought to be left to a future Slav Balkan state, allied with Italy, that would arise after the break-up of the Habsburg and Ottoman empires.[159]

Only after 1866 did the Italian political class, while nursing no specific designs on Dalmatia, start to grasp the strategic importance of this region. In general, the problem of the set-up in the Adriatic began to receive ever greater attention. The naval defeat at Lissa had painfully demonstrated Italy's military and strategic weakness in the Adriatic. Not surprisingly, in the years following Lissa, naval problems and the Adriatic became the subject of growing debate in Italy, which led to the rise of a solid tradition of maritime policy studies and the launch of an extensive program of naval rearmament.

At that time the Dalmatian coast was still considered a weak point of the Habsburg Empire, where an attack could be made in a future conflict. This view was shored up by the economic and social back-

---

158  Menabrea to Bertinatti, 26 February 1868, DDI, I, 10, doc. 128.
159  Mazzini, 'Politica internazionale,' pp. 306–8.

wardness of the region and, above all, the Ottoman presence in Bosnia and Herzegovina, which was considered a factor that greatly reduced the security of Austria's positions in the Adriatic. The very nature of Bosnian society, characterized by strong social, ethnic, and religious contrasts and continual revolts, was a source of instability for neighbouring Habsburg Dalmatia. The Italian consul in Serbia, Stefano Scovasso, sympathized with and supported the expansionistic designs of the Serbs on Bosnia and Herzegovina, showing no opposition to a possible future Serbian conquest of part of the Dalmatian coast. In the view of the Italian diplomat, a strong and vigorous Serbian state would constitute a continual political and military threat to Austria's Danubian and Adriatic dominions, while Austrian annexation of Bosnia and Herzegovina would have disrupted the Balkan situation and reinforced the Habsburg positions in the Adriatic. Scovasso was opposed to Italian designs on Dalmatia as these would have stirred hostility among the Serbs who, in his opinion, were the means by which Austria could be weakened and Italy could establish its influence in the Balkans.[160]

As confirmation of the new interest in the problems of the Adriatic, plans of territorial expansion into the eastern Adriatic coast began to be considered by the government in Florence from the end of the 1860s onward. The course of the 1866 war had proved the importance, in the event of military conflict, of conquering a strategic base on the Austrian or Ottoman coasts. During a war at sea, securing supremacy in the Adriatic could be a decisive factor for the fate of the Italian state; therefore, the control of ports in the eastern Adriatic (perhaps in Albania or Montenegro) would enormously strengthen Italian military power.

The Italian navy began to study the possibility of occupying a port or a coastal territory in the eastern Adriatic. Rather than on Dalmatia, however, attention in those years was focused on Albania, ruled by an Ottoman Empire for which it was easy to prophesy an imminent collapse or dismemberment. Acquisition of an Albanian port would have ensured the Italian fleet absolute control of the Strait of Otranto.[161]

---

160  Scovasso to the foreign minister, 15 April 1867, DDI, I, 8, doc. 381.
161  On Italian naval policy from unification to World War I, the studies of Mariano Gabriele remain fundamental: Gabriele, *La politica navale italiana dall'Unità alla vigilia di Lissa*; 'Sulla possibilità di una espansione strategica italiana,' pp. 399–427; 'Aspetti del problema adriatico,' pp. 460–512; *Le convenzioni navali della Triplice*; Gabriele and Friz, *La flotta come strumento di politica*; *La politica navale italiana dal 1885 al 1915*.

The negotiations over the conclusion of an alliance between France, Austria-Hungary, and Italy between 1868 and 1869 was another occasion that revealed the growing Italian sensibility to the Adriatic question. Among the territorial claims that were presented in Vienna and Paris as possible compensation for participation in the planned Franco-Austro-Italian alliance  was also the request for a territory on the Adriatic. In January 1869 the Menabrea government proposed to Austria-Hungary that, in the event of victory in a war fought by Italy and the Habsburg Empire as allies, with consequent major territorial gains for Vienna, Italy should obtain not just a new border on the Isonzo and the annexation of the Italian Tyrol but also 'a maritime base, in the interest of her commerce, on the coasts of the Eastern Adriatic.'[162]

As Renato Mori has rightly observed,[163] it was not the annexation of Dalmatian ports that the Italian government had in mind but, rather, the gaining of control of places in Albania like Durazzo (Durrës) and Valona (Vlorë). The Franco-Austro-Italian alliance never became an effective and active political grouping, but the negotiations for the triple alliance held in 1868–69 provided confirmation that the Italian government was beginning to take an interest in Adriatic matters and cultivate designs of expansion in that region.

This new attention to the strategic problem of the Adriatic did not translate, however, into a political interest in Dalmatia. In the years following 1866 Italy continued to avoid any involvement in the political struggles that were taking place in Dalmatian society, even though these gradually assumed the character of a conflict between a pro-Slav, anti-Italian Nationalist Party and an autonomist movement that defended the Italian language, a conflict in which citizens of the kingdom of Italy resident in that region sometimes became absorbed.

The spread of xenophobic and anti-Italian feelings throughout broad sectors of the Dalmatian rural population, stirred up by the National Party and the Catholic clergy, resulted in repeated incidents in which Italian subjects were the victims, and these could not fail to attract the attention of the Italian diplomatic corps and political class.

In July 1869 clashes broke out between sailors from the Italian ship *Monzambano* and Slav inhabitants of the Sebenico region, giving rise to

---

162 Enclosure I with Vimercati to Menabrea, 29 January 1869, DDI, I, 11, doc. 59. See too enclosure with doc. 121.

163 Mori, *Il tramonto del potere temporale*, pp. 357 et seq.

anti-Italian and xenophobic riots in a number of places in Dalmatia.[164] Brawls, incidents, and distinctly anti-Italian manifestations of xeno-phobia continued to occur in the following years, reaching their peak in June and July 1875 when the presence of several hundred work-men from the kingdom of Italy, employed on the construction of the railroad between Siverich and Spalato, led to clashes between Italian and Slav workers at Traù and an anti-Italian uprising by the local rural population, forcing the immigrants to make a hasty departure from Dalmatia.[165]

These outbursts of Italophobic sentiment stemmed from a variety of factors, which were duly pointed out by Italian diplomats. The political struggles between autonomist liberals (who were Habsburg loyalists, but culturally pro-Italian) and Croatian and Serbian nationalists had aroused in many supporters of the pro-Slav party an ideological hos-tility to the Italian language and culture and to the presence of Italian subjects in Dalmatia. On top of this came the economic reasons, which led many Dalmatians to see the foreign workers as dangerous com-petition, taking jobs away from the local population. Another element that could not be ignored was the hostile propaganda spread by the Catholic clergy against the Italian state as guilty of undermining papal independence.

The Italian government displayed great prudence and circumspec-tion in the face of these incidents involving its citizens in Dalmatia. The lack of political interest in the Dalmatian region and the desire, shared by all the governments of the Liberal Right, to establish close and friendly relations with the Habsburg Empire counselled playing down the significance of these clashes. Robilant tried to work out an amicable resolution of these incidents with the Habsburg government, asking Italian consuls to keep out of local politics.[166] The top officials at the Italian Foreign Ministry, Visconti Venosta and the secretary-

---

164  On the incidents at Sebenico in 1869: Pirjevec, *Niccolò Tommaseo*, pp. 244 et seq.; Grabovac, 'Preporod u Šibeniku i Afera "Monzambano,"' in *Dalmacija 1870*, pp. 255 et seq.; DDI, I, 11, docs. 513, 525.

165  The anti-Italian disturbances in central Dalmatia in 1875 are discussed in: Sandonà, *L'irredentismo*, vol. 1, pp. 115–16; DDI, II, 6, docs. 246, 251, 256, 274, 281, 284, 285, 288, and 292; Angiolini to the Italian Consular Agency in Spalato, 15 July 1875, ASMAE, Italian Consulate in Spalato, 1867–1915, portfolio 1; *Fanfulla*, 4, 5, 10, 11 and 12, 19 July 1875.

166  DDI, II, 6, docs. 246, 251, and 274.

general, Isacco Artom, supported Robilant's line of action.[167] In a private letter of 7 August 1875, Visconti Venosta declared himself perfectly in agreement with the conciliatory and moderate approach taken by the Italian minister in Vienna: 'We must avoid even the appearance of meddling in anything that might touch on internal questions of the empire and Dalmatia. The rivalry between races in the Dalmatian provinces, Austrian policy with regard to these rivalries, the inclinations of the present administration of Dalmatia and the relations of this administration with the Central Government, in all this we are and must remain uninvolved, even in the incident that concerns us.'[168]

This line of abstention from and political disregard of the Dalmatian question was also maintained publicly by Visconti Venosta. Replying in parliament on 23 November 1875 to questions on the incidents at Traù, the foreign minister minimized the political significance of such events, in essence denying that they could be attributed to national hostilities; he then stressed the Italian demand for the identification and punishment of those responsible, noting however that the government in Rome 'considered it necessary to remain completely outside any question related to the internal conditions of Dalmatia or to the parties that may exist there.'[169]

From the summer of 1875 onward Dalmatia began to attract the attention of European and Italian diplomacy, owing to the outbreak of bloody revolts against the Turks, first in Herzegovina and then in Bulgaria.

The emergence of a crisis in the Balkans caused great alarm in the Italian government led by Minghetti and Visconti Venosta.[170] For many

---

167  Artom to Robilant, 26 July 1875, DDI, II, 6, doc. 284.

168  Visconti Venosta to Robilant, 7 August 1875, DDI, II, 6, doc. 301.

169  AP, parliament, session of 23 November 1875, pp. 4640–2. The Habsburg diplomatic corps paid close attention to this statement by Visconti Venosta to parliament: Wimpffen to Andrássy, 24 November 1875, ber., HHSTA, PA, XI, portfolio 75; Wimpffen to Andrássy, 26 November 1875, ber., with the report of the speech made by the Italian foreign minister to the chamber enclosed.

170  On the policy of the last government of the Right on the Balkan question the analysis carried out by Gaetano Salvemini remains fundamental, drawing on documents belonging to the Robilant family that are only partly reproduced in the DDI: Salvemini, La politica estera italiana dal 1871 al 1915, pp. 165–97. Also useful to an understanding of the Italian handling of the crisis in the east between 1875 and 1878: Decleva, L'Italia e la politica internazionale, pp. 35–40; 'Destra e Sinistra di fronte alla crisi d'Oriente (1876–1878),' in L'incerto alleato, pp. 57–81; Sandonà, L'irredentismo, vol. 1; Petrignani, Neutralità e alleanza, pp. 107 et seq.; Biagini, 'La questione d'Oriente del 1875–78' in Memorie storiche militari, pp. 353–86.

exponents of the Right, Italy had to pursue a policy of peace and maintenance of the *status quo*, and thus of defence of Ottoman rule in the
Balkans. In this connection Visconti Venosta wrote to Robilant in March
1875: 'Our situation today, in this state of affairs, is extremely delicate.
Our interests in the East, as you know, are fairly conservative. And we
have a positive interest in making sure that, if the debacle is inevitable,
it does not happen now and is put off until a time when Italy has a
greater freedom of action and can protect itself better. The *status quo* is
for the moment the best that we can desire.[171]

Thus the policy followed by the Minghetti government between the
spring of 1875 and March 1876 was directed at trying to avoid aggravation of the crisis in the Balkans through a diplomatic and negotiated
solution, which would permit an improvement in the living conditions
of the Christian populations while preserving Ottoman rule over all the
territories affected by insurrections. Yet very little was achieved, as the
Italian desire for peace came into collision with Austria-Hungary's and
Russia's plans of expansion and the territorial ambitions of Serbia and
Montenegro.

The advent of the Liberal Left did not bring a radical change in Italian policy, in that Right and Left had their roots in the same liberal
national ideology. It did, however, result in a change in the make-up
of the government, with the exit of the group of politicians who had
worked directly with Cavour and the rise of new men to power, often
with different social and regional backgrounds to the central and northern liberal aristocracy and bourgeoisie that had been the real heart of
the Cavourian ruling class.

In the area of foreign policy generally, the men of the Left wanted
Italy to play an active and dynamic role in international politics, especially in the Mediterranean and the Balkans.[172] Many members of the
Liberal Left had once been followers of Mazzini; they still clung to their
former mentor's vision of Italy as a great European and Mediterranean
power and considered Austria the embodiment of values and interests
that were inevitably antithetical to those of their country.

---

171  Visconti Venosta to Robilant, 2 March 1875, DDI, II, 6, doc. 77.
172  On the view of the Italian Liberal Left held by Austrian diplomats: Ara, 'Le rip-
     ercussioni in Austria,' in *Fra Austria e Italia*, pp. 53 et seq. For an interpretation of
     the foreign policy of the Italian governments of the Left: Decleva, 'Il compimento
     dell'Unità e la politica estera,' pp. 169 et seq.; Andrè and Folchi, 'La politica estera
     dell'Italia liberale (1870–1915),' pp. 41 et seq.

It is not our aim to present a detailed picture of the general Italian approach to foreign policy in those years. Rather, what interests us here is to point out that after 1876 and the crisis in Ottoman rule in the Balkans there was a change in the perception of Dalmatia in Italian foreign policy. Up until that moment, as we have seen, Austrian control of Dalmatia had not assumed strategically a threatening character for the Italian ruling class, since the province lacked a hinterland, being surrounded by Ottoman dominions in Bosnia and Herzegovina that greatly weakened the Habsburg position in the eastern Adriatic; indeed, Dalmatia was regarded by many Italian politicians and military men as Austria's weak flank. Menabrea, former prime minister and then ambassador to London, wrote: 'The weak part of Austria, with respect to us, is Dalmatia, which only occupies a narrow strip of land on the eastern shore of the Adriatic, having at its back the Turkish provinces, i.e. Turkish Croatia and Herzegovina. This situation means that Austria would find it difficult to defend Dalmatia, if it were to be attacked from the sea, because its troops would have no support, and their retreat could easily be jeopardized.'[173]

The emergence of concrete Habsburg designs on Bosnia and Herzegovina altered this perspective and intimidated Italian diplomacy, as Austrian rule over those territories would have shifted the political balance in the Balkans and the Adriatic to Italy's disadvantage. The annexation of Dalmatia's Ottoman hinterland would have strengthened Austrian military power in the Adriatic.[174]

In August 1876, a few weeks after the Austro-Russian meeting at Reichstadt (Zákupy), Luigi Amedeo Melegari, foreign minister from March 1876 to December 1877, informed Robilant and Nigra, ambassador to St Petersburg, that Italy could not be indifferent to the possibility of Habsburg expansion into Bosnia and Herzegovina, precisely because its consequence would be the reinforcement of Austria-Hungary's position in the former Venetian possessions in Dalmatia.[175]

Melegari and Giuseppe Tornielli, secretary-general of the Foreign Ministry and the real shaper of Italian foreign policy, returned repeatedly to this theme over the following months, seeking to convince their

---

173  Menabrea to Melegari, 4 August 1877, DDI, II, 9, doc. 12.
174  For Menabrea's reflections on this: DDI, II, 9, docs. 12 and 21.
175  Melegari to Robilant, 8 August 1876, DDI, II, 7, doc. 307; Melegari to Nigra, 8 August 1876, doc. 308.

European counterparts of the damage that a Habsburg conquest of Bosnia and Herzegovina would cause to Italian interests by giving Austria hegemony in the Adriatic. As Melegari put it, 'for Italy, avoiding a shift in frontiers in the European provinces of Turkey to Austria's benefit is a question of security. What matters to us is that Austria's position in Dalmatia not be strengthened to the point where she can control the Adriatic from Venice to Bari from the provinces that border it.'[176] The same view of Dalmatia as a decisive element of a new Austrian domination of the Adriatic in the event of Habsburg expansion into Bosnia was expressed repeatedly by Tornielli over the course of 1877. According to the secretary-general of the Foreign Ministry, with Austrian annexation of the Bosnian province Dalmatia would have soon become a base of operations that could threaten the Italian peninsula.[177]

Naturally there was a manipulative side to this insistence on the threat offered to the balance of power in Europe and the Adriatic by Habsburg expansionism, and it was fully understood by European diplomats. The political consequences of possible Austrian conquests were exaggerated with the aim of justifying the Italian demands for exchanges of territory in Trentino and on the Isonzo.[178]

In any case, with the Balkan crisis of the years between 1875 and 1878 Italian foreign policy came to see Dalmatia as a crucial factor in the perception and determination of the balance of power in the Adriatic, a region whose control guaranteed the establishment of military hegemony in this sea that was so vital to Italian security.

The Italian concerns and the new importance of Dalmatia to the set-up in the Adriatic were precisely grasped by the French ambassador to Rome, Emmanuel Noailles, in a letter of August 1877: 'The crucial point of the Italian anxieties lies in the growing interest of Austria in Herzegovina and Bosnia. Perhaps they exaggerate their worries in this regard, but [it] is certain that the possession of Herzegovina and Bosnia

---

176 Melegari to Robilant, 10 February 1877, DDI, II, 8, doc. 135.
177 Tornielli to Menabrea, 18 February 1877, DDI, II, 8, doc. 154. Useful to an understanding of Tornielli's stance and of his role within the Foreign Ministry is the unpublished diary of the Piedmontese diplomat, covering the period from June 1876 to December 1877, conserved in ASF, Carte Tornielli, portfolio 2.
178 On Italian calculations of the possibility of exploiting Habsburg expansionism in the Balkans to its own advantage by obtaining the Italian territories of Austria in exchange: DDI, II, 8, docs. 51, 113, 123; DDI, II, 9, docs. 90, 102, 134; DDI, II, 10, docs. 169, 222.

would particularly increase the importance of the Dalmatian coast in the Adriatic.'[179]

The Italian political journalism that focused on maritime problems also began to point out the strategic and military importance of Dalmatia. Considering the strategic weakness of the Italian coasts, in the event of war the Savoy fleet would have to assume an offensive attitude and secure itself a base of operations in the eastern Adriatic at any cost, by conquering part of the Dalmatian shoreline.[180]

The changes in European and Mediterranean politics produced by the Balkan crisis,[181] which threatened the survival of the Ottoman Empire, prompted the government in Rome to make diplomatic moves aimed at attaining a number of territorial gains between 1876 and 1881. Faced with the risk of a radical disruption of the political set-up in the Balkans and the Mediterranean, which would have resulted in a weakening of Italy's strategic position, the Italian government sought to react to the actions of the other European powers. After carrying on with the policy of the maintenance of the *status quo* in the Balkans that had been pursued by Visconti Venosta, and after the outbreak of the Serbo-Turkish war and the news of the verbal agreement between Austria and Russia at Reichstadt in preparation for the division of the Ottoman territories in Europe, Melegari and Tornielli tried on several occasions between October and December 1876 to persuade the government in Vienna and the great powers that any change in the Balkan situation to the advantage of Austria-Hungary would disrupt the European balance of power and damage Italian interests. To borrow Melegari's words, 'we consider the enlargement, at the expense of Turkey, of the Power which is already preponderant in the Adriatic to be contrary to the interests of Italy.'[182] Implicit in this argument was an ill-concealed

---

179  Noailles to Decazes, 10 August 1877, DDF, I, 2, doc. 194.
180  See for example: Bonamico, *La difesa marittima dell'Italia*. On the evolution of Italian strategic naval thinking: Gabriele and Friz, *La flotta come strumento di politica*; Gabriele, *La politica navale italiana*.
181  Out of the very extensive international literature on the Balkan and Eastern crisis between 1875 and 1878 we recommend: Langer, *European Alliances*; Medlicott, *Bismarck, Gladstone and the Concert of Europe*; Diószegi, *Die Aussenpolitik*; Kos, *Die Politik Oesterreich-Ungarns*; Rupp, *A Wavering Friendship*; Sumner, *Russia and the Balkans*; Bridge, *From Sadowa to Sarajevo*, pp. 70 et seq.; Albertini, *The origins of the War of 1914*, vol. 1; Anchieri, *Costantinopoli e gli Stretti nella politica russa ed europea dal trattato di Qüciük Rainargi alla convenzione di Montreux*, pp. 53 et seq.
182  Melegari to Robilant, 14 October 1876, DDI, II, 7, doc. 483.

hope for territorial compensations on the part of Austria, for example the Trentino or the region of the Isonzo, a hope that was openly and loudly expressed by many Italian newspapers in the fall of 1876.[183]

Encountering Austrian hostility and German, English, and Russian indifference, the Italian attempts were a complete failure. The Austrian reaction to the Italian arguments was extremely tough. On 16 October 1876, Andrássy told Robilant that 'no territorial expansion of the [Austro-Hungarian] Monarchy, even if it were in the East, justified territorial claims on the part of Italy and that at the first sign of an annexationist policy Austria-Hungary would not limit itself to defence, but would go on the attack.'[184]

Menaced with war by Austria-Hungary, which had the support of Germany, Italy was also faced with the indifference of Russia, which was ready to concede Bosnia to the Habsburg Empire so long as the Turks were driven out of Europe.[185]

The more general causes of the failure of Italian diplomacy lay in its inability to grasp the dynamics of European politics rapidly and to react pragmatically. For a long time it nursed the illusion of a possible Italo-Russian and Italo-British collaboration in the maintenance of the *status quo* in the Balkans and in countering Austrian ambitions, without realizing that the Russians and British also harboured plans of expansion and were ready to go along with certain Habsburg designs if they were compatible with their own political aims.[186] At the same time there was no clear understanding of the shift in Austro-German relations and no awareness of the emergence of ever closer political co-operation between Vienna and Berlin. Francesco Crispi's visit to Germany in September 1877, with the naive hope of concluding an Italo-German anti-Habsburg alliance, showed the profound incomprehension of the

---

183 On the press campaign in favour of the surrender of unredeemed territories: Sandonà, *L'irredentismo*, vol. 1, pp. 130 et seq.; Chiala, *Pagine di storia contemporanea dal 1858 al 1892*, vol. 1, pp. 262 et seq.; Haines, 'Italian Irredentism during the Near Eastern Crisis 1875–1878,' pp. 23 et seq.

184 Andrássy to Gravenegg, 17 October 1876, quoted in Sandonà, *L'irredentismo*, vol. 1, p. 141.

185 Nigra to Melegari, 24 December 1876, DDI, II, 7, doc. 666; Petrignani, *Neutralità e alleanza*, pp. 126–7.

186 On Italo-British relations in 1878: Lee, 'The Proposed Mediterranean League of 1878,' pp. 33–45. Some reflections on the subject of relations between Italy and Russia in the nineteenth century in: Craveri, 'Costantino Nigra ambasciatore a Pietroburgo (1876–1882),' pp. 601 et seq.; Petracchi, *Da San Pietroburgo a Mosca*.

foreign policy of Bismarck and Andrássy in Italy.[187] Confronted by an Italy without allies and friends, Austria-Hungary could easily ignore the Italian requests for territorial and political concessions.[188]

The failure of attempts by Agostino Depretis, leader of the government in Rome, and Melegari to block Habsburg expansionism or obtain territorial concessions in Trentino led to the formation of the first Benedetto Cairoli government, in March 1878. The office of foreign minister was assumed by Luigi Corti, minister plenipotentiary in Constantinople.[189] A Lombard, Corti had played a direct part in the creation of the unified state, closely collaborating for many years with the Savoy minister in London, Emanuele d'Azeglio; in short, he was a fully paid-up member of the Cavourian Liberal Right. Like many diplomats of his generation Corti was skeptical about the solidity of the unified Italian state; in his view, Italy had to avoid any international initiative that would put its own survival at risk. He had given passionate expression to these ideas in 1875, declaring to Visconti Venosta his opposition to Italy's involvement in any new war: 'The outcome of armed conflict is always uncertain. Thanks to the marvellous patriotism of her peoples, the profound wisdom and energy of her statesmen, and the magnanimous heart of her Sovereign, Italy was created and the world was filled with admiration for the judgment and moderation she displayed after the triumph. And would it be worth risking her position now, at the very moment in which she is about to reap the harvest of so many heartbeats, so many efforts? ... Do we not now have the right and the duty to consolidate the great achievements made by our generation?'[190]

Corti's opinion had not changed in 1878. He considered that any military conflict would threaten the existence of the Italian state. 'Now

---

187  On Crispi's journey to Germany and other European capitals in 1877: DDI, II, 8, docs. 45, 64, 90, 102, 109, 111, 123, 129, 137, 139, 141, 145, 167, 178; DDF, I, 2, docs. 202, 205, 206, 211; Crispi, *Politica estera*, pp. 1–69; Petrignani, *Neutralità e alleanza*, pp. 130 et seq.; Duggan, *Francesco Crispi*; Chiala, *Pagine*, vol. 1, pp. 272 et seq.

188  Petrignani, *Neutralità e alleanza*, pp. 110 et seq.; Giglio, 'Il primo gabinetto Cairoli e il problema dei compensi all'Italia,' pp. 187 et seq.; 'Il secondo gabinetto Depretis e la crisi balcanica,' pp. 182 et seq.; Celozzi Baldelli, *L'Italia e la crisi balcanica 1876–1879*.

189  On the diplomatic action of the Cairoli-Corti government: DDI, II, 10; Albertini, *The Origins*, I, pp. 25 et seq.; Petrignani, *Neutralità e alleanza*, pp. 147 et seq.; Serra, 'La dottrina delle mani nette,' pp. 162–77; Sartori, 'Ruggero Bonghi e il congresso di Berlino in alcuni documenti inediti,' pp. 381–92.

190  Corti to Visconti Venosta, 10 December 1875, DDI, II, 6, doc. 499.

Italy has been made,' proclaimed the minister with conviction, 'I would rather cut off this hand than work toward creating a conflict that might take her to the brink of disaster.'[191]

Corti and Cairoli, aware of Italy's international isolation, abandoned the previous basically anti-Austrian strategy of Depretis and Melegari, which had its instigator in Tornielli,[192] and chose to make a wholesale retreat, ceasing to obstruct Austro-Hungarian policy and avoiding engagement in independent initiatives in the Balkans and the Mediterranean.

This passivity on Italy's part, however, came at the same time as a series of Russian, Habsburg, and British political initiatives that led to the disruption of the set-up in the Balkans over the course of 1878, with a reduction in the size of the Ottoman Empire and the establishment of the hegemony of Vienna and St Petersburg in the region. Austria-Hungary and Russia not only won direct control of important Balkan territories (Bosnia-Herzegovina, the sanjak of Novi Pazar, and southern Bessarabia) but also, thanks to the Treaty of Berlin and its long and difficult application, were able to assert their political and economic influence over the various more or less independent Balkan states.

The weakening of the Ottoman Empire that ensued from events in the Balkans and the Treaty of Berlin provided the opportunity for a change in the political set-up in North Africa over the following years. Ottoman powerlessness facilitated French and British actions in Tunisia and Egypt, that is, in territories nominally part of the Turkish empire. In Mediterranean politics too, Italy's isolation translated into impotence. Its attempts to counter French influence in Tunisia took the government in Rome to the brink of conflict with Paris, a possibility that the country preferred to avoid, given the lack of any international support for Italian positions. As for the Egyptian question, after having tried to preserve the autonomy of the khedivate of Egypt in the face of British and French interference,[193] the Depretis-Mancini government attempted to assert its own influence in Egypt, alongside the French and British, but then avoided a possible military intervention in support of Great Brit-

191  Corti to Cairoli, 30 June 1878, DDI, II, 10, doc. 231.
192  On the strong political disagreement between Corti and Tornielli: Tornielli to Launay, 3 June 1878; Tornielli to Ressman, 14 June 1878, ASF, Carte Tornielli, portfolio 1.
193  DDI, II, 7, doc. 11.

ain owing to the deterioration in Italy's domestic situation, the difficult relations with France, and the Austro-German refusal to back the Italian initiative.

The result of the Balkan crisis in the second half of the 1870s was, notwithstanding the attempts of the Cairoli and Depretis governments, a reduction in the influence and political role of Italy at an international level and the weakening of the country's strategic position in the Adriatic and the Mediterranean.

## 2.4. The Diplomacy of Irredentism: The Triple Alliance and the Problem of the Unredeemed Lands (1878–87)

The Habsburg Empire achieved great political success with the conquest of Bosnia, and it was followed over the course of the 1880s with the establishment of a substantial Austrian supremacy in the Balkans through the inclusion of Serbia, Romania, Greece, and later Bulgaria in a political and economic sphere of influence dominated by Vienna. The Austro-Serbian treaty of alliance in 1881, the Austro-Romanian alliance of 1883, and the ascent to the Bulgarian throne of Ferdinand of Saxe-Coburg were all stages in the creation of Habsburg hegemony in the Balkans.

The Balkan successes also contributed to modifying the internal set-up of the Austrian part of the Habsburg Empire. The year 1879 marked the beginning of rule by the Taaffe government, whose Catholic-conservative and Slavophile policy was regarded by Francis Joseph and top military men and diplomats as useful to the strengthening of imperial power and the role of the Habsburg state as a civilizing force in eastern Europe.

The pro-Slovene and pro-Croatian policy of the Taaffe government served to aggravate national conflicts in the eastern Adriatic, with a progressive reduction in the role of the Italian language and culture and a change in the political balance in Dalmatia.

Italian diplomacy quickly took note of this anti-Italian shift in Austrian domestic policy, which had its most serious consequences in Dalmatia with the decline of the Autonomist Party and the rise of Croatian nationalism. Between 1878 and 1882 the Croatian, Slovenian, and Czech press launched a series of harsh attacks on the Dalmatian autonomists, falsely accusing them of being *italianissimi* (that is, favouring union with Italy at any cost) and wanting to detach Dalmatia from the Habsburg Empire. The Italian consular agents in Trieste and Spalato called Rome's attention to this smear campaign several times, underlining its frequently specious and calculating character.[194]

An important role in the struggle against the Italian element in Dalmatia was played, according to the Italian consular agent in Ragusa, Luigi Serragli, by the Croatian clergy, who opposed the use of the Italian language: 'The Italian language has a powerful enemy here in the Croatized priests and friars who see it as a means for the spread of anticlerical ideas, and tell their congregations that the Italians are enemies of Catholicism, attempting in this way to destroy the age-old sympathies which had taken root as a result of the benefits of the culture and defence received from Italy. It is the same thing as the Croatian and Slovenian clergy do in Istria and Gorizia.'[195]

The possible consequences of this process of Slavicization in Dalmatia were quickly grasped by the government in Rome. As Serragli put it in 1884, with the complete Croatization of the Dalmatian schools it was clear that 'in ten or fifteen years Italian [would become] a foreign language like French or English.'[196]

The Adriatic question, the change in the Balkan set-up, the worsening of the living conditions of the Italian and Italian-speaking populations in the territories of the eastern Adriatic, and the perception and interpretation of all this by the ruling class of liberal Italy were elements that obviously influenced the foreign policy choices advocated and adopted by the various governments and Italian political elites over the course of the 1880s and 1890s.

The decision to establish ties with the Austro-German bloc, concluding in a defensive alliance with Austria-Hungary and Germany in May 1882, which came to be known as the Triple Alliance, was the political response that the liberal ruling class devised to react to the deep crisis in Italy's foreign policy at the end of the 1870s; it was also, as has been pointed out by Francesco Tommasini[197] and Pietro Pastorelli,[198] an at-

---

194  See, for example, the accusations made in the Czech press against Antonio Bajamonti, mayor of Spalato, of being *italianissimo* because he had staged a political demonstration on the day of the anniversary of the birth of King Umberto I of Italy: Bruno to Cairoli, 5 April 1880; Zink to Bruno, 30 March 1880, ASMAE, SP 1867–88, portfolio 1258.

195  Serragli to Mancini, 24 July 1884, ASMAE, SP 1867–88, portfolio 1262.

196  Ibid.

197  Tommasini, *L'Italia alla vigilia della Guerra*, vol. 1, pp. 37–9.

198  Pastorelli, 'Il principio di nazionalità nella politica estera italiana,' in *Dalla prima alla seconda guerra mondiale*, pp. 203–5

tempt to find a long-term political solution by diplomatic means to the problem of the Italo-Austrian border and the question of the Italians in Austria.

It is not our aim here to describe the political and diplomatic negotiations that led to the conclusion of the Triple Alliance, which have already been reconstructed in a detailed and thorough manner by several authors.[199] The decision to conclude a political and military alliance with Austria-Hungary and Germany met various general requirements of Italian foreign and domestic policy, such as the need to emerge from dangerous international isolation, the necessity to guarantee the internal and external security of the state, and the desire to exercise more influence on the course of European and Mediterranean politics. The problem of relations with the Habsburg Empire and the need to give them a new content and character remained, however, the fundamental factors that prompted Italian diplomacy to conceive the plan of a political rapprochement with Berlin and Vienna, long before the deterioration in Italo-French relations that resulted from the Tunisian question.

The crisis in bilateral relations between Rome and Vienna from 1876 to 1880 had been triggered, as has been pointed out, by the appearance of a series of territorial claims against Austria-Hungary in much of the Italian liberal press and by Italy's attempts to counter Austrian policy in the Balkans (through a collaboration with the Russians to obstruct Vienna's action over the course of the application of the Treaty of Berlin).[200] The deterioration in Italo-Habsburg relations took place in a situation of political isolation for Italy, which at that moment had very poor relations with Bismarckian Germany (which was impatient of Rome's independence)[201] and was not very friendly with France and Britain owing to Italian opposition to these countries' designs on Tunisia and

---

199  Among them: Chiala, *Pagine di storia contemporanea,* vol. 3, *La Triplice e la Duplice Alleanza (1881–1897),* (a still useful work as it draws on the Robilant papers); Salvemini, *La politica estera italiana;* Petrignani, *Neutralità e alleanza;* Pribram, *The Secret Treaties of Austria-Hungary;* Salata, *Per la storia diplomatica della Questione Romana,* pp. 83 et seq.; Langer, *European Alliances;* Salvatorelli, *La Triplice Alleanza;* Albertini, *The Origins of the War of 1914,* vol. 1; Fellner, 'Der Dreibund,' in *Vom Dreibund zum Völkerbund,* pp. 19–81; Afflerbach, *Der Dreibund.*

200  On Italian fears over presumed Austrian plans of expansion into Salonika and Albania: Tornielli to Maffei, 29 April 1879, ASF, Carte Tornielli, portfolio 1; DDF, I, 2, docs. 387, 460.

201  See Bismarck's outbursts of anger with Italy reported by the French ambassador, Saint-Vallier: DDF, I, 2, docs. 440 and 476.

Egypt. The Italo-Austrian tension, which looked as if it were going to turn into open military conflict several times between the summer of 1878 and the spring of 1880,[202] faced the Savoy government with a difficult choice: the pursuit of a foreign policy based on open antagonism with Austria-Hungary and aimed at support of the Balkan nationalities and creation of a Franco-Russian-Italian alliance against Austria; or the attempt to bring about an improvement in Italo-Habsburg relations through the conclusion of a treaty of political alliance and/or territorial guarantee that would entail the renunciation of claims to Habsburg lands in the short term but would allow Italy to establish close ties with the Austro-German bloc and influence its international course of action.

The influence of Tornielli, secretary-general of the Foreign Ministry from 1876 to 1878 and from the end of 1878 to the middle of 1879, stemmed from his close links with Agostino Depretis.[203] He advocated an openly anti-Habsburg policy, which gained little support among Italian diplomats, the majority of whom favoured a clear rapprochement with Austria-Hungary. According to Tornielli, the establishment of Habsburg supremacy in the Balkans was a violation of the principles of nationality and a threat to vital Italian interests, which Italy had to avert by seeking to maintain the *status quo* or by encouraging the formation of indigenous nation states opposed to Habsburg rule; it was necessary to counter Austria through the creation of close and special relationships with Romania and Serbia, countries that, in his view, were not prepared to accept Habsburg hegemony.[204]

---

202  Still useful in this connection: Chiala, *Pagine di storia*, vol. 2, pp. 1–72. See too: DDF, I, 3, docs. 11, 32, 33, 36, 38, 46, 54; Petrignani, *Neutralità e alleanza*.

203  Part of the correspondence between the Piedmontese diplomat and Depretis is conserved in the Tornielli Archives and shows the closeness of their relationship; Tornielli wrote Depretis's speeches on foreign policy and also collaborated with him on questions of domestic policy: Tornielli to Depretis, 9 and 19 October 1878, 4 November 1878, ASF, Carte Tornielli, portfolio 1. An exchange of letters between Tornielli and Depretis is also conserved in ACS, Carte Depretis, series I, portfolio 23.

204  On Tornielli's ideas: Tornielli to Depretis, 4 and 27 November 1879, 21 May 1880, ACS, Carte Depretis, series I, portfolio 23; Tornielli to Robilant, 19 April 1879, DDI, II, 11, doc. 523; Tornielli to Mancini, 26 June 1881, DDI, II, 14, doc. 63; Decleva, *L'Italia e la politica internazionale*, p. 78. Tornielli's hostility to the alliance with Austria and Germany made him the *bête noire* of the Habsburg and German diplomatic corps, who for decades tried, through all kinds of pressure, to impede his career and his appointment to important diplomatic posts: Wrede to Haymerle, 9 January

In opposition to the ideas of Tornielli, who remained faithful to the traditional 'Austrophobia' of the Risorgimento, the Italian ambassadors to Vienna (Robilant) and Berlin (Edoardo de Launay) proclaimed the need for closer ties with Austria, whose political weight was constantly growing as a result of its Balkan successes and the marked improvement in relations with Berlin; the latter relations had strengthened first, in 1878, with the abolition of the article in the Treaty of Prague referring to the possibility of a plebiscite in Schleswig-Holstein, and then, in 1879, with the stipulation of the Austro-German Dual Alliance, a pact of mutual defence against Russia and Italy. According to Launay and Robilant, Italy had to stop pursuing an anti-Austrian Balkan policy and begin instead to work with Vienna, with a view to exploiting Habsburg expansionism to its own advantage. Co-operation with the Habsburg Empire would make it easier to keep an eye on the empire's actions and, potentially, gain territorial advantages. In the view of Launay (writing in April 1879), in exchange for effective support Italy would be able to obtain better frontiers in the Alps and on the Isonzo in the near future.[205] Similar ideas were held by Robilant, for whom Italy was at that moment too weak to openly oppose Austria and Germany; a more opportune policy was to bide time, while strengthening the country economically and militarily and improving relations with Berlin and Vienna, in anticipation of future upheavals in an unstable European set-up that might redound to Italy's advantage. In a letter to the secretary-general of the Foreign Ministry, Carlo Alberto Maffei, in December 1879, Robilant declared: 'It is my firm conviction that Austria has ventured onto a particularly slippery slope, and the moment may come in which she will have need of us; if we are able to bide our time, our situation will change; ... [the Congress of Berlin] has created nothing stable; so the future remains open to all possible solutions.'[206]

The argument of the expediency of relying on the 'Eastward push' of the Habsburg Empire to solve the question of Italy's northern and eastern borders was a classic theme of the international thinking of the Italian Right (to which diplomats like Launay, Robilant, Corti, and

1880; Wimpffen to Haymerle, 30 April and 24 June 1880, ber., HHSTA, PA, XI, portfolio 93; Ludolf to Kálnoky, telegram, 6 November 1882, HHSTA, PA, XI, portfolio 95; Ludolf to Kálnoky, telegram, 2 November 1885; Ludolf to Kálnoky, 5 November 1885, HHSTA, PA, XI, portfolio 99; Sandonà, L'irredentismo, vol. 1, pp. 246–7.

205 Launay to Depretis, 8 April 1879, DDI, II, 11, doc. 492; see too doc. 550.
206 Robilant to Maffei, 26 December 1879, DDI, II, 12, doc. 510.

Alberto Blanc belonged), but it was foreign to the Garibaldian and Mazzinian tradition of the liberal monarchic Left that was now in power.
For left-wing liberalism, accepting the ideas of an alliance with Vienna
and of Austria's expansion to the east signified abandoning a traditionally negative perception of the Habsburg Empire.

A decisive part in the revision of the inspiring principles of the Liberal Left's foreign policy and the change in Italo-Austrian relations was
played by Pasquale Stanislao Mancini, a member of parliament and a
jurist from Campania who was foreign minister in the fourth Depretis
cabinet from 1881 to 1885.[207] Mancini was a statesman of great intelligence and pragmatism who had a primary role in the redefinition
of Italy's foreign policy, lending political weight to the idea of a rapprochement with Austria and Germany (advocated by diplomats close
to the Right), and personally heading the negotiations that led to the
conclusion of the treaty of alliance with Vienna and Berlin on 20 May
1882. His reputation has long suffered from rash and superficial judgments,[208] which have obscured the important role he played in Italian
foreign policy in the nineteenth century.

The Campanian politician carried out a personal and exhaustive re-
examination of Italian foreign policy that led him to outline a new program in which he sought to bring together ideas and themes drawn
from progressive as well as moderate liberalism.[209] He saw the creation
of an alliance with the Austro-German powers as a crucial factor if Italy
were to exercise effective international action; the alliance between Italy
and the Germanic states was now possible since there had been a 'complete cessation of the age-old hatred and rancour between the Italian
and German peoples, after the latter, with Italy restored to the complete
independence to which she is entitled, had forever crossed back over
the Alps.'[210] This relationship of alliance, which was established at the
same time as a marked political rapprochement with Great Britain, the

---

207  On the figure of Mancini and his career as a jurist and politician: Zecchino, *Pasquale
     Stanislao Mancini*; Droetto, *Pasquale Stanislao Mancini*; Zaghi, *P. S. Mancini*; Scovazzi,
     *Assab, Massaua, Uccialli, Adua*, pp. 74 et seq. See too the considerations of Affler-
     bach: Afflerbach, *Der Dreibund*, pp. 99 et seq.
208  Let us take, for example, the pages that Francesco Salata devoted to Mancini, accus-
     ing him of subservience to Austria: Salata, *Guglielmo Oberdan secondo gli atti segreti
     del processo*, pp. 203 et seq.
209  Mancini, *Discorsi parlamentari di Pasquale Stanislao Mancini*.
210  Speech at the session of 7 December 1881, ibid., vol. 8, p. 553.

major naval power in the Mediterranean, would permit the Savoy kingdom to increase its international weight and conduct a dynamic and effective foreign policy.

That Mancini, on his appointment as foreign minister, desired to break down the old barriers between Liberal Right and Left was made clear by his choice of Alberto Blanc as secretary-general of the Foreign Ministry. Blanc was a diplomat with close links to the circles of the Liberal Right;[211] a collaborator of Cavour, he had become Alfonso La Marmora's private secretary in 1864 and secretary-general at the Foreign Ministry from 1869 to 1870. Mancini's appointment and the choice of Blanc as secretary-general were indications that the need for a radical shift in Italy's foreign policy in the direction of an alliance with Vienna and Berlin was also strongly felt by King Umberto I of Savoy.[212] At the beginning of the 1880s the king, despite not having as strong a personality as his father, Victor Emmanuel II, exercised an important influence over the course of Italy's international action. It was often thanks to Umberto's support that, during the negotiations leading to the Triple Alliance, Mancini was able to prevail over the reluctance and indecisiveness of the prime minister, Depretis, who was fearful of the possible consequences for Italo-French relations of an alliance between Italy and Germany.

Mancini took into consideration the ideas of Launay and Robilant and forged ahead with the efforts to achieve a political rapprochement with Germany and Austria-Hungary that had already been initiated by the Cairoli government and the secretary-general of the Foreign Ministry, Maffei, between 1880 and the beginning of 1881.[213]

As early as the summer of 1881, with the aim of demonstrating his determination to put co-operation with Vienna on a sound and sincere footing, Mancini laid down the main points of a new Italian policy in the Balkans; it was a policy that was no longer antagonistic to Austria

---

211 On Blanc's life: Serra, *La questione tunisina da Crispi a Rudinì*, pp. 66 et seq.; 'Diplomatici del passato. Alberto Blanc,' pp. 840 et seq.

212 On this: Petrignani, *Neutralità e alleanza*, p. 277; Afflerbach, *Der Dreibund*, pp. 102 et seq. On the figure of Umberto I and his influence on Italian foreign policy: Farini, *Diario di fine secolo*; Paulucci, *Alla corte di re Umberto*.

213 On Cairoli and Maffei's attempts to bring about a political rapprochement with Austria-Hungary and Germany: DDI, II, 13, docs. 497 and 699; GP, 3, docs. 533, 534, 535; Pribram, *The Secret Treaties*; Petrignani, *Neutralità e alleanza*, pp. 271–4; Langer, *European Alliances*; Salvatorelli, *La Triplice Alleanza*, pp. 45 et seq.

but, on the contrary, tailored to go along with the designs and interests of the Habsburg Empire. In the minister's view, it was not possible to claim that the expansion of Austria-Hungary in the Balkans was the antithesis of any liberal aspiration and of that principle of nationality which, 'in the muddle of different races and languages that characterizes the Balkan peninsula, cannot find expression with the same simplicity and clarity of form that fortunately distinguishes it in Italy, for example.'[214] Indeed, it was in the Italian interest to promote Italo-Habsburg co-operation in the Balkan area with a view to exercising a beneficial and favourable influence on those populations. At bottom, the eastward impetus that Germany was imparting to Habsburg policy was not contrary to the essential interests of Italy, and it was better, 'rather than isolating ourselves in unproductive and spiteful aspirations of opposition, whose results, detrimental to our influence besides, could unfortunately by seen at the Congress of Berlin, to allow Austria-Hungary at this point to carry out the mission that within certain limits the Berlin accords have assigned it in part of the Balkan peninsula.'[215]

Discarding the old Mazzinian view of Austria as the absolute negation of Italian political values, Mancini regarded the Habsburg Empire as a positive factor, a civilizing force, in the Balkans. Over the following years, Italian diplomacy actually lent its support to the initiatives of the Habsburg government in the Balkan region, accepting Austrian hegemony in Serbia and backing Vienna's attempts to dispute Russian supremacy in Bulgaria.[216] This meant attempting to create a level of friendly co-operation between Italy and Austria-Hungary in the Balkans in order to bring the government in Rome out of its state of isolation and to facilitate, in the event of a future international crisis, the attainment of Italian territorial objectives – no longer in opposition to Vienna but as an ally of the Habsburg Empire.[217]

The visit of King Umberto and Mancini to Vienna in October 1881

214  Mancini to Tornielli, 28 July 1881, DDI, II, 14, doc. 119.
215  Mancini to Launay, 23 July 1881, DDI, II, 14, doc. 109.
216  On Italy's Balkan policy in the 1880s and 1890s: Tamborra, 'La crisi balcanica del 1885–1886 e l'Italia,' pp. 371–96; Salvatorelli, *La Triplice Alleanza*, pp. 101 et seq.; Petrignani, *Neutralità e alleanza*.
217  The Austrian diplomatic records present a positive view of Mancini, regarded as an Italian minister who wished to implement a policy of friendship with Austria-Hungary: Ludolf to Kálnoky, 7 May 1885, ber., HHSTA, PA, XI, portfolio 99. On this see too Salata, *Oberdan*, p. 267.

was a crucial step in the rapprochement between Italy, Austria-Hungary, and Germany and set the official seal on the Italian desire to improve relations with the Habsburg Empire. Mancini was instrumental in the decision to make this visit, overcoming the doubts of Depretis and the opposition of Robilant, who was reluctant to accelerate the reconciliation with Vienna and more inclined to sit on the fence. The foreign minister, with the collaboration of Blanc (who should, however, be considered the executor and not the instigator of the minister's policy), was able to prevail over resistance in the government and impose his own ideas, thanks in part to the support of the king.[218]

The negotiations for the conclusion of the Triple Alliance[219] (which were carried out over the course of the spring of 1882 and conducted on behalf of Italy mainly by Mancini, Blanc, and Robilant) and the text of the tripartite treaty signed on 20 May of that year clearly reflect the desire to impose co-operation in the Balkan area on Austria-Hungary and the attempt to create legal instruments (the treaty of alliance) that would oblige the Habsburg Empire to take Italian objectives and interests into account; thus was foreshadowed a scenario that would compel Austria to request Italy's military and political assistance at the cost of major territorial concessions.

The various articles of the treaty of the Triple Alliance signed in 1882, to a great extent conceived and inspired by Italy, created the conditions for Italo-Austrian negotiations in the event of war between Austria-Hungary and Russia or of conflict in the Balkans, on the basis of the hypothesis of Italian aid to Vienna in exchange for territory. The formulation of the *casus foederis* strongly favoured Italy; it provided for automatic Italian military intervention only in the event of an attack on Germany by France (article II) or on the contracting states by two or more great powers (article III), excluding the circumstances of a conflict involving only the small Balkan states, and rejecting the automatic extension of this military support, without a quid pro quo, in the event of a conflict between Russia and Austria-Hungary. The promise of simple

---

218 See for example: Mancini to Depretis, 4 and 11 October 1881, telegram, ACS, Carte Depretis, series I, portfolio 22, On the lead up to King Umberto's visit to Vienna and its effect: Decleva, 'Politica estera e politica interna alla vigilia della Triplice Alleanza,' in *L'incerto alleato*, pp. 103–7; Afflerbach, *Der Dreibund*, pp. 58 et seq.; DDF, I, 4, docs. 136, 168, 169, 171, 172, 176, 180, 182; DDI, II, 14, docs. 236, 241, 244, 254, 282, 308.
219 GP, 3, docs. 536 et seq.; DDI, II, 14.

neutrality in the event of a conflict stemming from the initiative of one member of the alliance (for instance, a war provoked by Vienna against Turkey, Serbia, or Russia) allowed for the possibility of negotiating Italian intervention, in exchange for concessions, if it was desired by the allied powers.

Another important article constraining the allies' freedom of action, and implicitly allowing for the possibility of Italy asking for compensation, was the fifth. This committed the contracting parties, in all cases of mutual participation in a war, to conclude armistices and peace treaties solely on the basis of a 'common accord' between the signatories of the Triple Alliance.

Mancini explained to Robilant that the articles of the pact gave Italy great freedom of action, while blocking any Austro-German attempt to exclude the government in Rome from possible peace talks:

> We have, in this way, the opportunity to protect ourselves against the possibility that accords might be reached, or territorial modifications arranged without our consent, and consequently without the necessary reservations or compensations to our benefit. Here, however, it is not out of place to recall, in the event of a successful conclusion, that, in everything concerning the *status quo* in the East, in accordance with what is already sanctioned and guaranteed by the Treaty of Berlin under the present terms of the agreements in force, and independently, therefore, of any further negotiation, Italy being one of the signatory powers of the Treaty, no territorial or political alterations to the present set-up in the Balkan peninsula could be made without the participation and the concurrence of Italy in any future possible accord.[220]

Thus it is possible to say that the rapprochement with Austria-Hungary and Germany signified not so much the abandonment of irredentism on the government's part as a desire to change the way of attaining certain territorial goals that could not be renounced. At the beginning of the 1880s the Italian government realized the impracticability of any plan to annex those regions of Austria inhabited by Italians, and taking account of the developments in the international context that strengthened the Habsburg state, chose to postpone any expansionistic design in the Alps and the Adriatic to a more distant future, without relinquish-

---

220  Mancini to Robilant, 20 April 1882, DDI, II, 14, doc. 686.

ing it definitively. At the same time, however, a system of alliances was concocted that at an unspecified date would facilitate the realization of Italy's traditional annexationist aims in Tyrol and the Adriatic.

In the light of the diplomatic action of the Depretis-Mancini government between 1881 and 1885, it is evident that on the occasion of the negotiations for the first renewal of the Triple Alliance, Robilant, Mancini's successor at the Foreign Ministry and foreign minister from 1885 to 1887, limited himself in essence to continuing the policy outlined by his predecessor. In an unstable international context, where the antagonism between France and Germany and the rivalry between Austria-Hungary and Russia might provoke conflicts that would permit implementation of the various provisions of the Triple Alliance, Robilant took advantage of the diplomatic work carried out by Mancini and succeeded in negotiating new and more stringent commitments with Vienna and Berlin.

Robilant was determined to continue with Mancini's scheme of offering Italy's co-operation with Austria in the Balkans to facilitate further expansion of the Habsburg possessions and asking for territorial rewards in exchange. He made this clear in a letter written to Nigra, ambassador in Vienna, in March 1886: 'Obviously the moment has not yet come to speak of this, but if the circumstances were such that Austria were to seriously consider altering the situation in the Balkan peninsula to its advantage, not a minute should be lost in putting our cards on the table ... The line of the Isonzo and Tyrol *feraient une affaire*, and with this, and on condition of taking Tripolitania from Turkey, I would have no difficulty in letting Austria go as far as Salonika.'[221]

The change in the international context, with the resurgence of French nationalism at the instigation of General Georges Boulanger and the outbreak of Austro-Russian rivalry in Bulgaria, persuaded Chancellor Bismarck to assign growing importance to the alliance with Italy. From 1886 until his replacement as chancellor in 1890, Bismarck pragmatically abandoned his previous attitude of coolness and hostility toward the Savoy monarchy and set about strengthening Italo-German relations, giving them an intensity and cordiality they had never had before.

Perceiving the shift in the international situation in a direction favourable to Italy, Robilant opened the negotiations for the renewal of the Triple Alliance by proposing to the allies in November 1886 the con-

---

221 Robilant to Nigra, 30 March 1886, DDI, II, 19, doc. 396.

clusion of an additional treaty to the accord of 20 May 1882.[222] This draft of a supplementary treaty envisaged a broadening of the *casus foederis* in Italy's favour: should France extend its occupation, sovereignty, or influence to Morocco or Tripoli, and Italy be forced to go to war in defence of its Mediterranean interests, then Germany and Austria-Hungary would play a military part in the conflict. Of particular importance was article II of the draft, which clearly expressed one of the political objectives that Italy had been pursuing since the beginning of the 1880s, that is, control of Austria-Hungary's Balkan policy and its link with Italy's aims of expansion. The first part of the article provided for the commitment of the contracting parties to avoid any territorial modification in the Ottoman-ruled coasts and islands of the Adriatic and the Aegean Sea that would damage the interests of one of the allied states. After this declaration of principles, however, the article declared that, should it prove impossible to maintain the *status quo* in these regions and if one of these territories were to be occupied to the advantage of Rome or Vienna, 'this occupation will only take place after a preliminary accord between the two aforesaid Powers, based on the principle of a mutual compensation satisfying the interests and well-founded needs of the two parties.'

Wary of a possible Italo-French rapprochement, Bismarck was extremely well disposed toward the Italian requests for modifications to the text of the Triple Alliance.[223] The Italian proposals met with strong resistance from Austria-Hungary. In addition to wishing to avoid military commitments in North Africa, Vienna had no desire to lose its own complete independence in the Balkan area and feared that Italy might ask for Habsburg territories inhabited by Italians as compensation for further Austrian expansion. However, German pressure and the usefulness to Austria-Hungary itself of preserving the alliance with Italy in order to avert the risk of co-operation between Italy and Russia in the event of war between Vienna and St Petersburg induced the Austrians to put aside their doubts and accept a great many of the Italian requests.

On 20 February 1887 a new series of accords was signed by the Triple Alliance. It comprised three treaties: one common to the three Powers,

---

222 Draft of supplementary treaty, 23 November 1886, enclosure with Robilant to Launay, 23 November 1886, DDI, II, 20, doc. 302. The text of the draft is also published in GP, 4, enclosure 1 with doc. 836.
223 On Bismarck's attitude: Rich, *Friedrich von Holstein*, vol. 1, pp. 193 et seq.; Petrignani, *Neutralità e alleanza*, pp. 395 et seq.; Afflerbach, *Der Dreibund*, pp. 201 et seq.

ratifying the renewal of the alliance; one between Italy and Germany; and one between Austria-Hungary and Italy.[224] The agreement between Italy and Germany, as well as committing both states to act against any change in the territorial *status quo* in the east that would damage one of them, guaranteed German military and political assistance to Italy in the event of a war between Italy and France over North Africa. In relation to the Italian Dalmatians, the Italo-Austrian treaty was highly significant. At its heart was article I (which would be denominated article VII on the occasion of the treaty's renewal in 1891). To a great extent it echoed Robilant's proposal of November 1886, in essence committing the two powers to concert their policies should it prove impossible to maintain the *status quo* in the Balkans and the Ottoman territories in the Adriatic and the Aegean, and to reach an agreement in advance on what to do in the case of a temporary or permanent occupation of some territory in the area. Such an agreement was to be founded on the principle of reciprocal compensation for any 'territorial or other' advantage that one of the contracting parties should obtain with respect to the existing *status quo*.

With the Italo-Austrian treaty of 1887 Italy appeared to have obtained an important recognition of its right to future conquests in the event of a change in the Balkan *status quo* that would be to the advantage of the Habsburg Empire. In those years no precise and detailed plans were outlined with regard to the possible territorial adjustments that Italy thought it might be able to require of Austria-Hungary. It seems clear that the men linked to the tradition of the Right, such as Robilant and Launay, still clung to the approach that the moderate liberal governments had taken to the problem of the country's frontiers after 1866, regarding as crucial the conquest of strategic borders that would lead to the annexation of the whole of the Italian Tyrol (Trentino and Alto Adige) and expansion as far as the line of the Isonzo. For them it was necessary to guarantee secure frontiers that would be acceptable to the Habsburg Empire, a political entity they considered solid and wanted to survive. Many men of the Left, from Giuseppe Zanardelli to Aurelio Saffi, traditionally closer to the irredentism of Venezia Giulia, were eager to annex Trieste and Istria as well.

The renewal of the Triple Alliance negotiations by Robilant in 1887,

---

224 *Testo del trattato separato tra l'Italia e l'Austria-Ungheria*, 20 February 1887, in DDI, II, 20, doc. 540; also published in GP, 3, doc. 571, and Pribram, *The Secret Treaties*.

however, left various problems unresolved. As Rinaldo Petrignani has pointed out, Robilant held that 'in the event of Austrian "annexation" of Bosnia-Herzegovina Italy would be entitled to compensation.'[225] This hypothesis was not accepted by the Austrians, and the Germans and Italians chose to fudge the issue so as not to wreck the negotiations.

Another major problem, in essence the shortcoming of the whole so-phisticated political program that the Italian ruling class had shaped over the course of the 1880s and that had given rise to the Triple Alliance, was that in the Italo-Austrian treaty of February 1887 Austria-Hungary limited itself to agreeing on vague and general principles of political co-operation without accepting in a precise and binding way the possibility of ceding to Italy those Habsburg territories inhabited by Italians. The diplomatic records indicate that the Italian ruling class had been well aware of this difficulty since the 1880s,[226] but over the course of the negotiations for the renewal of the Triple Alliance in 1886–7 Robi-lant chose to take the future acceptance of Italian requests for compen-sation for granted.

Yet the possibility of compensation to Italy in Albania was far from a foregone conclusion. During the military talks held between Italy, Ger-many, and Austria-Hungary in Berlin in 1888, which led to the conclu-sion of a military agreement for the transport of Italian troops to the Franco-German front in the event of war, the Habsburg foreign min-ister, Gustav von Kálnoky, opposed any possible Italian occupation of Albania. The Italian negotiator, Lieutenant Colonel Giovanni Goiran, was struck by the Austrian hostility to any suggestion of a landing on the Albanian coast: 'Austria does not trust us and wants freedom of action for herself on the eastern shore of the Adriatic. She understands very well that if we succeeded in installing ourselves in this region, we would be able at any point in the peace talks, or following a breakdown of the alliance, to counter her policy.'[227]

It could be foreseen even in those years that there would be difficul-ties when it came to concrete discussion of the problem of compensation to Italy in the event of a new Habsburg expansion in the Balkans. The Italian diplomatic corps believed it would be possible to surmount such difficulties through the mediation of the German government, which

225 Petrignani, *Neutralità e alleanza*, p. 411.
226 Robilant to Mancini, 17 June 1885, DDI, II, 17–18, doc. 973.
227 Goiran to Cosenz, 22 April 1888, DDI, II, 22, doc. 24. On the military negotiations within the Triple Alliance in 1888: Mazzetti, *L'esercito italiano nella Triplice Alleanza*, pp. 53 et seq.

was interested in the preservation of the Triple Alliance, and in the name of a political pragmatism that would permit the overcoming of certain conflicts of interest. It was hoped that Vienna would imitate Cavour and his decision to compensate France with the ceding of Nice and Savoy in exchange for the 'all clear' to Savoy's annexation of the duchies and Tuscany. However, Francis Joseph was not Cavour. When the occasion to discuss and apply the long-awaited article on compensation finally came in 1914, the government in Rome was met with an Austro-Hungarian refusal to accept the Italian interpretation of this clause and discovered that the leaders of the Habsburg Empire lacked the flexibility and pragmatism that was typical of Italian political culture.

The article on compensation turned out in the end to be an ineffective political mechanism, incapable of solving the Italian national question. However, the diplomatic solution to the problem of compensation was only one of the objectives of the new foreign policy initiated by Mancini and Depretis in the 1880s. The 'grand design' conceived by Mancini, that is, the redefinition of the overall strategy of Italian foreign policy with an end to isolation – the establishment of an alliance with Germany (the dominant power in Europe), the development of a real friendship with Great Britain, and the transformation of Italo-Austrian relations to place them on the footing of a competitive co-operation – aimed to provide Italy with the political means of undertaking an expansionistic policy in Europe, the Mediterranean, and Africa that would allow it to vie with the other great powers. In this general and long-term perspective Mancini's new strategy achieved a number of successes: the kingdom of Italy created its own colonial empire and won a certain influence in the Balkans and the Ottoman Empire. Thanks to Mancini, Depretis, and diplomats like Robilant, Blanc, Nigra, and Launay, the diplomatic foundations were laid for an increase in the kingdom of Italy's role in international politics over the following decades.[228]

### 2.5. The Dominance of Pan-Croatian Nationalism in Dalmatia and the Rise of an Italian National Ideology in the Autonomist Liberal Party

The 1880s marked a turning point in the history of Dalmatia. Croatian nationalism established a definitive hegemony, and, in general, na-

---

228 An interesting assessment of the usefulness of the alliance with Vienna and Berlin by Nigra in: DDI, II, 20, doc. 31, Nigra to Robilant, August 9–11, 1886.

tionalistic ideologies started to become the dominant form of political thinking throughout the region.

The rise of nationalism was not a phenomenon confined to Dalmatia; it affected the whole of Austria-Hungary, where liberalization, the broadening of suffrage, and the general economic development led to the emergence of a political life that involved growing numbers of people who found in national values the crucial element of their collective identity.[229] Granting a privileged position to the German and Hungarian elements, the Ausgleich was unable to bring political stability to the two parts of the empire, which in the closing decades of the century began to be troubled by fiercer and more intransigent national strife. Nationalism became the dominant ideology among the peoples of the empire, progressively influencing and shaping even those forces that were most alien or hostile to it. It suffices to think of the national divisions within the socialists of the Habsburg lands, which led, for example, to the emergence of a Czech socialist party that was distinct from the German one, and the strong national tensions in the socialist movements in Trieste and on the Adriatic coast.[230]

The structure of the imperial state, which was embodied in the figure of the emperor, the army, and the bureaucracy, remained the only element unifying the various peoples under Habsburg rule. The posthumous myth of the Austrian state as an even-handed protector of all its peoples is contradicted by a disenchanted historical analysis, which shows that it was the Habsburg state itself that fuelled internal and external national struggles and manipulated them to its own advantage, sometimes heavily influencing their outcome, as was the case in Dalmatia.

In the last two decades of the nineteenth century a political situation took shape in Dalmatia that was to last until the outbreak of World War I. The dominant element on the political and cultural plane was

229  On political and economic life in the Habsburg Empire in the last two decades of the nineteenth century: May, *The Hapsburg Monarchy*; Kann, *History of the Habsburg Empire*; Macartney, *The Habsburg Empire*; Dudan, *La monarchia degli Asburgo*, vol. 2, pp. 222 et seq.

230  On the national conflicts within socialist movements in the Habsburg Empire: Agnelli, *Questione nazionale e socialismo*; Droz, 'La socialdemocrazia nell'Austria-Ungheria (1867–1914),' pp. 84–135; Cattaruzza, *Socialismo adriatico*; Apih, *Il socialismo italiano in Austria*; Piemontese, *Il movimento operaio a Trieste*; Maserati, *Il movimento operaio a Trieste*; Schiffrer, 'La crisi del socialismo triestino nella prima guerra mondiale,' pp. 159 et seq.

Croatian nationalism, which until the 1880s had found a united expression in Hrvatska Narodna Stranka. Subsequently the more uncompromising exponents of pan-Croatian nationalism (Prodan, Biankini, and many of the younger generation including Frano Supilo and Ante Trumbić) began to criticize the legalistic and opportunistic approach of the National Party, which was eager to work closely with the government in Vienna and extremely loyal to the Habsburgs. They set up the Dalmatian section of the Party of Rights in the name of a more forceful and uncompromising struggle on behalf of pan-Croatian union.[231]

Different spirits and sensibilities continued to exist within pan-Croatian nationalism due to the heterogeneity and complexity of Dalmatian society. It was a movement whose leaders at the end of the nineteenth century still included people of Italian language and culture. This was the case with Bulat, the leader of Croatian nationalism in Spalato, and Ivan Machiedo, a nationalist member of parliament and a former member of the Dalmatian Autonomist Party who belonged to a family from Lesina (Hvar).[232] No one was shocked by this in a Dalmatia where national consciousness was still regarded as a cultural and political choice rather than an ethnic and biological fact. To Serbian accusations that many renegade Italians were to be found among the Croatian nationalists, the Croatian newspaper in Spalato, *Narod*, calmly responded in 1884: 'If there are Autonomists who speak Slav, and yet are enemies of the Slav, and do not want him in public life, is this not blameworthy on their part? If on the other hand there are Nationalists who as a result of a distorted education speak no Slav, and yet, out of a feeling of fairness and against their own interests, desire justice for the Slav language, are they not worthy of the highest praise?'[233]

---

231 On the subject of the birth of the Party of Rights in Dalmatia: Diklić, 'Pravaštvo don Ive Prodana,' pp. 361–411; 'Pojava Pravaštva i nastanak stranke prava u Dalmaciji,' pp. 5–107; *Don Ivo Prodan prvi čovjek dalmatinskog pravaštva*, pp. 243–54; *Pravaštvo u Dalmaciji do kraja prvoga svjetskog rata*. An analysis of the divisions within Croatian nationalism in Dalmatia can be found in OUS, 3, doc. 6, *Statthalterei Präsidium an Minister des Innern Graf Bylandt-Rheidt*, January 3, 1905.

232 The debates in the provincial diet are an interesting testimony to the national conflicts in the Dalmatian culture of the time: the autonomist and Serbian representatives often accused various Croatian nationalists of not being fluent in Croatian and of speaking Italian among themselves, prompting embarrassed responses from the majority in the diet: Session of 3 August 1889, ADP-BI, pp. 401 et seq.

233 *Narod*, 2 July 1884.

These Italian Dalmatians turned pan-Croatian nationalists were representatives of a section of the upper and middle classes in the coastal cities that was ethnically mixed and Italian-speaking or bilingual. With the shift in the political balance of the province, this section began increasingly, whether out of opportunism, conviction, or interest, to abandon Italo-Slav autonomism and embrace the new national Croatian ideology.

Within Croatian nationalism the Catholic and clerical element acquired ever greater strength. The vast majority of Catholic churchmen in Dalmatia had sided with the nationalists (with a few exceptions among the urban clergy, in Zara and Spalato for example) owing to the total identification of Catholicism with Croatian nationality. Some of the main leaders of Croatian nationalism were Catholic priests, including Miho Pavlinović,[234] Ivo Prodan,[235] and Jurai Biankini.[236] So closely did the Church identify with Croatian nationalism that it did not consider the formation of a Catholic party to defend its own principles and interests to be necessary, since the Croatian nationalist movement took on this responsibility with enthusiasm. Those prelates whose sympathies lay with the autonomists (such as the Orthodox bishop of Zara, Knezevich; the Catholic bishop of Zara, Maupas; and abbé Giovanni Devich, a close friend of Bajamonti and one of the autonomist leaders in Spalato) grew increasingly rare and were a distinct minority with respect to the great mass of the Dalmatian clergy, who were ardent supporters and moving spirits of the Croatian national movement.

The alliance between Croatian nationalism and Dalmatian Catholicism can be explained by certain elements of the identity of the Catholic Church in the region. In the first place, the great majority of the clergy were from the solidly Slav Dalmatian countryside, where the Italian language and culture was viewed as something foreign and imposed. To this must be added the peculiar nature of Catholicism in Dalmatia and the Croatian region; it was a frontier Catholicism, accustomed to holding its own in territories inhabited by various nations with different faiths, and for centuries subject to foreign domination and wars. One cannot overestimate the importance of the experience of Ottoman rule in the Balkans and in much of Dalmatia itself between the fifteenth

---

234  Diklić, 'Mihovil Pavlinović.'
235  Diklić, 'Don Ivo Prodan u dalmatinskom Saboru,' pp. 389–457.
236  On the figure of Biankini: Morović, 'Iz Korespondencije Jurje Biankinija urednike *Narodnog Lista*,' pp. 457 et seq.

and eighteenth centuries in shaping the identity of the Slav Catholics of the south; it had led to the development of a bellicose and passionate vision of religion, which was the fruit of much strife and of the many acts of violence inflicted and suffered.

The Catholic Church in Dalmatia, as in Venezia Giulia, was not therefore capable of playing the role of a bridge between the existing national and cultural communities. It did not exercise moderation; on the contrary, it was an active player in the assertion of nationalism, pushing the latter to assume more uncompromising positions with respect to the Italian and Serbian minorities.[237]

The other protagonist of Dalmatian political life in these decades remained the Austrian government. Habsburg rule enjoyed broad support in Dalmatia since the fact of belonging to the great empire was seen as a guarantee of the province's future economic and commercial development. Even if only to a marginal extent, Dalmatia too participated in the general process of economic modernization that characterized Austria between the last decades of the nineteenth century and 1914, benefiting in particular from the major investments in infrastructure made by Vienna in Bosnia and Herzegovina that facilitated Dalmatian communications and trade.

The Dalmatian Autonomist Liberal Party, while reduced to a secondary role in the politics of Dalmatia and Austria, managed to survive the disastrous defeats of the 1880s and 1890s. However, something began to change in its political and ideological identity. An antinationalistic political movement, in that it was founded on the promotion of a bilingual and multi-ethnic cultural tradition and therefore on a regionalistic particularism that rejected national conflict, liberal autonomism succumbed to the ever-growing strength of the Slav nationalist ideologies of the south and began slowly to delineate the elements of an Italian national discourse.

---

237 On the history of Catholicism in Croatia and the Adriatic coast in the nineteenth and twentieth centuries we shall mention just Vitezić, *Die römisch-katolische Kirche;* Malfer, 'Der Kampf um die slawische Liturgie in der österreichisch-ungarischen Monarchie – ein nationales oder ein religiöses anliegen?' pp. 165–93; Valdevit, *Chiesa e lotte nazionali;* Blasina, 'Santa Sede, Vescovi e Questioni nazionali,' pp. 471–502; 'Chiesa e problema nazionale,' pp. 129 et seq. See too the extensive references in: Novak, *Prošlost Dalmacije,* vol. 2; Engel-Janosi, *Österreich und der Vatikan,* vol. 1, pp. 268 et seq.; Džaja, *Bosnien-Herzegowina in der österreichisch-ungarischen Epoche,* pp. 46 et seq.

A crucial factor in this development was the policy of Croatization carried out by the National Party. The Croatian nationalist ideology became increasingly anti-Italian, abandoning any idea of accepting the Italo-Slav bilingualism that had been theorized by some nationalist writers in the 1860s. For many nationalists the persistence of a culture of Italian origin in Dalmatia constituted a threat to Croatian identity and might fuel forms of regionalism and autonomism that were considered antithetical to and incompatible with the existence of a unitary Croatian culture. Refusing to recognize the existence of either a specific cultural, linguistic, and ethnic Dalmatian character within the Yugoslav world or an Italian nationality in Dalmatia, they saw the Italians of Dalmatia as Italianized or Italophile Slavs (so-called *talijanaši*) who had abandoned and betrayed their original identity, or as immigrants from the peninsula who had to assume a new Slav identity or go back to Italy.[238]

From these ideological premises (which denied the reality of the bilingual and multi-ethnic Dalmatian cities) in the name of the Croatian national ideal, the transition to a policy of denationalization and assimilation of the Italian and Italophile Dalmatians was rapid. The question of education very soon became central, with the abolition of Italian as a medium of instruction in Dalmatian schools and the refusal of the nationalist provincial and municipal authorities to finance with public money the surviving schools that used Italian. This was a 'soft' and 'moderate' policy of denationalization, certainly not comparable with those policies implemented by Fascist Italy and Communist Yugoslavia but one which reflected an ideological rejection of linguistic and cultural pluralism. It was a repeatedly emphasized rejection, which the leader of the Croatian National Party, Klaić, reasserted to the Dalmatian provincial diet in 1886: 'In the name of the party to which I belong, I declare openly that we will always fight the plan of setting up Italian schools in Dalmatia, and what is more, we will strive by every means available to us to abolish the ones that do exist. We deny the existence of an Italian nationality in Dalmatia and consequently that it has any rights.'[239]

---

238 Innumerable were the declarations made by Croatian national representatives to this effect: cf. speeches by Biankini (pp. 443 et seq.) and Bulat (pp. 448 et seq.), session of 20 December 1886; speech by Buzolić, session of 31 January 1894, pp. 185 et seq.; speech by Bulat, session of 13 February 1894, pp. 398 et seq., ADP-BI.

239 Speech by Klaić, 18 December 1886, proceedings of the Dalmatian provincial diet, reproduced in *La Difesa*, 27 December 1886.

The assimilatory and xenophobic tendencies of the Croatian parties and the disappearance of a climate of peace and coexistence between the Dalmatian nationalities brought about a change in autonomist ideology. The extolling of a specific Dalmatian national and cultural character, capable of uniting Italians and Slavs in a single homeland, the spiritual heart of autonomist liberalism, was thrown into crisis by the growth of pan-Croatian nationalism in Dalmatia and the eruption of nationalistic struggles in Austria-Hungary. The policy of denationalization and xenophobia practised by the nationalists now made the defence of the use of the Italian language, which for many years had been just one of the various points of the autonomist program, a crucial theme of the autonomist struggle.

Commencing in the 1870, but growing in force over the two following decades, the call to defend the 'national rights' of Italians and Italophiles in Dalmatia started to appear in autonomist journalism. This new line coexisted with traditional Dalmatian autonomism and regionalism, but with the passing of the years the question of the defence of the Italian nationality in Dalmatia increased in importance. This is reflected in speeches made by autonomist representatives in the Dalmatian provincial diet, for whom the problem of the defence of Italian linguistic and cultural rights came to play a more central role in their political activity.[240] This was an important ideological and political shift in Dalmatian autonomism, which was slowly evolving from a multi-ethnic and multinational party into the defender of those Dalmatians who were beginning to call themselves 'Italians of Dalmatia' on the political plane as well. An Italian nationalism gradually started to emerge as a defence against the xenophobia of pàn-Croatian nationalism.

The political action and thinking of Antonio Bajamonti between the mid-1870s and 1891, the year of his death,[241] played a crucial part in the ideological evolution of Dalmatian autonomism into Italian nation-

---

240  We refer the reader, solely by way of example, to speech by Messa, session of 14
     December 1885, pp. 230 et seq.; speech by Bajamonti, session of 18 December 1886,
     pp. 399 et seq.; speeches by Vidovich (Vidovic) and Smirich (Zmiric), session of 31
     October 1890, pp. 444 et seq., ADP-BI. It should be stressed that from 1870, the year
     of the nationalist victory, the stenographers of the diet, while obliged by its regula-
     tions to reproduce the speeches of autonomist members in Italian, Croatized the
     spelling of their surnames in the published proceedings, with the aim of demon-
     strating that there were no Italians in the Dalmatian Assembly.
241  On this: Monzali, 'Dalmati o Italiani?' pp. 455 et seq.

alism. Bajamonti had been a follower of Tommaseo's arguments for the existence of a Dalmatian nation that was at once Italian and Slav. However, from the mid-1870s, in the face of the policy of Croatization implemented by the National Party, Bajamonti began to abandon these positions. In 1875 he founded his own newspaper, *L'Avvenire*, in Spalato, in which he set out the political program of the city's autonomist liberals. The mayor of Spalato decided to tackle the national question as well, declaring that it was time the autonomist movement changed its attitude toward it: 'Axioms are not open to dispute; and the existence of an Italian nationality in Dalmatia is in fact one of these indisputable axioms. The old Autonomist Party committed an error by not proclaiming this nationality at once, but wrapping it up instead in nebulous paraphrase and negative euphemism out of a desire for reconciliation. Today things have changed and the Italians of Dalmatia, following the example of their Slav brothers, loudly assert their own nationality.'[242]

According to Bajamonti, once the existence of two nationalities in Dalmatia, 'the Italian and the Slav,' had been established, the Autonomist Party had to become an alliance between Italian liberals and Slav liberals on a platform that aimed at parity between the languages, the strengthening of individual and municipal liberties, and material and intellectual progress.[243]

Bajamonti hardened his position over the course of the 1880s, declaring the existence of a Italian nationality in Dalmatia several times in public speeches. At the root of the decision to proclaim themselves no longer Dalmatians of Italian culture but 'Italians' of Dalmatia undoubtedly lay the rise of a new national consciousness provoked by Croatians attempts to stifle Italian culture in Dalmatia. Bajamonti passionately laid claim, in a speech in 1886, to the autochthonous character of the Italian language in Dalmatia: 'The Italian language, Gentlemen, was not imported, it is our own. It is the language of our fathers, in which for the first time we pronounced the revered name of mother, in which we said to our woman: *io t'amo* [I love you]. It is the language of an advanced civilization, which has brought culture, progress and prosperity to Dalmatia.'[244]

---

242  'Notizie provinciali e locali,' *L'Avvenire*, 18 March 1875. The article was published anonymously, but its content can without doubt be attributed to the inspirer and financier of the autonomist newspaper, that is, Bajamonti.
243  'Programma,' *L'Avvenire*, 4 March 1875. Article on the program of the autonomist liberals of Spalato, published anonymously but attributable to Bajamonti.
244  Bajamonti, *La società politica dalmata*, p. 10.

There was also a political calculation. Now reduced to a minority party controlling only the city of Zara, autonomists like Bajamonti saw intervention by the central Habsburg authority as a possible counterweight to the xenophobia of the Croatian nationalists. They proclaimed themselves Italians in order to enjoy the protection for minorities that the constitution of 1867, and article 19 in particular, guaranteed to all the nationalities of the empire. In 1886 this is what Bajamonti clearly told his followers in Spalato who were doubtful over whether to declare themselves Dalmatians of Italian culture or Italians:

> Woe betide us if we do not proclaim ourselves Italians! Woe betide us if we do not hold high the standard of our nationality! This alone, Gentlemen – absolutely this alone – gives us the right to live. The dispositions of article 19 of the constitution of the empire are explicit: not to cultures – note well – not to cultures, but to nationalities of the empire does the constitution guarantee equal rights. Describe yourselves as of Italian culture and repudiate our nationality, and you will have to resign yourselves to the fate to which they want to consign us: assimilation. But so long as there are, not the 70 to 80 000 Italians – add Dalmatian-Austrians if you like – that we are now but 40 – 30 – 20 – 10 thousand – even just one thousand, we will still have the right to invoke the provisions of article 19 of the Constitution.[245]

From this type of political discourse it can be seen that the emerging Dalmatian Italian nationalism theorized by Bajamonti had not yet assumed an anti-Habsburg tone; on the contrary, in the 1870s and 1880s the Italians of Dalmatia saw the Austrian empire as a potential defence and protection against the Croatian pressures for assimilation. In reality this was an illusion; Habsburg imperial power nurtured nationalisms and used them to its own advantage, ready to bend them to its strategic requirements and those of the survival of the state.

For the new Italian current within the Autonomist Party led by Bajamonti, however, the call for national solidarity among all the Italians of Austria became an increasingly important aspect of its political action. In an open letter to a group of Dalmatian students with autonomist leanings who were resident in Graz, Bajamonti wrote in 1887: 'For a long time two things have seemed absolutely necessary to me in order to save our nationality from the adversaries who are threatening it: declaring ourselves authentic Italians, thereby placing us under the

---

245  Ibid., pp. 11–12.

protection of article 19 of the empire's constitution; uniting ourselves as the Italians of the southern provinces that we are in a single thought, *the struggle for existence.*'[246]

In the mid-1880s the Dalmatian supporters of the new Italian national liberalism began to forge close political ties with the Italian liberal parties in Trentino and the Giulia region. Bajamonti and many of his Dalmatian followers gave a clear signal of their leanings by joining the Pro Patria association and setting up several sections of the organization in Dalmatia.

The Pro Patria association had been formed in Trentino in 1885 with the aim of defending the Italian language against attempts by pan-German groups to spread the use of German even in those parts of the Tyrol with a large Italian majority. The government in Vienna was not opposed to the gradual Germanization of part of the Italian Tyrol as it regarded this as a means of countering Italy's territorial designs on the Trentino; as a result, it encouraged the opening of German schools in the region.[247] The objective of Pro Patria was the creation of self-financing private schools in the Italian language wherever no Italian educational institutions existed.

Over the course of 1886 the association expanded not only through the Italian Tyrol but also into Venezia Giulia. The National Liberal Party of Trieste immediately grasped the cultural and political utility of Pro Patria and encouraged its spread on the Adriatic coast. One of the organizers of Pro Patria in Trieste was a Dalmatian, Professor Vincenzo Miagostovich, who was originally from Sebenico; in those years, together with numerous members of the Dalmatian community in the city he played an important role in the development of cultural and political contacts between the Autonomist Party and the national liberals of Venezia Giulia. Miagostovich suggested that the Trieste section of Pro Patria should also include Dalmatia in its area of activity, and Pro Patria's board of governors invited Bajamonti to open Dalmatian sections of the association.[248]

Bajamonti and his followers decided to set up a branch of Pro Patria in Spalato in August 1887, and they were soon followed by autonomists

---

246  *La Difesa,* 23 June 1887; italics in the original.
247  On the origins and development of the Pro Patria: Sandonà, *L'irredentismo,* vol. 2, pp. 127 et seq. On the Pro Patria in Dalmatia: Vrandečić, *Dalmatinski autonomistički pokret u XIX stoljeću,* pp. 250 et seq.
248  'Pro Patria,' *La Difesa,* 10 January 1887.

in Zara, led by Roberto Ghiglianovich, Giuseppe Sabalich, and the member of the provincial diet Giuseppe Messa, who opened a section of the society there in November of the same year. Bajamonti presented this initiative as the only way of ensuring the cultural survival of the Italian minority in Dalmatia. Through the foundation of private schools it was possible to counter the denationalizing policy of the Croatian nationalists; Pro Patria was to be the means of mobilizing and uniting the Dalmatian Italians in the defence of their national and linguistic rights. As Bajamonti's newspaper *La Difesa* put it: 'It is indispensable that the feeling of solidarity bond the Italian inhabitants of Dalmatia together in a single and united body so that, in the name of the Pro Patria, they can cement their union with their brothers in other provinces.'[249]

So the setting up of branches of Pro Patria formed part of the new strategy of the Italian national current of Dalmatian autonomism to form ties with the Italian liberal parties of Austria. Dalmatian representatives took part in the second congress of Pro Patria, held at Trieste in November 1888, and the third, staged at Trento in June 1890. When the government in Vienna dissolved Pro Patria later in the summer of 1890, accusing it of irredentist and anti-state tendencies,[250] the Dalmatians played a part in its rebirth, helping to organize the Lega Nazionale in 1891 and setting up branches in various parts of Dalmatia over the course of the 1890s.

As well as establishing links with other Italians in Austria, Dalmatian autonomism began to pay increasing attention to Italy. From the 1880s and 1890s onward the autonomist and Italian presses devoted more and more space to events in the kingdom of Italy, which were followed with growing interest.[251] Vienna was no longer the main centre of attraction, the exclusive point of reference for the Italians of Dalmatia. A weakening minority, the Italian Dalmatians started to look to Rome, to an Italy now allied with Austria-Hungary, an Italy viewed by many autonomists as a model of liberal society to be imitated and as a possible source of aid.

In 1887 *La Difesa* commended a speech by Francesco Crispi, praising the Sicilian statesman as a true liberal who knew how to govern,

---

249 'Pro Patria,' *La Difesa*, 25 August 1887.
250 On the dissolution of the Pro Patria: Sandonà, *L'irredentismo*, vol. 2, pp. 151–80; see too DDI, II, 23, docs. 631, 635, 641, 654, 667, 678.
251 By way of example we cite 'Pro Aris,' *La Difesa*, 9 May 1884; 6 January 1887, 24 February 1887 ('Eroismo italiano'), 3 March 1887.

respecting the law and the interests of all parties; going on to make a comparison between Italy and Austria-Hungary, the newspaper extolled the Italian political system.[252] Articles published in the kingdom's newspapers were quite frequently carried by the autonomist press, and developments in Italian foreign policy in the colonial field were followed with great attention.[253]

Yet it must be stressed that the shift toward Italian nationalism by Bajamonti and his supporters, who were especially numerous among the younger generation, was not accepted by the whole of the Autonomous Liberal Party. Many autonomists remained faithful to the values of Dalmatian particularism and multi-ethnic patriotism. Enunciations and commentaries reflecting the persistence of traditionalist positions continued to come out in autonomist newspapers. Even in the autonomist press of Spalato, which was dominated and inspired by Bajamonti, articles in the tradition of Dalmatian multi-ethnic patriotism appeared alongside those promoting the new Italian national liberal line; for example, in a historical evocation of the origins of Dalmatian civilization published in *L'Avvenire* in September 1875, it was declared that 'the present population [of Dalmatia], as a consequence of events in the past, of trade links, etc., is mixed, bilingual, with common rights in a common homeland, whose name is the one that it has always had and that serves to characterize its national autonomy. We are all *Dalmatians*, a name that recalls a glorious past. Neither Italians nor Slavs.'[254] Somewhat contradictorily, however, other articles set out to assert the existence of a Dalmatian nationality and of Italian national rights in Dalmatia at one and the same time.[255]

Dalmatian autonomism never succeeded in resolving these ideological contradictions throughout its subsequent political existence. From the end of the nineteenth century until the division of Dalmatia between Italy and the kingdom of Serbs, Croats, and Slovenes, a current was present in the Autonomist Party (despite its leaders' open support for Italian nationalism) that remained faithful to the tradition of the 'Dalmatian nation.' This ideological dualism between regionalism and Italian liberal nationalism was also reflected in the fact that in the 1890s Dalmatian autonomist liberalism began to define itself as the 'Autono-

---

252  'Teorie di governo,' *La Difesa*, 30 May 1887.
253  For example *La Difesa*, 3 March 1887.
254  'La Dalmazia terra slava!' *L'Avvenire*, 6 September 1875.
255  By way of example: 'Una frase-programma,' *La Difesa*, 8 December 1887.

mous Italian' Party, the party of those who struggled for the autonomy of Dalmatia and of those who fought for Italian national rights. All of this was a positive element for the autonomist movement as it avoided traumatic splits within the party and guaranteed a greater and more broad-based political appeal in a Dalmatian society where many still spurned simplifications of a nationalist character. Up until 1920 the Autonomous Italian Party remained a multi-ethnic party, comprising Slavs, Italians, Albanians, Dalmatian patriots, Italian national liberals, and *italianissimi* nationalists.

The multi-ethnic nature of the party was forcefully claimed by many autonomist politicians. The representative Emanuele Vidovich, who was a notary from Scardona and a friend of Bajamonti, clearly delineated the composition of the Dalmatian Autonomist Party in a speech to the provincial diet in 1890. The Autonomist Party was made up, according to Vidovich, in the first place of 'pure Italians,' descendants of indigenous Latin populations or of Italians who had emigrated to Dalmatia in the distant past. Then there were the 'Italianized': 'These Italianized members declare themselves Italians by sentiment and by language.' The last component of Dalmatian autonomism was the Dalmatian Slavs: 'In addition to these two fractions or parts of the Autonomist Party there is a third, which I declare and recognize as purely Slav and even ignorant of the Italian language, but which is inspired by Dalmatian patriotism, acknowledging the usefulness of the Italian language for culture and education, as well as its indispensability to our trade, our industry and our shipping. These, and they are certainly not few in number, are with us, not because they reckon themselves to be Italian or Italianized, but because they recognize the aforementioned necessity.'[256]

The existence of two spirits in autonomist liberalism, one Italian nationalist and the other Dalmatian regionalist, helps to explain its survival, if only as a minority party, in the whole of Dalmatia up until World War I and its peculiar and contradictory Italo-Slav character, which reflected the ethnic, cultural, and political complexity of Dalmatian society in the late Habsburg period.

---

256 Speech by Vidovich (Vidovic), session of 31 October 1890, pp. 444–6, ADP-BI. Even Ercolano Salvi, Bajamonti's successor as leader of the Italian Autonomous Party in Spalato, confirmed in 1894 that the Autonomist Party was made up of Italians, Italianized, and Slavs: speech by Salvi, session of 1 February 1894, ADP-BI, pp. 238–9.

## 2.6.  Francesco Crispi and the Relations Between Italy and Austria-Hungary

Francesco Crispi, one of the protagonists of Giuseppe Garibaldi's expedition to Sicily in 1860 and a prominent exponent of the Liberal Left for over two decades, re-entered government in April 1887 as minister of the interior in the Depretis cabinet after many years of political isolation.[257] He now appeared to be the only leader of the Liberal Left capable of taking on the mantle of Depretis, an ailing man who could no longer handle the government by himself, and of continuing to pursue the same domestic and foreign policy.

The representative from Sicily had agreed with Mancini's strategy of concluding a political and military alliance with Austria-Hungary and Germany, while criticizing some of his tactical choices and his excessive caution under certain circumstances; for example, Crispi considered Italy's failure to take part in the occupation of the Egypt a grave error.[258]

When Crispi assumed the leadership of the government and the post of foreign minister on Depretis's death in July 1887,[259] he committed himself to essentially following the lines of the international policy that had been laid down by Mancini and Depretis, with the consent of King Umberto I, and continued by Robilant. Crispi proclaimed himself a keen supporter of the Triple Alliance, which he regarded as a means of strengthening Italy's international influence, and devoted all his energies to giving this alliance a real cohesion and an internal solidity, elements that had in fact been lacking until 1887, and making it of greater use to Italy.

---

257  The best political biography of Francesco Crispi is the one by Duggan, *Francesco Crispi*; also useful are the pages devoted to Crispi by Gioacchino Volpe and Sergio Romano: Volpe, *Italia moderna*, vol. 1; Romano, *Crispi*; see too Fonzi, *Crispi e lo 'Stato di Milano.'*

258  Duggan, *Francesco Crispi*.

259  There still has been no full satisfactory study of Francesco Crispi's foreign policy between 1887 and 1891 and between 1893 and 1896; from the extensive existing literature we can cite Salvemini, 'La politica estera di Crispi,' in *La politica estera italiana*; Carocci, 'Alberto Blanc ministro degli Esteri (1893–1896),' pp. 545 et seq.; Mori, *La politica estera di Francesco Crispi*; Serra, *La questione tunisina da Crispi a Rudinì*; 'Le questioni di Cassala e di Adua nelle nuove fonti documentarie,' pp. 526 et seq.; Curato, *La questione marocchina*; Langer, *The Diplomacy of Imperialism*; Sandonà, *L'irredentismo*, vols. 2 and 3; Giglio, *L'articolo XVII del trattato di Uccialli*; 'Crispi e l'Etiopia,' pp. 71–83; Conti Rossini, *Italia ed Etiopia*; Salvatorelli, *La Triplice Alleanza*, pp. 131 et seq.; Albertini, *The Origins*, vol. 1; Lowe, *The Reluctant Imperialists*; Milza, *Français et italiens à la fin du XIXe siècle*, 2 vols.

Crispi's efforts to forge a concrete political co-operation with Berlin were an undeniable success. The German diplomatic corps and Bismarck showed that they appreciated the seriousness of intentions and the energy of the ex-Mazzinian, and at the end of the 1880s cordial relations were established between Berlin and Rome. These found public expression in the meetings between Bismarck and Crispi in Germany[260] and in the Italo-German military accords of 1888.

Crispi's attempts to establish close political collaboration and solidarity with Austria-Hungary proved less successful. The government in Rome tried to exploit the Bulgarian crisis and the resurgence of Austro-Russian rivalry in the Balkans to carry out an action of decided support for the Habsburg policy, in favour of Ferdinand of Saxe-Coburg, prince of Bulgaria.[261] At the same time, it used the bugbear of the threat of Russian expansionism to try to form an Italo-Austro-British alliance in defence of the territorial integrity of the Ottoman Empire and the independent Balkan states. Austrian acceptance of the Italo-British exchange of notes in February 1887, the Austro-Italo-British understanding of 12 December 1887, and the Italian adherence to the Austro-Romanian alliance in 1888 were the results of this intense diplomatic action on Crispi's part.

Notwithstanding Crispi's efforts, however, it proved impossible to persuade Vienna to conclude a secret bilateral understanding that would cover the eventuality of the Ottoman Empire's collapse. Nor were there any Italo-Austrian accords of military and naval co-operation against the Russians and the French; although greatly desired by Crispi,[262] they were not drawn up because of suspicions on the part of the Habsburg government.

Apart from the ritual declarations of defence of the *status quo*, the goal of Italy's pro-Austrian and anti-Russian Balkan policy was to create the juridical and political conditions for a future application of the article of the Triple Alliance on compensation. Austria's eastward drive, the possible Habsburg conquest of Ottoman territories, and a

---

260  On Italo-German relations between 1887 and 1890: Langer, *European Alliances*; Mazzetti, *L'esercito italiano nella Triplice Alleanza*, pp. 53 et seq.; Rich, *Friedrich von Holstein*, vol. 1, pp. 193–203, 247–8.

261  On this: Guida, *La Bulgaria dalla guerra di liberazione sino al trattato di Neuilly 1877–1919*; Guida, Pitassio, and Tolomeo, *Nascita di uno Stato balcanico*.

262  A detailed reconstruction of the Italo-Austrian military negotiations at the end of the 1880s in Mazzetti, *L'esercito italiano nella Triplice Alleanza*, pp. 95 et seq. On Italo-Habsburg relations under Crispi: Afflerbach, *Der Dreibund*, pp. 231 et seq.

Russian-Austrian war were situations that could have forced Vienna to seek Italy's military backing and thus allowed the government in Rome to demand in exchange some of the Austrian territories that were inhabited by Italians. Favouring Austria's influence in the Balkans signified shifting the course of Habsburg policy further to the east and fuelling the Austro-Russian rivalry that rendered Italy an indispensable partner for Vienna. In the light of these considerations, Crispi's attempt to broaden the Italian political and military commitments connected with the alliance with the Austro-German bloc and his pro-Austrian policy were parts of a plan to carry on with the policy, already outlined by Mancini and Robilant, of supporting Austria's eastward expansion in order to obtain territorial rewards. In Crispi's view, Italy and Austria needed one another:

> Austria in turn needs Italy, which, on certain occasions, could render her signal services. Austria, secure in the Alps and the Adriatic, would have full freedom of action to the East, where her true interests lie and where she may be assailed by her true enemies ... On our part I would say that it is in Italy's interest for Austria not to break up. She is a great barricade against potentially more dangerous adversaries, which are best kept faraway from our frontiers. In the light of this, there ought not to be any problems between Italy and Austria. That of the borders will, one day or the other, be solved amicably.[263]

The aim of favouring Austria's eastward drive, and through this an amicable solution to the problem of the Italo-Austrian borders, was nothing new for the Italian political tradition. Nonetheless, it continued to receive broad support in the Italian political world, from Crispi, for example, but also from his successor and opponent, Antonio di Rudinì, who in 1891 declared that he wanted to maintain the *status quo* in the Balkans. Rudini also proclaimed that if this were not possible, 'we will be prepared ... to support, under the right conditions, the Eastward expansion of Austria-Hungary. The possible aspirations of the Cabinet in Vienna in the Balkan peninsula cannot therefore be considered *a priori* contrary to the aims of Italian policy as we understand them and as they have found expression in the Triple Alliance.'[264]

---

263  Crispi to Nigra, 31 July 1890, doc. 654, DDI, II, 23. On Crispi's support for the Triple Alliance see the considerations of Pastorelli, 'Il principio di nazionalità,' p. 204.
264  Rudinì to Galvagna, 12 July 1891, DDI, II, 24, doc. 349.

In this general picture of Italo-Austrian relations, Crispi saw the un-redeemed lands as a question that would be resolved in a friendly man-ner in the future. In the meantime, in the view of Crispi and many of his colleagues, the existence of the Italo-Austrian alliance could improve the living conditions of the Italian populations. The policy of alliance conducted by the government in Rome should convince Vienna, and the Taaffe government in particular, that the Italians of Austria were not a threat to the empire and that the return to a pro-Italian domestic policy was in their common interest. 'If the Italians,' observed Crispi in October 1888, 'were to be well treated, if their autonomy were to be respected, the Italians of the kingdom would have no reason for com-plaint and there would be no pretext for irredentism.'[265]

The great difficulty that Italian policy encountered in dealing with Vienna derived first of all from the Habsburg refusal to accept a rela-tionship on equal terms with Rome in the Balkans, which was regarded as a region belonging exclusively to Austria-Hungary's sphere of influ-ence. Then the objectives of Crispi's pro-Austrian policy were clearly grasped by the Habsburg government. The Habsburg ambassador to Rome, Karl von Bruck, noted in June 1888 that at the root of Crispi's plans of military co-operation lay the dream of obtaining the Trentino as compensation for a successful expansion of Austria-Hungary in the Balkans.[266] All of this explains Kálnoky's rejection of the proposals to conclude military accords against the Russians and bilateral agree-ments on the political future of the Ottoman territories.[267] As Renato Mori has rightly pointed out, the opening of negotiations for a military accord might have provided Italy with an opportunity to advance terri-torial claims on the Trentino and the region of the Isonzo.[268] Moreover, while Crispi won approval in Vienna for his vigour in repressing public manifestations of anti-Habsburg irredentism, his personality remained troubling and ambiguous in the eyes of the conservative Catholic

265  Crispi, *Politica Estera*, p. 279.
266  Bruck to Kálnoky, 16 June 1888, in Sandonà, *L'irredentismo*, vol. 3, pp. 151–2; Albertini, *The origins of the War of 1914*, vol. 1. For more of Bruck's observations on Crispi's aims: Mazzetti, *L'esercito italiano*, pp. 79–80. On the fear, widespread in the Habsburg diplomatic corps, of having to cede much of the Italian Tyrol to Italy in the event of a military victory of the Triple Alliance against Russia or France, see Eulenburg to Hohenhole, 10 November 1895, GP, 10, doc. 2499.
267  On this: GP, 4, docs. 917, 920, 921; Mazzetti, *L'esercito italiano*, pp. 53 et seq.
268  Mori, *Crispi*, pp. 130–1.

Kálnoky, who accused him of having links with Freemasonry and republican circles.[269]

Moreover, Austria-Hungary's Balkan policy always sought to block any growth of Italian political, cultural, and economic influence in the region. For the Habsburg ruling class the 'civilizing' of the Balkan peoples was the exclusive responsibility of Austria-Hungary.[270]

Even after the conclusion of the Triple Alliance, the Austrian government carried on with its efforts to reduce the influence of the Italian and Italophile element in the Tyrol and the Adriatic regions by supporting the parties of the Slav nationalists, German Tyroleans, or Catholic loyalists. This was considered the best way of averting future claims by Italy in the Italian territories of Austria.

Austrian suspicion and Vienna's determination to carry on with a policy of national readjustment in Venezia Giulia and Dalmatia provoked a great deal of tension and a series of incidents (of which a thorough and well-documented analysis can be found in Augusto Sandonà's work on irredentism)[271] in the relations between Italy and Austria-Hungary even in the years of the Crispi government.

In general, Crispi, conscious of Austrian distrust, seemed to rely on the forging of a close relationship with Germany as a means of influencing Habsburg policy at the domestic as well as the international level.[272] Believing that the existence of good relations between the member states of the Triple Alliance was in the German interest, Crispi turned several times to German diplomacy with the hope that it could persuade the government in Vienna to adopt a more moderate and flexible policy toward the Italian element in Austria; examples of this were Crispi's appeal to Chancellor Bismarck at their meeting at Friedrichsruh in October 1887 for Germany to convince the government in Vienna to treat the Italians of Austria better;[273] and the Sicilian politician's requests for

---

269  Eulenburg to Caprivi, 20 December 1893, GP, 9, doc. 2138. Some comments on
       Crispi's entourage and collaborators in Serra, *Alberto Pisani Dossi diplomatico*.
270  On Austria-Hungary's Balkan policy in the 1880s and 1890s: Bridge, *From Sadowa*;
       Langer, *European Alliances*; Palotás, *Machtpolitik und Wirtschaftsinteressen*.
271  Sandonà, *L'irredentismo*.
272  On Crispi's attempts to win German support in moderating Austrian policy toward
       the Italian populations of the Habsburg Empire, first in 1888 and then in 1894:
       Crispi, *Politica estera*, p. 279; DDI, II, 26, docs. 662, 663, 665, 667, 668, 670, 678, 722;
       Afflerbach, *Der Dreibund*, pp. 281 et seq.
273  Crispi, *Politica estera*, p. 178.

German intervention in Vienna on the occasion first of the trial of the Triestine journalist Ferdinando Ullmann (November 1889)[274] and then of the issuing of the ordinance on languages in Istria by the Badeni government (fall 1894).[275]

Berlin then, in the eyes of the Italian ruling class, would be able to play the role of mediator. At the decisive moment of the negotiation of compensation in the event of a joint war or of Habsburg conquests in the Balkans, the German government would pressure Vienna to surrender some of the Italian territories of Austria. During Kaiser Wilhelm's visit to Rome in October 1888, Crispi spoke quite openly of this with Herbert Bismarck, the chancellor's son; in the view of the Sicilian politician, Italy did not have secure frontiers: 'It will be necessary for Germany to help us get them back at the first opportunity. For now let us remain united; let us keep the alliance of the three monarchies as close as possible.'[276]

The observation that the ceding of the Trentino to Italy by Austria in the future was actually regarded as a possible and desirable thing in some German political circles[277] greatly irritated the government in Vienna. In July 1888 the Habsburg foreign minister, Kálnoky, made it clear to Bruck that any talk of cession of the Trentino was unacceptable; Austria-Hungary was prepared to go along with Italy's aspirations for expansion in Africa, but if Italy also 'was nursing in secret the irredentist ideal and the hope of obtaining from us, under any circumstances, as an amicable surrender on the basis of the principle of nationality, territories that have been in the possession of the imperial house for centuries, then she was laying herself open to the greatest disappointment, even if on the German part the Hon. Crispi had been offered some hope that an *arrangement à l'amiable* could be reached with respect to the "Trentino."'[278]

Failing to understand the mentality and attitude of the Habsburg establishment, the Italian ruling class continued to regard the spontaneous and peaceful transfer of Italian territories on the part of Austria-

274  Sandonà, *L'irredentismo*, vol. 3, pp. 193–8.
275  On this: Crispi to Lanza, 5 November 1894, DDI, II, 26, doc. 662; docs. 670, 678, 722; Apollonio, *Autunno istriano*, pp. 123 et seq.; Riccardi, *Salata*, pp. 83–4.
276  Crispi, *Politica estera*, pp. 280–1.
277  Sandonà, *L'irredentismo*, vol. 3, p. 152.
278  Kálnoky to Bruck, 4 July 1888, reproduced in Sandonà, *L'irredentismo*, vol. 3, pp. 153–4.

Hungary as possible, and to see Germany as the interlocutor that could, thanks to Vienna's political and military dependence on the country, play a decisive role in such a political operation.

Crispi shared this hope and believed in a future German mediation on behalf of Italy. This fact can facilitate a better understanding of the Italian attitude on the occasion of the second renewal of the Austro-Italo-German treaty of alliance.

In the fall of 1890, seizing the opportunity of a visit by the German chancellor, Caprivi, to Italy,[279] Crispi began to present the Italian requests for possible modifications to the texts of the Triple Alliance treaties. According to Crispi, it was necessary to improve trade links between the three states by creating a sort of customs union. In addition, the three treaties concluded in 1887 should be merged into a single treaty; in the view of the Italian prime minister, 'the additional conventions of 1887, one between Austria and Italy and the other between Italy and Germany, are not identical; they differ, and it is certainly necessary to bring them closer in their means and aims, even if it is decided not to render them uniform.'[280]

These requests reflected the Italian desire to involve Germany more closely in Balkan policy and to make her the guarantor of application of the article on compensation that had been included in the separate Italo-Austrian treaty of 1887. This was an intention that could be read between the lines of Crispi's explanation of his proposals to Bruck. According to the Sicilian politician, the integration of the three treaties would result in improved co-operation and greater cordiality between the allies; furthermore, with a greater conformity of the accords any misunderstanding could be avoided, and the three states would move in the same direction – which was not the case at that moment, given the existence of minor difficulties that might grow worse under more serious circumstances.[281]

Naturally the Habsburg diplomatic corps was opposed to Crispi's plans, afraid of seeing Germany involve itself in the Balkan question and having to assume obligations on behalf of Italy in North Africa.[282]

279  On Caprivi's visit to Italy in November 1890: GP, 7, docs. 1394, 1395; DDI, II, 23, docs. 848, 849; Rich, *Friedrich von Holstein*, vol. 1, pp. 328–33
280  Crispi to Nigra, 4 December 1890, DDI, II, 23, doc. 875; GP, 7, docs. 1396, 1398; Afflerbach, *Der Dreibund*, pp. 310 et seq.
281  Bruck to Kálnoky, 18 November 1890, reproduced in Pribram, *The Secret Treaties of Austria-Hungary.*
282  Pribram, *The Secret Treaties of Austria-Hungary.*

With the fall of the Crispi government at the beginning of 1891, his successor, Rudinì, who was aware of Habsburg and German opposition to the idea of stepping up German commitments in the Balkan area,[283] continued the negotiations for the renewal of the Triple Alliance by asking for a simple formal union of the accords of 1887 into a single treaty and a greater safeguarding of Italian economic needs. He focused his attention chiefly on the Mediterranean, requesting a strengthening of Germany's support for Italian policy in Africa and a declaration that would confirm that the alliance was not anti-British in character.[284]

The Triple Alliance was renewed on 6 May 1891, in Berlin, thanks in part to the fact that the Germans and Austro-Hungarians accepted some of the Italian requests.[285] The three treaties of 1887, while keeping the different obligations between the contracting parties distinct, were conflated into a single text. In a new article (number IX) Germany agreed to support any Italian decision not to respect the *status quo* in North Africa and to occupy some territories in the region. A protocol was also signed in which the contracting parties pledged to introduce mutual trade concessions and proposed to encourage the development of closer political co-operation with Great Britain in the central and western Mediterranean.[286]

Thus can be seen that the Italian attempts to give greater force to the Triple Alliance, bringing it more into line with Italy's own interests, achieved only partial success. While gains were made in the commercial sphere with the Italo-Austrian and Italo-German trade agreements of 1891,[287] the negotiations failed to bring about effective and cogent

---

283 Rudinì to Launay and Nigra, 15 March 1891, doc. 124; Launay to Rudinì, 22–31 March 1891, doc. 144; Nigra to Rudinì, 2 April 1891, doc. 186, DDI, II, 24,; GP, 7, docs. 1398, 1399.

284 Rudinì to Launay, 6 April 1891, doc. 197; Rudinì to Launay, 15 April 1891, doc. 221, DDI, II, 24 (a French translation of the same dispatch is published in GP, 7, doc. 1410). On the negotiations that led to the renewal of the Triple Alliance: Pribram, *The Secret Treaties of Austria-Hungary*; Fellner, 'Der Dreibund'; Salvatorelli, *La Triplice Alleanza*, pp. 168 et seq.; Albertini, *The Origins of the War of 1914*, vol. 1.

285 On the last phase of the negotiations leading to the renewal of the Triple Alliance: GP, 7, docs. 1411, 1412, 1413, 1414, 1416, 1417; Pribram, *The Secret Treaties of Austria-Hungary*; Salvatorelli, *La Triplice Alleanza*, pp. 173 et seq.

286 The text of the treaty of the Triple Alliance signed on 6 May 1891, is reproduced in Pribram, *The Secret Treaties of Austria-Hungary*; GP, 7, doc. 1426.

287 On the commercial treaties between Italy, Austria-Hungary, and Germany: Cova, 'I rapporti di politica commerciale,' in *Commercio e navigazione*, pp. 195 et seq.; Del Vecchio, *La via italiana al protezionismo*, vol. 1, pp. 453 et seq.; 'Il regime doganale tra

political co-operation with Austria-Hungary in the Balkans and any real improvement in the living conditions of the Italian and Italophile populations in the Habsburg Empire. The political and commercial conflict with France, the poor relations with Russia, and the fruitlessness of Italo-British relations – with London hostile to Italian expansionistic designs in Africa[288] – rendered Italy's international action difficult and not very effective, thereby making the government in Rome highly dependent on Austria-Hungary and Germany. The attempts of the Rudinì, Giovanni Giolitti, and Crispi governments to improve relations with France between 1891 and 1894 were essentially a failure, largely because Paris, strengthened by the conclusion of the Franco-Russian defensive alliance at the beginning of the 1890s, desired the humiliation of Italy and its exit from the Triple Alliance.[289] The tariff war and French actions[290] to counter Italian interests in East Africa and the Mediterranean proved extremely effective and weakened the international position of the government in Rome, bringing Crispi's pro-Austrian policy and support for the Triple Alliance into question. Criticism of the foreign policy pursued by Crispi, who returned to power at the end of 1893, started to emerge in broad swathes of the Italian ruling class.[291]

The Austrian reluctance to strengthen the alliance with Italy emptied Crispi's policy of much of its potential significance, forcing the Sicilian statesman to imbue Italian diplomatic action with an initially unwanted ambiguity. Conscious of Austrian suspicions over Italy's influence in the western Balkans and the Adriatic, from 1894 onward Crispi and his foreign minister, Blanc, began to step up Italian cultural and economic penetration of Albania, Epirus, and Macedonia, showing interest in the national reawakening of the Albanians[292] and the Kouts-

l'Italia e l'Austria-Ungheria (1887–1892)'; 'Penetrazione economica italiana,' pp. 201 et seq.

288 On Italo-British relations in the 1890s: Lowe, *Reluctant Imperialists*; Lowe and Marzari, *Italian Foreign Policy 1870–1940*, pp. 28 et seq.; Silva, *Il Mediterraneo*, pp. 314 *et sqq*; Seton Watson, 'Adua 1896,' pp. 117 et seq.

289 On Italo-French relations: Guillen, *L'expansion 1881–1898*; Serra, *La questione tunisina*; Milza, *Français et italiens*, vol. 1, pp. 3–169, vol. 2, pp. 479–578; Billot, *La France et l'Italie*.

290 GP, 7, docs. 1462, 1463; Milza, *Français et italiens*, vol. 2, pp. 533 et seq.

291 Bonghi's attitude is interesting in this respect: Maturi, 'Bonghi e i problemi di politica estera,' in Bonghi, *Politica estera (1866–1893)*, pp. XI–XXXVII.

292 On the attitude of Italian diplomacy toward the Albanian question between 1890 and 1896 there is interesting documentation in DDI, II, 23, doc. 730; DDI, II, 24,

ovlach populations[293] as they were seen as pawns that could possibly be used to restrain or check Habsburg, Serbian, or Greek expansionism in the region. Another element of Crispi's Balkan policy that showed his awareness of the fragility of Italo-Austrian relations was the decision to strengthen relations with Montenegro through the marriage of the prince of Naples, Victor Emmanuel of Savoy, to the daughter of the king of Montenegro, Elena. The marriage, celebrated in October 1896 but strongly advocated by Crispi, had clear political motivations, that is, the need for Italy 'to have a base in the Balkan peninsula in the event of war in the East.'[294]

The Italian diplomatic records confirm the rise of a growing dissatisfaction on the part of the Crispi government over the alliance with Vienna and Berlin during the course of 1895 and the beginning of 1896. Crispi and Blanc harshly criticized Austria and Germany for their lack of support for Italy's colonial policy.[295] They attempted to create room for manoeuvre by trying to revitalize the Anglo-Italo-Austrian understanding of December 1887, which had remained purely theoretical until that moment.[296] The Sicilian politician's aim was to render the obligations and purposes of this understanding more precise in order to be ready for an eventual division of the Ottoman Empire. 'It is our desire,' Crispi told Nigra in January 1896, 'for the territorial *status quo* in the Balkan peninsula to remain the same. But if it were to change, if an apportionment of the Turkish empire were to take place, we want Italy to have its share.'[297] Crispi's plan came to nothing, encountering a lack of interest on the part of the British in bringing the Mediterranean ac-

docs. 293, 305, 335; DDI, II, 27, docs. 341, 456, 485, 644, 705; Crispi, *Questioni internazionali*, pp. 237 et seq.

293  On Italian support for the attempts by the Koutsovlach populations of Albania and Macedonia to give themselves an autonomous cultural and political organization: Catalani to Blanc, 18 March 1895, DDI, II, 26, doc. 979; Blanc to Catalani, 1 April 1895, DDI, II, 27, doc. 2; docs. 29, 60, 90; Carageani, 'Gli aromeni e la questione aromena,' in *Storia contemporanea*, pp. 929–1007.

294  Crispi, *Questioni internazionali*, pp. 240–1. Many references to Crispi's role in the marriage of the prince of Naples and the Montenegrin princess in Farini, *Diario*, vol. 1, pp. 636, 676, 724.

295  Blanc to Nigra, 12 January 1896, DDI, II, 27, doc. 739; docs. 782, 787; GP, 10, docs. 2369, 2370.

296  DDI, II, 27, docs. 779, 815.

297  Conversation between the prime minister and minister of the interior, Crispi, and the ambassador to Vienna, Nigra, 24 January 1896, DDI, II, 27, doc. 793.

cords of 1887 to life and in negotiating the future set-up of the Ottoman territories with Italy and Austria.[298]

While Crispi and Blanc were trying to forge an alliance with the Austrians and British in the Mediterranean, the events of the Italo-Ethiopian war carried the government in Rome toward military catastrophe.[299] The defeat inflicted on the Italian army by the Ethiopian forces at Adwa on 1 March brought an end to the political career of Francesco Crispi, who resigned as premier a few days later and was succeeded by Rudinì.

## 2.7.  A New Irredentism: The Dante Alighieri Association and Italian Foreign Policy at the End of the Nineteenth Century

The rethinking of Italian foreign policy carried out by the Depretis-Mancini government, leading to the conclusion of the Triple Alliance, received wide support from various sectors of Italian liberalism, but it also stirred criticism.

A number of officials in the Italian diplomatic corps, such as Alberto Pansa and, above all, Tornielli, who were linked to the anti-Habsburg tradition of the Italian national liberal movement, disapproved strongly of the shift in the kingdom's foreign policy that had been introduced by Mancini. According to Tornielli, the conclusion of the Triple Alliance exposed Italy to the dangers of a rupture with France, with which it was not possible to maintain a permanent state of hostility;[300] in addition, the deterioration in relations with France and the alliance with the Austro-German bloc weakened Italy's strategic position in the Mediterranean and undermined Italian prestige among the Balkan peoples, who saw the country as supinely carrying out the orders of others.[301] In a letter to Depretis in May 1883 Tornielli made a very harsh attack on Mancini's foreign policy, which had been accepted by the elderly prime minister, albeit with little conviction and enthusiasm. The Triple Alliance, in the view of the diplomat from Novara, had had no positive consequences for Italy's international action:

---

298  DDI, II, 27, docs. 852, 913.

299  On the conflict between Italy and Ethiopia in 1895–6: Conti Rossini, *Italia ed Etiopia*

300  In this connection see the passage from the diary of Alberto Pansa, dated 31 December 1882, in which he approvingly quoted some criticisms of the Triple Alliance by Tornielli, cited in Serra, 'Diplomatici del passato. Alberto Pansa,' pp. 532 et seq., citation p. 535.

301  Tornielli to Depretis, 18 July 1882, ACS, Carte Depretis, series I, portfolio 23.

We should not delude ourselves into thinking that we have grown in importance. It is the opposite that is true. We have returned to exactly the same situation in which we found ourselves prior to 1870, with the difference that then it was said that Italy wanted what France and Great Britain decided, and now it is said that to know our opinion, it is necessary to go to Berlin and Vienna ... Then we had Rome to acquire, and now no one understands what we want. When all that one wants is the right to be left in peace, one does not feel the need to strive to free other people's hands. Perhaps they are less suspicious of us in Vienna. But in return they are more suspicious of us everywhere else. The focus is, at this moment, on the great colonial questions. They lie outside the scope of our interests. Attention is beholden on us, but a vigilant attention, and vigilance is just what seems to me to have been made difficult by the widespread belief that Italy no longer has a voice of her own, nor any freedom of action.[302]

Within the Italian ruling class, many exponents of the Liberal Far Left with republican and radical leanings, faithful to the teachings of Mazzini, initially considered the alliance with Austria-Hungary to be a betrayal of the ideals of the Italian nation state. Aurelio Saffi, a politician from Romagna who had long been a close collaborator of Mazzini and one of the undisputed leaders of the Republican Party, denounced the Triple Alliance as a renunciation of the tradition of the Risorgimento, founded in his view on political ties with western states like France and Great Britain and on support for anti-Habsburg and anti-Ottoman national movements.[303] Similar views were held by Felice Cavallotti and Matteo Renato Imbriani,[304] leaders of the Radical Party and promoters of irredentist associations in Italy.

Fierce opposition to the Italo-Austro-German alliance also came from the irredentist circles of Trentino and Venezia Giulia that were present in the peninsula and had ties to the Liberal Far Left. They attempted to

---

302 Tornielli to Depretis, 23 May 1883, ACS, Carte Depretis, series I, portfolio 23. Part of the letter had been reproduced in Decleva, *L'Italia e la politica internazionale*, p. 78.

303 On the figure of Saffi and his stance with regard to Italian foreign policy: Quagliotti, *Aurelio Saffi*, pp. 208 et seq.; Volpe, *Italia moderna*, vol. 1, pp. 104–5; Barzilai, *Luci ed ombre del passato*, pp. 23–5. On the republican movement in the 1870s and 1880s: Spadolini, *I repubblicani dopo l'Unità*.

304 On the positions of Cavallotti and the radicals, opposed to the Triple Alliance: Galante Garrone, *I radicali in Italia 1849–1925*, pp. 208 et seq.; Cavallotti, *Lettere 1860–1898*, pp. 250–1, 264–5.

sabotage the alliance through agitations and acts of terrorism, culminating in plans by Guglielmo Oberdan (Oberdank) to assassinate Emperor Francis Joseph during a visit to Trieste in the summer of 1882.[305]

The failure of the attempts to sabotage the Italo-Austrian alliance, and the crisis in an openly irredentist political strategy (which went on tiredly repeating the principles of the Mazzinian and Garibaldian tradition that had been founded on national voluntarism and an oversimplified view of the nature of the Habsburg Empire, underestimating the solidity of a centuries-old state structure supported by broad sections of the population), led some exponents of the liberal and republican Far Left (Aurelio Saffi; the Masonic leaders Adriano Lemmi and Ernesto Nathan;[306] and the exiles from Venezia Giulia, Giacomo Venezian and Enrico Tedeschi) to rethink their attitude toward Italian foreign policy and the decision to make an alliance with Vienna and Berlin. The attempt to carry on with an open and total struggle against the Habsburg Empire, for example by making plans for expeditions of the Garibaldian type in Austria, was in the end unproductive and even counterproductive, as it brought greater repression of irredentism in the Tyrol and Venezia Giulia and put at risk the very survival and independence of the unified Italian state.[307] The exponents of the Far Left began to perceive instead that the existence of an alliance between Rome and Vienna could open up room in Austria for a different kind of political action that would be more fruitful in the long term, that is, an action of support and propaganda in defence of Italian and Italophile groups in the Habsburg Empire. All of this had the barely concealed

---

305 On the figure of Oberdank (Oberdan), the political agitations and the irredentist attacks of 1882: Salata, *Guglielmo Oberdan*; Coceani, *Riccardo Zampieri*, pp. 25–33. On the irredentist movement in Italy in the 1880s: Sandonà, *L'irredentismo*, vols. 2 and 3; Coceani, *Milano centrale segreta dell'irredentismo*; Veronese, *Ricordi d'irredentismo*.

306 On the important role of Ernesto Nathan in Italian foreign policy between the end of the nineteenth century and World War I: Levi, *Ricordi della vita e dei tempi di Ernesto Nathan*, pp. 137 et seq.; Pisa, 'Ernesto Nathan e la "politica nazionale,"' pp. 17 et seq.

307 On the subject of Aurelio Saffi's criticisms of attempts to organize acts of insurrection against Austria, and his ideas about the need for a new irredentist approach based on cultural means: Quagliotti, *Aurelio Saffi*, pp. 211–12. On Lemmi and Saffi's disagreement with the sort of publicly anti-government irredentist propaganda practised by the committees led by Imbriani: Lemmi to Saffi, 23 July 1889, DDI, II, 22, doc. 648.

objective of waiting for a future crisis in the Habsburg Empire, perhaps triggered by the succession to the imperial throne after the death of Francis Joseph or by an Austro-Russian war, and of preparing for the conquest of the unredeemed lands.

In short, acceptance of the Italo-Austrian alliance could provide a more effective, though less conspicuous, means of countering the anti-Italian tendencies that had become very strong in Austria-Hungary after the advent of Taaffe to power. The improvement in relations between Vienna and Rome and the dropping of an openly irredentist policy on the part of Italy could help to weaken the Italophobic sentiments of the Habsburg state structures, facilitating the return of the Austrian government to a more balanced and less anti-Italian attitude with regard to the national struggles in the Adriatic territories and the Tyrol. They would also permit Italy to organize a policy of cultural and political penetration in the border regions that would fortify the Italian populations and the pro-Italian liberal parties in the Tyrol and the eastern Adriatic. The survival of strong groups of Italians and Italophiles was in the interest of the government in Rome for it served to preserve political forces that could prove useful as a base on which to construct a future dominion if the time came to raise the problem of compensation to Italy for a change in the Balkan *status quo*.

These arguments had already been put forward in 1884 by Attilio Brunialti, a jurist from the Veneto and a member of parliament close to the Liberal Left, who had suggested looking at the Triple Alliance as a way of providing more effective protection of the Italian populations of Austria, which in his view were threatened by attempts at Slavicization in Istria and Dalmatia. Useful to this end could be the creation of an association for the spread of the Italian language that would be devoid of political aims and would send books, aid, and teachers across the Alps; the activity of such an association might be permitted by an Austrian government allied with Italy.[308]

From the 1880s onward the government in Rome began to advise the leaders of the Italian liberal parties in Austria to concentrate on the defence of their own national rights within and not against the Habsburg institutional system. According to the consul in Trieste, Cesare

---

308  Brunialti, 'Le scuole italiane fuori d'Italia,' pp. 627–53. On Brunialti: d'Amelio, 'Attilio Brunialti,' pp. 636–8.

Durando, the only remedy for the weakening of the positions of the Italian and Italophile element in the Habsburg Empire was for

> Austrian citizens of our race, the Italian, or who are Italianized by tradition, education and aspirations, to accept their Austrian citizenship and profess it in their conduct without displaying or revealing ambiguities; for them to lay claim to and defend their Italian nationality but within the limits and rights of the laws, laws which in Austria offer to each and every one of the empire's nationalities the broadest guarantees and the most effective means for their preservation and development. By placing themselves candidly and correctly on this terrain, Austrian Italians will no longer be faced with the opposition of the imperial government; they will no longer have to combat official and semi-official propaganda directed against them; they will be able to conserve and build up their strength for the future. Otherwise they will be the architects of their own defeat, they will commit the greatest betrayal of all, that of inexorably precluding any possibility of a future.'[309]

Similar ideas were put forward by Giuseppe Avarna, Nigra's assistant at the embassy in Vienna, in a lengthy memorandum devoted to the problem of the Italians in Austria, written in 1890. Avarna emphasized that in order to avert the threat of a Croatian and Slovenian hegemony in the Adriatic territories, it was necessary for 'the element Italian, following the example set by other nationalities, to renounce any idea of irredentism, and, placing themselves frankly on constitutional grounds, spare no efforts to obtain the autonomy that they need to safeguard their own nationality against the pretensions of its adversaries.'[310]

In those years the Italian press had begun to pay attention to the national struggles in Dalmatia, pointing out the deterioration of the living conditions of Italians in the eastern Adriatic. The publication of Giuseppe Marcotti's book *La Nuova Austria*[311] in 1885 contributed to the emerging public view of Dalmatia as not just a strategic problem but

---

309  Durando to Mancini, 3 September 1883, DDI, II, 15–16, doc. 679. Durando's moderate stance caused a rift between the Italian diplomat and exponents of Triestine irredentism: Veronese, *Ricordi d'irredentismo*, pp. 142 et seq.

310  Avarna to Crispi, 29 September 1890, DDI, II, 23, doc. 744.

311  Marcotti, *La nuova Austria*. Marcotti was commissioned by the Dante Alighieri to write a guidebook to the eastern Adriatic in 1899: Marcotti, *L'Adriatico orientale da Venezia a Corfù*.

also an Italian national one. Marcotti, a writer and historian from Friuli who was to become one of the moving spirits of the Dante Alighieri Society, painted a disquieting picture of the new political order in an Austria ruled by the conservative-Slav coalition led by Taaffe. Noting the vigorous growth of the Slovenian, Croatian, Serbian, and Czech national movements within the Habsburg Empire, Marcotti foresaw a future Slavicization of Austria and its transformation into a confederation dominated by Slav peoples. In this picture he presented the possible rise of a greater Croatia within the Habsburg state as a grave danger for the Italian nation, for in that case Italy would have to contend for the Adriatic not just with the Habsburg navy and with commerce based in Trieste and Fiume but also 'with the completely new forces of a young nation filled with cupidity and daring, vanguard of the Slav world in the Mediterranean basin.'[312]

Marcotti devoted many pages to analysis of the political situation in Dalmatia, denouncing the 'war on the Italian' that was being conducted in the region. Taking up the arguments of the autonomist movement, which he often called the 'Italian Party,' he observed that despite the absence of any irredentism in the Dalmatian Italian populations, the government in Vienna had assumed a hostile attitude to the Autonomist Party because it was afraid that the party would be 'dominated by the anti-Austrian spirit that already held sway among the Italians of Gorizia, Trieste, and Istria.'[313] The antagonism of the Austrian state authorities and the irresistible growth of the Croatian national movement had resulted in the application of a policy hostile to the Italian culture and language in Dalmatia and a worsening of the living conditions of the Dalmatian Italian-speaking populations.

Over the following years public opinion and the ruling class in Italy became increasingly sensitive and attentive to the fate of the Italian and Italophile populations in Dalmatia. It was often a superficial attention, fomented by sensationalistic reports that played up incidents and crimes in which the victims were Italian citizens, but there was also a genuine and sincere concern over the situation of the Italian Dalmatians, whose existence and political and national difficulties had now become visible. Often it was members of parliament from the Veneto or belonging to the Far Left and the Liberal and democratic Left who

---

312  Marcotti, *La nuova Austria*, p. 303.
313  Ibid., p. 290.

publicly denounced incidents involving fishermen from Chioggia in
Dalmatia and who drew attention to the difficult living conditions of
the Italian element on the Adriatic coast.[314] In March 1892, Salvatore
Barzilai, a member of parliament originally from Trieste and a representative of the Mazzinian and irredentist Far Left, denounced the ill
treatment that fishermen and workers from the kingdom had received
in Dalmatia for many years, blaming it on the anti-Italian policy of the
Austrian government and the Croatian nationalist parties; it was 'a no-
holds-barred struggle against the Italian national element, harassed
from all sides, by priests from the pulpit, by pan-Slavists in the streets,
by teachers in the schools, conducted tenaciously with the assistance
and support of government agents.' While the Italians in Trieste and
Istria were able for the moment to resist and fight back, Barzilai held
that 'in Dalmatia the campaign of pan-Slavism, of Croatism, backed by
the Imperial government, is already almost won.'[315]

In the circles of the liberal and republican Far Left and among the
irredentists of Venezia Giulia and Trentino the conclusion of the Triple
Alliance was seen as an opportunity to create new means for a more
effective policy of defence for the Italian inhabitants of Austria; consequently new political and cultural associations, the Giovanni Prati in
1887 and, following its dissolution, the Dante Alighieri Association in
1889, were founded.[316] These associations proposed a new type of irredentism based on cultural propaganda and the defence of the linguistic
and national rights of the Italians in Austria. They eschewed party politics and were open to the participation of Italian patriots of any ideology and affiliation so long as they were agreed on a common program of
foreign policy aimed at the creation of a Greater Italy and the reunion of
the unredeemed Austrian lands with the Italian fatherland in a distant
future. Ruggiero Bonghi described the purpose of the Dante Alighieri
Association as 'the fostering of the Italian spirit wherever it appears,

314  For example: question by Bernini with reply from Mancini, sittings on 23 January
     and 2 February 1884, parliament, AP, pp. 5356–8, 5622–37; speeches by Barzilai, Im-
     briani, Papadopoli, and Galli, sitting of 31 March 1892, pp. 7546–50. On this theme:
     Sandonà, L'irredentismo, vols. 2 and 3.
315  Speech by Barzilai, sitting of 31 March 1892, parliament, AP, pp. 7546–7.
316  On the origins of the Dante Alighieri: Guerrazzi, Ricordi d'irredentismo; Pisa, Nazione
     e politica nella Società 'Dante Alighieri'; Grange, L'Italie et la Méditerranée (1896–1911),
     vol. 1, pp. 661 et seq.; Levi, Ricordi della vita e dei tempi di Ernesto Nathan; Barbera, La
     Dante Alighieri; Boselli, 'Le origini della Dante,' in Per la 'Dante,' pp. 3 et seq.

and in the different forms in which it appears, however great or small it may be.'[317] Its objective was to aid those who wished to unite with the Italian fatherland and those who hoped only for the strengthening of relations between their new homeland and their old.[318]

The model from which the founders of the Dante Alighieri Association took their inspiration was that of the Società Nazionale, the patriotic association set up by Daniele Manin, Giuseppe La Farina, and Giorgio Pallavicino in 1857; it had carried out an intense activity of propaganda on behalf of unification and in support of the policy of Cavour and the kingdom of Sardinia in the years of the Risorgimento.[319] The ambition of the Dante Alighieri was to be a nimble and flexible instrument of Italian foreign policy and, at the same time, to influence its objectives by placing the question of the unredeemed lands and the problem of the Adriatic at the centre of Italy's diplomatic action.

The plan of the association's promoters to give rise to a new irredentism, capable of gathering wider support from Italian public opinion, quickly yielded results. Among the organizers of the Dante Alighieri were members of the most diverse currents and spirits of Italian liberalism; in addition to Nathan, Saffi, and others belonging to the most uncompromising and radical wing of the Liberal Left, many of whom had been followers of Mazzini in the recent past, the leaders of the Dante Alighieri included men linked to the tradition of moderate liberalism, such as Ruggiero Bonghi (first president of the association from 1890 to 1895),[320] Pasquale Villari (Bonghi's successor as president in the period from 1896 to 1903),[321] and Donato Sanminiatelli.[322] Members of parliament and ministers like Maggiorino Ferraris, Alessandro Fortis, Eduardo Pantano, and Luigi Rava joined the Dante Alighieri, as did important state officials like Bonaldo Stringher, who was president of the Bank of Italy and a Friulian very concerned about the fate of Italians

---

317  Bonghi, 'Per la società "Dante Alighieri,"' pp. 602–3.
318  Bonghi, *Discorso pronunciato da Ruggiero Bonghi*, p. 4.
319  Romeo, *Cavour*, vol. 3, pp. 277 et seq.
320  On the figure of Bonghi and his positions on foreign policy: Maturi, 'Bonghi e i problemi di politica estera,' pp. XI–XXXVII; di Ovidio, 'Ruggiero Bonghi,' pp. 5–45; Guerrazzi, *Ricordi d'irredentismo*, pp. 143 et seq.
321  On Villari's activity as president of the Dante Alighieri: Pisa, *Nazione e politica nella Società 'Dante Alighieri,'* pp. 85 et seq.; 'Pasquale Villari e la Dante Alighieri,' pp. 427 et seq.; Villari, *Scritti e discorsi per la 'Dante.'*
322  Bernardy, *Un diplomatico dell'irredentismo*.

in Austria (for many years he performed the function of treasurer of the Dante Alighieri). Thus it was an association of patriots with different and often opposing ideologies on the level of domestic policy but sharing the same aim of the defence of the Italian culture abroad and the strengthening of Italy at the international level.

The growth of the Dante Alighieri and its importance in the history of Italian foreign policy were in any case due to the development of a symbiotic relationship with the international action of the government in Rome. From the 1890s onward Rome began to view the Dante Alighieri as an answer to what remained one of the most serious problems in Italo-Austrian relations, the fate and treatment of the Italians of Austria. A political and financial collaboration between the government in Rome and the Dante Alighieri had already emerged under the premiership of Francesco Crispi. Notwithstanding the Italian renunciation of any open political irredentism and the existence of an alliance between Italy and the Habsburg Empire, Austria-Hungary continued its efforts to weaken the Italian national liberal parties in Trentino and the eastern Adriatic, and the government in Rome quickly realized the potential of the Dante Alighieri as an unofficial instrument to be wielded in a policy of influence and penetration in the unredeemed lands. Crispi himself took the decision to give the Dante Alighieri political and financial support; it was no coincidence that during the summer of 1890 when the Austrian government decided to abolish Pro Patria (accusing it of irredentist and anti-state designs) and publicly attacked the Dante Alighieri (holding it responsible for anti-Habsburg activities),[323] Crispi vigorously defended the work of the association headed by Bonghi, justifying its purpose in a letter to Nigra:

> The 'Dante Alighieri' association has no political aims. Its members belong to the moderate party and should not be confused with those who profess irredentism. In fact they would be the first to take exception to the charge. The 'Dante Alighieri' association exists to cultivate the Italian language in all the regions in which it is spoken and would not dare to do anything that might influence the Government's international policy or be prejudicial to its action abroad. The relations of the 'Dante Alighieri' association with the Government are such and so well known that I consider

---

323  On this: DDI, II, 23, docs. 627, 635, 641; Beust to Kálnoky, 28 July 1890, ber., HHSTA, PA, XI, portfolio 107.

an offence any accusation that might be made of factious tendencies or of acts that in any way or measure could harm the good relations that Italy maintains with its Empire neighbour.[324]

In 1890 the Crispi government started to give secret subsidies to the Dante Alighieri, which soon established regular relations with the national liberal leaders in Trentino and the Adriatic (Giovan Battista Tambosi, Felice Venezian, and Teodoro Mayer) and began to play an important political role as a source of funds for the Italian liberal parties in Austria and for educational institutions in the unredeemed lands. Thanks to the financial support of the Dante Alighieri, the association Lega Nazionale was created to set up private Italian schools in certain regions of mixed population like the Tyrol, Istria, and Dalmatia. From 1893 onward the electoral campaigns of the Italian liberal parties in Austria were fought with secret funding from the Dante Alighieri and therefore from the government in Rome.[325] At the same time the Dante Alighieri formed a network of correspondents and informers within the Habsburg Empire, who provided political and military intelligence.

Naturally the importance of the Dante Alighieri in Italian foreign policy gradually increased, especially after the defeat at Adwa and the reawakening of the Italian public's interest in Adriatic and Balkan questions at the end of the nineteenth century. The revival of an active Italian role in the Balkans made Italo-Austrian antagonism in the region increasingly evident, even if Italy's attitude toward the Habsburg Empire remained highly ambiguous in so far as it was influenced by the hope of a future application of the article on compensation in the treaty of the Triple Alliance.

The problems in Italo-Austrian relations and the aggravation of national tensions within Austria-Hungary, with the reinforcement of pro-Russian tendencies in many Czech, Croatian, Ruthenian, and Serbian national parties and the growth in sympathy for Germany in the Austrian political world, made the action of the Dante Alighieri Association indispensable to the support of the Italians and Italophile parties in the

---

324  Crispi to Nigra, 24 July 1890, DDI, II, 23, doc. 631; see too Crispi, *Questioni internazionali*, pp. 119 et seq.
325  Pisa, *Nazione e politica nella Società 'Dante Alighieri,'* pp. 111 et seq.; Guerrazzi, *Ricordi d'irredentismo*, p. 184.

political struggles against German, Croatian, and Slovenian nationalism and against the competing Catholics and socialists. It also proved
useful in gathering military intelligence for the leaders of the Italian
armed forces, who were concerned about the possibility of a war between Italy and Austria.

# 3 The Italians of Dalmatia Between the Habsburg Empire and Italy from 1896 to 1915

## 3.1. The Italians of Dalmatia, the Autonomist Party, and the Dante Alighieri Association at the End of the Nineteenth Century

As we have seen, the Dalmatian Autonomist Party saw a profound reduction in its political influence in Dalmatia over the course of the 1880s and 1890s. Victim of the shift in the Habsburg Empire's domestic and foreign policy, autonomist liberalism lost control of all the main Dalmatian cities except Zara and became a minority force with respect to pan-Croatian nationalism, which was now dominant at the regional level as well as in political representation at Vienna. The crisis in autonomism resulted in an important change in the nature of this movement. In the face of the emergence and growing strength of nationalism as a political ideology not just in Dalmatia but throughout Austria-Hungary, the municipalist and regionalist values of the Autonomist Party, rooted in local autonomy and the coexistence of different ethnic groups, began to seem inadequate and outdated, no longer answering to the needs of the majority of the Dalmatian peoples. The rise of Croatian nationalism and the determination of this movement to obliterate the specific cultural, linguistic, and administrative identities of the Dalmatians in the name of a common pan-Croatian ideal obliged the Autonomist Party to place the question of the defence of the Italian language and culture in Dalmatia at the centre of its political struggle. This was a decisive element in the emergence of a new Italian national liberal ideology within Dalmatian autonomism. From the 1880s onward, the followers of the Autonomist Party included not just Dalmatian, Italian, and Slav liberal municipalists but also people who now defined themselves politically as 'Italians of Dalmatia.' This Italian national liberal ideology gained

such widespread support in Lapenna's old movement that the autonomist militants and political leaders themselves began to call their party
'Italian Autonomist.'

Once again it must be stressed that not all Italian Dalmatians reacted
in the same way to the 'Croatization' of Dalmatian society. A section of
the Dalmatians of Italian language, culture, and origin preferred to accept and undergo denationalization. The motivations and reasons for
this were varied. Yugoslav and/or pan-Croatian national ideals had
gradually won support among some members of those urban classes
who were Italian in language and culture; the affirmation of such ideals was viewed by those Dalmatians, like Bulat, Monti, Morpurgo, and
Machiedo, as a way of unifying Dalmatian society, which for centuries
had been divided between Italian or Italian-speaking urban classes and
Serbian and Croatian rural populations. They regarded the Croatization of Dalmatia as a legitimate and inevitable phenomenon that, when
all was said and done, could coexist with the survival of the Italian
language in social life – a language, however, demoted to the rank of a
dialect and in a position of inferiority with respect to Croatian.

There was also a more concrete reason that induced many Italian
Dalmatians to accept the process of assimilation: the desire to avoid
discrimination on the social and political plane as members of a national minority. In a poor and patronage-ridden society like Habsburg
Dalmatia, work and career motivations led many Italians to declare
themselves Croatian in censuses and to vote for the dominant Croatian
parties. The humbler the social class and the lower the degree of economic independence, the stronger was the pressure for assimilation.[1]
As Graziadio Ascoli observed in 1895, 'by now the man of the people,
who is numbered among the Italians in Dalmatia, is unwilling to dare
the anger of the Serbo-Croatians, reluctant to profess himself for what
he is, and where he is capable of uttering a few words in Slav, allows the
census official to put him down as a Croatian.'[2]

This phenomenon of the Croatization of part of the Italian minority explains the progressive fall in the number of Italian Dalmatians
recorded in Austrian censuses over the course of the second half of the

---

1 On this: Monzali, 'La Dalmazia e la questione jugoslava negli scritti di Roberto Ghiglianovich durante la prima guerra mondiale,' pp. 429–41; Dudan, 'La Dalmazia di
  oggi,' in *La Dalmazia*, pp. 65–124.
2 Ascoli, 'Gli irredenti,' pp. 53–54. On Ascoli: Salimbeni, 'Graziadio Isaia Ascoli tra
  cultura e politica.'

nineteenth century and the early twentieth century. In the first Austrian unofficial statistical studies carried out in the 1860s and 1870s, the number of Italian Dalmatians varied between 40 000 and 50 000; in the official census of 1880, their number had fallen to 27 305; and in the following decades it declined drastically: 16 000 in 1890, 15 279 in 1900, and 18 028 in 1910 (out of a total Dalmatian population of 593 784 in 1900 and 645 646 in 1910).[3]

Alongside the Italians who fought for the defence of their own national and linguistic identity within the Italian Autonomous Party and those who chose to accept progressive Croatization, there were also groups of Italian Dalmatians who wanted to maintain a specific cultural and national identity but rejected the nationalistic conflict between pan-Croatian parties and Italian autonomous liberalism. They set up the first socialist associations in Dalmatia. It was certainly no accident that the early socialist trade union and political formations sprang from sections of the Autonomist Left, made up of a number of intellectuals and the Italian and Italian-speaking seafaring and working classes of Zara and Spalato.[4] Placing economic questions rather than national and religious divisions at the centre of social life, Marxist and internationalist socialism seemed to offer a possible solution and alternative to nationalistic strife. Over the course of the 1890s these Dalmatian socialist groups developed a well-defined organizational structure and were among the founders of the Adriatic Italian section of the Socialist Worker's Party in Austria, which held its first congress at Trieste in 1897.[5] Of note among the outstanding figures in this emerging Italo-Slav socialism, which supported the idea of a multi-ethnic Dalmatia, were Angelo Nani from Zara, Giacomo Lazzari from Spalato (a member of the political secretariat of the Socialist Party for the coast and Dalmatia), and above all, Luca Poduje Gicovich, who was the life and soul of socialism in Spalato and a candidate at the elections to the parliament in Vienna in 1901.[6] However, the Italo-Slav socialist movement was un-

---

3  De Castro, 'Cenno storico sul rapporto etnico tra italiani e slavi nella Dalmazia,' pp. 261–304.
4  Foretić, 'Socijalistički radnički pokret u Dalmaciji posljednjih godina XIX stoljeća,' pp. 5–34.
5  Maserati, *Il movimento operaio a Trieste,* pp. 135–45.
6  On the figure of Luca Poduje Gicovich, an Italo-Slav Dalmatian who emigrated to Italy after World War I: Poduje Gicovich, *Lettere politiche di un dalmata;* Russo, *La Dalmazia e il suo destino,* p. 215.

able to gain a political foothold in Dalmatia; the hostility of the government authorities and the Croatian parties and the flare-up of national
strife blocked its spread. The movement was given its *coup de grâce* by
a decision of the Socialist Party in Trieste to renounce representation of
the Dalmatian socialists in favour of a union with the Croatian Socialist
Party, which was ideologically opposed to the idea of a multi-ethnic
Italo-Slav Dalmatia; this occurred in spite of the opposition of many of
the Dalmatian socialists, led by Poduje, who would have preferred to
join the Socialist Party of the Adriatic coast owing to the close relations
between Dalmatia and Trieste and the internationalism of their com-
rades in that city.[7]

The definitive ideological and political shift of Dalmatian autonomism toward Italian nationalism coincided with the emergence of a
new generation of political leaders. After the death of Bajamonti and
Lapenna in 1891, the only surviving member of the old guard was Trigari, the mayor of Zara, who remained politically active until 1900. At
the end of the nineteenth century new and younger men took over the
reins of the party, men who were often inspired by a faith in Italian
nationalism that had been lacking in previous generations: Roberto
Ghiglianovich, Luigi Ziliotto, and Natale Krekich in Zara; Luigi Pini in
Sebenico; and Ercolano Salvi and Leonardo Pezzoli in Spalato.

The representatives from Zara assumed an undisputed role of leadership in the Autonomist Party after Bajamonti's death. Control of the
city's municipal administration gave the local autonomists a political
clout that the autonomists of Sebenico and Spalato had lost. From the
end of the 1890s and the time of the crisis in the coalition between Serbs
and autonomists in Ragusa and Cattaro (with the ousting of the latter
from the administration of the southern Dalmatian cities), Zara became
the autonomist and Italian stronghold in a Dalmatia now dominated by
Croatian and Serbian parties.

With a population of less than twenty thousand (19 463 according
to the census of 1910), Zara was, like all the coastal cities of Dalmatia,
home to many different peoples and nationalities. The suburbs were
inhabited chiefly by Serbs, Croats, and Albanians (the latter at Borgo
Erizzo), while the Italian and Italian-speaking element was dominant
in the city proper. Zara was unique in being the only city in Dalmatia

---

7 On this: 'Le parole di un socialista,' *Il Dalmata*, 17 March 1906.

where the Italian element was numerically superior to that of the Serbs and Croats; according to the censuses of the Habsburg period, in 1880, there were 6688 Italians and 4459 Slavs (Croats and Serbs) living in Zara; thirty years later, in 1910, the number of Italians in Zara had risen to 11 469, while there were still only 5705 Croats and Serbs.[8]

The fact that Zara was Dalmatia's capital facilitated the emergence of a strong middle class, Italian in culture and language or bilingual, that formed the backbone of the autonomist ruling class. The Autonomist Party was able to retain control of the municipality of Zara because it embodied the municipalist and particularist spirit of the city's inhabitants, who saw pan-Croatian nationalism as a threat to their identity and an attempt by the populations of the interior to dominate the city dwellers. For the autonomists of Zara, defence of the values of the municipal tradition came to coincide with the battle for the survival of the Italian spirit and a Venetian tongue whose roots in the city stretched back many centuries. The loyalist and conservative policy followed by the mayor, Trigari, who was careful not to identify with the Italian national liberal parties of the Trentino and Venezia Giulia and was remote from the political style of Bajamonti, had allowed the Autonomist Party to maintain good relations with the Austrian authorities, who refrained from open intervention in favour of the Croatian parties in the municipal elections held in the 1880s and 1890s. Another element that helps to explain the political dominance of the Autonomist Party in Zara until World War I is the accent that the autonomist municipal government placed on the city's economic development and on improvement of the living conditions of its population – policies that permitted the Italian Autonomous Party to find support not just among the Italian element but also in sections of the Slav and Albanian population.[9]

The dominant figures in the political life of the Italian Dalmatians between the end of the nineteenth century and First World War I were

---

8  De Castro, 'Cenno storico,' p. 302.

9  On the administrative and municipal policy of the autonomists in Zara between the second half of the nineteenth century and World War I: De' Benvenuti, *Storia di Zara dal 1797 al 1918*; Tacconi, 'Trigari'; Krekich, 'L'opera amministrativa e politica di Luigi Ziliotto,' pp. 43–106. For a description of Zara between the end of the nineteenth century and the beginning of the twentieth century: De' Benvenuti, *Storia di Zara dal 1797 al 1918*; Modrich, *La Dalmazia romana-veneta-moderna*, pp. 22 et seq.; Maserati, 'Simboli e riti nell'irredentismo dalmata,' pp. 63–78; 'Attività nazionali della comunità di Borgo Erizzo'; Battara, *Zara*; Sabalich, *Guida archeologica di Zara*; Coen, *Zara che fu*.

undoubtedly Luigi Ziliotto, Roberto Ghiglianovich, Natale Krekich, and Ercolano Salvi.

Luigi Ziliotto,[10] born in Zara on 8 February 1863, was the son of a state employee, and after attending high school in Spalato, he completed his studies at university in Graz. Subsequently he entered the legal profession and became involved in politics as a militant autonomist. In 1892 he was elected to the municipality of Zara, becoming a councillor in the city administration in 1894, and winning a seat in the Dalmatian provincial diet in 1895.

A similar political career was followed by Roberto Ghiglianovich,[11] who belonged to a family that had played a role in the history of autonomism in Zara; his father, Giacomo, a lawyer, had been elected to the Dalmatian provincial diet and was one of the most important members of the Autonomist Party. Ghiglianovich studied at the universities of Vienna and Graz before returning to Zara and devoting himself first to a legal career and then to politics, as an activist in the Autonomist Party.

Natale (Nade) Krekich, however, was a native of Scardona (Škradin), in the vicinity of Sebenico; after completing his studies at university, he too became a lawyer in Zara and embarked on a career in politics, first as a municipal councillor and then as a member of the diet.[12]

Ercolano Salvi was the man whom Antonio Bajamonti had chosen as his successor to the leadership of the autonomists in Spalato; also a lawyer, he had attracted attention during the course of the fierce political struggles that had taken place in the city.[13] From the death of Bajamonti

---

10 A great deal on Luigi Ziliotto in: Krekich, *L'opera amministrativa e politica di Luigi Ziliotto*, pp. 43 et seq.

11 On the life and figure of Roberto Ghiglianovich: Monzali, 'Un contributo alla storia degli italiani di Dalmazia,' pp. 192–217; 'La Dalmazia e la questione jugoslava negli scritti di Roberto Ghiglianovich'; Randi, 'Il senatore Roberto Ghiglianovich,' pp. 3–27; 'L'opera politica del Sen. Roberto Ghiglianovich'; 'Il Sen. Roberto Ghiglianovich. Mezzo secolo di storia dalmata.' Also useful are the memoirs that Ghiglianovich wrote over the course of World War I: BS, Carte Ghiglianovich, portfolio A, *Memorie autobiografiche*.

12 For information about Krekich: Ildebrando Tacconi, 'Natale Krekich,' in *Istria e Dalmazia*, vol. 2, pp. 475–6.

13 On Ercolano Salvi there are the commemorative and often eulogistic writings of some of his friends and colleagues: Krekich, 'L'opera di Ercolano Salvi nella Dieta di Dalmazia,' pp. 27 et seq.; Ildebrando Tacconi, *Per la Dalmazia con amore e con angoscia*, pp. 274–80; Randi, 'Dalla guerra a Rapallo,' pp. 18 et seq. See too Delich, *L'irredentismo italiano in Dalmazia*, pp. 21 et seq.; D'Alia, *La Dalmazia nella storia*, p. 81; Ziliotto,

to 1920, Salvi was the undisputed leader of the movement in Spalato, representing the city's autonomists at the Dalmatian provincial diet from 1891 onward. A passionate and effective orator – as his speeches in the diet show – and a notable capable of winning a degree of support in the old centre of Spalato inhabited by Italians and bilingual Slavs and in its suburbs, he led the Autonomist Party in a city that remained Italo-Slav and bilingual up until the years of World War I, notwithstanding the considerable expansion of its population as a result of an influx of people from the interior who were attracted by the growth of commerce in Spalato.

Ziliotto, Krekich, and Ghiglianovich formed a well-knit group that progressively gained influence within the Autonomist Party. Particularly important on this level was the election of Ziliotto and Ghiglianovich as municipal councillors in 1892 and as members of the Dalmatian provincial diet in 1895. Ziliotto and Ghiglianovich confirmed their political dominance of the Italian Autonomist Party of Zara at the end of 1899: Ghiglianovich engineered the ousting of Trigari from the post of mayor and had him replaced by Luigi Ziliotto.[14]

Trigari's replacement at the head of the Zara council marked the advent of a new leadership in the Italian Autonomous Party of that city. As Zara was now the only large urban centre in Dalmatia run by the autonomists, this guaranteed Ghiglianovich, Ziliotto, and Krekich a clear supremacy within the movement as a whole. Ercolano Salvi and the autonomist leaders of the other cities (Stefano Smerchinich in Curzola, Gian Antonio Botteri in Cittavecchia, Emanuele Fenzi and Luigi Pini in Sebenico, and Giovanni Avoscani in Ragusa) accepted this leadership and in essence went along with the political directives of the autonomists in Zara. The relations between Ghiglianovich, Ziliotto, and Krekich were characterized by a close harmony of ideas, strengthened by a sincere friendship, making the three of them a very strong power block within the Autonomist Party. They were shrewd and experienced politicians, driven by patriotic ideals and free of ulterior motives. Well educated, they were able to speak three or four foreign languages and

---

'Di Ercolano Salvi e del trattato di Rapallo,' pp. 21–33. On Salvi's political action in the 1880s much information can be found in Spalato's autonomist newspaper *La Difesa*: for example *La Difesa*, 25 April 1884.

14 A description of the events that led to the appointment of Ziliotto can be found in Monzali, '*Un contributo*'; Ghiglianovich, *Memorie autobiografiche*. See too De' Benvenuti, *Storia di Zara dal 1797 al 1918*, pp. 131 et seq.

The leaders of the Autonomist Party at the turn of the century. *From left, standing:* Stefano Smerchinich (Curzola), Luigi Ziliotto (Zara), Giovanni Lubin (Traù), Roberto Ghiglianovich (Zara). *Seated:* Count Marino Bonda (Ragusa), Nicolò Trigari (Zara), Ercolano Salvi (Spalato)

were accustomed to operating in a difficult and hostile political system like that of Habsburg Dalmatia at the beginning of the twentieth century. Ziliotto seems to have had the most forceful personality, the best political mind in the group, and an extensive knowledge not just of politics but also of literature and law. Ghiglianovich's capacities, were often limited by serious health problems, chiefly of a mental nature, so that he suffered from depression for many decades and was inclined to prefer a more reserved and less feverish activity than did Ziliotto; Ghiglianovich concentrated on the task of maintaining contact with the Italian national liberal parties in Austria and the political circles on the Italian peninsula. Krekich was always Ziliotto and Ghiglianovich's loyal second-in-command, an unobtrusive figure who let others monopolize the limelight but who played an important role as an able and prudent councillor with a deep understanding of local economic and administrative problems.

On the ideological and political plane, with the ascent of Ghiglian-ovich and Ziliotto, the Autonomist Party became a movement of Italian national liberal inspiration, similar to the liberal parties in Istria and Trieste. The concept of the Italian spirit took on the value of a specific political identity, with a consequent growth of interest in Rome and Trieste. This Italian national ideology also fostered the idea of politi-cal solidarity between Italian autonomists and the kingdom of Italy, which did not signify, at the end of the nineteenth century, proposing the annexation of Dalmatia to Italy but, rather, seeking in this solidarity a means of cultural and linguistic survival for an Italian minority that was being subjected to a process of forced assimilation; it was not, in short, political irredentism but cultural and national irredentism.

An important enunciation of the political platform of the new leaders of the Italian Autonomous Party came with the speech that Luigi Zili-otto made to the Dalmatian provincial diet on 3 February 1896. Ziliotto harshly condemned the boycott of Italian schools by the Croatian major-ity in the diet, who were motivated by the desire to erase all trace of the existence of an Italian minority in Dalmatia. This policy had in reality resulted in a more marked 'sense of being Italian' among many Italian Dalmatians. In the face of Croatian hostility some autonomist politi-cians, desperate to save the Italian language, were ready to settle for 'a wan Italian spirit.' 'I will tell you frankly, gentlemen,' declared Ziliotto, 'that I am not one of them. I demand to be able to state openly and with my head held high, I am Italian, without it being said that I am infring-ing anyone's rights by doing so. I insist in being allowed to develop the sense of my nationality to the highest degree.'[15] The development of the idea of nationality was, for Ziliotto, an indispensable moral and social requirement that gave an identity to the individual and made him part of a community. However, declaring oneself Italian in Dalmatia did not mean embracing a plan of political union with Italy; between declaring oneself Italian and 'leaning politically toward Italy there's a big dif-ference. The consciousness of our nationality is an absolute necessity for us, but suspecting us of irredentism is, in my view, tantamount to saying that we lack common sense. Separated from Italy by the whole of the Adriatic, we few scattered thousands, without any continuity of territory, amidst a population of not hundreds of thousands but several

---

15 Speech by Luigi Ziliotto, ADP-BI, 1896, pp. 479–82. On this speech by Ziliotto see the references in Salvemini and Maranelli, 'La questione dell'Adriatico,' pp. 364–5.

million Slavs, how could we think of a union with Italy?'[16] The destiny
of the Italians of Dalmatia – declared Ziliotto in 1896 – was with the
Slavs; the Autonomist Party was ready to collaborate on the realization of the ideals of the Slav nationalities of the South 'so long as our
national rights are explicitly recognized and respected.'[17]

Ziliotto subsequently commented on his speech in a letter sent to
Donato Sanminiatelli, one of the leading figures in the Dante Alighieri
Association, who had referred to it in one of his essays. The Dalmatian
politician thanked Sanminiatelli for having cited the speech and gave
sincere expression to his thoughts about the difficult situation of the
Italians of Dalmatia:

> Yet I would not like to pass for being more Austrian than I am. Unfortu-
> nately, so long as cold reflection predominates, we think as I put it in the
> speech you mentioned, but the heart cannot close itself to the hope that the
> Adriatic might once again become wholly Italian. Whatever the sceptical
> and the broken spirited may think, we have deep faith in the high destiny
> of our race. In any case, whether fortune holds in store what we most
> desire or it be our mission to serve as a link with the Slav world, in order
> to go on living we need to love intensely; and you can understand how
> beneficial to this love is the affection of our brothers in the Kingdom.[18]

This letter reveals the coexistence of contrasting sentiments and values
in some leaders of the Italian Autonomous Party. On the one hand, they
felt ever closer to Italy and hoped for a possible future political union
with the mother country. On the other hand, political realism and a cool
assessment of the nature of Dalmatian society prompted acceptance of
the *status quo* and collaboration with the Habsburg authorities. All this
confirms the uncertainty and ambiguity that characterized the political
action of the Italian Dalmatians at the end of the nineteenth century.
The sense of nationalism and the attraction to Italy grew, intensified by
the difficult cultural and political conditions in which the Italian minority found itself, but at the same time the autonomist leadership was
aware of the danger inherent in any design of political irredentism. The
only possible strategy was the defence of Italian national rights in the
legal sphere, accepting the reality of Habsburg rule and attempting to

16  Speech by Luigi Ziliotto, ADP-BI, 1896, pp. 479–82.
17  Ibid.
18  Ziliotto to Sanminiatelli, 12 June 1897, DA, file 1897, B. 51.

reduce the hostility of the Croatian parties by seeking forms of co-operation with them. Italy could play a fundamental role in this strategy by providing economic and political support to the struggles of the Italian Autonomous Party in defence of the rights of Italian Dalmatians.

The uncertainty also stemmed from the ideological diversity that survived in the Autonomist Party. If Ziliotto felt himself to be Italian above all, other members of the party kept alive the old multi-ethnic and Austrophile regionalist tradition. In a letter to Sanminiatelli in June 1897, Emanuele Fenzi, a notable of Sebenico, declared himself in favour of the maintenance of Habsburg rule and contrary to the hypothesis of an annexation of Dalmatia to Italy, since 'the economic and political conditions of Italy would promise a more unhappy future than our present conditions.'[19] Emanuele Vidovich, long an autonomist member of the provincial diet, felt himself to be primarily Dalmatian and laid claim to being one of those who 'whether Italian or Slav, still preserve intact the Dalmatian sentiment,' specifying that the struggle of the autonomists was merely aimed at ensuring the respect of the Austrian Constitution in Dalmatia.[20]

There was still, in short, an ideological and political ambivalence within the Dalmatian Italian Autonomous Party, in which the old regionalist autonomist tradition and the new Italian national liberal ideology coexisted; this ambivalence would last until the years of World War I.

Between the middle of the 1890s and 1914 Ghiglianovich and Ziliotto sought to maintain good and cordial relations with the Austrian state authorities, espousing officially the most unbending loyalty to the Habsburgs and the rejection of any irredentist dream. In Dalmatia the government exercised a decisive influence on local politics, being capable of determining the outcome of any electoral contest by its attitude. Therefore, if the Italians of Dalmatia wanted to retain control of the municipal council of Zara, they had to avoid alienating the Habsburg authorities, who were in a position to tilt the balance of the vote. Good relations with Vienna were also fundamental to the aim of heading off any political or administrative reform that went against the interests of the Dalmatian Italians. The leaders of the Italian Autonomist Party, for example, strove for a long time to persuade the Austrian government to

---

19 Fenzi to Sanminiatelli, 13 June 1897, DA, file 1897, B 53.
20 Vidovich to Sanminiatelli, 16 June 1897, DA, file 1897, B 44.

prevent the substitution of Italian by Croatian as the official language of public administration in Dalmatia, encountering a readiness on the part of the imperial institutions to find a compromise solution that would preserve the role of the Italian language in Dalmatian society. Ziliotto and Ghiglianovich's professed loyalty to the Habsburgs reinforced the strategy of dialogue with Vienna and reflected the conviction of many Italian Dalmatians that Austrian rule was a far lesser evil than the prospect of uncontested domination by Croats or Serbs.

For its part, at the beginning of the twentieth century the government in Vienna began to abandon the policy of open support for Croatian nationalism and assumed an attitude of cautious benevolence toward the Italians of Zara. It did not favour, for example, the attempts of the Croatian parties to win control of the municipal administration of the Dalmatian capital and repeatedly gave legal recognition to the Italian minority's right to have its own schools. This shift can be explained by the increasingly anti-German and pro-Serbian tone of the programs of the more radical segments of Croatian nationalism in Dalmatia; led by Ante Trumbić and Josip Smodlaka, these segments were determined to re-create a coalition between Serbs and Croats on the basis of a highly ambiguous political platform that combined the intransigent assertion of Croatian national rights with the extolling of a Yugoslav identity. Croatian nationalism was beginning to be no longer a docile instrument of Austrian policy, and Austria started to see an interest in containing the expansion of the Slavs in the south and to turn the opposing national antagonisms in Dalmatia to its own advantage, this time by giving up an excessive favouritism toward the Croatian parties.[21]

Another political objective pursued by Ghiglianovich and Ziliotto was the strengthening of relations with the Italian liberal parties of Austria and with Italy. Above all, through the organization and the diffusion of the Lega Nazionale in Dalmatia a strong and lasting political tie was forged between the Dalmatian autonomists and the National Liberal Party of Trieste and Istria. As we have seen, the need to preserve schooling in the Italian language had persuaded various members of the Autonomist Party to collaborate in the spread of Pro Patria in Dal-

---

21 On Habsburg policy in Dalmatia between the end of the nineteenth century and the beginning of the twentieth: *Statthalterei Präsidium an Minister des Innern Graf Bylandt-Rheidt*, 3 January 1905, OUS, 3, doc. 6; Schödl, *Kroatische Nationalpolitik und 'Jugoslavenstvo'*; Ganza Aras, 'Dalmacija u Austro-ugarskoj i unutrašnjoj politici početkom XX stoljeca,' pp. 309–42.

matia too. Disbanded by the Austrian government in 1890, Pro Patria was essentially reformed the next year under the name of the Lega Nazionale (National League). The Lega established a presence in Dalmatia in 1892 when Ghiglianovich and Ziliotto founded a branch in Zara.[22] The strong need to organize forms of private teaching of the Italian language throughout Dalmatia facilitated the diffusion of groups of the Lega Nazionale all over the region. In 1895 a report by the head office of the Lega on the activity of the association testified to the existence of Lega Nazionale groups in all the principal Dalmatian localities (Zara, Spalato, Sebenico, Cittavecchia, Lesina, Scardona, Arbe, Cattaro, Imoschi [Imotski], Curzola, and Dernis),[23] most of them organized and led by members of the Italian Autonomous Party.

In any case, the scarcity of the financial resources available to set up teaching facilities made a strengthening of the relations with the leaders of the National Liberal Party in Trieste and with the Italian government indispensable. In the first half of the 1890s a permanent and stable alliance was forged with the National Liberal Party of Trieste. Felice Venezian, able and intelligent leader of the Italian Liberals in Trieste and Istria, favourably received the requests from Dalmatia for assistance. Although convinced that Italy ended ideally and geographically at the Julian Alps and the gulf of the Quarnero, Venezian considered it the moral duty of the people of Trieste and the government in Rome to help 'those unhappy Dalmatians, abandoned by all (including ourselves, unfortunately) and who are working real miracles by themselves,' with the aim of preserving in Dalmatia 'an Italian minority, representing wealth and intelligence.'[24] The survival of this minority could help to strengthen Italy's political influence in the Adriatic and the Balkans. In November 1898 Venezian reminded his friend Nathan that Italy had to be prepared, in view of Francis Joseph's age, 'for the eventuality of a confused Austrian succession'; it needed to arm itself at its borders and

22  On this: 'Il congresso del gruppo di Zara della "Lega Nazionale,"' *Il Dalmata*, 11 January 1905.
23  *Rendiconto della Direzione generale Lega Nazionale*, gestione 1895 (Trent: Zippel, 1896), enclosed with Venezian to Galanti, 1 July 1896, DA, file 1896, B. 11. On the expansion of the Lega Nazionale in Dalmatia see too Ranzi to Villari, 11 September 1900, in *Dai carteggi di Pasquale Villari*, pp. 21–2.
24  On the figure of Venezian: Chersi, 'Felice Venezian alla difesa delle libertà municipali di Trieste 1882–1907,' pp. 332–7. On Felice Venezian's view of the Dalmatian question: Levi, *Ricordi della vita e dei tempi di Ernesto Nathan*, pp. 150 et seq.

rely on the understanding with Montenegro, which would be helpful in extending Italian influence over Albania and southern Dalmatia on the basis of a strategy of alliance with the southern, central, and northern Slavs that could guarantee Italy its natural borders and a strong economic and political influence in the Adriatic and Europe.[25] In such a possible strategy, which did not envisage the annexation of part or all of Dalmatia to Italy should the Habsburg Empire break up, the existence of Italian or pro-Italian political forces in the Adriatic territories could be extremely useful, according to Venezian, to Italy's foreign policy in the region and in the Balkans.

Ghiglianovich and Ziliotto, moreover, took Venezian's party as a model of political organization. Following the example of Venezia Giulia, the autonomists of Zara created sections of the Lega Nazionale in Dalmatia with the aim of opposing the educational policy of the Croatian nationalists, and they devised a unified party organization throughout the Dalmatian region by founding the Società Politica Dalmata (Dalmatian Political Association) in 1898. The leaders of the association included representatives of the various local groupings, even though the element from Zara, headed by Ziliotto and Ghiglianovich, was clearly predominant. The program of the Dalmatian Political Association reflected the coexistence of the Italo-Slav autonomist tradition and the new Italian ideology; the association's purpose was to 'foster the moral, economic, and political progress of Dalmatia, and especially to facilitate the civil coexistence of the two races of which it is composed, the Italian and the Slav, promoting the respect of their relative rights and obligations.' However, its prime objective was the 'restoration of the status that is due to the Italian nationality, civilization, and culture in Dalmatia.'[26]

The leaders of the Autonomist Party emphasized their aim of making themselves the representatives of both the races living in Dalmatia. However, by asserting that there was an 'Italian nationality' in Dalmatia, they showed that they wanted to follow the last teachings of Bajamonti and to abandon Tommaseo's old ideals concerning the existence of a 'Dalmatian nationality.'

---

25  Venezian to Nathan, 24 November 1898, DA, file 1898, B 34.
26  *Statuto della Società politica dalmata* (Zadar: Artale, 1898). For a different interpretation of the program of the Società Politica Dalmata: Vrandečić, *Dalmatinski autonomistički pokret u XIX stoljeću*, p. 277.

This strengthening of a national Italian consciousness among the leaders of the Dalmatian autonomists emerged simultaneously with the growth of Italy's interest in the fate of the Italian minority in Dalmatia, and during the 1890s out of this came a political collaboration between the Dalmatian Italian Autonomous Party and the government in Rome, whose hub and go-between was the Dante Alighieri Association.

In its early years the Dante Alighieri had avoided intervening directly in Dalmatia, leaving any support for the Dalmatian Autonomist Party to circles in Trieste.[27] The first direct political contact between members of the Dante Alighieri and of the Dalmatian Italian Autonomist Party took place in 1896 and was a meeting between interlocutors in search of one another. If the Dalmatian autonomists were seeking financial and political aid from Italy, the men of the Dante Alighieri saw Dalmatia as a real bridge to the world of the Balkans and Danubian Europe, an important region on the strategic and commercial plane where it was crucial for Italy to ensure the survival of friendly and pro-Italian forces.

Roberto Ghiglianovich, entering into direct contact with the Dante Alighieri at the end of 1896 and during 1897, presented the leaders of the association and, through them, the government in Rome with a series of requests for financial and political aid. According to Ghiglianovich, the government in Rome had to take an interest in the fate of the Italians in Dalmatia, financially supporting their political and cultural activities and taking diplomatic steps in Vienna, capital of an allied state, to protest 'against the ferocious witch hunt that is being carried out here against our element.'[28] In a letter to Nathan in August 1897, Ghiglianovich asked for money to maintain or open schools in Dalmatia, to set up a historical and literary magazine with the aim of demonstrating the existence of an Italian culture in Dalmatia (the *Rivista dalmatica* would be founded in 1899), and above all to reorganize the Autonomist Party, which had been financially depleted by the continual elections: the municipal elections of Zara in 1896 had been won with great expenditure, especially for the third constituency where the large

---

27  Some references to this role played by Venezian and his links with Ghiglianovich and the Italian Dalmatians in Levi, *Ricordi della vita e dei tempi di Ernesto Nathan*, p. 173–5. Also useful is Volpe, *Italia Moderna*, vol. 3, pp. 156 et seq.

28  Ghiglianovich to Sanminiatelli, 13 June 1897, DA, file 1897, B 14. For an analysis of the difficult situation of the Italian Autonomist Party in Dalmatia: Giacchi to the Foreign Minister, 7 March 1897, ASMAE, SP 1891–1916, portfolio 88.

majority of the electorate was made up of Croats and Serbs, 'since to get these Slavs to vote with us we have to pay them well.'[29]

Between 1897 and 1899 Ghiglianovich repeatedly asked the Dante Alighieri to persuade the government in Rome to intercede with the ruler of Montenegro so that in turn the latter would exert pressure on the Serbian party in Dalmatia to maintain a policy of collaboration with the Italian autonomists; thanks to the alliance between the two parties, Serbs and autonomists had gained control of the municipality of Ragusa, strengthening Italian influence in southern Dalmatia. Ghiglianovich observed: 'The fact that, as a result of this compromise, the Croatians cannot throw their weight about in that overwhelmingly Slav city, and vice versa, that we, who constitute a small minority there, have some say in the municipal administration ... is of extraordinary importance for our party.'[30]

The attitude of the directors of the Dante Alighieri toward the Dalmatian question and the requests for aid from the Italian Autonomous Party is clearly outlined in a memorandum that Sanminiatelli drew up over the course of 1897 after paying a visit to the Dalmatian coast and establishing the first contacts with autonomist political circles. In his memorandum he declared that the strength of the Croatian party had been growing since 1866 and had become preponderant. There were various reasons for the dominance of the Slavs in Dalmatian territory: 'in the first place the predominant number of them, since Dalmatia (it is worth recalling, to avoid possible misunderstandings) is at bottom a Slav land, unlike the Coast (Gorizia, Trieste, and Istria) which is truly an Italian land';[31] to this was added the political role of the clergy and the support of the Austrian government.

Sanminiatelli had gone to Zara and made contact with members of the Autonomist Party who asked for 'some assistance from Italy.' In his view, the Autonomist Party was still energetic and well organized in

---

29  Ghiglianovich to Nathan, 11 August 1897, DA, file 1897, B 15.
30  Ghiglianovich to Nathan, 26 November 1898, DA, file 1898, B 17; see too Ghiglianovich to Sanminiatelli, 1 March 1899, DA, file 1899, B 21.
31  Sanminiatelli, 'Promemoria sulle cose di Dalmazia,' n.d. (but written between the end of 1896 and the beginning of 1897), DA, file 1897, B 36. This memorandum formed the basis for an essay entitled 'Notarelle dalmate' that Sanminiatelli published in the *Nuova Antologia* in 1897. On his interest in Dalmatia see too Sanminiatelli, *In giro sui confini d'Italia*. On the figure of Sanminiatelli: Bernardy, *Un diplomatico dell'irredentismo, Donato Sanminiatelli*.

Dalmatia, and it was in Italy's interest to give it prudent support in order to guarantee Italian moral and commercial influence in the Balkans and the eastern Adriatic. Among the possible forms of this support, Sanminiatelli indicated intercessions with Nicholas of Montenegro to favour local alliances between Dalmatian autonomists and Serbs, and assistance for instruction in the Italian language, which had been boycotted by the provincial government; also urgent were financial aid to the autonomists for elections and the press, an increase in the number of direct sailings between Italy and Dalmatia, and the expansion of the Italian consular service.[32]

An important role in the decision to support the Italian Autonomous Party of Dalmatia was played by Pasquale Villari, president of the Dante Alighieri Association after Bonghi's death (1895). Villari took the cause of the Italian Dalmatians to heart, and over the course of his presidency, which lasted until 1903, Dalmatia became one of the regions on which the Italian patriotic association focused most attention. On more than one occasion at the congresses of the Dante Alighieri Villari pointed out the difficult situation of the Italian minority in Dalmatia and the need to help it. 'In Dalmatia,' declared Villari in 1901, 'the Italians constitute a weak minority, split into small and scattered groups in the midst of an ocean of Slavs, who are advancing, threatening to throw them into the sea. They defend themselves with a truly desperate heroism, but are continually losing ground. And if they do not receive aid, they will lose more and more.'[33]

At the urging of Villari and Nathan, whose Pesaro origin made him very sensitive to the problems of the Adriatic, the Dante Alighieri (which was funded chiefly by the Italian government and the royal family[34]) decided to meet the requests of the Dalmatian autonomists. The Dante Alighieri's funding to the Italian party in Dalmatia started to become continuous and abundant from 1898 onward and lasted up

---

32  Sanminiatelli, 'Memorandum.'

33  Villari, *Scritti e discorsi per la 'Dante,'* p. 165; see too pp. 90–1, 189–91, 198–207.

34  In this connection: Sanminiatelli to Villari, B 32; Villari to Sanminiatelli, 14 February 1897, B 45; Villari to Sanminiatelli, 10 May 1897, B 46, DA, file 1897. On government funding of the Dante Alighieri's aid to the Italian liberal parties in Austria: Giolitti, *Memoirs of My Life*; Rudinì, note, 6 February 1897, IVSLA, Carte Luzzatti, portfolio 39; in this note Rudinì stated that he had paid 60 000 lire to the Dante Alighieri – 20 000 drawn from the secret funds of the Ministry of the Interior, 20 000 from the secret funds of the Foreign Ministry, 5000 from the Finance Ministry and 15 000 from the Ministry of the Treasury. See too Rudinì to Luzzatti, 29 January 1897.

until Italy's intervention in World War I. This money was used for the creation and maintenance of Italian schools in Dalmatia, for the political and electoral activities of the Autonomist Party, and for the publication of newspapers and magazines in the Italian language. More specifically, the money from the Dante Alighieri and the government in Rome went into subsidizing schools in Zara and the boarding school for high-school students from outside that city, and founding Italian schools in Sebenico and Spalato.[35]

The results of this collaboration were undoubtedly positive for the Italian Dalmatians. Within a few years the conditions of cultural and national life of the Italian and Italophile minority in Dalmatia improved notably, with the opening of private schools in the Italian language at Sebenico and Spalato and an increase in the number of those already in existence at Zara. Thanks to the aid from Italy and Trieste the Italian Autonomous Party was able to withstand the serious difficulties produced by the rupture of the alliance with the Serbs, remaining a protagonist in the political life of Habsburg Dalmatia up until World War I.

The strengthening of the Autonomist Party, the improvement of the living conditions of the Italians in Dalmatia thanks to the opening of the private schools of the Lega Nazionale, and the political support of the Dante Alighieri for the Italians of Austria were facts noted by the Croatian nationalist parties. At meetings of the Dalmatian provincial diet in 1901 and 1902 numerous Croatian representatives, headed by the priest Biankini, attacked the Autonomist Party, accusing it of political irredentism and denouncing the opening of Italian schools in Dalmatia as an attempt to denationalize the Slav Dalmatians.[36] Campaigns were launched in the press against the Dante Alighieri and the autonomists, charging them with being a tool of Italian imperialism in

---

35 Information on this in Ghiglianovich to Sanminiatelli, 8 December 1897, B 14; Ghiglianovich to Nathan, 23 September 1897, B 16; Sanminiatelli to Villari, 1 March 1897, B 32, DA, fasc. 1897. Nathan to Villari, 16 February 1899, B 25; Willenik to Sanminiatelli, 4 January 1899, B 38, DA, file 1899. Ghiglianovich to Sanminiatelli, 1 October 1900, B 15, DA, file 1900. See too Grange, *L'Italie*, vol. 1, p. 679–81; Pisa, *Nazione e politica*, p. 251–5; Anonymous (but probably Roberto Ghiglianovich), 'Relazione del fiduciario per la regione dalmata,' 9 June 1915, BS, Carte Ghiglianovich, portfolio B.
36 For example: speech by Biankini, session of 14 July 1902, pp. 669 et seq.; speech by Biankini, session of 22 July 1902, pp. 965 et seq., ADP-BI. See too Italian consul in Zara to the Foreign Minister, 28 June 1901, ASMAE, SP 1891–1916, portfolio 89.

the eastern Adriatic and with seeking the denationalization of a land inhabited solely by Croats.[37]

For its part, the Austrian government, aware of Italian funding of the Autonomist Party and the Lega Nazionale but also anxious to avoid a grave crisis in relations with Italy, like the one that had broken out in 1890 with the dissolution of Pro Patria, kept an eye on these contacts and relations but allowed them to grow.

### 3.2.  Allies and Rivals: The Eastern Adriatic and the Balkans in the Relations Between Italy and Austria-Hungary from 1896 to 1903

The dramatic worsening in the international position of Italy in 1895, a position weakened by political and economic conflict with France, the coldness of Italo-British relations, and the outbreak of war in Ethiopia, deeply saddened Crispi. In January 1896, during various conversations with Nigra, Blanc, and Sidney Sonnino, Crispi complained of the lack of Austro-German support for Italian foreign policy[38] and declared that it was necessary for the two allied powers to be associated with Italy 'in all questions in which France will be our enemy.'[39] Also required were better guarantees if the Balkan *status quo* were to change; in the case of a division of Turkey, Italy ought to get its share.[40]

The defeat at Adwa and Crispi's political downfall thwarted his plan of imposing modifications on the alliance with Vienna and Berlin. His successor, Antonio di Rudinì, at the head of a government that brought together all the currents opposed to Crispi (with Onorato Caetani and then Emilio Visconti Venosta as foreign minister), was faced with a difficult political situation. For several months the principal aim of Rudinì's foreign policy was to bring the war with Ethiopia to an end, a goal that was not achieved until October 1896 with the Treaty of Addis Ababa.[41]

---

37  On this: Milazzo to the Foreign Minister, 5 October 1901, portfolio 89; Milazzo to the Foreign Minister, 11 and 24 September 1902, portfolio 90, ASMAE, SP 1891–1916.
38  DDI, II, 27, doc. 782.
39  DDI, II, 27, doc. 796.
40  DDI, II, 27, doc. 793. Further information on Crispi's intentions in GP, 11, docs. 2798, 2799, 2800; Pribram, *Les traités*, pp. 308–13; Salvatorelli, *La Triplice Alleanza*, pp. 203–4.
41  On the foreign policy of the Rudinì governments: Augusto Torre, *La politica estera dell'Italia*, pp. 50 et seq.; Salvatorelli, *La Triplice Alleanza*, pp. 215 et seq.; Curato, 'La politica estera italiana dopo la caduta di Crispi secondo i nuovi documenti

Another great question that confronted Rudinì was the renewal of the Triple Alliance. In a dangerous international situation Rudinì decided to abandon the plans of modification conceived by his predecessor and limited himself to declaring his readiness to renew the treaty as it stood. However, he asked for the reintroduction of the declaration that had been made with respect to Great Britain on the occasion of the first treaty of alliance, but which had been left out in the first renewal:[42] the so-called Mancini declaration, which had laid down that no stipulation of the treaty of the Triple Alliance was to be considered levelled against Great Britain. The Italian request was rejected by the government in Berlin, which did not desire to limit the scope of the alliance in any way.[43] Rudinì tried to assert his point of view and sent a new note to Berlin and Vienna that was not legally binding and required no answer but underlined the Italian vision of the scope of the alliance. The note declared that the Triple Alliance could have no anti-British purpose and that Italy, owing to its geographical position, was unable to take part in a conflict with the two strongest naval powers in the world.[44] Rudinì attempted, in short, to downplay the potentially anti-British and anti-French character of the alliance with the Austro-Germans.

The German government refused to recognize the Italian reservation proposed by Rudinì,[45] and Habsburg diplomacy reacted in the same way.[46] In the face of the allies' attitude, the Rudinì government renounced its requests. In need of their goodwill and co-operation to facilitate the conclusion of the war against Ethiopia, it chose to tacitly renew the treaty of the Triple Alliance without any modification by allowing the time to lapse for any denunciation.[47]

The negotiations for the renewal of the Triple Alliance confirmed that an improvement in the relations with the two great Mediterranean

diplomatici italiani,' in *Scritti di storia diplomatica*, pp. 351–79; Serra, *Camille Barrère e l'intesa italo-francese*; *La questione tunisina da Crispi a Rudinì*; Decleva, *Da Adua a Sarajevo*, pp. 15 et seq.; Monzali, *L'Etiopia nella politica estera italiana 1896–1915*; Francioni, *Medicina e diplomazia*; Giglio, 'Il trattato di pace italo-etiopico del 26 ottobre 1896, pp. 165–80; Afflerbach, *Der Dreibund*, pp. 413 et seq.
42  Caetani to Nigra and Lanza, 26 March 1896, DDI, III, 1, doc. 40.
43  Pribram, *The Secret Treaties of Austria-Hungary*, pp. 314 et seq.; Albertini, *The Origins of the War of 1914*, vol. 1.
44  Caetani to Nigra and Lanza, 26 April 1896, DDI, III, 1, doc. 87.
45  Lanza to Caetani, 1 May 1896, DDI, III, 1, doc. 92.
46  Pribram, *The Secret Treaties of Austria-Hungary*, p. 319.
47  DDI, III, 1, doc. 104.

powers, France and Great Britain, was an important plank of Rudinì's foreign policy. The period of Crispi's government had painfully demonstrated the untenability of a political and economic conflict with France; better relations with Paris were indispensable to strengthening the Italian position in the Mediterranean and Africa and to making the country less dependent on Berlin and Vienna.[48] The rapprochement with France was even more urgent in view of the fruitlessness of the so-called Italo-British friendship:[49] Great Britain had frowned on Crispi's attempts to create a major colonial empire in East Africa and was suspicious of Italy's desire to increase its influence in the Mediterranean, where the government in London was defending a highly favourable *status quo*.

The first signs of a change in the relations between Rome and Paris came over the course of 1896.[50] In September several agreements were reached on Tunisia, with Italy giving its recognition of the French protectorate in exchange for the concession of certain legal and cultural privileges to the Italian community in Tunisian territory. The peace treaty with Ethiopia was rapidly concluded thanks to the co-operation of French agents in Addis Ababa who gave the Italian negotiator, Cesare Nerazzini, considerable help over the course of the talks.[51] These were the first steps in a move toward an Italo-French reconciliation that would be continued over the following years and lead to the trade agreement of 1898, reached by the government led by Luigi Pelloux, and the Visconti Venosta–Barrère exchange of notes on Tripolitania and Morocco in December 1900.

In 1896 Italy also began trying to improve relations with London. It is from this perspective that we should interpret the Italian participation in the naval expedition of the great powers to Crete in 1897 and the pro-Greek attitude assumed in the negotiations over the future of the is-

48  In this connection: Billot to Berthelot, 13 March 1896, doc. 321; Billot to Hanotaux, 26 May 1896, doc. 390, DDF, I, 12.
49  On the difficult Italo-British relations in those years: DDF, I, 12, docs. 240, 245, 313, 405; Lowe, *The Reluctant Imperialists*; Glanville, *Italy's Relations with England*; Serra, *L'intesa mediterranea del 1902*; Marsden, 'Salisbury and the Italians in 1896,' pp. 91–117; Seton-Watson, 'Adua 1896,' pp. 117 et seq.; Lowe and Marzari, *Italian Foreign Policy 1870–1940*.
50  On the rapprochement between Italy and France from 1896 onward: Milza, *Français et Italiens à la fin du XIXe siècle*, vol. 2, pp. 579 *et sqq*; Decleva, *Da Adua*; Guillen, *L'expansion 1881–1898*.
51  Monzali, *L'Etiopia*, pp. 55 et seq.; Francioni, *Medicina e diplomazia*, pp. 347 et seq.

land.[52] However, the results of this Italian overture to London were not particularly positive. The British government, headed by Robert Salisbury, continued to attach little importance to relations with Italy, causing irritation in public opinion on the peninsula with the application of a policy hostile to the Italian language on Malta, paying no attention to Rome's claims on Tripolitania, and displaying coolness toward Italy's attempts to establish a colony of its own in China.[53]

In an international context in which, after 1896 and the improvement in Italo-French relations, the risk of a military conflict between France and Italy had faded, the Triple Alliance lost any function for the government in Rome as a means of defence against possible French aggression, but it retained its usefulness for other purposes. This explains the determination of the Francophile Rudinì to renew the alliance at any cost. In the first place, being part of an alliance with Germany and Austria-Hungary increased Italy's international influence, and abandoning the Triple Alliance without joining another one would have weakened the political role of the Italian state, causing France (eager to improve Italo-French relations chiefly in order to weaken Germany) to lose interest in a strong friendship with Italy.

Furthermore, Rudinì and the whole of the Italian ruling class were aware that the main purpose of the Triple Alliance was to facilitate a future diplomatic solution of the question of the eastern border. In a conversation with the speaker of the Senate, Domenico Farini, on 6 February 1897, Rudinì openly declared:

> Tripoli will be, is incontestably Italy's, but I go further, I am irredentist: we must push Austria into the East.
> [Farini:] Then we will have Trent, not Trieste ...
> [Rudinì:] And why not ...? We will have to see how great the size of the movement is and how much goes to each; and so I aspire to Trieste, in the case of a broad division ... Austria does not see us, for now, from this perspective, because it does not have Bosnia and Herzegovina.[54]

---

52  In this connection: Pastorelli, 'Albania e Tripoli nella politica estera italiana durante la crisi d'Oriente del 1897,' abstract; Langer, *The Diplomacy of Imperialism*; Volpe, *Italia moderna*, vol. 1, pp. 318 et seq.

53  On these questions: BD, 1, docs. 236, 246, 247, 251, 355, 356, 359; Glanville, *Italy's Relations with England*; Serra, *L'intesa mediterranea*; Borsa, 'La crisi italo-cinese del marzo 1899 nelle carte inedite del ministro Canevaro,' in *Europa e Asia tra modernità e tradizione*, pp. 292–326.

54  Farini, *Diario di fine secolo*, vol. 2, p. 1132.

Rudinì remained convinced, just as Mancini, Robilant, and Crispi had been, that the mechanism of compensations envisaged by the Triple Alliance could provide Italy with the opportunity to obtain much of the Italian lands possessed by Austria, in the case of a break-up of the Ottoman Empire and further Habsburg territorial expansion.

For that matter, the resurgence of national and religious conflicts in Ottoman Turkey since the middle of the 1890s (Armenian uprisings, the Greek revolt on Crete, and Bulgarian and Macedonian guerrilla warfare in Macedonia)[55] suggested a progressive decline in the solidity of the Ottoman Empire and rendered an imminent division of the Turkish territories among the European powers a likely prospect.[56]

In Habsburg military circles plans were circulating for the dismemberment of the Ottoman Empire. Famous is the memorandum of General Friedrich Beck, chief of staff, written in April 1897, in which he predicted the Russian conquest of the straits of Constantinople and the Dardanelles, the Habsburg annexation of Bosnia-Herzegovina and the sanjak of Novi Pazar, the creation of an independent Macedonia and Albania, and the establishment of nation states in the remaining Balkan territories (subdivided into Austrian and Russian spheres of influence).[57]

In such a context the maintenance of the Triple Alliance constituted an indispensable instrument of the Balkan policy of Italy (which was anxious to have an influence on the fate of the populations of that region) as well as a vital weapon for the protection of Italy's political and economic interests.

The subsequent evolution of Habsburg policy in the Balkans confirmed the usefulness of the Triple Alliance to Italian diplomatic action.

The new Habsburg foreign minister, the Polish count Agenor J. Golu-

---

55  An in-depth examination of the national conflicts within the Ottoman Empire and the attitude of the European powers in Langer, *The Diplomacy of Imperialism*. A fine study of the Armenian question is the one by Sidari, *La questione armena nella politica delle grandi poteri dalla chiusura*. See too *Documenti diplomatici italiani sull'Armenia*, series 2, vols. 1, 2, 3. On Macedonia: *Austro-Hungarian Documents Relating to the Macedonian Struggle, 1896–1912*; Adanir, *Die makedonische Frage, ihre Entstehung und Entwicklung bis 1908*; Dogo, *La dinamite e la mezzaluna*; *Lingua e nazionalità in Macedonia*; Ganiage, 'Terrorisme et guerre civile en Macedoine (1895–1903),' pp. 55–81.

56  Salvatorelli, *La Triplice Alleanza*, p. 198; Langer, *The Diplomacy of Imperialism*.

57  Albertini, *The Origins of the War of 1914*; Pastorelli, *Albania e Tripoli*, p. 390.

208 The Italians of Dalmatia

chowski,[58] concerned about the aggravation of the situation in the Balkans and stimulated by the political overtures of a Russia that was eager for peace in Europe so that it could concentrate on expansion in the Far East, agreed to make a reconciliation with the government in St Petersburg. On the occasion of Francis Joseph and Goluchowski's visit to St Petersburg in April 1897, Habsburg and Russian diplomats arrived at a verbal understanding on certain common principles and objectives that should govern their actions in the Balkans.[59] This understanding found written expression in an exchange of letters between Goluchowski and Michail Muravev in May.[60] The Austro-Russian understanding entailed a mutual obligation to maintain the Balkan *status quo* as long as possible; should this become impossible, the two states undertook to abstain from new conquests and to prevent them from being made by any other great power. There was a promise to collaborate in the prospect of a future joint agreement that would establish the political set-up in the Balkans, and some of the foundations for this possible agreement were laid, but here some discords emerged between the designs of the two states. Austria desired the annexation of Bosnia-Herzegovina and the sanjak of Novi Pazar, the creation of an independent Albania and various Balkan nation states, and a European solution to the Straits Question, while Russia, which had not given up its dream of conquering the straits, refused to recognize immediately and unconditionally the Habsburg annexation of the territories occupied in 1878 and the plans for an independent Albania.[61]

The understanding of April 1897 marked the resumption of Austro-Russian co-operation in the Balkans after decades of hostility and rivalry; it was a co-operation based on the idea that Austria-Hungary and Russia should be the states that would determine and control political developments in European Turkey. However, no binding decisions

---

58 On the appointment of Goluchowski: Engel-Janosi, *Österreich und der Vatikan*, vol. 1, pp. 254 et seq.
59 On the Austro-Russian verbal understanding of April 1897: Langer, *The Diplomacy of Imperialism*; Bridge, *From Sadowa to Sarajevo*, pp. 227 et seq.; 'Österreich(-Ungarn) unter den Grossmächten,' pp. 293 et seq.; Walters, 'Austro-Russian Relations under Goluchowski 1895–1906'; Pastorelli, *Albania e Tripoli*, pp. 391 et seq.; Albertini, *The Origins of the War of 1914*, vol. 1; Carlgren, *Iswolsky und Aehrenthal vor der bosnischen Annexionkrise*, pp. 7 et seq.; Afflerbach, *Der Dreibund*, pp. 465 et seq. See too DDS, 4, docs. 202, 238.
60 Text of the exchange of letters in Pribram, *The Secret Treaties of Austria-Hungary*.
61 Ibid.

were taken about what the future political set-up in the Balkans would be in the event of the break-up of the Ottoman Empire, and the whole matter was deferred to a subsequent bilateral Austro-Russian accord.

The Austrian government provided the German diplomatic corps with detailed and complete information on the contents and meaning of the agreement.[62] The information received by Italy, however, was vague and inaccurate:[63] nothing was said about the part of the understanding devoted to the territorial set-up to be established in the Balkans in the case of the collapse of Ottoman rule. This Austrian reticence is not surprising since the Austro-Russian understanding had a clearly anti-Italian purpose, that of excluding Italy from Balkan policy.

The Habsburg determination to keep Italy totally out of discussions on the future of the Balkans progressively relented over the course of the summer of 1897 due to various factors. First of all, Russian reservations on the future creation of an Albanian state and on an undisputed Austrian annexation of the occupied territories in 1878 rendered the Austro-Russian understanding fragile and ambiguous, prompting Vienna to seek a partial recognition of its own Balkan designs in Rome. Then, the growing Italian political, economic, and cultural penetration of Albania counselled the Ballhausplatz to try to curb Rome's initiatives through a bilateral political understanding.[64]

The government in Berlin was also favourably disposed to an Italo-Austrian understanding on Albania, conscious as it was of the growing attention paid by Italy to Adriatic problems.[65]

A verbal understanding on Albania was reached on the occasion of Goluchowski's visit to Monza between 6 and 8 November 1897 and his meeting with King Umberto I, Rudinì, and Visconti Venosta. This was put formally into writing a few years later with an exchange of letters between the two governments during December 1900 and January 1901, in which they agreed on the need to maintain the *status quo* in

---

62  GP, 12, part I, doc. 3126. See too GP 12, part I, docs. 3124 and 3125.
63  DDI, III, 2, docs. 8, 13, 20. In this connection: Pastorelli, 'Albania e Tripoli,' pp. 395–7; Duce, *L'Albania nei rapporti italo-austriaci 1897–1913*, pp. 30 et seq.
64  On the Italian penetration of Albania in those years, which gained impetus under the Crispi government: DDI, III, 1, doc. 228; III, 2, docs. 9, 174, 251; Duce, *L'Albania*; Maserati, 'L'Albania nella politica estera italiana degli anni 1896–1901,' in *Momenti della questione adriatica*, pp. 29–67; Schanderl, *Die Albanienpolitik Österreich-Ungarns und Italien 1877–1908*, pp. 59 et seq.; Volpe, *Italia moderna*, vol. 1, pp. 318 et seq., vol. 2, pp. 100 et seq.
65  GP, 12, part I, docs. 3129, 3130.

Albania and to co-operate in the event of a change in that *status quo*, in order to favour shifts in the direction of autonomy, while always seeking to reconcile their respective interests.[66]

We can make some observations on the nature of this agreement. As in later Italian and Austrian diplomatic papers on the Albanian question and the Balkan policy, there appears to be a declaration of support for the principle of autonomy and for the constitution of 'autonomous' Balkan states. In reality, these were abstract and theoretical declarations that served to prevent conquests by great powers for the moment and that, not coincidentally, always coexisted with promises by the contracting parties to find a common fulfilment of their own political interests. Naturally, in the event of conflict between the principle of autonomy and the pursuit of their own interests, the support for an autonomous Albanian or Serbian state would have yielded to Italian or Austrian reasons of state. On the Italian part, this signified that espousal of the principle of nationality would inevitably become a secondary factor in the event of the application of article VII of the Triple Alliance and in the event of any territorial compensation as a result of Habsburg expansion at the expense of the Serbs, Montenegrins, and Albanians. The principle of autonomy served as a formula that would not be prejudicial to the development of events, in anticipation of future agreements on dividing territories between Italy and the Habsburg Empire.

It is interesting to note, however, that while Habsburg diplomacy agreed to collaborate with Italy on the Albanian question, it refused to do so with regard to the problems of Macedonia and Serbia. There was an evident desire to maintain a hegemonic role in the region, justified by appeals to the view of the Balkans as the Habsburg monarchy's *Lebensraum* (habitat). The Italian attempts to initiate an exchanges of ideas and to create a political co-operation with Austria and Germany on the Eastern Question and – for example that of Visconti Venosta in October 1896[67] – were always met with indifference and rejection from the Austrians and Germans in those years.

66 On the Italo-Austrian negotiations on Albania, Goluchowski's visit to Monza, and the first verbal and then written understanding: DDF, I, 13, doc. 353; Pastorelli, 'Albania e Tripoli'.; Duce, *L'Albania*, pp. 35 et seq.; Serra, 'Note sull'intesa Visconti Venosta-Goluchowski per l'Albania,' pp. 441–52; Salvatorelli, *La Triplice Alleanza*, pp. 220–1.
67 Visconti Venosta to Lanza and Nigra, 9 October 1896, doc. 237; Lanza to Visconti Venosta, 16 October 1896, doc. 248, DDI, I, 1; GP, 12, part 1, docs. 3065, 3066, 3067, 3070.

The governments headed by Pelloux (1898–1900), with first Felice Canevaro and then Emilio Visconti Venosta as foreign minister, and by Giuseppe Saracco (1900–1901), with Visconti in the same post, essentially continued to follow the direction imparted to Italian foreign policy by Rudinì, that is, a marked improvement in relations with France and Great Britain and the maintenance of the Triple Alliance. This showed that the pro-Western shift in Italian foreign policy after 1896 found broad support across the whole liberal alignment in Italy.[68] Even Pelloux, a military man and a member of parliament with ties to court circles,[69] realized the need to give Italian diplomatic action free rein, going beyond Crispi's reliance on the Triple Alliance. In December 1898, the prime minister replied to Domenico Farini, who was critical of the Italo-French rapprochement: 'While we defend the left flank of the Triple Alliance, we alone bear its weight, not for the alleged increase in military expenditure, but for the economic war with France. The Triple Alliance on the other hand has not helped us, nor is it helping us in any way in the safeguarding of our other interests.'[70]

It was no coincidence that it was the Pelloux government that reached a trade agreement with France in November 1898.[71] The Pelloux and Saracco governments attempted, with mixed results, to exploit the improvement in relations with Paris to promote a more effective and ambitious Italian colonial policy. They succeeded in obtaining an expression of a lack of French interest in Tripolitania with the Barrère–Visconti Venosta exchange of notes dated from 14 to 16 December 1900,[72] and in taking advantage of Franco-British benevolence to impose the treaties of July 1900 on Ethiopia;[73] however, they failed miserably in their attempts to set up an Italian colony in China.[74]

Yet the Triple Alliance retained an undeniable usefulness for the Foreign Ministry. It was partly thanks to the alliance that Italian diploma-

---

68  On this see the observations of Decleva, *Da Adua*, pp. 81 et seq.
69  On Pelloux: Pelloux, *Quelques souvenirs de ma vie*.
70  Farini, *Diario di fine secolo*, vol. 2, p. 1401.
71  Milza, *Français et italiens à la fin du XIXe siècle*, vol. 2; DDF, I, 14, docs. 512, 527, 529, 535, 552.
72  On this: Peteani, *La questione libica nella diplomazia europea*; Silva, *Mediterraneo*, pp. 356 et seq.; Serra, *Barrère*, pp. 67 et seq.
73  On the genesis of the Italo-Ethiopian border agreements of July 1900: Monzali, *L'Etiopia*, pp. 146 et seq.
74  Borsa, 'La crisi italo-cinese del marzo 1899 nelle carte inedite del ministro Canevaro,' pp. 292–326.

cy had been able to wrest an understanding on Albania from Vienna. Many still saw the alliance with Germany and Austria as an element of stability for the Italian state and of peace in Europe. In this connection Visconti Venosta wrote to Luigi Luzzatti in September 1901: 'Leaving the Triple Alliance ... means losing our guarantees on the Adriatic, and it also means losing the cable that stops our ship from being carried away by who knows what currents into who knows what adventures.'[75]

Moreover, there was a still a strong hope that the Triple Alliance might serve as a means of preserving Italian positions in the so-called unredeemed lands and of moderating or blocking, perhaps through intervention by Berlin in Vienna, Austrian initiatives of domestic policy that were hostile to Italian populations. Adopting a tactic tried several times by Crispi, in January 1899 Canevaro made known to Goluchowski his grievances over the pro-Slav Austrian policy in Trieste, Istria, and Dalmatia, emphasizing the consequences that this had on bilateral relations between the states: 'It remains a fact, however, that the present agitations, in Trieste, in Friuli across the border, and in Istria, have not failed to arouse comment in the kingdom, and raise concerns among us that could become detrimental, perhaps even threatening, to the good and cordial relations that we firmly desire to maintain with our neighbouring empire. From this point of view, the struggle that is taking place, on our frontier, between Slavs and Italians cannot leave us indifferent.'[76] At the same time, the Italian foreign minister informed Berlin of his dissatisfaction with the policy of Slavicization pursued by the government in Vienna on the Adriatic coast and asked German diplomacy to support Italian efforts to persuade their Habsburg ally to change its conduct in domestic policy.[77]

Canevaro's initiative was essentially a failure, meeting with Habsburg hostility to foreign interference in its internal affairs and with German reluctance to exert pressure of this kind on Vienna.[78] However, it was indicative of the manner in which the alliance with Vienna was used

---

75  Visconti Venosta to Luzzatti, 14 September 1901, IVSLA, Carte Luzzatti, portfolio 48.
76  Canevaro to Nigra, 12 January 1899, DDI, III, 3, doc. 136.
77  *Der Staatssekretär des Auswärtigen Amtes Bernhard von Bülow an den Botschafter in Rom Freiherrn von Saurma*, 25 January 1899, GP, 13, doc. 3498.
78  DDI, III, 3, docs. 141 and 145. On Canevaro's initiative, see Tommasini, *L'Italia alla vigilia*, vol. 1, p. 95; Riccardi, *Salata*, pp. 84–5. On the attitude of the government in Berlin toward the national conflicts in Austria-Hungary: Kořalka, 'Deutschland und die Habsburgermonarchie 1848–1918,' pp. 1–158.

by Italian diplomacy in defence of the interests of Italian and Italophile populations and parties in Austria.

Paradoxically, it can be said that it was in those years (1896–1901), when Italian domestic policy was characterized by harsh political and social conflicts that seemed to threaten the very survival of the liberal and monarchic institutional system, that Italy's international role was greatly reinforced by the changes made to Italian foreign policy by the Rudinì, Pelloux, and Saracco governments.

This strengthening of the country's international standing prepared the ground for the ambitious attempt of the Giuseppe Zanardelli–Giulio Prinetti government to make Italy a leading power in European and Mediterranean politics.

Under the Zanardelli-Prinetti government, which came into office in February 1901, the management of Italian policy was once again in the hands of men who had no great liking for the Habsburg Empire. Highly significant in this respect is the figure of Zanardelli.[79] The Brescian politician, whose mother was from Trentino, had been active in Mazzini's movement and had played a direct part in the struggles against Austria in 1848–9 and 1859. Serving as a minister several times over the course of the 1870s and 1880s, he had been one of the leaders of the Liberal Left who were closest to the irredentists of Trentino and Venezia Giulia and most strongly opposed to a policy of subservient alliance with the Habsburg Empire. His criticism of Mancini's foreign policy, which he regarded as too submissive to Austria, had been one of the reasons for him leaving the government in 1883.[80] Zanardelli's concern for the Trentino and his ties with the world of irredentism were made manifest in 1893: asked by the king to form a new government, he intended to appoint General Oreste Baratieri, born in Trentino, as foreign minister; however, this led to protests from the government in Vienna (who saw in it a desire to challenge the territorial set-up resulting from the war in 1866) and to his failure to form an executive.[81]

---

79 Fundamental to an understanding of Zanardelli's ideas in the field of international politics is the fine essay by Decleva, 'Giuseppe Zanardelli: Liberalismo e politica estera,' in *L'incerto alleato*, pp. 109–44. On the figure of Giuseppe Zanardelli and his political thinking: Vallauri, *La politica liberale di Giuseppe Zanardelli dal 1876 al 1878*; Chiarini, *Giuseppe Zanardelli e la lotta politica nella provincia italiana*; Decleva, *Da Adua*, pp. 131 et seq.

80 Barzilai, *Luci ed ombre del passato*, pp. 34–5.

81 Farini, *Diario di fine secolo*, vol. 1, pp. 347 et seq.; Paulucci, *Alla corte di re Umberto*, pp. 85 et seq.; Sonnino, *Diario 1866–1912*, p. 173; Afflerbach, *Der Dreibund*, pp. 328 et seq.

Nor had Giulio Prinetti, a Milanese industrialist and a member of parliament, shown much fondness for Austria over the course of his political career. At the beginning of the 1890s he had caused a sensation with a public speech criticizing Crispi's pro-Austrian policy and raising doubts about the usefulness of the Triple Alliance to Italy.[82]

The reason for the formation of the Zanardelli-Prinetti government in 1901 was King Victor Emmanuel III's desire to take Italian politics in a more democratic and reformist direction after the fierce conflict of the preceding years that had culminated in the assassination of King Umberto I. Underlying this executive, however, were other important motivations of foreign policy. Unlike his father who was in favour of close co-operation with Austria and Germany, Victor Emmanuel nursed ambitions and plans that aimed to make Italy a decisive force in European politics, capable of competing with the other great powers. The new king showed a strong interest in Balkan policy, where he believed that Italy should play an important role and attempt to oppose Habsburg and Russian designs of hegemony. His marriage to Elena of Montenegro had brought him into direct contact with the turbulent reality of the Balkan and Slav nations, to which he would continue to pay close attention throughout his reign, often displaying an excellent grasp of the situation.[83]

In fact, Italian foreign policy took on an unprecedented dynamism and vigour with the Zanardelli-Prinetti government.[84] Italy's repositioning in the European political system with the improvement of Italo-French relations gave the government in Rome greater autonomy with respect to its allies and allowed it to try to grasp new opportunities

---

82  On this: Pastorelli, 'Giulio Prinetti ministro degli Esteri (1901–1902),' pp. 53–70, in particular pp. 55–6.

83  No satisfactory and well-documented political biography of Victor Emmanuel III has been written to date; however, see: Volpe, 'Principio di un regno,' in *Scritti su Casa Savoia*, pp. 155–81; Bertoldi, *Vittorio Emanuele III*, pp. 77 et seq.; Mack Smith, *Italy and Its Monarchy*; DDS, 4, docs. 345, 434. On the son of Umberto I's positions in international policy: BD, 1, docs. 286, 366; DDI, III, 7, doc. 11; Serra, *Barrère*; Afflerbach, *Der Dreibund*, pp. 431 et seq. On the young king's interest in the Adriatic and the Balkans: GP, 18, doc. 5775; DDF, I, 16, doc. 374; Bülow, *Memoirs of Prince von Bülow*.

84  On Prinetti as foreign minister see Decleva, *Da Adua*, pp. 145 et seq.; Pastorelli, 'Giulio Prinetti,'; Semper, 'Prinetti e l'Austria-Ungheria,' pp. 577 et seq.; Serra, *L'intesa mediterranea*; Tommasini, *L'Italia alla vigilia*, vol. 1, pp. 77–195; Salvatorelli, *La Triplice Alleanza*; Albertini, *The Origins of the War*, vol. 1; *Venti anni di vita politica*, part I, vol. 1; Behnen, *Rüstung-Bündnis-Sicherheit*, pp. 19 et seq.

for political and economic expansion in the Balkans and the Mediterranean.[85]

The person who played the leading role in Italian foreign policy during 1901 and 1902 was Giulio Prinetti. The appointment of the Milanese politician to the Foreign Ministry was, as Decleva has pointed out,[86] an element of novelty that could not be underestimated. Prinetti was an atypical figure for Italian and European diplomacy. Not the usual aristocrat or military man, but a dynamic and able industrialist – a manufacturer of bicycles *(Mailänder Fahrradfabrikant)*, as Bernhard von Bülow called him with contempt[87] – he entered politics early on and achieved a degree of success, becoming one of the leaders of the Liberal Right in Lombardy. From his diplomatic correspondence, which is characterized by a clear and concise style, emerges a personality of great intelligence and energy, an ambitious politician driven by the desire to bring about a change of direction in Italian foreign policy. Prime Minister Zanardelli gave him complete responsibility for diplomacy, limiting himself and the king to discussing and deciding with Prinetti the general lines of foreign policy.[88]

The objective of the Zanardelli-Prinetti government was, as has been pointed out, the conquest of new political and economic areas in the Balkans and the Mediterranean. To this end the government set out to consolidate relations with Paris and improve relations with Russia, which had been very cold since the 1880s as a consequence of Italian participation in the Triple Alliance. At the same time, however, Prinetti and Zanardelli wanted to preserve the Triple Alliance, making it better suited to their own aims, without renouncing a determined and fierce defence of Italian interests even at the expense of those of their allies. Hence Prinetti's policy was not opposed to the Triple Alliance; he did not want to abandon it but wanted to turn it into a more flexible instrument that would be of greater advantage to the Italian state.[89]

This new Italian foreign policy – which went on pursuing the traditional goals of Italy's international action but changed in its style and methods, becoming aggressive and uninhibited under Prinetti, ready

---

85  In this connection see the observations of the Swiss minister in Rome: Carlin to Brenner, 4 April 1901, doc. 359, DDS, 4.

86  Decleva, *Da Adua*, pp. 146–8.

87  Bülow to Alvensleben, 23 February 1902, GP, 18, part 2, doc. 5726.

88  DDI, III, 6, doc. 172.

89  On this: Decleva, *Da Adua*, pp. 173 et seq.; *Zanardelli*, pp. 130–5.

for open political conflict and the use of force, and thus more like those of a great power – did not always produce brilliant results. Undeniably the foreign minister achieved major diplomatic successes in the relations with Great Britain and France. Playing on the still existing Franco-British rivalry, Prinetti was able to obtain a formal recognition of the Italian right to a future conquest of Tripolitania and Cyrenaica from London (11 March 1902).[90] The Lombard politician also showed great skill in his dealings with France. Taking advantage of the French ignorance of the exact text of the Triple Alliance, with the Prinetti-Barrère exchange of notes (concluded in June 1902) he won major concessions in return for an Italian commitment to neutrality in the event of a Franco-German war provoked by Berlin, a promise which was perfectly compatible with the Triple Alliance; the concessions included an unconditional French green light for attempts to conquer Tripolitania and Cyrenaica and France's promise to remain neutral in the event of an Italo-Habsburg war. As Pietro Pastorelli has observed, in the case of a breaking of the Triple Alliance, with the Prinetti-Barrère accord 'Italy acquired the security of having a neutral France at her back and not a possible enemy.'[91]

The results achieved by the Zanardelli-Prinetti government in the area of relations with the powers of the Triple Alliance and Russia were much less satisfactory. The pursuit of greater influence in the Balkans very quickly led to a marked deterioration in the political relationship between Rome and Vienna. The government in Vienna reacted with concern to Zanardelli's rise to power and the uninhibited and hard-hitting style of the new foreign minister, so different from the caution and prudence of the elderly Visconti Venosta.[92] Over the following months various problems in the relations between the two states began to arise or worsen. Some of them were long standing. For instance, the fact that King Umberto's visit to Vienna in 1881 had not yet been returned by Emperor Francis Joseph, who refused to go to Rome out of respect for the Holy See,[93] remained a grave affront to Italian pride. Then there were the Balkans: the consolidation of Italian influence in Montenegro and Ottoman Albania, thanks to the intense efforts of economic, political, and cultural penetration, rang alarm bells in Vienna

---

90   BD, 1, docs. 352, 355, 356, 359, 360, 361; Serra, *L'intesa mediterranea*.
91   Pastorelli, 'Giulio Prinetti,' p. 69.
92   DDF, II, 1, doc. 120.
93   Tommasini, *L'Italia alla vigilia*, vol. 1, pp. 173–4; DDI, III, 7, doc. 8.

over Italy's aims.[94] The dissension between Italy and Austria was also aggravated by the fact that Italy demanded to be recognized by the Habsburg government as a primary interlocutor in Balkan policy, on a par with Russia. Prinetti made this clear to Nigra on 31 August 1901: 'Austria and Italy ought easily to find a basis for complete agreement over future eventualities that may emerge in the Balkan peninsula, and not just with regard to Albania; and this ought always to be one of the lynchpins of the Triple Alliance.'[95] However, as has already been pointed out, Habsburg diplomacy refused any recognition of Italy as a Balkan power equal to Austria-Hungary and Russia.

The Austro-Hungarian ruling class was also worried by the strong resurgence of anti-Austrian irredentism in Italy, in part due to the new Italian interest in Balkan policy and the Italo-French rapprochement. In fact, French diplomats did everything they could to fuel the antagonism between Italy and Austria, which was correctly regarded by Camille Barrère, French ambassador in Italy, and Théophile Delcassé, French foreign minister, as the weak point of the Triple Alliance.[96] However, the attention paid by public opinion on the peninsula to the fate of the Italians in Austria also stemmed from a genuine national sensitivity in the liberal establishment and from the aggravation of national conflicts in the Tyrol, Venezia Giulia, and Dalmatia. At the end of the nineteenth century and the beginning of the twentieth century, even among populations traditionally extremely loyal to the Habsburgs (such as the Italians of the Trentino and Gorizia), dissatisfaction began to emerge with the policy of the Austrian government, which was accused of failing to protect the national rights of Italians. This discontent was so widespread that the defence of Italian national rights, traditionally a concern of liberals alone, increasingly became a central theme of the political battles of theoretically 'non-national' forces like the Italian People's parties of Trentino and Gorizia or certain socialist groups.[97] All this prompted

---

94 On the Italian penetration of Albania and Montenegro: DDF, II, 1, docs. 4, 365; II, 2, doc. 201; II, 3, doc. 62.

95 Prinetti to Nigra, 31 August 1901, DDI, III, 5, doc. 751.

96 DDF, I, 16, docs. 373, 407; II, 1, doc. 12.

97 On political life in Trentino and South Tyrol and the attitude of the Liberal, Socialist and People's parties to the national question in these years, the writings of Umberto Corsini remain fundamental. The reader is referred to Corsini, *Problemi di un territorio di confine*; *Il colloquio Degasperi-Sonnino*, in particular pp. 117 et seq.; 'Problemi politico-amministrativi del Trentino nel nesso provinciale tirolese, 1815–1918,' pp.

growing attention on the part of public opinion in the kingdom to the situation of Italians in Austria. This attention was not confined to the liberal ruling class and exponents of the growing nationalism but was shared by many democratic and socialist intellectuals, such as the socialists Angiolo Cabrini, Gaetano Salvemini, and Leonida Bissolati who showed an interest in the Italian national question in Austria.[98]

From the viewpoint of our study, it is interesting to note that by this time, the beginning of the twentieth century, many citizens of the kingdom of Italy saw Dalmatia as one of the Italian lands of Austria. This attention paid to the Italian Dalmatians found clear expression in the kingdom's press in 1901, at the time of the incident of the college of St. Jerome in Rome. For centuries known as the 'Illyrian Asylum,' the college had served as a refuge for Illyrian pilgrims and priests, that is, Dalmatians, Croats, Slovenes and Serbs of the Catholic faith. The Vatican's decision to reorganize and place it in the hands of the Croatian clergy, renaming it the 'Croatian college,' prompted loud complaints from Italians in Dalmatia. As a gesture of protest a group of Italian Dalmatians resident in Rome decided to occupy the college. Their action received sympathetic treatment from the Italian press, which devoted a lot of space to the question and to the defence of the national rights of the Italian minority in Dalmatia.[99]

Italian diplomacy also paid growing attention to Dalmatia. The Italian consular representatives sent accurate analyses and reports on developments in the political situation in Dalmatia, displaying an ac-

213–57. See too *De Gasperi e il Trentino tra la fine dell'800 e il primo dopoguerra*; Garbari, *Vittorio de Riccabona (1844–1927)*; 'L'irredentismo nel Trentino,' pp. 307–46; Schober, 'Il Trentino durante il periodo di unione al Tirolo,' pp. 177–212; Benvenuti, *I principi vescovi di Trento fra Roma e Vienna*, pp. 273 et seq. On Venezia Giulia in the first decade of the twentieth century: Cattaruzza, *Socialismo adriatico*; Apih, Sapelli, and Guagnini, *Trieste*; Maserati, *Il movimento operaio*; Tamaro, *Storia di Trieste*, vol. 2; Millo, *L'élite del potere a Trieste*.

98  Unable to go further into the subject here, we only mention: Agnelli, 'Socialismo triestino, Austria e Italia,' pp. 221–80; Apih, 'La genesi di 'Irredentismo adriatico,'' pp. 263 et seq.; Millo, *Storia di una borghesia*, pp. 174 et seq. See too the interesting correspondence of Gaetano Salvemini, which shows that the scholar from Puglia was paying attention to the problems in the Adriatic many years prior to the outbreak of the world war: Salvemini, *Carteggio 1894–1902*, docs. 151, 162, 176; *Carteggio 1912–1914*.

99  On the question of the college of St Jerome: Engel-Janosi, *Österreich und der Vatikan*, vol. 1; DDI, III, 5, docs. 727, 760, 763, 787, 790, 793.

tivism that had not existed for many decades.[100] Among the most active were the consuls in Zara and the vice-consuls in Spalato, attentive observers of Dalmatian politics who were in contact with the leaders of the Italian Autonomous Party. The Italian diplomats, like the organizers of the Dante Alighieri Association, regarded the strengthening of the Italian Autonomous Party as useful to Italy even if the party did not support irredentist political ideas, because this would impede and prevent the total Croatization of Dalmatian society and permit the survival of an Italian and Italian-speaking minority in a region as strategically important as Dalmatia. In 1897, for example,[101] the vice-consul in Spalato, Giuseppe Giacchi, invited the government in Rome to put pressure on the Montenegrin court to get the Dalmatian Serb Party, which was close to the court in Cetinje, to allow the re-election of the autonomist representative Bonda to the parliament in Vienna. Bonda was loyal to the Habsburgs, and his electoral defeat would have gravely damaged the interests of the Italians in Dalmatia, for whose fate Italy ought to feel responsible.

As has been seen, the Italian government decided to give financial aid to the Italian Autonomist Party through the Dante Alighieri, which up until the outbreak of World War I was the main channel of contact between the kingdom's ruling class and the Italians in Dalmatia. Official diplomacy, on the other hand, tried not to appear in collusion with the Italian parties for fear of being accused of interference in Austrian internal affairs.

There were two principal motivations for the aid of the Italian state to the Italian minority in Dalmatia. In the first place, the national liberal ideology of the Italian ruling class created a sense of solidarity with the Italian populations of Austria; the grave situation of the Italians in Dalmatia made the concession of political and economic support to the Italian Autonomous Party seem almost like a moral obligation. It was feared that the Croatization of the Italian minority in Dalmatia might be the prelude to a further weakening of the Italian positions in Istria, Trieste, and Gorizia. Giuseppe Marcotti wrote of these fears to Pasquale Villari: 'My pessimistic predictions about Dalmatia do not, in my view, remove the need to hold out to the end so that the Croatians will not

---

100  On this, see for example: DDI, III, 5, docs. 876, 1064; 6, doc. 598; 7, docs. 30, 122, 149, 368, 719.

101  Giacchi to Visconti Venosta, 7 March 1897, ASMAE, SP 1891–1916, portfolio 88.

be free to act against Istria, as well as for moral reasons.'[102] Then there was the conviction that the survival of groups of Italians on the eastern shore of the Adriatic was a useful tool for Italy's foreign policy; according to one of the promoters of the Dante Alighieri, Donato Sanminiatelli, the Italian minority in Dalmatia could be a 'convenient link with the interior of the Balkan peninsula, should the day come when a favourable opportunity presents itself, and we do not lack the energy necessary to make our economic and perhaps even political influence felt over there.'[103]

Prompted by the desire to assert Italy's international influence with more force and vigour, the Zanardelli-Prinetti government was operating at a time when Italo-Austrian relations were not easy. The question of the renewal of the Italo-Habsburg commercial treaty of 1891,[104] the negotiations for the renewal of the Triple Alliance, and King Victor Emmanuel III's visit to Russia brought the relationship between Rome and Vienna to a point of grave crisis during the course of 1902.

Between the end of 1901 and the summer of 1902 feverish diplomatic negotiations were conducted for the renewal of the Italo-Austrian and Italo-German trade agreements and the Triple Alliance, negotiations that were characterized by a fierce clash of interests and points of view among the parties.[105] Prinetti wanted to renew the Triple Alliance but no longer to use it against the French. He saw it rather as a way of protecting Italian economic interests and, above all, a means of wielding influence in the Balkans and obtaining a future diplomatic solution to the Italian national question. So it was no accident that – apart from the demands on commercial matters and with regard to the Libyan question – the nub of the requests for modification of the treaty of the Triple Alliance presented by Prinetti concerned articles VI and VII, relating to the problems of the Balkans and territorial compensation for Italy. In February 1902 he proposed a new draft of those articles.[106] On the

---

102  Marcotti to Villari, 22 October 1903, DA, fasc. 1897, B 7.

103  Sanminiatelli to Pisani Dossi [?],22 July 1897, DA, file 1897, B 51.

104  DDF, II, 1, doc. 294; II, 2, doc. 535.

105  These events are already widely known, having been reconstructed in detail by numerous historians, including: Tommasini, *L'Italia alla vigilia*, I; Pribram, *The Secret Treaties of Austria-Hungary*; Fellner, 'Der Dreibund,' pp. 51 et seq.; Salvatorelli, *La Triplice Alleanza*.

106  *Nuovo testo per gli articoli VI e VII*, enclosed with Prinetti to Lanza, 26 February 1902, DDI, III, 6, doc. 182; GP, 18, part 2, doc. 5729.

one hand, he asked the two allied powers to commit themselves to opposing any attempt by 'any third great power' to alter the *status quo* in the Balkan region (and in particular the territories still under Ottoman rule) in a manner harmful to the interests of a member of the Triple Alliance. On the other, Prinetti rewrote article VII on compensation. He asked Austria-Hungary and Italy to undertake 'to apply their efforts to making sure that modifications of the *status quo* are made in the direction of autonomy'; however, if the two powers 'saw the need to modify the *status quo* in these regions,' the occupation of Balkan territories would only take place after an agreement in advance between Italy and Austria-Hungary that would be founded on the principle of mutual compensation for any territorial or other advantage that one party had obtained.[107]

We should not be misled by the reference to the principle of the autonomy of the Balkan nations contained in Prinetti's proposals, which recalled the contents of the notes on Albania in 1900–1; primarily it signified a desire to prepare for any future eventuality, including that of the expansion of existing Balkan states or the rise of new ones. In any case, the sense of the text drawn up by the minister showed clearly that the autonomy of the Balkan states was not the main objective pursued by Italy, since this possibility was strongly limited by the next paragraph of the article, which was devoted to providing, above and beyond political formalities, for the possibility of a Habsburg occupation of Balkan territories and territorial compensation for Italy.

Subsequently, in a letter to Nigra on 3 January 1903 Prinetti explained the meaning of his proposed modifications to the Triple Alliance. Complaining about the Habsburg refusal to agree with Italy in advance on the reforms to be introduced in Macedonia, the minister reminded him: 'Nor can it be said that I have neglected to point out to the Austro-Hungarian Government the great importance and significance that I attributed to that 7th art. in the event that the treaty be renewed ... In fact this 7th article is the expression of one of the most important objectives, perhaps the most important, that Italy sets herself with the Triple Alliance, i.e., that of not being faced with any surprise on the Balkan question, as happened in 1878, when she found herself completely in the dark and isolated at the Berlin Congress.'[108]

---

107  Ibid.
108  Prinetti to Nigra, 3 January 1903, DDI, III, 7, doc. 290.

Thus Prinetti viewed the Triple Alliance as an instrument for Italy's Balkan policy and for a diplomatic solution to the problem of the unredeemed lands. Prinetti did not introduce innovations into Italian political thinking on the Triple Alliance; rather, he was a new and skilled executor of the old plan devised by Mancini and Robilant.

The Austrians and Germans showed themselves to be of one accord in rejecting Prinetti's proposals. Germany was opposed to extending its political commitments to the Balkans;[109] Austria-Hungary was unwilling to accept new and more binding constraints and was reluctant to extend its co-operation with Italy to the whole of the Balkan region. Even when Prinetti withdrew the requests for modification of articles VI and VII, asking for the simple promise of a future Italo-Austrian understanding on Macedonia, similar to the one reached on Albania,[110] Goluchowski refused to make any separate agreement with Italy, on the specious argument that the Macedonian question, unlike the Albanian one, formed part 'of the big question of the East, regulated by international treaties comprising not just Italian and Austro-Hungarian interests, but European ones.'[111]

The outcome of the negotiations was not very positive for the Italian government, which was forced to accept the lapse of the commercial treaty with Austria-Hungary and a renewal of the complete text of the Triple Alliance without changes (30 June 1902); the only consolation for Prinetti was the Habsburg declaration of a lack of interest in Tripolitania, which was a further step in diplomatic preparations for the Italian conquest of the African region.

So Prinetti did not obtain significant results in the negotiations for the renewal of the Triple Alliance; on the contrary, the toughness and harshness of the negotiations aggravated relations between the powers of the Triple Alliance. Italo-Austrian relations deteriorated further in the second half of 1902 following the Italian government's decision to have the new king, Victor Emmanuel III, make his first journey abroad to Berlin and St Petersburg without stopping in Austria; this irritated Vienna, which saw a visit to Russia without first passing through the Austrian capital as an act of defiance and a snub.[112] Victor Emmanuel's

109  Bülow to Wedel, 9 March 1902, GP, 18, part 2, doc. 5731.
110  Prinetti to Nigra, 7 April 1902, DDI, III, 6, doc. 329.
111  Nigra to Prinetti, 15 April 1902, DDI, III, 6, doc. 379; see too docs. 389, 425.
112  On this Tommasini, L'Italia alla vigilia, vol. 1, pp. 173–86; DDI, III, 7, docs. 11, 22. On the worsening of Italo-Habsburg relations: Afflerbach, Der Dreibund, pp. 487 et seq.

visit to Russia was an attempt to improve Italo-Russian relations and to have Italy play a leading role in Balkan policy by broadening the Austro-Russian understanding. Prinetti accompanied the king to St Petersburg and had talks with the new foreign minister, Wladimir Lamzdorf, but these, apart from fine words, produced few concrete results. Lamzdorf was favourable to a strengthening and revival of the Austro-Russian understanding, in part because he was anxious to maintain good relations with Vienna in order to preserve the Balkan *status quo* in anticipation of major Russian military and political initiatives in the Far East at a time of growing tension with Japan.[113] Not coincidentally, Lamzdorf went to Vienna in December 1902 and began negotiations with Goluchowski to outline a program of reforms to be proposed to the signatory powers of the 1878 Treaty of Berlin concerning the pacification of Macedonia, which was tormented by continual guerrilla warfare and terrorism directed against the Turks and inspired and financed by the Bulgarian government.[114] Prinetti asked for an Italian representative to be allowed to participate in the Austro-Russian talks,[115] but this met with a double refusal; both Goluchowski and Lamzdorf preferred to first conduct confidential Austro-Russian negotiations and then communicate their results to the other signatory powers of the Treaty of Berlin, including Italy.[116] The joint determination of the Austrians and Russians not to give Italy a primary role in Balkan policy was clear.

Prinetti's policy was criticized and opposed by the Italian ambassador to Vienna, Costantino Nigra. Cavour's former aide, Nigra was one of the most highly respected diplomats in Europe at the time, and over the course of his long stay in Vienna, begun in 1885 as Robilant's successor, he had been able to win the trust of Austrian political circles, establishing good relations with Kálnoky, Goluchowski, and Emperor Francis Joseph himself, and had become a firm supporter of the preservation of the Triple Alliance.[117] In his view, the Triple Alliance had

---

113 On Lamzdorf's ideas: Bompard to Delcassé, 26 February 1903, DDF, II, 3, doc. 105.
114 DDI, III, 7, doc. 248; Tommasini, *L'Italia alla vigilia*, vol. 1, pp. 190–1; Bridge, *From Sadowa*, p. 258. On the results of the talks: GP, 18, part 1, doc. 5504.
115 DDI, III, 7, docs. 255, 264. See too GP, 18, part 1, doc. 5500; DDF, II, 2, docs. 542, 553.
116 DDI, III, 7, docs. 258, 271, 281; GP, 18, part 1, doc. 5502.
117 On Nigra's time in Vienna: Bonin Longare, 'Ricordi di Vienna nei primi anni della Triplice Alleanza,' pp. 145–68; Claar, 'Zwanzig Jahre habsburgischer Diplomatie in Rom. (1895–1915) Persönliche Erinnerungen,' pp. 539 et seq.; Tommasini, 'Erinnerungen an Wien (1900–1912),' pp. 469–78.

brought undeniable benefits to Italy and its international position.[118] Sceptical about the real strength and solidity of the unified state, he was convinced that it was in Italy's interest to see the maintenance of peace in Europe, and in particular the survival of the Habsburg Empire, which he believed to be internally fragile, anxious to preserve the *status quo* in the Balkans, and averse to any idea of new conquests. In the Italian diplomat's opinion, 'the Austro-Hungarian Government finds itself in enormous difficulties owing to the coexistence of different nationalities in the empire. Adding a new element of division to those already in existence would be more than imprudent, it would be disastrous to the Empire. Austria-Hungary is a conservative country in its essence. It has no conquering tendencies. It wants the *status quo* at its gates.'[119] According to Nigra, the Habsburg state was an easy going and peaceful neighbour that left its Italian populations undisturbed; it would be a grave error to want to replace it with a large Slav state, which would persecute the Italian element.[120] Nigra did not agree with Prinetti's designs and with his harsh and direct style. He criticized the minister's actions during the negotiations for the renewal of the commercial treaty and the Triple Alliance, as well as in the area of Balkan policy.[121] In his view, Prinetti's lack of a spirit of reconciliation and political toughness, along with the resurgence of irredentism in Italy fostered by the government in office, was leading to a marked worsening in the relations between Vienna and Rome and to the risk of a war. Unable to support the actions of the government, Nigra asked to be recalled from the embassy in Vienna.[122]

Italo-Austrian relations continued to deteriorate even after Prinetti's retirement from the office of foreign minister following a serious stroke in January 1903 and his replacement by Admiral Enrico Costantino

---

118  On this see Nigra to Robilant, 9–11 August 1886, DDI, II, 20, doc. 31; DDI, II, 27, doc. 769; DB, 2, doc. 34.
119  Nigra to Prinetti, 19 June 1902, DDI, III, 6, doc. 579.
120  In this connection see the report of a conversation between Bülow and Nigra in September 1903: *Aufzeichnung des Reichskanzlers Grafen von Bülow, z.Z. in Wien*, 20 September 1903, GP, 18, part 2, doc. 5780; Bülow, *Memoirs of Prince von Bülow*.
121  DDI, III, 6, docs. 193, 353; 7, docs. 258, 271; GP, 18, part 2, docs. 5716, 5723; Tommasini, *L'Italia alla vigilia*, vol. 1, pp. 295–6.
122  Interesting in this respect are the memories of Francesco Tommasini, Nigra's aide at the Italian embassy in Vienna in those years: Tommasini, *L'Italia alla vigilia*, vol. 1, pp. 295–6; *Erinnerungen*, pp. 472–3.

Morin, first pro tempore and then permanently.[123] With the appointment of Morin, Zanardelli's influence on foreign policy grew, maintaining a continuity with respect to the direction imparted to it by Prinetti, even though Morin lacked the personality and the political skills of the Milanese minister.

The aggravated problem of the creation of an Italian university in Austria-Hungary as a political question contributed to the anti-Austrian shift in Italian public opinion.[124] The attempts to set up a faculty of Italian law at Innsbruck University and the anti-Italian reactions that this stirred among Tyrolean Germans triggered innumerable anti-Habsburg and irredentist demonstrations in Italy in May 1903, of an intensity and scale that had not been seen for many decades;[125] these demonstrations were repeated in November in protest against the anti-Italian riots that had taken place in Innsbruck on the occasion of the inauguration of the Italian faculty in the Tyrolean capital. Anti-Austrian irredentism had again become widespread and popular among Italian students and intellectuals, rendering the handling of bilateral relations between Rome and Vienna even more complicated.

Spectacular proof of the spread of Austrophobic feelings was provided by the irredentist demonstrations that were held in Udine in August that same year on the occasion of the visit by the Italian king and queen to the annual manoeuvres of the army. Many Austrian Italians went to Udine and publicly fêted the king. As Luigi Carlo Schiavi, head of the Udine section of the Dante Alighieri Association, wrote to Pasquale Villari, 'people from Trieste, Istria, and Dalmatia rallied around national flags flying at half-mast, with noisy expressions of love for Italy and hatred for Austria, and found broad support among our people.'[126]

In Austria-Hungary these events aroused great irritation,[127] despite Morin's attempts to play them down.[128] On the occasion of German

---

123  DDF, II, 3, docs. 57, 115; Tommasini, *L'Italia alla vigilia*, vol. 1, pp. 194–7.
124  On this, Ara, 'La questione dell'università italiana in Austria,' in *Ricerche sugli austro-italiani e l'ultima Austria*, pp. 9 et seq.
125  DDI, III, 7, docs. 493, 495, 498, 507, 511, 515, 519, 520, 554; DDF, II, 3, docs. 266, 270; Tommasini, *L'Italia alla vigilia*, vol. 1, pp. 204 et seq.
126  Schiavi to Villari, 28 September 1904, DA, file 1904, B 7. On the irredentist demonstrations in Udine see Del Bianco, *La guerra e il Friuli*, vol. 1, pp. 145 *et sqq*; Mantegazza, *L'altra sponda*, pp. 482–3.
127  GP, 18, part 2, doc. 5779.
128  GP, 18, part 2, doc. 5777.

Emperor Wilhelm II's visit to Vienna from 18 to 19 September, Golu-chowski complained to Chancellor Bernhard von Bülow about the Italian attitude: the irredentist demonstrations were real provocations that, when added to the action in Albania of the Rome government, had anti-Austrian aims; if Italy did not change its behaviour, Goluchowski would not renew the Triple Alliance without guarantees of better con-trol over irredentism and a less adventurous policy in Albania. Emperor Francis Joseph also showed his concern; the irredentist demonstrations were trying his patience, and in his view, Italo-Austrian relations had worsened after the death of King Umberto as a result of the Austropho-bia of King Victor Emmanuel III, an ambitious and proud man whose sympathies lay with the irredentists and who had an excessive interest in Balkan policy.[129]

Italo-Austrian relations deteriorated in those months to a degree that had not been seen for many decades. Nigra pointed out with grave concern that the irredentist demonstrations had had a deleterious effect on the relationship between Italy and Austria-Hungary:

> Officially there is an alliance, and there is no hostility in the relations be-tween the two Governments. However, not only is there no friendship between the populations of the two countries, but its place has been taken by a marked aversion. What popular feelings toward Austria are in Italy, and especially among the young in the schools, Your Excellency knows better than I. In Austria, among the German and Slav population, the ir-ritation with irredentist demonstrations is very widespread and is all the deeper the less it is outwardly expressed ... If this state of mutual irritation on the part of a substantial section of opinion in the two countries were to continue for a long time and were to be exacerbated it would not be with-out danger for peaceful relations between the two neighbouring states.[130]

The reaction of the Austrian government was twofold. On the one hand, diplomatically it sought to consolidate relations with Russia, working closely with it in the Balkan area and preparing two plans of reform for Macedonia over the course of 1903 (the February Memo-randum and the Mürzsteg Pact); the plans excluded Italy and aimed to create an Austro-Russian supremacy in the Ottoman territories in

---

129  *Aufzeichnung des Reichskanzlers Grafen von Bülow, z. Z. in Wien,* 20 September 1903.
130  Nigra to Morin, 5 September 1903, DDI, III, 7, doc. 707.

question[131] and to ensure Russian friendship in the event of war with Italy. On the other hand, the government in Vienna decided to build up its military forces on the Italo-Austrian border, preparing itself for the eventuality of just such a war.[132]

The Austrian rearmament was naturally detected and noted[133] and helped to increase the level of political tension in Italy, further weakening the Zanardelli government. This executive had lost strength over the course of 1903, first with Prinetti's illness and then with the resignation of Giovanni Giolitti as minister of the interior in June. A series of major failures in foreign policy led to its progressive disintegration. Following on the deterioration in relations with Vienna and the presentation of the Austro-Russian program of reforms in Macedonia, the cancelling of Tsar Nicholas's planned visit to Italy[134] was a heavy blow for the Zanardelli government as it marked the failure of its attempt to find an alternative interlocutor to Vienna in the area of Balkan policy. These were all facts that underlined Italy's political weakness at a time of grave tension with Austria-Hungary and Germany.

Attacked from many sides and being seriously ill, Zanardelli handed in his resignation on 21 October 1903. His successor was Giovanni Giolitti, who found himself confronting a difficult international situation: while Italy had achieved a rapprochement with France, it had not succeeded in creating a political co-operation with Russia and faced a grave crisis in relations with the states of the Triple Alliance.

### 3.3. The Italian Autonomist Party and the Croatian 'New Course' in Dalmatia (1903–7)

The Austrian political system went through a profound crisis between the last decade of the nineteenth century and the first decade of the twentieth. In Hungary conflict grew between the dominant nationality, the Magyars, and the oppressed Croatian, Slovak, and Romanian

---

131 On this: DDI, III, 7, docs. 360, 362, 363, 366, 387, 389, 391; DDF, II, 3, docs. 87, 89, 103; GP, 18, part 1, docs. 5507, 5508, 5514, 5522, 5539, 5612, 5621, 5626; Tommasini, *L'Italia alla vigilia*, vol. 1, pp. 211 et seq.; Bridge, *From Sadowa*, pp. 257 et seq.
132 Bridge, *From Sadowa*, pp. 257 et seq.
133 Baccelli to Nigra, 2 February 1903, DDI, III, 7, doc. 328.
134 In this connection: Tommasini, *L'Italia alla vigilia*, vol. 1, pp. 211–16; Donnini, 'Un momento dei rapporti italo-russi all'inizio del secolo,' pp. 447 et seq.; DDF, II, 3, docs. 132, 143.

minorities, while in Cisleithania the crisis of the Taaffe government in 1893 had marked the beginning of a long period of instability. The strengthening of the more radical and hard-line tendencies in the various national parties made it increasingly difficult to form a multinational parliamentary coalition that would support the actions of the Austrian government.[135] With the Iron Ring coalition thrown into crisis by the Taaffe government's plans for electoral reform, the radicalization of the unrest between Germans and Czechs in Bohemia and Moravia aggravated the conflict in the Austrian political system. The Czech-German clash over a bill on the use of languages in Bohemia, which was presented by the government headed by the Pole Kazimierz Badeni, triggered violence in the streets and fierce disputes in parliament, with the German representatives of the most varied factions turning to obstructionist practices to prevent approval of the law.[136] The crisis of November 1897 brought down the Badeni government and marked the beginning of a paralysis of the Austrian parliamentary system. From 1897 onward national conflict broke out with ever greater frequency in parliament, finding expression in continual recourse to an obstructionism that had the effect of blocking the normal activity of the Abgeordnetenhaus. This resulted in an interruption of the evolution of the system of government in a parliamentary direction, and the establishment of a situation in which the executive, appointed by the emperor, enjoyed broad and unlimited powers on the basis of the resort to imperial emergency decrees that allowed it to pass laws independently of the parliament. Ernst Koerber, a high state official, headed the Austrian government from 1900 to 1904 essentially without the co-operation of a stable parliamentary majority. His aim was to build consensus in the country through a program of economic development that would meet the concrete needs of the different populations.[137] All this was done on

135  For an overview of the political and national conflicts within the Habsburg Empire between the end of the nineteenth century and World War I: Boyer, *Culture and Political Crisis in Vienna*; Valiani, *The End of Austria-Hungary*; Hantsch, *Die Geschichte Österreichs*, vol. 2, pp. 457 et seq.; May, *The Hapsburg Monarchy*; Macartney, *The Habsburg Empire*; Kann, *History of the Habsburg Empire*; Höbelt, *Kornblume und Kaiseradler*, pp. 106 et seq.; 'Parties and Parliament,' pp. 41–61; 'Parteien und Fraktionen im Cisleithanischen Reichsrat,' pp. 954 et seq.

136  Höbelt, *Kornblume und Kaiseradler*, pp. 150 et seq.; Sutter, *Die Badenischen Sprachenverordnungen von 1897*, 2 vols.; Afflerbach, *Der Dreibund*, pp. 472 et seq.; DDS, 4, doc. 240.

137  On the Koerber government: May, *The Hapsburg Monarchy*; Redlich, *Emperor Francis Joseph of Austria*.

the basis of continual political horse-trading with the various parties present in the parliament. The result was an extremely bizarre political system, with a parliament that existed on the legal plane but was incapable of legislating because of obstructionism; its members regarded extra-parliamentary negotiations with ministers as the crucial part of their activity, aimed at obtaining favours for their own constituencies or parties. As the Austro-German historian and politician Josef Redlich has pointed out, while there was seemingly a constitutional government in Austria, what existed in practice was a 'bureaucratic absolutism' legitimized by the authority of the emperor.[138]

Despite the existence of an executive able to function by disregarding parliament, national conflict continued to worsen. The elections of 1901 indicated a strengthening of the more radical nationalist parties. The German national parties with a pan-German outlook increased their representation. In Bohemia the anti-German and pro-Russian Young Czechs, led by Karel Kramář, became the biggest party.[139] Other national conflicts grew worse in Austria in those years: unrest over the question of university teaching in Italian exacerbated the national rivalry between Germans and Italians in the Tyrol, as was shown by the repeated riots in Austrian university cities and at Innsbruck in particular in 1903 and 1904; and the conflicts between Ukrainian/Ruthenians and Poles in Galicia and between Italians, Slovenes, and Croats in Venezia Giulia showed no signs of losing their intensity.

Even the confessional and Marxist parties took on increasingly national and nationalistic connotations. In the German Catholic world the strength of Karl Lueger's Christian Socialists grew, becoming the main party representing Austrian Germans. Lueger's movement was capable of putting down roots among the masses of German Austria thanks to a political message that combined Catholic conservatism, a sensitivity to social problems, anti-Semitism, and a vigorous defence of German national rights.[140]

---

138 Redlich, *Emperor Francis Joseph of Austria*, p. 453. An interesting record of political life in Austria in the first two decades of the twentieth century can be found in Redlich's diary: Fellner, ed., *Schicksalsjahre Österreichs 1908–1918*, 2 vols.

139 A commentary on the result of the Austrian elections of 1901 in de Clarapède to Brenner, 28 January 1901, DDS, 4, doc. 352.

140 On the Austrian Christian Socialists, a political party that has had a great influence on political Catholicism in Europe, the works of John Boyer are fundamental: Boyer, *Political Radicalism in Late Imperial Vienna; Culture and Political Crisis in Vienna*.

The socialist movement, which was gaining increasing electoral support in those years, was not able to maintain a unified political structure as it was undermined by national antagonisms, with the Czechs at odds with the Germans and progressively more independent of them.[141]

The political situation in Austria was not particularly reassuring even in the eyes of observers who nursed a great admiration for the Habsburg Empire, such as the Italian ambassador in Vienna, Costantino Nigra. The Italian diplomat did not fail to inform his government about the crisis in Austrian domestic policy and its gravity, reporting the exacerbation of national conflicts and the progressive paralysis of parliamentary activity following the fall of the Badeni government;[142] however, in his view, the fierce national struggles did not threaten the survival of the Habsburg state. In March 1901 Nigra wrote: 'In any other country this state of affairs might provoke momentous changes in the body of the state. But Austria possesses two conditions that rescue it from this danger. One of these conditions is the attachment of the population not just to the person of the current Emperor, who is venerated everywhere, but also to the monarchic tradition. The other consists in the disciplined and loyal structure of the army, which remains intact so far.'[143]

As in the rest of Austria-Hungary, political life in Dalmatia was increasingly dominated by the nationalist parties in the last decades of the nineteenth century. The 1880s and 1890s saw the undisputed supremacy of the old Croatian National Party, with a majority both in the provincial diet and among the Dalmatian parliamentary representatives in Vienna. The 'opportunistic' policy of Klaić and Bulat had been founded on total and sincere co-operation with the Habsburg authorities and a pragmatic acceptance of the separation between Dalmatia and Croatia, which was sanctioned by the constitutional laws of 1867, in the hope of a trialist reorganization of the empire in the distant future that would lead to the creation of a Habsburg Greater Croatia. However, this policy now provoked the rise of new intransigent and radical Dalmatian Croatian nationalist groups, which broke away from the old

141 On Austrian social democracy see Agnelli, *Questione nazionale e socialismo*; Droz, 'La socialdemocrazia nell'Austria-Ungheria.'
142 Nigra to the Foreign Minister, 3 April, 5 April, and 18 December 1897, 3 September 1899, ASMAE, SP 1891–1916, portfolio 88; Nigra to Visconti Venosta, 20 January 1901, DDI, III, 4, doc. 688; DDI, III, 5, docs. 66, 1113.
143 Nigra to Prinetti, 18 March 1901, DDI, III, 5, doc. 138.

National Party. They found ideological and organizational expression in the Party of Rights, which was set up in Croatia by Ante Starčević in opposition to the policy of compromise with Hungary and in favour of an uncompromising struggle for the unification of the so-called Croatian lands into a single state.[144]

The Dalmatian section of the Party of Rights was founded, as has been seen, by some members of the most anti-Serbian and Italophobic wing of Croatian nationalism, Don Juraj Biankini and Don Ivo Prodan, and a number of young militants, including the lawyer Ante Trumbić from Spalato,[145] the judicial officer and lawyer Josip Smodlaka,[146] and Frano Supilo[147] (originally from Cavtat) who worked as a journalist first in Ragusa and then in Fiume (Rijeka).

There were two factions within the Dalmatian Party of Rights. The first, represented by Biankini and Prodan, was characterized by a xenophobic Croatian nationalism, steeped in Catholicism and clericalism, and fiercely anti-Serbian and anti-Italian. In the second, a strong sense of pan-Croatian nationalism coexisted with a secular liberal ideology, typical of the Dalmatian middle classes, who had previously supported the autonomists but in the closing decades of the nineteenth century had in part sided with the Croatian nationalists. The representatives of this new Dalmatian-Croatian nationalism were men like Trumbić, Smodlaka, and Supilo, young notables and intellectuals eager to reconcile the principal components of Dalmatian culture (Italo-Slav municipalism and Slavophile nationalism) in order to place Dalmatia at the head of the Croatian national revival.

Trumbić, Smodlaka, and Supilo became the leading figures of Croatian politics in Dalmatia, carving out the roles of uncompromising defenders of Croat national rights and critics of the nationalist establishment dominated by an Austrophile Italian Dalmatian like Bulat. In their efforts to win support they did not refrain from attacking the Italian Autonomous Party. Supilo was a fierce adversary of the Autonomist

---

144  On Starčević, refer to Banac, *The National Question in Yugoslavia*, pp. 85 et seq.; Gross, *Die Anfänge*, pp. 137 et seq.

145  On the figure of Trumbić: Perić, *Ante Trumbić na dalmatinskom političkom poprištu*; Trumbić, *Izabrani Spisi* and *Suton Austro-Ugarske i Riječka rezolucija*.

146  On the figure of Smodlaka: Smodlaka, *Izabrani Spisi* and *Zapisi dra Josipa Smodlaka*; Schödl, *Kroatische Nationalpolitk und 'Jugoslavenstvo*,' pp. 156 et seq.

147  On Supilo: Šepić, 'Političke koncepcije Frana Supila,' in Supilo, *Politički Spisi*, pp. 7–95; Petrinović, *Politička misao Frana Supila*; Valiani, *The end of Austria-Hungary*.

Party in Ragusa during the years he edited the *Crvena Hrvatska* news-paper, while Trumbić and Smodlaka distinguished themselves in the Dalmatian provincial diet with attacks on the Autonomist Party and the private Italian schools founded by the Lega Nazionale.[148] At the same time, however, the two lawyers from Spalato maintained good personal relations with the city's autonomist leaders, Ercolano Salvi and Leonardo Pezzoli.

It was among these young Dalmatian *pravaši* (followers of the Party of Rights) that a new Croatian national program took form between the end of the 1890s and the early years of the 1900s. An unprecedented element in the ideology of this new Croatian nationalism was its grow-ing hostility to the German world and culture.[149] Under the ideologi-cal influence of the Germanophobic nationalism of the Young Czechs, Trumbić and Supilo regarded German culture as the greatest threat to the Slavic world of the south. They considered the Habsburg Empire to be a tool of Germany's effort to carry out a cultural and economic Germanization of the Slav populations of the Danubian and Balkan re-gions; the government in Vienna was seen as an enemy of the Croatian nation, which was oppressed and divided up within the Habsburg Empire. It was a Germanophobia of a chiefly ideological nature, which could be explained by the reawakening of pan-Slav and Russophile feelings and tendencies in these Croatian politicians, who dreamed in a very abstract way of future Balkan federations of the Slav peoples and underestimated the strength of national particularism. In addition to the rekindling of Slavophile tendencies, another return to the past of the Dalmatian nationalist tradition was the assertion that Croats and Serbs were a single nation, inasmuch as the religious differences were not considered sufficient to separate the two peoples. For the young members of the *pravaši* movement it was necessary for Croats and Serbs in Dalmatia and all the Habsburg lands to find unity and co-operate politically under the banner of a common program that would make Croatia the hub and guide for all the Habsburg southern Slavs.

---

148  For example: speech by Trumbić, session of 16 February 1898, pp. 744–55; speech by
      Trumbić, session of 15 July 1902, pp. 731–5, ADP-BI.
149  On this: Ganza-Aras, 'Il rapporto della politica croata in Dalmazia,' pp. 173 et seq.;
      Ganza-Aras, *Politika 'Novog Kursa' dalmatinskih pravaša oko Supila i Trumbića*, pp. 83
      et seq. Very interesting, for their analysis of the anti-German and anti-Habsburg
      component of the new Croatian Dalmatian nationalism, are Trumbić's memoirs:
      Trumbić, *Suton Austro-Ugarske.*

An innovative element in the thinking of Trumbić and his friends with respect to the tradition of Croatian nationalism in Dalmatia was the desire to seek friendship with Italy and a national compromise with the Italians of Dalmatia, Istria, and Quarnero.

It is interesting to note that for Trumbić, Smodlaka, and Supilo it was important to try to link the national struggles of the southern Slavs with the interests and objectives of some of the European great powers, which were regarded as a potential source of international support for Croatian national rights that might be useful in the event of the break-up of the Habsburg state. Once again following the example of the Czech nationalists, who were careful to publicize and plead their own national cause in France, Great Britain, and Russia from the end of the nineteenth century onward,[150] the Croats started to see European public opinion as a political battlefield. However, the great attention paid to Italy was peculiar to the Croatian Dalmatians, and this explains in part the desire to adopt a new policy toward the Italians of Dalmatia.[151] In the early twentieth century Italy was a rising power on the international scene. After overcoming the trauma of the war with Ethiopia and the instability at home, the Italian state had embarked on a process of economic growth that had strengthened the country on the international plane. Supilo and Trumbić believed that Italy, historic adversary of the Habsburg Empire, whose foreign policy in the years of the Zanardelli government was clearly anti-Austrian, could become a point of reference and an ally of the new Croatian nationalism. The political need for an Italo-Croatian national compromise stemmed from the aim of creating an alliance between pan-Croatian nationalism and Italy. In the first place, in order to reinforce the drive for a pan-Croatian union it was necessary to improve relations with the Italians of Dalmatia, Fiume, and Istria and bring about a political agreement that would facilitate, in exchange for the recognition of some Italian cultural rights, the union of those lands with the rest of the Croatian lands. Secondly, overcoming Italo-Croatian antagonism in Venezia Giulia and Dalmatia

---

150 In those years the Young Czechs launched a propaganda campaign in France: GP, 13, docs. 3488, 3495, 3499, 3500. On the close political and ideological ties between Czech and Croat nationalists: Agičić, *Hrvatsko-češki odnosi na prijelazu iz XIX u XX stoljeće.*

151 Ganza-Aras, *Politika 'Novog Kursa' dalmatinskih pravaša*; Trumbić, *Suton Austro-Ugarske.*

was an indispensable condition for winning the support of the government in Rome and Italian public opinion.

The New Course in Croatian politics and the dialogue with the Italian autonomists got under way in 1903 as a reaction to the disturbances that had broken out in Croatia and in Zagreb. In the first few months of 1903 anti-Hungarian demonstrations organized at Zagreb and many other places in Croatia and Slavonia triggered numerous disturbances and riots, with deaths and hundreds of arrests among the Croatian demonstrators.[152]

These events – which were followed a few months later, in June, by the *coup d'état* in Serbia, with the massacre of the ruling Obrenović family and the ascent of the Karadjordjević dynasty to the throne,[153] and the subsequent new anti-Austrian course taken by Serbian foreign policy – prompted protests in all the Habsburg Slav territories and finally persuaded many Croat and Serb politicians of the need for a change in political direction that would lead to the overcoming of Serbo-Croatian conflict in the name of a common collaboration against Magyars and Germans.

The leaders of the Party of Rights, Trumbić and Supilo, provided the firm guidance for this change, exploiting the fact that their political control of Dalmatia gave the pan-Croatian nationalists greater freedom of action. First of all, numerous demonstrations were staged in Dalmatia to protest against the events in Croatia.[154] Then Trumbić and various Croatian Dalmatian members of the parliament tried to obtain an audience with the emperor in Vienna in order to express their disagreement with the policy of the Hungarian government and their solidarity with their fellows in Croatia and Slavonia, but this was disdainfully refused.[155]

Discontent with the imperial government grew in Dalmatia as a result of the policy of the province's governor, Erasmus von Handel, who was eager to bolster the influence of German culture through the crea-

---

152  On the disturbances in Croatia in 1903: Miller, *Between Nation and State*, pp. 60 et seq.; Lebrecht to the Foreign Minister, 7 May 1903; Cusani to the Foreign Minister, 12 May 1903, ASMAE, SP 1891–1916, portfolio 90.

153  On the events in Serbia in 1903: Tommasini, *L'Italia alla vigilia*, vol. 1; DDI, III, 7, docs. 552, 555, 556, 561.

154  Tritonj to the Foreign Minister, 6 June 1903, ASMAE, SP 1891–1916, portfolio 90.

155  Tritonj to the Foreign Minister, 23 May 1903, ASMAE, SP 1891–1916, portfolio 90.

tion of a German high school in Zara[156] and a project of public administration reform that made German the main language to be used in the Dalmatian bureaucracy.

Outraged at the behaviour of the Habsburg government in Croatia and Dalmatia, Supilo and Trumbić made a series of contacts with Italian political and cultural circles with the aim of making Italy aware of the Croatian question and preparing the ground for an Italo-Croatian alliance. On these contacts between Italians and Croats in the years 1903 and 1904 there is only scanty and confused information.[157] It is evident, however, that in the heated climate of 1903 – the year of the repression in Croatia, as well as the Italo-Austrian clashes at Innsbruck and the irredentist demonstrations in Udine, which had brought the relations between Rome and Vienna to the brink of military conflict – these Dalmatian politicians were convinced that an Italo-Austrian and European war was likely and that it was therefore necessary to prepare the ground for the birth of an independent Croatian state should the Habsburg Empire disintegrate. A national Italo-Croatian accord in Dalmatia and Istria was important at that juncture precisely to lay the political foundations for collaboration between the government in Rome and the Croatian nationalists in the event of such a war. In this respect Trumbić noted: 'Our not very numerous Italians belong to the greater Italian community. They are supported by the entire Italian people. To have them against us means taking on Italy and the whole national Italian community.'[158] That the hypothesis of an Italo-Austrian war lay at the root of the plans for Italo-Croatian reconciliation in Dalmatia in 1903 is demonstrated by the fact that the Dalmatian *pravaši* made contact with the circles of the republican and irredentist Far Left that were led by Ricciotti Garibaldi and with members of the radical wing of the National Liberal Party in Trieste, as well as with a number of Italian liberal and socialist intellectuals such as Ferrero, Morgari, and Pavia. Forging political links with the most intransigent sectors of Italian ir-

---

156  Camicia to the Foreign Minister, 12 October 1903, ASMAE, SP 1891–1916, portfolio 90.
157  On the contacts between the Croatian-Dalmatian Party of Rights and Italian political circles: OUS, 2, docs. 30, 33, 56, 208, 256, 285; Ganza-Aras, 'Il rapporto della politica croata' ; Ganza-Aras, *Politika*; Šepić, 'Gli slavi del sud e l'irredentismo italiano,' pp. 237 et seq.; Petrinović, *Politička misao*, pp. 59 et seq.
158  Trumbić, *Izabrani spisi*, p. 179; Ganza-Aras, 'Il rapporto della politica croata,' p. 180.

redentism signified that they were pursuing a radically anti-Habsburg political objective.[159]

The Italians of Dalmatia were in favour of improving the relations with the Croatian parties dominant in the region. A national compromise with the Croat majority might lead to an improvement in the living conditions of the Italian and Italophile element, which had suffered from discrimination in its linguistic and cultural rights for decades. A crucial role in the contacts with the Dalmatian Party of Rights was played by Ercolano Salvi, a colleague and personal friend of Smodlaka and Trumbić. Over the course of the summer of 1903 political talks were held between Salvi and several Croatian representatives in Zara and Spalato. The Italian member of the diet declared that his party was ready for dialogue with the Croats as long as they were disposed to respect Italian national rights; in exchange the Italian autonomists would agree to the union of Dalmatia with Croatia.[160]

Many difficulties, however, lay in the way of an Italo-Slav national compromise in Dalmatia. The Croatian nationalists wanted the compromise with the Dalmatian Italians to be part of wider accord between all the Croats and Italians in Austria-Hungary, and thus including those of the Quarnero and Istria. They were ready to make concessions in Dalmatia, not as a unilateral gesture in the name of the recognition of the principles of liberty and national pluralism but in order to obtain, in compensation and consideration, advantages for the Croats of Istria and Fiume; moreover, many Croatian Dalmatians were not willing to recognize and accept a complete Italo-Croat bilingualism in Dalmatia and an equality of rights for the Italian language and culture.

In November 1903, while the Dalmatian provincial diet was in session, the quest for an Italo-Slav national compromise found public expression in a long speech[161] in which Trumbić outlined the new policies of Dalmatian Croatian nationalism. To the member from Spalato the greatest threat for the Croats was the German expansionism that aimed to subjugate the Slav and Balkan peoples. Rather than providing a place of refuge and protection for the small nations of central Europe, the

159 Šepić, 'Političke koncepcije Frana Supila,' in Supilo, *Politički Spisi*; Šepić, 'Gli slavi del sud e l'irredentismo italiano'; Trumbić, *Suton Austro-Ugarske*.
160 Ganza-Aras, 'Il rapporto della politica croata,' p. 181.
161 Speech by Trumbić, session of 7 November 1903, ADP-BI, pp. 651 et seq., reproduced in Trumbić, *Izabrani spisi*, pp. 37–58. On this speech: Ganza-Aras, *Politika*, pp. 205 et seq.

Habsburg monarchy had become a means of oppression. The creeping Germanization that the Habsburg administration was trying to bring about in Dalmatia proved that the government in Vienna was a tool of Germany. For the defence of their own rights and the realization of their own national aspirations the Croatians needed allies, and one of these was Italy. Relations with Italy had to be improved and strengthened; to this end and in the name of higher interests it was necessary to resolve and overcome the linguistic conflicts between the Italians and Croats and lay the foundations for their peaceful coexistence. 'We Croatians are not thinking about conquering Italy, and I hope that no Italian politician, worthy of the name, would lay claim to our coasts for his people, coasts that nature has separated through the sea, that at the same time keep us apart and unite us.'[162]

Another natural ally for the Croats were the Magyars, who had obtained great privileges from the Habsburgs with the system of dualism. In Trumbić's view, however, the Hungarians had to understand that their own liberty could not be rooted in the slavery of other peoples. Croatians and Hungarian patriots could fight together for their common freedom against an increasingly oppressive and despotic Habsburg rule.[163]

Smodlaka also spoke in the diet, making a speech on 8 November that offered an opening to the Italians and Serbs. After denouncing the repression of Croats in Hungary, the representative called for national reconciliation with Italy and the Italian Dalmatians and declared himself in favour of guarantees for the Italian language in Dalmatia. It was also necessary to overcome the differences with the Serbs, with whom a political collaboration had to be undertaken: 'This task is becoming even easier for us now that Serbia is ruled by a king, a friend of concord and peace with the Croatians, just as our friendship with the Italian nation has been made easier for us now that a queen sits on the throne of Italy in whose veins flows the blood of our nation.'[164]

Not all the Croatian members of the diet agreed with the arguments put forward by Trumbić and Smodlaka. The idea of opening up to the Italians clashed with an Italophobic political tradition that was hard for

162  Trumbić, *Izabrani spisi*, p. 51.
163  Ibid., pp. 52–7.
164  Speech by Smodlaka, session of 8 November 1903, ADP-BI, pp. 683 et seq., reproduced in Italian translation in *Il Dalmata*, 11 November 1903.

them to abandon; thus some members, like the Ragusan Pero Čingrija (Cingria), although in favour of the New Course, clung to the usual arguments that there was no Italian nationality in Dalmatia.[165]

The autonomist members reacted favourably but with a degree of caution to Trumbić's overtures. After all, the policy of Italo-Croatian reconciliation was being proposed by the same men who only the year before had been putting up a hard fight, in the diet, against the Italian schools of the Lega Nazionale at Spalato. On 8 November, Ercolano Salvi made a long speech praising Trumbić's new arguments in favour of Italo-Croatian friendship. For Salvi too it was time for the new generations of Dalmatians to set aside old prejudices and hostilities in the name of common values; the longstanding aversions to the Italian language had to be dropped, and the people had to unite in their struggle against Germanization:

> It was fair and just to recognize, as the Hon. Trumbich has done, that in this country of ours, Italian, vehicle of civilization, of culture, does not dilute the character of the Slavs, but gives them the weapons they need to rise, to invigorate the virgin national disposition, to illuminate it with a brighter flame; that Italian, freely adopted in these lands, ancestral and domestic heritage of Dalmatian intellectuals, cannot be compared to the slipknot of German bureaucratization that stifles, that freezes every vital impulse of moral independence, binding to the thralldom of the foreign imposition those who are called to head the government of public affairs, to preside over the development of our economic and political future.[166]

According to Salvi, the Autonomist Party was ready to work with the Croat and Serb nationalists of Dalmatia and, if necessary, re-examine its opposition to union with Croatia if the national rights of the Italian minority were to be recognized by the Croatian majority.[167]

Even the autonomist newspaper *Il Dalmata* published articles in favour of a national compromise between Slavs and Italians in Dalmatia.[168] The need for Italo-Croatian-Serbian collaboration against the

---

165  Speech by Cingria in the Dalmatian provincial diet on 8 November 1903, reported in *Il Dalmata*, 11 November 1903.
166  Speech by Ercolano Salvi, 8 November 1903, ADP-BI, 1903, pp. 679–83; the text of the speech is also reproduced in *Il Dalmata*, 11 November 1903.
167  Ibid.
168  'Dopo il voto,' in *Il Dalmata*, 14 November 1903.

Germans seemed to take on more significance after the clashes between Italian and German students at Innsbruck on the occasion of the opening of the department of Italian law at the local university.[169]

An initial, partial co-operation between the different Dalmatian parties, after decades of harsh and bitter struggle, took place over the course of the diet's proceedings when the Italian, Croat, and Serb representatives joined in opposition to the proposal by Governor Erasmus von Handel for regulation of the use of languages in the offices of the Dalmatian region, which envisaged the introduction of German as the obligatory language for use in the internal affairs of the public administration.[170]

Over the following months, however, while Croatian-Serbian contacts in Dalmatia and Croatia developed and were consolidated,[171] the plans for an Italo-Croatian accord in Dalmatia stalled. The only temporary result was a partial softening of the tones in the controversies between Italians and Croats.

The change in the international situation and in the relations between Rome and Vienna then obliged Supilo and Trumbić to modify the objectives of their political strategy. Convinced that a war in Europe was imminent, Trumbić met Ricciotti Garibaldi and, in the spring of 1904, went to Italy to make contact with the Foreign Ministry and Victor Emmanuel III with the aim of consolidating and giving substance to a possible Italo-Croatian collaboration against the Habsburgs. However, he did not succeed in his intention since both Foreign Minister Tommaso Tittoni and the king, anxious not to fuel suspicion in Vienna, refused to meet him and to enter into such a negotiation.[172] The improvement in relations between Italy and Austria-Hungary brought about by the Giolitti government, which wanted to preserve the Triple Alliance, averted the possibility of an Italo-Habsburg war and an opening of the Croatian question at the international level. For the time being, Trumbić and his friends renounced any hope of the immediate and rapid creation of an independent Croatian-Yugoslav state, limiting themselves to legal political activity within Austria-Hungary. The plan for an Italo-

---

169  'Nuove violenze teutoniche,' Il Dalmata, 28 November 1903; 'Per la libertà di tutti,' Il Dalmata, 5 December 1903.
170  Camicia to the Foreign Minister, 1, 10, and 16 November 1903, ASMAE, SP 1891–1916, portfolio 90.
171  On this: Miller, Between Nation and State, pp. 73 et seq.
172  Trumbić, Izabrani spisi, p. 185.

Croatian national compromise was not dropped but became a secondary element in a new legalistic strategy that was built around an
agreement with the supporters of Magyar national independence and
the Serbian parties of Austria-Hungary to obtain the unification of Dalmatia and Croatia within Transleithania, a preliminary step on the road
to a greater Croatian autonomy.

The persistence of an interest by the leaders of the Dalmatian Party of Rights in a political accord with the Italian autonomists derived
from the fact that the support of all the province's national components
would make it easier to bring about the union of Dalmatia with Croatia;
after all, the Autonomist Party had been the main obstacle to attempts
at pan-Croatian union in 1860–1. However, the Italo-Croatian negotiations made no progress since the *pravaši*, pursuing their pan-Croatian
goals, wanted them to include and resolve the national controversies in
Fiume, Istria, and Trieste, where, unlike in Dalmatia, the Italian and Italophile Liberal and Autonomist parties held power. Ziliotto gave Salvi
the task of conducting the negotiations with the Croatians and going to
Trieste to discuss the question with the leaders of the National Liberal
Party. The Italian leadership of the party in Istria, which held a majority
in the Istrian provincial diet, had been in direct political conflict with
the Croatian and Slovenian parties for many years, desiring to preserve
the Italian cultural and linguistic dominance of the region;[173] they were
opposed to making concessions as part of a general Italo-Slav accord.[174]

According to Romolo Tritonj, the Italian vice-consul in Spalato, there
were various reasons for the failure to achieve an Italo-Croatian deal.[175]
In the first place, the policy of opening to Italians was not shared by
the old leaders and by many militant Croatian nationalists, who were
faithful to their traditional Italophobia, and the clergy and the Austrian
government were hostile too; secondly and above all, it was difficult to
reach an agreement between Croats and Italians in Dalmatia because,

173 On the political situation in Istria at the beginning of the twentieth century and the
   attempts at an Italo-Slav national compromise in that region: Riccardi, *Salata*; Ara,
   'Le trattative per un compromesso nazionale in Istria (1900–1914),' pp. 247–328.
   On the national conflicts in Fiume in those years: Italian Consulate in Fiume to the
   Foreign Ministry, 6 October 1904, ASMAE, SP 1891–1916, portfolio 94; Ghisalberti,
   *Da Campoformio a Osimo*, pp. 201 et seq.; Capuzzo, 'Fiume tra storia e storiografia,'
   pp. 277 et seq.; Ballarini, *L'Antidannunzio a Fiume*.
174 Ganza-Aras, 'Il rapporto della politica croata,' pp. 182–9.
175 Tritonj to the Foreign Minister, 21 September 1904, ASMAE, SP 1891–1916, portfolio
   91.

in the view of the Italian diplomat, there was no possibility of an exchange of equivalent mutual interests:

> If the Croats had been willing to make concessions by agreeing to funding
> from the province for Italian schools or representation of the Italian minor-
> ity on the municipal councils, etc., what could they have been offered in
> compensation by the Italians in Dalmatia, who are by now only in shaky
> control of the municipality of Zara? At the most something practical in this
> regard could have been obtained with concessions by the Italians of Istria
> to the local Slavs, but it seems that the few steps in this direction that have
> been attempted have produced a wholly negative result in that region.
>
> So what remained was a purely sentimental concord that probably en-
> tailed the sacrifice by one of parts of what it had already won and held
> with confidence.[176]

Yet the worsening of the political conflict between the provincial governor and Croatian nationalists in 1904 seemed to recreate the conditions
for a rapprochement between Italian autonomists and Croat and Serb
parties. Over the course of the year the Croatian press in Dalmatia continued its campaign against Handel, who was accused of fostering the
Germanization of the Dalmatian public administration and of being a
German who did not give opportunities to Dalmatian officials.  Suspecting that the press campaigns were being stoked by functionaries
of the provincial government, Handel accused some Croat Dalmatian
civil servants of being responsible for the leaking of official secrets and,
in the face of their denials, let slip the phrase 'You already know what
I think of the word of honour of Dalmatians!' This unfortunate remark
was publicized by the newspapers and deepened the hostility of the
Croatian nationalists toward the governor. During the summer and fall
they launched a hard-hitting political campaign to force Handel's resignation.[177] The Italian autonomist and Serb parties joined this campaign
against Handel, unwilling to leave a monopoly of the defence of Dalmatian pride to the Croatian nationalists.

Matters reached a climax with the incident that took place at the
inauguration of the Dalmatian diet at the beginning of October 1904.

---

176  Ibid.
177  Tritonj to the Foreign Minister, 3 and 15 September 1904, ASMAE, SP 1891–1916,
    portfolio 91.

242 The Italians of Dalmatia

When the time came for Handel to make the opening speech, Pero Čin-grjia, in the name of all the members (who belonged to the Serb, Italian, Opportunist Croatian, and Radical Croatian parties), read first in Croatian and then in Italian 'a declaration announcing that none of the members would play any more part in the proceedings of the diet while Baron Handel remains governor of Dalmatia.'[178] All the representatives left the assembly immediately, and Handel proclaimed the diet closed. Over the following months public protests against Handel continued, and the governor was obliged by the police authorities to not make journeys in the province as he might trigger hostile demonstrations.[179] In January 1905 Handel was recalled to Vienna and in January 1906 was replaced in the post of governor by the Dalmatian Nikola (Niccolò) Nardelli, who had previously been deputy governor of the province.[180]

The opposition to Handel had produced a new situation. For the first time after many decades, Croatian and Italian autonomist representatives had publicly collaborated on the political plane. The Croatian members, who for many years had refused to recognize the political legitimacy and existence of an Autonomist and Italian Party, which was kept in a state of total isolation, had been willing to hold meetings with the Italian leaders and agree with them on a joint line of conduct in opposition to the governor of the province.[181]

Thus the common struggle against the governor of Dalmatia opened a new phase in the relations between the region's parties, characterized by a decrease in national tensions that lasted until the middle of 1906. This was reflected in the municipal elections of August 1905, which were unusual for their moderate tones; applying an unofficial agreement, the Italian autonomists refrained from electioneering outside Zara, while the Croat and Serb parties stayed aloof of the contest in the provincial capital, allowing the autonomists to win.[182]

At the same time as a national reconciliation between Italians and Croats seemed to be taking shape in Dalmatia, there was a rapproche-

---

178 Tritonj to the Foreign Minister, 6 October 1904; Avarna to the Foreign Minister, 8 October 1904, ASMAE, SP 1891–1916, portfolio 91.
179 Tritonj to the Foreign Minister, 14 January 1905, ASMAE, SP 1891–1916, portfolio 92.
180 Camicia to the Foreign Minister, 11 January 1906, ASMAE, SP 1891–1916, portfolio 93.
181 For Tritonj's views on the matter: Tritonj to the Foreign Minister, 6 October 1904.
182 Camicia to the Foreign Minister, 2 September 1905, ASMAE, SP 1891–1916, portfolio 92.

ment between Serbs and Croats in Croatia and Slavonia and on the Dalmatian coast, and between the Croats and the Hungarian Independence
and 1848 Party, led by Ferenc Kossuth, which wanted a stronger Hungary with more autonomy from central dynastic rule. As Leo Valiani
has rightly pointed out, a decisive factor in the birth of a Croatian-Ser-
bian-Hungarian alliance was the electoral victory of the Independence
Party and its allies in Hungary in January 1905: 'The victory of the "Independence and '48 Party" and its allies in the Hungarian general elections of January 1905 and the consequent conflict with Francis Joseph
... gave Supilo and his friends the impression that Hungary was about
to set out again on the path it had taken in 1848 and that this time the
Croatians should take advantage of this to attain their emancipation,
instead of again serving as the dynasty's policemen.'[183]

The victory of the Independence and 1848 Party, at the head of a
Hungarian 'national coalition,' put an end to the dominance of the Liberal Party and opened a period of fierce political conflict with the imperial rulers, who were opposed to the Hungarian nationalist demands
for the Magyarization of part of the Habsburg army and to increasing
the political and economic autonomy of Transleithania. Francis Joseph
refused to recognize the electoral victory of the supporters of the Independence Party and appointed a loyalist extraparliamentary government headed by General Géza Fejérváry, who administered Hungary
in opposition to the parliamentary majority for the whole of 1905.[184]

In this climate of open conflict between the Habsburg authorities and
Hungarian nationalists, the policy of the New Course emerged and
took on substance. *New Course* was the name given to the co-operation
between Magyars, Croats, Serbs, and Italians to reduce and counter imperial authoritarianism, which was regarded by the Croat nationalists
as a tool of Germanization.

In an article published in *Narodni List* on 11 March 1905,[185] Trumbić
publicly revived the idea of an alliance between the Hungarian independence coalition and the Croatian parties. In exchange for support of
the Hungarian struggle for Dual Monarchy reform to bring it more into
line with Magyar demands, the Croatians would be granted a genuine

---

183 Valiani, *The End of Austria-Hungary.*
184 On this: Valiani, *The End of Austria-Hungary.*
185 Trumbić, 'Dalmacija u borbi izmedju Ugarske i Austrije,' reproduced in Trumbić,
    *Izabrani spisi*, pp. 59–65.

autonomy of government and the unification of Dalmatia and Croatia within the kingdom of Hungary.

In those months Trumbić and Supilo established links with Kossuth's party and with Serbian political groups in Croatia and Dalmatia. To promote rapprochement between Croats and Serbs, Supilo went to Belgrade to meet the leaders of Serbia and persuade them to accept the plan for a Serbo-Croatian understanding and an alliance with the Hungarian independence movement. As Nicholas J. Miller has observed, the support of the government in Belgrade was decisive in the launching of the policy of the New Course and in Croatian-Serbian reconciliation.[186]

To speed up the moves toward a new Croatian political strategy, a congress was held in Spalato in April 1905 that ratified the merger of the Dalmatian Party of Rights and the old National Party to form the Croatian Party (Hrvatska Stranka), with the mayor of Ragusa, Čingrija, as president and Trumbić as vice-president.[187] The new party's platform was characterized by a return to the old idea of the Dalmatian Narodnjaci that Croats and Serbs were a single nation by blood and language (po krvi i jeziku) and that they should abandon any form of antagonism and work together politically. The party's overall objective was the unification of Croatia, Dalmatia, and Bosnia-Herzegovina under a single autonomous Croatian government, in which Serbs would have equal rights, within the kingdom of Hungary.[188]

The congress in Fiume (Rijeka), organized by the Croatian Party and held at the beginning of October that same year, and its public resolution were further steps in this process of political reorganization in the Yugoslav world. The Croatian parties of Dalmatia and Croatia took part in the congress, with the exception of the Party of Rights led by Josip Frank, which was opposed to the pro-Serb and pro-Magyar policy of Trumbić and Supilo and inclined instead to collaborate with Austrian political circles favourable to trialism.[189] The congress gave a mandate to the Croatian parties to negotiate a political alliance with the Hungarian Independence Party and passed a resolution on 3 October proclaiming the objectives and demands of the Croatian nation. The Croatian parties declared their support for the political and national demands

186  Miller, *Between Nation and State*, pp. 80–2.
187  On this: Perić, *Ante Trumbić*, p. 96; Ganza-Aras, *Politika*, pp. 277 et seq.
188  Perić, *Ante Trumbić*, pp. 97–100; Trumbić, *Izabrani spisi*, pp. 75–101.
189  On Frank: Banac, *The National Question*, pp. 94–5.

of the Hungarians and their readiness to collaborate with them so long as the unification of Croatia and Dalmatia was guaranteed and the Croatians were granted a free and autonomous government, with political freedom, freedom of the press and assembly, and an independent judiciary.[190]

The fact that the resolution did not deal with questions relating to the Serb and Italian populations that would be included in this new Croatian state envisaged by the politicians of Spalato and Zagreb meant that the attitude of the Serbian and Italian autonomist parties to the Rijeka Resolution was a cautious one.

The leaders of the Serb parties of Croatia (Independent and Radical) and Dalmatia met at Zara in mid-October and published a response to the Croatian resolution. They declared themselves ready to work with the Hungarians and the Croatians and to accept the union of Dalmatia with Croatia and Slavonia if the Magyars undertook to improve the treatment of the non-Hungarian populations of the kingdom of Hungary and if the Croatian parties accepted the equality of rights of the Serbian nation with the Croatian one (*ravnopravnost srpskoga naroda s hrvatskim*).[191]

The Italian Autonomous Party decided to take a stand with regard to the Rijeka Resolution. Meeting in Zara, the Italian autonomist members of the provincial diet, Ghiglianovich, Ziliotto, Krekich, Salvi, Pini, and Smerchinich, made public a statement dated 16 October 1905:

> The club of the Italian members of the diet of Dalmatia, having weighed the tone of the resolution adopted by the majority of the delegates of the Croatian people at the recent conference in Fiume and considered the gravity and importance that the aforementioned event assumes with regard to the political position of the province, which, in the sought-for understanding with the legitimate representatives of the Hungarian nation, expounds a new and freely evolutionist program of action, expresses its own assessment of the situation in the following way:

> The Italians of Dalmatia are focused exclusively on the preservation of their Italian national character and the recognition and implementation

---

190  The text of the Rijeka Resolution is in Trumbić, *Izabrani spisi*, pp. 192–5.
191  The text of the Serbian resolution of Zara, dated 17 October 1905, is published in Trumbić, *Izabrani spisi*, pp. 199–201; see too Miller, *Between Nation and State*, pp. 83–4.

of the rights that derive from it, in suitable proportion not only to their number but to the general requirements of agriculture, of the facility of trade relations, and of protection from vehement Germanism, their own immutable objective in public life.

They recall that the Autonomist platform embraced by the party in 1860 was an act of political expediency, suggested by a loyal concern for the destiny of the fatherland, in relation to the times and the conditions. Austria did not prove worthy of the trust placed in her.

The mangling of a centuries-old civilization and the abnormality of the social, moral, and economic conditions into which the most culpable neglect has plunged this historic coastal province would be sufficient in itself to condemn any attempt to maintain the intolerable present state.

The uniformity of judgment on the conditions of Dalmatia had brought the parties together over the course of the 1903 session of the diet, in the hope of a practical understanding that would make feasible a common emancipation from the prejudices of the past and from ruinous racial rivalries.

Except that the facts have not kept in step with the theories. The Croatian Party neglected to make any mention of changing its failure to recognize the country's Italian minority even in the administrative field.

These facts and the absence of any guarantee that in the movement now promoted unilaterally by the Croatians, while involving the common interest, the national rights of the Italians of Dalmatia would be given their due consideration, imposes on them, however much sympathy the beginning of a crystallization of the other national individualities may inspire, the most absolute reservation and freedom of action.[192]

The Italian response was cautious and non-committal and made the acceptance of a new unified Croatian-Slavonian-Dalmatian state conditional on the recognition of the linguistic, political, and cultural rights

192 Enclosure with Camicia to the Foreign Ministry, 17 October 1905, Asmae, SP 1891–1916, portfolio 92. The communiqué was also published in *Il Dalmata*, 18 October 1905. A Croatian translation of the communiqué is given in Trumbić's memoirs, *Suton Austro-Ugarske*, p. 92 et seq.

of the Italians and Italophiles of Dalmatia. Mario Camicia, the Italian consul in Zara who was in close contact with Ghiglianovich and Ziliotto, noted that 'the Dalmatian Autonomist Party is content for now to await events, as it quite rightly seems too imprudent to them to commit themselves straightaway and without an exit to a struggle whose consequences are so difficult to predict and in which the good faith of one or the other ally, judging by past experience, is so uncertain and unreliable.'[193]

Yet, as Trumbić has written, with the Zara Resolution the Italian autonomists declared publicly for the first time since 1860 that they were ready to abandon their opposition to the union of Dalmatia with Croatia.[194]

At the November session of the Dalmatian provincial diet, Salvi and Krekich repeated the arguments put forward in the Zara Resolution in the name of the Autonomist Party. Trumbić responded by publicly declaring the readiness of the Croatian Party to reach a political agreement with the Italian autonomists, who no longer seemed unwilling to compromise over the question of annexation.[195]

In those days during the sittings of the diet the Croats and Serbs of Dalmatia reached an accord. The Croatian representatives declared that they recognized the equality of the Serbian nation with the Croatian one, and in exchange the Dalmatian Serbs abandoned any opposition to the unification of Croatia and Dalmatia.[196] After more than twenty years of political antagonism, the old alliance between Dalmatian Croats and Serbs, which had been the foundation of the original National Party, was reformed. The alliance between *pravaši* liberals, Narodnjaci, and Serbs would last in Dalmatia until the constitution of the kingdom of the Serbs, Croats, and Slovenes.

However, no agreement was reached between Croats and Italians. Between the end of 1905 and the summer of 1906 lengthy negotiations and talks were held between some members of the Croatian Party (headed by Trumbić) and Ziliotto, Salvi, and Krekich, but they were unable to reach an Italo-Croatian national compromise. There were various reasons for this failure. First of all, the Italian demands were unacceptable to many Croatian politicians. The autonomist representatives were ask-

193  Camicia to the Foreign Ministry, 17 October 1905.
194  Trumbić, *Suton*, pp. 94 et seq.
195  In this connection: *Il Dalmata*, 19 November 1905.
196  Miller, *Between Nation and State*, p. 86.

ing for equality of rights for the Italian language in institutions and schools, where it would be treated as a compulsory subject; in addition, the Italian schools would be funded by the public authorities. As Tereza Ganza-Aras has pointed out, the Italian autonomists were demanding the recognition of Dalmatia as a binational, Italian and Serbo-Croatian province.[197] Many Croat politicians had built their careers on anti-Italian xenophobia, and it is no coincidence that attacks on the Italians by the opponents of an accord with the Autonomist Party recommenced over the course of 1906, with the precise aim of sabotaging the Italo-Croat negotiations.[198]

A second complication in the Italo-Croatian talks was the problem of electoral reform. Over the course of 1906 the Austrian parliament, on the initiative of the government, debated and approved an electoral reform that introduced universal suffrage and redefined the electoral constituencies.[199] The Dalmatian Italians, supported by the Italian parties of the Trentino and Venezia Giulia, asked for the creation of an electoral constituency comprising the city of Zara alone in order to guarantee the Italian minority in Dalmatia parliamentary representation in Vienna. In February 1906, at the height of the debate over electoral reform, Salvi and Ziliotto proposed to Trumbić that all the Dalmatian parties request an Italian parliamentary mandate for Zara; in exchange, the autonomists would be 'passive' on the question of the incorporation of Dalmatia into Croatia. Trumbić's willingness to go along with the Italian idea clashed with a firm refusal by the majority of the party and the Croatian representatives in Vienna; during the parliamentary debate on electoral reform, Biankini and Vičko Ivčević in particular opposed the hypothesis of an Italian seat in Dalmatia, a hypothesis supported by the Italian representatives Giorgio Pitacco, Valeriano Malfatti, and Matteo Bartoli.[200]

In the end, the Austrian electoral reform reserved eleven parliamentary seats for Dalmatia, whose electoral districts were drawn up in such

---

197  Ganza-Aras, 'Il rapporto della politica croata,' p. 194.

198  On this see: *Il Dalmata*, 31 March 1906; 'A proposito di uno sfogo,' *Il Dalmata*, 4 April 1906; 'Rispondendo,' *Il Dalmata*, 20 June 1906.

199  In this connection: Jenks, *The Austrian Electoral Reform of 1907*; Höbelt, *Parteien und Fraktionen*, pp. 970 et seq.; Ara, 'La Dalmazia e la riforma elettorale austriaca del 1906–1907,' pp. 27–45.

200  Ara, 'La Dalmazia e la riforma elettorale austriaca del 1906–1907'; Salvi, 'Questione di 'correttezza,'' *Il Dalmata*, 25 August 1906.

a way as to permit the election of nine Croatian and two Serbian representatives, leaving the Italian minority without representation and rousing the fury of the Autonomist Party.[201]

The negotiations over an Italo-Slav national compromise in Dalmatia were brought to a complete halt after clashes in Zara between 31 August and 5 September 1906. At a time when groups of gymnasts were passing through the city on their way back from a Croatian national demonstration held in Zagreb, many militant nationalist supporters of Frank's Party of Rights and numerous farmers from the hinterland came into Zara, where Croatian nationalist demonstrations were organized, leading to clashes and brawls with the Italian inhabitants.[202] The parade was inspired and organized by Don Prodan (leader of the most xenophobic and anti-Italian wing of the *pravaši*, and editor of the newspaper *Hrvatska Kruna*, who was resident in Zara and opposed to Trumbić's moderate policy toward the Italians) with the clear objective of sabotaging any possible political rapprochement between Italians and Croats; incidents of a nationalistic character were provoked in the stronghold of the Italian autonomists. In the view of the Italian consul in Zara, the Austrian government, which was hostile to Italo-Croatian reconciliation, had encouraged these clashes by permitting the nationalist demonstration in the city.[203]

In addition, the policy of the New Course devised by Trumbić and Supilo, which was an attempt to create a grand political anti-Habsburg and anti-German alliance of Croats, Serbs, Italians, and Magyars, was brought to a standstill in the area of relations with the Hungarians. After gaining power in 1906, the Hungarian Independence Party did not keep its promises of liberalization and resumed its policy of Magyarization in Croatia, blocking any prospect of collaboration with the Croatian and Serbian parties.[204] In the end the only lasting success of the New Course was the reconciliation between Croats and Serbs in Croatia and Dalmatia.

However, not all Croats agreed with the policy of rapprochement

---

201  Salvi, 'I soli sacrificati!,' *Il Dalmata*, 1 August 1906; Salvi, 'Questione di 'correttezza.''

202  On the incidents in Zara: 'La Cronaca,' *Il Dalmata*, 5 September 1906; 'Dopo il funesto passar dei croati,' *Il Dalmata*, 7 September 1906; Tommasini, *L'Italia alla vigilia*, vol. 3, pp. 78–80.

203  Camicia to the Foreign Ministry, 20 September 1906, ASMAE, SP 1891–1916, portfolio 94.

204  On this see Valiani, *The End of Austria-Hungary*.

between Serbs and Croats. Frank's Party of Rights, with ties to Austrian conservative circles and strong support in the Catholic world, consistently opposed any pro-Serbian policy and remained loyal to the Habsburg dynasty. Also critical of the policy of Croatian-Serbian alliance was the Peasant Party led by the Radić brothers,[205] but this was not to become the main Croatian political force until after World War I.

Seen from the perspective of the history of the Autonomist Party, the Italo-Croatian political negotiations between 1903 and 1906 clearly indicate that in those years the Italian leadership was still a long way from placing political irredentism at the centre of its strategy, that is, the design for a union of Dalmatia with Italy. The efforts of Ziliotto, Ghiglianovich, and Salvi were focused on the struggle for the defence of the national and cultural rights of the Italians of Dalmatia and the Italophile Italo-Slav Dalmatians. In order to obtain this they were ready to accept being part of a Croatian state that was respectful of the rights of minorities and willing to recognize the Italo-Slav character of Dalmatia. The political and financial relationship with Italy served to strengthen the Italian minority and ensure the survival of its schools and did not signify hostility to the full acceptance of a non-Italian sovereignty over Dalmatia. In short, in the first decade of the twentieth century the Italian Dalmatians pursued a national and cultural irredentism, rooted in defence of the Italian national identity, not a *political* irredentism. The latter did not emerge until the outbreak of World War I, as a product of the further deterioration in the living conditions of the Italian element in Dalmatia and the evolution of European politics after 1914.

As far as the general history of Dalmatian society is concerned, the failure of the Italo-Croatian national compromise was a great missed opportunity to halt the process of regression toward an extreme nationalism that had characterized Dalmatia for decades and that was to dominate Dalmatian political life for many years to come. The inability to find a political balance among its various races and nationalities, to a great extent the result of an unwillingness by the Croatian parties to respect the rights of the Dalmatian Italian minority, was to have grave consequences, degrading the life of a society that was in many ways one of the most advanced in the whole of central and eastern Europe and preventing the establishment of an internal order that would have

205  Banac, *The National Question*, pp. 104 et seq.; Biondich, 'Stjepan Radić, Yugoslavism and the Habsburg monarchy,' pp. 109–31; Biondich, *Stjepan Radić*; Perić, *Stjepan Radić 1871–1928*.

permitted steady economic and political progress while preserving its rich Italo-Slav cultural legacy.

## 3.4. The Problem of the Italians of Austria and the Relations Between Italy and the Habsburg Empire in the Giolittian Era (1903–14)

When Giovanni Giolitti[206] became prime minister in November 1903, he was faced with a difficult international situation. While Italy had regained the friendship of France, it had not succeeded in creating a political collaboration with Russia. In addition, the improvement in Italo-French relations, the attempts at rapprochement with Russia, and the rise of anti-Austrian irredentism had worsened relations within the Triple Alliance, obliging the government in Rome to deal with Austrian hostility and German irritation. Senator Urbano Rattazzi Junior, a close aide to the king, described the international situation of Italy in October 1903 as follows: 'We are passing through one of the saddest periods in Italian public life as far as foreign policy is concerned. France has embraced us, but *far too much* and *does not trust us*; Austria is offended, irritated by irredentism, our Albanian policy, and all the Adriatic questions, and is waiting at the pass to give us a thrashing; Germany distrusts us for our flirtations with France; now we are annoying Russia too – and what are we left with? The streets, demonstrations, buffoonery. Through these rowdy but ineffectual demonstrations and rash actions we have ended up with the Treaty of Berlin and Adwa.'[207]

Giolitti had not agreed with Zanardelli's decision to allow irredentist agitations to be staged in Italy, and this had been one of the reasons that had prompted the Piedmontese politician to resign as minister of the

---

206 Still useful on the figure of Giolitti and his ideas, even if full of inaccuracies, are his memoirs: Giolitti, *Memoirs of My Life*; see too *Dalle carte di Giovanni Giolitti*. His political activity has been studied and discussed at great length by historians, but there is no truly complete and satisfactory biography, nor any close examination of Giolitti's thought and action in the international field. However, refer to Romano, *Giolitti lo stile del potere*; Valeri, *Giovanni Giolitti*; Spadolini, *Giolitti: un'epoca*, in particular pp. 14–77; Carocci, *Giolitti e l'età giolittiana*; Albertini, *Venti anni*, vols. 1 and 2; Romeo, *L'Italia liberale*, pp. 323 et seq.; Aquarone, *L'Italia giolittiana*, pp. 178 et seq.; Volpe, *Italia moderna*, vols. 2 and 3; Candeloro, *Storia dell'Italia moderna*, vol. 7; Gentile, *Le origini dell'Italia contemporanea*, pp. 24 et seq.; Mola, *Giolitti*.
207 Rattazzi to Giolitti, 23 October 1903, in *Dalle carte di Giovanni Giolitti*, vol. 2, doc. 561.

interior.[208] In general, he regarded the regression in Italo-Austrian relations as dangerous, having already led to a crisis in the relations with
Berlin and the questioning of the survival of the Triple Alliance. As a
result he decided to work forcefully for an improvement in the relations
with Vienna and to avoid a possible war. Not that Giolitti had any particular liking for Austria and the German world, or was ideologically a
pacifist; rather, he was a realist who thought that Italy was unprepared
for war and therefore had need of a period of peace to strengthen itself
politically and economically.[209] Giolitti agreed with the need for greater
flexibility and independence in Italian diplomatic action, but he considered the tough and brazen style that Prinetti had imparted to Italian international action to be dangerous since behind this aggressiveness lay
a serious military weakness due to economic and technological back-
wardness and the fragility of the defences on the border with Austria.

Giolitti's international strategy had the support of the new foreign
minister, Tommaso Tittoni, and, most importantly, of Victor Emmanuel
III, who had been the instigator of Prinetti and Zanardelli's policy. The
king, offended by the tsar's refusal to pay a visit to Italy and to bring
about an Italo-Russian rapprochement,[210] was aware of the risks that
Zanardelli's Francophile and Austrophobic policy entailed and of the
fact that for the moment the Triple Alliance remained an indispensable
instrument of Italian foreign policy; therefore, he supported Giolitti's
new line.

In relation to this phase in the relations between the powers of the
Triple Alliance, Francesco Tommasini[211] has praised 'Tittoni's remedial
action' in dealings with Vienna and Berlin between 1903 and 1905, almost as if the Roman politician had been the only protagonist of Italian
foreign policy at that moment. In reality Tittoni was an unknown figure
on the international plane with little experience of diplomacy when he
was appointed foreign minister. For many months it was Giolitti (in
addition to the king and the influential minister of the treasury, Luigi
Luzzatti) who handled relations with Berlin and Vienna; Giolitti was an
experienced man who had been familiar to European diplomats since
the time he was prime minister between 1892 and 1893, and he had

---

208  Decleva, 'Zanardelli,' pp. 137–8.
209  See Barrère's observation on this: Barrère to Delcassé, 20 December 1903, DDF, II, 4,
     doc. 132.
210  Barrère to Delcassé, 21 December 1903, DDF, II, 4, doc. 134.
211  Tommasini, L'Italia alla vigilia, vol. 1.

· excellent relations with Bülow, the German chancellor and former diplomat and ambassador in Rome.[212]

The Piedmontese politician – whose strong points were his possession of a brilliant political mind as well as a thorough grasp of law and administration and a great pragmatism – had little taste for the daily handling of diplomatic affairs, which he preferred to delegate to men he trusted. However, he was too intelligent and shrewd not to be aware of the significance of certain international questions in the life of a nation. When particular diplomatic problems assumed great political importance, he did not hesitate to take personal responsibility for their management and solution. Faced with the risk of the dissolution of the Triple Alliance and the waging of a preventive war by Austria-Hungary, the prime minister was obliged to devote much of his attention to foreign policy for several months.

As soon as he was appointed prime minister in November 1903, Giolitti received the German and Austrian ambassadors in Rome, Anton von Monts and Marius Pasetti von Friedenburg, and informed them that his government had the firm intention of remaining faithful to the Triple Alliance and was willing to put a stop to all demonstrations against Austria; the members of the government were in agreement with him on this, especially Tittoni.[213] Tittoni and Giolitti called for German mediation in the political and economic disputes between Italy and Austria-Hungary, declaring their determination to keep the Triple Alliance alive and to improve relations with the Habsburg Empire.[214]

It was in Germany's interest to avoid an open split in the alliance, and German diplomats worked to prevent a worsening in Italo-Habsburg relations.[215] On the part of Austria, Francis Joseph and Goluchowski, while exasperated with irredentism and suspicious of Italian diplomacy, showed that they were eager to improve relations with Rome and avert the risk of war, which, despite Habsburg military superiority, presented great uncertainties.[216] A clear signal of the determination of the parties not to aggravate the crisis was the opening of Italo-Habsburg trade talks in Rome at the end of November 1903, leading to the conclusion of a provisional accord on 31 December of the same year (which

---

212  In this connection: DDF, II, 4, docs. 64, 99, 291, 304.
213  GP, 18, part 2, doc. 5785; Tommasini, *L'Italia alla vigilia*, vol. 1, pp. 268 et seq.
214  For example: GP, 18, part 2, docs. 5786, 5787, 5788; 20, part 1, doc. 6389.
215  GP, 18, part 2, doc. 5790.
216  Avarna to Tittoni, 25 February 1904, ASMAE, SP 1891–1916, portfolio 91.

would be transformed into a definitive commercial treaty on 21 September 1904). Averting economic warfare between Italy and Austria-Hungary was fundamental to avoiding the breakdown of bilateral political relations.[217]

Giolitti and Tittoni's desire to improve relations with Vienna was confirmed in the choice of the successor to Nigra, the outgoing ambassador to Vienna. In February 1904, on Nigra's suggestion, the post of ambassador in Austria-Hungary was given to Giuseppe Avarna,[218] a Sicilian aristocrat who had worked for a long time with his predecessor in the Austrian capital and shared his sympathies with Austria. Culturally alien to the irredentist tradition, Avarna made great efforts to cement the ties between the two countries during his time in Vienna. Similarly, the Habsburg representatives in Rome, Pasetti[219] and, from the beginning of 1904, Heinrich von Lützow,[220] strove to bring about an improvement in Austro-Italians relations. They reflected a stance favourable to the maintenance of good Italo-Austrian relations that could be found in some sections of the diplomatic corps and Austro-German liberalism; however, these relations had often succumbed to the hostility toward Italy that was widespread in the aristocracy, the army, and the conservative and Slav parties of the Habsburg monarchy.

To demonstrate the good intentions of the new government and reduce the tension between the two states triggered by rumours of a possible Habsburg military action against Italy or in the Balkans,[221] Tittoni proposed a meeting to Goluchowski, declaring himself ready to go to Austria. The Habsburg minister agreed to the Italian proposal and met Tittoni at Abbazia (Opatija), a resort town on the gulf of Quarnero, in April 1904. The meeting served to reassure both governments that nei-

---

217  Tommasini, *L'Italia alla vigilia*, vol. 1, pp. 281–3; GP, 18, part 2, doc. 5791.
218  On the personality and ideas of Avarna: GP, 18, part 2, doc. 5794; Aldrovandi Marescotti, *Guerra diplomatica*, pp. 19–27; De Vergottini, 'Missione Avarna a Vienna (1904–1915),' pp. 73–102; Lützow, *Im diplomatischen Dienst der k.u.k. Monarchie*; Tommasini, *L'Italia alla vigilia*, vol. 1, pp. 295 et seq.; Tommasini, *Erinnerungen an Wien*, pp. 474 et seq.
219  GP, 18, part 2, doc. 5793; Tommasini, *L'Italia alla vigilia*, vol. 1, pp. 298–99; Claar, 'Zwanzig Jahre.'
220  In this connection: Lützow, *Im diplomatischen Dienst der k.u.k. Monarchie*, pp. 112 et seq. On the appointment of Lützow as ambassador in Rome see the considerations of Avarna: Avarna to Tittoni, 27 February 1904, ASMAE, SP 1891–1916, portfolio 91.
221  On this: GP, 18, part 2, doc. 5796; 19, part 1, docs. 5999, 6013; DDF, II, 4, docs. 241, 284 and 319; Tommasini, *L'Italia alla vigilia*, vol. 1, pp. 302–3.

ther Italy nor Austria-Hungary had any intention of or interest in further aggravating their bilateral relations. Tittoni criticized the foreign policy of the Zanardelli government and assured Goluchowski of his and Giolitti's desire to maintain cordial relations with Vienna and oppose any demonstration hostile to the Habsburg Empire. Goluchowski reassured the head of the Italian diplomatic corps that Austria-Hungary had no plans for expansion in the Balkans and wanted to maintain the *status quo* in the region, reserving solely the possibility of an occupation of the sanjak of Novi Pazar; this possibility was a hypothesis envisaged by the Treaty of Berlin and for which Vienna was not prepared to consider the possibility of compensation for Italy. Tittoni listened to Goluchowski's observations without raising objections but also without making any precise and stringent commitments. The two ministers then agreed on the need to maintain the territorial integrity of Ottoman Albania and avoid foreign occupations in that region.[222]

The Giolitti-Tittoni government managed to partly repair the rift that had opened up in the Triple Alliance at the time of Prinetti and Zanardelli. Despite the Italian attempts to win back Austrian trust, however, suspicion of and hostility to Italy persisted in Habsburg political circles.[223] As Maximilian Claar has pointed out,[224] the crisis in bilateral relations of 1902–3 had revived the still latent anti-Italian feelings of a large section of Austrian military leaders that was always skeptical about the political value of the alliance with Rome and eager to assert Habsburg hegemony in the Balkans.[225]

With the possibility of a war against Italy, the government in Vienna tried to strengthen Austro-Russian co-operation and conclude a secret pact of neutrality with Russia. On 15 October 1904, Aloys Lexa Aehrenthal, the Habsburg ambassador in St Petersburg, and Lamzdorf,

---

222  The Austrian account of the meeting at Abbazia in 1904 is published in OUS, 2, doc. 132, *Aufzeichnung über eine Unterredung Seiner Excellenz des Herrn Ministers Grafen Goluchowski mit dem königlich italienischen Minister des Äußern Tittoni*. See too Wedel to Bülow, 14 April 1904, GP, 20, part 1, doc. 6401; Barrère to Delcassé, 17 April 1904, DDF, II, 5, doc. 26; Duce, *L'Albania*, pp. 79–80; Tommasini, *L'Italia alla vigilia*, vol. 1, pp. 353 et seq.

223  See Barrère's observations on this: Barrère to Pichon, 30 October 1906, DDF, II, 9, part 1, doc. 250; Barrère to Pichon, 21 January 1907, DDF, II, 10, doc. 396.

224  Claar, 'Zwanzig Jahre,' p. 548.

225  De Laigue to Delcassé, 6 February 1904, DDF, II, 4, doc. 241.

the tsar's foreign minister, signed a secret treaty[226] that committed the two countries to continuing with their political collaboration, based on the desire to preserve the *status quo* in the Balkans. Most important was the mutual undertaking to maintain steadfast and absolute neutrality in the event that one of the contracting parties found itself 'alone, without provocation on its part, in a state of war with a third power, that sought to undermine its security and the *status quo*.'[227]

Russia needed this accord to guarantee peace in Europe while it was engaged in the conflict with Japan; Austria-Hungary, however, had signed it in view of a possible Italo-Austrian war, with the aim of avoiding the rise of an Italo-Russian alliance and the opening up of two fronts. The anti-Italian purpose of the pact was clearly explained by Francis Joseph in a letter that was sent to King Wilhelm II to inform him of the conclusion of the treaty; the risks and dangerous surprises that Italy might have in store obliged him to cover his back (*Rückendeckung*) in the event of war.[228]

The fact is that for the whole of the first decade of the twentieth century Italo-Austrian relations, notwithstanding the undoubted improvements since 1904, remained ambiguous and characterized by suspicion, bad faith, and a complete lack of intimacy.

On the Italian side, there was a desire for an improvement in relations with Vienna to avert the risk of a war for which the country was not ready and to restrain Habsburg initiatives in the Balkans, which had become a crucial area for Italian foreign policy in those years. Tittoni tried to impose on Vienna and St Petersburg the participation of all the European great powers in the policy of reforms in Macedonia, but he ran up against the Russian and Habsburg determination to keep a dominant and preponderant role with regard to reforms within the Ottoman Empire and thereby to guarantee the survival of the understanding of 1897 and the Mürzsteg Pact.[229]

---

226  There is interesting documentary material on the negotiations that led to the Austro-Russian pact in OUS, 2, docs. 112, 162, 186, 195, 197, 204, 221, 234.
227  Tommasini, *L'Italia alla vigilia*, vol. 1, pp. 432–3. On the Austro-Russian treaty see too Albertini, *Venti anni*, vol. 1, 1, pp. 185 et seq.
228  Francis Joseph of Austria to Wilhelm II, 1 November 1904, GP, 22, doc. 7344.
229  On the Italian attempts to counter Austro-Russian collaboration on the introduction of reforms in Ottoman Macedonia: BD, 5, docs. 23, 33, 150; DDF, II, 4, docs. 230, 277, 283, 295, 303, 307, 308; 6, doc. 62; GP, 19, part 1, docs. 5996, 5999; 22, docs. 7394, 7397, 7417, 7507, 7720; Tommasini, *L'Italia alla vigilia*, vol. 1, pp. 409 et seq., vol. 2, pp. 15 et seq., vol. 3, pp. 489 et seq.; Torre, *La politica estera dell'Italia dal 1896 al 1914*, pp. 216 et seq.; Biagini, 'Italia e Turchia (1904–1911),' pp. 207–28.

Not trusting Austria-Hungary, Italian diplomacy also set out to improve the country's relations with individual Balkan states (Serbia, Bulgaria, Montenegro, and Romania), often by pressing them to develop forms of political and economic co-operation.

At the same time, it stepped up a policy of Italian cultural and economic penetration of Ottoman Albania and Montenegro that was aimed at creating concrete ties between the indigenous populations and Italy and countering similar actions carried out by Austria-Hungary. Elements of this economic and political penetration of the Balkans[230] – part of a broader strategy of expansion that the government in Rome was trying to implement in the eastern Mediterranean, North Africa, and Ethiopia[231] – were the opening of Italian post offices and schools in Albania and Macedonia; the winning of mining, railroad, and industrial concessions (such as the construction of a railroad and the management of the tobacco monopoly in Montenegro by a Venetian consortium headed by Volpi and subsidized by the Italian state);[232] the sale of arms and granting of loans to the Balkan states; and the creation of cultural institutions.

The strengthening of the Balkan states and nations provided Italy with another card to play in its complicated political game of competition with Habsburg expansionism in the eastern Adriatic. The Italian strategy was to try to control forces with contrasting plans and tendencies (Austria, Russia, Turkey, the Balkan nations) in order to emerge as the decisive element.

Rearmament was another problem that poisoned relations between Rome and Vienna. The Italian government's decision to move the bulk of its armed forces from the French frontier to the Habsburg one and the major programs of navy and army rearmament that the Giolitti, Ales-

---

230 A great deal of information on this in: Grange, *L'Italie*, vol. 2, pp. 1203 et seq.; Tamborra, 'The Rise of Italian Industry and the Balkans (1900–1914),' in *Studi storici sull'Europa orientale*, pp. 281 et seq.; Webster, *Industrial Imperialism in Italy*; Sori, 'La penetrazione economica italiana,' pp. 217–69.

231 On this: Vigezzi, 'L'imperialismo e il suo ruolo nella storia italiana del primo Novecento,' in *L'Italia unita e le sfide della politica estera*, pp. 55–81; Petricioli, *Archeologia e Mare Nostrum*; Petricioli, 'Le missioni archeologiche italiane nei paesi del Mediterraneo,' pp. 9–31; Grange, *L'Italie*; Monzali, *L'Etiopia*, pp. 301 et seq.; Tommasini, *L'Italia alla vigilia*, vol. 2, pp. 57 et seq., vol. 3, p. 199.

232 On the activity of the Compagnia di Antivari: Romano, *Giuseppe Volpi*; Tamborra, 'The Rise of Italian Industry,' pp. 290 et seq.; Tamborra, 'Mondo Turco-balcanico e Italia,' pp. 323–54; Grange, *L'Italie*, vol. 2, pp. 1205 et seq.; Webster, *Industrial Imperialism in Italy*, pp. 375 et seq.

sandro Fortis, and Sidney Sonnino governments launched with broad parliamentary support were all elements that worried the Habsburg ruling class.[233]

Throughout the Giolittian period great attention was paid to the problem of the build-up of the navy, which was regarded as a fundamental tool of Italian expansion in the Mediterranean and, above all, a crucial factor in a future conflict with Austria-Hungary. From the beginning of the twentieth century onward a conflict with the Habsburg Empire was treated as an ever more likely possibility in the strategic plans of the Italian navy,[234] and this increased the strategic importance of Dalmatia to Italy. In January 1904 the general staff of the navy once again underlined the strategic significance of the Dalmatian coast in any possible Italian military attack on the Habsburg Empire:

> Austria-Hungary enjoys a privileged position in the Adriatic with respect to Italy. In fact, while the latter has only a weak naval base in that sea, Venice, situated at the far north of the long undefended coast and easily bombarded from the sea, Austria, with Pola [Pula] easily defended from the sea and from the land, with the archipelago of Dalmatia and with Cattaro, which can be regarded as impregnable, possesses naval bases of indisputable strategic superiority ... In order for us to launch a successful naval action against Austria, therefore, it is necessary for our fleet to have a much greater superiority over the opposing one than it does at present, and since the nature of our coasts gives us no advantage, we will have to conquer our real base of operation right at the beginning of the war, with a rapid and energetic offensive on the enemy coast.[235]

The Italian navy began to lay plans for a landing in Dalmatia in the

---

233  For example: Wedel to Bülow, 11 July 1907, GP, 21, part 2, doc. 7171. The Italian rearmament and the redeployment of the Italian army on the Austrian border are described with precision in: *Bericht des Militaerattachés in Rom Majors Freiherrn von Hammerstein-Equord*, 20 March 1906, and 26 July 1906, GP, 21, part 2, docs. 7175 and 7176. On Italian rearmament in these years and the tensions it created between Italy and Austria-Hungary: Albertini, *Venti anni*, vol. 1, 1, pp. 199 et seq.; Ruffo, *L'Italia nella Triplice Alleanza*, pp. 81 et seq.; Gabriele, *Le convenzioni navali della Triplice*, p. 285; Mazzetti, *L'esercito italiano*, pp. 208 et seq.; Afflerbach, *Der Dreibund*, pp. 518 et seq.; Biagini and Reichel, *Italia e Svizzera durante la Triplice Alleanza*, pp. 62 et seq.
234  On this: Grange, *L'Italie*, vol. 1, pp. 350 et seq.
235  'Confronto tra la Flotta italiana e quella austro-ungarica secondo uno studio dello S.M. della Marina del gennaio 1914,' in Gabriele, *Le convenzioni navali della Triplice*, pp. 509–14.

event of war with Austria, with the aim of occupying a position that could serve as a naval base for gaining military supremacy in the Adriatic.[236] Antonio Baldissera, one of the best Italian generals, considered the occupation of a base in Dalmatia indispensable to defeating the Habsburg Empire: 'The strategic point that we lack in the Adriatic and that we must have at any cost, being an absolute and organic necessity for our fleet, will inevitably have to be found on the Dalmatian coast.'[237]

The difficult relations with the Habsburg Empire and Italy's desire for expansion on the international plane were to increase the strategic importance of Dalmatia to the military and foreign policy of the government in Rome. Italy's interest in Dalmatia was motivated not just by feelings of national solidarity with an oppressed Italian minority but also by military and strategic requirements.

The growing strength of the Italian state and the unpleasant realization of its vitality led to the rise of activist impulses in certain Habsburg political and military circles that betrayed a growing sense of weakness. These groups found their leader in General Franz Conrad von Hötzendorf, chief of staff of the Habsburg army from November 1906 up until World War I (except for a short period during 1911 and 1912).[238] Conrad had served much of his military career in Tyrol and Venezia Giulia and was convinced that Italy represented a mortal threat to the Habsburg Empire. Appointed chief of staff thanks to the support of the heir to the throne, Francis Ferdinand, he began to call for the launch of a preventive war against Italy before it could complete its own programs of rearmament and while Russia remained weakened by the conflict of 1904–5.[239] The lack of political sense that characterized Conrad's plans, which paid no attention to the international context and offered no clear indications of the concrete and long-term gains that Austria might make from a victory over Italy, explains why the bellicose arguments of the chief of staff were rejected by the emperor and the Austro-Hungarian governments for a long time.

---

236  Gabriele, *Le convenzioni navali della Triplice*, pp. 310–11.

237  Gabriele and Friz, *La politica navale italiana*, p. 164.

238  Useful on Conrad remain his memoirs, in reality largely a collection of documents: Conrad, *Aus meiner Dienstzeit*, in particular, for the period that concerns us, the first three volumes. See too Sondhaus, *Franz Conrad von Hötzendorf*; Ritter, *Staatskunst und Kriegshandwerk*; Afflerbach, *Der Dreibund*, pp. 600 et seq.

239  For example: Conrad, 'Denkschrift vom 6 April 1907 mit Zusatz und Anhang vom 8 April 1907,' in Conrad, *Dienstzeit*, vol. 1, pp. 503–10; OEU, 2, *Zuschrift des Chefs des Generalstabs, Conrad*, 2 July 1909, doc. 1666. A thorough analysis of Conrad's attitude toward Italy in Albertini, *The Origins of the War*, vol. 1.

Naturally Conrad's warmongering ideas[240] and the support they received from Francis Ferdinand were well-known facts in both countries[241] and fuelled mutual distrust and fear. The resurgence of anti-Austrian irredentism in Italy, in particular among the young and the intellectuals, and the aggravation of political conflict in Tyrol and the eastern Adriatic caused continual public debate, as well as sparking many incidents that were often of very little significance in themselves but attracted considerable diplomatic attention. The historical archives of the Italian Foreign Ministry contain extensive documentation of the innumerable incidents that took place in Dalmatia, Trentino, and Venezia Giulia and upset Italo-Habsburg relations in those years: brawls between Italian and Croatian workers, ill treatment of Italian fishermen in Dalmatia, insults to the Italian flag,[242] et cetera. These incidents had political repercussions as they were reported in Italian newspapers, making them known to the public. They were events that reflected both an exacerbation of local political struggles, which were increasingly dominated by nationalistic sentiments, and an undeniable spread of anti-Italian feelings. However, Ambassador Avarna and the Italian consular representatives noticed a tendency of the Italian press to exaggerate these incidents and report them inaccurately in order to criticize the government in Vienna.[243]

Particular interest was stirred by the incidents at Fiume and Zara in August and September 1906 that were provoked by the transit of Croatian athletes through the two cities governed by Italophile autonomist parties; Croatian and anti-Italian nationalist demonstrations

---

240  An assessment of Conrad by Helmuth von Moltke, chief of the German general staff, in GP, 21, part 2, doc. 7169.

241  GP, 21, part 2, doc. 7170. In 1911 the Italian government obtained copies of a large number of Austrian military documents, including various memorials by Conrad, and gained a precise understanding of the anti-Italian ideas of the Habsburg chief of staff: DDI, V, 2, doc. 772.

242  For example: Italian consulate in Zara to the Foreign Ministry, 11 and 16 October 1902, 10 June 1904, 4 January 1906, portfolio 92; Italian vice-consul in Spalato to the Foreign Ministry, 30 October 1907, portfolio 94; Avarna to the Foreign Ministry, 19 November 1908, portfolio 96, ASMAE, SP 1891–1916; Galli, *Diarii e lettere. Tripoli 1911 Trieste 1918*. A fairly accurate account of the many Italo–Austrian clashes in the period between 1903 and 1909, based on Italian diplomatic records, can be found in Tommasini, *L'Italia alla vigilia*.

243  Avarna to the Foreign Ministry, 19 and 21 June 1904, ASMAE, SP 1891–1916, portfolio 92.

resulted in riots and fights. These disturbances received extensive cov-
erage in the Italian and Austro-Hungarian press and were even discussed in the Rome and Vienna parliaments.[244] The Italian press, as the
Italian consuls in Zara (Mario Camicia) and Fiume (Vittorio Lebrecht)
noted, exaggerated the story, speaking of massacres of Italians, when in
reality there had been just a few blows and some property damage.[245]
The space devoted by the press to these events, however, was proof of
the great interest that public opinion and the Italian ruling class had in
those regions and peoples.

A predominant role in the attacks on Austria that appeared in the
newspapers was played by the question of the Italian university in
Austria. The fact that Austrian Italians had been prevented from setting
up a university using the Italian language was something that struck a
deep chord in liberal Italy, which saw it as a clear denial of the rights of
liberty and nationality on which Italian national liberalism was founded. For the Italian parties in Austria, not just the National Liberal Party
but also the People's and Socialist parties, the creation of the Italian university became a crucial theme of their political battle in the parliament
of Vienna over the course of the first decade of the twentieth century.
Various Italian governments tried many times to persuade the Austrian
government to allow the establishment of an Italian university but met
with obstructionism and refusals that were partly the result of domestic policy (the desire not to fuel conflict between pan-Germanists and
Slovene and Croat nationalists) and partly due to the vision of the Italian university as a means of spreading irredentist ideas and desires for
union with Italy.[246]

Toward the Italians of Dalmatia, Tittoni and Giolitti (like Francesco
Guicciardini and Sonnino)[247] continued with the policy of their pred-
ecessors. They supported the financial efforts of the Dante Alighieri Association on behalf of the Italian Autonomous Party, limiting the action
of official diplomacy to the provision of information on political developments in the region, and careful not to give the Austrians any excuse

---

244 In this connection: Avarna to the Foreign Ministry, 21 and 26 September 1906,
    ASMAE, SP 1891–1916, portfolio 94; DDF, II, 10, doc. 230.
245 Camicia to the Foreign Ministry, 13 September 1906, ASMAE, SP 1891–1916, portfo-
    lio 94; Tommasini, *L'Italia alla vigilia*, vol. 3, pp. 78–80.
246 On this, Ara, 'La questione dell'Università italiana in Austria,' pp. 9 et seq.
247 On the attention already paid by Sonnino to Dalmatia in the first decade of the
    twentieth century: Bergamini, 'Sonnino e la Dalmazia,' pp. 3 et seq.

for accusations of interference in their internal affairs. While Avarna, who had good contacts in Viennese diplomatic and aristocratic circles, did not show much interest in national struggles in the various regions of the empire, the correspondence of the Italian consuls in Dalmatia and the rest of Austria-Hungary make it clear that the Foreign Ministry received detailed and thorough analyses of political developments in the allied state, frequently of high intellectual and political quality. It is no coincidence that some of the most talented young Italian diplomats were operating in Austria-Hungary in those years: Carlo Galli, Carlo Sforza, Vittorio Cerruti, and Francesco Tommasini. In the specific case of Dalmatia the consuls in Zara and Spalato, Silvio Milazzo, Giuseppe Giacchi, Mario Camicia, Giovanni Cesare Majoni, and Romolo Tritonj, accurately described the political and national conflicts in Dalmatian society, emphasizing two contrasting aspects. On the one hand, there was the growing strength of a new pro-Serbian and basically anti-Habsburg Croatian nationalism, led by Trumbić, Supilo, and Smodlaka, that aimed at a political rapprochement with the Serbs in the name of the ideal of a unitary south Slav nation. On the other hand, there was the persistence of cultural and national particularism among the Slav and Italian Dalmatians that, in the view of the Italian diplomats, rendered the Slav Dalmatians something completely different from the Croats, Serbs, and Slovenes. According to the consul in Zara, Majoni, the Croatization of the Dalmatian Slav element was merely 'the artificial product of an adroit and self-serving propaganda, inspired by a somewhat doubtful pan-Croatism.'[248]

On the political plane, Italian diplomacy looked with favour on the attempts of the Croat, Italian, and Serb parties to reach a national compromise in Dalmatia between 1903 and 1906 that would take the heat out of the nationalistic conflicts, in which the Italian element was the weakest and most defenseless part. As well as improving the conditions of the Dalmatian Italians, such an accord would have reduced Austrian influence in Dalmatia and strengthened politicians like Trumbić and Smodlaka whose anti-Habsburg designs were already discernible; once the local Italo-Croatian conflict had been resolved, pan-Croatian nationalism could become a useful instrument of Italy's foreign policy.[249]

248  Majoni to Avarna, 14 October 1910, ASMAE, SP 1891–1916, portfolio 97.
249  On the attitude of Italian diplomacy toward the attempts at an Italo-Slav national compromise in Dalmatia: Tritonj to the Foreign Ministry, 6 June 1903; Camicia to

When the possibility of a national compromise in Dalmatia evaporated, the Italian diplomatic corps could not fail to notice the deterioration in the living conditions of the Italian minority. In a situation of growing political difficulty, the leaders of the Italian Autonomist Party sometimes placed their hopes in an open and direct intervention by the government in Rome on their behalf. In 1909, during the course of a difficult negotiation with the Dalmatian Slav parties and the government in Vienna over the use of the Italian language in the civil service, the autonomist leaders, anxious to strengthen their own positions, requested diplomatic intervention by the government in Rome. In April, Ghiglianovich repeatedly asked Majoni, consul in Zara, for 'a friendly intercession by Italy with her allied state' in support of the arguments of the Italian Dalmatians.[250] Tittoni and the Italian diplomatic corps did not take up these requests; Tittoni explained to Majoni that the Italian Dalmatians had to be aware that the existing relations between Italy and Austria-Hungary did not permit 'one state to meddle in any way whatsoever in the domestic policy of the other.'[251]

The Italian government's refusal to intervene openly in favour of the Italian minority in Dalmatia caused bitterness among the autonomist leaders. Majoni reported that in his talks with the leaders of the Italian Autonomous Party he seemed 'to be able to detect a sense of grievance toward the R. Government, believing themselves to have been deserted by it, despite being aware of the extremely delicate position in which it finds itself.'[252]

In reality the Italian state, through the Dante Alighieri Association, played a discreet but active role in domestic policy in the regions of the Tyrol and the eastern Adriatic, and even Tittoni and Giolitti's support for the Triple Alliance, accompanied as it was by major programs of naval rearmament and a skilful political and cultural penetration of the Italian regions of Austria, proved highly ambiguous. Yet the Habsburg

---

the Foreign Ministry, 16 November 1903, ASMAE, SP 1891–1916, portfolio 90; Tritonj to the Foreign Ministry, 21 September 1904, ASMAE, SP 1891–1916, portfolio 91; Camicia to the Foreign Ministry, 17 October 1905, ASMAE, SP 1891–1916, portfolio 92; Majoni to the Foreign Ministry, 26 April 1908, ASMAE, SP 1891–1916, portfolio 96.

250 Majoni to the Foreign Ministry, 4, 14, and 21 April 1909, ASMAE, SP 1891–1916, portfolio 96.

251 Tittoni to Majoni, 2 November 1909, ASMAE, SP 1891–1916, portfolio 96.

252 Majoni to the Foreign Ministry, 18 October 1909, ASMAE, SP 1891–1916, portfolio 96.

government tolerated all of this because it regarded the alliance with Italy as an indispensable element of its foreign policy.

The attention paid by Italy to the unredeemed lands and Dalmatia was partly spontaneous and partly fostered by government leaders, sections of the body politic, or pressure groups that wanted to justify certain political decisions or to press for them to be taken.[253] Associations like the Italian Naval League, the Freemasons, and the Dante Alighieri carried out intense propaganda activity aimed at sensitizing public opinion about the importance of the Adriatic question to the nation's political and economic future. In those years, the first nationalist groups also focused much of their propaganda on drawing Italian society's attention to the questions of the unredeemed lands and the Adriatic.[254] Even the Italian national liberal parties of Austria carried out their own propaganda activity in Italy with the aim of drumming up greater support; they were conscious of the importance of aid from the government in Rome if they were going to survive in an ever more hostile and difficult context. In Venezia Giulia an important role was played by Teodoro Mayer, publisher of *Il Piccolo* of Trieste and one of the leaders of that city's National Liberal Party; he moved to Rome in order to be able to develop better political contacts and exercise a greater influence on Italian public opinion.[255]

As we have seen, the Italian Autonomous Party of Dalmatia also tried to carry out political activity in Italy. This consisted of not just an effort to make contact with members of the kingdom's ruling class but also the sensitization of public opinion through writings, pamphlets, and articles. Roberto Ghiglianovich was able to publish articles and essays on the Italian minority in Dalmatia in journals like *Rassegna contemporanea* and *Italia all'Estero* and to get books by Italian Dalmatian authors like Oscar Randi and Vitaliano Brunelli published in Italy.[256]

---

253 Capuzzo, 'L'irredentismo nella cultura italiana del primo Novecento,' pp. 59 et seq.
254 Still fundamental on the development of the Italian nationalist movement is Volpe, *Italia moderna*, vol. 2, pp. 341 et seq., vol. 3, p. 274 et seq. See too Gaeta, *Il nazionalismo italiano*; Perfetti, *Il movimento nazionalista in Italia 1903–1914*; Sabbatucci, 'Il problema dell'irredentismo'; Roccucci, "Il Carroccio' e la formazione del gruppo nazionalista romano,' pp. 421–71; Roccucci, *Roma capitale del nazionalismo (1908–1923)*.
255 On Teodoro Mayer: Monzali, 'Tra irredentismo e fascismo,' pp. 267–301; Riccardi, *Salata*, pp. 85 et seq.; Benco, 'Il Piccolo' di Trieste.
256 Monzali, 'Oscar Randi,' pp. 650 et seq.; Ghiglianovich to Sanminiatelli, 26 June 1913, DA, file 1913, B 11 bis.

In the first decade of the twentieth century, in short, a new political, economic, and cultural assertiveness at the international level emerged in the Italian ruling class and in a substantial part of the country's public opinion, which led to a strong interest in the regions of the Adriatic and the Balkans, considered natural areas of Italian influence. This expansionistic spirit was partly the product of the revival of economic development in Italy, which had given the country's middle and ruling classes back their confidence and energy; and partly it was a response to the tendencies of the international system and the behaviour of the other large European nations, which was guided by power politics and an imperialist culture.[257] It is important to grasp the connection that existed between the new Italian expansionism, the Italian element in Austria, and the question of the Italo-Habsburg border. Many Italian politicians and intellectuals realized that Italy would not be able to safely conduct a policy of expansion and become a great power if it did not acquire secure borders, capable of protecting it from easy invasion. The existence of Italian and Italian-speaking populations that were dissatisfied with Austrian rule in part of those Alpine and Adriatic territories and whose control would have guaranteed the strategic security of the state made the solution of this territorial problem even more important and vital. Therefore, the policy of expansion in the Mediterranean, East Africa, and the Balkans pursued by Italy under Giolitti had the consequence of rendering urgent the solution of the question of the Alpine border and the set-up in the Adriatic. This would naturally drive the Italian state toward conflict with the Habsburg Empire, unless, as many hoped in Italy, it were possible to reconcile Italian territorial requirements with an Austrian policy of expansion in the Balkans, based on article VII of the Triple Alliance.

The representatives of the European great powers present in Italy were aware of the new spirit of aggrandizement embraced by the ruling class and the desire to exercise Italian influence in the Adriatic, which found expression on the literary and journalistic plane in the growing popularity of Gabriele d'Annunzio, a bard and an apostle of the Italian mission of domination over the Adriatic.[258] In a report made in July 1906, the German military attaché in Rome, Arnold von Hammer-

---

257 On these themes refer to: Volpe, *Italia moderna*, vol. 2, pp. 369–81.
258 On this: Solmi, *Gabriele D'Annunzio e la genesi dell'impresa adriatica*; Ghisalberti, *Da Campoformio a Osimo*, pp. 147 et seq.; Grange, *L'Italie*, vol. 2, pp. 965 et seq.

stein-Equord, noted the spread of the idea that the Italian state should embark on a policy of conquest (*Eroberungspolitik*), focusing on the liberation of national territories still under foreign rule in the east and on hegemony in the Adriatic.[259] The most acute and intelligent foreign ambassadors in Rome, the Briton Rennell Rodd[260] and the Frenchman Camille Barrère, also perceived these new Italian moods and designs, interpreting them as a sign of the strengthening of the Italian state. Barrère, in particular, saw great advantage in supporting the Italian objectives in the Adriatic and in stirring up the antagonism between Italy and Austria as ways of enfeebling and undermining the Triple Alliance; he intelligently realized that the Italo-Habsburg conflict of interests was the weak point of the alliance, given that serious disagreements were unlikely to arise between Germany and Italy.

German diplomats were aware of these attempts to weaken the Triple Alliance but did very little to try to foil them. German diplomatic records between 1903 and 1909 show a complete lack of interest on the part of the government in Berlin in studying initiatives (for example, an improved specification of article VII of the Triple Alliance that would indicate with greater clarity the compensation to be made to Italy in the event of Habsburg conquests) that might allow an overcoming of the antagonism between Italy and Austria and the emergence of a real closeness between the allied states. Conscious of the Austrian opposition to the idea of ceding territories under Habsburg rule in compensation, the German leaders preferred to follow a passive policy focused exclusively on the short term. The overestimation of its own strength and a short-sighted view of the international situation, which was not considered alarming owing to the weakness of Russia (exacerbated by the defeats inflicted on it in the war with Japan in 1904–5 and the internal political crisis of 1905), led Germany to undervalue the importance of the alliance with Italy.[261]

---

259  *Bericht des Militaerattachés in Rom Majors Freiherrn von Hammerstein-Equord*, 26 July 1906.
260  On James Rennell Rodd: Rodd, *Social and Diplomatic Memoirs*, in particular vols. 2 and 3; Bosworth, 'Rennell Rodd e l'Italia,' pp. 420–36.
261  On the foreign policy of Bülow, state secretary for the Foreign Department from 1897 to 1900 and chancellor from 1900 to 1909: Rich, *Friedrich von Holstein*, vol. 2, pp. 540 et seq.; Albertini, *The Origins of the War of 1914*, vol. 1; Tommasini, *L'Italia alla vigilia*; Hildebrand, *Das vergangene Reich*, pp. 200 et seq.; Gooch, *Before the War*, pp. 187 et seq.

Even the relations between Italy and Germany in the period of Bülow's chancellorship were marked by disagreements and difficulties. The spread of rumours about the existence of an Italo-French pact (the Prinetti-Barrère accord) guaranteeing Paris that Italy would remain neutral in the case of German aggression aroused feelings of anger in Berlin, even though such a commitment was not in conflict with the defensive nature of the Triple Alliance. Similarly, the moderate and conciliatory conduct of Italy during the Moroccan crisis and at the Algeciras Conference (1905–6)[262] and the conclusion of an Italo-Franco-British agreement on Ethiopia (13 December 1906)[263] drew attacks on and criticisms of the government in Rome, as if membership of an alliance were not compatible with the independent pursuit of a country's own political and economic interests.

The underestimation of the international significance of Italy and the growing hostility toward its political independence became clear during the discussions on the advisability of renewing the treaty of the Triple Alliance, which was due to expire in 1907; it was a debate that went on within the German diplomatic corps over the course of 1906. In June, Ambassador Monts proposed various modifications to the treaty of the Triple Alliance to his government[264] that were aimed at reducing German obligations to Italy, on the grounds that the alliance was almost useless given the unlikelihood of an Italian intervention in the event of conflict between France and Germany. For the German diplomat, it was Italy that had derived the greatest advantages from the Triple Alliance. Its political independence, demonstrated in the Moroccan crisis, should be regarded as incompatible with participation in an alliance. If Italy would not agree to any modifications of the treaty of the Triple Alliance that would limit its freedom of action, this would be proof of

---

262 On the Moroccan crisis of 1905–6: Torre, *Alla vigilia della guerra mondiale 1914–1918*, pp. 138 et seq.; Nava, *La spartizione del Marocco*, vol. 1, pp. 177 et seq.; Tommasini, *L'Italia alla vigilia*, vol. 2; Serra, *Barrère*, pp. 184 et seq.; Salvatorelli, *La Triplice Alleanza*, pp. 296 et seq.; Albertini, *Le origini della guerra*, vol. 1, pp. 169 et seq.; Monzali, 'Sidney Sonnino e la politica estera italiana dal 1878 al 1914,' pp. 397–447, in particular pp. 422–4; Afflerbach, *Der Dreibund*, pp. 538 et seq.

263 On the tripartite accord of 1906: Monzali, *L'Etiopia*; Buccianti, *L'egemonia sull'Etiopia (1918–1923)*, pp. 161 et seq.

264 Monts to Tschirschky, 8 June 1906, with two enclosures, doc. 7156; *Aufzeichnung des Botschafters in Rom Grafen Monts*, 16 June 1906, doc. 7158, GP, 21, part 2. In this connection: Afflerbach, *Der Dreibund*, pp. 568 et seq.; Skřivan, *Deutschland und Österreich-Ungarn*, pp. 31 et seq.

its untrustworthiness, to the point where it would be better to get rid of such a weak and disloyal ally.[265] Monts's ideas reflected feelings that were widespread in the German diplomatic corps, but they were not taken up by the government in Berlin chiefly because of the Austrian refusal to alter or denounce the treaty of the Triple Alliance.[266] For its part, the government in Rome decided not to try to improve the treaty of the Triple Alliance; the poor state of relations with Germany and Austria-Hungary suggested that it would be better not to add new sources of disagreement within an alliance that it wished to maintain. Therefore, in the summer of 1907 the automatic renewal of the Triple Alliance up until June 1914 took place with the consent of all the contracting parties.[267]

In the following years, the evolution of relations between the great powers considerably increased the international importance of Italy. The Moroccan crisis and the German attempts to build a large navy cemented the political co-operation between France and Great Britain, which had been born after the understanding of April 1904 that had eliminated the colonial conflicts between the two countries.[268] The Russo-British accord of August 1907 and the diplomatic clash between the Austro-German and Russian powers that was provoked by Vienna's decision to unilaterally proclaim the annexation of Bosnia-Herzegovina in October 1908 further weakened the international position of Germany; by supporting the Austrian stance, Germany lost its friendship with Russia for good. In a Europe that was becoming more rigidly split into two opposing political blocs (Austria-Hungary and Germany on the one hand, and Great Britain, France, and Russia on the other), Italy's policy, which was founded on its ability to work with all the great powers, became increasingly influential and significant.

The international position of the Habsburg monarchy, however, worsened considerably. The replacement of Goluchowski at the Foreign Ministry[269] with Aloys Lexa Aehrenthal, ambassador to St Peters-

---

265  *Aufzeichnung des Botschafters in Rom Grafen Monts*, 16 June 1906.

266  On this: GP, 21, part 2, docs. 7160, 7162, 7164, 7165. See too the detailed description of the German discussions with Vienna in Tommasini, *L'Italia alla vigilia*, vol. 3, pp. 110 et seq.

267  Salvatorelli, *La Triplice Alleanza*, p. 320.

268  Gooch, *Before the War*, pp. 34 et seq.; Torre, *Alla vigilia*, pp. 55 et seq.

269  On Goluchowski's replacement by Aehrenthal, resulting from Hungarian aversion to the Polish minister who had proved hostile to the Magyar requests during the difficult renewal of the Ausgleich: Avarna to the Ministry of Foreign Affairs, 14 and

burg, was not a very happy choice. Aehrenthal did indeed impart a
new dynamism to Habsburg foreign policy, but he also brought about a
progressive deterioration in relations with Russia, reviving the antagonism between the two powers in the Balkans. The new foreign minister
abandoned Goluchowski's Balkan policy, which had been founded on
respect of the *status quo* and the understanding with Russia, and embarked on a new strategy that aimed to assert Habsburg hegemony in
the region at the expense of a tsarist Russia; the former ambassador
in St Petersburg considered Russia to have been seriously weakened
by its defeats in the Far East and the internal political crisis.[270] A solution to the Serbian question was central to this strategy. The Habsburg
minister saw pan-Serbian nationalism, which was capable of gathering support from the southern Slav peoples by appealing to the ideals
of Yugoslav liberty and independence, as a mortal threat to Austria-
Hungary. To avert this danger it was necessary for the unity of the Yugoslav peoples to be realized under the aegis of the Catholic Croatians
within the Habsburg Empire. The annexation of Bosnia-Herzegovina
was to be the first step toward an internal reorganization of the empire
in a trialistic sense that would create an autonomous Serbo-Croat entity
alongside Cisleithania and Transleithania. A future Balkan war would
then have permitted, Aehrenthal hoped, a division of Serbia between
Austria and Bulgaria, with the new conquests ready to be absorbed by
the Habsburg Triple Monarchy.[271]

The international crisis triggered by the annexation of Bosnia in Oc-

---

28 June, 13, 29, and 30 October 1906, ASMAE, SP 1891–1916, portfolio 93; Ourous-
soff to Iswolsky, 27 July / 9 August 1906, in Isvolsky, *Au service de la Russie*, vol. 1,
pp. 126–8; DDF, II, 10, docs. 19, 20, 124, 240; DB, 3, doc. 52.

270 On the change in Austro-Russian relations after the appointment of Aehrenthal see
the observations of the Russian ambassador to Vienna, Urossov (Ourossoff): Ourous-
soff to Iswolsky, 29 April / 12 May 1907, in Isvolsky, *Au service de la Russie*, vol. 1,
pp. 156–8.

271 A vast amount of Austrian diplomatic documentation of Aehrenthal's foreign
policy has been published: see first of all vols. 1, 2, 3, and 4 of the OEU collection;
the recent publication *Aus dem Nachlass Aehrenthal*; also very useful are the memoirs
of Conrad, *Dienstzeit*, vols. 1 and 2, and Musulin, *Das Haus am Ballplatz*, pp. 155
et seq., as well as Redlich's diary, *Schicksalsjahre Österreichs*, vol. 1. Among the
historiographical works: Albertini, *The Origins of the War of 1914*, vol. 1; Tommasini,
*L'Italia alla vigilia*, vol. 3; Carlgren, *Iswolsky and Aehrenthal*, pp. 99 et seq.; Bridge,
*From Sadowa*; Bridge, 'Österreich(-Ungarn) unter den Grossmächten,' pp. 309 et
seq.; Gooch, *Before the War*, pp. 365 et seq.; Afflerbach, *Der Dreibund*, pp. 615 et seq.

tober 1908, and brought to an end in March 1909 when Germany forced
Russia to accept the fait accompli and Serbia recognized Habsburg sovereignty over that territory, is a subject that has been studied exhaustively and in depth by many historians, including Francesco Tommasini,
Alessandro Duce, Bernadotte Schmitt, Momtchilo Nincić, and Luigi Albertini.[272] Yet it has to be stressed that the consequences of the Bosnian
crisis were catastrophic for Austrian foreign policy and changed the nature of Italo-Habsburg relations. Contrary to Aehrenthal's expectations,
the annexation of Bosnia had sparked an international crisis that resulted in a radical deterioration in the relations with Russia, definitively
destroying any hope of the sort of collaboration between the two states
that had existed between 1897 and 1908, and rekindling a marked antagonism toward both Austria and Russia in the Balkans. The Bosnian
crisis also produced a worsening of the relations with Great Britain,[273]
which was opposed to Aehrenthal's diplomatic action and methods.
The deterioration in Vienna's relations with St Petersburg and London
progressively induced France, interested in maintaining the collaboration with these governments as a counterbalance to Germany, to pursue
an anti-Austrian policy in the Balkans.[274] In short, a grave consequence
of Aehrenthal's foreign policy between 1906 and 1909 was a marked
worsening in the international position of the Habsburg empire; increasingly the alliance with Germany and the Triple Alliance became
the only props for its foreign policy.

Naturally all this increased the importance of Italy, to the foreign
policy of the Habsburg Empire, as a power whose role in the Balkans
became decisive once the Austro-Russian understanding had broken
down. It is no coincidence that from 1909 onward the relationship with
Italy became a crucial factor in the diplomatic action of both Aehrenthal
and his successor, Leopold Berchtold.

The Bosnian crisis also resulted in a sharp deterioration in Germa-

272  Tommasini, *L'Italia alla vigilia*, vols. 4 and 5; Albertini, *The Origins of the War of 1914*,
     vol. 1; Nintchitch (Nincić), *La crise bosniaque (1908–1909)*, 2 vols.; Duce, *La crisi bos-
     niaca del 1908*; Schmitt, *The Annexation of Bosnia 1908–1909*; Skřivan, *Deutschland und
     Österreich-Ungarn*, pp. 76 et seq.
273  On this, see the British documentation of the Bosnian crisis published in BD, 5, for
     example docs. 430, 503, 504, 585. Cf. Bridge, *Great Britain and Austria 1906–1914*.
274  On Franco-Austrian relations: Berenger, 'Die Österreichpolitik Frankreichs von
     1848 bis 1918,' in particular pp. 532 et seq.; Girault, 'Les Balkans dans les relations
     franco-russes en 1912,' pp. 155 et seq.

ny's relations with St Petersburg. The growing political co-operation between Russia, Great Britain, and France meant that the maintenance of Italian benevolence and the preservation of the Triple Alliance were no longer marginal factors in Berlin's foreign policy.

Thus, after the Bosnian crisis and despite the confused and contradictory action of Tittoni, Italy's international position was considerably reinforced. The conclusion of the Italo-Russian agreement at Racconigi (24 October 1909)[275] and the Italo-Austrian exchange of notes on the sanjak of Novi Pazar (19 December 1909)[276] provided confirmation of the growing international clout of the Italian state and set the seal on its role as a Balkan great power.

These two accords gave Italy a lot of room for manoeuvre, allowing it to adopt, depending on events, the policy in the Balkans that would best suit its own interests. The seeming contradiction between the support of the development of the Balkan states as a counterweight to Habsburg hegemony in the Racconigi Agreement, and the understanding reached with Vienna that Italy would be compensated for giving a green light to new conquests by Austria-Hungary in the Balkans, was the means of maintaining its own freedom of action and decision up until the moment of the dissolution of the Ottoman Empire in Europe. Tittoni explained the Italian policy as follows:

> The contradiction is only apparent. For what we are asking from Austria-Hungary in the first place is to come to an agreement with us before proceeding with that occupation. Now we ... are going to seek, friendlily but firmly, to oppose the realization of such a plan in every way possible; and only when our opposition has not produced any effect, only then can we resign ourselves to a compensation in the agreed forms. In other words, we want and believe ourselves to be in agreement with Austria in desiring: firstly, the preservation of the *status quo* in the Ottoman Empire; secondly, should this no longer be possible, the development of the Balkan states on the basis of the principle of nationality; thirdly, should neither

---

275 On Italo-Russian relations and the conclusion of the Racconigi Agreement: Tommasini, *L'Italia alla vigilia*, vols. 4 and 5; Donnini, *L'accordo italo-russo di Racconigi*; Anchieri, *Costantinopoli*, pp. 114 et seq.; Isvolsky, *Au service de la Russie*, vol. 1, pp. 266–9, 284–8; Siebert, *Entente Diplomacy*, docs. 178, 179, 180, 181.

276 On the negotiations that led to the exchange of notes between Italy and Austria: Tommasini, *L'Italia alla vigilia*, vol. 5, pp. 355 et seq.; Donnini, *L'accordo italo-russo di Racconigi*, pp. 89 et seq.; Monzali, 'Sidney Sonnino,' pp. 431–3.

one nor the other prove possible and an Austro-Hungarian occupation take place, in spite of everything, the assurance of an adequate compensation for Italy.[277]

This letter makes it clear that the very man who had negotiated the Racconigi Agreement would have been quite happy to see Austria expand in the Balkans so long as particular territorial compensations were peacefully obtained.

This hope in the future application of article VII of the Triple Alliance was very widespread in the Italian ruling class. It was, for instance, shared by the leaders of the liberal opposition to Giolitti, Sidney Sonnino and Francesco Guicciardini. The Austrian annexation of Bosnia-Herzegovina had troubled Sonnino, who was aware of the risk that, in the event of a break-up of the Ottoman Empire, Italy would find itself faced with faits accomplis to Austria's advantage, without the government in Rome being able to defend its own interests effectively. In June 1909, at a meeting with Gottlieb von Jagow, Monts's successor at the German embassy in Rome, the Tuscan politician expressed his concerns and declared the necessity for agreements to be made in advance between the states of the Triple Alliance that would provide Italy with precise guarantees about the application of article VII in the event of a crisis in the Balkans.[278]

Returned to power in December 1909, Sonnino and his foreign minister, Guicciardini, decided the time had come to raise the problem of a better specification of article VII of the Triple Alliance with its allies. Meeting the Austrian ambassador, Heinrich von Lützow, on 2 January 1910, Guicciardini declared that it would be opportune to improve article VII by 'settling what is meant by compensations.' In the event of war in the Balkans it was likely that Austria-Hungary would occupy and annex Serbia; therefore it was necessary to 'provide for this eventuality and regulate its consequences.'[279] The Habsburg diplomat listened to the Italian government's arguments and then dropped the subject.[280]

---

277 Tittoni to Avarna, 7 November 1909, document cited in Donnini, *L'accordo italo-russo di Racconigi*, pp. 262–5, and in Tommasini, *L'Italia alla vigilia*, vol. 5, pp. 546–9.
278 Jagow to Bülow, 10 June 1909, GP, 26, part 2, doc. 9550. On Guicciardini's action with regard to the question of compensation: Duce, *L'Albania*, pp. 201 et seq.; Monzali, 'Sidney Sonnino,' pp. 430 et seq. See too the documents published in DDI, IV, 5–6.
279 Guicciardini, 'Cento giorni alla Consulta,' pp. 154–73.
280 Lützow to Aehrenthal, 3 January 1910, OEU, 2, doc. 1935.

On 9 January, Guicciardini received Avarna in Rome and instructed him to prepare for negotiations with Aehrenthal on a further specification of article VII. The exchange of notes of December 1909 was an extension of the treaty of the Triple Alliance, but to make it perfect, 'one more step' was needed: 'defining what was meant by compensations.' It was necessary to tackle the question at that moment since 'when things come to a head, there is no more discussion of compensation.' Guicciardini was ready to accept a future Habsburg conquest of Serbia, but Italy had to receive territorial compensations in Europe, as 'we will never be able to consider Tripolitania a compensation.'[281] Having been given the go-ahead by the king and Sonnino, Guicciardini decided to raise the question with Bülow's successor, Theobald Bethmann Hollweg, on the latter's visit to Rome. On 22 March he told the German chancellor that the accord of the Triple Alliance should be completed and improved and that the precise compensations for Italy in the event of application of article VII had to be established; it was necessary for 'the compensations to be defined at a time of calm before that calm ceases to be.'[282]

Bethmann Hollweg declared himself to be in agreement with Guicciardini but pointed out the difficulties involved. To fix the compensations it was necessary to foresee which territories Austria would occupy, and this was not an easy thing to do at that moment.[283]

The fall of the Sonnino government on 21 March 1910, and its replacement by the Luzzatti executive, which chose Antonio di San Giuliano as foreign minister, slowed down and then blocked the negotiations over the compensations. San Giuliano agreed with Guicciardini's ideas, and in talks with Bethmann Hollweg in Florence made this known to the government in Berlin. San Giuliano told the German chancellor that the aim of the Italian government was the maintenance of the *status quo* in the Balkans; should this prove impossible, however, it would be necessary to apply the clause in the treaty of the Triple Alliance concerning compensations.[284] San Giuliano sought to raise the question of

---

281  Guicciardini, 'Cento giorni,' pp. 161–2; DDI, IV, 5–6, doc. 59.

282  Meeting of the foreign minister, Guicciardini, with the German chancellor, Bethmann Hollweg, 24 March 1910, DDI, IV, 5–6, doc. 185; Guicciardini, 'Cento giorni,' pp. 168–9; Monzali, 'Sonnino,' p. 434.

283  Meeting of the foreign minister, Guicciardini, with the German chancellor, Bethmann Hollweg; Guicciardini, 'Cento giorni,' pp. 168–9; *Aufzeichnung des Reichskanzler von Bethmann Hollweg*, 5 April 1910, GP, 27, part 1, doc. 9859.

284  Report on the talks between the marchese of San Giuliano and Herr Bethmann Hollweg in Florence on 2 April 1910, ASMAE, ARG, portfolio 5; DDI, IV, 5–6, doc. 197. Bethmann's account is published in GP, 27, part 1, doc. 9859.

the definition of compensation in the event of a change in the Balkan *status quo* with the Habsburg diplomatic corps as well. At a meeting with the new Austro-Hungarian ambassador to Rome, Kajetan Merey, on 12 May 1910, the minister mentioned the spread of rumours about the Habsburg intention to reoccupy the sanjak of Novi Pazar; in the face of Merey's denials, he referred only to the question of compensation, declaring that for Italy the maintenance of the *status quo* in the Balkans would be a thousand times better than a possible concession of compensation by Austria in the event of the sanjak's reoccupation.[285] Reporting on the talks with Merey to Avarna, the minister recalled that, in the event of Habsburg reoccupation of the sanjak of Novi Pazar, it would be necessary to agree on compensation for Italy before the Austro-Hungarian action took place, and he invited the ambassador in Vienna to consider whether it might not be opportune to declare this to the Austro-Hungarian foreign minister.[286]

In those months Avarna showed himself unwilling to open negotiations on compensation. In a long letter of March 1910[287] the Italian diplomat analysed the question in depth. Avarna agreed with Guicciardini that neither the text of the Triple Alliance nor that of the agreement on the sanjak, while envisaging territorial compensations for Italy, specified their nature; however, he felt that beginning negotiations with Vienna on the question of specific compensations for Italy was dangerous as it was likely that Austria-Hungary would be opposed to the request for the cession of the Trentino and a territorial adjustment on the Isonzo. According to the ambassador in Vienna, it was advisable to tackle the question when the time came for the renewal of the Triple Alliance. While conscious of the distrust and hostility toward Italy in Vienna, Avarna declared his confidence in the possibility of reaching an agreement in this respect with the Habsburg Empire through the mediation of Germany. To this end it was necessary, in the first place, to dispel Austrian suspicions, with a 'frank and open' policy, one 'capable of demonstrating to the cabinet in Vienna our firm intention not to thwart but to support its designs in the Balkans.' The basis of the agreement could be the Italian willingness to place its own military and naval forces at the

---

285  Merey to Aehrenthal, 13 May 1910, OEU, 2, doc. 2171.
286  San Giuliano to Avarna, 11 May 1910, DDI, IV, 5–6, doc. 261.
287  Avarna to Guicciardini, 2 March 1910, DDI, IV, 5–6, doc. 150; also published in Avarna di Gualtieri, *L'ultimo rinnovamento della Triplice*, pp. 87–101.

disposal of Austria for an action of expansion in the Balkan peninsula, but on condition '(1) that she give us a fitting compensation with the cession of regions of Austria inhabited by Italian-speaking populations; (2) that she reach a precise agreement with us on Albania, that will establish her neutralization, so that the country is forever safe from any Austro-Hungarian dominance or further occupation.' If the eastward expansion of Austria were to be carried out under these conditions, 'it would certainly not be to our disadvantage. Indeed, Italy would have more interest in facilitating it than Germany.'[288]

When San Giuliano asked him in May 1910 to raise the question of compensations with the government in Vienna, Avarna declared himself against such an initiative. Given the mistrust that continued to exist between Rome and Vienna, opening this question might entail dangers if it were to lead to the perception of the existence of an irreconcilable difference between the two governments.[289]

Fearful of a possible break-down of the negotiations on compensation and having probably already decided to resolve the Libyan question with dispatch, San Giuliano chose to put off the controversial question. In the meantime he sought to pursue a friendly policy toward Austria-Hungary in order to dispel the hostility and distrust, and in this he had a degree of success. Aehrenthal met San Giuliano several times over the course of 1910 and formed a good opinion of him. The Italian minister declared that the central theme of his foreign policy would be the maintenance of good and close relations with Austria-Hungary.[290] Undoubtedly during the time Antonio di San Giuliano held the post of foreign minister, under the Luzzatti, Giolitti, and Antonio Salandra governments from March 1910 to October 1914,[291] a policy of Italo-Austrian

---

288  Ibid. On this letter from Avarna see the observations of Albertini, *The Origins of the War of 1914*, I.

289  Avarna to San Giuliano, 12 May 1910, DDI, IV, 5–6, doc. 269. See too Avarna to San Giuliano, 18 May 1910, DDI, IV, 5–6, doc. 287.

290  On the meetings between San Giuliano and Aehrenthal in Salzburg and Turin: OEU, 2, doc. 2244; *Aufzeichnung des österreich-ungarischen Ministers des Äussern Grafen von Aehrenthal*, n.d., GP, 27, part 1, doc. 9864; DDI, IV, 5–6, docs. 433, 436, 489, 492.

291  On the figure and international political activity of San Giuliano: Bosworth, *Italy, the Least of the Great Powers*; Bosworth, *Italy and the Approach of the First World War*; Volpe, *Italia moderna*, vol. 3; Petricioli, *L'Italia in Asia minore*; Albertini, *The Origins of the War of 1914*; Albertini, *Venti anni*, vol. 2, 2; Monzali, *L'Etiopia*, pp. 357–90; Longhitano, *Antonio di San Giuliano*; Cataluccio, *Antonio di San Giuliano*; Sertoli Salis,

co-operation in the Balkans was progressively consolidated. In those years San Giuliano, faithful executor of the decisions taken by the king and Giolitti, tried to turn to Italy's advantage the evolution in European politics, which was now characterized by the formation of two opposing blocs of powers: on the one hand, Germany and Austria-Hungary and, on the other, the collaboration between Great Britain, France, and Russia that was not yet a military alliance but an effective political structure that tended to co-ordinate its activities on the international plane.[292] In this context of opposition, and exploiting the desire of the great powers to maintain good relations with the government in Rome, Italy was able to strengthen its own positions in the Mediterranean through the conquest of Libya and the Dodecanese and the creation of its own economic and political interests in Anatolia and Albania.

The policy of good relations with Austria was also intended to facilitate the improvement of living conditions for the Italians of the Tyrol, Venezia Giulia, and Dalmatia. The establishment of close relations with Vienna allowed San Giuliano to hope for a possible shift in Austrian domestic policy in a direction more favourable to Italians.[293] This shift and the continuation of financial aid to the Italian liberal parties would have permitted a strengthening of the positions of the Italian populations in Austria. Where Dalmatia was concerned, San Giuliano went on using the Dante Alighieri Association as an informal tool of Italian foreign policy, it being both a source of information and a means of contact with Dalmatian politicians who had close relations with the leaders of the association, such as Sanminiatelli.[294] On the official plane, however, the foreign minister preached a total lack of interest in Dalmatian political affairs. In March 1912, San Giuliano responded to requests from the republican member of parliament Napoleone Colajanni for Italy to press the Austrian government for better treatment of the Italians in Dalmatia, by saying that 'no government may interfere in the internal

Le isole italiane dell'Egeo; Ferraioli, 'Il marchese di San Giuliano deputato'; Ferraioli, 'Giolitti e San Giuliano di fronte alla questione della chiusura dell'impresa di Libia,' pp. 325 et seq.; Ferraioli, 'L'apprendistato di un ministro degli Esteri,' in Clio, no. 4, 2001, pp. 621–48, no. 1, 2002, pp. 25 et seq. A fine portrait of San Giuliano in Rodd to Grey, 16 October 1914, CP, series H, 1, doc. 249.
292 For an analysis of international politics in the years preceding the outbreak of World War I refer to Fay, The Origins of the World War, 2 vols.; Albertini, The Origins of the War of 1914, vol. 1; Hildebrand, Das vergangene Reich, pp. 249 et seq.
293 DDI, IV, 5–6, docs. 355, 444, 491, 560.
294 For example: Sanminiatelli to San Giuliano, 10 July 1913, DA, file 1913, B 4.

affairs of another state, and the solid and steady relations of friendship and alliance between Italy and Austria-Hungary gave no reason to deviate from this principle.'[295]

In the years following the Habsburg annexation of Bosnia, the conditions of the Italian minority in Dalmatia deteriorated owing to the stepped-up attacks on it by the Croat and Serb parties, who were eager to conquer the last Italian autonomist stronghold, the municipality of Zara. The consul in Zara, Majoni, praised the moderation and political sense of the leaders of the Italian Autonomous Party who, aware of their weakness, tried to not fall victim to provocations and to avoid any talk of irredentism.

> The Italian party was left with no better alternative than to abstain from pointless demonstrations, of any character, and resign itself to provocations. This language, however disagreeable, the leaders of the party are preaching to their fellows, risking unpopularity. For this they should be praised on all accounts; only in this way will they be able to forestall the game played by their adversaries, impatient to compel the Government, under the pretext of Italian agitations, to support them in making a bid for the Municipality. This would constitute a cruel blow to the Italian culture in Dalmatia, which is still able to derive new vigour from the unequal struggle for the maintenance of its noble ideal.'[296]

In Majoni's view, a paradoxical effect of the anti-Italian policy of the Croat and Serb parties in Dalmatia was the reinvigoration of the Italian spirit in Dalmatia. The Italian Autonomist Party was organized and combative. 'Indeed, one would say from the growing number of adherents, reflected in the more numerous enrolments in the schools this year, that the Croatian excesses are taking on, for them, the aspect of persecutions, with the usual consequences that these bring with them. This is true not just in Zara but throughout the region.'[297] An element of weakness, however, remained the scarcity of financial resources available. 'The Italians of Dalmatia – many of them clerical workers on meagre salaries, having been kept out of high positions – unflagging in their struggle out of pride in their traditions and race, have now reached the

---

295  San Giuliano to Avarna, 28 March 1912, ASMAE, SP 1891–1916, portfolio 99.
296  Majoni to Tittoni, 22 August 1909, ASMAE, SP 1891–1916, portfolio 96.
297  Majoni to Tittoni, 18 October 1909, ASMAE, SP 1891–1916, B. portfolio 96.

peak of their sacrifices ... So things are not going well, and the leaders of the party are rightly worried about the future that such circumstances may hold in store for the cause.'[298] Consequently the financial aid that arrived from Italy through the Dante Alighieri Association grew in importance.

During the period in which San Giuliano was at the Foreign Ministry the relations between Italy and the Italian Autonomous Party of Dalmatia were further strengthened. Finding it increasingly difficult to counter the Croat and Serb parties, now to a great extent allied in the name of a Yugoslav program, the leaders of the Italian Autonomous Party stepped up their efforts to consolidate and boost collaboration and contacts with the Italian government and ruling class. Roberto Ghiglianovich took charge of this part of autonomist strategy. He paid increasingly frequent visits to Italy to develop relations with Rome. From the documents preserved in the historical archives of the Dante Alighieri Association, we know that he went to Italy in the summer of 1912,[299] meeting among others Sanminiatelli and Paolo Boselli, a former minister and the president of the association, who was an enthusiastic supporter of the cause of the Italian Dalmatians. After his meeting with Ghiglianovich, Boselli wrote to Sanminiatelli: 'I repeat it with all my heart: I am a passionate admirer of the Dalmatians. If it were possible, more ought to be done for them. So I should be sparing in other places.'[300]

Ghiglianovich returned to Italy in December 1913. During this visit he managed to obtain a meeting with the foreign minister, San Giuliano, who promised him political solidarity and additional financial assistance; he saw old friends of the Dalmatians like Stringher, Nathan, and Sanminiatelli and went to the Roman offices of *Il Corriere della Sera*, where he talked to Andrea Torre and Roberto Forges Davanzati.[301]

In general we can say that the points of reference of the Dalmatian Italian autonomists were the members of the liberal ruling class who, whether conservative or progressive, had a certain appreciation of the problems of the Italian populations of Austria and believed that it was in Italy's interest to support the survival of an Italian-speaking minority in Dalmatia. Other people to whom Ghiglianovich talked were the nationalists, in particular Piero Foscari and the groups in the Veneto;

298  Ibid.
299  Sanminiatelli to Boselli, 26 July 1912, DA, file 1912, B 7.
300  Boselli to Sanminiatelli, 27 July 1912, DA, file 1912, A 6.
301  Ghiglianovich to Sanminiatelli, 10 January 1914, DA, file 1914, B 9 bis.

however, the support that the Italian Nationalist Association gave to the extremist and *italianissimo* group of Raimondo Desanti and Girolamo Italo Boxich, a dissident faction that emerged in Zara after 1908, caused considerable irritation among the leaders of the Autonomist Party. Ghiglianovich complained about this several times to the leaders of the Dante Alighieri, criticizing the conduct of the Italian nationalists and raising doubts about Desanti's grasp of politics. In a letter of June 1913 the member of the Dalmatian diet declared in a critical and sceptical tone: 'The ones who have a great trust in and liking for Desanti, evidently because he edits the *Risorgimento* with a markedly nationalistic intonation, are the members of the nationalist group in Rome, and especially De Frenzi.'[302]

The reopening of the Moroccan question and the rapid moves made toward its peaceful solution thanks to the negotiations between France and Germany during the course of 1911 obliged the Italian government to think carefully about what it should do in Tripolitania. The government in Rome was fully aware of the possible repercussions in Europe and the Balkans of a military venture in Tripolitania and Cyrenaica.[303] The Italian diplomatic corps feared not the possibility of an action by the Balkan states against the Ottoman Empire but that Austria-Hungary, taking Italy's initiative as a pretext, would carry out a *coup de main* in Albania, Macedonia, or the sanjak of Novi Pazar. In July of 1911 Avarna himself, although convinced that Austria-Hungary wanted to maintain the *status quo* in the Balkans, pointed out to Rome the potentially grave consequences of a military conquest of Tripolitania: 'I am equally convinced that, if the maintenance of the *status quo* were to become impossible in the Balkans, the Monarchy would proceed without hesitation with the occupation of the Sanjak of Novi Pazar and the other territories that interest us, should they be threatened by an isolated or combined action of Serbia and Montenegro.'[304]

---

302  Ghiglianovich to Sanminiatelli, 26 June 1913, DA, file 1913, B 11 bis.
303  In this connection: Memorandum by the foreign minister, San Giuliano, 28 July 1911, in *Dalle carte di Giovanni Giolitti*, vol. 3, doc. 49; San Giuliano to Giolitti, 4 September 1911, portfolio 23; Antonio di San Giuliano, memorandum, 13 September 1911, enclosure with San Giuliano to Giolitti, 13 September 1911, portfolio 22, ACS, Carte Giolitti.
304  Avarna to San Giuliano, 28 July 1911, ACS, Carte Giolitti, portfolio 22. Very useful on the genesis of the Italian decision to conquer Tripolitania and Cyrenaica is Malgeri, *La guerra libica (1911–12)*, pp. 97 et seq. See too Serra, 'I diplomatici italiani, la guerra di Libia e l'imperialismo,' in Serra and Seton-Watson, *Italia e Inghilterra nell'età dell'imperialismo*, pp. 146–64.

The decision to go to war in Libya without consulting or warning its allies stemmed from the Italian desire to confront Austria-Hungary, Germany, and the other great powers with a *fait accompli* in order not to be obstructed in the conquest of Tripolitania and Cyrenaica and above all to avert the possibility of a Habsburg initiative in the Balkans.

The attitude of the European powers to the invasion of Tripolitania and Cyrenaica was a clear confirmation of the growing international weight of Italy.[305] The desire of the various powers to maintain good relations with Italy gave the government in Rome great leeway during the war against the Ottoman Empire, which was exploited in order for Italy to occupy the Libyan coast and the islands of the Dodecanese. The attempts at mediation and finding a negotiated solution to the conflict, often concocted with the aim of curbing Italian designs, proved ineffective in the face of the Giolitti government's decision to go ahead with its own plans (the unprovoked attack on Turkey in September 1911, the proclamation of the annexation of Tripolitania and Cyrenaica in November 1911, and the broadening of military operations to the Aegean and the eastern Mediterranean in the spring of 1912).

It is interesting to note that the Italo-Turkish War aroused fierce debate in the Austrian government on the opportunity that the Italian initiative offered Austria-Hungary. With the spread of rumours of a possible Italian attack on Turkey, Conrad von Hötzendorf sent a famous note to Aehrenthal on 24 September 1911,[306] proposing that the Habsburg monarchy launch a war either against Italy or to conquer Balkan territories and eliminate the Serbian state. In the view of the Austrian chief of staff, Italy was a rising state on the political and economic plane; it was necessary to take advantage of the outbreak of the Italo-Turkish War to attack Italy from the rear and cut it down to size, or to carry out an action of force in the Balkans, conquering the territories

---

305 On the diplomatic history of the war in Libya in 1911–12 Askew's work remains fundamental: Askew, *Europe and Italy's Acquisition of Libya 1911–1912*; see too Albertini, *Venti anni*, vol. 1, 2; Salvatorelli, *La Triplice Alleanza*; Volpe, *Italia moderna*, vol. 3; Malgeri, *La guerra libica 1911–1912*; Childs, *Italo-Turkish Diplomacy and the War over Libya 1911–1912*; Christopher Seton–Watson, 'British Perceptions of the Italo-Turkish War 1911–12,' in *Italia e Inghilterra*, pp. 111–45; Lowe, 'Grey and the Tripoli War, 1911–1912,' pp. 315 et seq.; Afflerbach, *Der Dreibund*, pp. 686 et seq.

306 *Note des chefs des Generalstabs Conrad*, 24 September 1911, doc. 2644, OEU, 3; Conrad, *Dienstzeit*, vol. 2, pp. 172 et seq.; Skřivan, *Deutschland und Österreich-Ungarn*, pp. 247 et seq.

needed to establish Habsburg hegemony in the region and confronting the Italians with a *fait accompli*.

Aehrenthal refuted Conrad's arguments in a memorial of 22 October 1911,[307] declaring a war against Italy to be unwise. In his opinion, the country was distracting its attention from the Adriatic question by embarking on a venture in the Mediterranean and coming into conflict with the Western powers, making it increasingly in need of good relations with Vienna and Berlin. The foreign minister also affirmed that it was not the right moment to spark a Balkan conflict. In fact, his entire diplomatic action in those months was oriented toward avoiding a spread of the Italo-Turkish War into the Balkans.

The disagreement between Conrad and Aehrenthal soon turned into an institutional conflict between the Foreign Ministry and the leaders of the armed forces. Conrad was accused of intruding into the Ballhausplatz's area of competence and carrying out a propaganda campaign in the Austrian press in an attempt to influence the policy of the government in Vienna. The emperor decided to back Aehrenthal and ordered Conrad's replacement as chief of staff of the army on 30 November 1911.[308]

The nature of Italo-Austrian relations over the course of the war in Libya shows that it was Aehrenthal's intention to avoid, in the event of a change in the Balkan *status quo*, the application of article VII of the Triple Alliance in the sense desired by the Italians, that is, the future concession of Austrian territory to the government in Rome. At the end of 1911 Aehrenthal tried to invoke the application of that clause in the event of an Italian military initiative in the Aegean. After protesting loudly against the Italian military actions in the Adriatic Sea,[309] he informed Avarna on 6 November that any Italian occupation of islands in the Aegean would violate the commitment to maintenance of the *status quo* in the Ottoman Empire and be inconsistent with article VII.[310] It was made clear that, should the Habsburg interpretation of the clause be infringed, the government in Vienna would consider itself no longer

---

307 *Denkschrift*, 22 October 1911, doc. 2809, OEU, 3.
308 Salvatorelli, *La Triplice Alleanza*, p. 410; Conrad, *Dienstzeit*, vol. 2, pp. 281 et seq.; OEU, 3, doc. 3056; BD, 9, part 1, doc. 338 and enclosure; Choffat to Forrer, 29 February 1912, DDS, 5, doc. 306.
309 Avarna to San Giuliano, 1 October 1911, portfolio 15; Avarna to San Giuliano, 4 and 7 October 1911, portfolio 14, ACS, Carte Giolitti; OEU, 3, docs. 2713, 2714, 2738.
310 OEU, 3, doc. 2878.

bound by it and seek its cancellation when the time came for renewal of the Triple Alliance.[311]

Invoking article VII and bringing it into question at the height of the Italo-Turkish War and at the moment when discussions were getting underway on the renewal of the Triple Alliance served to curb Italy's military initiatives and reinforce Vienna's bargaining position within the alliance.[312] Above all, it was the beginning of a diplomatic operation that attempted to link the Italian conquests in the Mediterranean with a future Habsburg action of conquest in the Balkans, by putting forward an interpretation of article VII that saw the Italian violation of the territorial integrity of the Ottoman Empire in the Aegean as a change in the *status quo*, for which Vienna was entitled to request territorial compensation in the future. Aehrenthal's next step was to try to weaken the legal value of the clause, with the aim of cancelling any Italian right to territorial compensations; in this regard, Heinrich Tschirschky, the German ambassador in Vienna, noted that Aehrenthal would have been very happy if article VII were to be cancelled, eliminating once and for all the awkward question of compensation, which had led Italian politicians to harbour obscure and dangerous illusions.[313]

Aehrenthal's sudden death in February 1912 prevented the implementation of his design. The new head of the Habsburg diplomatic corps was Leopold Berchtold, the former ambassador in St Petersburg and a man lacking a strong political personality,[314] who tried to pursue the strategy of his predecessor.

The foreign minister also showed himself to be little disposed to the idea of compensation to Italy in the event of Austrian expansion in the

---

311 Tschirschky to Bethmann Hollweg, 10 November 1911, GP, 30, part 1, doc. 10938. See too GP, 30, part 1, docs. 10965, 10967.

312 OEU, 3, docs. 2932, 2996, 3123, 3139.

313 Tschirschky to Bethmann Hollweg, 10 November 1911.

314 On Berchtold's appointment as foreign minister: Avarna to San Giuliano, 20 February 1912, ASMAE, SP 1891–1916, portfolio 99. On Berchtold's actions as a whole see the contrasting judgments of Albertini and Hantsch: Albertini, *The Origins of the War of 1914*, vol. 1; Hantsch, *Leopold Graf Berchtold*, 2 vols. Also of value on Berchtold's foreign policy is the work of the Czech historian Skřivan: Skřivan, *Deutschland und Österreich-Ungarn*, pp. 255 et seq. Interesting, because it cites the harsh criticisms levelled at Berchtold (accused of having little interest in political questions, having ignorance and little appetite for work) in Austrian diplomatic circles, is the following letter from Avarna: Avarna to San Giuliano, 31 July 1913, ACS, Carte Giolitti, portfolio 19.

Balkans, and his diplomatic actions during the spring of 1912 betrayed his intention to reinterpret article VII of the Triple Alliance in a way favourable to Vienna. Initially Berchtold continued to follow the uncompromising line of a rejection of any initiative by Italy in the Aegean Sea.[315] Subsequently, under pressure from Berlin, the Austrian minister conceded Italy the right to occupy some islands in the Aegean temporarily, which cleared the way for the Italian occupation of Rhodes and the Dodecanese in May 1912, proclaimed temporary and justified by the needs of war.[316]

From his statements to Avarna and the German government, as well as several memoranda, we can tell that Berchtold was determined to follow and defend his own peculiar interpretation of the content and value of article VII that would, if necessary, have allowed Austria-Hungary to act in isolation in the Balkans and without conceding compensation to Italy. In Berchtold's view, with the war against Turkey, Italy had changed the *status quo* and the balance of power in the Aegean Sea and the Mediterranean to its own advantage and without adequate consultation with its allies in advance, thereby violating the provisions of the Triple Alliance; this justified the granting of compensation to Austria-Hungary. When Avarna asked, at the end of May, for his consent to the occupation of the island of Chios, the foreign minister vetoed the move and repeated several times that Italy's military actions and occupations in the Aegean Sea had violated article VII and gave Austria the right to demand compensation. At that moment the government in Vienna did not call for compensation but threatened to do so and to conduct itself in a way similar to Italy, 'at a later moment.'[317]

In a memorandum of 3 June 1912 Berchtold stated clearly that the moment for invoking compensations in favour of Austria-Hungary to make up for the violation of article VII resulting from the Italian actions in the Aegean would come in the event of a change in the *status quo* in the Balkans. If the Italian occupation of Turkish islands were to be repeated, the government in Vienna should reserve the right to act in the same way, that is, without the agreement of Italy and without *Kompensationsbestimmung*. This signified reserving complete freedom

---

315  GP, 30, part 2, doc. 11076.
316  Sertoli Salis, *Le isole italiane dell'Egeo*, pp. 12 et seq.
317  For example: *Tagesbericht über einen Besuch des ital. Botschafters*, 21 May 1912, doc. 3534; *Aufzeichnung über die in Berlin in der Zeit vom 24 bis 26 Mai 1912 geführten Unterredungen*, n.d., doc. 3540, OEU, 4.

284 The Italians of Dalmatia

to act, without obligations to Italy. 'Should complications arise in the Balkans, we will not be bound to come to an agreement with Italy on our plan of expansion but will have a free hand in the pursuit of our interests without regard for Italy.'[318]

In short, as early as 1912 Habsburg diplomacy had decided not to accept the Italian interpretation of article VII, which linked any Austrian expansion in the Balkans to the concession of territorial compensations to Italy. For Berchtold the change in the political set-up of the Turkish empire to Italy's advantage justified Austria-Hungary's freedom of action in the Balkans.

The repeated Austrian attempts to manipulate and predetermine the possible future application of article VII in a sense unfavourable to Italy were noted by the Italian government and created a resentment that had its repercussions on the negotiations for the renewal of the Triple Alliance.

Naturally people in Italy were aware of the Austrian reluctance to accept the Italian plans underlying the formulation of article VII of the Triple Alliance.[319] Yet San Giuliano continued to be hopeful of the future application of the article. Italy's membership in the Triple Alliance was also motivated by its fear of Germany's power and its certainty about the utility of remaining allied to Berlin and Vienna. The Sicilian minister was convinced of the indispensability of the Triple Alliance: 'On the usefulness of our renewing the Triple Alliance I have no doubts ... The accession of Italy to the Triple Entente (which moreover only exists in a very limited sense), if it were, and for now it is not, desired by those three powers, would not perhaps be sufficient to wholly overturn the military superiority of the Austro-German bloc, and would not be compensated by our new allies with sufficient regard to our interests.'[320]

This firm Italian belief in the usefulness of the Triple Alliance was shared by Germany. Contrary to the renewal negotiations of 1902 and 1907, the government in Berlin now displayed a strong interest in maintaining the alliance with Italy and made considerable efforts to obtain that objective. The worsening of relations with Great Britain and the

---

318 *Mémoire über die durch die italienischen Inselbesetzungen im ägäischen Meere geschaffene Lage*, 3 June 1912, OEU, 4, doc. 3551; Hantsch, *Berchtold*, vol. 1, p. 274.
319 On this, see San Giuliano's long memorandum: Antonio di San Giuliano, memorandum, 13 September 1911.
320 San Giuliano, memorandum, 13 September 1911.

continuing risk of war with France rendered the alliance with Italy of vital importance to Germany. It was the secretary of state, Alfred Kiderlen-Wächter (although he was to die suddenly at the end of 1912), who was the keenest supporter of maintaining close relations with Italy.[321]

After the official opening of the negotiations for the renewal of the Triple Alliance in September 1911, the government in Rome continued with internal consultations to establish its official requests. San Giuliano, determined to focus Italian policy on the Libyan question, had given up the plan to raise the question of the specification of article VII at the time of the renewal of the Triple Alliance.[322] After long talks and various contacts, the Italian government made known its requirements with regard to the renewal of the alliance to its allies in March 1912: Italy was ready to renew the treaty of alliance without modifications; however, it asked for the incorporation of the Italo-Austrian accords of 1900–1 and 1909 into the treaty through an additional protocol and the recognition by the allies of Italy's full sovereignty over Libya.[323]

The request for a link between the Italo-Austrian bilateral accords and the treaty of the Triple Alliance clearly betrayed a growing Italian distrust of the government in Vienna and Italy's desire to involve Germany and bind it to the respect and possible implementation of these pacts. Berchtold's opposition to the demands of the government in Rome, and the cooling of Italo-Austrian relations as a result of the dispute over the application of article VII in the Aegean and the Italian right to carry out acts of war in that region without the consent of Vienna, blocked the negotiations for the renewal of the Triple Alliance for several months.

The German government, worried about the consequences of a deterioration in Italo-Austrian relations, tried to mediate between the two states. However, a marked improvement in the relations between Vienna and Rome did not come until the end of the Italo-Turkish War and the outbreak of the first Balkan War. Vienna's and Rome's need to exercise control over the action of the Balkan states and make their

---

321  On the figure of Kiderlen-Wächter: Fay, *The Origins of the World War*, vol. 1, pp. 260 et seq.

322  San Giuliano, memorandum, 13 September 1911; San Giuliano to Giolitti, 20–23 September 1911, ACS, Carte Giolitti, portfolio 12.

323  GP, 30, part 2, docs. 11258, 11260, 11261, 11265; OEU, 4, docs. 3375, 3379, 3384, 3437; Avarna to San Giuliano, April 1, 1912, ACS, Carte Giolitti, portfolio 15; Salvatorelli, *La Triplice Alleanza*, pp. 428 et seq.

respective influence in the Balkans more incisive rendered it even more urgent to break the deadlock in the talks over the renewal of the Triple Alliance. The conclusion of the war in Libya with the signing of the Peace Treaty of Ouchy (18 October 1912) made it easier to meet the demand for the recognition of Italian sovereignty over Tripolitania and Cyrenaica. The request for the inclusion of the Italo-Austrian treaties of 1900–1 and 1909 in the Triple Alliance remained the major obstacle to renewal. The government in Vienna held that the insertion of the Italo-Austrian accords in an additional protocol to the text of the Triple Alliance would constitute an extension of a treaty 'which imposed greater obligations on Austria-Hungary than it did on Italy';[324] in addition, in Berchtold's view, the Italian insistence on inserting the two agreements in the additional protocol could be seen as a sign that Italy did not trust 'Austria-Hungary to fulfil the obligations assumed with the pacts in question.'[325]

In the Italian government it was Giolitti in particular who insisted on the importance of the connection between the Italo-Austrian accords and the Triple Alliance. Suspicious of Austrian policy, he wrote to San Giuliano on 2 November that the Habsburg determination to oppose the Italian requests made it even more necessary to persevere in them. 'For us these accords are now the essential thing; if we were to agree not to include them in a protocol we would be implicitly admitting that they have lost their value.'[326]

The difficulties in the negotiations were overcome thanks to the mediation of Berlin and to insistent German pressure on Berchtold. In November 1912 the government in Vienna, anxious to preserve the Triple Alliance at the height of the Balkan War, agreed to attach a protocol to the treaty of alliance (drawn up by Kiderlen-Wächter and San Giuliano) that in addition to recognizing Italian sovereignty over the Libyan territories, declared that the accords of 1900–1 and 1909 were not modified by the renewal of the treaty of alliance between Italy, Austria-Hungary,

---

324  Avarna to San Giuliano, 31 October 1912, ACS, Carte Giolitti, portfolio 12; OEU, 4, doc. 4220.
325  Avarna to San Giuliano, 2 November 1912, ACS, Carte Giolitti, portfolio 12; OEU, 4, doc. 4246.
326  Giolitti to San Giuliano, 2 November 1912, ACS, Carte Giolitti, portfolio 12. On Giolitti's stance during the negotiations for the renewal of the Triple Alliance: Giolitti to San Giuliano, 31 October 1912; Bollati to San Giuliano, 6 November 1912, ACS, Carte Giolitti, portfolio 12; GP, 30, part 2, docs. 11269, 11270.

and Germany.[327] The renewed treaty was finally signed in Vienna on 5 December 1912[328] and was to come into force on the expiry of the existing treaty, that is, on 8 July 1914 and to last theoretically until 1920.[329]

The reaffirmation of the validity of the bilateral Italo-Austrian treaties at the time of the renewal of the Triple Alliance confirmed the Italian distrust of Austria-Hungary's policy in the Balkans; it also reflected the desire of the government in Rome to involve Berlin as closely as possible in the relations between Italians and Austrians, almost making the survival of the alliance dependent on the respect for the 1900–1 and 1909 accords (and therefore for Italian interests) by Austria-Hungary.

Notwithstanding the efforts of the European powers to circumscribe the Italo-Turkish War, the Italian conquest of Libya inflicted a heavy blow on the Ottoman Empire, weakening it further and providing the Balkan Christian states with the opportunity for a definitive confrontation with the Turkish enemy. Under the pressure of tsarist diplomacy, Greece, Bulgaria, Montenegro, and Serbia concluded a series of defensive and offensive alliances in the first few months of 1912 aimed at preparing a war of liberation against Turkey, and they embarked on a military conflict in the fall of the same year.[330] The Turkish army proved incapable of resisting the offensive of the Balkan League, which in a short space of time conquered much of the European territories of the Ottoman Empire.

The arrival of Serbian, Montenegrin, Greek, and Bulgarian troops in the Ottoman territories prompted the Austrians and Italians to co-operate in order to establish a new political order in the Balkans. Crucial

---

327  GP, 3, part 2, docs. 11272, 11273, 11275, 11277; OEU, 4, docs. 4424, 4505, 4522, 4524; San Giuliano to Bollati, 5 November 1912, ACS, Carte Giolitti, portfolio 12; Pansa to San Giuliano, November 15, 1912, and San Giuliano to Giolitti, 15 November 1912, ACS, Carte Giolitti, portfolio 22; Pribram, *The Secret Treaties of Austria-Hungary*; Salvatorelli, *La Triplice Alleanza*, p. 457; Albertini, *The Origins of the War of 1914*, vol. 1; Volpe, *Italia moderna*, vol. 3, pp. 457 et seq.

328  Avarna to San Giuliano, 5 December 1912, ACS, Carte Giolitti, portfolio 12.

329  Pribram, *The Secret Treaties of Austria-Hungary*. The text of the treaty is reproduced ibidem.

330  On the origin and course of the Balkan Wars: Helmreich, *The Diplomacy of the Balkan Wars*; Albertini, *The Origins of the War of 1914*, vol. 1; Duce, *L'Albania*; Biagini, *Momenti di storia balcanica (1878–1914)*, pp. 209 et seq.; Biagini, *L'Italia e le guerre balcaniche*; Hantsch, *Berchtold*, vol. 1, pp. 276 *et sqq*; Afflerbach, *Der Dreibund*, pp. 721 et seq.; Poincaré, *Au service de la France*, vols. 1 and 2; Treadway, *The Falcon and the Eagle*; Skřivan, *Deutschland und Österreich-Ungarn*, pp. 255 et seq.; Boeckh, *Von den Balkankriegen zum Ersten Weltkrieg*.

for Vienna and Rome was the future of the Albanian territories; both governments were opposed to an excessive expansion of Serbia and Greece at the expense of Albania, as the Serbs and Greeks were regarded as tools and allies of hostile powers like Russia and France.[331] This situation revitalized the old exchange of notes (of 1900 and 1901) that had envisaged the possible emergence of an Albanian state in the event of a change in the *status quo*. Despite many doubts about the survival of an independent Albania, the government in Rome, fearful of Serbian, Greek, or Austro-Hungarian plans to annex the Albanian coasts, embarked on a strategy of collaboration with Vienna, with the ill-concealed objective of keeping a close eye on Habsburg foreign policy and influencing it.

Over the course of the long negotiations that sought to determine the set-up in the Balkans between the end of 1912 and the summer of 1913, Italy went along with Austria-Hungary's anti-Serbian policy, while attempting to curb some of its excesses. Thus Italian diplomacy worked for the compensation of the renunciations made by Belgrade in Albania, with support for the Serbian conquest of Kosovo, the sanjak of Novi Pazar, and much of Macedonia; in the same way, it tried to moderate Austrian hostility to the Montenegrin designs on Scutari (Shkodër), attempting to find other territorial or at least financial compensation for the government in Cetinje.[332] In addition, the Italian government was not opposed to Austro-German attempts to preserve Romania's ties with the Triple Alliance, seeking in favour of Bucharest to obtain territorial concessions from Bulgaria in exchange for the award of Salonika.[333] Sensitive to problems in the Mediterranean, San Giuliano strove to contain the territorial expansion of Greece, fearful of its in-

---

331 On this: San Giuliano to Legation in Athens, 3 April 1913, ASMAE, TEL GAB, outgoing, portfolio 369.
332 San Giuliano to the embassies in Vienna, Berlin, and London, 13 January 1913; San Giuliano to the embassies in Berlin, Vienna, London, and St Petersburg, 8 February 1913, ASMAE, TEL GAB, outgoing, portfolio 369; BD, 9, part 2, docs. 64, 87, 123, 148, 164, 167, 453, 675; GP, 33, docs. 12272, 12370, 12382, 12390, 12391, 12419, 12460, 12484; GP, 34, part 1, docs. 12536, 12610, 12701, 12715, 12816; GP, 34, part 2, docs. 12973, 12998, 13011, 13228, 13245; OEU, 4, docs. 4276, 4325, 4469, 4504, 4638 and enclosure; OEU, 5, docs. 4732, 4869, 4964, 5056, 5480; Duce, *L'Albania*, pp. 309 et seq.
333 San Giuliano to the embassy in St Petersburg, 1 March 1913, ASMAE, TEL GAB, outgoing, portfolio 369; GP, 34, part 2, docs. 12949, 12950, 13012; OEU, 5, docs. 6057, 6105, 6153.

fluence in southern Albania and Valona (Vlorë).[334] In his attempts to attain these results, he brought the country closer to Austria-Hungary, establishing a totally unprecedented level of collaboration between the two governments.

The effort by San Giuliano to create a sense of trust and intimacy between Rome and Vienna induced him to accept the renewal of Italy's adherence to the Austro-Romanian alliance in March 1913[335] and declare the country's readiness to collaborate in any Habsburg military initiatives against the Serbs and the Montenegrins, with the aim of restraining its ally and ensuring Vienna's support against the designs of Greece.[336] However, the foreign minister's enthusiasm for the Triple Alliance and his warmongering tendencies clashed repeatedly with the caution of the prime minister, who was responsive to the mood of Italian public opinion (favourable to the expansion of the Balkan states) and was anxious to avoid the involvement of Italy in a new military conflict.[337]

San Giuliano's support for the Triple Alliance can be explained in part by the conviction that the division of Asiatic Turkey among the European great powers was imminent and that Italy therefore needed the backing of the Triple Alliance to defend its own interests in the eastern Mediterranean.[338] Yet article VII remained at the centre of San Giuliano's pro-Austrian policy. The Italian minister was afraid that Austria would seize the opportunity of the Balkan War to carry out *coups de main* aimed at the occupation of the sanjak of Novi Pazar and Macedonia, refusing to grant compensation; in the event of a change in the Balkan *status quo* to the advantage of the great powers, Italy reserved the right to its own freedom of action and to ask for territorial compensation. San Giuliano declared this candidly to Jagow, who

---

334  GP, 34, part 2, docs. 13257, 13287, 13319; BD, 9, part 2, docs. 851, 878, 976; BD, 10, part 1, docs. 145, 173, 179; OEU, 5, docs. 6045, 6153, 6367 and enclosure; Duce, *L'Albania*, p. 330 et seq.

335  San Giuliano to the legation in Bucharest, 29 January 1913 and 8 February 1913, ASMAE, TEL GAB, outgoing, portfolio 369; San Giuliano to Giolitti, 21 January 1913, portfolio 15, ACS, Carte Giolitti; OEU, 5, docs. 5991, 6013, 6016, 6038.

336  Mazzetti, 'L'Italia e la crisi albanese del marzo–maggio 1913,' pp. 219–62.

337  In this connection Giolitti, *Memorie*, vol. 2, pp. 475 et seq.; Giolitti to San Giuliano, 28 March 1913, ACS, Carte Giolitti, portfolio 19; Mazzetti, 'L'Italia e la crisi albanese,' pp. 230 et seq.; OEU, 5, doc. 6277.

338  André, *L'Italia e il Mediterraneo alla vigilia della prima guerra mondiale*, pp. 147 et seq.; Petricioli, *Italia in Asia Minore*.

claimed that Italy's only interest in the Balkans was that Austria should not occupy Albania: 'I replied to him that it was not just a question of Albania, but that if Austria made territorial gains or reoccupied the sanjak of Novi Pazar, we have, as a consequence of our accords, right to compensations, and these compensations are necessary to us to ensure that the current balance of size and forces between Austria and Italy is not modified to our detriment.'[339]

Over the following months the Italian government restrained and hindered Habsburg initiatives, with the aim of making Italy's collaboration and benevolence more valuable to Austria-Hungary in order to derive political, economic, and territorial advantages from it. It was a policy that had some effect, curbing Austria-Hungary's expansionistic initiatives. One of the reasons given to military leaders by Berchtold to justify his policy of renouncing territorial conquests was the need to avoid raising the question of compensation to Italy, provided for by the Triple Alliance.[340]

In reality the Italo-Austrian collaboration that developed in the Balkan area from the end of 1912 onward presented some unresolved problems. The greatest of these was undoubtedly the question of the application of article VII. The Austrian government did not agree with the Italian interpretation of that clause and would have opposed its application in the way desired by Italy. In spite of the growing evidence of Austria's real intentions with regard to article VII, Italy's poor relations with France and Great Britain, its designs on part of Asiatic Turkey,[341] and the unstable situation in the Balkans were factors that induced the government in Rome to keep the Triple Alliance alive. The conclusion of a new Italo-Austro-German naval convention in June 1913[342] was an indication of San Giuliano and Giolitti's determination to remain allied to Germany and Austria-Hungary and to use that alliance as a tool of Italy's foreign policy, partly with a view to reinforcing Italy's position with respect to France, which was perceived as a dangerous rival.[343]

---

339  San Giuliano to the embassies in Vienna, Berlin, London, Paris, and St Petersburg, 1 November 1912, ACS, Carte Giolitti, portfolio 12.

340  Berchtold, *Note an den Chef des Generalstabs*, 26 October 1912, OEU, 4, doc. 4183; Albertini, *The Origins of the War of 1914*, vol. 1.

341  On the French fears of Italian expansion in the eastern Mediterranean: DDF, III, 8, docs. 81, 163; DDF, III, 9, doc. 422.

342  On the genesis of the naval convention: Gabriele, *Le convenzioni navali della Triplice*, pp. 324 et seq.

343  On the Italian vision of the Triple Alliance: Decleva, *Da Adua a Sarajevo*, pp. 416 et

From the summer of 1913, however, the Austrophobic attitude of much of Italian public opinion became an increasingly important factor in the relations between Rome and Vienna, in particular when the news of the so-called Hohenlohe decrees broke.[344] For many years the Austrian government had sought to undermine the powers and the political and economic strength of the municipality of Trieste (which was controlled by the Italian national liberals), rightly regarding it as the heart of Italian national liberalism in Austria and of irredentist tendencies. The decrees (decided by the governor of Trieste, Konrad Hohenlohe) called for the dismissal of all Italians not in possession of Austrian citizenship who were working for the city council of Trieste, with the aim of severing the strong political, cultural, and social connections between the liberals in Trieste and Italy. The fact that the Austrian government decided to make such a move at a time of close political co-operation with Rome provoked a very harsh reaction in Italy; even those Italian newspapers, such as *Il Corriere della Sera* and *La Stampa*, that had hitherto been particularly favourable to the maintenance of good relations with the Austrian ally launched attacks on the government in Vienna.[345] Despite the pressing demands of San Giuliano and Giolitti to Berchtold for the decrees of the governor of Trieste to be revoked, the government in Vienna refused to repudiate and rectify the actions of Hohenlohe, who was a prominent member of the Habsburg establishment; it limited itself to applying the decrees in a partial and pragmatic manner, favouring the acquisition of Habsburg citizenship by all the staff of the municipality of Trieste and avoiding attention-grabbing dismissals. However, this did not satisfy the government in Rome and, above all, the Italian public opinion, where an Austrophobic mood once more held sway and strong irredentist sentiments had again been roused.[346]

---

seq.; Vigezzi, *Da Giolitti a Salandra*, pp. 3–52; Volpe, *Italia moderna*, vol. 3, pp. 457 et seq.; André, *L'Italia e il Mediterraneo*, pp. 147 et seq.

344  On the crisis in Italo-Austrian relations triggered by the Hohenlohe decrees: André, *L'Italia e il Mediterraneo*, pp. 175 et seq.; Volpe, *Italia moderna*, vol. 3, pp. 556 et seq.; Afflerbach, *Der Dreibund*, pp. 793 et seq.; San Giuliano to Avarna, 1 September 1913; San Giuliano to Bollati and Avarna, 6, 11, and 23 October 1913, ASMAE, TEL GAB, outgoing, portfolio 369; GP, 39, docs. 15742, 15743, 15744, 15745, 15746, 15747, 15748, 15749, 15750; DDF, III, 8, docs. 100, 174.

345  Flotow to Bethmann Hollweg, 17 April 1914, GP, 39, doc. 15727; Monzali, 'Introduzione,' in Albertini, *I giorni di un liberale*, pp. 27 et seq.

346  Volpe, *Italia moderna*, vol. 3, pp. 559 et seq.

Between September 1913 and the summer of 1914 there was a marked increase in the attention paid by public opinion in Italy to the conditions of Italians in Austria, and in particular the Italian populations of Venezia Giulia and Dalmatia. Important journalists like Luigi Barzini and Virginio Gayda wrote long stories on this theme in which they pointed out the existence of an Italian minority in Dalmatia that was oppressed by the southern Slav nationalist parties and neglected by the government in Vienna. For Barzini,[347] principal correspondent of *Il Corriere della Sera*, the Italians of Dalmatia had been the first victims of the Habsburg government's anti-Italian policy, and the conditions in which this minority found itself foreshadowed what was going to happen in Istria and Trieste in the near future. Using language of great emotional intensity, Barzini foresaw a tragic future for the Italians in the eastern Adriatic: 'The scheme for the destruction of the Italian spirit, to the benefit of an inferior race, offends not just us, but humanity. The treasures of Italian art, the signs of Italian glory, the vestiges of Italian history lavished on those lands, form a living and breathing whole ... And it is this Italian spirit that is being attacked. They want to sever a history like one severs a head. They want the monuments to the Italian spirit, so alive, to turn into mute tombstones in the Slav world and, as in Croatized Dalmatia, to demolish the greatest, most precious, and most glittering monument of the people: its soul.'[348]

For Virginio Gayda, *La Stampa*'s correspondent in Vienna, the Italians of Dalmatia had been the victims of a 'national massacre' carried out by the Austrian government, which was anxious to annihilate the Italians in the provinces of the eastern Adriatic. In his book, *L'Italia d'oltre confine* (Italy Across the Border),[349] Gayda recounted the political history of the Italian minority in Dalmatia with a wealth of details, extolling its spirit of sacrifice, idealism, and national values. According to the Roman journalist, Italy could not wash its hands of the Dalmatian Italians, because their fate would be decisive for the future of the Adriatic. 'The Italian problem of the Eastern Adriatic ... is such that it presumes a continuity of Italian culture between its two furthest points. It admits no gaps. Dalmatia cannot claim to be wholly Italian, but her coast cannot be exclusively Slav. It is a problem of life. One province depends on the

---

347  Barzini, *Le condizioni degli italiani in Austria*.
348  Ibid., pp. 42–3.
349  Gayda, *L'Italia d'oltre confine*.

other. If the Italians of Dalmatia finally fall, the threat to those of Istria, and then those of Trieste, is increased. An army cannot stand without covering flanks and vanguards. Dalmatia guards Istria and Trieste from the south and carries their spirit as far as the coast of Albania. She is a bridge and a bulwark. This shows you the heroic and vital mission of her surviving Italian culture.'[350]

In Gayda's view, the Italians of Dalmatia and Venezia Giulia had to form a bulwark against the rise of Slav expansionism in the Balkans and the Adriatic. 'Austria is not definitive. She can change, she can vanish ... The Slav people of the south, in their slow, inner development, are preparing a radical transformation of the Empire, perhaps into a new Empire. An immense Slav unity is being crystallized. Thus the national onslaught of today can turn into a political onslaught by states tomorrow. Whatever solution is found to the problem, if the Italian culture of the coast falls, this formidable Slav bloc that is advancing up from the Balkans and is under Russian influence will immediately appear on the shore of the Adriatic and press directly, in a solid mass, against the borders of the kingdom.'[351]

Thus it is clear that in the months preceding the outbreak of World War I the Dalmatian question and the wider problem of the Italians in Austria were topics of which Italian public opinion was keenly aware, with the result that it was increasingly swayed by anti-Habsburg feelings and tendencies that inevitably influenced foreign policy. After the Balkan Wars, however, a new potential enemy began to emerge – Yugoslav nationalism – which was now led by a Serbia that had come out of the conflicts of 1912–13 with a new strength and a desire to assert its own hegemony in the eastern Adriatic. In April 1914, the Italian consul in Zara, Antonino D'Alia, reported that the Croats, in favour of Serbia, had renounced the role of being a unifying magnet for the Slavs of the south. 'The latest idea that guides the Serbs is the one that aims at the formation of a single Serb-Montenegrin state embracing not only their own territories but also those of Bosnia-Herzegovina, Croatia-Slavonia, and Dalmatia ... And since, in politics, it is easy to move on from one aspiration to another, more ambitious one, it will not be long before the Serbs start to believe they can include in the Serbian-Montenegrin state all the countries of the hypothetical and prospective third state of the

---

350  Ibid., pp. 292–3.
351  Ibid., pp. 340–1.

Austro-Hungarian Monarchy, dreaming in this manner of the formation of a great Yugo-Slav-Serb state.'[352]

In such a political situation Serb and Croat hostility toward the Italians of Dalmatia could only intensify:

> Today the tactics of the Serbo-Croatians are
> (1) to stir up ever greater Yugo-Slav fanaticism to the point of irredentism
>     and calls for independence;
> (2) to get the Italians of the Austro-Hungarian coast to cling to close
>     agreements and relations with those of Italy, so that Italy, by this
>     means, should keep alive a hotbed of irredentism which, sooner or
>     later, might be of use to her aspirations; and
> (3) to strive to eliminate, by all tricks and means, including immoral ones,
>     any trace of Latin civilization throughout the region.
> The raging of the newspapers, the attacks on and boycott of the Italian
> traders of the empire, only represent one part of the plan that the Serbo-
> Croatians intend to carry out.[353]

According to D'Alia, in Dalmatia the Austrian government had shown
itself incapable of reacting and had chosen to go down the road of concessions in order to please Serbs and Croats; this did nothing but reinforce pan-Serbism, which threatened to become a dangerous enemy for
Italy in the Adriatic in the future.

In the summer of 1913 the Italian national question in Austria once
again became the focus of Italo-Austrian relations and was to remain
so. The worsening of national conflicts and the recurrence of clashes on
the Adriatic coast between Croats, Slovenes, and Italians contributed to
making relations between the two states difficult, even against the will
of the Italian government, which wanted close ties between the two
countries. San Giuliano was convinced of the usefulness of the existence of the Habsburg Empire to Italy and held that the Italo-Austrian
alliance was the best means of countering the new pan-Serbian and Yugoslav threat. In November, San Giuliano complained to the German
ambassador, Hans Flotow, about the Austrian attitude: he had made his
government's priority the creation of close relations with the Habsburg
Empire, but he was realizing that Austria did not wish to establish a

---

352  D'Alia to Avarna, 9 April 1914, ASMAE, EMB VIENNA, portfolio 236.
353  Ibid.

lasting friendship with the Italian nation; Austrian domestic policy, which encouraged the Slavicization of Venezia Giulia and Dalmatia, was removing one of the principal advantages that Italy derived from the alliance and was destroying the function of Austria as a bastion against the Slav menace.[354]

The deterioration in relations between Italy and Austria-Hungary, while not desired by the Foreign Ministry, was further aggravated by the Albanian question. The concrete organization of the Albanian state and the struggle for supremacy in that country increasingly divided the two governments; the Italian and Habsburg representatives competed fiercely to win the favour of the local populations and to lay the foundations for a domination of particular parts of the Albanian territory by their own state in the event of the disintegration of the principality of Albania.[355]

In fact, at the beginning of 1914 Italy found itself in a difficult position on the international plane, one of partial isolation in spite of its membership in the Triple Alliance and its efforts to maintain relations with the Triple Entente.[356] The Austro-Germans and the French, British, and Russians were mistrustful of Italy.[357]

In an atmosphere increasingly dominated by the conflict between the Central Powers and the Triple Entente and by hostility toward Italian policy, the government in Rome felt obliged to stick to the Triple Alliance, notwithstanding the difficult relations with Austria, in order to preserve some international influence, however minimal. In Italy many continued to have hope in a friendly understanding with Austria-Hungary that, as in 1904, would allow the grave sources of disagreement to be overcome. It was with such hopes that San Giuliano agreed to meet

---

354 Flotow to Bethmann Hollweg, 9 November 1913, GP, 39, doc. 15752.

355 A vast amount of Austrian and Italian documentation of the troubled existence of the Albanian principality and the Italo-Austrian rivalry in Albania between the end of 1913 and the outbreak of World War I has been published: OEU, vols. 6, 7, 8; DDI, IV, 12. See too Salandra, *La neutralità italiana 1914–1915*, pp. 38 et seq.; Biagini, *Storia dell'Albania*, pp. 90 et seq.; Albertini, *Venti anni*, vol. 1, 2, pp. 471 et seq.; Swire, *Albania*; Skřivan, *Deutschland und Österreich-Ungarn*, pp. 321 et seq.

356 André, *L'Italia e il Mediterraneo*, pp. 232 et seq.; DDF, III, 8, docs. 408, 601; DDF, III, 9, docs. 324, 330. On Italo-French relations between 1912 and 1915: Keiger, *Raymond Poincaré*, pp. 132 et seq.; Keiger, *France and the Origins of the First World War*, pp. 56 et seq. On the subject of the relations between Italy and Russia: IB, I, 1, doc. 312; IB, I, 2, doc. 80; IB, I, 3, doc. 32; Petracchi, *Da San Pietroburgo*, pp. 90 et seq.

357 Volpe, *Italia moderna*, vol. 3, pp. 604–5.

Berchtold at Abbazia in April 1914, but the talks between the two men went nowhere. Both San Giuliano and Berchtold stressed their desire to pursue a policy of friendship and close relations between the two countries, but no progress was made in specific matters. San Giuliano insisted on the importance of the cessation of the Vienna government's policy of Slavicization in the Adriatic territories, in order to improve the image of Austria in the eyes of the Italian public. The Austrian government's response was not encouraging. San Giuliano reported that Berchtold, 'while beginning to understanding the Italian government's need to have a more favourable public opinion than it has today for the policy of accord with Austria, and promising me ... to try to do something about it, denied that Austria's Italian subjects are less well treated than other subjects of the Monarchy.'[358]

With respect to the Albanian question they confined themselves to repeating their mutual commitment to an independent Albania, but without finding any way of overcoming the rivalry between the local representatives of the two powers. San Giuliano then tried to raise the thorny question of the possibility of territorial changes in the Balkans. When Berchtold reminded him of the unacceptability to Austria of a union between Serbia and Montenegro, the Italian minister declared that Italy was ready for a genuine agreement, to be drawn up as soon as possible, that would clearly establish a common approach for the two countries in the Balkans; the government in Rome was waiting for Austria, the power most directly interested, to communicate 'her ideas on this in the most concrete manner.' The Habsburg representatives refused to make binding commitments and only stressed that they would do everything possible to ensure that Italy and Austria-Hungary acted in concert on these important questions.

So the meeting at Abbazia did not permit a friendly solution to be found to the problems between the two countries, whose relations deteriorated further in May following the disturbances that broke out between Slovenes and Italians in Trieste, which led to many anti-Austrian demonstrations in Italy,[359] and the staging of a revolt against the rule of

---

358  enclosure with the Foreign Ministry to Avarna, 30 April 1914, ASMAE, EMB
     VIENNA, portfolio 238; San Giuliano to Victor Emmanuel III, 14 April 1914, BL,
     Carte Salandra, C–II-42. Berchtold's account of the talks at Abbazia is published in
     OEU, 7, doc. 9592. See too GP, 39, docs. 15729, 15730; DDF, III, 10, docs. 126, 129, 167.
359  GP, 39, docs. 15761, 15762, 15763, 15764, 15765; DDF, III, 10, docs. 219, 260, 316;
     Salandra, La neutralità, pp. 31 et seq.; San Giuliano to Salandra, 7 and 19 May 1914;
     Avarna to San Giuliano, 11 May 1914, BL, Carte Salandra, C-1-5.

Prince Wilhelm zu Wied in Albania (which Vienna suspected of having been inspired by Italy).[360]

The aggravation of Italo-Austrian relations began to worry some German diplomats who were afraid that the rivalry between Rome and Vienna would put an end to the Triple Alliance. Flotow, who had good contacts in Rome and close relations with San Giuliano, sent reports to Berlin in which he expressed his concern about the rise of increasing hostility to the Habsburg Empire in broad swathes of Italian society.[361] During the first few months of 1914 Italo-Austrian relations continued to deteriorate over the Albanian question, prompting the government in Berlin and the Austrian representatives in Rome to make greater efforts to improve the relationship between the two allied states.

In April 1914 Flotow, convinced that maintenance of the alliance with Italy was of great value to Germany, began to discuss the objectives of Italian Balkan policy with San Giuliano on his own initiative. The aim of these talks was to prepare the ground for negotiations that would lead to an Italo-Austrian accord on the territorial set-up in the Balkans. On 4 April Flotow asked San Giuliano what the Italian attitude would be in the event of a union between Serbia and Montenegro and of an Austrian action against the government in Belgrade to prevent it gaining an access to the sea. The minister replied that Italy was opposed to an Austrian expansion at the expense of Montenegro, but that it would be possible to avoid a conflict by coming to an agreement on the compensation to be assigned to Italy for the Habsburg conquest of the Montenegrin coast.[362] In a conversation in June, San Giuliano was more explicit: should Albania lose its independence, he declared that the government in Rome would drop its opposition to Austrian control of northern Albania only if Austria-Hungary ceded the Italian provinces of Austria to Italy.[363] The minister said the same thing to Flotow on 10 July: an Austrian expansion in the Balkans could only be tolerated if compensation were to be made to Italy; if the Habsburg Empire

---

360  On the Italo-Austrian rivalry in Albania: Salandra to San Giuliano, 24 May 1914, BL, Carte Salandra, C-II-42; GP, 36, part 2, docs., 14373, 14439, 14440, 14443, 14445, 14446, 14450, 14451; GP, 38, doc. 15553; OEU, 6, 7, and 8.

361  GP, 39, docs. 15744, 15752.

362  San Giuliano to Avarna and Bollati, 4 April 1914, ASMAE, TEL GAB, outgoing, portfolio 391.

363  San Giuliano to Avarna, Bollati, and Carlotti, 13 June 1914, ASMAE, TEL GAB, outgoing, portfolio 391.

were to assume control of the Lovćen massif, it would have to cede the Trentino to Italy.[364]

For an Italian government in increasing difficulty on the international plane, the search for a territorial agreement with Austria-Hungary within the Triple Alliance remained the ideal and logical solution. Notwithstanding all the differences and rivalry, Flotow was right in perceiving, even in the months preceding the outbreak of World War I, the existence of an Italian desire to stay loyal to the Triple Alliance and a willingness to accept an Austrian expansion at the expense of Serbia, Montenegro, or Albania in exchange for the acquisition of part or all of the Italian provinces of Austria.[365]

However, the Italian aspirations to a deal with Austria-Hungary on the future of the Balkans and on the application of article VII in the first half of 1914 came to nothing. The government in Vienna, more and more dominated by the bellicose and Italophobic ideas of Conrad, did not consider Italy a reliable partner and was not willing to agree to the territorial exchange desired by the head of the Foreign Ministry. The idea of a new cession of Austrian territories to Italy was unacceptable to almost the whole of the Habsburg establishment. Vienna was by now determined to resolve the Serbian question unilaterally and by force, presenting Italy with a *fait accompli*. Germany failed to make its views clear. Much of the responsibility for this can be laid at the door of Kiderlen's successor, Gottlieb von Jagow, whose experience as ambassador in Rome had left him with the impression that Italy was militarily weak and internally fragile and therefore almost obliged to follow the course of action taken by Germany; in any case, it was an Italy of no great importance on the international plane.

### 3.5.  Dalmatia in the Treaty of London, and the End of the Triple Alliance

In the light of the nature of Italo-Habsburg and Italo-German relations in the years preceding the outbreak of the Austro-Serbian War, it is easy to understand the origins of the crisis in the Triple Alliance in July and August 1914.

---

364  Flotow to Bethmann Hollweg, 10 July 1914, GP, 38, doc. 15555; DDI, IV, 12, doc. 124.
365  See Luigi Albertini's observations on this: Albertini, *The Origins of the War of 1914*, vol. 1.

Borders before the end of World War I, 1918
The Dalmatian coast according to the Treaty of London, 26 April 1915

0    50 km

On the origins of the Austro-Serbian War and its widening to a European and then worldwide level there are some extremely well-documented works, such as those by Luigi Albertini,[366] Sidney B. Fay,[367]

366  Albertini, *The Origins of the War of 1914*, 3 vols.
367  Fay, *The Origins of the World War*, 2 vols.

Pierre Renouvin,[368] Bernadotte Schmitt,[369] Gerhard Ritter,[370] Fritz Fischer,[371] and Klaus Hildebrand,[372] that have carefully reconstructed the events of those days and their causes. The assassination of Francis Ferdinand and his wife by pan-Serbian nationalists was the pretext used by the government in Vienna to realize a plan that a section of the Habsburg leadership had been cherishing for many years: the violent suppression of independent Serbia and the annexation of many Serbian territories that were destined to become part of a future Yugoslav entity dominated by the Croats and integrated into the Habsburg Empire. On the Habsburg side, the war against Serbia was conceived as a unilateral action to be carried out without consultations with Italy. The government in Vienna wanted to face the Italians with a *fait accompli*. It wished to follow the tactics adopted by Aehrenthal on the occasion of the annexation of Bosnia-Herzegovina, a stratagem that after all had been copied by Italy at the time of the war for the conquest of Tripolitania. It was believed that in this way, with Berlin's backing of Austria's war objectives and mode of achieving them, Italian demands for compensation could be resisted; the Italian government, regarded as weak and timid, would not have the courage to declare war on Austria if the latter had Germany's support, especially if Serbia were easily defeated. At the root of this choice lay Austria's distrust of its Italian ally and the very poor political relations between the two states since the issuing of the Hohenlohe decrees, which had undermined the co-operation and close relationship that San Giuliano had tried to create.

The broadening of the conflict into a European war and the inability of Austria and Germany to gain a rapid victory wrecked Habsburg calculations. However, these Habsburg plans and German support for them explain the failure of Austro-German diplomacy to involve Italy in the fighting. As Bernhard von Bülow himself noted,[373] the Italian government was ready to support the military initiatives of Austria-Hungary politically and even to consider intervening in the war on the

---

368  Renouvin, *The Immediate Origins of the War*; Renouvin, *La crise européenne et la première guerre mondiale*.

369  Schmitt, *The Coming of the War, 1914*, 2 vols.

370  Ritter, *Staatskunst und Kriegshandwerk*, 3 vols.

371  Fischer, *Germany's Aims in the First World War*.

372  Hildebrand, *Das vergangene Reich*.

373  Bülow, *Memoirs*, 3.

side of its allies.[374] Such was the advice of the Italian ambassadors in Berlin and Vienna, Riccardo Bollati and Giuseppe Avarna, and it was a hypothesis that the government in Rome considered seriously. This is demonstrated by the letter that San Giuliano wrote to Victor Emmanuel III on 24 July (the day after the Austrian delivery of an ultimatum to Belgrade), in which he proposed the following line of conduct, approved by Salandra:

> 1st) making it clear to our allies that we are not obliged to participate in the prospective war for the reasons put forward in the outgoing telegrams;
> 2nd) making sure before supporting our allies even diplomatically that they accept our interpretation of art. 7 of the treaty of the Triple Alliance;
> 3rd) ensuring that there will be compensation for any territorial aggrandizement of Austria;
> 4th) ensuring that there will be compensation in the unlikely event of our participation in the war, a participation that we will be free to decide for or against when the time comes;
> 5th) if possible also ensuring that there will be compensation although on a much lesser scale, or at least guarantees that our interests will not be damaged, for any diplomatic backing we give to our allies.[375]

In the light of the history of the Triple Alliance, there was nothing strange or surprising about the Italian stance, which was consistent with the decades of effort that had gone into obtaining application of article VII and a diplomatic solution to the problem of the Italians in Austria. Bollati, in a conversation with Jagow on 24 July, took an even more matter-of-fact approach, informing him of a plan he had for agreement that was very similar to the one desired by the Foreign Ministry: 'On the one hand, she [Austria-Hungary] would have to cede us part

---

374 On the Italian attitude toward the international crisis of July 1914: Albertini, *The Origins of the War of 1914*, vols. 2 and 3; Toscano, 'L'Italia e la crisi europea del luglio 1914,' in *Pagine di storia diplomatica contemporanea*, vol. 1, *Origini e vicende della prima guerra mondiale*, pp. 125 et seq.; Pastorelli, *Dalla prima alla seconda guerra mondiale*, pp. 15 et seq.; Vigezzi, *L'Italia di fronte alla prima guerra mondiale*; Vigezzi, *L'Italia unita e le sfide della politica estera*, pp. 129 et seq.; Renzi, *In the Shadow of the Sword*; Monticone, *La Germania e la neutralità italiana*; Valiani, *The End of Austria-Hungary*; Bosworth, *Italy and the Approach of the First World War*, pp. 121 et seq.; Salandra, *La neutralità*, pp. 63 et seq.; Repaci, *Da Sarajevo al 'maggio radioso,'* pp. 66 et seq.

375 San Giuliano to Victor Emmanuel III, 24 July 1914, DDI, IV, 12, doc. 470: also published in Salandra, *La neutralità*, pp. 78–80.

of the Italian provinces in exchange for an enlargement of her territory gained at the expense of Serbia or Montenegro; on the other, she would have to commit herself to accepting the acquisition by Italy of Valona [Vlorë] and southern Albania in the event that she seized control of northern Albania.'[376]

The refusal by the government in Vienna to agree to the cession of Habsburg territories to Italy and the short-sightedness of German diplomacy made Italian collaboration with the Austrian war plans impossible and threw the Triple Alliance into political crisis. Over the course of the second half of July Berchtold countered the Italian demands for compensation by reiterating the old Austrian arguments about article VII: this clause concerned exclusively changes in the *status quo* of the Ottoman territories and not Serbia and Montenegro;[377] and the Habsburg Empire did not wish to annex Serbian territories, which would be occupied only temporarily, and therefore article VII was not applicable.[378] Between the end of July and the first few days of August the Austro-Hungarian minister, under German pressure, agreed to consider the possibility of applying the clause in the event of conquests by Austria-Hungary but rejected any hypothesis of ceding Austrian territories to Italy.[379]

On the German side, as Luigi Albertini has clearly shown,[380] the importance of Italy's co-operation was initially underestimated. Bethmann Hollweg, Wilhelm II, and Jagow went along fully with the Austrian plans, including those of presenting Italy with a *fait accompli* to avoid the question of compensation; only Tschirschky, on his own initiative on 3 July, tried to remind the government in Vienna of the importance of a collaboration with Italy, but without any result.[381]

The leaders of the German government did not begin to take steps

---

376   Bollati to San Giuliano, 25 July 1914, DDI, IV, 12, doc. 524.

377   *Notiz des Gesandten Grafen Albert Nemes*, n.d. [but around 19 July 1914], OEU, 8, doc. 10392; DDI, IV, 12, doc. 565.

378   *Tagesbericht über einen Besuch des deutschen Botschafters*, 20 July 1914, doc. 10398; Berchtold to Merey, 26 July 1914, doc. 10746, OEU, 8; DDI, IV, 12, doc. 681.

379   DDI, IV, 12, docs. 839, 848, 882; Berchtold to Merey, 28 July 1914, doc. 10909; docs. 11165, 11172, 11203, OEU, 8.

380   Albertini, *The Origins of the War of 1914*, vol. 2. On the German attempts to influence Vienna in a way favourable to Italy in July 1914 see too Monticone, *La Germania e la neutralità italiana*, pp. 15–40; Hantsch, *Berchtold*, vol. 2, pp. 654 et seq.

381   *Tagesbericht über eine Unterredung mit dem deutschen Botschafter*, 3 July 1914, OEU, 8, doc. 10006.

to foster an Italo-Austrian accord on the basis of compensations until the middle of July,[382] after Flotow's anxious messages about the Italian intention not to recognize the validity of the *casus foederis* in the event of a Habsburg attack on Serbia and the possibility of Italy leaving the Triple Alliance.[383] However, there was no time left for such a difficult negotiation, and the German attitude was fairly ambiguous, more concerned with creating a temporary impression of the alliance's solidarity and gaining time than with reaching a definitive political and territorial accord with Italy. The fact is that the German government also viewed a transfer of Austrian territories to Italy as a negative step, considering it a weakening of the Habsburg Empire, and for months tried to bring the Italians into the conflict with promises of Albanian or French territories.[384]

The impossibility of reaching a territorial agreement with Austria-Hungary induced the Italian government to remain neutral in a conflict that, at the end of July and the beginning of August, saw Germany enter the field on the side of Austria-Hungary and saw Russia, France, and Great Britain enter in defence of Serbia and of a Belgian state whose neutrality had been violated by the German army.

From the beginning of August until the death of San Giuliano in October 1914 there was a de facto phase of stagnation and lull in Italian foreign policy, partly as a result of deterioration in the health of San Giuliano, who was gravely ill and unable to handle a heavy burden of work; chiefly it derived from the Italian desire to await the outcome of the military conflict and to carry out a major build-up of arms before taking a final decision.[385]

Up until the first French successes in September 1914, most of the Italian ruling class believed a military victory by Germany to be imminent, and this prompted the government to try to preserve good relations with Berlin and Vienna. The idea of a future Austro-German

---

382  Jagow to Tschirschky, 15 July 1914, in Kautsky, *Die Deutschen Dokumente*, 1, doc. 46; Tschirschky to Jagow, July 26, 1914, in Kautsky, *Die Deutschen Dokumente*, 2, doc. 326; OEU, 8, docs. 10398, 10448, 10715; Albertini, *The Origins of the War of 1914*, vol. 2.

383  Kautsky, *Die Deutschen Dokumente*, 1, docs. 42, 51, 64; Albertini, *The Origins of the War of 1914*, vol. 2.

384  Kautsky, *Die Deutschen Dokumente*, 1, docs. 212, 269; 2, docs. 326, 363.

385  In this connection: San Giuliano to Salandra, 4 August 1914, DDI, V, 1, docs. 54 and 55; Salandra, *La neutralità*.

victory explains the Italian coolness with regard to the Russian proposals of intervention by Italy on the side of the Triple Entente in exchange
for the Italian conquest of the Tyrol, Venezia Giulia, and a not clearly
defined part of Dalmatia, proposals that had been prompted by Andrea
Carlotti, ambassador to St Petersburg, in August 1914.[386]

It was not until after the German failure to break French resistance
and the Habsburg defeats in Galicia that serious consideration was giv-
en to the possibility of a war against Austria-Hungary.

Italian foreign policy regained momentum with the appointment of
Sidney Sonnino as minister of foreign affairs.[387] On the one hand, the
choice of Sonnino as the man in charge of Italian diplomacy reflected
Salandra's desire to play a primary role in the direction of foreign policy
through the appointment of a great friend in whose government he had
already served, someone who fully agreed with the prime minister's
plan and who at that moment seemed devoid of personal ambitions; on
the other hand, it was a choice that could hardly be avoided since, apart
from Giolitti, Sonnino was the only Italian politician to possess the necessary range of qualities (experience, a thorough grasp of international
questions, energy, tough negotiating skills, and the capacity to make
decisions) to guide Italian diplomacy in that grave political situation.

Sonnino's appointment was favourably received in Berlin as his sympathies for German culture and the Triple Alliance were well known.[388]
In effect, in the months between November 1914 and February 1915
Salandra and Sonnino, with the approval of the king and Giolitti, who
controlled the parliamentary majority that supported the government,
reopened negotiations with Vienna and Berlin with the aim of finding
an accord on the basis of article VII. The objective was to obtain the
surrender of Austrian territories inhabited by Italians or considered
necessary to the strategic security of the state as compensation for the

---

386  DDI, V, 1, docs. 65, 100, 133, 179, 198; CP, series H, 1, docs. 11, 14, 21, 33, 46, 72; DDF
     1914, docs. 20, 21, 22, 35, 52; IB, II, 6, part 1, docs. 24, 25, 35, 42, 54, 63, 77, 86, 117;
     Iswolsky to the Foreign Ministry, 23 July / 5 August 1914 and 25 July / 7 August
     1914, LN, 3, pp. 1–2; L'Intervento dell'Italia, pp. 10–11; Petracchi, Da San Pietroburgo a
     Mosca, pp. 111 et seq.; Pastorelli, Dalla prima alla seconda guerra, pp. 18 et seq.
387  On the figure of Sidney Sonnino: Carlucci, Il giovane Sonnino fra cultura e politica
     (1847–1886); Guido Biagi, 'Sidney Sonnino,' in Passatisti, pp. 173–214; Jannazzo,
     Sonnino meridionalista; Monzali, 'Sidney Sonnino e la politica estera italiana'; Nieri,
     Costituzione e problemi sociali; Ballini, Sidney Sonnino e il suo tempo; Bergamini, 'Son-
     nino e la Dalmazia.'
388  Monticone, La Germania e la neutralità italiana, pp. 58 et seq.

Sidney Sonnino, the Italian Minister of Foreign
Affairs who negotiated the Treaty of London with
England, France, and Russia, April 1915

new Habsburg conquests and for Italy's neutrality. At the same time the
Italian government continued to work on defining its own plans of territorial expansion in the eventuality of either a compensated neutrality
or a military intervention on the side of the Triple Entente.

Once the Austro-Hungarian unwillingness to give serious and concrete consideration to the Italian demands for compensation had become clear, in February 1915 Salandra, Sonnino, and the king decided
in favour of a military intervention against Vienna, and in March they
commenced talks with the powers of the Triple Entente to determine
the nature of Italy's future participation in the world war.

The fundamental stages in the evolution of Italian foreign policy during 1914 and 1915 are now widely known. The researches conducted by Luigi Albertini,[389] Alberto Monticone,[390] Mario Toscano,[391] Brunello Vigezzi,[392] Leo Valiani,[393] Hugo Hantsch,[394] Friedrich Engel-Janosi,[395] Pietro Pastorelli,[396] and Italo Garzia[397] have exhaustively reconstructed the long negotiations between Italy and the Austrians and Germans in their search for an agreement on Italian neutrality and the simultaneous diplomatic talks that led to the conclusion of the Treaty of London on 26 April 1915[398] and the subsequent declaration of war on Austria in May.

During 1914 and early 1915, while bloody war was waged in Europe, and Italy stayed neutral, there was a debate among Italian politicians and diplomats over the decisions to be taken with regard to Italy's attitude to the belligerents and the nature of any plan of conquest in the event of intervention in the war against Austria-Hungary or of an agreement of compensated neutrality with Vienna and Berlin. The debate dealt at length with the Adriatic question, had numerous public expressions, and continued in the following years, after the conclusion of the Treaty of London and Italy's entry into the war.[399]

389  Albertini, *Venti anni di vita politica*, vol. 2, 1.
390  Monticone, *La Germania e la neutralità italiana*.
391  Toscano, *Il patto di Londra*; *La Serbia e l'intervento in guerra dell'Italia*; 'Le origini diplomatiche dell'art,' pp. 342 et seq.; 'Rivelazioni e nuovi documenti sul negoziato di Londra,' in *Nuova Antologia*, August 1965, pp. 433–57, September 1965, pp. 15–37, October 1965, pp. 150–7, November 1965, pp. 295–312; 'Il negoziato di Londra del 1915,' pp. 295–326; 'L'Intervento dell'Italia nella prima guerra mondiale,' pp. 303–23, 461–73; 'Imperiali e il negoziato per il patto di Londra,' pp. 177–205; 'Il libro verde del 1915,' pp. 157–229.
392  Vigezzi, *L'Italia di fronte alla prima guerra mondial*; *Da Giolitti a Salandra*.
393  Valiani, *The End of Austria-Hungary*.
394  Hantsch, *Berchtold*, vol. 2, pp. 617 et seq.
395  Engel-Janosi, *Österreich und der Vatikan*, vol. 2, pp. 190 et seq.
396  Pastorelli, *Dalla prima alla seconda guerra mondiale*.
397  Garzia, 'Le origini dell'articolo 15 del Patto di Londra,' pp. 523–49; Garzia, *La questione romana durante la prima guerra mondiale*.
398  On the negotiations between Italy and the Entente in the spring of 1915 see too Burgwyn, *The Legend of the Mutilated Victory*, pp. 16 et seq.; Renzi, *In the Shadow of the Sword*; Petrovich, 'The Italo-Yugoslav Boundary Question 1914–1915,' p. 178 et seq.; Gottlieb, *Studies in Secret Diplomacy during the First World War*, pp. 135–401.
399  A large amount of journalistic and historical writings on the Adriatic question in Italian foreign and domestic policy over the course of World War I and after has been published; here are mentioned just: Valiani, *The End of Austria-Hungary*;

It is interesting to note that this time, unlike in 1866, Dalmatia was included in the Italian plans of territorial conquest. The political and strategic interest in this region had existed, as has been amply demonstrated, for many decades. Ever since the Habsburg conquest of Bosnia-Herzegovina, Italian military and political circles had believed that the control of Dalmatia was crucial to determining the outcome of military conflicts in the Adriatic. The rise of an Italian national consciousness in many of the Italians of Dalmatia had permitted the creation of political and economic ties between the government in Rome and the Dalmatian Italian Autonomous Party from the end of the nineteenth century onward.

A few weeks after the outbreak of war in Europe, calls for the government in Rome to remember Italy's right to control of Dalmatia in the future began to appear in the Italian press. Among the initiators of this Dalmatian campaign were the leaders of the nationalist movement: Luigi Federzoni; Enrico Corradini; Piero Foscari; the Dalmatian writer and teacher of Italian in London, Antonio Cippico; and Gabriele d'Annunzio.

At a number of rallies held in September 1914 Federzoni stressed that the Adriatic question was a crucial problem for Italy, which had to become the dominant power in that sea,[400] while Corradini called for the liberation of not just Trent and Trieste but also Dalmatia.[401] The nationalist position on Dalmatia was expressed in a definitive and complete way by Foscari in an article in *Il Giornale d'Italia* on 24 September.[402] According to the Venetian member of parliament, the approach of Serbs and Montenegrins to the heart of Bosnia represented a grave threat to

---

Albertini, *Venti anni di vita politica*, vol. 2, parts 1, 2, 3; Vivarelli, *Storia delle origini del fascismo*; Monteleone, *La politica dei fuorusciti irredenti nella guerra mondiale*; Salvemini and Maranelli, 'La questione dell'Adriatico' ; Tamaro, *Italiani e slavi nell'Adriatico*; Tamborra, *L'idea di nazionalità e la guerra 1914–1918*; Monzali, 'Tra irredentismo e fascismo' ; 'Un contributo alla storia degli italiani di Dalmazia'; 'La Dalmazia e la questione jugoslava' ; 'Introduzione,' in Albertini, *I giorni di un liberale*, pp. 155 et seq.; Micheletta, 'Pietro Silva storico delle relazioni internazionali,' pp. 497 et seq.; Bucarelli, '"Manicomio jugoslavo,"' pp. 467 et seq.; De Felice, *Mussolini il rivoluzionario 1883–1920*; Riccardi, *Salata*; Caccamo, *L'Italia e la 'Nuova Europa.'*

400 'Nazionalisti, repubblicani e socialisti discutono gl'interessi dell'Italia nell'ora presente,' *Il Giornale d'Italia*, 9 September 1914.
401 'I nazionalisti reclamano l'annessione di Trento e Trieste all'Italia,' *Il Giornale d'Italia*, 20 September 1914.
402 Odenigo, *Piero Foscari*, pp. 104–7.

the interests of Italy, which could defend itself adequately in the Adriatic only if Dalmatia came under Italian control.

> As well as for inescapable strategic necessities, Northern Dalmatia was and is ours for geological, historical, and ethnic reasons, not only in Italy's most Italian city, the indomitable Zara, marvellous in its martyrdom and resistance, but down along the Dinaric Alps, at least as far as the Narenta [Neretva]. And with this we take nothing away from the valorous Serbian people who should live fraternally with us in the same sea, since they are left with the magnificent economic outlets of Ragusa and Antivari and the formidable position of Cattaro ... Dalmatia in the hands of others is a continual and grave threat to our heart and too short a distance from it, while in our hands it is our necessary defence without threatening anyone.[403]

Again in *Il Giornale d'Italia*, during September and October and at the probable instigation of some officials at the Foreign Ministry, Antonio Cippico[404] published a series of articles designed to reawaken the interest of Italian public opinion in the Adriatic question and Dalmatia. In Cippico's opinion, Italy had to follow the example of the republic of Venice and conquer Dalmatia in order to ensure its hegemony and security in the Adriatic Sea: 'Whoever possesses Venice has to possess Vallona [Vlorë] and Dalmatia and Istria and Trieste.'[405] In addition, the control of Dalmatia would put a stop to the work of denationalization in the Italian lands.[406]

Gabriele d'Annunzio also began to make public proclamations in the summer and fall of 1914, calling on Italy to intervene in the war on France's side with the aim of conquering Istria and Dalmatia.[407]

The demand for the annexation of part of Dalmatia was widely supported not just among the nationalists led by Federzoni and the na-

---

403 Foscari, 'Salviamo la Dalmazia!' *Il Giornale d'Italia*, 24 September 1914.
404 Pastorelli, *Dalla prima alla seconda guerra*, p. 23.
405 Cippico, 'La polemica nazionale. Gli interessi economici,' *Il Giornale d'Italia*, 25 September 1914. See too Cippico, 'L'Adriatico dell'Italia. Gl'interessi strategici,' *Il Giornale d'Italia*, 27 September 1914; 'L'Adriatico dell'Italia. La libertà del mare e la Nazione,' *Il Giornale d'Italia*, 1 October 1914; 'L'Adriatico dell'Italia. La chiave del Mare,' *Il Giornale d'Italia*, 3 October 1914.
406 Antonio Cippico, 'L'Adriatico dell'Italia. II. Gl'interessi politici,' in *Il Giornale d'Italia*, September 21, 1914.
407 'Un appello di Gabriele d'Annunzio,' *Il Corriere della Sera*, 1 October 1914; Solmi, *Gabriele d'Annunzio*, pp. 75 et seq.

tional liberals who took their inspiration from Giovanni Borelli[408] but also in more traditional Italian liberal circles. In 1914–15 *Il Corriere della Sera* showed determination in claiming Italy's right, in the event of intervention in the war against the Habsburg Empire, to guarantee itself military hegemony in the Adriatic Sea once and for all. In October 1914, responding to attacks in the *Times* on possible Italian claims to Dalmatia, *Il Corriere della Sera* defended Italy's right to make conquests in that region: 'Italy has many rights in Dalmatia founded on ethnography, language, and history, but she also has very powerful claims to assert on the day when the new strategic and commercial balance in the Adriatic is established. Since, on that day, Europe will not be able to insist on reconstituting, on the Peninsula's flank, the threat of a state that possesses the whole of the Dalmatian coast with the substantial protection of the island barrier, and will have to recognize Italy's right to shatter that threat, ensuring for herself a permanent sense of security.'[409]

The campaign on behalf of Dalmatia was partly inspired by circles close to the government that were interested in demonstrating to the European powers, and Vienna and Berlin in particular, the existence of strong expansionistic forces in Italy; it suffices to think of the role played by Sonnino's *Il Giornale d'Italia* in the Dalmatian campaign. There was, however, also a genuine political sensitivity to the Dalmatian question in important sectors of liberal Italy. Associations and organizations like the Lega Navale, the Dante Alighieri, and the Freemasons, representing influential sectors of the ruling Italian political and military class, were favourable to a program of national demands that comprised much of Dalmatia, a favour that stemmed, as has been pointed out many times, from a now long-standing interest in the Italian minority in Dalmatia and the Adriatic question.

Not all the ruling and intellectual class was persuaded of the Italian interest in controlling part of Dalmatia. Among the dissenting voices as early as 1914 was that of Gaetano Salvemini from Puglia, who was at the time an intellectual and a politician occupying a position somewhere between liberalism and reformist socialism. Salvemini too was convinced that Italy had to secure strategic supremacy in the Adriatic and annex the majority of the Italian lands of Austria; however, in his opinion, all that was needed to achieve military security was Italian

---

408  On this: Caroncini, *Problemi di politica nazionale*, pp. 255 et seq.
409  'Il problema dell'Adriatico e l'Italia,' *Il Corriere della Sera*, 6 October 1914.

rule over Trieste and Istria, the creation of a Greater Serbia, and the political weakening of the Habsburg Empire. An Italian annexation of part of Dalmatia would have inflicted serious damage on Italy by creating a Slav colony of the Italian state in which Croat and Serb irredentism held sway; Italian Dalmatia would be, according to Salvemini, 'an eternal cause of friction and resentment between Italy and Serbia. And we must oppose this with all our strength.'[410]

In the view of the writer from Puglia, the formation of a Greater Serbia, comprising Dalmatia and Bosnia, was to Italy's advantage as it would weaken the Habsburg positions in the Adriatic; therefore, an Italo-Serbian accord was needed that would guarantee Italy control of the Trentino and the whole of Venezia Giulia while conceding Dalmatia to the Serbs.[411] The creation of a Greater Serbia would speed up the Slavicization of Dalmatia, but for Salvemini this was inevitable: 'It's high time for it to be said loud and clear that the cause of the Italian culture in Dalmatia has been irretrievably lost for some time now and that it is absurd to subordinate our foreign policy to the vain hope of stopping the inevitable.'[412]

A position fairly close to Salvemini's, if more prudent and non-committal, was taken in those months by Benito Mussolini. Leaving the Socialist Party in the fall of 1914 because of his disagreement with the neutralist stand adopted by the majority of socialists, Mussolini became one of the leaders of the interventionist Left.[413] On the question of Dalmatia, he used his newspaper, *Il Popolo d'Italia*, to put forward ideas very similar to those of Salvemini. For Mussolini, Italy had to support the development of the Slav nation and free it from the rule of the Habsburg Empire by going to war against the Austrians and Germans; Italy's principal war aim should be the Trentino and Venezia Giulia.[414] On 6 April 1915 Mussolini addressed the theme of Dalmatia specifically, asserting the importance of an accord with Serbia and contesting the maximalist demands of the nationalists. According to the politician

410 Salvemini, 'Postilla,' *L'Unità*, 26 March 1915.
411 Salvemini, 'Austria, Italia e Serbia,' *L'Unità*, 18 December 1914, reprinted in Salvemini, *Come siamo andati in Libia*, pp. 414–20; Salvemini, 'La Dalmazia,' in *Come siamo andati in Libia*, pp. 370–3.
412 Salvemini, 'Fra la grande Serbia ed una più grande Austria,' *L'Unità*, 7 August 1914, reprinted in Salvemini, *Come siamo andati in Libia*, pp. 344–50.
413 On this: De Felice, *Mussolini il rivoluzionario*, pp. 221 et seq.
414 Mussolini, 'Il monito di Oriani,' *Il Popolo d'Italia*, 14 March 1915, included in *Opera omnia di Benito Mussolini*, vol. 7, pp. 253–5.

from Romagna, Serbia had the right to an extensive access to the sea, and this did not constitute a threat for Italy; he then expressed doubts on the wisdom of annexing Dalmatia:

> It is necessary to proceed with discretion and restraint, keeping our dis-
> tance from dangerous imperialist infatuations. The 'hunger for square kil-
> ometres' has already given us unpleasant surprises ... Like all principles,
> that of nationality should not be understood and practised in an 'absolute'
> sense but in a relative one. For this reason we cannot expect to annex the
> 'whole' of Dalmatia just because the people on the coast speak Italian,
> especially if such an annexation were to create a state of enmity between
> Italy and Serbia and thus the Slav world. So should we sacrifice the sur-
> viving Italian spirit of Dalmatia and abandon to rampant Slavicization
> forever cities dear to the heart of every Italian like Zara, Sebenico, Spalato,
> and Ragusa? No! On the contrary! *We believe that Italian culture must be
> saved and safeguarded.* But to do this is it necessary to 'conquer' Dalmatia
> militarily and politically? We think not, until the contrary is proved.[415]

In Mussolini's opinion, the question of Dalmatia was to be resolved through an Italo-Serb understanding, avoiding the extreme measures of the nationalists:

> We think that the linguistic and cultural Italianness of Dalmatia can and
> should be guaranteed and preserved by a peaceful and open understand-
> ing between Italy and the Serbia. If this understanding should lead for
> reasons of a strategic nature to a more or less extensive possession of the
> Dalmatian coast and archipelago by Italy, there is no objection, especially
> with regard to the archipelago; but if, by this possession, we were to create
> a Serbo-Croatian irredentism and arouse the hostility of the Slavs, the Dal-
> matian hinterland and – most important! – the Istrian hinterland, it would
> be better to forego it and to limit ourselves to demanding from Serbia the
> defence of the Italian culture in Dalmatia from the assaults of an official
> and forced Slavicization.[416]

It is interesting to note that the question of Dalmatia acquired political significance in part because it was a central factor in Italy's future

---

415 Mussolini, 'Italia, Serbia e Dalmazia,' *Il Popolo d'Italia*, 6 April 1915, included in
   *Opera omnia di Benito Mussolini*, vol. 7, pp. 308–10.
416 Ibid.

relations with the Serbian state. In 1914 and 1915 the interventionist left-wing parties (Liberals, Social Democrats, and Socialist Revolution-aries) hoped for the creation of a Greater Serbia as a counterweight to the Habsburg Empire. Precisely because they saw the relationship with Serbia as an element of great importance for Italian foreign policy, Salvemini and Mussolini declared themselves willing to renounce con-trol of Dalmatia, a land inhabited not just by Italians and Croats but also by a large Serb minority.

It should also be stressed that both the 'Dalmatomanic' and 'Dal-matophobic' interventionists had one objective in common, that of es-tablishing Italian political and military hegemony in the Adriatic. The disagreements were over the way to bring about this hegemonic design in which the Dalmatian problem was just one aspect. All were aware that to guarantee Italy's security and supremacy it would be necessary to make a compromise between strategic requirements and the princi-ple of nationality. For the interventionists on the Left, the renunciation of Dalmatia was motivated not so much by a desire to apply the nation-al principle in a rigid way as by the interest in reaching an agreement with the Serbs that, in exchange for dropping all Italian claims to the Dalmatian coast, would facilitate the conquest of the whole of Venezia Giulia as far as Monte Nevoso (Mount Sněžník) and Monte Maggiore (Mount Učka), with the inclusion of the Slovene and Croat Istrians in the kingdom of Italy.

In 1914, for the Italian liberal ruling class and much of public opinion in the country, Dalmatia was also a *terra irredenta*, an 'unredeemed land' inhabited by Italians who wanted political unification with Italy. Was a political presence of Italy in Dalmatia opportune, however, or could the Dalmatian coast become a new 'Ticino,' an Italian part of another state willing to accept the survival of an Italian population and the inevitable influence of Italy in that region?

In the case of the desire to exercise political control over Dalmatia, the question arose of defining the limits of Italy's presence in the future: was it better to rule the whole of Dalmatia or just one part of it? Could Italian control be limited to a number of cities on the coast or simply to the Dalmatian islands? In the determination of Italian territorial claims, should more weight be given to the principle of strategic security or to that of nationality?

Just as in Italian public opinion, there were different views over the future of Dalmatia within the government in Rome. Study of the Italian diplomatic records shows that initially a minimalist approach prevailed. For several months the idea that it was sufficient to ensure control of the islands in the gulf of Quarnero  and some of those in Dalmatia, in particular Pelagosa (Palagruza), Lissa, Lesina, and others nearby, seemed to predominate.[417] To avoid the emergence of a strong Croat and Serb irredentism it was advisable, according to San Giuliano and Tittoni (at that time ambassador in Paris), to renounce the annexation of portions of the Dalmatian coast; the Italian minority living in the coastal cities would be protected through international accords safeguarding its linguistic, cultural, and political rights.[418]

Even military circles considered a territorial plan based on control of the Dalmatian islands alone to be acceptable. Leone Viale, vice-admiral and navy minister, sent a memorandum to Sonnino on 15 November 1914 that outlined Italy's possible 'minimal aspirations' in the eastern Adriatic.[419] While declaring that command of the Adriatic was held by whomever controlled the eastern shore and that from a military viewpoint 'the occupation of that shore would therefore be advantageous and all the more so, the more extensive it were,' Viale claimed it would also be possible to guarantee Italy a position of strength through the implementation of a moderate territorial plan aspiring to '(1) Istria as far as beyond Abbazia or the current Austro-Hungarian border; (2) the outer islands that stretch from Istria as far as off Sebenico; and (3) some islands in the Curzola group, especially Lesina, Lissa, Curzola, Lagosta [Lastovo], and Meleda [Mljet].'[420]

Over those months the idea that Italian territorial demands should be determined largely by motivations of a strategic and military nature, especially in the event of war against Austria-Hungary,  prevailed in the government in Rome. The secretary-general of the Foreign Ministry, Giacomo De Martino, stated it clearly:

> The program of natural borders is a minimal program, but it is not a sufficient program in the event of our participation in the war ... Waging war, we must set ourselves the objective of not only the conquest of Italian lands

---

417 On the thinking in the Italian government with regard to the claims on Dalmatia: Pastorelli, *Dalla prima alla seconda guerra*, pp. 27 et seq.

418 Salandra to Sonnino, 8 November 1914, with enclosures 1 and 3, DDI, V, 2, doc. 164; Tittoni to San Giuliano, September 28, 1914, DDI, V, 1, doc. 834.

419 Sonnino, *Carteggio 1914–1916*, Leone Viale, *Coste istriane e dalmate ed isole prospicienti nei riguardi bellici*, enclosure with doc. 44, Viale to Sonnino, 15 November 1914.

420 Ibid.

but also *supremacy in the Adriatic*: otherwise it is not worth making war ...
As for islands of the Quarnero Gulf and Dalmatia, the question should be
considered from a primarily political and strategic perspective. Since they
are islands, the danger of Slav irredentism is less great, while the strategic
factor is absolutely predominant. Given the fact of our own flat Adriatic
coast without naval bases, we cannot leave to others those safe havens that
are the channels of the Dalmatian islands, from which even a mediocre
force of torpedo boats can constantly threaten our coast.[421]

For several weeks Sonnino, Salandra, and Victor Emmanuel III en-
dorsed the plan of limiting claims on Dalmatia to the islands, but this
later came to be regarded as a minimal program, acceptable only if it
were to be realized within the ambit of a territorial accord with Austria-
Hungary that would allow Italy to remain neutral and not enter the
war. In fact, a draft Italo-Austrian agreement prepared by Sonnino in
February 1915 contained the request for the 'surrender to Italy of the
Curzola group of islands,' a definition by which was meant a series
of islands off the coast of central Dalmatia: Lissa and its neighbouring islands, Lesina, Torcola (Šcedro), and Curzola; and Lagosta and its
nearby islets, Cazza, Meleda, and Pelagosa.[422] This request was repeated in the program of territorial demands that the government in Rome
presented to Austria-Hungary and Germany on 8 April 1915.[423]

The idea of pursuing a territorial program in Dalmatia limited to the
islands, even in the event of Italian intervention on the side of the Triple Entente in the war, was abandoned by the government in Rome
between the end of 1914 and February 1915. Sonnino wrote in his diary on 27 December 1914 that in the future *telegrammone* (the telegram
of instructions to be sent to Imperiali, the ambassador in London, for
opening negotiations on Italy joining the Entente) it was necessary to
'reserve Dalmatia as far as the Narenta and the islands offshore from
Meleda to Melata, as well as Lussino [Lošinj] and Cherso [Cres]. For
(mainland) Dalmatia we could stick to the old Austrian administrative
division.'[424]

---

421 De Martino to Salandra, 31 October 1914, enclosure IV with doc. 164, DDI, V, 2.
422 Sonnino to Avarna, [? February 1915], doc. 781, DDI, V, 2.
423 Sonnino to Avarna and Bollati, 8 April 1915, doc. 293, DDI, V, 3. On the demands
    presented by Italy see Salandra, *L'Intervento [1915]*, pp. 116 et seq.; Monticone, *La
    Germania*, pp. 331 et seq.
424 Sonnino, *Diario 1914–1916*, p. 54.

From Salandra's memoirs it is known that during December and January the prime minister and Sonnino discussed at length the territorial claims in the eastern Adriatic and Dalmatia, which would then be defined in articles 4 and 5 of the Treaty of London. According to Salandra, the broadening of Italian territorial plans was due to clear strategic and military requirements:

> The reaffirmation and liberation of Italian Trieste, a non-negotiable objective for us, was not enough ... It was necessary to guarantee us exclusive military supremacy in the future in a sea that is too narrow to hold two powers without inevitably turning them into rivals and potential enemies, with an obvious natural advantage for the one that occupies the eastern coast and its offshore islands. For the maritime defence of Italy, with too long a coastline in relation to its continental area, it would be necessary to make efforts out of proportion to our means if they always had to be carried out on three seas. Whence the aspiration to absolute security in the eastern sea. It was needed, for their tranquility, by Rome and Venice, much greater naval powers, for their time, than we were or could be. Absolute security can only be attained with material command.[425]

It was decided to make territorial claims to a significant part of the Dalmatian coast and the hinterland as well. The outline of political and territorial requests that the government presented to the Entente powers at the beginning of March 1915 as a basis for negotiations for Italy's intervention in the war included the annexation of the whole of central and northern Dalmatia as far as the Narenta River, the peninsula of Sabbioncello (Pelješac), and 'all the islands lying to the north and west of Dalmatia herself.'[426]

In the new Italian territorial program there was a clear reference to Venice's former colonies; it asked for the annexation of territories with borders that almost coincided with those of Venetian Dalmatia at the time of the Treaty of Passarowitz in 1718. Also taking into account the claim to Istria and Valona, it appeared evident that Italy wanted to turn the Adriatic Sea back into a 'Gulf of Venice.'

---

425  Salandra, L'Intervento, p. 191.
426  Sonnino to Imperiali, 16 February 1915, doc. 816, DDI, V, 2. For an interpretation of the Italian territorial plan: Salandra, L'Intervento, pp. 149 et seq.; Albertini, Venti anni, vol. 2, 1; Toscano, Il patto di Londra, pp. 82 et seq.

What had prompted the Italian government to expand its territorial plans in Dalmatia between October 1914 and February 1915? The motivations of a strategic and military nature referred to by Salandra were important, and they were made more urgent by the course of the war. The protraction of the military conflict in Europe and the increasingly devastating and difficult character that it was assuming for the belligerents made a deep impression on the Italian ruling class. Italian diplomats, journalists, and military representatives informed the government and the public about the ferocity of the fighting, the great losses of human lives, and the material costs of the war. If future Italian intervention in a war whose outcome was still very uncertain was considered indispensable, it had to be done on the basis of a territorial program that fully satisfied both national demands and the strategic and power requirements of the Italian state. From this stemmed the idea that the war should not just unify the greatest possible number of Italians in Austria with Italy but also lay the foundations for the definitive security of the Italian state – which signified control of the Alpine divide and supremacy in the Adriatic, with the control of part of Dalmatia and part of Albania.

The territorial demands with regard to Dalmatia were also the result of a reflection on Italian history. The sad memories of the war of 1866 and its disastrous diplomatic preparations occupied the minds of Italian politicians and induced them to put forward maximalist territorial demands to their future allies. The failure of the La Marmora government to secure the conquest of the Italian Tyrol and Istria in the negotiations with Prussia that had led to the treaty of alliance in April 1866 had been one of the reasons for Italy's inability to fully realize its territorial aspirations; the Italian government, defeated by the Austrians at Custoza and Lissa, had been forced to accept the Prussian impositions, conclude an armistice with Vienna, and renounce the complete fulfilment of its designs of expansion, contenting itself with just the Venetian part of the Lombardo-Venetian kingdom.

On the basis of this historical precedent, of which all Italian politicians and Sonnino,[427] Salandra, and the king in particular were well

---

427  There are numerous references to 1866 in Sidney Sonnino's diaries: for example: Sonnino, *Diario 1866–1912*, pp. 10 et seq.; Sonnino, *Diario 1914–16*, pp. 95–6. On the influence of the events of the 1866 war on Sonnino's political and cultural development: Haywood, *Failure of a Dream*, pp. 29 et seq.

aware, the request for and agreement to a much wider range of territorial conquests than was considered indispensable was not just a normal diplomatic tactic at the beginning of a negotiation but also a political necessity to protect the state in the event of an unfavourable outcome of the war and a break-down in friendly relations with the Allies. Obtaining much in the treaty of alliance, unlike in 1866, would fortify the government at the time of the conclusion of the preliminaries and the peace treaty, guaranteeing Italy a stronger negotiating position. Salandra explained this to the minister for the colonies, Ferdinando Martini, in April 1915: 'It is a good idea to ask for a great deal in order to have something to give up at a future congress.'[428]

However, it was also true that once certain territorial aspirations had been advanced, it became politically very difficult to make concessions and renunciations. The Italo-Yugoslav border negotiations after the war, heavily conditioned by the London agreement of 1915, were to make this abundantly clear.

That the Italian requests in Dalmatia were in part a negotiating tactic and exceeded Italy's minimal expectations was demonstrated by the course taken by the talks with the Triple Entente.[429] Russia, which was anxious to guarantee Serbia extensive access to the sea in Dalmatia, strongly opposed the Italian requests to control the Dalmatian coast as far as the Narenta River., As a result, the government in Rome agreed to cut back on its territorial program, renouncing the region of Spalato and Sabbioncello. Signed on 26 April 1915, the Treaty of London guaranteed Italy, in exchange for its intervention in the war against the Austrians, Germans, and Turks, not just the Italian Tyrol, Venezia Giulia, and Valona but also Dalmatia from the north of the Zara region as far as Capo Planka, as well as all the numerous islands of northern Dalmatia (apart from Veglia and Arbe), along with Lissa, Lesina, Curzola, La-

---

428  Martini, *Diario 1914–1918*, p. 397.
429  Documentary material on the negotiations for the Treaty of London is published in IB, II, 7, tomes 1 and 2; LN, 3, pp. 77 et seq.; *L'Intervento dell'Italia*, pp. 84 et seq.; DDI, V, 3. On the plane of historiographical research: Renzi, *In the Shadow of the Sword*, pp. 197 et seq.; Petrovich, 'The Italo-Yugoslav Boundary Question 1914–1915,' pp. 178 et seq.; Solmi, 'Le origini del patto di Londra,' pp. 129–84; Gottlieb, *Studies in Secret Diplomacy*, pp. 135–401; Toscano, *Il patto di Londra*, pp. 82 et seq.; Lowe, 'Italy and the Balkans, 1914–1915,' pp. 411 et seq.; Lowe, 'Britain and Italian Intervention 1914–1915,' pp. 533–48; Pingaud, *Histoire diplomatique de la France pendant la grande guerre*, pp. 257 et seq.

gosta, Meleda, Cazza (Sušac), Sant'Andrea (Sv. Andrija), Busi (Biševo), Torcola, and Pelagosa.[430]

The Treaty of London was a great success for Italian diplomacy. Unlike in 1866, the government in Rome was preparing to go to war with the support of a treaty that guaranteed the future possession of a group of territories that in the Adriatic amply exceeded the minimum expectations of the Italian ruling class. This was, for example, the case with Dalmatia where the recognition of Italian sovereignty over not just the majority of the Dalmatian islands but also the mainland from Zara to Capo Planka put Italy in a formidable negotiating position at any future peace conference, whatever the outcome of the fighting for the Italian army.

The signing of the Treaty of London induced the Italian government to cut off negotiations with Austria and Germany, which had continued up until then in order to prevent Vienna and Berlin from grasping Italy's real intentions despite the decision having been taken to intervene in the war on the side of the powers of the Triple Entente in February.[431] A clear signal of the Italian desire to go to war with Austria-Hungary came with the denunciation of the Triple Alliance on 4 May.

The Salandra government's decision to enter the field against the Austro-Germans resulted in a rift in the ranks of Italian liberalism, leading Giolitti to oppose the choices made by Sonnino and the prime minister. Giolitti had given his political support to the government's actions since the summer of 1914 and had agreed with its choice to conduct parallel negotiations with Austria and Germany and with the Entente. However, unlike Sonnino and Salandra, he thought haste should be avoided in taking decisions and that preference should be given to the strategy of the accord with Vienna and Berlin in order to obtain the compensation envisaged in article VII in exchange for Italy's benevolent neutrality.[432] Giolitti made his position known in February 1915 in no uncertain terms by publishing in *La Tribuna* a letter he had written to Camillo Peano, a member of parliament and the chief of his ministerial

430  Text of the Treaty of London in DDI, V, 3, doc. 470.
431  On this: Sonnino, *Carteggio 1914–1916*, docs. 133, 151, 155.
432  On Giolitti's attitude over the course of 1914–15: Giolitti, *Memoirs*; Malagodi, *Conversazioni della guerra 1914–1919*, vol. 1; Monticone, *La Germania e la neutralità italiana*; Salandra, *La neutralità italiana*; Salandra, *L'intervento*; Albertini, *Venti anni di vita politica*, vol. 2, 1; De Biase, *L'Italia dalla neutralità all'intervento nella prima guerra mondiale*.

staff when he was in government. In this letter Giolitti denied having close relations with Bülow (while describing him as a man of intelligence and character, as well as a 'friend of Italy') and being a supporter of neutrality under any circumstance:

> My adherence to the party of absolute neutrality. Another legend.
>
>   Certainly I do not consider war a good thing, as the nationalists do, but a misfortune, which must be embarked on only when it is necessary to the honour and the overriding interests of the country.
>
>   I do not believe it admissible to take the country into war out of a sentimental attachment to other peoples. One can throw away one's own life out of sentiment, but not the country's. But when it is necessary I would not hesitate to go to war, and I have proved this.
>
>   It may be and does not appear unlikely that, under the present conditions in Europe, a great deal could be obtained without a war, but on this those who are not in government do not have the facts on which to base a complete judgment.[433]

Giolitti's stand, which was the same as the one taken by the Salandra government until February 1915, was certainly not surprising; it was consistent with the policy of his governments, which were always committed to maintaining good relations with Austria-Hungary within the framework of the Triple Alliance in order to be able to apply article VII and thereby attain better borders in the Alps and the Adriatic and a peaceful solution to the Italian national question in Austria without a new war. The policy of compensated neutrality, of obtaining 'a great deal,' was nothing but Mancini, Robilant, and Launay's old plan to link Habsburg expansion in the Balkans with Italian territorial claims, a plan that had produced article VII of the Triple Alliance.

Even Giolitti thought it was necessary to exploit the conflict in Europe to correct the unsatisfactory Italo-Austrian borders produced by the war of 1866. This is the gist of what he told the British ambassador, Rodd, in March 1915: looking at Italy's future prospects, it was essential not to repeat the compromise that had been made in 1866. All Italy's subsequent problems with Austria, in Giolitti's view, had been due to

---

433 Giolitti to Peano, 24 January 1915, letter published in *La Tribuna*, 2 February 1915, passage reproduced in Salandra, *L'Intervento*, p. 39, and, with a few formal changes, in Giolitti, *Memoirs*, and in De Biase, *L'Italia dalla neutralità all'intervento nella prima guerra mondiale*, 1, pp. 259 et seq.

the fact that a certain number of Italians had been left under Austrian rule and had not been treated justly. Ridding itself of them would have strengthened Austria.[434]

Giolitti's disagreement with the government of Salandra came into the open at the moment of the composing of the Treaty of London and the Italian denunciation of the Triple Alliance, which were hasty decisions in the eyes of the Piedmontese politician who was convinced that it was still possible to obtain much from Austria-Hungary by diplomatic means through the mediation of his old friend Bülow. Urged on by his political supporters and informed of the government's intentions, Giolitti decided to leave his retreat in Piedmont and arrived in Rome on 9 May. That day and the next, in repeated talks with the minister Paolo Carcano, Pietro Bertolini, the king, and Salandra, he declared that in his view the army and the country were too weak to wage a war against Austria and Germany for which there was not even broad popular support; instead, Giolitti advised resuming negotiations with Austria and exploiting the threat of the imminent application of the Treaty of London to secure the best conditions possible.[435]

Aware of the signing of an accord between Italy and the Entente and the emergence of divisions in the Italian ruling class over the wisdom of taking the country to war, the Austrians and Germans, with the support of the Holy See (which favoured the survival of the Habsburg Empire and was eager to achieve a political success that would increase its prestige), made offers of major territorial concessions in exchange for Italian neutrality. Having refused to make such offers for many months, they presented them with the aim of averting Italian intervention and gaining time, with the not-very-secret intention of deferring the actual handing over of the territories in question for as long as possible and, if necessary, taking them back by force once the war with the Entente had been won. These proposals were made formally in a memorandum of 10 May that Bülow and Karl von Macchio signed and sent to Sonnino and Salandra. The offers were extremely vague and ambiguous in that they promised Italy very generically the Tyrol 'that is of Italian nation-

---

434  Rodd to Grey, March 14, 1915, CP, series H, 1, doc. 511.
435  On this: Salandra, *L'Intervento*, pp. 247 et seq.; Giolitti, *Memoirs*; Albertini, *Venti anni*, vol. 2, 1; Monticone, *La Germania*, pp. 559 et seq.; Sonnino, *Diario 1914–1916*, pp. 132 et seq.; De Biase, *L'Italia dalla neutralità all'intervento nella prima guerra mondiale*, 2, pp. 75 et seq.

ality,' 'the whole of the west bank of the Isonzo that is of Italian nationality, with Gradisca,' full municipal autonomy and a university for
Trieste, the area of Valona, and Austrian disengagement from Albania;
there were also purely theoretical promises to safeguard the national
interests of Italian subjects in Austria and to sympathetically examine
'any other wishes that Italy will put forward on the whole of the territories that are the subject of the negotiations (in particular Gorizia and
the islands).'

Germany guaranteed the conclusion of the Italo-Austrian agreement
on the basis of these territorial offers, and its implementation.[436]

The vague and uncertain nature of many of the promises contained
in the memorandum, which in the following days was revised by the
Austrians to include the promise of the possible surrender of the Dalmatian island of Pelagosa, showed that the Austrian offers were made
with quite different purposes in mind. Their aim was not to reach a
serious and lasting agreement with Italy but to bring the government
down, prevent the application of the Treaty of London, and gain time
in the hope that a shift in the course of the war in favour of Austria and
Germany would frighten Italy and persuade it to remain neutral.

The decisive factor in the failure of these Austro-German attempts
was not so much the demonstrations in the streets by groups advocating
intervention,[437] as it was the question of the immediate handing over
of the promised territories. This had been a non-negotiable condition
for Italy over the course of the long talks with Vienna and Berlin, but
not even in May 1915 was Austria willing to accept this demand, argu-
ing that the surrender of the territories should take place only after the
setting up of commissions composed of Italians and Austrians (which
would have defined the accord in a more specific manner), the conclusion of the work of these bodies, and the approval of the whole matter
by the governments in question. This meant putting off the handing
over of the territories to Italy to some undefined time in the future.[438]

Sonnino and Salandra saw the trap laid for them by Austria and Ger-

---

436  Text of the memorandum in DDI, V, 3, doc. 653. On the subject: Monticone, *La Ger-
     mania*, p. 527.
437  Volpe, *Il popolo italiano tra la pace e la guerra (1914–1915)*, p. 239.
438  In this connection: Salandra, *L'Intervento*, pp. 257–60; Pastorelli, *Dalla prima alla se-
     conda guerra mondiale*, pp. 70–1; Renzi, *In the Shadow of the Sword*, p. 193; Monticone,
     *La Germania*, pp. 569 et seq.

many with the new offers[439] and, refusing to reopen the question of the Treaty of London, tendered the government's resignation on 13 May.

The king proposed to Giolitti and some of his political allies (Carcano, Giuseppe Marcora, and Paolo Boselli) that they should take on the job of heading a new government that would reverse the decision to declare war on Austria-Hungary taken by Salandra and Sonnino and the sovereign himself, but they refused. It is likely that Giolitti, a shrewd politician and a great realist, also realized the unreliability of the Austrian promises and the grave risks entailed in such a radical reversal of direction in Italian foreign policy as a repudiation of the Treaty of London. The dream of using the Triple Alliance to achieve the long-standing national claims on Austria had vanished forever.

On 16 May, Victor Emmanuel III rejected the resignation of the Salandra government; on 20 May, parliament voted by an overwhelming majority to give full powers to the government; and in the following days Italy declared war on Austria-Hungary.

The Triple Alliance was dead. But Italy saw its intervention in the war from the perspective of the Risorgimento, that is, as a war against the Habsburg Empire. It had nothing against Germany; the decision was taken to conclude an agreement with Berlin on 21 May 1915 on the treatment of their respective subjects during the war,[440] and no war was declared on Germany. This declaration was not to come until the summer of 1916, in the wake of heavy pressure from Britain, France, and Russia.[441]

Italy entered the war for the same reasons that had prompted it to devise and sign the alliance with the Habsburg Empire and Germany in the 1880s: a reinforcement of its own international role and the search for a new way of obtaining secure borders and the union of a great many of the Italians in Austria with the motherland. In essence the Treaty of London did not represent a change in the strategy and the fundamental directions of Italian foreign policy, just a new tactical choice. After failing to solve diplomatically the question of the Italians in Austria through exploitation of the hoped-for eastward shift of the Habsburg Empire, the Italian government returned to the modus operandi that had been adopted by Cavour and his successors: using the

---

439  Sonnino, *Diario 1914–16*, pp. 145–8.
440  On the Italo-German treaty of May 1915: DDI, V, 3, docs. 724, 736, 746; Solmi, 'L'intervento italiano e le sue conseguenze politiche (maggio–agosto 1915),' pp. 500–17; Renzi, *In the Shadow of the Sword*, pp. 195–6.
441  In this connection: Riccardi, *Alleati non amici*.

struggle between the great powers for hegemony in Europe to Italy's advantage with the aim of making new territorial gains through an alliance between the Savoy state and Austria's enemies.[442]

Italy's war against Austria-Hungary was in reality a Risorgimento conflict as it was inspired and waged in the name of those values of liberty, independence, and unity of the nation and the Italian state that had been typical of the national liberalism of the nineteenth century. In 1915, as in 1860, the Italian national liberal leaders strove to reconcile the values of nationality with the strategic and military needs of the state when conceiving the borders of unified Italy, taking into account the political necessities imposed on them by the international context. Naturally doing this in 1915 meant acting in a European situation that had changed greatly with respect to the mid-nineteenth century; consequently there was the appearance of Dalmatia in the Italian territorial programs in 1914–15 although it had been absent in the years of the Risorgimento. If, for Terenzio Mamiani, Cavour, and Mazzini, Italy could be content with borders in the Alps, comprising the whole of the Italian Tyrol and Istria, for their political heirs (Nathan, Salandra, Sonnino, and Giolitti), the naval disaster of Lissa, the Habsburg conquest of Bosnia, the end of Ottoman rule in the Balkans, and the worsening of the living conditions of the Dalmatian Italians were all motives that drove them to demand the inclusion of part of Dalmatia among the lands to be conquered – a Dalmatia in which the Italian cultural, linguistic, and national presence was undoubtedly stronger than in Alto Adige and the upper valley of the Isonzo, which were traditionally regarded as lands whose annexation was vital to the future of the Italian state.

### 3.6. The Struggle for Survival: The Aggravation of National Conflicts in Dalmatia and the Affirmation of Political Irredentism Among the Italian Dalmatians (1907–15)

The failure to reach a national compromise with the Croats and Serbs and the electoral reform in the parliament in Vienna further weakened

---

442 Among the different interpretations of the Treaty of London it is worth mentioning: Mosca, 'La politica estera italiana dall'intervento alla vittoria,' in *Le relazioni internazionali nell'età contemporanea*, pp. 19 et seq.; Salvemini, *La politica estera italiana dal 1871 al 1915*, pp. 538 et seq.; Solmi, 'Le origini del patto di Londra,' ; Albrecht-Carrié, 'Italian foreign Policy 1914–1922,' pp. 328 et seq.; Albrecht-Carrié, *Italy at the Paris Peace Conference*, pp. 19 et seq.; Toscano, *Il patto di Londra*; Pastorelli, *Dalla prima alla seconda guerra*.

the political position of the Italian Autonomist Party at the end of the first decade of the twentieth century. The emergence of a strong Serbo-Croat coalition in Dalmatia increased the isolation of the autonomists at the regional level; although they were present in all the main Dalmatian cities, the only council they controlled was that of Zara. The lack of success in the attempt to have an electoral district covering Zara alone, in order to guarantee parliamentary representation of the Italian minority in the Reichsrat, confirmed the final demotion of Dalmatian autonomist liberalism (once the most influential Italophile and Italian political formation in Austria) to the level of a small regional party.

In reaction to this growing political weakness, the autonomist leaders stepped up their collaboration with the other Italian parties in Austria that had been underway for a long time. In the years from the beginning of the twentieth century to the outbreak of World War I, the Italian liberal members of the parliament in Vienna from Trentino and Venezia Giulia often served as spokesmen for the demands and protests of the Italian Dalmatians, seeking to defend their aspirations and interests with the authorities in Vienna.[443]

The solidarity of the liberals from Trieste and Istria with the Italians of Dalmatia found a significant expression in the decision to nominate Ziliotto as a candidate for the Reichsrat in an electoral constituency of Trieste in 1907. However, Ziliotto's candidature in Trieste, during the first Austrian elections on the basis of universal suffrage, came to nothing, foundering in the resounding defeat of the liberals of Trieste by the Socialist Party, which won all the parliamentary seats.[444] Ziliotto stood for parliament in Dalmatia too but, despite reaching the second ballot, was defeated by the leader of the Dalmatian Party of Rights, Don Ivo Prodan.[445] As predicted, the autonomists were unable to win a single seat in the parliament in Vienna.

From 1907 onward, the Italian Autonomist Party developed political ties not just with its now traditional Italian liberal allies but also

---

443  See, for example, Pitacco's speech in the Reichsrat in defence of the Italians of Dalmatia in September 1906: on this, Avarna to the Foreign Ministry, 21 September 1906, ASMAE, SP 1891–1916, portfolio 94. On the defence of Italian Dalmatian political rights by the representatives of Venezia Giulia during the debate on the electoral reform of 1907: Ara, 'La Dalmazia e la riforma elettorale.'

444  On Ziliotto's candidature in Trieste and the results of the 1907 elections: Tamaro, *Storia di Trieste*, vol. 2; Winkler, *Wahlrechtsreformen und Wahlen in Triest 1905–1909*; Maserati, *Il movimento operaio a Trieste*, pp. 219 et seq.

445  De' Benvenuti, *Storia di Zara dal 1797 al 1918*, p. 139; Perić, *Dalmatinski Sabor*.

with the People's parties. The Italian People's parties of Trentino and Venezia Giulia, while rejecting any idea of political irredentism and retaining their traditional loyalty to the Habsburgs, were progressively obliged to engage in battles in defence of Italian national rights, which were under threat from the increasingly aggressive German, Slovenian, and Croatian nationalisms and from a not very friendly government policy toward the Italians of Austria, who were regarded as a potential fifth column of Italy.[446]

Between 1907 and 1914, the People's Party representative Giuseppe Bugatto, a native of Zara but elected in the Gorizia region,[447] was very active in the defence of the national and political rights of the Italians of Dalmatia. In the parliament in Vienna and at public meetings Bugatto repeatedly denounced the measures taken against the Italian minority by the Croats of Dalmatia, whose abolition of every public school that used Italian as a medium of instruction was aimed at the total assimilation and Croatization of the Italian Dalmatians; he also pointed out the difficult living conditions that they faced. In a speech to his Friulian electors in 1907 Bugatto declared: 'It is easy, gentlemen, to be Italian here in our countries, where there is no one who questions your nationality, but there in our most troubled land, on the furthest limb of Italian culture in the Adriatic, there it is heroic to declare yourself Italian, there it is openly military martyrdom for your own language, there the heart bleeds to see the children of our people forced into schools in another language, forgetting Italian and becoming, against their will, Croatian!'[448]

Bugatto worked intensely with the leaders of the Italian Autonomist Party on the long and difficult negotiations over the question of the use of languages in the civil service.

The failure of the policy aimed at reaching a national compromise led, from 1908 onward, to a resumption of the efforts to undermine the rights of Italians by the Croat and Serb parties. For many years the focus of these efforts was the demand for the abolition of the use of Italian as

---

446 On this: Avarna to the Foreign Ministry, 3 July 1912, ASMAE, SP 1891–1916, portfolio 100; Benvenuti, *La Chiesa trentina e la questione nazionale 1848–1918*; Benvenuti, *I principi vescovi di Trento*, pp. 293 et seq.

447 On Bugatto: Santeusanio, 'Lettere inedite di Roberto Ghiglianovich e Gino de Benvenuti,' pp. 79–88; Santeusanio, *Giuseppe Bugatto il deputato delle 'Basse' (1873–1948)*, in particular pp. 185 et seq.

448 Santeusanio, *Giuseppe Bugatto il deputato delle 'Basse' (1873–1948)*, p. 186.

a language in public administration in the province. Once the possibility of a policy of Italo-Croatian friendship had evaporated, the plan for an agreement on the linguistic question that had been devised jointly by Italians and Croats in 1906 was abandoned, and the Croatian members of parliament began again to pressure the government in Vienna to Croatize the civil service in Dalmatia completely. After much dithering, the Austrian government decided to act to meet the demands of the Croatian Dalmatians. The enthusiastic support of Croat public opinion for the imperial decision to annex Bosnia-Herzegovina in October 1908 had breathed new life into the Habsburg establishment's old design of using Croatian nationalism to counter Serbian expansionism. It was politically convenient for the government in Vienna, headed at the time by Richard Bienerth, to fulfil the linguistic demands of the Croats in Dalmatia as a sign of imperial interest in and benevolence toward pan-Croatian nationalism.

During 1908 and 1909 Ghiglianovich, Ziliotto, and Krekich engaged in a long and gruelling political battle over the language question, seeking to limit as much as possible the government's concessions to the Croatian parties. The problem of the language used in the civil service had enormous symbolic value for the Italian Dalmatians: after the abolition of Italian public schools the elimination of Italian from the state administration would have meant doing irreparable harm to the status of the Italian language as an indigenous element of Dalmatian society; in addition, total Croatization would have opened the way to a vast influx of Croats into the civil service, where the Italian and Italophile element, representing much of the province's middle and upper classes, was still strong. In this connection Majoni, the Italian consul in Zara, declared:

> The Slavicization of the bureaucracy would make things very difficult for civil servants who have a poor grasp of Croatian and for all those who work under the same conditions in government departments handling administrative, judicial, or any other matters. Considering too that in Dalmatia, where commerce is scant and industry virtually non-existent, the majority of the sons of the best families choose to become employees of the imperial civil service after finishing their studies or passing the state exams instead of going in for independent occupations, and that for many of them it would be very difficult to gain a perfect knowledge of a language absolutely indispensable to their career, it is easy to imagine that the

planned reform is'destined to meet fierce opposition among Italians while favouring the entry of Croat speakers into the posts.[449]

With the complete Croatization of the civil service and the consequent need for old and new officials to have a perfect grasp of Croatian, many of the Italian Dalmatians themselves would be obliged to attend Croat schools, and this would lead to the final collapse of Italian educational institutions in Dalmatia. 'Perhaps too,' observed Majoni, 'if Italian is dispensed with as a vivid source of intellectualism, it may be forced, if no remedy is found, to withdraw into commerce, doomed to the same humble, however practical, function as the Levantine Italian spoken in the ports of the East, while by tradition, and by sentiment, and by propagation of intellectuality the function of the Italian language and culture in Dalmatia is very different.'[450]

To counter the pressure from the Croatian parties and the intentions of the government in Vienna, the Italian Autonomous Party tried to get the help of Italian members of the Austrian parliament and mobilize the support of the Italian and German press in Austria and on the peninsula. As has been pointed out, the representative of the People's Party Bugatto fought vigorously in defence of the linguistic rights of the Italian Dalmatians,[451] as did many liberals, especially Valeriano Malfatti from Trentino.[452]

To impose a rapid solution on the linguistic controversy in Dalmatia, the Bienerth government summoned the leaders of the various Dalmatian parties to Vienna during March and April 1909 and held a series of discussions with the aim of reaching a mutual understanding that would reconcile the demands of the Croatian majority with those of the Italian minority.[453] The Austrian government intended to resolve the language problem through an ordinance providing for the complete

---

449  Majoni to the Foreign Ministry, 3 March 1909, ASMAE, SP 1891–1916, portfolio 96.
450  Majoni to the Foreign Ministry, 4 April 1909, ASMAE, SP 1891–1916, portfolio 96.
451  Extensive documentation of the relations between the Italian autonomists of Dalmatia and Bugatto in Santeusanio, *Giuseppe Bugatto il deputato delle 'Basse,'* pp. 200 et seq.
452  On this: Avarna to the Foreign Ministry, 26 June, 17 July, and 22 July 1908, ASMAE, SP 1891–1916, portfolio 95.
453  Zanotti Bianco to the Foreign Ministry, 3 March 1909, ASMAE, SP 1891–1916, portfolio 96.

Croatization of the offices of the state in Dalmatia. The only concessions envisaged for the Italian Dalmatians were the possibility of filing applications in Italian and receiving responses in the same language, and the maintenance of bilingualism for decisions and ordinances concerning the entire Dalmatian region, along with the bilingual character of ordinances and other proceedings of the district and local authorities in Zara, Arbe, and Curzola alone.[454]

The decisive phase in the negotiations on the question of language in the Dalmatian public service was reached between 20 and 23 April 1909 over the course of a long conference called by Prime Minister Bienerth in Vienna in which Bienerth himself, Minister of the Interior Guido Haerdtl, Minister of Religion and Education Karl Stürgkh, and Governor Nardelli of Dalmatia took part, along with the Croat representatives Vičko Ivčević and Juraj Biankini, the Serb Dušan Baljak, and the Italians Krekich and Ziliotto.[455] The result of the conference was a ministerial ordinance on the use of languages in the imperial civil authorities and state offices in Dalmatia, dated 26 April 1909.[456] The ordinance was a compromise because, while accepting many of the Croatian demands, it conceded more rights to the Italian minority than had initially been planned. The ordinary language to be used in the civil service became Croatian, but the possibility of filing an application and receiving a response in Italian, if the official in charge knew that language, was recognized. The Italian language could be used in official correspondence, the internal handling of affairs, and any official or technical legal document; in addition, official summonses, signs, and stamps would be bilingual in twenty-four districts on the Dalmatian coast where the Italian communities were concentrated.[457]

At a meeting with Majoni, Ghiglianovich and Ziliotto declared themselves dissatisfied with the accord, which dealt a heavy blow to the idea of a perfect and equal Italo-Croat bilingualism in Dalmatia. The minimum Italian demands were the use of both languages in all district proceedings – now it has been limited to twenty-four districts;

---

454 Majoni to the Foreign Ministry, 4 April 1909

455 Avarna to the Foreign Ministry, 24 April 1909, ASMAE, SP 1891–1916, portfolio 96.

456 The text of the ordinance is published in the *Objavitelj Dalmatinski/Avvisatore Dalmato*, 28 April 1909, copy enclosed with Majoni to the Ministry of Foreign Affairs, 30 April 1909, in ASMAE, SP 1891–1916, portfolio 96.

457 Ibid.; Majoni to the Foreign Ministry, 26 April 1909, ASMAE, SP 1891–1916, portfolio 96.

that the subsequent handling of dealings with parties would have to be in Italian if the application was made in Italian – now it is left to the official to decide, which in fact means that the language used will almost always be Slav as the vast majority of the officers are Croat either by origin, or by sympathy, or in compliance with higher political policy.'[458] It could be predicted that the accord would not last long, as the Croat nationalists would try to modify it to their own advantage as soon as possible.

In the view of the Italian consul in Zara, the ordinance of 26 April was in part a political victory for the Italian Dalmatians: 'The agreement has, in my opinion, sanctioned in favour of the Italians a de facto truth that the Croatians wanted to keep suppressed, that is to say, the recognition by the Government of an Italian nationality that, despite the undeniable hostility from above and the vicious war waged on it, has been solemnly affirmed.'[459]

The prudent and moderate policy followed by the leaders of the Italian Autonomous Party and their search for a dialogue with the Habsburg authorities were the grounds for their acceptance of the language ordinance but caused irritation among the militant extremists of the Italian autonomist movement, who wanted to engage in a noisier and more intransigent campaign in defence of the Italian culture in Dalmatia. This dissatisfaction led to the emergence of a dissident group, led by Girolamo Italo Boxich, Raimondo Desanti, and Gino de Benvenuti, who wanted to abandon the traditional reconciliation between Italo-Slav Dalmatian autonomism and the defence of Italian national rights on order to espouse a pure Italian nationalism.

Among these, Boxich is a particularly interesting figure. An Italo-Slav Dalmatian born in Signi and a lawyer who emerged in the early years of the twentieth century as one of the most dynamic and brilliant of the autonomist politicians, he was endowed with uncommon intellectual gifts, which he displayed in numerous political writings in *Il Dalmata*. Boxich became famous in Zara for taking part in the irredentist demonstrations at Udine in August 1903, and for years he was the leader of the hard-line and nationalist wing of the Italian autonomist movement. However, after World War I he declared his opposition to the annexation of Dalmatia by Italy and, following the Treaty of Rapallo, opted

---

458  Majoni to the Foreign Ministry, 26 April 1909.
459  Ibid.

for Yugoslav citizenship.[460] His was an emblematic story that symbolized the complexity of the Dalmatian politics and society before the Great War, a multi-ethnic society in which Italians headed pan-Croatian nationalist parties and Dalmatians of Slav origin like Boxich declared themselves Italian nationalists.

In 1908 the dissident group of critics of the Dalmatian Italian party founded a weekly newspaper in Zara called *Il Risorgimento*, which was published by Boxich, edited by Desanti, and issued until 1914. The weekly proclaimed itself the 'organ of the Italian Democratic Party,' which was a slap in the face to the leaders of the Italian Autonomist Party, who were accused of being members of the propertied and oligarchic classes as well as strangers to the needs of the Italian-speaking lower-middle classes of the Dalmatian population. However, the predominant tone of the newspaper was that of a visceral Italian nationalism, which in part imitated the style and message of the Party of Rights and in part took its inspiration from the rising anti-liberal nationalism of Enrico Corradini and Luigi Federzoni.[461]

This Italian nationalist group in Zara found its support chiefly among students and the younger activists of the Autonomist Party, with which it maintained a relationship of political dissent but electoral co-operation; given the political weakness of the Italian and Italophile Dalmatians, the liberal and national autonomists agreed to field joint candidates at elections. Nonetheless, between 1908 and 1914 a strong rivalry developed between the traditional Autonomist Party, led by Ziliotto and Ghiglianovich, and the newly formed Italian nationalist group headed by Desanti and Boxich. Desanti was able to establish political ties with nationalist circles in Rome, led by Federzoni and Forges Davanzati, which allocated large subsidies to his group and newspaper.[462] Ghiglianovich and Ziliotto displayed hostility toward Desanti and Boxich, repeatedly accusing them of superficiality and extremism. For Ghiglianovich, Desanti was unreliable and irresponsible; certainly he was an Italian Dalmatian who was fighting for the right cause; 'however, the form that this fight takes does not at all convince me, Ziliotto,

460  Delich, *L'irredentismo italiano in Dalmazia secondo i documenti segreti della polizia austriaca*, p. 43.
461  See, for example, 'Il nazionalismo italiano,' *Il Risorgimento*, 9 May 1914; 'Nazionalismo sociale,' *Il Risorgimento*, 6 June 1914.
462  Ghiglianovich to Sanminiatelli, 26 June 1913, DA, file 1913, B 11 bis; Millo, *Storia di una borghesia*, p. 279.

and our party.' The representative from Zara wrote to Sanminiatelli in January 1914: '*Il Risorgimento*, in fact, promotes a nationalism that is too zealous, often verging on irredentism; its attacks on the Austrian government, on Austria, on its opponents are often violent, too violent. We believe this can, in the extreme difficulty of our situation, sometimes be harmful. However, *Il Risorgimento* is attractive to the younger element, which does not have to bear the weight of responsibility. It is good that this should be so, but it ought to be more disciplined and diplomatic.'[463]

The consuls in Zara were also critical of Desanti, Boxich, and the Dalmatian Italian nationalists. Majoni described Boxich as 'a brilliant, but quirky, literary mind, in love with words, with applause, and governed by an extremely dangerous impulsiveness and emotionalism.'[464]

The failure of national compromise in Dalmatia, the Habsburg annexation of Bosnia-Herzegovina, and the exacerbation of national conflict in Austria and Hungary were all elements that influenced the Dalmatian political situation, causing it to deteriorate. In those years Croatian nationalism was at the heart of Austro-Hungarian policy. On the one hand, the governments in Vienna and Budapest were deeply hostile to the Yugoslav and pro-Serbian tendencies of the Serbo-Croat coalition in Croatia and Trumbić's Hrvatska Stranka in Dalmatia. The result was an action of harsh repression, which led to the famous Zagreb trial of a number of Austrian Serbs who were members and supporters of the Serbo-Croatian coalition and charged with anti-Habsburg activities and propaganda, and to the accusations made by the historian Heinrich Friedjung that the Serbo-Croatian coalition was collaborating with Serbia.[465] On the other hand, certain sectors of the Habsburg establishment as well as Aehrenthal and Francis Ferdinand wanted to support and exploit the anti-Serbian and pro-Austrian currents in pan-

---

463 Ghiglianovich to Sanminiatelli, 12 January 1914, DA, file 1914, B 9 bis.
464 Majoni to the Foreign Ministry, 19 January 1911, ASMAE, SP 1891–1916, portfolio 98.
465 In this connection: Schuster, *Henry Wickham Steed und die Habsburgermonarchie*, pp. 79 et seq.; Hugh and Christopher Seton-Watson, 'R.W. Seton-Watson and the Yugoslavs,' in *R.W. Seton-Watson and the Yugoslavs: Correspondence 1906–1941* (London and Zagreb: British Academy; University of Zagreb, Institute of Croatian History, 1976), vol. 1, pp. 14 et seq.; Hugh and Christopher Seton-Watson, *The Making of a New Europe*, pp. 57 et seq.; Robert W. Seton-Watson, *The Southern Slav Question and the Habsburg Monarchy*; Albertini, *The Origins of the War of 1914*, vol. 1; Cartwright to Grey, 21 December 1909, BD, 9, part 1, doc. 87; Tommasini to the Foreign Ministry, 24 December 1909, ASMAE, SP 1891–1916, portfolio 96.

Croatian nationalism as a counter to Serb and Italian irredentism; they also wanted to weaken Hungarian autonomist ambitions and reorganize the empire on a trialistic basis, that is, by creating a Croatian entity within the Habsburg state that would comprise Croatia, Dalmatia, and Bosnia-Herzegovina. Therefore, close political links were forged between Frank's Party of Rights and the Austrian political groups close to Francis Ferdinand and the leaders of the army.[466]

After sabotaging the policy of Italo-Slav national compromise, Frank's Party of Rights, with the support of important members of the government who were eager to undermine the alliance between Hrvatska Stranka and the Serbian party, continued a fierce campaign against the Italians and the autonomists for several years.[467] The other Croatian parties, Trumbić's Hrvatska Stranka and Smodlaka's Hrvatska Pučka Napredna Stranka, afraid of losing support to the *pravaši*, also went along with this anti-Italian policy, abandoning the moderation of previous years.

From 1906 onward, the focus of the struggle of the Croatian and Serbian parties against the Italian autonomists was the attempt to gain control of the municipal administration of Zara. The exacerbation of national conflicts in Dalmatia first found expression in the resurgence of political incidents in the form of brawls and clashes between Croat militants, Serbs, and Italian autonomists that sometimes led to the killing of political opponents. Commenting on some disturbances that took place in Zara in 1909, the consul Majoni declared that the causes of these fights and clashes were usually insignificant matters that would not have had serious consequences in another country. 'But here politics has invaded even the smallest social event, every little individual act; it has become a mania for all, an industry for many, and has created an irksome environment, filled with tension, at times verging on fever pitch. Thus the playing of a piece of music, the wearing of a badge, a stroll by participants in a conference of any kind spark off huge demonstrations, at times triggering bloody clashes.'[468]

According to Majoni, the state authorities were usually passive in the

466  Albertini, *The Origins of the War of 1914*, vol 1, II; Chlumecky, *Erzherzog Franz Ferdinands Wirkens und Wollen*, pp. 176 et seq.; Valiani, *The End of Austria-Hungary*; Conrad, *Dienstzeit*, vol. 1; Adler, *L'Union forcée*, pp. 54 et seq.
467  On Frank's Party of Rights: Stranieri to the Foreign Ministry, 21 August 1911, ASMAE, SP 1891–1916, portfolio 98.
468  Majoni to the Foreign Ministry, 22 August 1909, Asmae, SP 1891–1916, portfolio 96.

face of these events and showed a bias in favour of the Croatian nationalists, who controlled the provincial government.[469]

The strategy of the hard-line nationalists was to assert the Croatian identity of Zara and Dalmatia by organizing demonstrations or parades of Croatian sporting and religious associations in the autonomist city. In March 1908 Ghiglianovich explained to Sanminiatelli that the Croatian nationalists hoped to bring down the Italian administration of Zara in this way: '[The Croats] do not let a week go by, as it were, without attempting to stage some little demonstration here in the hope that it will incite the citizens, who are deeply attached to their Italian culture, to acts of reaction, to resort to violence, and thereby induce the Government to intervene, and to dismiss the Council, which by law is' responsible for policing the city.'[470]

The Croatian nationalists hoped to repeat the political manoeuvre that had succeeded against Bajamonti in Spalato at the time of Taaffe: using political incidents to de-legitimize the autonomists in the eyes of the government and induce it to dissolve the administration of Zara and then oust them from the municipality. Aware of the precedent of Spalato, the Italian autonomist leaders tried to resist the provocations of the Croats by carrying out a policy of moderation and attempting to win the goodwill of the government. As Ghiglianovich put it: 'Conscious of all these dangers, we implement the most legalistic policy that can be imagined in the Municipality and seek, as far as possible, to avoid conflicts between Croats and Italians.'[471]

Sometimes incidents occurred nonetheless, and discussions with the government authorities became vitally important. 'Fortunately we have as Governor and Vice-Governor quite well-bred people who, for a whole set of circumstances, are not personally on good terms with the leaders of the Croatian party today and, on the contrary, have fairly cordial relations with us. They know what we think, but they know that we save appearances, for which they hold us in regard and act today with sufficient fairness even in political questions.'[472]

The year 1911, the date of the next municipal elections for Zara, became an important deadline in the political struggles of the Autonomist Party. To weaken the position of the autonomists, the Dalmatian

---

469  Ibid.
470  Ghiglianovich to Sanminiatelli, 29 March 1908, DA, file 1908, B 11.
471  Ibid.
472  Ibid.

provincial diet passed several resolutions favourable to the Croatian parties between 1909 and 1910: special allocations were voted for Croatian nursery schools in Zara; the constitution of the state police, controlled by the Croatian provincial government, was approved for the Dalmatian city; and finally, with the aim of strengthening Croatian representation on the Zara city council, the electoral regulation concerning the third block of voters, that of the surrounding countryside, was reformed to make it easier for Croatian peasants living in the rural areas and on the islands of the Zara district to vote.[473]

Nonetheless, in July 1911 the Italian Autonomous Party managed to win the municipal elections of Zara again, and the city council re-elected Luigi Ziliotto as mayor.[474] This success could be attributed to the strongly Italian and autonomist feelings of the population of Zara, to the fact that the Italian Autonomous Party was able to receive financial aid from the government in Rome, and to a more cautious attitude on the part of the Habsburg state authorities toward the Croatian nationalist parties in Dalmatia (Vienna was worried about the spreading pro-Serbian and Yugoslav sympathies among them). The survival of an Italian Autonomous Party in Dalmatia and of an Italian council in Zara had now became a positive element for Habsburg policy. It was no coincidence that in those years the Austrian administration, while pursuing a policy very hostile to the Italian National Liberal Party in Venezia Giulia, assumed a more impartial attitude in the Italo-Croatian national conflict on the Dalmatian coast.[475] Significant in this respect was the choice of Nardelli's successor as governor of Dalmatia in 1911: Mario Attems, a member of the Gorizian aristocracy who was very loyal to the Habsburgs and linguistically and culturally Italo-German. In the years of his administration he pursued a moderate and friendly policy toward the Italian minority in Dalmatia.[476]

---

473  On this: Majoni to the Foreign Ministry, 18 October 1909, portfolio 96; the deputy of the consulate of Zara to the Foreign Ministry, 19 January 1911, portfolio 98, ASMAE, SP 1891–1916.

474  Majoni to the Foreign Ministry, 31 July 1911, ASMAE, SP 1891–1916, portfolio 98; 'La solenne seduta del consiglio per la nomina del podestà e degli assessori,' Il Dalmata, 25 November 1911.

475  On the political situation in Dalmatia in the early years of the twentieth century: Schödl, Kroatische Nationalpolitk und 'Jugoslavenstvo'; D'Alia, La Dalmazia, le terre limitrofe e l'Adriatico; D'Alia, La Dalmazia nella storia e nella politica, nella guerra e nella pace; Dudan, 'La Dalmazia di oggi'; Gayda, L'Italia d'oltre confine; Delich, L'irredentismo italiano in Dalmazia secondo i documenti segreti della polizia austriaca.

476. De' Benvenuti, Storia di Zara dal 1797 al 1918, p. 149.

   The last years before the outbreak of the world war were characterized by a strengthening of the desire for a unified Yugoslav state and
by growing anti-Habsburg and pro-Serbian sentiments in the Croat and
Serb parties of the Dalmatian region and amongst the Slav population
of the coastal cities. The start of the first Balkan War in the fall of 1912
and the unexpected victories of the Slav states over the hated Turks
excited incredible enthusiasm among the inhabitants of the cities of
coastal Dalmatia. Numerous public demonstrations of support for the
Balkan nations (and in particular the fellow southern Slav states, Serbia
and Montenegro) were staged in Sebenico, Spalato, and Ragusa, demonstrations that, considering the hostile attitude of the government in
Vienna toward the Balkan League, also took on anti-Habsburg tones.
The Italian consul in Zara, Antonino D'Alia, wrote to Rome about this
in November 1912:

> On the outbreak of hostilities between the Balkan states and Turkey, the
> first moment of astonishment was followed by great enthusiasm on the
> part of the Slav populations of Dalmatia. Turcophiles turned into Turco-
> phobes, and there was a rapid shift from obedience and deference to the
> organs of the state to covert aversion and rebellion such as the Govern-
> ment in Vienna never dreamed of in this province ... Every steamship
> that passed through bringing Serbs or Montenegrins back from overseas
> sparked off great demonstrations of support for the *brothers*, and Slav
> songs from all parts of the empire and the Balkan states were interspersed
> with cries of *up with* directed at the states themselves and the occasional
> *down with* aimed at Austria. Even the motifs of the Marseillaise could be
> heard at each of these demonstrations. The battle of Kumanovo raised
> even more the sympathies of all the Southern Slav peoples of the Mon-
> archy for Serbia: *the little Piedmont* as they call it. The idea of trialism has
> been abandoned; everyone now looks to Serbia as the centre of common
> aspirations. Even the Croats, who wanted to draw the South toward the
> North, feel that they have lost their cause irrevocably and, even though
> Catholics, are beginning to accept the new program. The masses do not
> want to hear of war against their Slav brothers of the South, and even go
> so far as to suggest to soldiers that they desert or refuse to obey outright.[477]

---

477  D'Alia to the Foreign Ministry, 27 November 1912, ASMAE, SP 1891–1916, portfolio
     100. See too D'Alia to the Foreign Ministry, 9 December 1912, ASMAE, SP 1891–
     1916, portfolio 100.

In those days Josip Smodlaka wrote to his friend Robert Seton-Watson to tell him that the enthusiasm for Serbia and the Yugoslav cause in Dalmatia was very great: 'Even the *pravaši* of Dalmatia are enthusiasts for the cause of Balkan freedom. The only sad exception are the ones in Zagreb. But they count for little. Croatian youth in its entirety (even the *pravaši*) are fervent *jugoslavi*. This war is a world-shaking event for the whole of Europe. For us it is national resurrection. Austria will be forced to change her policy. Serbia has displayed not just great military valour but also a surprising political maturity. Now we are sure that we will not be trampled on by the Magyars. The future of 17 million Yugoslavs is guaranteed.'[478]

These outbursts of sympathy for Serbia and of Yugoslav sentiment in the Dalmatian cities, which often turned into demonstrations against Austria, frightened the government in Vienna; in those months it was in the grip of total confusion and fear, in part because these events co-incided with simultaneous pro-Serbian and pro-Slav demonstrations in the regions inhabited by Czechs, Slovenes, and Slovaks in all the Slav lands of the empire.[479] In response Vienna decided to dissolve the municipal councils of Spalato and Sebenico, which were controlled by the parties of Trumbić and Smodlaka, provoking angry reactions on the part of the Dalmatian Slav parties and further strengthening the Serbo-Croat alliance in Dalmatia.[480]

Thus the Balkan Wars resulted in a radicalization and further diffu-sion of Yugoslav, pro-Serbian, and as a result pan-Slav nationalistic feel-ings in Dalmatia. All of this had negative consequences for the Italian minority and the Autonomist Party, which were increasingly viewed as an unacceptable foreign presence in the heart of a land regarded as purely Slav. Even Italy's foreign policy helped to foster Italophobia among the Slav parties of Dalmatia. While the Italy of the early twen-tieth century had been perceived by southern Slav public opinion as a liberal, anti-Austrian power that represented the values of nationality and as a friend of the Balkan peoples, the foreign policy of the Giolitti–San Giuliano government, founded on close collaboration with Aus-

---

478 Smodlaka to Seton-Watson, 6 November 1912, in *Seton Watson and the Yugoslavs*, vol. 1, doc. 57.

479. Rogel, *The Slovenes and Yugoslavism 1890–1914*, pp. 90 et seq.

480 Peric, *Dalmatinski Sabor*, pp. 160–1; Živanović, 'Dve demonstracije u Splitu i Šibeniku 1912 godine,' pp. 327–52; Smodlaka to Seton-Watson, 8 December 1912, in *Seton Watson and the Yugoslavs*, vol. 1, doc. 62.

tria-Hungary, had stirred profound anti-Italian feelings in Serbia and the southern Slav world. Italy's opposition to granting Serbia access to the sea, its support for the birth of an Albanian state (which was seen by the Serb and Croat public as a puppet of Italian and Austrian imperialism), and its defence of Albanian national rights against Montenegrin and Serbian claims were all elements that had spread the perception in the Yugoslav world and, more in general, among the Habsburg Slavs that Italy was a hostile power.[481]

The result was an intensification of the struggle of the Serbo-Croat parties against the Italian autonomists in Dalmatia. The situation became particularly difficult for Italians and Italophiles in the cities governed by Croatian parties, such as Spalato. Despite decades of Croat rule, the Italian presence had remained strong in Bajamonti's city. The Autonomist Party had deep roots in the city thanks to its ability to gather support among anti-Croatian bilingual Slavs with autonomist leanings as well as among the Italian minority; this was reflected in the numerous autonomist and Italian associations in Spalato (the Società Operaia, the Società del Bersaglio, the Società di Ginnastica e Scherma, the Filarmonica, and the Teatrale). The autonomist influence was boosted by the continued use of the local Venetian dialect by all strata of the population, and by the fondness for Italian culture that was widespread in the city among the middle and urban classes, whether Italian or Slav; in short, Spalato was still a multi-ethnic and bilingual Italo-Slav city in the years before the world war.

The radicalization of Croatian-Yugoslav nationalism at the time of the Balkan Wars, especially among the younger generations, prompted a growing impatience with the survival of the Italian culture and minority in Spalato on the part of the most extreme nationalists. This intolerance found expression in numerous acts of hooliganism and intimidation directed at stores with Italian signs[482] and the houses of supporters of the Italian autonomists. Children attending the Italian school of the Lega Nazionale were insulted and occasionally attacked. Every public event that had an Italian or autonomist character (from funerals to musical performances) was challenged and disrupted by students and young Croat militant nationalists.[483] During the end of 1913 and

---

481 On this: DDF, III, 10, docs. 145, 260, 316.
482 'Cronaca della Provincia,' Il Risorgimento, 9 May 1914.
483 'Cronache della Provincia,' Il Risorgimento, 27 June 1914.

the beginning of 1914 the campaign launched by some extremists for the boycott of the stores in Spalato owned by citizens of the kingdom or people of Italian nationality,[484] and the incidents triggered by the city council's ban of autonomist music bands taking part in the traditional parade in honour of Saint Doimus, caused a great outcry and much unrest in the Italian minority.[485]

These episodes were not particularly serious in themselves, but in the context of a Dalmatia in which national conflicts were rife and the Italian element had for decades been subjected to a policy of forced assimilation, they gave many Italian Dalmatians the impression that their living conditions were passing the point of no return, deteriorating irremediably. The mood of many Italian Dalmatians in those months is made clear in a letter that Roberto Ghiglianovich sent to Sanminiatelli on 9 April 1914. According to the member of the Dalmatian diet, Serbs and Croats were emboldened by the victories in the Balkans and were being mollycoddled by the Austrian government, which hoped to win back their favour.

> [The Serbs and Croats] are engaged in an extremely violent struggle against the Italian element of the Adriatic regions; and, against us, more exposed than the others, on a level that it had never reached before. You will have read over and over again about the events in Spalato. Even the boycott! In an attempt to seize control of Zara at the next municipal elections (three years away) all the different Croat and Serb political fractions have recently formed a coalition. And the ones who have played a particularly violent part in this assault, unlike in the past, are the Serbs, evidently as a result of Italy's Balkan policy with regard to Serbia. Under these circumstances, it is necessary that you do not abandon us. It is in the interest of Istria, Trieste, Friuli, Albania, and Italian policy in the Adriatic to keep us here on the eastern coast of the Gulf of Venice.[486]

The pressure exerted by the Croat and Serb parties on the Italian minority must inevitably have led to a deepening of the splits and the nation-

---

484  In this connection: D'Alia to Avarna, 9 April, 1 and 22 May 1914, ASMAE, EMB VIENNA, portfolio 236; Battara, 'Cronaca di vita italiana fuori del regno,' in *Rassegna contemporanea*, 1914, no. 7, pp. 142–7, no. 11, pp. 853–4; 'L'assalto slavo alla Dalmazia. Il disperato appello all'italianità,' *L'Idea Nazionale*, 7 May 1914.
485  *Il Risorgimento*, 16 and 30 May 1914.
486  Ghiglianovich to Sanminiatelli, 9 April 1914, DA, file 1914, B. 9 bis.

al divisions within Dalmatian society, which were to deteriorate still further during the World War and the years following it. The reaction of many Italian Dalmatians and autonomists to this policy of forced denationalization, which tended to turn into the political oppression of a minority, was a strengthening of their own feeling of Italianness – a visceral and emotional sentiment, typical of a population that felt its cultural and linguistic identity to be under threat. At the same time there was a growing sense of closeness and belonging to Italy, a state that, after the conquest of Libya, looked more and more like a great European power and a nation of increasing economic, cultural, and political stature.[487]

The outbreak of the Austro-Serbian War, its subsequent widening into a European conflict, and the choice of the government in Rome to remain neutral were events that put the autonomist leadership in a serious quandary, throwing the party of the Italian Dalmatians into confusion. A decisive influence was exercised on the positions taken by the Italian Dalmatians by what they believed to be the direction of Italy's foreign policy. From Ghiglianovich's memoirs,[488] it is known that the outbreak of the World War sparked a political debate in the Italian Autonomous Party. Taking account of the close Italo-Habsburg collaboration in recent years and the Austrophile leanings of San Giuliano, many leaders of the Autonomist Party (Ziliotto, Salvi, and Krekich) felt that a victory of Austria-Hungary and Germany against Serbia, Russia, and Slavism was to be desired. As Roberto Ghiglianovich recalled, 'all were more in favour of Germany and Austria than of the Triple Entente, which included Slav Russia with her Serbian appendage. The Italian party of Dalmatia laboured under the illusion that an Austria victorious over Slavism would have changed course in the future, that the Triple Alliance would have been strengthened, and that persecution of the Italian element in the Adriatic province would have ceased and the Slavs been persecuted in its place.'[489]

The protraction of the war and the emergence of more and more marked interventionist and anti-Austrian tendencies in Italian public opinion began to make the Italian Dalmatians realize that a war be-

---

487  In this connection: Monzali, 'Oscar Randi scrittore di storia dalmata,' pp. 654 et seq.
488  Roberto Ghiglianovich, *Appunti del 1915*, BS, Carte Ghiglianovich, portfolio A, issue 2. See too Monzali, 'Un contributo,' pp. 202–3.
489  Ghiglianovich, *Appunti del 1915.*

Roberto Ghiglianovich

Luigi Ziliotto

Natale Krekich

Ercolano Salvi

Antonio Tacconi

Antonio Cippico

Leonardo Pezzoli

Alessandro Dudan

tween Italy and Austria was likely.[490] The Italian consul in Zara, D'Alia, declared himself to be certain of future intervention by Italy against Austria-Hungary,[491] and the articles in favour of the Italians in Dalmatia published by Antonio Cippico and the Venetian nationalist member of parliament Foscari in *Il Giornale d'Italia* in the fall of 1914 made a great impression. In those months Ghiglianovich wrote a letter to San Giuliano and another to his successor at the Foreign Ministry, Son-

---

490  On this: Albertini, *Venti anni*, vol. 2, 1; Vigezzi, *L'Italia di fronte alla prima guerra mondiale*, pp. 143 et seq.; Volpe, *Il popolo italiano*, pp. 51 et seq.
491  D'Alia, *La Dalmazia nella storia e nella politica*, pp. 92 et seq.

nino, in which he stressed the feelings of Italianness shared by many Dalmatians and the importance to Italy of gaining political control of the former Venetian colony of Dalmatia, from the Dinaric Alps to the Narenta River, if it wanted to establish hegemony in the Adriatic.[492]

In the fall of 1914 Ercolano Salvi, the leader of the Italian party in Spalato, went to Italy and, after receiving medical treatment in Bologna, arrived in Rome, where he had meetings with Gayda (a journalist of *La Stampa*), Boselli and Sanminiatelli (the leaders of the Dante Alighieri Association), and De Martino (the secretary-general of the Foreign Ministry). Salvi was given the impression that Italy was going to enter the war against Austria sooner or later and that Dalmatia was included in its territorial plans.

In view of this prospect, the Italian Autonomous Party decided to send one of its members, a well-known and representative figure, to Italy to defend the interests of the Italian Dalmatians in the event of war between Austria-Hungary and Italy. Ghiglianovich recalls the moment of that choice as follows: 'The logic of things, the impossibility of Austria ceding to Italy what she would have had to demand, Sonnino, and the speeches of Salandra reinforced the conviction that Italy would, against her will, be forced to intervene ... Ziliotto, D'Alia, and my cousin Barbieri held a council of ... war. We weighed up the pros and cons, the dangers and advantages, and decided that I should go, and Ziliotto's influence was decisive in this.'[493]

On 16 March 1915 Roberto Ghiglianovich left Zara for Trieste, and from there, on 22 March, crossed the Italo-Austrian frontier. It was the beginning of an exile that would last until the end of World War I, in 1918.

With the decision to send Roberto Ghiglianovich to Italy, the Italian Autonomous Party made a clear choice, that of political irredentism. A very different choice had been made by the autonomist leaders in 1866, that of siding unambiguously with the Habsburg state. However, Dalmatia and the Habsburg Empire had changed profoundly between 1866 and 1915. The evolution in Austria's domestic policy and the rise of Croatian nationalism had turned the Italian and Italo-Slav Dalmatians into a persecuted minority whose fundamental cultural and national rights were oppressed: the right to a free public school in their

492 Ghiglianovich, *Appunti del 1915*; Monzali, 'Un contributo.'
493 Ghiglianovich, *Appunti del 1915*.

own language, the right to cultural and linguistic freedom, and the recognition of an equality of treatment with respect to the majority of the country. Under such oppression there is nothing surprising about the slow emergence of a political sentiment of Italian national identity in Dalmatia between the nineteenth and twentieth century, a sentiment that first took the form of a simple cultural irredentism and then was, in a European context dominated by the most unbridled nationalism and by the struggle for power, transformed into political irredentism. For the Italian minority the annexation of Dalmatia to liberal Italy became the only hope of warding off a fate that seemed inevitable: denationalization.

The battle for the liberty of the Italian Dalmatians, merging with Italian foreign policy, inexorably assumed more complex and ambiguous connotations, becoming part of a program of expansion that was aimed at securing for the government in Rome the hegemony in the Adriatic that the republic of Venice had once had. As a result, Italy's policy in the eastern Adriatic over the course of World War I and afterward was complicated, being at once a defence of the right of the Italians of Austria to their nationality and a struggle for the aggrandizement of the Italian state.

# Bibliography

**Archival Sources**
Archivio Centrale dello Stato (Central State Archive), Rome
- Agostino Depretis Papers
- Giovanni Giolitti Papers
Archivio di Stato di Forlì (State Archive of Forlì)
- Giuseppe Tornielli Papers
Archivio Storico della Società Dante Alighieri (Archive of Dante Alighieri
    Society), Roma
- Dante Alighieri Society Papers
Archivio Storico del Ministero degli Esteri Italiano (Archive of the Italian
    Ministry of Foreign Affairs), Rome
- Ambasciata Italiana a Vienna
- Archivio Politico (1861–1887)
- Archivio Riservato di Gabinetto
- Archivio Telegrammi di Gabinetto
- Serie Politica (1891–1916)
Biblioteca Comunale di Lucera (Town Library of Lucera)
- Antonio Salandra Papers
Biblioteca del Senato (Senate Library), Rome
- Roberto Ghiglianovich Papers
Haus-, Hof und Staatsarchiv, Vienna
- Karl Macchio Papers, Vienna
- Kartei des Informationsbüros
- Politisches Archiv, Länderberichte: Italien
Istituto Veneto di Scienze, Lettere e Arti (Venetian Institute of Sciences,
    Literature and Arts), Venice
- Luigi Luzzatti Papers

Kriegsarchiv, Vienna
- Gabriel Rodich Papers

**Published Documents**

Alberi, Eugenio, ed. *Relazioni degli ambasciatori veneti al Senato*. Series 3.
   Florence: Tipografia all'insegna di Clio, 1839–.
*Atti della Dieta Provinciale Dalmata/Brzopisna Izvješća Zasjedanja Pokrajinskoga
   Sabora Dalmatinskoga*. Zara, 1861–.
*Atti parlamentari. Camera dei deputati*. Rome, 1861–.
*Aus dem Nachlass Aehrenthal: Briefe und Dokumente zur österreichisch-ungarischen
   Innen und Aussenpolitik 1885–1912*. Graz: Neugebauer, 1994.
*Austro-Hungarian Documents Relating to the Macedonian Struggle, 1896–1912*.
   Thessaloniki: Institute for Balkan Studies, 1976.
*British Documents on Foreign Affairs: Reports and Papers from the Foreign Office,
   Confidential Print*. Washington: University Publications of America, 1983–.
*British Documents on the Origins of the War, 1898–1914*. London: HMSO, 1927–.
*Carteggi di Bettino Ricasoli*. Rome: Istituto Italiano per la Storia Moderna e
   Contemporanea, 1963–.
*Carteggio Cavalletto-Luciani, 1861–1866*. Padua: Marsilio, 1962.
*Carteggio Cavalletto-Meneghini, 1865–1866*. Padua: Marsilio, 1967.
*Carteggio Volpe-Cavalletto, 1860–1866*. Padua: Marsilio, 1963.
Cavallotti, Felice, *Lettere, 1860–1898*. Milan: Feltrinelli, 1979.
*Cavour e l'Inghilterra: Carteggio con V. E. D'Azeglio*. Bologna: Zanichelli, 1933.
*Cavour, la liberazione del Mezzogiorno e la formazione del Regno d'Italia*. Bologna:
   Zanichelli, 1954.
Chiala, Luigi, ed. *Camillo Cavour: Lettere edite ed inedite*. Turin, 1883–87.
Crispi, Francesco. *Politica estera: Memorie e documenti*. Milan: Treves, 1912.
- *Questioni internazionali*. Milan: Treves, 1913.
*Dai carteggi di Pasquale Villari. La Società 'Dante Alighieri' e l attività nazionale nel
   Trentino (1896–1916)*. Trent: Comitato trentino dell'Istituto per la storia del
   Risorgimento italiano, 1963.
*Dalle carte di Giovanni Giolitti: Quarant'anni di politica italiana*. Milan: Feltrinelli,
   1962.
*Die Auswärtige Politik Preußens, 1858–1871*. Berlin: Stalling-Oldenbourg,
   1933–9.
*Die Belgischen Dokumente zur Vorgeschichte des Weltkrieges, 1885–1914*. Berlin:
   Deutsche Verlagsgesellschaft für Politik, 1925.
*Die Grosse Politik der Europäischen Kabinette, 1871–1914*. Berlin: Deutsche Ver-
   lagsgesellschaft für Politik und Geschichte, 1922–7.
*Die Internationalen Beziehungen im Zeitalter des Imperialismus*. Berlin, 1934–42.

*Die politiche Korrespondenz der Päpste mit den oesterreichischen Kaisern, 1804–1918.* Edited by Friedrich Engel-Janosi. Vienna: Herold, 1964.

*Die Protokolle des Österreichischen Ministerrates, 1848–1867. V Abteilung: Die Ministerien Rainer und Mensdorff; VI Abteilung: Das Ministerium Belcredi.* Vienna: Österreichischer Bundesverlag für Unterricht, Wissenschaft und Kunst, 1971–.

*Die Rheinpolitik Kaiser Napoleons III. von 1863 bis 1870 und der Ursprung des Krieges von 1870/1871.* Osnabrück: Biblio Verlag, 1967. First published 1926.

*Diplomatic Documents Relating to the Outbreak of the European War.* New York: Oxford University Press, 1916.

*Documenti diplomatici italiani.* Rome: Libreria dello Stato-Istituto Poligrafico dello Stato, 1952–.

*Documenti diplomatici italiani sull'Armenia.* Second series, vols. 1, 2, 3. Florence, 1999–2000.

*Documents diplomatiques français, 1871–1914.* Paris : Imprimèrie Nationale, 1929–.

*Documents diplomatiques suisses / Documenti diplomatici svizzeri / Diplomatische Dokumente der Schweiz, 1848–1945.* Bern: Benteli Verlag, 1979–.

*Il carteggio Cavour-Nigra dal 1858 al 1861.* 2nd. ed. Bologna: Zanichelli, 1961.

*Il Diritto d'Italia su Trieste e l'Istria. Documenti.* Milan: Bocca, 1915.

*Il problema veneto e l'Europa, 1859–1866.* Venice: Istituto Veneto di Scienze, Lettere e Arti, 1966.

*Izvještaji italijanskog konzulata u Sarajevu (1863–1870).* Sarajevo: Naučno društvo nr Bosne i Hercegovine, 1958.

Izvol'skij, Aleksandr (Isvolsky, Alexandre). *Au service de la Russie : Correspondence diplomatique, 1906–1911.* Paris: Les Editions Internationales, 1937.

Kautsky, Karl, ed. *Die Deutschen Dokumente zum Kriegsausbruch, 1914.* Berlin: Deutsche Verlagsgesellschaft für Politik, 1921. First published 1919.

*La campagna del 1866 nei documenti militari austriaci: operazioni terrestri.* Edited by Angelo Filipuzzi. Padua: Università di Padua, 1966.

*La conferenza e la pace di Zurigo nei documenti diplomatici francesi.* Rome: Istituto Italiano per la Storia Moderna e Contemporanea, 1965.

*La guerra del 1859 nei rapporti fra la Francia e l'Europa.* Rome: Istituto Italiano per la Storia Moderna e Contemporanea, 1960–1.

*Le lettere di Vittorio Emanuele II.* Edited by Francesco Cognasso. Turin: Deputazione subalpina di storia patria, 1966.

*Les origines diplomatiques de la guerre de 1870–1871.* Paris : Imprimèrie Nationale, 1910–32.

*L'Intervento dell'Italia nei documenti segreti dell'Intesa.* Rome: Rassegna Internazionale, 1923.

Mancini, Pasquale Stanislao. *Discorsi parlamentari di Pasquale Stanislao Mancini.* 8 vols. Rome: Camera dei Deputati, 1896–7.

Minghetti, Marco. *Discorsi parlamentari.* Rome: Tipografia del Parlamento, 1889–.

*Monumenta spectantia historiam slavorum meridionalium: Commissiones et Relationes Venetae.* Zagreb: Academy of Sciences and Arts, 1876–.

Morović, Hrvoje. 'Pisme Miha Klaića uredniku "Narodnog Lista" Jurju Biankiniju.' In *Radovi instituta jugoslavenske Akademije Znanosti i Umjetnosti u Zadru* 6/7 (1960).

*Opera omnia di Benito Mussolini.* vol. 7. Florence: La Fenice, 1951.

*Österreich-Ungarns Aussenpolitik von der Bosnischen Krise 1908 bis zum Kriegsausbruch 1914.* Vienna: Österreichischer Bundesverlag, 1930–.

*Österreich-Ungarn und Serbien, 1903–1918: Dokumente aus Wiener Archiven.* Belgrade: Historisches Institut, 1973–89.

*Quellen zur deutschen Politik Österreichs, 1859–1866.* Osnabrück: Biblio Verlag, 1967. First published 1934–8.

Salvemini, Gaetano. *Carteggio, 1894–1902.* Bari: Laterza, 1988.

– *Carteggio, 1912–1914.* Bari: Laterza, 1984.

Seton-Watson, Hugh, and Christopher, eds. *R.W. Seton-Watson and the Yugoslavs: Correspondence, 1906–1941.* Zagreb: British Academy, London-University of Zagreb, Institute of Croatian History, 1976.

Siebert, B. de, trans., and George Abel Schreiner, ed. *Entente Diplomacy and the World: Matrix of the History of Europe, 1909–1914.* London: Allen and Unwin, 1921.

Šišić, Ferdo, ed. *Korespondencija Rački-Strossmayer.* Zagreb: Jugoslavenska Akademija Znanosti i Umjetnosti, 1928–.

Sonnino, Sidney. *Diario, 1866–1912.* Bari: Laterza, 1972.

– *Carteggio, 1914–1916.* Bari: Laterza, 1974.

*Stenographische Protokolle des Hauses der Abgeordneten.* Vienna, 1861–.

*Un Livre Noir: Diplomatie d'avant-guerre et de guerre d'après les documents des archives russes (1910–1917).* Paris: Librairie du Travail, n.d.

**Newspapers**

*Il Costituzionale*, Zara (Zadar)

*Il Dalmata*, Zara (Zadar)

*Il Nazionale (Narodni List)*, Zara (Zadar)

*La Difesa*, Spalato (Split)

*L'Avvenire*, Spalato (Split)

*Narod*, Spalato (Split)

**Memoirs and Diaries**

Albertini, Luigi. *I giorni di un liberale: Diari, 1907–1923*. Bologna: Il Mulino, 2000.

Aldrovandi Marescotti, Luigi. *Guerra diplomatica: Ricordi e frammenti di diario (1914–1919)*. Milan: Mondadori, 1936.

Barzilai, Salvatore. *Luci ed ombre del passato: Memorie di vita politica*. Milan: Treves, 1937.

Benco, Silvio. *'Il Piccolo' di Trieste: Mezzo secolo di giornalismo*. Milan: Treves, 1931.

Bergamini, Alberto. 'Sonnino e la Dalmazia.' *La Rivista dalmatica*, 1955, no. 2.

Beust, Adolf. *Trois quarts du siècle: Mémoires du comte de Beust*. Paris: Westhausser, 1888.

Billot, A. *La France et l'Italie: Histoire des années troubles, 1881–1899*. Paris: Plon, 1905.

Bonin Longare, Lelio. 'Ricordi di Vienna nei primi anni della Triplice Alleanza.' *Nuova Antologia*, 1932, no. 1456.

Bülow, Bernhard Von. *Memoirs of Prince von Bülow*. Boston: Little, Brown and Company, 1931–2.

Claar, Maximilian. 'Zwanzig Jahre habsburgischer Diplomatie in Rom. (1895–1915) Persönliche Erinnerungen.' *Berliner Monatshefte*, 1937.

Conrad, Franz Von Hötzendorf. *Aus meiner Dienstzeit*. Vienna and Berlin: Rikola, 1921–.

D'Alia, Antonino. *La Dalmazia nella storia e nella politica, nella guerra e nella pace*. Rome: Optima, 1928.

Farini, Domenico. *Diario di fine secolo*. 2 vols. Rome: Bardi, 1962.

Fellner, Fritz, ed. *Schicksalsjahre österreichs, 1908–1918: Das politische Tagebuch Josef Redlichs*. Graz: Böhlau, 1953.

Galli, Carlo. *Diarii e lettere: Tripoli 1911 Trieste 1918*. Florence: Leonardo-Sansoni, 1951.

Giolitti, Giovanni. *Memoirs of My Life*. London: Sydney, Chapman and Dodd, 1923.

Guerrazzi, Gian Francesco. *Ricordi d'irredentismo: I primordi della 'Dante Alighieri' (1881–1894)*. Bologna: Zanichelli, 1922.

Guicciardini, Francesco. 'Cento giorni alla Consulta.' *Nuova Antologia*, 1942, no. 1697.

Höbelt, Lothar, ed. *Österreichs Weg zur Konstitutionellen Monarchie: Aus der Sicht des Staatsministers Anton von Schmerling*. Frankfurt: Lang, 1994.

Lützow, Heinrich von. *Im diplomatischen Dienst der k.u.k. Monarchie*. Munich: Oldenbourg, 1971.

Malagodi, Olindo. *Conversazioni della guerra 1914–1919*. Milan and Naples: Ricciardi, 1960.

Martini, Ferdinando. *Diario, 1914–1918*. Milan: Mondadori, 1966.

Musulin, Alexander. *Das Haus am Ballplatz: Erinnerungen eines österreichisch-ungarischen Diplomaten*. Munich: Verlag für Kulturpolitik, 1924.

Paulucci, Paolo. *Alla corte di re Umberto: Diario segreto*. Milan: Rusconi, 1986.

Pelloux, Luigi. *Quelques souvenirs de ma vie*. Rome: Istituto per la storia del Risorgimento, 1967. Poincaré, Raymond. *Au service de la France: Neuf années de souvenirs*. Vols. 1 and 2. Paris: Plon, 1926.

Rodd, James Rennell. *Social and Diplomatic Memoirs*. London: Arnold and Co., 1925.

Salandra, Antonio. *La neutralità italiana, 1914–1915*. Milan: Mondadori, 1928.

– *L'Intervento [1915]: Ricordi e pensieri*. Milan: Mondadori, 1930.

Semper. 'Prinetti e l'Austria-Ungheria.' *Nuova Antologia*, 1909, no. 900.

Smodlaka, Josip. *Zapisi dra Josipa Smodlaka*. Zagreb, 1972.

Tommaseo, Niccolò. *Venezia negli anni 1848 e 1849: Memorie storiche inedite*. Edited by Paolo Prunas. Florence: Le Monnier, 1931.

Tommasini, Francesco. 'Erinnerungen an Wien (1900–1912).' *Berliner Monatshefte*, 1941.

Trumbić, Ante. *Suton Austro-Ugarske i Riječka rezolucija*. Zagreb: Tipografija, 1936.

Veronese, Leone. *Ricordi d'irredentismo*. Trieste: Spazzal, 1929.

– *Vicende e figure dell'irredentismo giuliano*. Trieste: Tipografia triestina, 1938.

**Other Sources**

Adanir, Fikret. *Die makedonische Frage, ihre Entstehung und Entwicklung bis 1908*. Wiesbaden: Steiner, 1979.

Adler, Jasna. *L'Union forcée: La Croatie et la création de l'Etat yougoslave (1918)*. Chêne-Bourg: Georg, 1997.

Afflerbach, Holger. *Der Dreibund: Europäische Grossmacht-und Allianzpolitik vor dem Ersten Weltkrieg*. Vienna: Böhlau, 2002.

Agičić, Damir. *Hrvatsko-česki odnosi na prijelazu iz XIX u XX stoljeće*. Zagreb: Ibis, 2000.

Agnelli, Arduino. *La genesi dell'idea di Mitteleuropa*. Milan: Giuffrè, 1971.

– *Questione nazionale e socialismo: Contributo allo studio del pensiero di K. Renner e O. Bauer*. Bologna: Il Mulino, 1969.

– 'Mazzini e le giovani nazioni nel centenario della morte di Giuseppe Mazzini,' in *Atti del Centro di ricerche storiche di Rovigno*, III (1972).

– 'Socialismo triestino, Austria e Italia.' In *Il movimento socialista e operaio in Italia e Germania dal 1870 al 1920*. Bologna: Il Mulino, 1978.

Alacevich, Giuseppe. 'Il forte di Clissa ed il conte Nicolò Cindro.' In *Biblioteca storica di Dalmazia*, vol. 4. 1882–3.

Albertini, Luigi. *The Origins of the War of 1914*. 3 vols. London and New York: Oxford University Press, 1952–7.

– *Venti anni di vita politica*. Edited by Luciano Magrini. Bologna: Zanichelli, 1950–3.

Albrecht-Carrié, René. 'Italian Foreign Policy, 1914–1922.' *Journal of Modern History*, 1948.

– *Italy at the Paris Peace Conference*. New York: Columbia University Press, 1938.

Alföldy, Geza. 'La Dalmazia nella storia dell'impero romano.' In *Atti e Memorie della Società dalmata di storia patria*. Vol. 14. Rome, 1990–1.

Anchieri, Ettore. *Costantinopoli e gli Stretti nella politica russa ed europea dal trattato di Qüciük Rainargi alla convenzione di Montreux*. Milan: Giuffrè, 1948.

– *Il sistema diplomatico europeo, 1814–1939*. Milan: Angeli, 1977.

André, Gianluca. *L'Italia e il Mediterraneo alla vigilia della prima guerra mondiale: I tentativi di intesa mediterranea (1911–1914)*. Milan: Giuffrè, 1967.

André, Gianluca, and Guglielmo Folchi. 'La politica estera dell'Italia liberale (1870–1915).' In *Saggi storici sul liberalismo italiano*. Rome: Historia, n.d. [but 1953].

Apih, Elio. *Il socialismo italiano in Austria (1888–1918): Saggi*. Udine: Del Bianco, 1990.

– 'La genesi di "Irredentismo adriatico."' in Angelo Vivante, *Irredentismo adriatico*. Trieste: Italo Svevo, 1984.

Apih, Elio, Giulio Sapelli, and Elvio Guagnini. *Trieste*. Bari and Rome: Laterza, 1988.

Apollonio, Almerigo. *Autunno istriano: La 'rivolta' di Pirano del 1894 e i dilemmi dell'irredentismo*. Trieste: Italo Svevo, 1992.

Aquarone, Alberto. *L'Italia giolittiana*. Bologna: Il Mulino, 1988.

Ara, Angelo. *Fra Austria e Italia: Dalle Cinque Giornate alla questione alto-atesina*. Udine: Del Bianco, 1987.

– 'La Dalmazia e la riforma elettorale austriaca del 1906–1907.' In *Atti e Memorie della Società dalmata di storia patria*. Vol. 17. 1985.

– *Ricerche sugli austro-italiani e l'ultima Austria*. Rome: Elia, 1974.

Ascoli, Graziadio. 'Gli irredenti.' *Nuova Antologia*, 1895, no. 13.

Askew, William C. *Europe and Italy's Acquisition of Libya, 1911–1912*. Durham: Duke University Press, 1942.

Avarna di Gualtieri, Carlo. *L'ultimo rinnovamento della Triplice (5 dicembre 1912)*. Milan: Alpes, 1924.

Bajamonti, Antonio. *Dell'amministrazione del Comune di Spalato dal 9 gennaio 1860 al 6 giugno 1864*. Trieste: Tipografia del Lloyd Adriatico, 1864.
– *Discorso pronunziato alla Camera dei deputati dall'on: Bajamonti nella seduta del 9 dicembre 1876*. Spalato: Zannoni, 1876.
– *La società politica dalmata: Discorso inaugurale 4 luglio 1886*. Spalato: Russo, 1886.
– *Nello inaugurare la pubblicità delle sessioni municipali in Spalato il giorno 9 giugno 1862*. Trieste: Tipografia del Lloyd Adriatico, 1862.
Ballarini, Amleto. *L'Antidannunzio a Fiume: Riccardo Zanella*. Trieste: Italo Svevo, 1995.
Ballini, Pier Luigi, ed. *Sidney Sonnino e il suo tempo*. Florence: Olschki, 2000.
Banac, Ivo. *The National Question in Yugoslavia: Origins, History, Politics*. Ithaca: Cornell University, 1988.
Barbera, Piero. *La Dante Alighieri: Relazione storica al XXV Congresso (Trieste-Trento 1919)*. Rome: Dante Alighieri, 1919.
Bartoli, Matteo. 'Due parole sul neolatino indigeno di Dalmazia.' *La Rivista dalmatica*, 1900, no. 2.
– *Il Dalmatico*. Edited by Aldo Duro. Rome: Istituto per l'Enciclopedia Italiana, 2001.
Barzini, Luigi. *Le condizioni degli italiani in Austria*. Milan: Dante Alighieri, n.d. [but 1913].
Battara, Antonio. *Zara*. Trieste: Maylander, 1911.
Bauer, Ernst. *Drei Leopardenköpfe in Gold*. Vienna and Munich: Herold, 1973.
Beer, Adolf. *Die orientalische Politik Oesterreichs seit 1774*. Prague and Leipzig: Tempsky-Freytag, 1883.
Behnen, Michael. *Rüstung-Bündnis-Sicherheit: Dreibund und informeller Imperialismus, 1900–1908*. Tübingen: Niemeyer, 1985.
Beiche, Friedrich. *Bismarck und Italien: Ein Beitrag zur Vorgeschichte des Krieges 1866*. Berlin: Ebering, 1931.
Bellumore. *I nostri onorevoli: Schizzi biografici, fisiologici, critici, parlamentari fatti in dieta, in istrada, al caffè*. Zara: Battara, [1869?].
Benedikt, Heinrich. 'Le relazioni italo-austriache dal 1861 al 1870.' *Rassegna storica toscana*, 1957, nos. 3–4.
Benvenuti, Sergio. *I principi vescovi di Trento fra Roma e Vienna*. Bologna: Il Mulino, 1988.
– *La Chiesa trentina e la questione nazionale, 1848–1918*. Trent: Temi, 1987.
– *L'autonomia trentina al Landtag di Innsbruck e al Reichsrat di Vienna: Proposte e progetti, 1848–1914*. Trent: Società di Studi trentini di Scienze storiche, 1978.

Berchtold, Klaus. 'Die politischen Parteien und ihre parlamentarischen Klubs bis 1918.' In *Österreichs Parlamentarismus: Werden und System*. Berlin: Dunckler Humblot, 1986.

Berenger, Jean. 'Die Österreichpolitik Frankreichs von 1848 bis 1918.' In *Die Habsburgermonarchie, 1848–1918*. Vol. 6, part 2. Vienna: Österreichischen Akademie der Wissenschaften, 1989.

Berger, Peter, ed. *Der österreichisch-ungarische Ausgleich von 1867: Vorgeschichte und Wirkungen*. Vienna: Herold, 1967.

Bernardy, Amy A. *Un diplomatico dell'irredentismo: Donato Sanminiatelli*. Rome: Casini, 1953.

Berselli, Aldo. *Il governo della Destra: Italia legale e Italia reale dopo l'Unità*. Bologna: Il Mulino, 1997.

Berti, Giuseppe. *Russia e stati italiani nel Risorgimento*. Turin: Einaudi, 1957.

Bertoldi, Silvio. *Vittorio Emanuele III*. Turin: UTET, 1989.

Biagi, Guido. *Passatisti*. Florence: La Voce, 1923.

Biagini, Antonello. 'Italia e Turchia (1904–1911): gli ufficiali italiani e la riorganizzazione della gendarmeria in Macedonia.' In *Memorie storiche militari*, 1977.

– 'La questione d'Oriente del 1875–78 nei documenti dell'archivio dell'ufficio storico dello Stato maggiore dell'Esercito.' In *Memorie storiche militari*, 1978.

– *L'Italia e le guerre balcaniche*. Rome: Ufficio Storico dello Stato Maggiore dell'Esercito, 1990.

– *Momenti di storia balcanica (1878–1914): Aspetti militari*. Rome: Ufficio Storico dello Stato Maggiore dell'Esercito, 1981.

– *Storia dell'Albania*. Milan: Bompiani, 1998.

Biagini, Antonello, and Daniel Reichel. *Italia e Svizzera durante la Triplice Alleanza: Politica militare e politica estera*. Rome: Ufficio Storico dello Stato Maggiore dell'Esercito, 1991.

Bianchi, Nicomede. *Storia documentata della diplomazia europea in Italia dall'anno 1814 all'anno 1861*. Turin: Unione Tipografico Editrice, 1865–72.

Biondich, Mark. *Stjepan Radić, the Croat Peasant Party and the Politics of Mass Mobilization, 1904–1928*. Toronto: University of Toronto Press, 2000.

– 'Stjepan Radić, Yugoslavism and the Habsburg monarchy.' In *Austrian History Yearbook*, 1996.

Blaas, Richard. *Die italienische Frage und das österreichische Parlament*. In *Mitteilungen des Österreichischen Staatsarchivs*. Vol. 22. 1969.

– 'L'Austria di fronte al problema veneto.' In *Atti del XLII Congresso di Storia del Risorgimento Italiano*. Rome: Istituto per la storia del Risorgimento italiano, 1968.

– 'L'Austria e la proclamazione del regno d'Italia.' *Archivio Storico Italiano*, nos. 431–2, 1961.

– 'Vom Friauler Putsch in Herbst 1864 bis zur Abtretung Venetiens 1866.' In *Mitteilungen des Österreichischen Staatsarchivs*. Vol. 19. 1966,

Blasina, Paolo. 'Chiesa e problema nazionale, il caso giuliano, 1870–1914.' In *Regioni di frontiera nell'epoca dei nazionalismi: Alsazia e Lorena / Trento e Trieste, 1870–1914*. Bologna: Il Mulino, 1995.

– 'Santa Sede, Vescovi e Questioni nazionali: Documenti vaticani sull'episcopato di A.M. Sterk a Trieste (1896–1901).' *Rivista di storia e letteratura religiosa*, 1988, no. 3.

Bled, Jean-Paul. *François Joseph*. Paris: Fayard, 1987.

Boeckh, Katrin. *Von den Balkankriegen zum Ersten Weltkrieg : Kleinstaatenpolitik und ethnische Selbstbestimmung auf dem Balkan*. Munich: Oldenbourg, 1996.

Bogović, Mile. *Katolička Crkva i pravoslavlije u Dalmaciji za mletačke vladavine*. Zagreb: Kršcanska Sadašnjost Školska Knjiga, 1993.

Bonamico, Domenico. *La difesa marittima dell'Italia*. Rome: Barbera, 1881.

Bonghi, Ruggero. *Discorso pronunciato da Ruggiero Bonghi il 19 Novembre in Spoleto nella inaugurazione di un comitato della Società Dante Alighieri*. Siena: Tipografia cooperativa, 1893.

– 'Per la società "Dante Alighieri."' *Nuova Antologia*, 1895, no. 24.

– *Politica estera (1866–1893)*. Rome: Istituto italiano per la storia moderna e contemporanea, 1958.

Borsa, Giorgio. *Europa e Asia tra modernità e tradizione*. Milan: Angeli, 1994.

Boselli, Paolo. 'Le origini della Dante.' In *Per la 'Dante': Discorsi e scritti*. Rome: Dante Alighieri, 1932.

Bosworth, Richard J. *Italy and the Approach of the First World War*. London: Macmillan Press, 1983.

– *Italy, the Least of the Great Powers: Italian Foreign Policy Before the First World War*. Cambridge and New York: Cambridge University Press, 1979.

– 'Rennell Rodd e l'Italia.' *Nuova Rivista Storica*, nos. 3–4, 1970.

Boyer, John W. *Culture and Political Crisis in Vienna: Christian Socialism in Power, 1897–1918*. Chicago: University of Chicago Press, 1995.

– *Political Radicalism in Late Imperial Vienna: The Origins of the Christian Social Movement, 1848–1897*. Chicago: Chicago University Press, 1981.

Brauneder, Wilhelm. 'Die Entstehung des Parlamentarismus 1861/1867 und seine Weiterentwicklung.' In *Österreichs Parlamentarismus: Werden und System*. Berlin: Dunckler Humblot, 1986.

– 'Die Verfassungsentwicklung in Österreich 1848 bis 1918.' In *Die Habsburgermonarchie, 1848–1918*. Vol. 7, part 1. Vienna: Österreichischen Akademie der Wissenschaften, 2000.

Bridge, Francis Roy. *From Sadowa to Sarajevo: The Foreign Policy of AustriaHungary, 1866–1914*. London: Routledge and Kegan Paul, 1972.

- *Great Britain and Austria, 1906–1914: A Diplomatic History.* London: Weidenfeld and Nicolson, 1972.
- 'Österreich(-Ungarn) unter den Grossmächten.' In *Die Habsburgermonarchie, 1848–1918.* Vol. 6, part 1. Vienna: Österreichischen Akademie der Wissenschaften, 1989.
Broucek, Peter. 'Konservativismus in den Armeen des Hauses Österreich und der Republik Österreich.' In *Konservativismus in Österreich: Strömungen – Ideen – Personen und Vereinigungen von den Anfängen bis Heute.* Graz: Stocker, 1999.
Brunelli, Vitaliano. *Storia della città di Zara.* Trieste: Lint, 1974. First published 1913.
Brunialti, Attilio. 'Le scuole italiane fuori d'Italia.' *Nuova Antologia,* 15 April 1884.
Bucarelli, Massimo. '"Manicomio jugoslavo": L'ambasciatore Carlo Galli e le relazioni italo-jugoslave tra le due guerre mondiali.' *Clio,* 2002, no. 3.
Buccianti, Giovanni. *L'egemonia sull'Etiopia (1918–1923): Lo scontro diplomatico tra Italia Francia e Inghilterra.* Milan: Giuffrè, 1977.
Buczynski, Alexander. 'Der Dalmatinische Landtag.' In *Die Habsburgermonarchie, 1848–1918,* vol. 7, part 2. Vienna: Österreichischen Akademie der Wissenschaften, 2000.
Budak, Neven. 'Elites cittadine in Dalmazia nel Tre-Quattrocento.' In *Atti e Memorie della Società dalmata di storia patria.* Vol. 26. Venice, 1997.
Bulat, Gajo Filomen. *Izabrani spisi.* Split: Književni Krug, 1995.
Burgwyn, H. James. *The Legend of the Mutilated Victory: Italy, the Great War and the Paris Conference, 1915–1919.* Westport: Greenwood Press, 1993.
Caccamo, Francesco. *L'Italia e la 'Nuova Europa': Il confronto sull'Europa orientale alla conferenza della pace di Parigi (1919–1920).* Milan: Luni, 2000.
Camizzi, Corrado. 'Figure dell'irredentismo dalmata: Antonio Bajamonti il Podestà mirabile.' *L'Esule,* 25 October 1977.
- 'Il dibattito sull'annessione della Dalmazia alla Croazia.' *La Rivista dalmatica,* 1973, no. 3.
- 'La Dalmazia e il Risorgimento italiano (1815–1866).' *La Rivista dalmatica,* 1982.
Candeloro, Giorgio. *Storia dell'Italia moderna.* Milan: Feltrinelli, 1974.
Capuzzo, Ester. 'Fiume tra storia e storiografia.' *Clio,* 1999, no. 2.
- 'L'irredentismo nella cultura italiana del primo Novecento.' *Clio,* 2001, no. 1.
Carageani, Gheorghe. 'Gli aromeni e la questione aromena nei documenti dell'archivio storico diplomatico del Ministero degli affari esteri italiano (1891–1916),' *Storia contemporanea,* 1987.

Carlgren, W.M. *Iswolsky und Aehrenthal vor der bosnischen Annexionkrise: Russische und österreichisch-ungarische Balkanpolitik, 1906–1908*. Uppsala: Almqvist and Wiksells, 1955.

Carlucci, Paola. *Il giovane Sonnino fra cultura e politica (1847–1886)*. Rome: Istituto di Storia del Risorgimento Italiano-Archivio Izzi, 2002.

Carocci, Giampiero. 'Alberto Blanc, ministro degli Esteri (1893–1896).' *Clio*, 2003.

– *Giolitti e l età giolittiana*. Turin: Einaudi, 1971.

Caroncini, Alberto. *Problemi di politica nazionale*. Bari: Laterza, 1922.

Case, Lynn M. *Franco-Italian Relations, 1860–1865*. Philadelphia: University of Philadelphia Press, 1932.

Cataluccio, Francesco. *Antonio di San Giuliano e la politica estera italiana dal 1900 al 1914*. Florence: Le Monnier, 1935.

Cattaruzza, Marina. *Socialismo adriatico: Là socialdemocrazia di lingua italiana nei territori costieri della Monarchia asburgica, 1888–1915*. Manduria: Lacaita, 2001.

Cella, Sergio. 'Studi, pregiudizi e polemiche della fine del '700: i 'viaggi scientifici' di Alberto Fortis e di Lazzaro Spallanzani in Dalmazia e Istria.' In *Atti e Memorie della Società dalmata di storia patria*. Vol.17. Venice, 1989.

Celozzi Baldelli, Pia G. *L'Italia e la crisi balcanica, 1876–1879*. Galatina: Congedo, 2000.

Cervani, Giulio. *La borghesia triestina nell'età del Risorgimento: Figure e problemi*. Udine: Del Bianco, 1969.

– *Momenti di storia e problemi di storiografia giuliana*. Udine: Del Bianco, 1993.

Cessi, Roberto. *Campoformido*. Padua: Messaggero, n.d. [but 1942].

– *La Repubblica di Venezia e il problema adriatico*. Naples: Edizioni Scientifiche Italiane, 1953.

– *Storia della Repubblica di Venezia*. Florence: Giunti, 1981. First published 1944–6.

Chabod, Federico. *Italian Foreign Policy: The Statecraft of the Founders*. Princeton: Princeton University Press, 1996.

Chersi, Ettore. 'Felice Venezian alla difesa delle libertà municipali di Trieste, 1882–1907.' In *Rassegna storica del Risorgimento*, 1951.

Chiala, Luigi. *Ancora un po' più di luce sugli eventi politici e militari dell'anno 1866*. Florence: Barbèra, 1902.

– *Pagine di storia contemporanea dal 1858 al 1892*. Vol. 1, *Dal convegno di Plombières al Congresso di Berlino*. Turin: Roux, 1892.

– *Pagine di storia contemporanea dal 1858 al 1892*. Vol. 2, *Tunisip*. Turin: Roux, 1895.

– *Pagine di storia contemporanea*. Vol. 3, *La Triplice e la Duplice Alleanza (1881–1897)*. Turin: Roux, 1898.

Chiarini, Roberto. *Giuseppe Zanardelli e la lotta politica nella provincia italiana: il caso di Brescia (1882–1902)*. Milan: Sugarco, 1976.

Childs, Timothy W. *Italo-Turkish Diplomacy and the War over Libya, 1911–1912*. Leiden and New York: Brill, 1990.

Chlumecky, Leopold von. *Erzherzog Franz Ferdinands Wirkens und Wollen*. Berlin: Verlag fuer Kulturpolitik, 1929.

Cialdea, Basilio. *L'Italia nel concerto europeo (1861–1867)*. Turin: Giappichelli, 1966.

Ciampini, Raffaele. *Vita di Niccolò Tommaseo*. Florence: Sansoni, 1945.

Clark, Chester Wells. *Franz Joseph and Bismarck: The Diplomacy of Austria Before the War of 1866*. Cambridge, MA: Harvard University Press, 1934.

Clewing, Konrad. *Staatlichkeit und nationale Identitätsbildung: Dalmatien in Vormärz und Revolution*. Munich: Oldenbourg, 2001.

Coceani, Bruno. *Milano centrale segreta dell'irredentismo*. Milan: La Stampa Commerciale, 1962.

– *Riccardo Zampieri: Mezzo secolo di lotte a Trieste per l'unità italiana*. Milan: La Stampa Commerciale, 1961.

Coen, Gastone. *Zara che fu*. Rijeka and Trieste: Unione Italiana-Università Popolare di Trieste, 2001.

Conti Rossini, Carlo. *Italia ed Etiopia dal trattato di Uccialli alla battaglia di Adua*. Rome: Istituto per l'Oriente, 1935.

Coons, Ronald E. *Steamships, Statesmen and Bureaucrats: Austrian policy Towards the Steam Navigation Company of the Austrian Lloyd, 1836–1848*. Wiesbaden: Steiner, 1975.

Corsini, Umberto. 'Deputati delle terre italiane ai Parlamenti viennesi.' In *Problemi di un territorio di confine: Trentino e Alto Adige dalla sovranità austriaca all'accordo Degasperi-Gruber*. Trent: Comune di Trento, 1994.

– *Il colloquio Degasperi-Sonnino: I cattolici trentini e la questione nazionale*. Trent: Monauni, 1975.

– 'Problemi politico-amministrativi del Trentino nel nesso provinciale tirolese, 1815–1918.' In *Austria e province italiane 1815–1918: Potere centrale e amministrazioni locali*. Bologna: Il Mulino, 1981.

Cova, Ugo. *Commercio e navigazione a Trieste e nella monarchia asburgica da Maria Teresa al 1945*. Udine: Del Bianco, 1992.

Craveri, Marta. 'Costantino Nigra ambasciatore a Pietroburgo (1876–1882).' *Clio*, 1992, no. 4.

Cronia, Arturo. *Storia della letteratura serbo-croata*. Milan: Nuova Accademia, 1956.

Curato, Federico. *La questione marocchina e gli accordi italo-spagnoli del 1887 e del 1891*. Milan: Comunità, 1961.

– *Scritti di storia diplomatica*. Milan: Giuffrè, 1984.

Cusin, Fabio. *Appunti alla storia di Trieste*. Udine: Del Bianco, 1983.

Cvitanic, Antun. *Pravno uredjenje splitske komune po statutu iz 1312 godine (Srednjovjekovno pravo Splita)*. Split: Izdanje Muzeja Grada Splita, 1964.

D'Alia, Antonino. *La Dalmazia, le terre limitrofe e l'Adriatico*. Bologna: Zanichelli, 1914.

D'Amelio, Giuliana 'Attilio Brunialti.' In *Dizionario biografico degli italiani*. Vol. 14.  Rome: Istituto dell'Enciclopedia Italiana, 1972.

Dassovich, Mario. *I molti problemi dell'Italia al confine orientale. I – Dall'armistizio di Cormons alla decadenza del patto Mussolini – Pašić (1866–1929)*. Udine: Del Bianco, 1989.

De' Benvenuti, Angelo. 'I riflessi della crisi dell'impero in Dalmazia.' In *La crisi dell'impero austriaco dopo Villafranca*. Trieste: Monciatti, [1960?].

– *Storia di Zara dal 1409 al 1797*. Milan: Bocca, 1944.

– *Storia di Zara dal 1797 al 1918*. Milan and Rome: Bocca, 1953.

De Biase, Corrado. *L'Italia dalla neutralità all'intervento nella prima guerra mondiale*. Modena: STEM/Mucchi, 1965–6.

De Castro, Diego. 'Cenno storico sul rapporto etnico tra italiani e slavi nella Dalmazia.' In *Studi in memoria della prof. Paola Maria Arcari*. Milan: Giuffrè, 1978.

Decleva, Enrico. *Da Adua a Sarajevo: La politica estera italiana e la Francia, 1896–1914*. Bari: Laterza, 1971.

– 'Il compimento dell'Unità e la politica estera.' In *Storia d'Italia*. Vol. 2. Bari: Laterza, 1995.

– *L'incerto alleato: Ricerche sugli orientamenti internazionali dell'Italia unita*. Milan: Angeli, 1987.

– *L'Italia e la politica internazionale dal 1870 al 1914: L'ultima fra le grandi potenze*. Milan: Mursia, 1974.

De Felice, Renzo. *Mussolini il rivoluzionario, 1883–1920*. Turin: Einaudi, 1965.

*De Gasperi e il Trentino tra la fine dell'800 e il primo dopoguerra*. Trent: Reverdito, 1985.

Degli Alberti, Gianlorenzo. *Memoria intorno lo scioglimento del municipio di Spalato*. Trieste: Herrmanstorfer, 1864.

Del Bianco, Giuseppe. *La guerra e il Friuli*. Udine: Del Bianco, 1937.

Delich, Silvio, ed. *L'irredentismo italiano in Dalmazia secondo i documenti segreti della polizia austriaca*. Rome: La Vita Italiana, 1924.

Del Vecchio, Edoardo. 'Il regime doganale tra l'Italia e l'Austria-Ungheria (1887–1892).' *Clio*, 1972.

– *La via italiana al protezionismo: Le relazioni economiche internazionali dell'Italia (1878–1888)*. Rome: Camera dei deputati, 1979.

- 'Penetrazione economica italiana nell'area degli slavi del Sud (1878–1896).' In *Storia delle relazioni internazionali*, 1985, no. 2.

Der Bagdasarian, Nicholas. *The Austro-German Rapprochement, 1870–1879: From the Battle of Sedan to the Dual Alliance*. Rutherford: Farleigh Dickinson University Press, 1976.

De' Robertis, Anton Giulio. *La diplomazia italiana e la frontiera settentrionale nell'anno 1866*. Trent: Istituto di studi trentini di scienze storiche, 1973.

Dethan, Georges. 'La France et la question de Venise en 1966.' In *Atti del XLIII Congresso di Storia del Risorgimento italiano*. Rome, 1968.

Deutsch, Wilhelm. *Habsburgs Rückzug aus Italien: Die Verhandlungen von Villafranca und Zürich, 1859*. Leipzig: Luser, 1940.

De Vergottini, Tomaso. 'Missione Avarna a Vienna (1904–1915).' *Rivista di Studi Politici Internazionali*, 1992, no. 1.

Devich, Giovanni. 'Documenti per la storia di Spalato.' *La Rivista dalmatica*, 1932, no. 3.

Diklić, Marjan. 'Don Ivo Prodan prvi čovjek dalmatinskog pravaštva.' *Radovi, Zavod za povijesne znanosti HAZU u Zadru*, no. 39 (1997).

- 'Don Ivo Prodan u dalmatinskom Saboru'. *Radovi, Zavod za povijesne znanosti HAZU u Zadru*, no. 43 (2001).

- 'Mihovil Pavlinović i pojava pravaštva u Dalmaciji.' *Radovi Instituta jugoslavenske Akademije Znanosti i Umjetnosti u Zadru*. no. 31 (1989).

- 'Pojava Pravaštva i nastanak stranke prava u Dalmaciji.' *Radovi, Zavod za povijesne znanosti HAZU u Zadru*, no. 32 (1990).

- 'Pravaštvo don Ive Prodana.' *Radovi, Zavod za povijesne znanosti HAZU u Zadru*, no. 40 (1998).

- *Pravaštvo u Dalmaciji do kraja prvoga svjetskog rata*. Zadar: Hrvastke Akademije Znanosti i Umjetnosti u Zadru, 1998.

Di Nola, Carlo. 'La Venezia nella politica europea dalla pace di Zurigo (November 1859) alla pace di Vienna (ottobre 1866).' *Nuova Rivista Storica*," nos. 1 and 2, 1961.

Di Nolfo, Ennio. 'Austria e Roma nel 1870.' *Rassegna storica del Risorgimento*, 1971, no. 3.

- *Europa e Italia nel 1855–1856*. Rome: Istituto per la storia del Risorgimento italiano, 1967.

- 'Il problema di Roma nella politica dell'Italia.' In *Atti del XLI Congresso di storia del Risorgimento italiano*. Rome, 1971.

- 'Monarchia e governo durante la crisi diplomatica dell'estate 1870.' In *Un secolo da Porta Pia*. Naples: Guida, 1970.

Diószegi, István. *Bismarck und Andrássy: Ungarn in der Deutschen Machtpolitik in der 2; Hälfte des 19. Jahrhunderts*. Munich and Budapest: Oldenbourg-Teleki László, 1999.

- *Die Aussenpolitik der Oesterreichisch-Ungarischen Monarchie, 1871–1877.* Vienna: Boehlau, 1985.
- *Österreich-Ungarn und der französich-preussische Krieg 1870–1871.* Budapest: Akademiai Kiado, 1974.

Di Ovidio, F. 'Ruggiero Bonghi.' *Nuova Antologia*, 1895.

Di Vittorio, Antonio, Sergio Anselmi, and Paola Pierucci. *Ragusa (Dubrovnik) una Repubblica adriatica: Saggi di storia economica e finanziaria.* Bologna: Cisalpino, 1994.

Dogo, Marco. *La dinamite e la mezzaluna: La questione macedone nella pubblicistica italiana, 1903–1908.* Udine: Del Bianco, 1983.

- *Lingua e nazionalità in Macedonia: Vicende e pensieri di profeti disarmati (1902–1903).* Milan: Jaca Book, 1985.

Donnini, Guido. *L'accordo italo-russo di Racconigi.* Milan: Giuffrè, 1983.

- 'Un momento dei rapporti italo-russi all'inizio del secolo: La mancata restituzione della visita a Vittorio Emanuele III da parte di Nicola II nel 1903.' *Il Politico*, 1978.

Droetto, Antonio. *Pasquale Stanislao Mancini e la scuola italiana di diritto internazionale del secolo XIX.* Milan: Giuffrè, 1954.

Droz, Jacques. 'La socialdemocrazia nell'Austria-Ungheria (1867–1914).' In *Storia del socialismo*, vol.2. Rome: Editori Riuniti, 1974.

Duce, Alessandro. *L'Albania nei rapporti italo-austriaci, 1897–1913.* Milan: Giuffrè, 1983.

- *La crisi bosniaca del 1908.* Milan: Giuffrè, 1977.

Dudan, Alessandro. 'La Dalmazia di oggi.' In *La Dalmazia: Sua italianità, suo valore per la libertà d'Italia nell'Adriatico.* Genoa: Formiggini, 1915.

- *La monarchia degli Asburgo: Origini, grandezza e decadenza.* Rome: Bontempelli, 1915.

Dudan, Bruno, and Antonio Teja. *L'italianità della Dalmazia negli ordinamenti e statuti cittadini.* Milan: ISPI, 1943.

Duggan, Christopher. *Francesco Crispi, 1818–1901: From Nation to Nationalism.* London and New York: Oxford University Press, 2002.

Duplancić, Arsen. 'Dopune zivotopisu i bibliografiji Julija Bajamontija.' *Gradja e prilozi za povijest Dalmacije*, no. 13 (1997).

Džaja, Srećko M. *Bosnien-Herzegowina in der österreichisch-ungarischen Epoche (1878–1918): Die Intelligentsia zwischen Tradition und Ideologie.* Munich: Oldenbourg, 1994.

Engel-Janosi, Friedrich. *Geschichte auf dem Ballhausplatz: Essays zur österreichischen Aussenpolitik, 1830–1945.* Graz: Verl. Styria, 1963.

- *Graf Rechberg: Vier Kapitel zu seiner und Österreichs Geschichte.* Munich, 1927.
- *Österreich und der Vatikan, 1846–1918.* Graz: Verl. Styria, 1958.

Erber, Tullio. 'La colonia albanese di Borgo Erizzo presso Zara: Cenni storici raccolti dai documenti dell'I.R. Archivio luogotenenziale.' In *Biblioteca storica di Dalmatia*, vol. 6, 1883.

– 'Storia della Dalmazia dal 1797 al 1814.' In *Atti e Memorie della Società dalmata di storia patria*, vol. 18. Venice, 1990.

Fay, Sidney B. *The Origins of the World War*. New York: Free Press, 1966. First published 1928–30.

Fellner, Fritz. 'Der Dreibund: Europäische Diplomatie vor dem Ersten Weltkrieg.' In *Vom Dreibund zum Völkerbund: Studien zur Geschichte der internationalen Beziehungen, 1882–1919*. Salzburg and Munich: Oldenbourg, 1994.

Ferluga, Jadran. *L'amministrazione bizantina in Dalmazia*. Venice: Deputazione di Storia Patria per le Venezie, 1978.

Ferraioli, Gianpaolo. 'Giolitti e San Giuliano di fronte alla questione della chiusura dell'impresa di Libia: annessione o protettorato?' *Africa*, 2001, no. 3.

– 'Il marchese di San Giuliano deputato, ambasciatore e ministro degli Esteri (1852–1914),' PhD diss., 'La Sapienza' University, Rome, 2000.

– 'L'apprendistato di un ministro degli Esteri: Antonino di San Giuliano ambasciatore a Londra e Parigi (1906–1910).' *Clio*, 2001, no. 4.

Fischer, Eric. 'New Light on German-Czech Relations in 1871.' *Journal of Modern History*, 1942.

Fischer, Fritz. *Germany's Aims in the First World War*. London: Chatto and Windus, 1967.

Fonzi, Fausto. *Crispi e lo 'Stato di Milano.'* Milan: Giuffrè, 1972.

Foretić, Dinko. 'Socijalistički radnički pokret u Dalmaciji posljednjih godina XIX stoljeća.' *Radovi instituta jugoslavenske Akademije Znanosti i Umjetnosti u Zadru*, nos. 6 and 7, 1960.

Foretić, Dinko, ed. *Dalmacija 1870*. Zadar, 1970.

Foretić, Miljenko. 'L'uomo dell'illuminismo in Dalmazia con particolare riferimento a Dubrovnik.' In *Homo Adriaticus: Identità culturale e autocoscienza attraverso i secoli*. Reggio Emilia: Diabasis, 1998.

Franchi, Bruno. 'Per la storia della Dalmazia nel Risorgimento (con documenti inediti).' *La Rivista dalmatica*, 1938, no. 4.

Francioni, Andrea. *Medicina e diplomazia: Italia ed Etiopia nell'esperienza africana di Cesare Nerazzini (1883–1897)*. Siena: Nuova Immagine, 1997.

Funaro, Lidia F. *L'Italia e l'insurrezione polacca: la politica estera e l'opinione pubblica italiana nel 1863*. Modena: Mucchi, 1964.

Gabriele, Mariano. 'Aspetti del problema adriatico con particolare riguardo al primo rinnovo della Triplice (1887).' Rome: Ufficio storico della Marina militare, 1981.

– *La politica navale italiana dall'Unità alla vigilia di Lissa.* Milan: Giuffrè, 1958.
– *Le convenzioni navali della Triplice.* Rome: Ufficio storico della Marina militare, 1969.
– 'Sulla possibilità di una espansione strategica italiana nel Basso Adriatico e nello Ionio durante la crisi d'Oriente del 1875–1878.' *Storia e Politica*, 1965, no. 3.
Gabriele, Mariano, and Giuliano Friz. *La flotta come strumento di politica nei primi decenni dello Stato unitario italiano.* Rome: Ufficio storico della Marina militare, 1973.
– *La politica navale italiana dal 1885 al 1915.* Rome: Ufficio storico della Marina militare, 1982.
Gaeta, Franco. *Il nazionalismo italiano.* Bari: Laterza, 1981.
Galante Garrone, Alessandro. *I radicali in Italia, 1849–1925.* Milan: Garzanti, 1973.
Gall, Lothar. *Bismarck, the White Revolutionary.* London and Boston: Allen and Unwin, 1986.
Ganiage, Jean. 'Terrorisme et guerre civile en Macedoine (1895–1903).' *Guerres mondiales et conflits contemporaines*, no. 201 (2001).
Ganza-Aras, Tereza. 'Dalmacija u Austro-ugarskoj i unutrašnjoj politici početkom XX stoljeca.' In *Radovi Instituta Jugoslavenske Akademije Znanosti i Umjetnosti u Zadru*, 1981.
– 'Il rapporto della politica croata in Dalmazia nei confronti degli italiani nel periodo della grave crisi che investì il dualismo austro-ungarico agli inizi del XX secolo.' In *Atti del Centro di ricerche storiche di Rovigno*, 1984–5.
– *Politika 'Novog Kursa' dalmatinskih pravaša oko Supila i Trumbića.* Split: Matica Hrvatska, 1992.
– 'Prilog upoznavanju društva splitskog kraja u doba pohrvacenja splitske opcine.' In *Hrvatski narodni preporod u Splitu.* Split: Logos, 1984.
Garbari, Maria. 'L'irredentismo nel Trentino.' In *Il nazionalismo in Italia e in Germania fino alla prima guerra mondiale.* Bologna: Il Mulino, 1983.
– *Vittorio de Riccabona (1844–1927): Problemi e aspetti del liberalismo trentino.* Trent: Società di Studi trentini di Scienze storiche, 1972.
Garzia, Italo. *La questione romana durante la prima guerra mondiale.* Rome: ESI, 1981.
– 'Le origini dell'articolo 15 del Patto di Londra.' In *Storia e Politica*, 1975.
Gayda, Virginio. *L'Italia d'oltre confine (Le provincie italiane d'Austria).* Turin: Bocca, 1914.
Gentile, Emilio. *Le origini dell'Italia contemporanea: L età giolittiana.* Bari: Laterza, 2003.

Ghisalberti, Carlo. *Da Campoformido a Osimo: La frontiera orientale tra storia e storiografia*. Naples: ESI, 2001.

Giannini, Amedeo. 'I rapporti italo-ellenici (1860–1955).' *Rivista di studi politici internazionali*, 1957.

Giglio, Carlo. 'Crispi e l'Etiopia.' *Rassegna storica toscana*, 1970, no. 1.

– 'Il primo gabinetto Cairoli e il problema dei compensi all'Italia (marzo–giugno 1878).' In *Annali pavesi del Risorgimento*, 1963.

– 'Il secondo gabinetto Depretis e la crisi balcanica.' *Rivista storica Italiana*, 1955.

– 'Il trattato di pace italo-etiopico del 26 ottobre 1896.' In *Studi storici in memoria di Leopoldo Marchetti*. Milan: Direzione dei Musei del Risorgimento e di Storia contemporanea, 1969.

– *L'articolo XVII del trattato di Uccialli*. Como: Cairoli, 1967.

Ginsborg, Paul. *Daniele Manin and the Venetian Revolution of 1848–49*. Cambridge: Cambridge University Press, 1979.

Girault, René. 'Les Balkans dans les relations franco-russes en 1912.' *Revue Historique*, no. 513 (1975).

Giusti, Wolfango. *Mazzini e gli Slavi*. Milan: ISPI, 1940.

Glanville, James L. *Italy's Relations with England, 1896–1905*. Baltimore: Johns Hopkins University, 1934.

Gooch, G.P. *Before the War: Studies in Diplomacy*. London: Longmans, Green, and Co., 1936.

Goodman, Carey. 'The Nachlass of Karl Ludwig Freiherr von Bruck in the Austrian National Library.' In *Austrian History Yearbook*, vol. 25, 1994.

Görlitz, Walter. *Jelačić Symbol für Kroatien: Die Biographie*. Vienna: Amalthea, 1992.

Gottlieb, W.W., *Studies in Secret Diplomacy During the First World War*. London: Allen and Unwin, 1957.

Grabovac, Julije. *Dalmacjia u oslobodilačkom pokretu hercegovačko-bosanske raje, 1875–1878*. Split: Književni Krug, 1991.

Grange, Daniel J. *L'Italie et la Méditerranée (1896–1911)*. Rome: Ecole française de Rome, 1994.

Gross, Mirjana. *Die Anfänge des modernes Kroatien: Gesellschaft, Politik und Kultur in Zivil-Kroatien und Slawonien in den ersten dreissig Jahren nach 1848*. Vienna: Boehlau, 1993.

Guida, Francesco. *La Bulgaria dalla guerra di liberazione sino al trattato di Neuilly, 1877–1919: Testimonianze italiane*. Rome: Bulzoni, 1984.

Guida, Francesco, Armando Pitassio, and Rita Tolomeo. *Nascita di uno Stato balcanico: la Bulgaria di Alessandro di Battenberg nella corrispondenza diplomatica italiana, 1879–1886*. Naples: ESI, 1988.

Guillen, Pierre. *L'expansion 1881–1898*. Paris: Imprimèrie Nationale, 1984.

Haines, C. Grove. 'Italian Irredentism During the Near Eastern Crisis, 1875–1878.' *Journal of Modern History*, 1937.

Halperin, S. William. *Diplomat Under Stress: Visconti Venosta and the Crisis of July 1870*. Chicago: University of Chicago Press, 1963.

– *Italy and the Vatican at War: A Study of Their Relations from the Outbreak of the Franco-Prussian War to the Death of Pius IX*. New York: Greenwood Press, 1968. First published 1939.

Hantsch, Hugo. *Die Geschichte Österreichs*. Graz: Styria, 1964.

– *Leopold Graf Berchtold: Grandseigneur und Staatsmann*. Graz: Verl. Styria, 1963.

Haselsteiner, Horst. 'Zur Haltung der Donaumonarchie in der orientalischen Frage.' In *Der Berliner Kongress von 1878: Die Politik der Grossmächte und die Probleme der Modernisierung in Südosteuropa in der zweiten hälfte des 19. Jahrhunderts*. Wiesbaden: Steiner, 1982.

Haywood, Geoffrey A. *Failure of a Dream: Sidney Sonnino and the Rise and Fall of Liberal Italy, 1847–1922*. Florence: Olschki, 1999.

Helmreich, Ernst Christian. *The Diplomacy of the Balkan Wars, 1911–1912*. Cambridge, MA: Harvard University Press, 1938.

Hildebrand, Klaus. *Das vergangene Reich: Deutsche Aussenpolitik von Bismarck bis Hitler, 1871–1945*. Stuttgart: Deutsche Verlags-Anstalt, 1995.

Höbelt, Lothar. 'Die Deutschliberalen Altösterreichs als Verfassungsbewegung, 1848–1918.' Abstract. *L'istituzione parlamentare nel XIX secolo: Una prospettiva comparata*. Bologna: Il Mulino, 2000.

– 'Die Linken und die Wahlen von 1891.' In *Mitteilungen des Österreichischen Staatsarchiv*, vol. 40, 1987.

– 'Die Vertretung der Nationalitäten im Reichsrat.' In *Österreichs Parlamentarismus: Werden und System*. Berlin: Dunckler Humblot, 1986.

– *Kornblume und Kaiseradler: Die deutschfreiheitlichen Parteien Altösterreichs, 1882–1918*. Munich: Oldenbourg, 1993.

– 'Parteien und Fraktionen im Cisleithanischen Reichsrat.' In *Die Habsburgermonarchie, 1848–1918*. Cit., vol 7, part 1. Vienna: Österreichischen Akademie der Wissenschaften, 2000.

– 'Parties and Parliament: Austrian Pre-war Domestic Politics.' In *The Last Years of Austria-Hungary: Essays in Political and Military History, 1908–1918*. Exeter: University of Exeter Press, 1990.

Hocquet, Jean-Claude. *Il sale e la fortuna di Venezia*. Rome: Jouvence, 1990.

Holodik, Ludovit, ed. *Der österreichisch-ungarische Ausgleich 1867*. Bratislava: Verlag der slowakischen Akademie der Wissenschaften, 1971.

Holzer, Josef Jakob. 'Erzherzog Albrecht, 1867–1895: Politisch-militärische

Konzeptionen und Tätigkeit als Generalinspektor des Heeres.' Dissertation, Universität Vienna, 1974.

Ivanišević, Frano. *Narodni Preporod u Dalmaciji: Spalato u Narodnoj Borbi*. Split: Tisak Leonove Tiskare, 1932.

Jacov, Marko. 'Le guerre veneto-turco del XVII secolo in Dalmazia.' In *Atti e Memorie della Società dalmata di storia patria*, vol. 20. Venice, 1991.

Jannazzo, Antonio. *Sonnino meridionalista*. Bari: Laterza, 1986.

Jelavich. Charles. 'The Croatian Problem in the Habsburg Empire in the Nineteenth Century.' In *Austrian History Yearbook*, vol. 3, 1967.

Jenks, William A. *Austria Under the Iron Ring, 1879–1893*. Charlottesville: University Press of Virginia, 1965.

– *The Austrian Electoral Reform of 1907*. New York: Columbia University Press, . 1950.

Jirecek, Costantin. 'L'eredità di Roma nelle città della Dalmazia durante il Medioevo.' in *Atti e Memorie della Società dalmata di storia patria*, vol. 9. Rome, 1984.

Kann, Robert A. *History of the Habsburg Empire, 1526–1918*. Berkeley: University of California Press, 1974.

Kasandric, Pietro. *Il giornalismo dalmato dal 1848 al 1860*. Zadar: Artale, 1899.

Kečkemet, Duško. 'Associazione dalmatica' i pad Ante Bajamontija.' In *Hrvatski narodni preporod u Splitu*. Split: Logos, 1984.

– *Bajamonti I Split*. Split: Slobodna Dalmacija, 2007.

– *Prošlost Splita*. Split: Marjan Tisak, 2002.

– *Vid Morpurgo i Narodni Preporod u Splitu*. Split, 1963.

– *Židovi u povijesti Splita*. Split, 1971.

– 'Židovi u Splitu.' In *Dva stoljeca povijesti i kulture Židova u Zagrebu i Hrvatskoj*. Zagreb: Židovska opcina Zagreb, 1998.

Keiger, John F.V. *France and the Origins of the First World War*. New York: St Martin's Press, 1983.

– *Raymond Poincaré*. Cambridge: Cambridge University Press, 1997.

Kiszling, Rudolf. *Die Revolution im Kaisertum Österreich, 1848–49*. Vienna: Universum, 1948.

– 'Gabriel Freiherr von Rodich.' In *Neue Oesterreichische Biographie ab 1815*. Vol. 11, *Grosse Oesterreicher*. Vienna and Zurich: Amalthea, 1957.

Knauer, Oswald. *Das oesterreichische Parlament von 1848–1966*. Vienna: Bergland, 1969.

Kolmer, Gustav. *Parlament und Verfassung in Österreich*. Graz: Verlag Sanstalt, I, 1972. First published 1902–.

Kořalka, Jiří. 'Deutschland und die Habsburgermonarchie, 1848–1918.' In *Die Habsburgermonarchie, 1848–1918*, vol. 6, part 2. Vienna: Österreichischen Akademie der Wissenschaften, 1987.

Kos, Franz-Josef. *Die Politik Oesterreich-Ungarns während der Orientkrise, 1874/75–1879: Zum Verhaeltnis von politischer und militärischer Führung*. Vienna: Boehlau, 1984.

Kratzik, Johann. *Die nationalen Auseinandersetzungen in Dalmatien während der Zeit der italienischen Landtagsmehrheit 1860–1870, Diplomarbeit zur Erlangung des Magistergrades der Philosophie*. Vienna: Vienna University, 1989.

Krekić, Bariša. *Dubrovnik, Italy and the Balkans in the Late Middle Ages*. London: Variorum Reprints, 1980.

– 'Venezia e l'Adriatico.' In *Storia di Venezia dalle origini alla caduta della Serenissima*, vol. 3. Rome: Istituto dell'Enciclopedia Italiana, 1997.

Krekich, Natale. 'L'opera amministrativa e politica di Luigi Ziliotto.' *La Rivista dalmatica*, nos. 1–2, 1932.

– 'L'opera di Ercolano Salvi nella Dieta di Dalmazia.' *La Rivista dalmatica*, 1931, no. 3.

Krizman, Bogdan. 'The Croatians in the Habsburg Monarchy in the Nineteenth Century.' In *Austrian History Yearbook*, vol. 3, 1967.

Langer, William L. *European Alliances and Alignments, 1871–1890*. New York: Knopf, 1931.

– *The Diplomacy of Imperialism, 1890–1902*. New York: Alfred A. Knopf, 1935.

Lanza, Francesco. *Sopra le relazioni dell'amministrazione del comune di Spalato dal 9 gennaio al 6 giugno 1864 del d.r. A. Bajamonti: Osservazioni*. Spalato: Soregotti, 1865.

Ledel, Eva-Katharin. 'Konservativismus und das Haus Habsburg.' In *Konservativismus in Österreich: Strömungen – Ideen – Personen und Vereinigungen von den Anfängen bis Heute*. Graz: Stocker, 1999.

Lee, Dwight E. 'The Proposed Mediterranean League of 1878.' *Journal of Modern History*, 1931.

Lefebvre d'Ovidio, Francesco. 'Napoleone III, l'Austria e la questione del Veneto: Aspetti diplomatici della terza guerra di independenza.' *Storia delle relazioni internazionali*, 1988, no. 2.

Levi, Alessandro. *Mazzini*. Florence: Barbera, 1955.

– *Ricordi della vita e dei tempi di Ernesto Nathan*. Florence: Le Monnier, 1945.

Lill, Rudolf. 'L'alleanza italo-prussiana.' In *Atti del XLIII Congresso di Storia del Risorgimento italiano*. Rome, 1968.

Lill, Rudolf, and Matteucci Nicola, eds. *Il liberalismo in Italia e in Germania dalla rivoluzione del '48 alla prima guerra mondiale*. Bologna: Il Mulino, 1980.

Lippert, Stefan. *Felix Fürst zu Schwarzenberg: Eine politische Biographie*. Stuttgart: Steiner, 1998.

Longhitano, Rino. *Antonio di San Giuliano*. Milan: Bocca, 1954.

Lowe, C.J. 'Britain and Italian Intervention, 1914–1915.' *The Historical Journal*, 1969, no. 3.

– 'Grey and the Tripoli War, 1911–1912.' In *British Foreign Policy under Sir Edward Grey*, edited by F.H. Hinsley. Cambridge: Cambridge University Press, 1977.

– 'Italy and the Balkans, 1914–1915.' In *British Foreign Policy under Sir Edward Grey*, edited by F.H. Hinsley. Cambridge: Cambridge University Press, 1977.

– *The Reluctant Imperialists: British Foreign Policy, 1878–1902*. London: Macmillan, 1967.

Lowe, C.J., and Frank Marzari. *Italian Foreign Policy, 1870–1940*. London and Boston: Routledge and Kegan Paul, 1975.

Lucio, Giovanni. *Storia del regno di Dalmazia e di Croazia*. Trieste: Lint, 1983.

Lutz, Heinrich. *Österreich-Ungarn und die Gründung des Deutschen Reiches: Europäischen Entscheidungen, 1867–1871*. Frankfurt: Propyläen, 1979.

– *Zwischen Habsburg und Preussen: Deutschland, 1815–1866*. Berlin: Siedler, 1985.

Luzio, Alessandro. 'La missione Malaguzzi a Vienna nel 1865–66 per la cessione del Veneto.' *Il Risorgimento Italiano*, nos. 1–2 and 3–4, 1922, and nos. 1–2, 1923.

Macartney, C.A. *The Habsburg Empire 1790–1918*. New York: Macmillan, 1969.

Mack Smith, Denis. *Italy and Its Monarchy*. New Haven and London: Yale University Press, 1989.

Mackenzie, David. *The Serbs and Russian Panslavism, 1875–1878*. Ithaca: Cornell University Press, 1967.

Madirazza, Francesco. *Storia e costituzione dei comuni dalmati*. Spalato: Morpurgo, 1911.

Malfer, Stefan. 'Der Kampf um die slawische Liturgie in der österreichisch-ungarischen Monarchie - ein nationales oder ein religiöses anliegen?' *Mitteilungen des Österreichischen Staatarchivs*, no. 44 (1996).

Malgeri, Francesco. *La guerra libica (1911–12)*. Rome: Edizioni di Storia e Letteratura, 1970.

Malinverni, Bruno. *La Germania e il problema italiano nel 1859 (Dalla crisi diplomatica a Villafranca)*. Milan: Marzorati, 1959.

– 'L'Unificazione italiana e la politica prussiana (giugno 1860–giugno 1861).' *Rassegna storica toscana*, nos. 3–4, 1957.

Mamiani, Terenzio. *Scritti politici di Terenzio Mamiani*. Florence: Le Monnier, 1853.

Manfroni, Camillo. *Storia della Marina italiana*, I. Milan: Periodici Scientifici, 1970. First published 1897–1902.

Mantegazza, Vico. *L'altra sponda: Italia ed Austria nell'Adriatico*. Milan: Libreria editrice lombarda, 1905.

Marchesi, Vincenzo. *Storia documentata della Rivoluzione e della Difesa di Venezia negli anni 1848–49 tratta da fonti italiane ed austriache*. Venice: Istituto veneto di arti grafiche, [1913?].

Marcocchia, Giacomo. 'Lineamenti della storia di Spalato.' *La Rivista dalmatica*, 1929, no. 2–3.

– 'Sessant'anni di storia della scuola in Dalmazia.' *La Rivista dalmatica*, nos. 2 and 3, 1928.

Marcotti, Giuseppe. *L'Adriatico orientale da Venezia a Corfù*. Florence: Bemporad, 1899.

– *La nuova Austria: Impressioni*. Florence: Barbera, 1885.

Marsden, Arthur. 'Salisbury and the Italians in 1896.' *Journal of Modern History*, 1968.

Maschek, Luigi. *Manuale del regno di Dalmazia per l'anno 1873*. Zadar: Battara, 1873.

Maserati, Ennio. *Il movimento operaio a Trieste dalle origini alla prima guerra mondiale*. Milan: Giuffrè, 1973.

– *Momenti della questione adriatica (1896–1914): Albania e Montenegro tra Austria ed Italia*. Udine: Del Bianco, 1981.

– 'Simboli e riti nell'irredentismo dalmata.' in *Atti e Memorie della Società dalmata di storia patria*, no. 14. Rome, 1990–1.

Maver, Giovanni. 'Discorso sul dalmatico.' *La Rivista dalmatica*, 1995, no. 2.

May, Arthur. *The Hapsburg Monarchy, 1867–1914*. Cambridge, MA: Harvard University Press, 1951.

Mazzetti, Massimo. *L'esercito italiano nella Triplice Alleanza: Aspetti della politica estera 1870–1914*. Naples: ESI, 1974.

– 'L'Italia e la crisi albanese del marzo-maggio 1913.' *Storia contemporanea*, 1973, no. 2.

Mazzini, Giuseppe. *Scritti di politica e di economia*, II. Milan: Sonzogno, 1966.

– *Scritti politici*. Einaudi: Turin, 1976.

Medlicott, William Norton. *Bismarck, Gladstone and the Concert of Europe*. London: University of London, 1956.

Micheletta, Luca. 'Pietro Silva storico delle relazioni internazionali.' *Clio*, 1994, no. 3.

Miller, Nicholas J. *Between Nation and State: Serbian Politics in Croatia Before the First World War*. Pittsburgh: University of Pittsburgh Press, 1997.

Millo, Anna. *L'élite del potere a Trieste: Una biografia collettiva, 1891–1938*. Milan: Angeli, 1989.

– *Storia di una borghesia: La famiglia Vivante a Trieste dall'emporio alla guerra mondiale*. Gorizia: Libreria Editrice Goriziana, 1998.

Milza, Pierre. *Français et italiens à la fin du XIXe siècle: Aux origines du rapprochement franco-italien de 1900–1902*. Rome: Ecole française de Rome, 1981.

Mitic, Ilija. *Dubrovačka država u medjunarodnoj zajednici (od 1358 do 1815)*. Zagreb: Nakladni zavod Matice Hrvatske, 1988.

Modrich, Giuseppe. *La Dalmazia romana-veneta-moderna: Note e ricordi di un viaggio*. Turin: Roux, 1892.

Mola, Aldo A. *Giolitti: Lo statista della nuova Italia*. Milan: Mondadori, 2003.

Monteleone, Renato. *La politica dei fuorusciti irredenti nella guerra mondiale*. Udine: Del Bianco, 1972.

Monti, Lorenzo (Lovre). *Considerazioni sull'annessione del regno di Dalmazia a quelli di Croazia e Slavonia*. Spalato: Morpurgo, 1861.

– *Zašto sam istupio iz Sabora i iz Carevinskoga Vijeća*. Vienna, 1882.

Monticone, Alberto. *La Germania e la neutralità italiana, 1914–1915*. Bologna: Il Mulino, 1971.

Monzali, Luciano. 'Dalmati o Italiani? Appunti su Antonio Bajamonti e il liberalismo autonomista a Spalato nell'Ottocento.' *Clio*, 2002, no. 3.

– 'La Dalmazia e la questione jugoslava negli scritti di Roberto Ghiglianovich durante la prima guerra mondiale.' *Clio*, 1998, no. 3.

– *L'Etiopia nella politica estera italiana, 1896–1915*. Parma: Università di Parma, 1996.

– 'Oscar Randi scrittore di storia dalmata.' *Clio*, 2000, no. 4.

– 'Sidney Sonnino e la politica estera italiana dal 1878 al 1914.' *Clio*, 1999, no. 3.

– 'Tra irredentismo e fascismo: Attilio Tamaro storico e politico.' *Clio*, 1997, no. 2.

– 'Un contributo alla storia degli italiani di Dalmazia: Le carte Ghiglianovich,' *La Rivista dalmatica*, 1997, no. 3.

Mori, Renato. *Il tramonto del potere temporale, 1866–70*. Rome: Edizioni di Storia e Letteratura, 1967.

– *La politica estera di Francesco Crispi (1887–1891)*. Rome: Edizioni di Storia e Letteratura, 1973.

– *La questione romana, 1861–1865*. Florence: Le Monnier, 1963.

Morović, Hrvoje. 'Iz Korespondencije Jurje Biankinija urednike *Narodnog Lista*.' *Radovi, Zavod za povijesne znanosti HAZU u Zadru*, no. 25 (1978).

Mosca, Rodolfo. *Le relazioni internazionali nell'età contemporanea: Saggi di storia diplomatica (1915–1975)*. Florence: Olschki, 1981.

Mugnaini, Marco. *Italia e Spagna nell'età contemporanea: Cultura, politica e diplomazia (1814–1870)*. Alessandria: Dell'Orso, 1994.

Mustilli, D. *La conquista romana della sponda orientale adriatica.* Naples, 1941.

*Namen-Verzeichniss der p.t. Herren Mitglieder des Abgeordnetenhauses. III Session (1864–1865).* Vienna: Staatsdruckerei, 1865.

Nava, Santi. *La spartizione del Marocco: Sue vicende politico-diplomatiche.* Florence: Marzocco, 1939.

Nicolich, E. 'Colonie di slavi di Dalmazia nell'Istria.' In *Biblioteca storica di Dalmatia,* vol. 4, 1882–3.

Nieri, Rolando. *Costituzione e problemi sociali: Il pensiero politico di Sidney Sonnino.* Pisa: ETS, 2000.

Nintchitch (Ninčić), Momtchilo. *La crise bosniaque (1908–1909) et les Puissances européennes.* Paris: Costes, 1937.

Novak, Grga. 'Kako je došlo do pobjede Hrvata u Splitu god. 1882 (prilikom 80-godišnjce).' *Radovi Instituta Jugoslavenske Akademije Znanosti i Umjetnosti u Zadru,* no. 9 (1962).

– 'Političke prilike u Dalmaciji, 1862–1865.' *Radovi Instituta Jugoslavenske Akademije Znanosti i Umjetnosti u Zadru,* nos. 4–5 (1959).

– 'Političke Prilike u Dalmaciji G. 1866–76.' *Radovi Instituta Jugoslavenske Akademije Znanosti i Umjetnosti u Zadru,* nos. 6–7 (1960).

– *Povijest Splita.* Split, 1957–65.

– *Prošlost Dalmacije.* Zagreb, 1944.

Obad, Stijepo. *Dalmacija revolucionarne 1848/49 Godine.* Rijeka: Izdavački Centar, 1987.

Obolensky, Dimitri. *The Byzantine Commonwealth: Eastern Europe, 500–1453.* London: Weidenfeld and Nicolson, 1971.

Odenigo, Armando. *Piero Foscari.* Bologna: Cappelli, 1959.

*Onoranze funebri ad Antonio Bajamonti.* Zara: Artale, 1892.

Ostrogorsky, Georg. *History of the Byzantine State.* New Brunswick, NJ: Rutgers University Press, 1969.

Paci, Renzo. *La 'Scala' di Spalato e il commercio veneziano nei Balcani fra Cinque e Seicento.* Venice: Deputazione di Storia patria per le Venezie, 1971.

Paladini, Filippo M. *Un caos che spaventa: Poteri, territori e religioni di frontiera nella Dalmazia della tarda età veneta.* Venice: Marsilio, 2002.

Palotás, Emil. *Machtpolitik und Wirtschaftsinteressen: Der Balkan und Russland in der österreichisch-ungarischen Aussenpolitik, 1878–1895.* Budapest: Akademiai Kiado, 1995.

Pantić, Miroslav. 'Illuminismo a Ragusa nel Settecento.' In *Atti e Memorie della Società dalmata di storia patria,* vol. 14. Rome, 1990–1.

Paoli Palcich, Germano. 'Vincenzo Duplancich: Lettere e documenti, tra autonomia e irredentismo.' *La Rivista dalmatica,* 1986, no. 3.

Pastorelli, Pietro. 'Albania e Tripoli nella politica estera italiana durante la crisi d'Oriente del 1897.' *Rivista di Studi Politici Internazionali*, 1961, no. 3.
– *Dalla prima alla seconda guerra mondiale*. Milan: LED, 1997.
– 'Giulio Prinetti ministro degli Esteri (1901–1902).' *Nuova Antologia*, no. 2197 (1996).
Pavlinović, Mihovil. *Misao Hrvatska i Misao Srbska u Dalmaciji*. Spalato: Laus, 1994. First published 1882.
– *Izabrani politički spisi*. Zagreb: Golden Marketing, 2000.
Pederin, Ivan. *Mletačka uprava, privreda i politika u Dalmaciji (1409–1797)*. Dubrovnik, 1990. Perfetti, Francesco. *Il movimento nazionalista in Italia, 1903–1914*. Rome: Bonacci, 1984.
Perić, Ivo. *Ante Trumbić na dalmatinskom političkom poprištu*. Split: Izdanja Muzeja Grada Splita, 1984.
– *Dalmatinski Sabor 1861-1912 (1918) God*. Zadar: Centar Jugoslavenske Akademije Znanosti i Umjetnosti, 1978.
– *Politički portreti iz prošlosti Dalmacije*. Split: Književni Krug, 1990.
– *Stjepan Radić, 1871–1928*. Zagreb: Dom i Svijet, 2003.
Peričić, Sime. 'Vranski feud i obitelj Borelli.' *Radovi instituta jugoslavenske Akademije Znanosti i Umjetnosti u Zadru*, no. 18 (1971).
Peteani, Luigi. *La questione libica nella diplomazia europea*. Florence: Cya, 1939.
Petracchi, Giorgio. *Da San Pietroburgo a Mosca: La diplomazia italiana in Russia, 1861/1941*. Rome: Bonacci, 1993.
Petricioli, Marta. *Archeologia e Mare Nostrum: Le missioni archeologiche nella politica mediterranea dell'Italia, 1898–1943*. Rome: Levi, 1990.
– 'Le missioni archeologiche italiane nei paesi del Mediterraneo: uno strumento alternativo di politica internazionale.' In *L'archeologia italiana nel Mediterraneo fino alla seconda guerra mondiale*. Catania: Centro di studi per l'Archeologia greca, 1986.
– *L'Italia in Asia minore: Equilibrio mediterraneo e ambizioni imperialiste alla vigilia della prima guerra mondiale*. Florence: Sansoni, 1983.
Petrignani, Rinaldo. *Neutralità e alleanza: Le scelte di politica estera dell'Italia dopo l'Unità*. Bologna: Il Mulino, 1987.
Petrinović, Ivo. *Politička misao Frana Supila*. Split: Književni Krug, 1988.
Petrović, Rade. 'Il problema dell'Unione della Dalmazia con la Croazia nel 1848.' *Archivio Storico Italiano*, 1976, no. 1–2.
– *Nacionalno pitanje u Dalmaciji u XIX stoljeću: Narodna stranka i nacionalno pitanje 1860–1880*. Sarajevo: Svjetlost, 1968.
Petrovich, Michael Boro. 'The Italo-Yugoslav Boundary Question, 1914–1915.' In *Russian Diplomacy and Eastern Europe, 1914–1917*, edited by Henry I. Roberts. New York: King's Crown Press, 1963.

Piemontese, Giuseppe. *Il movimento operaio a Trieste: Dalle origini all'avvento del fascismo*. Rome: Editori Riuniti, 1974.

Pincherle, Marcella. *Moderatismo politico e riforma religiosa in Terenzio Mamiani*. Milan: Giuffré, 1973.

Pingaud, Albert. *Histoire diplomatique de la France pendant la grande guerre*. Paris: Alsatia, n.d.

Pirjevec, Jože (Pierazzi, Giuseppe). 'Studi sui rapporti italo-jugoslavi (1848–49).' *Archivio Storico Italiano*, 1972, no. 2:181–249.

– *Niccolò Tommaseo tra Italia e Slavia*. Venice: Marsilio, 1977.

Pisa, Beatrice. 'Ernesto Nathan e la "politica nazionale."' *Rassegna storica del Risorgimento*, 1997, no. 1.

– *Nazione e politica nella Società 'Dante Alighieri.'* Rome: Bonacci, 1995.

– 'Pasquale Villari e la Dante Alighieri: considerazioni su sette anni di mandato presidenziale.' *Storia contemporanea*, 1992, no. 3.

Poduje Gicovich, Luca. *Lettere politiche di un dalmata*. Florence: Rassegna nazionale, 1903.

Praga, Giuseppe. 'Elementi neolatini nella parlata slava dell'insulario dalmato.' In *Atti e Memorie della Società dalmata di storia patria*, vol. 10. Venice, 1982.

– *History of Dalmatia*. Pisa: Giardini, 1993.

– *Povijest Hrvata u vrijeme narodnih vladara*. Review of Ferdo Šišić (Zagreb, 1925). In *Atti e Memorie della Società dalmata di storia patria*, vol. 2. Zara, 1927.

– *Storia di Dalmazia*. Milan: Dall'Oglio, 1981.

Praga, Giuseppe, and Arrigo Zink. 'Documenti del 1848–49 a Zara e in Dalmazia.' In *La Venezia Giulia e la Dalmazia nella rivoluzione nazionale del 1848–49*. Udine: Del Bianco, 1950.

Preto, Paolo. *Venezia e i Turchi*. Florence: Sansoni, 1975.

Pribram, Alfred Francis. *The Secret Treaties of Austria-Hungary, 1879–1914*. Cambridge, MA: Harvard Press University, 1921.

Quagliotti, Giovanni. *Aurelio Saffi: Contributo alla storia del mazzinianesimo*. Rome: Edizioni Italiane, 1944.

Quarantotto, Giovanni. *Figure del Risorgimento in Istria*. Trieste: CELVI, 1930.

– *Uomini e fatti del patriottismo istriano*. Trieste: CELVI, 1934.

Rajčić, Tihomir. 'Odnos "Srpskog Lista (Glasa)" prema autonomašima u Dalmaciji 80-ih godina XIX stoljeća.' *Radovi, Zavoda povijesne znanosti HAZU u Zadru*, no. 43 (2001).

Randi, Oscar. *Antonio Bajamonti, 'il mirabile' podestà di Spalato*. Zara: Società dalmata di Storia Patria, 1932.

– 'Dalla guerra a Rapallo.' *La Rivista dalmatica*, 1931, no. 3.

– 'Il senatore Roberto Ghiglianovich: Profilo aneddotico.' *La Rivista dalmatica*, 1930, no. 2.

- 'Il Sen. Roberto Ghiglianovich: Mezzo secolo di storia dalmata.' *La Rivista dalmatica*, 1963, 1965–8, 1979, 1981–4, 1986, 1991.
- 'L'opera politica del Sen. Roberto Ghiglianovich.' Abstract. *La Rivista dalmatica*, 1935.
- 'Luigi Lapenna e l'autonomia dalmata.' Abstract. *La Rivista dalmatica*, 1941.

Raukar, Tomislav, Ivo Petricioli, Franjo Švelec, and Šime Peričić. *Zadar pod Mletačkom upravom 1409–1797.* Zadar: Narodni List, 1987.

Redlich, Joseph. *Emperor Francis Joseph of Austria: A Biography.* Hamden: Archon Books, 1965.

*Reichsraths-Almanach für die Session 1867.* Prague: Satow, 1867.

*Relazione della Congregazione municipale di Spalato letta all'onorevole Consiglio riunito nel dì 23 dicembre 1860 sulla condotta da essa tenuta a tutela della provinciale autonomia garantita dall'imperiale diploma 20 ottobre 1860.* Spalato: Oliveti e Giovannizio, 1860.

Renouvin, Pierre. *La crise européenne et la première guerre mondiale.* Paris: PUF, 1948. First published 1934.
- *The Immediate Origins of the War (28th June–4th August 1914).* New Haven: Yale University Press, 1928.

Renzi, William A. *In the Shadow of the Sword: Italy's Neutrality and Entrance into the Great War, 1914–1915.* New York: Peter Lang, 1987.

Repaci, Antonino. *Da Sarajevo al 'maggio radioso': L'Italia verso la prima guerra mondiale.* Milan: Mursia, 1985.

Riccardi, Luca. *Alleati non amici: Le relazioni tra l'Italia e l'Intesa durante la prima guerra mondiale.* Brescia: Morcelliana, 1992.
- *Francesco Salata tra storia, politica e diplomazia.* Udine: Del Bianco, 2001.

Rich, Norman. *Friedrich von Holstein: Politics and Diplomacy in the Era of Bismarck and Wilhelm II.* Cambridge: Cambridge University Press, 1965.

Rinaldi Tufi, Sergio. 'La Dalmazia.' In *Storia di Roma*, vol. 3, part 2. Turin: Einaudi, 1993.

Ritter, Gerhard. *Staatskunst und Kriegshandwerk: Das Problem des 'Militarismus' in Deutschland.* Munich: Oldenbourg, 1954–68.

Roccucci, Adriano. '"Il Carroccio" e la formazione del gruppo nazionalista romano: Imperialismo democratico ed antidemocratico nel primo nazionalismo romano.' *Storia contemporanea*, 1991, no. 3.
- *Roma capitale del nazionalismo (1908–1923).* Rome: Istituto di Storia del Risorgimento Italiano-Archivio Guido Izzi, 2001.

Rogel, Carole. 'The Slovenes and Yugoslavism, 1890–1914.' *East European Quarterly* (Columbia University Press, Boulder), 1977.

Rogge, Walter. *Oesterreich von Vilagos bis zur Gegenwart.* Vol. 2. Leipzig and Vienna: Brockhaus, 1872.

Rohrbacher, Robert J. 'Bishop J.J. Strossmayer's Yugoslavism in the Light of the Eastern Crisis of 1875–1878.' *East European Quarterly*, 2001, no. 3.

Romanin, Samuele. *Storia documentata di Venezia*. Venice: Filippi, 1972–5. First published 1853–.

Romano, Sergio. *Crispi: Progetto di una dittatura*. Milan: Bompiani, 1973.

– *Giolitti lo stile del potere*. Milan: Bompiani, 1989.

– *Giuseppe Volpi: Industria e finanza tra Giolitti e Mussolini*. Milan: Bompiani, 1970.

Romeo, Rosario. *Cavour e il suo tempo*. Rome and Bari: Laterza, 1969–84.

– *L'Italia liberale: sviluppo e contraddizioni*. Milan: Il Saggiatore, 1987.

Rothenberg, Gunther E. 'Jelačić, the Croatian Military Border, and the Intervention Against Hungary in 1848.' In *Austrian History Yearbook*, I, 1965.

Ruffo, Maurizio. *L'Italia nella Triplice Alleanza: I piani operativi dello Stato Maggiore verso l'Austria Ungheria dal 1885 al 1915*. Rome: Ufficio Storico dello Stato Maggiore, 1998.

Rupp, George Hoover. *A Wavering Friendship: Russia and Austria, 1876–78*. Cambridge, MA: Harvard University Press, 1941.

Russo, Mario. *Antonio Bajamonti*. Milan: Il Mare Nostro, 1934.

– *La Dalmazia e il suo destino*. Milan: Renon, 1952.

– *L'epopea dalmatica e il suo Eroe: Storia aneddotica di un cinquantennio*. Milan: Trevisini, 1925.

Sabalich, Giuseppe. *Guida archeologica di Zara*. Zara: Woditzka, 1907.

Sabbatucci, Giovanni. 'Il problema dell'irredentismo e le origini del movimento nazionalista in Italia.' *Storia contemporanea*, 1970, no. 3.

Salata, Francesco. *Guglielmo Oberdan secondo gli atti segreti del processo, carteggi diplomatici e altri documenti inediti*. Bologna: Zanichelli, 1924.

– *Per la storia diplomatica della Questione Romana: Da Cavour alla Triplice Alleanza*. Milan: Treves, 1929.

Salimbeni, Fulvio. 'Graziadio Isaia Ascoli tra cultura e politica.' Abstract. In *Studi goriziani*, 1986.

Salvatorelli, Luigi. *La Triplice Alleanza: Storia diplomatica, 1877–1912*. Milan: ISPI, 1939.

Salvemini, Gaetano. *Come siamo andati in Libia e altri scritti dal 1900 al 1915*. Milan: Feltrinelli, 1963.

– *Dalla guerra mondiale alla dittatura (1916–1925)*. Milan: Feltrinelli, 1964.

– *La politica estera italiana dal 1871 al 1915*. Milan: Feltrinelli, 1970.

Salvemini, Gaetano, and Carlo Maranelli. 'La questione dell'Adriatico,' in Gaetano Salvemini, *Dalla guerra mondiale alla dittatura (1916–1925)*. Milan: Feltrinelli, 1964.

Salvi, Beniamino. *Il movimento nazionale e politico degli sloveni e dei croati: Dall'illuminismo alla creazione dello Stato jugoslavo (1918)*. Trieste: ISDEE, 1971.

Sandonà, Augusto. *L'irredentismo nelle lotte politiche e nelle contese diplomatiche italo-austriache*. Bologna: Zanichelli, 1932.

Sanminiatelli, Donato. *In giro sui confini d'Italia*. Rome and Turin: Bocca, 1899.

Santeusanio, Italo. *Giuseppe Bugatto il deputato delle 'Basse' (1873–1948)*. Udine and Gorizia: La Nuova Base / Istituto di storia sociale e religiosa, 1985.

– 'Lettere inedite di Roberto Ghiglianovich e Gino de Benvenuti all'on. Giuseppe Bugatto sulla questione linguistica in Dalmazia tra il 1908 e il 1912.' *Quaderni giuliani di Storia*, 1988, no. 1.

Santini, Giovanni. *Dall'Illirico romano alla Jugoslavia moderna*. Milan: Giuffré, 1997.

Sanzin, Luciano Giulio. *Federico Seismit Doda nel Risorgimento*. Bologna: Cappelli, 1950.

Sarti, Roland. *Mazzini: A Life for the Religion of Politics*. Westport, CT: Praeger, 1997.

Sartori, Federica. 'Ruggero Bonghi e il congresso di Berlino in alcuni documenti inediti.' In *Rassegna storica del Risorgimento*, 2000.

Schanderl, Hanns Dieter. *Die Albanienpolitik Österreich-Ungarns und Italien, 1877–1908*. Wiesbaden: Harrassowitz, 1971.

Schiffrer, Carlo. 'La crisi del socialismo triestino nella prima guerra mondiale.' In *Il movimento nazionale a Trieste nella prima guerra mondiale*. Udine: Del Bianco, 1968.

– *Le origini dell'irredentismo triestino (1813–1860)*. Udine: Del Bianco, 1978.

Schmidt, Rainer F. *Graf Julius Andrássy: Vom Revolutionär zum Außenminister*. Göttingen: Muster-Schmidt, 1995.

Schmitt, Bernadotte E. *The Annexation of Bosnia, 1908–1909*. New York: Fertig, 1970. First published 1937.

– *The Coming of the War, 1914*. New York: Fertig, 1966. First published 1930.

Schober, Richard. 'Il Trentino durante il periodo di unione al Tirolo.' In *Austria e province italiane, 1815–1918: Potere centrale e amministrazioni locali*. Bologna: Il Mulino, 1981.

– 'L'arciduca Alberto alla corte d'Asburgo: militare di rango e politico sottovalutato.' In *Il luogo di cura nel tramonto della monarchia d'Asburgo: Arco alla fine dell'Ottocento*. Bologna: Il Mulino, 1996.

Schödl, Günther. *Kroatische Nationalpolitk und 'Jugoslavenstvo': Studien zu nationaler Integration und regionaler Politk in Kroatien-Dalmatien am Beginn des 20. Jahrhunderts*. Munich: Oldenbourg, 1990.

Schroeder, Paul W. *Metternich's Diplomacy at Its Zenith, 1820–1823*. Austin: University of Texas Press, 1962.

- 'Metternich Studies Since 1925.' *Journal of Modern History*, 1961.
Schuster, Peter. *Henry Wickham Steed und die Habsburgermonarchie*. Vienna: Böhlau, 1970.
Scovazzi, Tullio. *Assab, Massaua, Uccialli, Adua: Gli strumenti giuridici del primo colonialismo italiano*. Turin: Giappichelli, 1998.
Selem, Alessandro. 'Tommaso Arcidiacono e la storia medievale di Spalato.' In *Atti e Memorie della Società Dalmata di storia patria*, vol. 16. Venice, 1988. First published 1933.
Semi, Francesco, and Vanni Tacconi, eds. *Istria e Dalmazia: Uomini e tempi*. Udine: Del Bianco, 1992.
Šepić, Dragovan. 'Gli slavi del sud e l'irredentismo italiano.' *Rivista di Studi Politici Internazionali*, 1980, no. 2.
Serra, Enrico. *Alberto Pisani Dossi diplomatico*. Milan: Angeli, 1987.
- *Camille Barrère e l'intesa italo-francese*. Milan: Giuffrè, 1950.
- 'Diplomatici del passato: Alberto Blanc.' In *Affari Esteri*, 1992.
- 'Diplomatici del passato: Alberto Pansa.' In *Affari Esteri*, 1991.
- 'La dottrina delle mani nette.' *Nuova Antologia*, no. 2181 (1992).
- *La questione tunisina da Crispi a Rudinì ed il ' colpo di timone' alla politica estera dell'Italia*. Milan: Giuffrè, 1967.
- 'Le questioni di Cassala e di Adua nelle nuove fonti documentarie.' *Storia e Politica*, 1966, no. 4.
- *L'intesa mediterranea del 1902: Una fase risolutiva nei rapporti italo-inglesi*. Milan: Giuffrè, 1957.
- 'Note sull'intesa Visconti Venosta-Goluchowski per l'Albania.' *Clio*, 1971, no. 3.
Serra, Enrico, and Christopher Seton-Watson, eds. *Italia e Inghilterra nell'età dell'imperialismo*. Milan: Angeli, 1990.
Sertoli Salis, Renzo. *Le isole italiane dell'Egeo: Dall'occupazione alla sovranità*. Rome: Istituto per la storia del Risorgimento italiano, 1939.
Sestan, Ernesto. 'Le riforme costituzionali austriache del 1860–61.' In *La crisi dell'impero austriaco dopo Villafranca*. Trieste: Monciatti, [1960?].
- *Venezia Giulia: Lineamenti di una storia etnica e culturale e il contesto storico-politico in cui si colloca l'opera*. Udine: Del Bianco, 1997.
Seton Watson, Christopher. 'Adua 1896: timori e perplessità britanniche.' In *Studi piacentini*, 1993.
Seton-Watson, Hugh, and Christopher Seton-Watson. *The Making of a New Europe: R.W. Seton-Watson and the Last Years of Austria-Hungary*. Seattle: University of Washington Press, 1981.
Seton-Watson, Robert W. *The Southern Slav Question and the Habsburg Monarchy*. New York: Fertig, 1969. First published 1911.

Sidari, Francesco. *La questione armena nella politica delle grandi poteri dalla chiusura del Congresso di Berlino del 1878 al trattato di Losanna del 1923.* Padua: CEDAM, 1962.

Šidak, Jaroslav. 'Josip Juraj Strossmayer.' In *Enciklopedija Jugoslavije*, vol. 8. Zagreb: Jugoslavenski leksikografski zavod, 1971.

Silva, Pietro. *Figure e Momenti di storia italiana.* Milan: ISPI, 1939.

– *Il 1848.* Rome: Il Faro, 1948.

– *Il Mediterraneo dall'Unità di Roma all'impero italiano.* Milan: ISPI, 1942.

– *Il Sessantasei: Studio storico.* 2nd. ed. Milan: Treves, 1935.

– 'La politica italiana di Napoleone III.' *Nuova Rivista Storica*, 1927, no. 1/2: 1–51; no. 3/4: 242–85.

Šišić, Ferdo. *Pregled povijest hrvatskoga naroda.* Zagreb: Matica Hrvatska, 1962.

Sked, Alan. 'Jelačić in the Summer of 1848.' *Südost-Forschungen*, no. 57 (1998).

– *The Decline and Fall of the Habsburg Empire, 1815–1918.* London: Longman, 1989.

Skřivan, Aleš. *Deutschland und Österreich-Ungarn in der europäischen Politik der Jahre, 1906–1914.* Hamburg: Dölling und Galitz, 1999.

Skunca, Mirjana. *Glazbeni život Splita od, 1860–1918.* Split: Književni Krug, 1991.

Skup, Znanstveni. *Splitski Polihister. Julije Bajamonti.* Split: Književni Krug, 1996.

Smerchinich, Stefano. *Antonio Bajamonti.* Trieste: Nigris e Morpurgo, 1922.

Smodlaka, Josip. *Izabrani Spisi.* Split: Književni Krug, 1989.

Solitro, Giuseppe. *Antonio Bajamonti il podestà mirabile di Spalato (nel quarantesimo anniversario della morte) (1891–1931).* Padua: Comitato d'azione dalmatica, 1931.

Solmi, Arrigo. *Gabriele D'Annunzio e la genesi dell'impresa adriatica.* Milan: Rizzoli, 1945.

– 'Le origini del patto di Londra.' *Politica*, nos. 50–51 (November–December 1923).

– 'L'intervento italiano e le sue conseguenze politiche (maggio–agosto 1915).' *Nuova Antologia*, no. 1466 (1933).

Somogyi, Eva. *Der gemeinsame Ministerrat der österreichisch-ungarischen Monarchie, 1867–1906.* Vienna: Böhlau, 1996.

– *Vom Zentralismus zum Dualismus: Der Weg der Deutschösterreichischen Liberalen zum Ausgleich von 1867.* Wiesbaden: Steiner, 1983.

Sondhaus, Lawrence. *Franz Conrad von Hötzendorf: Architect of the Apocalypse.* Boston: Humanities Press, 2000.

Soppelsa, Giancarlo. 'Antonio Bajamonti.' In *Istria e Dalmazia.* Vol. 2, *Uomini e tempi.* Edited by Sergio Cella and Vanni Tacconi. Udine: Del Bianco, 1992.

– 'Luigi Lapenna.' In *Istria e Dalmazia*. Vol. 2, *Uomini e tempi*. Edited by Sergio Cella and Vanni Tacconi. Udine: Del Bianco, 1992.

Sori, Ercole. 'La penetrazione economica italiana nei territori degli Slavi del Sud (1896–1914).' *Storia contemporanea*, 1981, no. 2.

Sosnosky, Theodor von. *Die Balkanpolitik Österreich-Ungarns seit 1866*. Stuttgart: Deutsche Verlags-Anstalt, 1913.

Spadolini, Giovanni. *Giolitti: un'epoca*. Milan: Longanesi, 1985.

– *I repubblicani dopo l'Unità*. Florence: Le Monnier, 1972.

Spellanzon, Cesare, and Ennio Di Nolfo. *Storia del Risorgimento e dell'Unità d'Italia*. Milan: Rizzoli, 1933–.

Spremić, Momčilo. 'La migrazione degli Slavi nell'Italia meridionale e in Sicilia alla fine del Medioevo.' *Archivio Storico Italiano*, no. 1 (1980).

Srbik, Heinrich von. *Aus Österreichs Vergangenheit von Prinz Eugen zu Franz Joseph*. Salzburg: Müller, 1949.

– *Deutsche Einheit: Idee und Wirklichkeit vom Heiligen Reich bis Königgratz*. Munich: Bruckmann, 1935–42.

– *Metternich: Der Staatsmann und der Mensch*. Munich: Bruckmann, 1925–54.

Stančić, Nikša. 'Das Jahr 1848 in Kroatien: unvollendete Revolution und nationale Integration.' *Südost-Forschungen*, no. 57 (1998).

Stefani, Giuseppe. *Cavour e la Venezia Giulia: Contributo alla storia del problema adriatico durante il Risorgimento*. Florence: Le Monnier, 1955.

Stickler, Matthias. *Erzherzog Albrecht von Österreich: Selbstverständnis und Politik eines konservativen Habsburgers im Zeitalter Kaiser Franz Josephs*. Husum: Matthiesen, 1997.

Stojanović, Mihailo D. *The Great Powers and the Balkans, 1875–1878*. Cambridge: Cambridge University Press, 1968. First published 1939.

Sumner, B.H. *Russia and the Balkans, 1870–1880*. London: Archon, 1962. First published 1937.

Supilo, Frano. *Politički Spisi: Lanci, govori, pisma, memorandumi*. Zagreb, 1970.

Suppan, Arnold. 'Die Kroaten.' In *Die Habsburgermonarchie*, vol. 3. Vienna: Verlag der Österreichischen Akademie der Wissenschaften, 1980.

Sutter, Berthold. *Die Badenischen Sprachenverordnungen von 1897: Ihre Genesis und ihre Auswirkungen vornehmlich auf die innerösterreichischen Alpenländer*. Graz: Böhlau, 1960.

Swire, Joseph. *Albania: The Rise of a Kingdom*. London: Williams and Norgate, 1929.

Tacconi, Ildebrando, ed. 'Biografia di Vitaliano Brunelli, desunta dal manoscritto delle sue "Memorie."' *La Rivista dalmatica*, 1934, no. 2.

– *Per la Dalmazia con amore e con angoscia: Tutti gli scritti editi ed inediti di Ildebrando Tacconi*. Udine: Del Bianco, 1994.

Tacconi, Vanni, ed. *Antonio e Ildebrando Tacconi: Due paladini della civiltà latino-veneto-italica in Dalmazia.* Venice: Fondazione Tacconi, 1997.

Tamaro, Attilio. *Histoire de la Nation italienne sur ses frontières orientales.* Vol. 2, *La Vénétie Julienne et la Dalmatie.* Rome: Unione Editrice, 1918–19.

– *Italiani e slavi nell'Adriatico.* Rome: Atheneum, 1915.

– *Storia di Trieste,* vol. 2. Trieste: Lint, 1976. First published 1924.

Tamborra, Angelo. *Cavour e i Balcani.* Turin: ILTE, 1958.

– *Imbro I. Tkalac e l'Italia.* Rome: Istituto per la storia del Risorgimento italiano, 1966.

– 'La crisi balcanica del 1885–1886 e l'Italia.' *Rassegna storica del Risorgimento,* 1968.

– *L'Europa centro-orientale nei secoli XIX e XX (1800–1920).* Milan: Vallardi, 1973.

– *L'idea di nazionalità e la guerra 1914–1918.* Abstract. Rome: Istituto per la storia del Risorgimento italiano, 1965.

– 'Mondo Turco-balcanico e Italia nell'età giolittiana (1900–1914).' *Rassegna storica del Risorgimento,* 2002, no. 3.

– 'Problema sociale e rapporto città-campagna in Dalmazia alla fine del sec. XVIII.' *Rassegna storica del Risorgimento,* 1972.

– 'Russia, Prussia, la questione polacca e il riconoscimento del regno d'Italia (1861–1862).' In *Rassegna storica del Risorgimento,* fols. II–III, 1959.

– *Studi storici sull'Europa orientale.* Rome: Edizioni dell'Ateneo, 1986.

Teke, Susanna. 'L'Ungheria e l'Adriatico all'epoca del re Sigismondo.' In *Atti e Memorie della Società dalmata di storia patria,* vol. 26. Venice, 1997.

Tenenti, Alberto, and Branislava Tenenti. *Il prezzo del rischio: L'assicurazione mediterranea vista da Ragusa (1563–1591).* Rome: Jouvence, 1985.

Thomae Archidiaconi Spalatensis. 'Historia salonitarorum pontificum atque spalatensium a s. Domnio usque ad Rogerium.' In *Atti e Memorie della Società dalmata di storia patria.* Supplement to vol. 16. Venice, 1988.

Tombor, Tibor. 'La formazione e lo sviluppo dell'autonomia comunale delle città dalmate nel medioevo.' In *Atti e Memorie della Società dalmata di storia patria,* vol. 13. Venice, 1985.

– 'L'alleanza della Repubblica di Genova con l'Ungheria nel secolo XIV contro la Repubblica di Venezia per il dominio della Dalmazia e l'impero del mare.' In *Atti e Memorie della Società dalmata di storia patria,* vol. 11. Venice, 1983.

Tommaseo, Niccolò. *Ai Dalmati.* Zara: De Marchi, 1861.

– *La questione dalmatica riguardata ne' suoi nuovi aspetti.* Zara: Battana, 1861.

– *Via Facti: La Croazia e la fraternità; Di nuovo ai Dalmati.* Trieste: Coen, 1861.

Tommasini, Francesco. *L'Italia alla vigilia della guerra: La politica estera di Tommaso Tittoni.* Bologna: Zanichelli, 1934–41.

Torre, Augusto. *Alla vigilia della guerra mondiale, 1914–1918*. Milan: ISPI, 1942.
– *La politica estera dell'Italia dal 1896 al 1914*. Bologna: Patron, 1960.
Toscano, Mario. 'Il libro verde del 1915.' *Clio*, 1968, no. 2.
– 'Il negoziato di Londra del 1915.' *Nuova Antologia*, November 1967.
– *Il patto di Londra: Storia diplomatica dell'intervento italiano (1914–1915)*. Bologna: Zanichelli, 1934.
– 'Imperiali e il negoziato per il patto di Londra.' *Storia e Politica*, 1968, no. 2.
– *La Serbia e l'intervento in guerra dell'Italia*. Milan: Giuffrè, 1939.
– 'Le origini diplomatiche dell'art. 9 del patto di Londra relativo agli eventuali compensi all'Italia in Asia Minore.' *Storia e Politica*, 1965, no. 3.
– 'L'Intervento dell'Italia nella prima guerra mondiale: Le carte Imperiali e la preparazione del negoziato.' *Nuova Antologia*, 1968.
– *Pagine di storia diplomatica contemporanea*. Milan: Giuffrè, 1963.
– 'Rivelazioni e nuovi documenti sul negoziato di Londra per l'ingresso dell'Italia nella prima guerra mondiale.' *Nuova Antologia*, August 1965, September 1965, October 1965, November 1965.
Treadway, John D. *The Falcon and the Eagle: Montenegro and Austria-Hungary, 1908–1914*. West Lafayette : Purdue University Press, 1983.
Trumbić, Ante. *Izabrani Spisi*. Split: Književni Krug, 1986.
Valdevit, Giampaolo. *Chiesa e lotte nazionali: il caso di Trieste (1850–1919)*. Udine: ARIES, 1979.
Valeri, Nino. *Giovanni Giolitti*. Turin: Utet, 1972.
Valiani, Leo. *The end of Austria-Hungary*. New York: Knopf, 1973.
Vallauri, Carlo. *La politica liberale di Giuseppe Zanardelli dal 1876 al 1878*. Milan: Giuffrè, 1967.
Valsecchi, Franco. *L'Europa e il Risorgimento: L'alleanza di Crimea*. Florence: Vallecchi, 1968.
– *L'Italia del Risorgimento e l'Europa delle nazionalità: L'unificazione italiana nella politica europea*. Milan: Giuffrè, 1978.
Venturi, Franco. *Settecento riformatore*, vol. 5, part 2. Turin: Einaudi, 1989.
Vigezzi, Brunello. *Da Giolitti a Salandra*. Florence: Vallecchi, 1969.
– *I problemi della neutralità e della guerra nel carteggio Salandra-Sonnino (1914–1917)*. Milan and Naples: Ricciardi, 1962.
– *L'Italia di fronte alla prima guerra mondiale*. Vol. 1, *L'Italia neutrale*. Milan and Naples: Ricciardi, 1966.
– *L'Italia unita e le sfide della politica estera dal Risorgimento alla Repubblica*. Milan: Unicopli, 1997.
Villari, Pasquale. *Scritti e discorsi per la 'Dante.'* Rome: Dante Alighieri, 1933.

Vitezić, Ivan. 'Die roemisch-katholische Kirche bei den Kroaten.' In *Die Habsburgermonarchie*, vol. 4. Vienna: Österreichischen Akademie der Wissenschaften, 1985.

Vivarelli, Roberto. *Storia delle origini del fascismo: L'Italia dalla grande guerra alla marcia su Roma*. Bologna: Il Mulino, 1991.

Vocelka, Karl. 'Das osmaniche Reich und die Habsburgermonarchie, 1848–1918.' In *Die Habsburgermonarchie, 1848–1918*, vol. 6, part 2. Vienna: Österreichischen Akademie der Wissenschaften, 1993.

Volpe, Gioacchino. *Il Medioevo*. Rome and Bari: Laterza, 1990. First published 1926.

– *Il popolo italiano tra la pace e la guerra (1914–1915)*. Milan: ISPI, 1940.

– *Italia moderna*, Florence: I. Sansoni, 1973. First published 1943–51.

– *L'Italia che nasce*. Florence: Vallecchi, 1968.

– *Scritti su Casa Savoia*. Rome: Volpe, 1983.

Vrandečić, Josip. *Dalmatinski autonomistički pokret u XIX stoljeću*. Zagreb: Dom i Svijet, 2002.

– 'What Did the Merchant's Son Francis of Assisi Say to Thomas, a Student from Spalato? Protonationalism in early-modern Venetian Dalmatia (1420–1797).' Abstract. *Annals for Istrian and Mediterranean Studies*, no. 24 (2001).

Vuličević, Ludovico. *Partiti e lotte in Dalmazia*. Trieste: Tergesteo, 1875.

Walters, Eurof. 'Austro-Russian Relations Under Goluchowski, 1895–1906.' *The Slavonic and East European Review*, nos. 76–9 (1952–4).

Wandruszka, Adam. *Schicksaljahr 1866*. Graz: Verl. Styria, 1966.

Wawro, Geoffrey. *The Austro-Prussian War: Austria's War with Prussia and Italy in 1866*. Cambridge: Cambridge University Press, 1996.

Webster, Richard A. *Industrial Imperialism in Italy, 1908–1915*. Berkeley: University of California Press, 1975.

Wertheimer, Eduard von. *Graf Julius Andrássy: Seine Leben und Seine Zeit*. Stuttgart, 1910–13.

Wilkes, John. *Dalmatia*. London: Routledge and Keegan Paul, 1969.

– *The Illyrians (The Peoples of Europe)*. London: Blackwell, 1992.

Winkler, Eduard. *Wahlrechtsreformen und Wahlen in Triest 1905–1909: Eine Analyse der politischen Partizipation in einer multinationalen Stadtregion der Habsburgermonarchie*. Munich: Oldenbourg, 2000.

Wolff, Larry. *Venice and the Slavs: The Discovery of Dalmatia in the Age of Enlightenment*. Stanford: Stanford University Press, 2001.

Zaghi, Carlo. *P.S. Mancini, l'Africa e il problema del Mediterraneo, 1884–1885*. Rome: Casini, 1955.

Zamboni, A. 'Note linguistiche dalmatiche.' In *Atti e Memorie della Società dalmata di storia patria*. Venice, 1976.

Zecchino, Ortensio, ed. *Pasquale Stanislao Mancini: l'uomo, lo studioso, il politico*. Naples: Guida, 1991.

Ziliotto, Giuseppe. 'Di Ercolano Salvi e del trattato di Rapallo.' *La Rivista dalmatica*, 1973, no. 1.

Živanović, Milan. 'Dve demonstracije u Splitu i Šibeniku 1912 godine.' *Radovi Instituta Jugoslavenske Akademije Znanosti i Umjetnosti u Zadru*, 1957, no. 3.

Zorić, Mate. *Dalle due sponde: Contributi sulle relazioni letterarie italo-croate*. Rome: Il Calamo, 1999.

– *Književni dodiri hrvatsko-talijanski*. Split: Književni Krug, 1992.

# Index of Names and Places

Paulucci, Paolo, 143, 213, 350
Pavia, Luigi, 235
Pavissich, Luigi Cesare, 107
Pavlinović, Mihovil, 46, 65, 67, 76, 87,
   101, 102, 154
Peano, Camillo, 318, 319
Pederin, Ivan, 11
Pelagosa/Palagruza, 313, 314, 318,
   321
Pellegrini-Danieli, Cesare, 89
Pelloux, Luigi, 205, 211, 213, 350
Pepoli, Gioacchino Napoleone, 119,
   124
Perasto/Perast, 17
Perfetti, Francesco, 264
Perić, Ivo, 64, 68, 87, 89, 91, 100, 103,
   109, 231, 244, 324, 336
Peričić, Šime, 101
Pesaro, 30, 31, 201
Petacco, Arrigo, xiii
Peteani, Luigi, 211
Petracchi, Giorgio, 134, 295, 304
Petricioli, Marta, 257, 275, 289
Petrignani, Rinaldo, 105, 106, 118,
   121, 123, 129, 134, 135, 139, 140,
   143, 144, 148, 150
Petrinović, Ivo, 231, 235
Petrović, Rade, 26, 64, 66, 102, 103
Petrovich, Michael Boro, 306, 317
Petrovich/Petrovic, Spiridione, 45,
   49, 54
Pezzi, Enrico, 109
Pezzoli, Leonardo, 188, 232, 341
Pichon, Stephen, 255
Piedmont/Piemonte, ix, 320
Piemontese, Giuseppe, 152
Pierazzi, Giuseppe. *See* Pirjevec, Jože
Pietro II Orseolo, 11
Pilo, Giuseppe Maria, xv
Pincherle, Marcella, 30

Pingaud, Albert, 317
Pini, Luigi, 188, 191, 245
Piperata, Giuseppe, 63, 90
Pirjevec/Pierazzi, Jože/Giuseppe, 29,
   35, 38, 44, 124, 128
Pisa, Beatrice, 176, 180, 181, 183, 202
Pisani Dossi, Alberto, 220
Pitacco, Giorgio, 248, 324
Pitassio, Armando, 165
Plener, Ignaz von, 42, 51, 108
Po River, 22
Poduje Gicovich, Luca, 187
Poincaré, Raymond, 287
Pola/Pula, x, 258
Poland, 17, 72
Potocki, Alfred, 81, 82, 85
Pozza, Raffaele, 101
Pozzobon, 24
Praga, Giuseppe, xii, xv, 3, 6, 7, 9–11,
   17, 18, 19, 26, 28, 61
Prague, 92, 104, 141
Preto, Paolo, 14
Pribram, Alfred Francis, 139, 143,
   149, 170, 171, 203, 204, 208, 220,
   287
Prinetti, Giulio, 213–17, 220–5, 227,
   230, 252, 255, 267
Prodan, Ivo, 67, 102, 153, 154, 231,
   249, 324
Prussia, 40, 41, 71, 73, 78, 116, 119,
   120, 316
Pučisća, 66
Puglia, 51, 309, 310
Pulić, Juraj/Đuro, 46, 65, 67

Quagliotti, Giovanni, 175, 176
Quarantotto/Quarantotti, Giovanni,
   47, 74
Quarnero/Kvarner, 31, 43, 197, 233,
   236, 254, 313, 314